An Anthology of Philosophy in Persia

بچشم نهان بین، نهان جهان را   که چشم عیان بین نبیند نهان را
نهان در جهان چیست آزاده مردم   نبینی نهان را، ببینی عیان را
جهان را بآهن نشایدش بستن   بزنجیر حکمت ببند این جهان را

See with the inner eye, the inner dimension of the world
For the outward looking eye cannot see the inward.

What is the inward in the world, men who are free,
Thou doest not see the inward, but seeth the outward.

One cannot bind this world with iron,
Thus bind this world with the chain of philosophic wisdom

Nāṣir-i Khusraw

An Anthology of Philosophy in Persia

VOLUME II

SEYYED HOSSEIN NASR

with

MEHDI AMINRAZAVI

OXFORD
UNIVERSITY PRESS

2001

OXFORD
UNIVERSITY PRESS

Oxford New York
Athens Auckland Bangkok Bogotá Buenos Aires Calcutta
Cape Town Chennai Dar es Salaam Delhi Florence Hong Kong Istanbul
Karachi Kuala Lumpur Madrid Melbourne Mexico City Mumbai
Nairobi Paris São Paulo Shanghai Singapore Taipei Tokyo Toronto Warsaw

and associated companies in
Berlin Ibadan

Published by Oxford University Press, Inc.
198 Madison Avenue, New York, New York 10016

Library of Congress Cataloging-in-Publication Data
An anthology of philosophy in Persia / [edited by] Seyyed Hossein
Nasr, Mehdi Aminrazavi.
p. cm.
Includes bibliographical references and index.
ISBN 0-19-512700-5
1. Philosophy, Iranian. I. Nasr, Seyyed Hossein. II. Aminrazavi,
Medhi, 1957– .
B5072.A48 1999
181'.5—dc21 98-36440

The figure on the cover is that of Sīmurgh, a mythical bird that,
according to ancient Persian mythology, resided on top of the cosmic
mountain (Alborz) and symbolizes divine wisdom. Later it became identified
with the Logos and Intellect by Persian Islamic philosophers.

1 3 5 7 9 8 6 4 2

Printed in the United States of America
on acid-free paper

ACKNOWLEDGMENT

The editors wish to express their gratitude to the Iranian Academic Society, the Institute for Ismāʿīlī studies, Institut International de Philosophie (under the auspices of UNESCO) and especially its former president, professor Raymond Klibansky, and the Foundation for Traditional Studies for making this publication possible.

CONTENTS

CONTRIBUTORS

SEYYED HOSSEIN NASR received his early education in Iran and completed his studies at Massachusetts Institute of Technology and Harvard University. Nasr is the author of over three hundred articles and thirty books. He has taught at a number of universities, both in the Middle East, especially Tehran University, and in the United States; and he has lectured widely on Islamic philosophy. He is currently the University Professor of Islamic Studies at The George Washington University.

MEHDI AMINRAZAVI received his early education in Iran and received his master's degree in philosophy from the University of Washington in Seattle and his doctorate from Temple University. He is the author and editor of numerous books and articles on Islamic philosophy in Iran. He is now an Associate Professor of Philosophy and Religion at Mary Washington College and the codirector of the Center for Asian Studies.

FAQUIR MUHAMMAD HUNZAI undertook his postgraduate studies in philosophy, Arabic and Persian languages and literatures at Karachi University, and subsequently obtained his Ph.D. degree in Islamic studies from McGill University, Montreal. He is at present a Research Associate at the Institute of Ismāʿīlī Studies in London.

HERMANN LANDOLT has studied philosophy, Greek philology, cultural anthropology, and Islamic studies at Basle University and Sufism at Paris, Ecole Pratique des Hautes Etudes (Sorbonne). He has published extensively in Islamic studies and Ismāʿīlī thought and has taught at the McGill University Branch in Tehran, the Institute of Ismāʿīlī Studies in London, as well as in Indonesia and France. He is currently Professor of Islamic Studies at the Institute of Islamic Studies at McGill University.

LATIMAH PARVIN PEERWANI was educated at the American University of Beirut and the University of Tehran and has taught at the Institute of Ismāʿīlī Studies in London and at the Pontifical Institute of Islamic Studies in Rome. Her main areas of research and publications are in Shiʿite and Ismāʿīlī philosophy and Sufism.

DANIEL C. PETERSON studied Greek, philosophy, and the history of the Middle East at Brigham Young University and the American University in Cairo before receiving a doctorate in Near Eastern Languages and culture from the University of California at Los Angeles. He is an Associate Professor of Islamic Studies and Arabic, managing editor for the Islamic Translation Series, and director of the Center for the Preservation of Ancient Religious Texts at Brigham Young University.

EVERETT K. ROWSON has studied at Princeton and Yale and is Professor of Arabic literature at the University of Pennsylvania. He has written extensively on Islamic philosophy and literature and is a specialist on ʿĀmirī.

LIST OF REPRINTED WORKS

Jābir ibn Ḥayyān *Kitāb al-aḥjār* (Book of Stones), translated by Seyed Nomanual Haq (Boston: Kluwer Academic Publishers, 1994), pp. 163–202.

Nāṣir-i Khusraw, *Dīwān*, translated by P. L. Wilson and Gh. R. Aavānī (Tehran: Imperial Iranian Academy of Philosophy, 1973) pp. 31–43.

Nāṣir-i Khusraw *Gushāyish wa rahāyish* (Knowledge and Liberation) translated by F. M. Hunzai (London: The Institute of Ismāʿīlī Studies, 1998), pp. 24–53.

Rasāʾil Ikhwān al-Ṣafāʾ (*Treatise of the Brethren of Purity: On Numbers*). The first Treatise of the division of the abstract sciences, translated by Bernard Goldstein, Cairo, Dar al-fikr Press, 1347. Reprinted from *Centaurus 10*, (1964): 135–160.

Rasāʾil Ikhwān al-Ṣafāʾ (Treatise of the Brethren of Purity: Animals versus Man), translated by Lenn E. Goodman, Boston: Twayne Press, 1978, pp. 51–77 and 198–202.

Al-Muʾayyad bi-Llāh Shīrāzī's *Khuṭbah* (sermons), edited and translated by J. Muscati and A. M. Moulvi, (Karachi: Islamic Association Press, 1969), pp. 78–91, 141–153, and 174–178.

Ṭūsī, Naṣīr al-Dīn, *Sayr wa sulūk* (Contemplation and Action) translated by S. J. Badakhshani, (London: I. B. Tauris and the Institute for Ismāʿīlī Studies, 1998), pp. 26–47.

LIST OF TRANSLITERATIONS

Arabic characters

ء	’
ب	b
ت	t
ث	*th*
ج	j
ح	ḥ
خ	*kh*
د	d
ذ	*dh*
ر	r
ز	z
س	s
ش	*sh*
ص	ṣ
ض	ḍ
ط	ṭ
ظ	ẓ
ع	‘
غ	*gh*
ف	f
ق	q
ك	k
ل	l
م	m
ن	n
ه	h
و	w
ي	y
ة	ah; at (construct state)
ال	(article) al- and ’l- (even before the anteropalatals)

long vowels

ا ى	ā
و	ū
ي	ī

short vowels

ـَ	a
ـُ	u
ـِ	i

Diphthongs

ـَو	aw
ـَي	ai (ay)
ـيّ	ayy (final form ī)
ـوّ	uww (final form ū)

Persian letters added to the Arabic alphabet

پ	p
چ	*ch*
ژ	*zh*
گ	g

ISMĀʿĪLĪ AND HERMETICO-PYTHAGOREAN PHILOSOPHY

GENERAL INTRODUCTION

The second volume of the *Anthology of Philosophy in Persia* deals with some major schools of thought in the early history of Islamic Persia that were not treated in the first volume. In the first volume, in addition to pre-Islamic thought in Persia, special attention was paid to the Peripatetic school associated most of all with the name of Ibn Sīnā (Avicenna). This much better known school of Islamic philosophy is usually identified in the West as Islamic philosophy; and in most general treatments of the history of Islamic philosophy, little attention has been paid until recently to other schools of thought of that period that are of philosophical significance. In the early centuries of Islamic history, Ismāʿīlī philosophy and philosophies influenced by Pythagorean and Hermetic ideas—also usually associated with Shiʿite thought in general and Ismāʿīlism in particular—stand out especially as schools of great philosophical significance if philosophy be understood in its traditional and time-honored sense.

Ismāʿīlism, which is a branch of Shiʿism that shares the first six Imams with the mainstream form of Shiʿism known as the Ithnā ʿashariyyah or Twelve-Imam Shiʿism, began to formulate its philosophical and theological teachings earlier than any other form of Shiʿism with which it has always shared a common concern for the central role of *ʿaql*, or intellect, in the understanding of religious doctrines. Already one can see the propensity toward intellectual discourse, the significance of *ʿaql*, and use of demonstration or *burhān* in the *Nahj al-balāghah* (Path of Eloquence), which is a collection of the sayings and teachings of ʿAlī ibn Abī Ṭālib, the first Shiʿite Imām, presented in its present form by Sayyid Sharīf al-Raḍī. The Shiʿite Imāms also held occasional discourse with those knowledgeable in Greco-Alexandrian philosophies and sciences, as can be seen in the meeting between the eighth Shiʿite Imām of the Twelve-Imām School, ʿAlī al-Riḍā, and ʿImrān al-Ṣābī, who belonged to the "Sabaean" community of Harran known to have been a center where more esoteric currents of Greco-Alexandrian thought were cultivated and preserved into the Islamic period. Moreover, the sixth Imām Jaʿfar al-

Ṣādiq—the last person to be accepted by both Twelve-Imām Shiʿites and Ismāʿīlīs as Imām—was associated with currents of Hermeticism, and Jābir ibn Ḥayyān, the first Muslim alchemist who is a historical figure despite having gained a "mythological" dimension, was a student of Imām Jaʿfar. These and many other characteristics of Shiʿism and events in Shiʿite sacred history created a more favorable ambience for the propagation of the intellectual sciences of which philosophy is the heart in Shiʿite circles than in most (but not all) climates dominated by later Sunni theological thought. The survival of Islamic philosophy during later centuries in Persia and its reflowering during the Safavid period, when Persia had become predominantly Shiʿite of the Twelve-Imām School, is related to this reality as is the central significance of philosophy for the religious thought of Ismāʿīlism.

There is another cardinal point that must be remembered, and that is the esoteric dimension of Shiʿism that therefore links it at its very roots with Islamic esoterism as such, of which it is a manifestation along with Sufism, which is the central expression of that esoterism. Moreover, Islamic esoterism is based essentially on knowledge of a principial order (*al-maʿrifah/ʿirfān*) and is therefore more than anything else gnostic, if this term be understood in its original sense and not confused with the sectarian views of historical gnosticism. From the beginning Shiʿism was concerned with gnosis, and throughout history one can observe the manifestation of Shiʿite gnosis in various forms, with many of which we shall deal in later volumes of this series, especially those associated with Twelve-Imām Shiʿism. Meanwhile, in early Islamic history Ismāʿīlī gnosis began to manifest itself through a number of works that are both gnostic and philosophical or one could say theosophical in nature, if this latter term be understood in its authentic sense as *theo-sophia* or *al-ḥikmat al-ilāhiyyah* in Arabic and *ḥikmat-i ilāhī* in Persian, terms which are its exact and literal equivalent.

Ismāʿīlī thought associated philosophy/theosophy with the esoteric dimension of the religion and the instructions of the Imāms, who according to both Twelve-Imām and Ismāʿīlī Shiʿism possess knowledge of the esoteric (*bāṭinī*) truths of religion. During Islamic history many Muslims in fact referred to the Ismāʿīlīs as *bāṭinīs*, sometimes in a pejorative sense accusing them of denying the outward (*ẓāhir*) form of the revelation. Without entering into this theological discussion which has had a long history, it suffices here to emphasize that for the Ismāʿīlīs philosophy possesses essentially an esoteric, gnostic, and soteriological character and is not simply meant to be mental learning. It is related to the *ḥaqīqah* or truth at the heart of the Quranic revelation, and therefore can be attained only after proper training of not solely the mind but also the whole of one's being, which then makes one worthy of receiving knowledge from the representative of true gnosis who is none other than the Imām or his representatives. The role of the Imām and the hierarchy of those who know at whose head he stands is, therefore, essential in the disciple's gaining of authentic knowledge.

Understanding the true nature of this esoteric knowledge is related to grades of initiation and the attainment of spiritual virtues. The *Rasāʾil Ikhwān al-Ṣafāʾ* (Treatises of the Brethren of Purity), composed in the fourth/tenth century, which the Ismāʿīlīs have claimed over the centuries as their own (but which it might be said reflects the wider climate of Shiʿism in general), a work that had much influence in the Islamic world at large, is based more than anything else on the link between philosophy and the virtuous life. The Ismāʿīlīs emphasized from the beginning the fact that a philosopher or *ḥakīm* had to be a sage in the traditional sense of the term, in whom perfection of knowledge and being were wed. They thereby propagated a view that the whole of Islamic tradition was also to embrace as the major intellectual schools of that tradition were crystallized. Such later masters of Islamic thought in Persia as Suhrawardī and Mullā Ṣadrā, although not Ismāʿīlī, never ceased to emphasize the inalienable link between knowing and being and the moral and spiritual qualifications necessary for the understanding of philosophy. The Ismāʿīlīs and later schools of thought also often made a distinction between *falsafah* as the fruit of ratiocination and *ḥikmah* as true philosophy, adding that the first was attainable through the training of the mind and the second only through the training of one's whole being. This distinction was not, however, absolute and there are a number of authors who use *falsafah* and *ḥikmah* practically interchangeably and as closely associated terms, enumerating the same conditions for the mastering of *falsafah* as they do for *ḥikmah*.

In any case, Ismāʿīlī philosophy with its gnostic nature was able to integrate readily into its perspective other schools of thought of a gnostic and esoteric character with which it came into contact. These included not only the esoteric strands of Greco-Alexandrian thought such as Hermeticism and Neopythagoreanism, but also certain cosmological ideas associated with Mazdaeism and Manichaeism. Nor were the Ismāʿīlī philosophers indifferent to Neoplatonism. On the contrary, they showed great interest in this last major metaphysical synthesis of the Greek tradition, but they did not display the same degree of interest in Aristotelianism as did the Muslim Peripatetics. It is true that both the Peripatetics and the Ismāʿīlī philosophies integrated elements of Greco-Alexandrian thought into their perspectives drawn essentially from the Islamic worldview and created philosophies that for this very reason were Islamic. But precisely because of the difference in emphasis and the type of Greco-Alexandrian thought that they integrated into different dimensions of the Islamic intellectual universe, they created different and distinct schools of philosophy that interacted with each other in many ways and that must be considered fully in any serious study of philosophy in Persia. This claim holds true especially since nearly all the major early Ismāʿīlī philosophers, although associated with the Fāṭimids and their capital in Cairo, were Persians.

The selections of Ismāʿīlī philosophy presented in this volume cover some five centuries, from the second/eighth to the seventh/thirteenth, starting with the enigmatic *Umm al-kitāb* (The Archetypal Book), the earliest Ismāʿīlī philosophical text that was written in archaic Persian, to the writings of Naṣīr al-Dīn Ṭūsī, who was devoted to the study of Ismāʿīlism while in the service of the Ismāʿīlī rulers of Alamut, but who was a Twelve-Imām Shiʿite who wrote the first systematic work of theology in this branch of Shiʿism, entitled *Kitāb al-tajrīd* (The Book of Catharsis). The period considered in the present volume was marked by the ascendance of the Fāṭimids, and later on the period was punctuated by the "Resurrection of Alamut," announced in 559/1164 by the Ismāʿīlī Imām of the time and associated with the name of Ḥasan Ṣabbāḥ and the establishment of Ismāʿīlī states in the mountainous regions of northeastern Persia, especially Quhistan in

Khurasan. This period came abruptly to an end with the Mongol invasion of western Asia by Hülāgū. Henceforth in Persia Ismāʿīlism took another form, going for the most part underground and becoming intermingled with certain forms of Sufism. In effect, the "golden age" of Ismāʿīlī philosophy is the very period treated in this volume, that from the point of view of philosophy came to an end with Ṭūsī, although Ismāʿīlī thought continued to produce works of mystical and theological significance and even some of a philosophical nature, especially in Yemen and India.

Of special interest regarding philosophy in Persia is the fact that this early period of Ismāʿīlī philosophy, which also marks in many ways its peak, especially involved cultivation of the Persian language as a medium for philosophical discourse. This tendency can be seen from the *Umm al-kitāb* onward and culminates, from the point of view of the beauty and maturity of language, in the works of Nāṣir-i Khusraw. Usually Ibn Sīnā is credited with writing the first philosophical work in Persian, the *Dānish-nāma-yi ʿalāʾī* (The Book of Science Dedicated to 'Alā' al-Dawlah). This statement is certainly true for Peripatetic philosophy, but if we look at philosophy in general, including other schools of thought, then the major contribution of Ismāʿīlī writers to the very foundation of philosophical Persian must be given serious consideration. Moreover, perhaps the only figure in the history of Persia who was at once a major poet and a major philosopher is the Ismāʿīlī figure Nāṣir-i Khusraw, ʿUmar Khayyām being the only other possible candidate for such an honor. There were of course other Persian philosophers who were also poets, such as Afḍal al-Dīn Kāshānī, Mīr Dāmād, Mullā Ṣadrā, and Sabziwārī, but none held the same position of eminence in poetry as did Nāṣir-i Khusraw, who is considered by most authorities to be one of the seven greatest poets in the Persian language. At the same time he was a major philosopher who wrote all his works in Persian.

The Ismāʿīlī philosophers under consideration in this volume did not simply repeat the same philosophical ideas. While they were all concerned with the soteriological function of knowledge, the esoteric character of philosophy, the relation between religion and philosophy, the development of an esoteric cosmology and anthropology, the study of the philosophical significance of the presence of the Imam as the source of infallible knowledge, and many other issues, one can see as well a gradual unfolding over the centuries of ideas concerning other matters. For example, the development of a metaphysics based upon not Being but the Beyond-Being, of which Being is the First Act, and the incorporation of the Neoplatonic idea of emanation into the Ismāʿīlī worldview took place gradually.

The centuries under consideration here also reveal extensive interaction between Ismāʿīlī philosophy on the one hand and various schools of Islamic philosophy and theology as a whole on the other, as can be seen in Abū Ḥātim Rāzī's criticism of Muḥammad ibn Zakariyyāʾ Rāzī, the interaction between Ibn Sīnā's synthesis and systematization of Peripatetic philosophy and the writings of Ḥamīd al-Dīn Kirmānī, and the response of Sunni thinkers to the *Rasāʾil* of the Ikhwān al-Ṣafāʾ, read extensively by many of these thinkers including such a major figure as Abū Ḥāmid Muḥammad Ghazzālī, who at the same time wrote against Ismāʿīlism.

In any case, the tradition of Ismāʿīlī philosophy, developed mostly in Persia during the earlier centuries of Islamic history, is of much philosophical interest and is certainly one of the important schools of philosophy that developed during the Islamic period. Its treatment of such subjects as the relation of time and eternity; cosmic cycles; the nature of the *anthropos*; a metaphysics based not on Being but the Absolute as Beyond-Being whose first manifestation is Being; a cosmology related to the hierarchy of spiritual beings; the relation between religion in its formal aspect and philosophy, reason, and revelation; and many other philosophical themes are of innate philosophical value as well as of great significance for the in-depth understanding of Islamic philosophy in general.

The selections chosen for this volume begin with the *Umm al-kitāb* (The Archetypal Book), meaning literally "Mother of all Books," which is one of the names of the Quran itself. The work purported to be the result of certain questions posed to the fifth Shiʿite Imam, Muḥammad al-Bāqir, contains many themes of philosophical interest that were to be expanded in many later works of Ismāʿīlī philosophy. There is an explanation of the letters of the Divine Name Allah interpreted according to Shiʿite esoterism. This concern with the symbolism of letters, which is also found in the Kabbala, is in evidence among numerous Shiʿite as well as Sufi authors and is said to go back to the science of the esoteric meaning of letters and their numerical values or *jafr* associated with ʿAlī ibn Abī Ṭālib and taught by him to those who were inheritors of his esoteric knowledge.

The *Umm al-kitāb* also discusses the relationship between the Prophet and ʿAlī, the legislating aspect of revelation and its esoteric aspect, and delves into the technical Ismāʿīlī terminology of the silent (*ṣāmit*) and the enunciator (*nāṭiq*). This whole section points to the sharp delineation made by Ismāʿīlī thought between the exoteric and esoteric dimensions of religion and the association of philosophy as *ḥikmah* with the esoteric dimension. It is in light of this esoteric view of philosophy that the text deals with the correspondence between macrocosm and microcosm, astrological symbolism, and the explanation of sacred history based on the number 7, which is central to the Ismāʿīlī perspective to the extent that they were sometimes referred to as the Seveners. Those ideas reveal the early integration of certain elements of Hermeticism, Pythagoreanism, and other strands of esoteric ideas in the Greco-Alexandrian world into the perspective of early Shiʿism in general and Ismāʿīlism in particular.

The selections from the *Umm al-kitāb* include also a section dealing with the esoteric significance of events and realities of Islamic sacred history, specifically the seven prophets and major spiritual figures of this cycle—Adam, Noah, Abraham, Moses, Jesus, the Prophet of Islam, and ʿAlī—and what has been the most important event or object associated with them, namely, in consecutive order, the *bayt al-maʿmūr* (the heavenly prototype of the temple of Mecca), the Ark, the bird (mentioned in the Quran in association with Abraham), Mount Sinai, the birth of Jesus, and the Dhuʾl-fiqār (the two-pronged sword of ʿAlī). All of these realities of Islamic sacred history are treated from the point of view of their esoteric meaning. The *Umm al-kitāb* also analyzes chapters of the Quran according to the early Ismāʿīlī cosmology, identifying various chapters with stages in the cycle of prophecy. The same symbolic approach is used in the study of the tenets of the *Sharīʿah*. It is of particular interest to note how the five daily prayers are shown to be correlated with both the external senses of man and his inner constitution. This type of study was to be pursued by many later Sufis and philosophers, and we find extensive studies in works concerned with "secrets of worship" (*asrār al-ʿibādāt*) in later centuries by such figures as Qāḍī Saʿīd Qummī and Ḥājjī Mullā Hādī Sabriwārī, both of whom will be treated in the last volume of this anthology.

There is a body of writings in Arabic attributed to Jābir ibn Ḥayyān al-Ṭūsī al-Ṣūfī, which has caused a great deal of debate among scholars in both East and West. Some Western scholars have gone so far as to deny that there ever was such a figure as Jābir, while most Muslim scholars accept the traditional account that such a figure actually did exist and that he was a disciple of the sixth Shiʿite Imam Jaʿfar al-Ṣādiq. Most likely the latter view is correct and many of the treatises attributed to him are by him, while many other titles within the vast Jābirean Corpus were written by later authors of mostly Ismāʿīlī background inspired by him. In any case, the body of works associated with Jābir who hailed from Khurasan forms an important chapter in Islamic intellectual history in general and that of Persia in particular.

Jābir is the founder of Islamic alchemy and its most famous practitioner, while he also exercised vast influence in the West where he was known as Geber and where because of his authority some Latin works were written and attributed to him. The Jābirean Corpus deals naturally to a great extent with Hermetic philosophy. But it also deals with many other subjects, including the philosophy of science in general and the philosophy of language. The vastly diverse domains that form the subject matter of the Corpus are united by the central concept of the balance (*al-mīzān*), which Jābir applies in both a quantitative and a qualitative manner to nearly every realm of existence and its study ranging from alchemy to the science of the soul, which constitutes its inner dimension, to the study of language. He also establishes correspondences between these and other realms in the manner that one finds in Hermetic philosophy in both East and West.

The selection from the writings of Jābir consists of the *Kitāb al-aḥjār* (The Book of Stones), where he seeks to clarify the views of Balīnās (Apollonius of Tyana) on the balance, complementing his own studies on the subject in the series of works he wrote under the title *Books of Balances*. The text reveals Jābir's mastery of the sciences of language (concerning Arabic) as well as alchemy and his acceptance of the traditional idea, later expounded by other Persian thinkers, that the name of a thing is related to that thing's nature and reality. For most authors this view involves the sacred language of Arabic and not just any language, and within the Islamic world this view is ultimately based on the Quranic verse that God taught Adam the names of all things by virtue of which he and his progeny were able to gain knowledge of them. In this perspective the name of a thing is not simply a manmade word having nothing to do with the nature of that thing. Rather, each letter of that name corresponds to a nature or quality and also to numerical symbols. Through the balance, these numbers and qualities determine the outward and inward nature of a thing, as the term *nature* is understood in ordinary language and not in its alchemical connotation.

Hermeticism and the alchemical philosophy of nature, the philosophy of language in its relation to the study of the natural world, the idea of correspondences between various orders of reality, and many other ideas to be found in the Jābirean Corpus are all of great significance for the history of science as well as philosophy. One cannot in fact understand the depth and breadth of philosophy in Persia and the many different issues with which it was concerned without at least some sampling of the vast Jābirean Corpus whose origin and many works certainly go back to the historical figure of Jābir, at once a Sufi, a man from the famous Khurasani city of Tus, and a disciple of the sixth Shiʿite Imām after whom the Twelve-Imām Shiʿite Law (the Jaʿfarī) that has dominated Persia since the tenth/sixteenth century is named.

With Abū Yaʿqūb Sijistānī, we reach perhaps the earliest systematic expositor of Ismāʿīlī philosophy. The Persian text of his *Kashf al-maḥjūb* (Unveiling of the Hidden) included in this volume is based on an earlier fourth/tenth century text in Arabic that has been lost, but the survival of this early Persian translation attests to the role played by Persian in the whole tradition of Ismāʿīlī philosophy. The work is composed of seven treatises on divine knowledge, making use of the central sacred number of Ismāʿīlism. In the first discourse, Sijistānī deals with Divine Unity (*tawḥīd*) in the language of the radical apophatic theology that characterizes this phase of Ismāʿīlī thought. He also deals with the angelic ranks and degrees of creation so central to Ismāʿīlī cosmogony and cosmology. Sijistānī emphasizes also the seven cycles of prophecy, each cycle beginning with a prophet and the last with the imam, who becomes enunciator (*nāṭiq*) of the next cycle.

In the selections from Sijistānī's other major work, *Kitāb al-yanābīʿ* (The Book of Wellsprings) the discussion of *tawḥīd* continues, but most of the material is devoted to the intellect (*ʿaql*)—its rapport with the Divine Origin (*Mubdiʿ*) on the one hand and with the soul (*nafs*) and the natural world on the other. A definition is given of the intellect and its primacy emphasized. The knowledge acquired by *ʿaql* is discussed in relation to divine assistance (*taʾyīd*) and as inspired by divine guidance (*muʾayyid*). These are specifically Ismāʿīlī terms that help to define the Ismāʿīlī understanding of *ʿaql*, which plays such a pivotal role in Ismāʿīlī philosophy as well as theology.

Many Ismāʿīlī philosophers were knowledgeable in the doctrines of other religions and showed keen interest in comprehending their meaning, which according to their perspective they usually sought on the esoteric level. The section on Sijistānī terminates with a text that belongs to the field now often called comparative religion. Therein Sijistānī discusses the symbolism of the cross and why it is venerated by Christians. He also explains why its veneration for them is like the veneration of the *shahādah* for Muslims. Here again early Shiʿite thought in general, and Ismāʿīlism in particular, displays interest in issues later treated in Sufism, often in similar or parallel fashion. The Sufi doctrine of the symbolism of the cross has become well known in the West thanks to the classical work of René Guénon, *The Symbolism of the Cross*, which deals in a much more extensive and thorough manner with a subject for which concern is nevertheless present in this early work of Sijistānī written a millennium earlier.

Abū Ḥātim Rāzī's *Aʿlām al-nubuwwah* (Science of Prophecy) is not only a major text of Ismāʿīlī thought but also an important text of Islamic philosophy concerned with what is today called the philosophy of religion. Like Sijistānī, Rāzī was deeply interested in the universal reality of religion and revelation within as well as across the religious frontiers of Islam, and he dealt with many issues that lie at the heart of the current discussion in the West on religious diversity, or what many now call religious pluralism. This seminal work also deals, however, with another subject of great importance to Islamic thinkers—namely, the origin of the sciences. Rāzī considers the sciences including astronomy and pharmacology, especially knowledge of the medical properties of herbs, to have been originally revealed knowledge. Rāzī writes that in teaching Adam the names of all things, as asserted in the Quran, God also taught him the medicinal properties of plants. Rāzī in fact presents a kind of sacred history of science that was shared by many other Muslim thinkers and is also found in traditions such as Hinduism, as well as among certain Christian and Jewish authors. His views are, needless to say, of much importance for the Islamic understanding of the sciences of nature themselves.

With Ḥamīd al-Dīn Kirmānī, we reach the most systematic treatment of early Ismāʿīlī philosophy. Kirmānī, whose systematic treatment of that philosophy caused him to be called by some later authorities the Ismāʿīlī Ibn Sīnā, wrote a number of works, among which *Rāḥat al-ʿaql* (Repose of the Intellect) stands out as the best known and most influential. In pages chosen for this anthology from this work, arguments for the existence of God, the nature of the intellect, the system of emanation reaching down to the world of nature, and other major philosophical issues developed in Ismāʿīlī philosophy are treated in a logical and systematic fashion that bears comparison with the Peripatetic theses of masters such as Fārābī and Ibn Sīnā. In a comparison and contrasting of Ismāʿīlī and *mashshāʾī* philosophies, the *Rāḥat al-ʿaql* serves as a particularly valuable text that reveals the richness and diversity of philosophical thought in Persia in the early Islamic period.

The selections from the works of Kirmānī include also his treatise *al-Risālat al-durriyyah* rendered by its translator as *The Brilliant Treatise* while it literally means *The Pearly Treatise*. In this concise work, Kirmānī deals with the question of unity and the different meanings that technical Arabic terms such as *wāḥid, aḥad, fard* as well as *muwaḥḥid* and *muwaḥḥad* have in the context of Ismāʿīlī philosophy and theology. It is well known that Ismāʿīlī thought considers the Divine Reality the Originator (*al-Mubdiʿ*) to stand even above Being. Kirmānī follows the same doctrine in this treatise in considering God as the Originator to stand even above *tawḥīd*, since He is the Originator of both *wāḥid* and *aḥad*, Names of God associated with unity. Kirmānī also deals briefly with numerical symbolism in relation to his discussion of the relation between the unifier and the unified and the manifestation of unity in the domain of contingency. This treatise represents a summary of Kirmānī's views on the central subject of Islamic thought and was written in his later life after his major philosophical masterpiece *Rāḥat al-ʿaql* to which he refers in this text.

The *Rasāʾil* (Epistles or Treatises) of the Ikhwān al-Ṣafāʾ, the enigmatic Brethren of Purity who lived in Iraq in the fourth/tenth century in the Shiʿite milieus of Basra and perhaps Baghdad, are not the product of a single figure, Arab or Persian, but a group nurtured in a climate dominated by both Arab and Persian elements. Even their Ismāʿīlī affiliation has been doubted by some scholars in favor of a more general Shiʿite character. They were, however, claimed later specifically by the Ismāʿīlīs; the treatise entitled *Risālat al-jāmiʿah* (The Treatise of Summation), which summarizes the teachings of the *Rasāʾil*, and the even more esoteric *Jāmiʿat al-jāmiʿah* (The Summation of the Summation) especially were not only Ismāʿīlī texts but were also used as esoteric works taught only to those who had reached the higher levels in the hierarchy of Ismāʿīlī initiation. They were not even available to the general public until fairly recently. The *Rasāʾil*, therefore, belong to any general treatment of Ismāʿīlī philosophy as it developed in Persia, although their influence went far beyond the Ismāʿīlī, or even the general Shiʿite world, and there were few major Shiʿite or Sunni figures of later Islamic thought, concerned with the esoteric dimension of Islam, who were not familiar with it, including such colossal figures as Ghazzālī, Ibn ʿArabī, and Mullā Ṣadrā.

What is of particular interest in the *Rasāʾil* is not only their assertion of the esoteric nature of true philosophy, grades of initiation, and degrees of knowledge and the wedding between philosophy and spiritual realization combined with moral rectitude so characteristic of Ismāʿīlī philosophy in general, but their clear exposition of Islamic Pythagoreanism and Hermeticism. No single treatise in Islamic philosophy is in fact more impregnated with Pythagorean ideas integrated into the Islamic perspective as are the *Rasāʾil*. This is to be seen especially in the treatise on arithmetic, which is without doubt one of the major sources for understanding the Islamic philosophy of mathematics, but also in the treatises on music, geometry, astronomy—in fact, practically throughout the fifty-one treatises that constitute the *Rasāʾil*. Herein is to be found an exposition in depth of the *quadrivium* and the *trivium* as these disciplines were understood in the medieval West and going back to Greek philosophy and the *artes liberales* of Cicero.

The selections chosen from the *Rasāʾil* deal not only with this Pythagorean philosophy but also with the Hermetic idea of the relation between the microcosm and macrocosm, which Muslims trace back to ʿAlī ibn Abī Ṭālib. Extensive correspondences are described by the Ikhwān between the structure of the human state and the structures of the heavens and the earth; detailed resemblances are shown between man and the three kingdoms of minerals, plants, and animals, which are synthesized in man's being.

The selections from the *Rasāʾil* conclude with a section on the debate between man and the animals, who argue about their respective rights before the king of the *jinn*. This writing by the Ikhwān is one of the most pertinent in the annals of Islamic philosophy as far as the current environmental crisis is concerned. At a time when man is usurping the rights of other creatures and destroying the natural environment on the assumption of his absolute rights over creation, the philosophical arguments provided by the Ikhwān concerning the rights of animals are of incredible timeliness and display an "ecological philosophy" that is of the greatest significance for the formulation of an Islamic philosophy of the environment and a response to the current environmental crisis.

Of all the Ismāʿīlī figures presented in this volume, Muʾayyad fiʾl-Dīn Shīrāzī is in a sense the least philosophical. Yet, as one of the greatest figures of Fāṭimid Ismāʿīlism, his expositions of the tenets of Ismāʿīlī teachings are both authoritative and revealing as far as the philosophical dimensions of Ismāʿīlī theological doctrines are concerned. Shīrāzī deals, in the selections from his *Jāmiʿat al-ḥaqāʾiq* (The Sum of Truths), first of all with *taʾwīl*, which means literally taking something back to its source, based on the metaphysical principle that all that is manifested or revealed has an inward (*bāṭin*) and an outward (*ẓāhir*) aspect and issues from the inward to the outward. *Taʾwīl* is therefore a casting aside of the veil of outwardness or *kashf al-maḥjūb*, a term used by both Sufis and Shiʿites to denote not arbitrary rejection of the outward form but of reaching the inward through the outward with the aid of a science, which comes from the dimension of inwardness associated with the Imam in Shiʿism. *Taʾwīl* can be said to be a hermeneutic interpretation if the term hermeneutics is understood in its original sense as dealing with the inner mystery of things which was the function of Hermes to reveal or unveil according to Hermeticism.

With this understanding in mind, Shīrāzī, then, deals with the "initiatic power" (*walāyah/wilāyah*) associated in the Islamic revelation with ʿAlī and the necessity of the Imam, who is the inheritor of the power of *walāyah/wilāyah*, and the guide for those who aspire to carry out *taʾwīl* with respect to both revelation in the sense of sacred scripture and that primordial revelation which is the cosmos. As an example, Shīrāzī applies the method of *taʾwīl* to the understanding of the famous *ḥadīth* of the Prophet, "I am the city of knowledge and ʿAlī is its gate," in which the "gate" itself is identified as the science of *taʾwīl*. He also follows the teachings of the sixth Shiʿite Imam, Jaʿfar al-Ṣādiq, in providing a profound metaphysical interpretation of another well-known *ḥadīth*, "he who knows himself knows his Lord," in which Shīrāzī has recourse to specifically Ismāʿīlī ideas and terms such as *ḥadd* (pl. *ḥudūd*) or limit(s), which is associated by Ismāʿīlism with the hierarchy of being and which he calls "the parents of the soul." It needs hardly to be emphasized how significant these ideas are for the understanding of Ismāʿīlī philosophy and theosophy and also how fecund they are philosophically speaking even independent of the Ismāʿīlī matrix within which they were cultivated.

With Nāṣir-i Khusraw we reach in many ways the peak of Ismāʿīlī philosophy. Some Persian scholars have even gone so far as to consider him the most challenging of Persian philosophers. The selection presented in this volume deals most of all with the relation between religion and philosophy or faith and reason, which has been of concern to all Islamic philosophers. Like other Ismāʿīlī philosophers, Nāṣir-i Khusraw identifies philosophy with the inner dimension of religion and seeks to harmonize what he calls the *ḥikmatayn* or two philosophies/wisdoms (that is, philosophy and wisdom derived from the intellect and from revelation), this harmonization being the basic theme of his most important work, the *Jāmiʿ al-ḥikmatayn* (The Sum of the Two Wisdoms). To this end he elaborates on the correspondences between man and the cosmos, cycles of prophecy, and the history and grades of Ismāʿīlī initiation. He speaks of the seven angelic lights and the seven prophets, and provides a philosophical explanation of such realities as angels, *parīs* (fairies), and devils—all of whom possess a specifically religious significance and play a major role in the religious cosmos. Through these explanations one gains a glimpse of a rhapsodic Ismāʿīlī vision of reality dominated by the number 7 so central to Ismāʿīlī philosophy and theology and mentioned in the Quran and Ḥādīth in relation to the structure of both the heavens and the earth.

Nāṣir-i Khusraw also delves deeply into the meaning and significance of the intellect (*ʿaql*) and its relation to knowledge. He accentuates the general Shiʿite emphasis on the significance of the intellect, an emphasis central to an understanding of why—as already mentioned in general, although not necessarily always—Shiʿite theology and jurisprudence were more favorable to the intellectual sciences, of which philosophy is the heart, than were the majority of Sunni theologians and jurists and why an antiphilosophical *kalām* such as the Ashʿarites did not have its equivalence in Shiʿite theology despite the deep interaction between Sunni and Shiʿite theologies

The section on Nāṣir-i Khusraw includes a discussion of cosmology drawn from his *Gushāyish wa rahāyish* (Knowledge and Liberation), which contains a most penetrating example of early Ismāʿīlī thought concerned with the complicated questions of the genesis of the world, its newness or eternity, and similar issues that have been of concern to philosophers and theologians in Persia over the ages. Being the great moralist and philosophical poet that he was, Nāṣir-i Khusraw could not be included in this volume without a sample of his poetry. A few philosophical poems are therefore presented to bring to a close the selection of his writings.

Selections from the Ismāʿīlī writings of Naṣīr al-Dīn Ṭūsī who was not only an expositor of Ismāʿīlī teachings, but also a leading Peripatetic (*mashshāʾī*) philosopher as well as the founder of Twelve Imam Shiʿite rational theology, brings this volume to a close. This section begins with a segment of Ṭūsī's *Sayr wa sulūk* ("Contemplation and Action"), which has an autobiographical element within it although also dealing with philosophical issues. The title of the work means literally "spiritual wayfaring" and is associated especially with Sufism. But in this work Ṭūsī deals more with his intellectual journey rather than with personal spiritual matters. Because he is one of the greatest intellectual figures in Persian history, at once supreme philosopher, theologian, and scientist, his own account of his intellectual journey is of great interest for the understanding of the tradition of Islamic philosophy in Persia in general.

In the *Sayr wa sulūk* Ṭūsī explains his early attraction, after studying *Uṣūl* or the principles of religion and the Sacred Law, to the intellectual sciences and his study of theology and philosophy. But in turning to the study of the supreme object of metaphysics, that is the Divine Reality, Ṭūsī gives an account of how he realized that ordinary philosophy was not enough and that there was the necessity of a "truthful instructor" and "instruction" (*taʿlīm*) from an infallible teacher who had received knowledge of God from God Himself. Herein lies the specifically Ismāʿīlī nature of this treatise for this view of receiving instruction (*taʿlīm*) from the infallible Imam was so characteristic of the Ismāʿīlīs that they came to be known in Islamic society at large also as "those who receive instruction" (*taʿlimiyān*). In discussing the necessity of instruction in the particular sense given to it by Ismāʿīlī doctrines, Ṭūsī also discusses the nature of the Divine Intellect in its relation to the human intellect and the whole act of intellection.

As for selections of Ṭūsī drawn from his *Taṣawwurāt* (Notions), they begin with the definition of the soul (*nafs*) in its various levels of reality and distinct from the intellect. Ṭūsī emphasizes the supreme importance of knowledge (*ʿilm*), which is the ultimate goal of the soul and whose realization marks the soul's perfection. He also discusses the level of intelligence within human beings, going back to Ibn Sīnā's enumeration of the four stages of the intellect. Ṭūsī then turns to the human body and why the soul becomes attached to it. In the manner of the Ikhwān al-Ṣafāʾ, Ṭūsī compares the body to a city while he also considers the stages of the growth of the body from its inception in the womb until its birth, a process governed at each stage by one of the planets.

In a section of particular interest for understanding the continuities and discontinuities of the philosophical tradition of Persia, Ṭūsī discusses the nature of good and evil and points out that they are not ontologically equivalent. He explicitly rejects the usual understanding of Zoroastrian dualism in which Yazdān and Ahrīman, to use Ṭūsī's language, are opposite forces of good and evil that seem to possess the same ontological status. Throughout its long history, Persian thought has been concerned with the question of good and evil, but with the advent of Islam, which emphasizes unity above all else, the metaphysical background of the ethical discussion changed and even those such as Suhrawardī who supported the wisdom of the ancient Persian philosophers (*ḥukamā-yi furs*) asserted that these sages were unitarians and did not believe in dualism and the ontological equivalence of good and evil.

Ṭūsī then turns to *taʾwīl*, in the time-honored sense of the term as already discussed, to deal with the thorny issue of the newness or eternity of the world. He asserts that time is cyclic and in each cycle there is a new world that did not exist before. Therefore, *this* world is not eternal but new (*ḥādith*). Yet, there is always *a* world but not *this* world that did not exist in the last cycle and will cease to exist in the next cycle. As there is always *a* world, there is also always *a* humanity but not the humanity of this cycle. In each world man must be present because he is the final purpose of the world. Ṭūsī also deals in greater detail with the seven smaller cycles of cosmic history, each cycle consisting of seven thousand years after which—that is, after forty-nine thousand years—the Great Resurrection takes place and the whole of present creation reaches the end of its cycle.

The subjects and themes treated by the major Ismāʿīlī philosophers of Persia in this volume constitute the heart of Ismāʿīlī philosophy as such and have been treasured by later Ismāʿīlī thinkers of not only Persia itself but also of the Yemen, India, Syria, and other lands where much of the later Ismāʿīlī writings saw the light of day. But it must be remembered that this Ismāʿīlī philosophical tradition is not to be identified solely with the Ismāʿīlī branch of Shiʿism. Rather, it belongs to the integral tradition of Islamic philosophy as well as Shiʿite thought in general. Like Sufism, Ismāʿīlism and Twelve-Imam Shiʿism drew their inspiration, knowledge—in fact their very existence—from the esoteric dimension of the Islamic tradition, and their philosophy bears the imprint of that source. That is why Ismāʿīlism shared certain ideas with Sufism and after the Mongol invasion it went underground in Persia to appear in many places as a form of Sufism. In this context it is noteworthy that one of the greatest masterpieces of Persian Sufi poetry, the *Gulshan-i rāz* (The Secret Garden of Divine Mysteries) of Maḥmūd Shabistarī had not only later Sufi commentators but also Ismāʿīlī ones.

Ismāʿīlī philosophy also shares much with later Islamic philosophy as it developed in Persia in the Twelve-Imam Shiʿite milieu created by the Safavids. It is true that it was most of all Mullā Ṣadrā who, in the eleventh/seventeenth century, drew the full implications of the philosophical saying of the Shiʿite Imams, as one observes in his commentary upon Kulaynī's *Uṣūl al-kāfī* (The Sufficient Principles). But long before Mullā Ṣadrā, the early Ismāʿīlī philosophers drew to a large extent from the teachings of the Shiʿite Imams whom, up to and including the sixth Imam Jaʿfar al-Ṣādiq, they shared with the Twelve-Imam Shiʿites. That is why they must be considered as being among the predecessors of Mullā Ṣadrā from the point of view of the exposition of the philosophical dimension of the esoteric teachings of the Imams. It should be added that Mullā Ṣadrā was in fact familiar with some of their writings. In any case, Ismāʿīlī philosophy is an important manifestation of philosophical thought in Persia related in profound ways to Sufism on the one hand and the later flowering of philosophy in the Shiʿite Persia of the Safavid period on the other. The Ismāʿīlī philosophical tradition also created some of the most important philosophical works in the Persian language and left an indelible mark upon the development of Persian as a vehicle for philosophical discourse, a vehicle that was to be used continuously by Persian philosophers through the centuries continuing in fact up to today.

Ismāʿīlī philosophy provides teachings of great depth about time and eternity, cosmic cycles, the nature of the *anthropos*, a metaphysics based not on Being but the Absolute as Beyond-Being whose first manifestation is Being, a cosmology related to the hierarchy of spiritual beings, the relation between religion in its formal aspect and philosophy or reason and revelation and many other basic philosophical themes. It is certainly one of the major schools of Islamic philosophy associated in its early centuries nearly completely with Persia and also to a large extent with the Persian language. Although Ismāʿīlism went underground in Persia after the Mongol Invasion, its influence in later schools of philosophy, theology and even certain strands of Sufism is evident while the major philosophical works written by such figures as Abū Ḥātim Rāzī, Ḥamīd al-Dīn Kirmānī and Nāṣir-i Khusraw, not to speak of the *Rasāʾil* of the Ikhwān al-Ṣafāʾ written by both Arabs and Persians, are among outstanding monuments of the long tradition of philosophy in Persia.

—*S. H. Nasr*

I

UMM AL-KITĀB

Written in archaic Persian, *Umm-al-kitāb* is a major work of the early Shiʿi Imāmī tradition that addresses an array of religious and philosophical issues. While its author is unknown, the date of its authorship is said to be anywhere from the second half of the second/eighth century to the end of fourth/tenth century. Recent scholarship attributes the book to a Shiʿite sect called al-Mukhammasah, and was preserved among the Ismāʿīlīs of Central Asia. This is evident not only in the doctrinal and cosmological features of the treatise but also because of such nuances as attributing a major role in the rise of Islam to Salmān al-Fārsī, whose gnostic name here is al-Salsāl. He is also regarded as a gate through whom one could have access to Muḥammadan Light.

The treatise contains a discourse of the fifth Shiʿite Imām, Muḥammad al-Bāqir (d. 114/732), who appears here as a five-year-old child, the situation strongly resembling certain apocryphal Gospels relating to Jesus. Imām al-Bāqir responds in this treatise to thirty questions raised by a group of disciples among whom Jābir ibn ʿAbd Allāh Anṣārī, Jaʿfar al-Jūʿfī, Abuʾl-Khaṭṭāb, Abuʾl-Khālid Kābilī, and Muḥammad ibn Mufaḍḍal can be named.

Umm al-kitāb offers an esoteric hermeneutics (taʾwīl) of the nature of man and his place in the universe, as well as of questions concerning cosmology, epistemology, and Islamic worship within a Quranic context. The analysis and interpretations offered in this treatise seem to be a synthesis of many different religious traditions and schools of thought, such as Manichaeanism, Buddhism, Ismāʿīlism, and Valentinian gnosticism.

The central idea in the work is the psychological and philosophical interpretation of cosmological symbols, and the faithful are asked to engage themselves in acts of inner purification and transformation. Throughout the work, the "theology of light" pervades every doctrine. An extraordinary number of colors are displayed to symbolize different theurgies and the corresponding levels of consciousness that man must realize within himself.

This text, which remains part of the corpus of the Ismāʿīlī intellectual literature to this day, is held in high esteem particularly by the Nizārī Ismāʿīlī community surviving in Afghanistan, Wakhan, and Chitral in the upper Oxus and more generally in the Pamir range. The selection treats primarily the subject of man and the esoteric and philosophical significance of the Quran and the symbolic significance of worship in Islam.

—*M. Aminrazavi*

Umm al-kitāb

THE MOTHER OF BOOKS

[4] This book is called the "Mother of Books" (*Umm al-kitāb*), because it is the capital (*sarmāyah*) of all the books. Every kind of knowledge which exists in this world is extracted from this book. This book is called the "Mother of the Books" (*Umm al-kitāb*), [5] that means whoever reads this book it is such that once for all he becomes independent of every science. This book is called the "Spirit of the Books" (*rūḥ al-kitāb*), for it is the spirit of all the books, and essence (*maʿnī*) of all the books. There is insight [about everything] in this book. It is called the "Light of the Books" (*nūr al-kitāb*), because the [the explication of the] light of the heavens and the earth is given in it. It is called the "All-embracing doctrines" (*wāṣiʿ al-maqālāt*), because it reveals the seven divine doctrines. [6] It is called the "Seven Disputes" (*sabʿ al-mujādalāt*), because the seven disputes between Iblīs and Adam are given in it. It is called the "Exalter of Degrees" (*rafīʿ al-darajāt*) [Qurʾān, 40:15], because the degree and the essence of the believers and the infidels and those spirits are known by this book. It is called the "Bearer of good tidings" (*bashīr al-mubāsharāt*), because it is the herald of good tidings to the believers who attain liberation and salvation by [following] this book. It is called the "Ten Articles" (*ʿashr al-maqālāt*), because the attribute of ten cosmic palaces and the mode of ten spirits is known through this book. It is called the "Seven Manifestations" (*sabʿ al-ẓuhūrāt*), because the attribute of seven physical and spiritual cycles in its real sense is given in this book. It is called the "Book of Reward" (*Kitāb al-mujāzāt*), because the reward and punishment for the believers and infidels of the microcosm and macrocosm are described in it. It is called the "Book of Mothers" (*Kitāb al-ummahāt*), because it is the root and essence of Tawrāt, Injīl, Zabūr, Furqān [Qurʾān], and [the essence of] every scripture which exists in the world [8] is given in this book.

This book was composed in the city of Mecca in the locality of Quraysh b.Hāshim, in the house of ʿAbd al-Manāf, and was found in the treasury of Bāqir

This translation is based on the *Ummuʾl-kitāb*, edited by W. Ivanow, *Der Islam*, 23 (1963), pp. 1–32.

al-Salām. Jaʿfar [al-] Juʿfī[1] brought it to Kufa. In the time of Hārūn [al-Rashīd], ʿAlī ibn ʿAbd al-ʿAẓīm brought it to Iraq. After his death it was handed over to the believers and [his] apostles as a trust to be safeguarded from the undeserving. The believers, the unitarians (*muwaḥḥidān*) and [9] the chiefs have not exposed it to any dissident person, nor have they spoken about it to any creature. That is because not every believer can comprehend this knowledge, for this is that category of knowledge which transcends our comprehension and imagination and we are not receptive to it except he who is a unified believer, or a dispatched prophet or a cherub. That is why their hearts are full of the light of divine unity. [Apart from them] no other believer has any capacity to stomach this knowledge of the realm of Mysteries. [If he endeavors in it] he only wastes his life and thereby suffers the loss of life. [10]

The attribute of the unity of the Creator, glorified be His majesty, is known through this book. Also, the realities of God's creation from behind the highest veil, the veil of the believer, the attribute of the Throne, the Pedestal, the Tablet, the Pen, the veils of the spirits of believers, unbelievers and the dissidents and 'how' and 'why' [they are so] are known through this book. Moreover, [the account of] existence, non-existence, the knowledge of the Exalted Lord, glorified be His majesty, five angels in the seven divine and human cycles is known [11] through this book. Also, the seven debates between Iblis and Adam and the total creation whether it is possible or impossible to comprehend and imagine, has been revealed in this book from the discourses of Bāqir, may peace be upon us from him, for "He it is Who has revealed unto thee the Book wherein are clear signs—they are the *umm al-kitāb*, and others are *mutashābihāt*" [Qur'ān, 3:7]. This book is named the *Umm al-kitāb* of Bāqir, and is the *Umm al-kitāb* of Bāqir al-ʿIlm, may peace be upon us from him. [12]

When Bāqir was born and came into existence, he said to [his mother] Āminah, the 'mother of all believers', "The *āyāt* (signs) which are clear are the *umm al-kitāb*" [Qurʾān, 3:7]. When he was sent to school, the divine power (*farrah-i īzadī*) of wisdom and inspirational knowledge (*ʿilm-i taʾyīdī*)[2] manifested through him which no teacher knew. Jābir ibn ʿAbdallāh al-Anṣārī narrates that when Bāqir al-ʿIlm, may peace be upon us from him, was only a child of five he was sent for education to ʿAbdallāh Ṣabbāḥ. ʿAbdallāh, according [13] to the custom of the teachers, gave him a clean silver tablet on which twenty-nine letters of the alphabets were written. He said to him. "Recite *alif* [the first letter of the Arabic alphabet]." Bāqir said, "*Alif*." Then ʿAbdallāh said "recite *bāʾ* [the second letter of the Arabic alphabet]." Bāqir said, "Until you explain to me the meaning of *alif* I will not recite *bāʾ*." ʿAbdallāh said, "O the delight of the eyes of believ-

1. Jābir (or) Jaʿfar al-Juʿfī, (d.128/746), known as one of the noteworthy *ghulāt* in the circle of the sixth Shīʿīte Imam Jaʿfar al-Sādiq. Cf. W. Madelung, "Djābir al-Djuʿfī", in *EI2*, Supplement, pp. 232–33.

2. The term *taʾyīd* is a verbal noun derived from the verb *ayyada*. The notion of *taʾyīd* conveys the idea of assistance and divine inspiration which is a source of supernatural wisdom. This notion is derived from the two verses of the Qurʾān (2:87 and 253) in which God says about Jesus, "We inspired him (*ayyadnāhu*) with the Holy Spirit."

ers, O Bāqir, recite *alif*." Then he said, "*Alif* is for Allāh, 'there is no deity save Him the Ever-living the Self-subsistent' [Qur'ān, 2:255]'." [Bāqir] said O ʿAbdallāh, "*Alif* [or A in the word] Allāh stands for God and [the letter] *lām* stands for Muḥammad. *Alif* signifies the spirit of Muḥammad. It consists of three letters and a [diacritical] point, [14] which are *alif, lām, fāʾ* and the *nuqṭah* [the point]. *Alif* stands for Muḥammad, *lām* for ʿAlī [ibn Abī Ṭālib], *fāʾ* for Fāṭimah, and *nuqṭah* for Ḥasan and Ḥusayn. [The two names] Ḥasan and Ḥusayn end with *nuqṭah* so does *alif*.

ʿAbdallāh was astonished to hear [this explanation] and said, "O the light of the eyes of believers, this [knowledge] is strange. What thou art saying regarding the description and characteristics of *alif* is not from any book written by a man." Bāqir replied, "That is how the book of us, the *ahl al-bayt* [the family of the Prophet], has been in every cycle and period. O ʿAbdallāh, *alif* [corresponds to] the place of the throne and seat of God, the Mighty and Majestic. [15] It is called the Vital Rational Spirit (*rūḥ al-ḥayāt-i nāṭiqah*) which [dwells] in the brain of the believers. *Lām* [corresponds to] the Luminous Spirit (*rūḥ-i rawshanī*), *fāʾ* to the Spirit of Invincibility (*rūḥ al-jabarūt*), and *nuqṭah* to the Reflective Spirit (*rūḥ al-fikr*). Above the non-spherical *alif* there is a spirit which is the veil of ʿAlī, may peace be upon us from him. *Alif* also [corresponds to] the spirit of ʿAlī, *lām* to the radiance of ʿAlī, *fāʾ* to the reflection of the spirit of revelation of ʿAlī, and *nuqṭah* to the luminous speech of ʿAlī which encompasses the thirty letters [of the alphabet]."

ʿAbdallāh Ṣabbāḥ was greatly astonished [to hear such an explanation] so he said, "O son of the Messenger of God, by God, indeed by God the most exalted, this is the divine guidance. I have never heard such knowledge from any master before. How strange that thou hast been sent to learn from me! How strange that thou who hast never been sent to any teacher before, nor hast read a book nor hast seen any learned man [to speak of such astonishing knowledge]! O the fruit of the heart of the believers, what kind of situation is this. For it is not lawful for anyone to teach a science to people when he himself is ignorant of it. I wanted to teach thee *alif*, I never knew that I will end up learning from thee. O the eyes of Muḥammad and ʿAlī, complete [thy] favor by giving me the explanation of [the letters] *bāʾ* and *tāʾ*. May [God's] mercy be upon thy parents." [17]

Bāqir replied, "O my learned teacher, *bāʾ* is the threshold of *alif*. *Alif* [corresponds] to Muḥammad, and *bāʾ* to ʿAlī. The [diacritical] point [under] *bāʾ* [corresponds to] the speech of ʿAlī. *Alif* [is like] the Luminous Spirit, and *bāʾ* the Vital Spirit of the brain, whereas the diacritical point is like the speech (*nuṭq*). O my learned teacher, tell me what is the first letter of the alphabet?" ʿAbdallāh replied, "*Alif*." Bāqir said, "By what reasoning?" ʿAbdallāh replied, "O the eyes of the believers, I do not know more than this." Then Bāqir said, "O ʿAbdallāh, all these learned people [18] are really ignorant teachers. They really do not know whether *alif* is the first [letter of the alphabet] or *bāʾ*. The first letter of the alphabet is *bāʾ*, then comes *alif*. *Bā* stands for ʿAlī, and *alif* stands for Muḥammad. Outwardly Muḥammad is prior [to ʿAlī] and ʿAlī is the threshold (*bāb*) of Muḥammad. [Just as] in order to enter the house one has to go through the gate, [similarly] in order to reach Muḥammad [one has to go] through ʿAlī. Both Muḥammad and ʿAlī are one [reality, as] *alif* and *bāʾ* are one [reality]. The [diacritical] point of *alif* is hidden, [similarly] the speech of Muḥammad is [in the] veiled [form]. But the [diacritical] point of *bāʾ* is manifest [like] the speech of ʿAlī which is manifest by [19] the light of knowledge. These infidels who are from the nest of Ahrīman know the way (*sharīʿah*) of Muḥammad, and they protect it, but as for the way (*sharīʿah*) of ʿAlī, they have no knowledge about it. For Muḥammad is [like] this world and ʿAlī the next world. The truth of this matter is affirmed by the saying of Him the Exalted, "They know the outward significance of the life of this world, but of the next world they are heedless" [Qurʾān, 30:7].

[Bāqir continued, and said,] "O ʿAbdallāh, is the first letter of the alphabet the point or *bāʾ*?" ʿAbdallāh replied, "O the eyes of Muḥammad I do not know unless I hear from you." Bāqir said, "the first letter of the [Arabic, or Persian] alphabets [20] is the 'point'. The point [corresponds] to the speech of the believers who are attributed with speech. *Bāʾ* [corresponds to] the Spirit which [dwells] between the two eyebrows, and *alif* [corresponds to] the physical body. So [the alphabets] begin by the point, followed by *bāʾ* and then *alif*. O ʿAbdallāh, you are my learned teacher, [tell me] out of the two which one is bigger *alif* or camel." ʿAbdallāh replied, [21] "I know neither the *alif* nor the camel unless I hear from you." Bāqir said, "The *alif* [is bigger.] It is the Luminous Spirit (*rūḥ-i rawshanāʾī*). The love and brotherhood amongst the believers are due to it. The camel is [also] a spirit. In spirituality its name is 'rational soul' (*nafs-i nāṭiqah*)." Then ʿAbdallāh said, "O the fruit of the heart of the believers, is it true, what they say, that *alif* is bigger [than the camel] because in writing it is possible to stretch *alif* as much as one could?" Bāqir replied, "*Alif* [corresponds to] the Spirit [whose seat is] the brain. It is called the Spirit of Faith (*rūḥ-i īmān*) and is above the Vital Conscious Spirit (*rūḥ al-ḥayāt-i nāṭiqah*). It testifies to eight other Spirits which are above it and are interconnected within the Spirit of Faith which englobes [everything] from the earth to the heaven. The first one is the Spirit of Preservation (*rūḥ-i ḥifẓ*) of the Guarded Tablet of the Exalted King. It is concealed within the Spirit of Faith. [22] The next one is the Spirit of Reflection (*rūḥ-i fikr*) of the Pen of the [Guarded] Tablet. It is concealed within the Spirit of Preservation. Then comes the Spirit of Invincibility (*rūḥ-i jabarūt*) which is concealed within the Spirit of Reflection. The next one is the Spirit of Knowledge (*rūḥ al-ʿilm*) which is concealed within the Spirit of Invincibility. Then there is the Spirit of Intellect (*ruḥ al-ʿaql*) which is concealed within the Spirit of Knowledge. Then there is the Sacred Spirit (*rūḥ-i-quddūs*) which is concealed within the Spirit of Intellect. The next one is the Supreme Spirit (*rūḥ al-akbar*) which is the Universal Spirit (*rūḥ-i kullī*); it is hidden in the Sacred Spirit. Finally there is the Sublime Spirit (*rūḥ-i aʿẓam*) which is hidden in the Supreme Spirit. [23] O ʿAbdallāh, all of them are interconnected, hence it is said alif is bigger [than the camel]."

Question XII

Then Jābir said, "O [251] my Lord, what is the Qurʾān?"

Bāqir replied, "The Qurʾān is the Eloquent Spirit (*rūḥ-i nāṭiqah*), as the Exalted Sovereign said, 'This is our Book which speaks to you the Truth' [Qurʾān, 45:28].

It signifies that our Book is the true Word and Speech. In the macrocosm Salmān al-qudrah is the chant of the Exalted Sovereign. [This chant] is his speech from the Spirit of Enunciation. Salmān is also the Last Day and the Great Day. 'The Qur'ān is the Speech (*kalām*) of God which is uncreated, so whoever says it is created is an unbeliever in God, the Almighty.' That is to say, this Salmān al-qudrah[3] is [252] the Qur'ān and the chant of God. Whosoever does not testify to it is an unbeliever in God. O Jābir, the significance of this discourse is that the Qur'ān is the speech of God which is the uncreated Salmān. Likewise, the chant (*āwāz*) of the Exalted Sovereign is uncreated unlike the Dissident Spirits, so 'whoever says it is created is an unbeliever in God the Sublime.' It signifies that these unbelievers have been manifested by the chant of ʿAzāzīl and have [therefore] become unbelievers in the Exalted Sovereign, both in the Macrocosm and in the Microcosm. When the Exalted Sovereign said, 'He is the Lord of those who believe, and the disbelievers have no Lord', [Qur'ān, 47:12] He indicated that, He was not the Lord [253] of the concupiscent soul, nor of the reproved anima.

"The Eloquent Spirit also effuses benevolence, quietude and compassion upon the Pacified Spirit (*rūḥ-i muṭma'innah*). But it does not benefit the Captive Spirit (*rūḥ-i ḥabsī*), the Concupiscent Soul (*nafs-i ḥissī*) and the dissident Adam; rather [it causes] their destruction. Muḥammad to whom the Qur'ān was revealed is the Pacified Spirit [which dwells] in this heart which is placed at the center of the seven firmaments and twelve constellations."

Then Jābir said, "O my Lord, do elucidate its meaning." Bāqir replied, "This earth which is called the 'heart' [254] is placed amidst the four natures. The water is wetness, the air is sanguine, the fire is yellow bile and the earth is black bile. The sphere of the moon is the bone-marrow, the sphere of Venus is the fat, the sphere of the sun is the blood-vessels, the sphere of Mars is the blood, the sphere of Jupiter is the flesh, the sphere of Saturn is the skin, and the Outermost Sphere is the Eloquent Vital Spirit (*rūḥ al-ḥayāt-i nāṭiqah*) which glories Him [the Exalted Sovereign] in all the spheres. 'Everything in the sphere glorifies [Him]' [Qur'ān, 21:33].

From the twelve constellations, six rotate [255] above the earth which are: Aries which [corresponds] to the head, Taurus to neck, Gemini to hands, Cancer to chest, Leo to abdomen, Virgo to back. These six constellation signs are placed above the heart. Six [constellations] are below the heart which are naval [corresponding] to Libra, the genitals to Scorpio, thighs to Saggitarius, knees to Capricorn, legs to Aquarius, and feet to Pisces. These constellations are placed below the heart.

The Pacified Spirit is [the symbol] of Muḥammad. The Light of Effulgence (*nūr-i rawshanā'ī*) passes from the Eloquent Spirit to all parts of the body via the white vein and then enters the heart and awakens the Dissident Spirit (*rūh-i muʿtariḍah*) from the slumber of heedlessness. This Spirit-Light is connected to the White Sea of the Macrocosm and Microcosm and from there to the heart."

3. Here Salmān al-qudrah is the gnostic name of Salmān al-Fārisī. He was a Persian who was taken into the household of the Prophet. Later he became the model of spiritual adoption and mystical initiation in Shiʿism and Sufism. Cf. Louis Massignon, "Salmān Pāk et les prémices spirituelles de l'Islam iranien", *Société des études iraniennes*, 7, (1934).

Question XIII

Then Jaʿfar-i Juʿfī got up and said, "O my Lord, what kind of state is this that at times I see dreams which cannot be narrated to anyone; at times I see strange things in the dreams which have not been seen in the waking state?"

Bāqir al-ʿIlm replied, "If you see any dream of the moon, the sun, the angels, the cherubs in this azure dome, [then know that] that is seen by the Luminous Spirit. A dream of the Prophets, the Imams, and the heavens is seen by the Spirit that has been tested (*rūḥ-i mumtaḥanah*); a dream about the state and condition of the world is seen by the Pacified Soul, and the dream which depicts murder, killing, adultery with women and pollution is seen by the Concupiscent Soul. Any time the Luminous Spirit transfers itself and departs from the summit of the Spirit that has been tested, the Spirit of the heart enters into the slumber of heedlessness. When the Conscious Spirit leaves the brain the Spirit of the heart goes into the sleep of ignorance. When the Pacified soul departs the whole body dies including the Concupiscent Soul and everything that is there in the body."

Question XV

Abuʾl-Khaṭṭāb[4] got up and recited the prayer of benediction and then said, "O my Lord, if it is not heavy for you then [please] explain [the meaning of] the Throne of the Exalted Sovereign as well as Bayt al-maʿmūr of Adam, the Ark of Noah, the birds of Abraham, the Mount Sinai of Moses, the birth of Jesus, the ascension (*miʿrāj*) of Muḥammad, and the [sword] Dhuʾl-fiqār of ʿAlī, to this weak servant and illuminate his rusted heart so that this servant is liberated by Thy [knowledge] and becomes Thy well-wisher."

Bāqir al-ʿIlm replied, "O Abū Khālid Kābilī (sic) [266], these seven cycles constitute the seven manifestations [whose knowledge] with such clarity was not given to anyone by the Exalted King except to Muḥammad, as He said, 'Say: the knowledge is with God only' [Qurʾān, 67:26]. [It means] 'O Muḥammad, only God and those who are proximate to Him know the knowledge of Resurrection.' There are many learned and enlightened theologians but they have no access to this knowledge. [I seek] protection [with God]! Attention! We have not read about this discourse in any book; nor have we written it in any book. This discourse has not been revealed to any prophet. You should safeguard it [267] as much as you can. Read it day and night to the believers and the obedient ones. The believers to whom this book reaches in inheritance should safeguard it and read it alone by themselves.

The first temple [of God], al-Bayt al-maʿmūr, was revealed to Adam. Adam is the Lord; He is the Spirit whose seat is the frontal lobe of the brain. One wall of the temple al-Bayt al-maʿmūr is made of pure silver, one is of red gold, one is of

4. Abūʿ l-Khaṭṭāb, a Kufan from the tribe of Asad, was one of the chief *dāʿīs* of Imām Jaʿfar al-Ṣādiq. He died around 145/762. Cf. *EI2*.

verdant chrysolite, and one is made of [268] red ruby. Its floor is made of yellow carnelians and its roof is made of white pearl. These are [the symbols of] six Spirits of different colors. The silver wall is [the symbol] of the Spirit of Faith; the gold wall [symbolizes] the Spirit of Preservation (*rūḥ al-ḥifẓ*); the chrysolite wall that of the Spirit of Invincibility; the ruby wall that of the Sacred Spirit. The floor which is made of carnelians is [the symbol of] the Spirit of Knowledge; the roof of the temple which is made of white pearl is the [symbol of the] Supreme Universal Spirit (*rūḥ al-akbar-i kull*), as [He] the most exalted says, 'By the Mount and the scripture inscribed on fine parchment unrolled, and the al Bayt al-maʿmūr and the exalted roof and the sea kept filled' [Qurʾān, 52:1–6]."

Question XVI

Abūʾl-Khālid Kābīlī [269] said, "O my Lord, what is the meaning of the Ark of Noah?"

Bāqir replied, "The Ark is also a [symbol] of the Spirits. The four walls of the Ark [symbolize] the Spirit of Faith, the Spirit of Preservation, the Spirit of Reflection and the Spirit of Knowledge. The roof of the Ark [symbolizes] the Luminous Consciousness (*nuṭq-i nūr*); the anchors . . . the sail of the Ark is the Extreme Temperament (*mizāj-i ghāyatī*); Noah is the Conscious Spirit, as [He] The Exalted said, 'And we carried him upon a thing of planks and nails' [Qurʾān, 54:13].

As for the four birds of Moses, one of them was the eagle, one was the peacock, one was the vulture, [270] and one was the heron. Abraham [symbolizes] the Vital Conscious Spirit which [dwells] in the frontal lobe of the brain and is the Lord of the Sublime Spirit. The eagle is the Spirit of Faith; the heron is the Reflective Spirit; the august Humā is the Sacred Spirit; and Vulture is the Spirit of Intellect which is the life of the Spirit of hearts (*rūḥ al-qulūb*). Whereas the Reflective Spirit is their captive, as He the Exalted said, 'Take four birds and cause them to incline unto thee, then place one of them on each hill, then call them, they will come to thee in haste' [Qurʾān, 2:260].

[271] Moses is the Vital Conscious Luminous Spirit. The rod of Moses is speech (*nuṭq*); Mount Sinai is the Spirit of Faith. [As He said,] 'We caused the Mount to tower above them.' [Qurʾān, 4:154]. The Pen is the Reflective Spirit; Gabriel is the Spirit of Invincibility; and God is the Sacred Spirit. Moses desired to see the beauty of the Exalted Sovereign, but He said, 'O Moses, you cannot see. Go and look at the Mount so that you see My power [Qurʾān, 7:143].' Moses looked at the Mount. The Exalted King emanated His splendor on the Mount which was shattered to pieces and Moses went into prostration. It means the Vital Spirit [272] of the brain is Moses. It is possible to see God by the Spirit of Faith, and Mount [Sinai] is the Spirit of Faith. The Splendor of the divine manifestation cannot settle on anything but the Spirit of Faith; it settles on the mount, [i.e.,] the heart of the believer. The splendor is the divine manifestation in the heart through the vein of Solar wind in which there is no blood. It signifies the manifestation of the Sublime Spirit, as He the Exalted said, 'And when Moses came to Our appointed tryst and his Lord had spoken unto him, he said, 'My Lord, show me [Thy

self], that I may gaze upon Thee.' He said 'Thou wilt not see Me, but gaze upon the Mountain. If [273] it stands still in its place, then thou wilt see Me'. And when his Lord revealed [His] glory to the Mountain, He sent it crashing down. And Moses fell down senseless' [Qurʾān, 7:143].

In reality [the word] Sinai is composed of seven letters and three dots. They [symbolize] the seven Spirits [dwelling] over the brain of the believers about which it has already been explained in many places.

There are three other Spirits beyond [those seven] whose names cannot be written in any book. The Pacified Soul ascends to this place through the vein of the Solar wind for the inner litany (*munājāt*) and [274] converses with the Sublime Spirit on this Mount Sinai which is an ensemble of seven mountains standing over each other. These are the seven spirits of seven colors from the seven thresholds and spheres (*dīwān*). They are: the Unified Spirit of Faith, the Spirit of Preservation, the Reflective Spirit, the Spirit of Invincibility, the Spirit of Knowledge, the Spirit of Intellect, and the seventh one is the Sacred Spirit.

The three Spirits above it are: the Supreme Spirit, the Sublime Spirit and the Extreme Temperament which is above everything. Moses is the Spirit of hearts; the Scripture Torah is the Vital Conscious Spirit [275]; the Israelites [symbolize] the Spirit in the liquid chamber [of the heart] and the Awaiting [Spirit] in the chamber of blood. The Spirit of Faith dwells above the Conscious Spirit. Those [Spirits] which are in the heart accept [the Spirit of Faith]. When it detaches from them, they fall in the sleep of heedlessness. He the Exalted said, "'When we shook the mount above them as it were a covering, and they supposed that it was going to fall upon them [and we said]' 'Hold fast that which We have given you and remember that which is therein, that ye may be pious.'" [Qurʾān, 7:171]

Jesus [symbolizes] [276] the Spirit of the brain; his mother Mary is the Spirit of Faith. At the time of giving birth [to Jesus] she went to the Siloan fountain. At the edge of the fountain was a palm tree which was dried up. The fountain which was also dried up, started flowing with water by the grace of Jesus, and the tree also became green and fresh. Jesus could not separate from his mother, so God the Exalted and Sublime sent His Spirit of Revelation to Jesus that he should tell his mother to shake the palm tree so that the ripe dates fall down which she should eat so that her labor pain eases. So Jesus called his mother from the womb and said, 'O [277] mother, shake this tree so that the ripe dates fall; then eat those dates so that I am born without incurring any pain to you.' So Mary shook the palm tree, the ripe dates fell down which she ate and Jesus was born [without much pain].

Jesus [is the symbol of] the Vital Conscious Luminous Spirit which calls from beneath the Spirit of Faith by the power of the Extreme Temperament which is Gabriel. After every hour it kicks the tree which is the Spirit of Reflection, and drops different kinds of knowledge which become sustenance for the Spirit [of Reflection] and [for many other] Spirits. Mary is the Spirit of Faith. The green tree is the Spirit of Reflection which is of verdant color [278]. It contemplates upon the divine sciences without having read or heard [any sciences], and comes to fruition like a date. Gabriel is the Spirit of Invincibility. It is connected with the coming and going between the Conscious [Spirit] and the Azure Dome, and is the

Lord of the Extreme Temperament. Beneath it is Jesus, the Sacred Spirit. Mary is the Conscious Spirit (*rūḥ-i nāṭiqah*); the palm-tree is the Spirit of Faith, and the fountain is the Light of God, the Sublime Spirit. As He the Exalted said, "And she conceived him, and she withdrew with him to a far place. And the pangs of childbirth drove her unto the trunk of the palm-tree. She said 'O, would I that I had died ere this and become a thing of naught, forgotten.' Then [one] cried unto her from below her, saying: Grieve not. Thy Lord hath placed a brook beneath thee. And shake the trunk of the palm-tree toward thee, thou wilt cause ripe dates to fall upon thee' [Qur'ān, 19:22–25]."

Question XVII

Abū'l-Khālid Kābilī said, "O my Lord, what is [the significance of] Muḥammad and his Ascension (*mi'rāj*)?"

Bāqir replied, "As for the Ascension of Muḥammad, first of all the Exalted King sent Gabriel to the earth. Muḥammad was sleeping. [Gabriel] said [to him], "Wake up. This is not the time of the night [280] for you to sleep. 'O thou wrapped up in thy raiment! Rise, the night . . .'" [Qur'ān, 73:1–2]. Muḥammad sat on Burāq and went to the Sacred Precinct (*al-Bayt al-muqaddas*). There he put his foot on the rock, and from there he crossed the seven heavens and reached at 'two bows'-length'. From there he ascended to the throne, then to the Pedestal, Tablet, Pen and then he crossed five thousand veils and reached in the presence of the Exalted King where he spoke and listened to ninety thousand words. Then he returned to his house. His bed was still warm. The news [of his ascension] spread among the Arabs [281] who did not believe it.

[Its interpretation:] The Sublime Spirit sent the revelation to the heart of Muḥammad, that means to the heart of the believer. Muḥammad is that Spirit which dwells in the right half of the heart in the house of the Pure Wind. The Burāq signifies the fulguration of Light; the ascension (*mi'rāj*) is the ascension of the vein of Solar Wind which connects the heart to the brain and bifurcates in seven ramifications. In this vein and nerve [?] there is no blood but Pure Wind and the passage for the Light and illumination of the Sublime Spirit. It is connected to the heart [and the brain] which is [like] the ascension from the earth to the sky. Whatever [282] the seven organs—the [organs] of sight, hearing, smell, touch and speech—do the information reaches the heart sooner than the twinkling of an eye [like] 'be, and it becomes'. This vein is called the jugular vein. As He the Exalted said, '[We] are nearer to him than his jugular vein' [Qur'ān, 50:16]. The color of this vein is similar to white milk. The manifestation of the Spirit of the Light of Gabriel reaches the heart through this vein to the Pacified Soul and awakens this Spirit from the sleep of heedlessness and resurrects it [283] whereby it accepts the manifestation of the Spirit of Faith while sitting on Burāq. Its coming to this vein means the ascension (*mi'rāj*). Its coming to the lips, mouth and tongue means reaching the Sacred Precinct (*Bayt al-muqaddas*). Its reaching the teeth is like putting the feet on the Rock; when it crosses the seven lights which are on the face of man, it is like crossing the seven heavens, as He the Exalted said, 'He stood poised again being on the higher horizon' [Qurʾān, 53:6–7]. When it comes between the eyebrows, it is like reaching the two bows'-length, [284] 'two bows'-length away or nearer' [Qurʾān, 53:9]. When it reaches the Vital Spirit of the frontal lobe of the brain, it is like reaching the Throne; when it reaches the Spirit of Faith it is like reaching the Pedestal; when it reaches the Spirit of Preservation it is like reaching the Tablet; when it reaches the Reflective Spirit it is like reaching the Pen; when it crosses the Spirit of Invincibility, the Spirit of Knowledge, the Spirit of Intellect, the Sacred Spirit, the Supreme Spirit, it is like crossing five hundred thousand veils. When it reaches the Sublime Spirit it is like reaching the Lord of eighteen thousand worlds. The manifestation of piety, [285] humility, fear [of God], hope, [and] trust [in God], certainty and love from the Pacified Spirit are like speaking seventy thousand words.

The Extreme Temperament, the Divine Breath, the Solar Illumination, the Divine communion, the Credent Look, the Trumpet of Isrāfīl [proceed] from the Spirit that has been Tested. [It reaches] the Spirit of the Heart and illuminates the [Pacified] Spirit which is like listening to seventy thousand words. When it returns to the heart [it is like returning] to his bed which was still warm. When the [Spirit] narrates the significance [of this ascension], the Sensitive Spirit—the Dissident Captive Adam—does not believe it for it is [286] constantly preoccupied with doing evil and satanic insinuation and is dumb and deaf. Whoever is preoccupied with the [satanic] whispering holds a primal grade [in the matters pertaining to evil]. So this is the significance of the Ascension.

The [the sword] Dhuʾl-fiqār of ʿAlī signifies the Luminous Vital Conscious Spirit. Dhuʾl-fiqār is the Spirit of Faith, the Lord of the believers, the oppressed ones, the worthy ones and the paupers. Samsām is the Spirit of Preservation; Qamqām is the Reflective Spirit; and Dargām is the Spirit of Knowledge. Islam and the [state] of being a Muslim becomes complete by the four swords of ʿAlī, [287] as the Prophet, peace be upon him, said, 'Islam becomes complete by the four swords of ʿAlī.' A Muslim is the one who follows Islam. The four swords [of ʿAlī], Ḥasan, Ḥusayn, [and] Muḥammad ibn Ḥanafiyyah, the meaning of the Qāʾim (Resurrector, or Messiah), the miracles of the Qāʾim also signify the Vital Spirit of the brain. The miracle of the fire means the manifestation of the [Spirit of] Faith. The Qāʾim will carry a red flag which signifies the Sacred Spirit. He will brandish a white sword that means, the Conscious Spirit having three hundred and thirteen emissaries who will form the army of the Resurrector. They are the same seven Spirits which are above the Spirit of Faith about which it has been explained in several places [288]. They are three hundred and three [in number]; that is thirteen and three, plus ten which is one [make fourteen divided by two]. The result is seven which signify the seven manifestations of the Prophets."[5]

5. This is in reference to the concept of Ismāʿīlī sacred history of religion which is divided into seven cycles, each cycle founded by a speaker-prophet, *Nāṭiq*. The seven *Nāṭiqs* are: Adam, Noah, Abraham, Moses, Jesus, Muḥammad, and Qāʾim (or Messiah). The first six are the revealers of the divine *sharāʾiʿ*, the last one would unveil the inner truths of all the *sharāʾiʿ* revealed to the speaker-prophets. Cf. H. Corbin, *Cyclical Time and Ismaili Gnosis*, English trans. by R. Manheim and J. W. Morris (London, 1983), especially pp. 84–99.

Question XX

Then Muḥammad ibn Mufaḍḍal got up and said, "I render my gratitude to the Sublime, the Sacred, [and] the Sacred, the Sublime. [303] Indeed Muḥammad and ʿAlī are truly worthy of praise by God [and] are the chosen ones, so are his progeny, [Salmān] al-Salsāl and Abū'l-Khaṭṭāb." Then Jaʿfar-i Juʿfī said, "How does one interpret the verse of God in which He said, 'Are then they who disbelieve not aware that the heavens and the earth were [once] one single entity, which We then parted asunder?' [Qur'ān, 21:29]."

Bāqir replied, "God says, 'O the heedless, the intolerant and the unbelievers, aren't you aware that the earth and the heavens at the beginning of the creation were one-entity; then We divided it into two halves. From the one half we created seven levels [304] of the heaven, and from the other half We created seven levels of the earth. This signifies the quality of the semen (*nuṭfah*) which in its primal nature is a drop of liquid, from which [it is transformed into] a human seed, then to a clot, and a lump of flesh until from half of it the head is created with eyes, ears, nostrils and mouth [which correspond to the seven heavens]. From the other half, the lower part [of the body] is created [which constitutes] the heart, lungs, liver, spleen, the bladder, pancreas and kidneys which [correspond to] the seven [levels] of the earth. The earth in reality is the heart which is centered amidst the seven humors, [as He said], 'And the earth, He expanded it after that' [Qur'ān, 79:30]."

Jaʿfar-i Juʿfī said, "O my Lord, they say that this earth stands on the back of the cow. [Is it true?]"

Bāqir replied, "Yes it is true. The earth stands on the back of the cow; the cow stands on the fish and the fish is in the water; the water is on the stone and that stone is held on the palm of the hand of an angel. The seven heavens and the earth are held in suspension [by the angel]. O Jaʿfar-i Juʿfī, the earth [corresponds to] the heart; the seven levels of the earth are [like] the seven humors which are located from above the heavens till their base. The cow is the Awaiting Spirit (*rūḥ-i muntaẓirah*) which is inside the oceans. The fish is the feet and the ocean [306] is the Universal Spirit which pervades [the whole body] from the top of the head till the nails of the toes. The stones are these bones which are the resting place of the Spirit, and the Spirit is the movement (*raftār*) of the angel who holds everything in the palm of his hand and moves it wherever he wishes."

Question XXVII

Abū Khālid said, "O Walī of the time (*walī al-zamān*), if it is not too heavy for you then enlighten me on the meaning by inner interpretation and real meaning [of the chapters of the Qur'ān and the places where they were revealed]."

Bāqir al-ʿIlm, peace be upon us from him, replied, "The first [*sūrah*] *al-Ḥamd* was revealed in Mecca; *Sūrat al-Baqarah* was revealed in Mecca; *Āl al-ʿImrān* was revealed in Medina; *Sūrat al-Nisā'* in Basra; *Sūrat al-Mā'idah* in Damascus; *Sūrat al-Anʿām* in Jerusalem; *Sūrat al-Aʿarāf* in Yemen and Yathrib; *Sūrah al-*

Anfāl in Kufa and the remaining hundred and five chapters were revealed in all parts of the universe. The *Sūrat al-Baqarah, Alif. Lām. Mim.* This is the Scripture in which there is no doubt, a guidance unto those who are pious' [2:1–2], is the Vital Spirit of the frontal lobe of the brain symbolizing the cycle of Adam. Mecca is the forehead, because the Vital Spirit descends from the azure [celestial] dome to the frontal lobe of the brain. *Sūrah Āl al-ʿImrān, Alif. Lām. Mim.* Allah! There is no God save Him' [Qurʾān, 3:1–2] is the Spirit of Audition symbolizing the cycle of Noah. It descends from the spheres of stars to these ears. The ears symbolize Medina. *Sūrat al-Nisāʾ*, 'O mankind, [357] be pious to your Lord' [4:1] is the Spirit of Vision and symbolizes the cycle of Abraham. It was revealed in Basra, and Basra [in Arabic] means vision. This Spirit descends from the sun to the vision (*baṣrah*). *Sūrat al-Māʾidah*, 'O ye who believe, fulfill your undertaking' [4:1], was revealed in Syria. This is the Olfactory Spirit. It descends from the wind and joins the sense of smell, and symbolizes the cycle of Moses. *Sūrah al-Anʿām*, 'Praise be to God, Who has created the heavens and the earth' [6:1], is the Spirit of Speech. It was revealed in Jerusalem. [358] [It descends] from the thunder and lightning. Jerusalem is the tongue and lips and symbolizes the Cycle of Jesus. *Sūrah al-Aʿrāf, Alif. Lām. Mim. Ṣād.* It is a Scripture' [Qurʾān, 7:1–2], is the Spirit of Touch. It manifests from the air in the hands for revealing Islam. All the books, [as well as] writing and learning manifest through the hands. It symbolizes the cycle of Muḥammad in Yemen and Yathrib. *Sūrat al-Anfāl*, 'They ask thee about the spoils of war' [8:1], is the Spirit of Movement, it is the symbol of the cycle of ʿAlī. It was revealed in Kufa that is, in the sole of the feet. It comes down from the Moon and joins [359] the sole of the feet. Out of one hundred and five *sūrah*s, one hundred are [equal] to one and when five are added to it, the [total] becomes six. They [symbolize] the Spirit of Taste, the Vegetative Soul which pervades the whole body, and four other [Spirits] which reside in the heart about which it has already been explained. They descended upon Muḥammad of the Microcosm, [i.e.,] upon the Pacified Spirit which is the particular servant of the Exalted Sovereign about which the saying of Allah the Mighty and Sublime confirms, 'Blessed is He Who hath revealed unto His servant the Furqān' [Qurʾān, 25:1]. The seven verses of [*Sūrat al-*] *Ḥamd* which are prior to *Sūrat al-Baqarah* are the seven [360] Spirits which are above the Vital Conscious Spirit. They are of seven colors and have descended from the seven spheres upon Mecca, that is, the frontal [lobe of the brain] which is the seat of the Divine. Their seven legatees such as, piety, humility, reliance [upon God], trustworthiness, faithfulness, certitude [in God], and illumination form twice-[repeated] seven [legatees] as He the Exalted, said, 'We have given thee seven of the twice-[repeated verses] and the great Qurʾān" [Qurʾān, 15:87].

Physically, this heart, and the Spirit which is in it, is *Sūrat* [361] *al-Baqarah* and [symbolizes] the Cycle of Adam. It proceeds from the celestial sphere of the Resistant Spirits. *Āl al-ʿImrān* is the Cycle of Noah. It symbolizes the [sense of] touch which proceeds from the celestial sphere of the Noble ones (*najībān*). *Surat al-Nisāʾ* is the Cycle of Abraham. It symbolizes the [faculty of] speech. It proceeds from the celestial sphere of the Chiefs (*naqābān*). *Sūrah al-Māʾidah* is the

Cycle of Moses. It symbolizes the [sense of] smell and proceeds from the celestial sphere of Bā-Dharr [i.e., Abū Dharr Ghifārī]. *Sūrat al-Anʿām* symbolizes the [sense of] sight and is the Cycle of Jesus. [It proceeds from] the celestial sphere of Miqdād. *Sūrat al-Aʿrāf* is the Cycle of Muḥammad and symbolizes the [sense of] hearing. It proceeds from the celestial sphere of Salmān al-qudrah. *Sūrat al-Anfāl* [362] is the symbol of the Cycle of the Resurrector (Qāʾim). It is the Conscious Spirit and symbolizes the Exalted Sovereign. This Microcosm becomes complete by those six Spirits and six celestial spheres as He the Exalted said, 'Lo, your Lord is Allah Who created the heavens and the earth in six days then He mounted the Throne' [Qurʾān, 7:54].

O Abū Khālid, this Spirit which is called the Conscious [Spirit] is the Celestial Dome; its speech is the Sun; [its] mouth is Bayt al-maʿmūr, for the Sun rises from the Bayt al-maʿmūr [363], and the six stars which constantly rotate are Nashīdar, Nashīdar-i Māh, Nashīdar-i Tābān, Samīʿā, Bahman and Kafū. Once in thirty years one of them glances at this world and manifests luminous hair in such a way that the whole world could see it."

Question XXVIII

Then Abū Khālid said, "O my Lord, do complete Thy gratitude upon me by revealing [the meaning of] this doctrine to me."

Bāqir replied, "The Sun is the Consciousness (*nuṭq*) which is manifested through the Spirit of the brain. The Nashīdar, the Nashīdar-i Māh and the Nashīdar-i Tābān are the right eye, right ear and the right nostril. The Samīʿā, Bahman and Kafū are the left eye, left ear and the left nostril. Thirty years signify thirty letters from which the speech is formulated, and their recognition is through these thirty letters. The Universe is the heart. The two Spirits in the heart realize [their plight] and yearn for their salvation. They cause affliction to the other two Spirits and turn their face upward. The sun which is going to rise from the west on the Day of Resurrection is the Spirit which [dwells] in the heart which is the House of Pure Wind. The moon is the Captive Vital Spirit. [365] When this Spirit reaches the moon it is cultivated by the light of the moon. The six lights are connected to the six veins which are the locus of smell, hearing, sight, speech, which in turn are connected to the heart, and from there to the arteries of the head which surround this Spirit. They persist in that state so that outwardly they see, hear and speak everything, and also inwardly they see and hear things and speak. When this Spirit rises from the heart, it is like rising from the Occident of the horizon. When it arrives at the top of the chest, it is like mounting [the Throne]. When it arrives at the lips, tongue and mouth, it is like reaching the Orient [366]. When it reaches the brain, it is like reaching the veil of the Celestial Dome, as He the Exalted said, 'Therefore pray unto God making religion pure for Him, however much the disbelievers be averse. The Exalter of the ranks, the Lord of the Throne. He casteth the Spirit of His command' [Qurʾān, 40:14–15]. This [verse] signifies that the Lord of the Microcosm evokes the Conscious Spirit by the illumination of the Spirit of Faith of the Devotees who dwell in the right half of the heart. Also, it reveals to it the Light of Prophecy so that it loathes and humiliates the dissident Concupiscent [Spirit], [367] and rises to a higher degree which is the Divine Throne, [i.e.,] the [vital] Spirit of the brain, by the [Divine] command and order. All the [Divine] commands and prohibitions are for the [Concupiscent] Spirit. Canonical prayer, fasting, pilgrimage, and poor-tax are obligatory for this Spirit so that it fulfills them in the required order and as a consequence becomes obedient and docile."

Question XXIX

Then Jābir ibn ʿAbdallāh Anṣārī said, "O my Lord, how does one know the meaning of this doctrine?"

Bāqir replied, "Five canonical prayers (*namāz*) render the witness to the five stations: a believer is the one who performs his noon prayer with the assembly of the Najīb, [368] the evening prayer with the assembly of the Naqīb, the prayer after sunset with the assembly of Bā-Dharr[6], the night prayer with the assembly of Miqdād and the early morning prayer with the assembly of Salmān. [Then] he stands behind the prayer niche and recites the supplication (*duʿā*)."

Then Jābir ibn ʿAbdallāh Anṣārī said, "O my Lord, may my life, possession and blood be sacrificed for Thee. Can you please enlighten me with the meaning of what you said so that the utmost desire of us, the servants, is fulfilled?"

Bāqir replied, "By Muḥammad Muḥammad, by ʿAlī ʿAlī. We have not related this discourse anywhere, nor have we written it in any book. It is difficult [to believe], [369] so you should have confidence [in me]. O Jābir, any time the Pacified Spirit faces upwards and reaches the [sense] of touch, and from there to the Spirit which is enjoined by the Wind and gives its testimony, it is like reaching the assembly of the Najīb. When it reaches the [faculty of] speech, it is like reaching the assembly of the Naqīb; when it reaches the olfactory [sense] it is like reaching the assembly of Bā-Dharr; when it reaches the sense of sight it is like reaching the assembly of Salmān. When it reaches the brain and reposes on the Spirit of Faith, it manifests the cosmos of Light. The noon canonical prayer is the [symbol of the sense of] touch; the evening canonical prayer [symbolizes the faculty of] speech; [370] the canonical prayer after sunset [symbolizes] the olfactory [sense]; the night canonical prayer signifies [the symbol of] the [sense] of sight; and the morning canonical prayer [symbolizes the sense of] hearing. When the Pacified Spirit traverses these five stations [i.e., five senses] and renders testimony [to God in all these stations] it attains salvation. If not, then it remains in the troubled state, as He the Exalted said, 'Ah, woe unto worshipers who are heedless of their prayer [Qurʾān, 107:4–5].'"

6. Bā-Dharr or Abū Dharr al-Ghifārī, Salmān al-Fārisī, Ammār ibn Yāsir and Miqdād are acclaimed by *Shiʿas* as the chief supporters of ʿAlī ibn Abī Ṭālib's candidature for the caliphate. Cf. *An Introduction to Shīʿī Islam* by M. Momem (New Haven, 1985). p. 20.

Question XXX

Jābir said, "O my Lord, what is the meaning of fasting?"

Bāqir replied, "The Spirit must fast for thirty days which are like thirty letters [of the alphabet]. [In those thirty days] one should not speak to anyone, nor associate with those who are unworthy of this Knowledge of Light which is communicated through the thirty letters [of the alphabet]; nor should he segregate from the Brothers of Religion to whom the truth must be revealed; nor should he commit any act of betrayal or dishonesty against them; otherwise its consequence will be grave. After every thirty years, one should fast for twelve months. These thirty letters are constituted of light by which twelve organs [or limbs of the body] are recognized. [After fasting for twelve months] one should fast again for thirty days; detach from everything that is unworthy, and should not associate with infidels, unjust and bigoted people. One should not talk to anyone so that the fasting is proper, [as He the Exalted said,] 'That ye fast is better for you' [Qur'ān, 2:184].

Moreover, participating in the battle is incumbent upon the Spirit of the heart. It should prepare itself with the shield, spear and arrow; wear the iron coat; make its bow ready and put the arrow of thirty wooden freckles in its holder and wear it on the waist. Then he should march toward the infidels for waging the holy war (*jihād*) against them, and then annihilate them. The spear [symbolizes] the speech and knowledge of Light; the shield [symbolizes] humility; the iron coat the fear of God; the armor the gentleness, the bow [symbolizes] the lips; the arrow-holder the mouth; the arrow of thirty wooden freckles [symbolizes] the thirty letters [of the alphabet] through which [God] is glorified and [His invocation], 'There is no god but God', is recited day and night so that the infidels who have taken hold of the left side of the heart are annihilated [373] together with their soldiers and army such as jealousy, envy, hate, rancor, anger, enmity and greed. This battle [is fought] with humility, as He the Exalted said, 'And you should fight for the cause of God with your wealth and your lives' [Qur'ān, 61:11].

When he has completed [the above worship] then he should go for the pilgrimage. He must take the provision and the riding camel, and he should have thirty dinars of gold of the caliphate in order to cross the desert. Then he should cross the ʿAqabā of Satan, the robbers, the desert nomads and reach the House of God and pray with six hundred thousand people.

The Spirit which resides in the heart has six limits (*ḥudūd*). In one respect the House of God [resembles] the heart which has six limits signifying six thousand people. But in the true sense the House of God [374] is the station of the Conscious Spirit. When this Spirit reads, speaks and commands the divine spiritual knowledge through the medium of thirty letters [of the alphabet], it is like having thirty (thousand?) dinars of the caliphate. When it has crossed the rebuked Adam, it is [like] having crossed the ʿAqabā of Satan and the other half [of the heart] which is below the ʿAqabā of Satan. When it has transcended the [qualities such as] recalcitrance, violence, disunity, anger, enmity, and rancor, it is like having crossed the robbers and the desert nomads. When it reaches the white vein in which there is no blood and is connected to the brain and the heart, it is like reaching the way to Medina. [375] When it reaches the mouth it is like crossing a distance of one thousand *farsangs* and reaching the House of God—the station of speech which manifests from a thousand places every day in cold, warm and piquant ways. When it reaches the Spirit of taste, it is like reaching the well of Zamzam. When it reaches the tip of the tongue, it is like reaching the [mount ʿArafāt. When it reaches the six parts of the mouth and becomes preoccupied with divine knowledge, it is like standing for the canonical prayer with six hundred thousand people. When it reaches the [sense of] smell, it is like reaching Marwah. When it reaches the [sense of] sight, it is like reaching Ṣafā. Seven times running from Ṣafā to Marwah and from Marwah to Ṣafā [376] [symbolizes traversing] seven layers of the eye. When it reaches the forehead, it is like reaching Mecca. Then it circumambulates around six Spirits near the Divine Throne, and after that it becomes peaceful and pacified as He the Exalted said, 'And whosoever entereth it is safe. And pilgrimage to the House is a duty unto Allah for mankind, for him who can find a way thither' [Qurʾān, 3:97]."

—Latimah Parvin Peerwani, translator

References

Daftari, F. *The Ismāʿīlīs: Their History and Doctrines*. Cambridge: 1990.

Fillipani-Ronconi, P. *Umm al-kitāb*. Naples: 1966.

Ivanow, W. *A Guide to Ismāʿīlī Literature*. London: 1933.

———. "Early Shiʿite Movements." *Journal of the Bombay Branch of the Royal Asiatic Society*, 17 (1941):1–23.

———. "A Forgotten Branch of the Ismāʿīlīs." *Journal of the Royal Asiatic Society*, 1938: 57–79.

———. *Studies in Early Persian Ismāʿīlism*. Leiden: 1948; 2nd ed., Bombay: 1955.

———. *Studies in Early Ismāʿīlism*. Leiden: 1983.

———. *Ummuʾl-kitāb*, ed. by W. Ivanow, *Der Islam*, 23 (1936) : 1–132.

Poonawala, I. K. *Bibliography of Ismāʿīlī Literature*. California: 1977.

Quhistānī, Abū Isḥāq. *Haft bāb-i Bābā Sayyidnā*, ed. by W. Ivanow, in his *Two Early Ismāʿīlī Treatises*. Bombay: 1959, pp. 4–44. English trans. in M. G. S. Hodgson, *Order of Assassins*. The Hague: 1955, pp. 279–324. Second ed. New York: 1980. Persian trans. F. Badraʾī. *Firqa-yi Ismāʿīliyyah*. Tabriz: 1343AH.

Sykes, P. M. *Ten Thousand Miles in Persia*. New York: 1902.

Tajdin, N. *A Bibliography of Ismāʿīlism*, Delmar: 1985.

2

JĀBIR IBN ḤAYYĀN

One of the most mysterious figures in the intellectual history of Islam is Jābir ibn Ḥayyān, at once so famous and so little known that some scholars have even doubted his historical existence. His full name is Abū Mūsā Jābir ibn Ḥayyān al-Kūfī al-Ṭūsī al-Ṣūfī al-Azdī, and he has also been referred to in some texts as Abū ʿAbd Allāh. His name reveals that he was originally from the Arab tribe of Azd, that he was associated with Tus in Khurasan as well as with Kufa in Iraq, and that he was a Sufi. Traditional sources claim that he was a disciple of the sixth Shiʿite Imam Jaʿfar al-Ṣādiq and lived in the early Abbasid period, that is in the second/eighth century. The German scholars of alchemy, Julius Ruska and Paul Kraus, cast doubt on the link between Jābir and the Imam and even upon the historical authenticity of the figure of Jābir, whose most important student in the modern West—that is, Kraus—even believed the Jābirean corpus to have been composed a full century later than when Jābir was supposed to have lived. But many of the arguments offered by Kraus in his monumental study of Jābir concerning the date of the corpus, as well as arguments presented by Ruska concerning the denial of the relationship between Jābir and Imam Jaʿfar as it involved the art of alchemy, have now been refuted. Documents have revealed that texts belonging to the Jābirean corpus existed before the third/ninth century date set for them by Kraus, and that some of the earliest Shiʿite sources mention that Jābir was a disciple of Imam Jaʿfar al-Ṣādiq.

In any case, we believe that there is no reason to doubt the historical reality of Jābir, the father of Islamic alchemy and one of the most influential figures in Latin alchemy as well. He was probably a Khurāsānī of Arab origin and without doubt associated with the earliest phase of Shiʿism and especially the period when the early Ismāʿīlī movement was born. There are, however, some statements in his corpus that do not accord with certain Ismāʿīlī tenets. Interestingly enough, his name also included the epithet al-Ṣūfī, which indicates his association with very early sufism as well. Taking all the historical references as well as the content of his works into consideration, he must be considered a member of the early Shiʿite community immersed particularly in Islamic gnosis (*ʿirfān*) in which Imam Jaʿfar, who was also the pole of Sufism in his day, was the undisputed master. In the sciences Jābir probably also drew much from the Ḥarrāneans also known as the Sabaeans, who, however, should not be confused with the real Sabaeans who still survive in southern Persia and Iraq.

Although very little is known about the life of Jābir, there is an enormous body of works ascribed to him and known as the Jābirean corpus. This corpus was already well known in the fourth/tenth century and is mentioned by Ibn Nadīm in his *al-Fihrist*. Kraus studied this corpus in which he counted 2,982 works and sought to classify them. The extraordinarily large number of treatises was itself one of the main reasons given by Kraus to doubt that they could all have been written by a single person. He believed, on the contrary, that they were written by a group of Ismāʿīlīs over many years. Yet they possess a unity of style and a single philosophy dominates all of the texts within the corpus. Seyed Nomanul Haq has shown that this number is in fact more around 500 rather than 2,982 and that even then many of the titles are but one or two pages long. The Jābirean corpus therefore, although immense, is not beyond the power of a single individual to compose. It is enough to turn to the literary output of Ibn ʿArabī and Mullā Muḥammad Bāqir Majlisī to confirm this fact. Some have even claimed that the "authors" of Jābirean corpus were the same as the Ikhwān al-Ṣafāʾ or Brethren of Purity who composed the famous *Rasāʾil* ("Epistles or Treatises") selections of which are to be found in this volume. This thesis also cannot be true for many reasons and has been refuted by other scholars already.

Kraus divided the Jābirean corpus into several collections including the CXII books on practical alchemy with reference to ancient alchemists such as Zosimus, Democritus, and Hermes; the CXLIV books called *Kutub al-mawāzīn* (Books of Balances) dealing with the philosophical foundations of alchemy and the other occult sciences and the D books that investigate more fully certain questions posed in the *Kutub al-mawāzīn*. To these collections must be added smaller ones dealing with philosophy, astronomy/astrology, arithmetic, music, medicine, magic, the religious sciences, and even the generation of living beings.

There are many references in the Jābirean corpus to Ismāʿīlī and more specifically Qarmaṭī ideas such as the usage of the terms *nāṭiq* (speaking) and *ṣāmit* (silent), degrees of initiation, the significance of the Imam, and the division of the history of the world into seven periods. But as already mentioned there are also points in which he does not follow known Ismāʿīlī teachings.

It is interesting to note that although alchemy is the application of Hermeticism to a particular realm and has been closely associated with "The Hermetic Philosophy" in both the Islamic world and the West, Jābir, who is the founder of Islamic alchemy and indirectly Latin alchemy, does not usually use the language of Hermeticism. His philosophical perspective and language are more Aristotelian although symbolic while his alchemy is primarily an "experimental science" based on that philosophy (if one does not reduce the term experimental simply to the sensuous and empirical). He does not use the usual arcane language of the alchemist yet succeeds in hiding the teaching as do other alchemists but in a different manner. His recourse is to what is called "dispersion of knowledge" (*tabdīd al ʿilm*), which means placing various parts of the exposition of a particular teaching in different works. This method was not unique to Jābir but is to be found in other Islamic figures as well as in other traditions, as one can see in the works of Maimonides and Roger Bacon.

The vast Jābirean corpus, which is indeed encyclopedic and includes even many lost Greek sciences, has been rightly compared in its encyclopedic character to the *Rasāʾil* of the Ikhwān al-Ṣafāʾ. But whereas the *Rasāʾil* are bound together by a Hermetico–Neo-Pythagorean philosophy, the Jābirean corpus is unified by a philosophy drawn from Aristotle as well as Islamic sources and based on the concept of the balance or *mīzān*, which is a Quranic term. Jābir sees everything, not only the physical world but also language, thought, ethics, and the world of the spirit in terms of the *balance* of qualities both inward and outward. Even words are seen by him to be constituted of letters on the basis of the science of "the balance of letters" (*mīzān al-ḥurūf*). Moreover, he combines this central concern with the balance with numerical symbolism drawn from the traditional Islamic science of numerical symbolism of letters called *al-jafr*, as well as Neo-Pythagorean ideas probably associated with Ḥarrān, which remained a repository of the more esoteric currents of Greco-Alexandrian thought into the early Islamic period. Altogether it can be said that Jābir is the father of a whole "philosophy of nature" that was to possess a long life in the annals of Islamic thought.

One cannot be concerned with philosophy in Persia without at least dealing to some extent with Jābir and his works because, although he is studied usually in the context of either the history of science or the history of religion or both, he is also of much philosophical importance. His influence can be seen not only in later Ismāʿīlī thought but also in many later religious movements with a philosophical perspective, such as the Nuqṭawiyān. Also, this archetypal figure has hovered over all those Persian theologians and philosophers of the later centuries who were concerned with alchemy, *jafr*, or the occult sciences in general ranging from Suhrawardī to Mīr Findiriskī to Ḥājj Muḥammad Karīm Khān Kirmānī, who died only over a century ago.

In this section, the first part of the Jābir ibn Ḥayyān's *Kitab al-aḥjār* (Book of Stones) has been included. In this section, Jābir discusses the symbolism of numbers and the significance in regard to the concept of balance.

—S. H. Nasr

Kitāb al-aḥjār

THE BOOK OF STONES

The First Part of the Book of Stones According to the Opinion of Balīnās

[*1*]

In the name of God, the Compassionate, the Merciful

Praise be to God for perpetually bestowing upon us His gifts and favors, and for His benevolence. After this follow our prayers for our lord Muḥammad and his family. Peace be upon them!

In several books belonging to the *Books of Balances*, we had promised you an account of the views of Balīnās, particularly with regard to the Science of Balance. Accordingly, we now proceed at once with an exposition of those aspects of his doctrine which are in agreement [with our views] and those which are not.

[*2*]

Balīnās said, "To expound the wisdom which was dispensed to me after my exit from the cave and taking hold of the Book and the Tablet,[1] I declare:[2] That which belongs in common to all things is the natures. These natures are simple not compound. And if something is common to all things, it would be absurd to suppose that it does not possess quantity." We have already elucidated [all] this in a number of books on this Art.[3]

He went on to say, "The weights which are common to all animals, plants, and stones conform to the proportion of 17. And as for the elixirs, they are not like this"—[4] again, this is something which we have already explained in several books of ours.

This translation is based on Jābir ibn Ḥayyān's *Kitāb al-aḥjār* (The Book of Stones), translated by Seyed Nomanul Haq (Boston: Kluwer Academic Publishers, 1994), pp. 163–202.

1. This is one of the several legendary accounts of the discovery of the writings attributed to Hermes. Some accounts, such as that of Abū Maʿshar (d. 273/886), have it that in order to preserve revealed wisdom Hermes had left inscriptions on the walls of temples and caves which were subsequently discovered by sages. Hermes had himself received his knowledge, so a legend goes, from a book written on sapphire tablets delivered to him by an angel. (Cf. Pingree [1968]. For a general survey of Arabic *Hermetica* see Plessner [1954]; Affifi [1951]; for specific accounts in the Arabic tradition see Scott [1936], IV, pp. 248–276; Massignon's "Appendix" to Festugière [1944]).

2. This entire quotation of Jābir (namely, "To expound the wisdom . . . I declare"), comes practically verbatim from the *Sirr* of Balīnās where one reads, "*aqūlu ʿalā ithri kitābī hādhā wa aṣifu'l-ḥikmata'l-latī uyidtu bihā* . . ." (Weisser ed. [1979], 1:3–4). Indeed, the legend of the cave in which Hermes revealed his Tablet to Balīnās is also found in the *Sirr* (Weisser ed. [1979], pp. 5–7).

3. The Art = alchemy.

4. In other words, elixirs vary according to the objects to which they are applied (see below).

Then Balīnās determined the quantities of these weights; [these quantities are] in accordance with what we have already set forth in the *Book of Morphology*, namely: 1 in the First [Degree of intensity], 3 in the Second, 5 in the Third, and 8 in the Fourth.

[*3*]

Balīnās said, "As for the effective weight [of the natures],[1] I believe that its lower limit is the *ʿashīr*, that is, ¾ *ḥabba*." By this he means that the fifth [in the First Degree of intensity] has the value of 1 *ʿashīr*. Then he arrived at the necessary conclusion that the fourth is 1 *dirham* [*dir.*], the third 60 *dir.*, and the second 3,600 [= 60^2] *dir.*; the minute is the product of 3,600 and 60, so that it becomes 216,000 [= 60^3] *dir.*

The grade is the product of 216,000 and 60, thus it is 12,960,000 [= 60^4] *dir.*; and [finally], the degree is the product of 12,960,000 and 60, so that the degree in the First Degree[2] [of intensity] of any nature is 777,600,000 [= 60^5] *dir.*

Likewise, [the degree in] the Second Degree [of intensity] is 2,332,800,000 [= 3×60^5] *dir.*, the grade in the Second Degree is 38,880,000 [= 3×60^4] *dir.*, the minute in the Second Degree is 648,000 [= 3×60^3] *dir.*, the second in the Second Degree is 10,800 [= 3×60^2] *dir.*, the third in the Second Degree is 180 [= 360] *dir.*, the fourth in the Second Degree is 3 *dir.*, and [finally], the fifth in the Second Degree is 2½ *ḥabbas*, that is, 3 [= ¾ × 3] *ʿashīrs* . . .

To continue the fifth in the Third Degree is, according to the doctrine of Balīnās, 15/4 [= 5 × ¾] *ḥabbas*, or 5 *ʿashīrs*; the fourth in this Degree is 5 [= 5 × 1] *dir.*, the third 300 [= 5 × 60] *dir.*, the second 18,000 [= 5×60^2] *dir.*, and the minute 1,080,000 [= 5×60^3] *dir.* The grade in this [Degree] is 64,800,000 [= 5×60^4], and, following this pattern . . . , the degree in the third Degree is 3,888,000,000 [= 5×60^5] *dir.*

Similarly, the fifth in the Fourth Degree is 8 *ʿashīrs* or 6 [= 8 × ¾] *ḥabbas*, the fourth 8 [= 8 × 1] *dir.*, the third 480 [= 8 × 60] *dir.*, and the second 28,800 [= 8×60^2] *dir.* The minute in the Fourth Degree is 1,728,000 [= 8×60^3] *dir.*; the grade in this Degree is 103,680,000 [= 8×60^4] *dir.*, and [finally], the degree in the Fourth Degree is 6,220,800,000 [= 8×60^5] *dir.*

So God protect you, certain ideas of Balīnās have been sufficiently elucidated. Let us now work out how, according to his views, these weights are applied to all things.

1. *Ṣanja* is the term sued for standard weights used as counterpoise in balances. Thus, "*al-wazn bi'l-ṣanja*" would mean the measured weight, or the effective weight.

2. It should be noted that Jābir uses the term "degree" in two different senses: (i) in the Galenic sense of *taxeis*, and (ii) as the largest subdivision of (i) which latter seems to have been borrowed from astronomy. To distinguish the two, the 'd' in (i) has been capitalized, thus "the degree in the First Degree, the degree in the Second Degree," etc.

[*4*]

Balīnās claimed that animals, plants and stones each possess a characteristic Balance which was created in the First Generation by God, may He be glorified and exalted. Further, he said that animals have a Balance besides the First, and likewise [plants] and stones; and that the generation of this Second Balance depends on us. So know that!

He also claimed that the Supreme Elixir in particular has a Balance of its own. . . . And as for theurgical works, he believed that they possess different Balances according to their characteristic diversity. Then, in broad outline, Balīnās specified each of these Balances which we shall thoroughly explicate in the course of these four books as we have repeatedly promised elsewhere. Also, we shall establish our objectives concerning those Balances which we have ourselves discovered.

You ought to know that anyone who has not read our prior writings on the subject of Balances will derive from the present four books no benefit at all, for all these are intimately interdependent. However, we now proceed with our explication as we have promised you, God the Most High willing!

[*5*]

Know, may God protect you, that after attributing a Balance to all things we have enumerated, and after having spoken of the quantitative values which we have mentioned, Balīnās also made a pronouncement on the letters which is in conformity with what we have [ourselves] taught you in the *Book of the Result*.

Next, he said, "When two letters of identical appearance follow each other in one word, only the first is taken into account considering its type and the value characteristic of its Degree. To the second is ascribed a minimal value which does not enter into the computation made with the letters of the alphabet. An example is " ʾ ʾ " or " b b ". By God the Great, this I have already taught you in the *Book of the Arena of the Intellect*.

After that, he said, "Let us consider the Arabic language in particular. For it is obvious that the practitioner of Balance need take into account no other language." Then Balīnās said, "As for the First Balance of animals [etc., etc.]"—here I need not repeat [his words], for what he said is in accordance with, and nothing other than, what I have myself set forth in the *Book of Morphology*.[1] The same applies to [his assertions concerning the First Balance of] plants and stones. So we are done with it, and there is no obscurity nor doubt in it, nor do we present to you a confused account. And [yet], as always, we deliberately abrogate in one book what we say in another. The purpose is to baffle and lead into error everyone except those whom God loves and provides for!

With regard to [the weights governed by] the Second Balance of animals, plants and stones, they range—as we have said in the beginning of this book—

1. The text 4:8–9 is somewhat ambiguous due to the author's broken style.

from [the maximum to the minimum, that is from] 1 *ʿashīr* in the fifth [in the First Degree], and this is the minimum value, to the [degree in the] Fourth Degree which is of the value 6,220,800,000 *dir.*, [this being the maximum]. . . .[2]

[*6*]

The reason why we are furnishing an account of stones in these [four] books, setting these books apart from all other writings, is that Balīnās said, and it is the truth, that among the letters which occur in drugs and in other things belonging to the three kingdoms of nature, there are those which signify the internal [natures], but not the ones which are external; those which do the opposite, in that they signify the external [natures], but not the internal; those in which all of them [sc. internal as well as external] are found; and those which signify [not only] all that is in the thing, [but also] the excesses which need to be discarded and thrown away—just as one needs to augment and complete what is deficient. . . .[1]

Further, Balīnās believed that the name of gold truly conforms to the Balance, for its signifies two natures. Nay, the correct judgment in this case is that the name of gold is that which is necessitated by all [four of] its natures. . . .[2]

Balīnās continued, "I only say that all things ought to be named according to the reality of their Balance, with a view to practical applications, not verbal usage. And, may God protect you, it behooves you to know that whoever in this world discovers a new language, he is a great man!"—what Balīnās is here referring to is the bringing forth of another language of which mankind in general does not know, for precise application of names is not a matter of common knowledge. Such knowledge is found only in exceedingly rare cases.

In order to discover the natures by means of letters, you ought to follow what we taught you in the *Book of the Elite*, so that we lead you at the initial stages not into the precise determination of things, but into their nature. And this is also what we taught you in the *Book of the Result*, except that, for the purposes of learning, the *Result* is better than the *Elite*. This is so because the *Elite* is like the aroma which emanates from things, whereas the *Result* is like their essence: the absence of the latter is the absence of the source.[3]

Thus, these accounts make it known that the extraction of the mere external nature of an object is of no use—if we do this, we have practically let the thing slip away from our hands. Rather, you must, may God protect you, weigh every-

2. See the table in [3] above.

---

1. If the weights of the natures in a thing did not conform to the proportion 1:3:5:8, one had to discover it by intuition: thus, if these weights fell short, one made additions; if the weights were in excess, then, again by means of intuition, "separations" had to be carried out.

2. This is strange, for "*dh*^{a}*h*^{a}*b*" has only three letters: how can it signify four natures? One notes also that our author himself does not seem to agree with the view that the nature of gold "truly conforms to the Balance," for a little later we are told that gold is "excessive" (see [26] below).

3. Note the eulogy here.

thing whose weight you desire and attain it, away from everything else,[4] in the interior of the thing, and in its exterior.

As for the different ways of the removal of excesses, you need at this point what is set forth in the *Book of Morphology* and elsewhere in these [four] books, namely that you must necessarily remove from all things whose weight you desire what is added to their primitive structure, and what has entered into this structure due to reasons other than additions.[5] It is known that the [word which denotes the] name of gold, (*al-*) $Dh^{a}H^{a}B$, exists in its primitive form, since it is free from additions; and the spelling of the [word which names] silver, *fiḍḍa*, becomes *FḌ*, since the *hāʾ* enters in it for the sake of feminine designation, and it does not admit of masculine gender. Thus, after removing the additions from the name of silver, you ought to augment it according to the need.

So know, O brother, that when you obtain only one letter, like "ʾ" or "b" or whatever else you obtain, you must make the total conform to 17 . . . , but with one proviso: you ought to separate the result obtained through the analysis of letters from that obtained by means of intuition. You try to work out the latter in relation to the form,[6] so that the two figures form one unique figure. By my Master! I have already explained to you that which you need not augment, in it there is a third thing—but I am not happy with it unless you make in one day one thousand animals, one thousand plants, and one thousand stones.[7] God is our Guide, may His blessings be upon you. Indeed, He is Generous and Kind.

[7]

[A]

My brother! you ought to know that additions to the primitive root of a word may be in the form of prefixes, suffixes or infixes. You ought to know, further, that some of these additions are represented by inflexions, and should therefore be discarded and disregarded: for example, $Z^{a}YD^{un}$, $Z^{a}YD^{an}$ and $Z^{a}YD^{in}$, [which are the inflected forms of the primitive noun $Z^{a}YD$] in the nominative, accusative and genetive cases [respectively][1]; and $Z^{a}YD^{\bar{a}n}$ and $Z^{a}YD^{\bar{u}n}$ in the dual and the plural forms. So, my brother, pay no attention to this, and restore the word to its singular core, such as *ZᵃYD* from $Z^{a}YD^{ayn}$, and ʿ$UM^{a}R^{ayn}$, and so on.

4. It is not clear what the author means by "away from everything else."

5. Jābir very likely means inflections, feminine designations and plural forms.

6. Form = 17 (see [13] below).

7. Indeed, through the method of artificial generation, the adept could accomplish this (see [4] above).

---

1. Jābir specifies two terms for the genitive case, *khafḍ* and *jarr*. This betrays a terminological eclecticism, for the former term was used by the grammarians of Baghdad, the latter by those of Kufa.

[B]

It behooves you to know that some letters are such that if they appear at the beginning of the word, they are additions to the primitive root, while these same letters function as radicals when they occur in the middle of the word or at its end. On the contrary, the final letter of a word may be an addition to the root, whereas this same letter, when it is medial or initial in a word, may be a radical, I mean an essential part of the primitive core. Similarly, a medial letter may be a radical, while as an initial or final letter it may either be an adjunct or a radical.

You ought to know that there are ten letters which function as adjuncts and these are: *hamza, lām, yāʾ, wāw, mīm, tāʾ, nūn, sīn, alif,* and *hāʾ*. But, then, these letters keep changing their places of occurrence and their positions in words, whence we need to establish morphological paradigms which govern these changes.

[C]

So, seeking assistance from God, may He be exalted and glorified, we proceed: The basic units of speech consist in three structures, namely: triliteral, quadriliteral, and quinqueliteral. As for the triliteral, they are divided into twelve paradigms. Out of these, ten are in use; while one is the basis only for one word; and one exists only in theory, nothing is ever built on it, and it is practically nonexistent.

Concerning these paradigms, one of them is *FAʿL*, exemplified in *fahd*, and [nine others are these]: *FIʿL*, such as *ḥiml*; *FUʿUL*, such as *dubur*; *FUʿL*, such as *ʿunq*; *FAʿAL*, such as *rasan*; *FIʿIL*, such as *ibil*; *FUʿAL*, such as *ṣurad*; *FIʿAL*, such as *qimaʿ*; *FAʿIL*, such as *kabid*; and *FAʿUL*, such as *sabuʿ*. So these are ten paradigms into which the triliteral structure multiples. As for the paradigm which generates only a unique example, it is *FUʿIL*: the insect *duwaybba* is called "*duʾil*." Finally, the structure on which nothing could possibly be based is *FIʿUL*.

As for the quadriliteral structure, it has five morpological paradigms, namely: *FAʿLAL*, such as *ʿaqrab*; *FUʿLUL*, such as *burquʿ*; *FIʿLIL*, such as *zibrij*; *FIʿLAL*, such as *hijraʿ*; and *FIʿALL*, such as *qimaṭr*.

The quinqeliteral is divided into four paradigms, they exist in accordance with: *FAʿALLAL*, such as *safarjal*; *FAʿLALIL*, such as *jaḥmarish*; *FUʿALLAL*, [such as . . . ?; and *FIʿLALL*] such as *jirdaḥl*.

[D]

All else is nothing but adjuncts to the primary core. As for the recognition of the additions so that everything is restored to its true structure, there are, as we have mentioned above, ten [letters which function as] adjuncts. Among these, *mīm* and *lām* are specific to nouns: *lām* is accompanied by *alif*, and [the addition of] these two are meant for definition, as in *AL-ʿabd*, *AL-ghulām*, *AL-dawāʾ*, and the like. And all nouns admit of a gender. The letter *lām* is added also between *alif* and *kāf* in order to specify the grammatical third person alluded to,[1] although

1. Indeed, *lām* is added in "*dhāk^{a}*" so that it becomes "*dhāl^{i}k^{a}*."

it is more appropriate with the *hamza*.[2] Similarly, [a third] *lām* is added between the second *lām* and *dhāl* in *alladhī*.[3] This is done in order that it [sc. the third *lām*] can carry the a-vowel, and that a distance is introduced between the vowelessness of the [second] *lām* and the i-vowel of the *dhāl*. As for *mīm*, it is added in [such nouns as] *makrum* and *mustaḍrab*, and in others like these. This letter is not endowed to verbs except very rarely, such as [its occurrence in] the verb *makhraqa*.

With regard to *hamza*, *wāw*, *yāʾ*, *tāʾ*, *nūn*, *sīn*, *alif*, and *hāʾ*, *hamza* is added in *Aḥmad*, and in *Afḍal*, [these two] being nouns; and in *aḥsana*, and in *akrama*, and these two are verbs. To be sure, our purpose is not to teach you grammar. In fact, we are showing you all this only because in [the appellations applied to] stones, plants and animals, [some have the form of a primitive noun], others have the form of a verbal noun. Thus, we show you those letters which occur [a] as additions to [the primitive root] of verbs, as well as to [the primitive core] of nouns; or [b] as additions to nouns, but as radicals of verbs; or [c] as primary elements of nouns, but as additions to verbs. We do so in order that you apply these rules to all things in general, God willing!

The letter *yāʾ* is added in the word *yāʿmalu*, and this is a noun; and in *yaḍribu*, and this is a verb. *Wāw* is added in *jawhar*^{un}, and this is a noun; and in *hawqala*, and this is a verb. The letter *tāʾ* is added in the word *tanḍubu*, this being a noun, and in *taḍribu* which is a verb. [Similarly], *nūn* is added in *narjis*^{un}, and this is a noun; and in *naḍribu* which is a verb.

The letter *sīn* is added in *mustaḍrab*^{un} which is a noun; and in *istaḍraba*, and this is a verb. The letter *alif* is added in *muḍārib*^{un} which is a noun; and in the word *ḍāraba* which is a verb. [Finally], *haʾ* is added in *qāʾimat*^{un}, and this is for feminine designation—thus, [in the apocopate form], the word is [pronounced] *qaʾima*. *Hāʾ* is added also in *irmih*, and this is for [phonetic] pause. So know [these rules], and apply them in dealing with all such paradigms you come across. . . .

[*8*]

When we say that rhythm is defined as a numerical composition, then [we explain it by saying that] this composition exists by virtue of [sequences of] motion and rest. And as for the moving and quiescent [letters] when they are composed in speech or in rhythm, the maximum number of moving letters that can cluster in a row is four—metricians exemplify it by the paradigm, *FAʿALATUN*; and the maximum number of quiscent letters that can cluster in a row is [two], represented by their paradigm *FĀʿILĀN*—here the letter *alif* and the letter *nūn* are quiescent. This [latter] would have been impossible were it not for the softness which is in

2. This is not clear.

3. The case Jābir has in mind is that of the relative pronoun for the dual, e.g., *all*^{a}*dhān*^{i} (masc. nom.) and *all*^{a}*dh*^{a}*yn*^{i} (masc. acc. and gen.)—these words are, indeed, spelt with three *lāms*, and the same applies to the feminine forms.

alif. Such clustering of quiescent letters is inadmissible except in the case of soft letters, and these are three: *wāw, yā'*, and *alif*. So know that![1]

Since, in speech and hearing, numerical composition [= rhythm] is based solely on motion and rest, the total number of metrical feet is eight; two of them are quinary, the remaining six septenary. As for the quinary, they are *FA'ŪLUN* and *FĀ'ILUN*. And as for the six septenary ones, they are *MAFĀ'ĪLUN*, *FĀ'ILATUN*, *MUSTAF'ILUN*, *MUTAFĀ'ILUN*, *MUFĀ'ALATUN*, and *MAF'ŪLĀTUN*. Then, from these, practically unlimited number of feet are generated through additions and subtractions. So it is their doctrine concerning the definition of rhythm, namely that it is governed by numbers, which has yielded all these elaborations.

[9]

Here we need something else, for rhythm, when viewed in terms of numbers, may either be odd or even. Now, even and odd numbers are of different types: even even, even-odd, odd-odd, or odd-even. Odd numbers are 1 and its sisters;[1] even numbers are 2 and its sisters.[2] The even-even number is like 8: it arises out of the pairing of 6, of 4, and of 2.[3] As for the even-odd numbers, they are [the even numbers] like 6 which is contained in [an odd number] 9; and the sisters of 6, like [the even number] 4 contained in [the odd number] 5, and so on.[4] As for the odd-

1. For an extensive study of Arabic phonetics see Bravmann [1934]. An excellent brief account is to be found in Fleisch *s.v.* "Ḥurūf al-Hidjā'," [EI²], III, p. 596 ff.

---

1. Jābir defines odd numbers before defining even numbers. This reverses the order one finds in Euclid's *Elements* (Def. 7 and 8, Heath tr. [1956], II, p. 277). In fact it was a logical necessity for Euclid to define even numbers first, since he defines odd numbers in terms of even numbers. As for the rest of the definitions, Jābir follows the order of Euclid.

But perhaps the most significant feature of this definition of Jābir is his use of the term "*wāḥid*" for unit, rather than "*waḥda*," for this is one of the identifying traits of the Arabic Euclid tradition which derives from, *inter alia*, the Ḥajjāj text (see De Young, *op. cit.*, pp. 565–567). According to De Young (*loc. cit.*) the difference between the two terms hinges on whether the unit is considered odd or not. As we can see, Jābir does, indeed, consider the unit to be an odd number. Thus, we can legitimately place him in a pre-Isḥaq-Thābit environment.

2. One would have thought that by 'sisters' Jābir means 'multiples,' but, then, he used the same word in his definition of odd numbers where it had a different sense! This definition, like his first one, is totally dissimilar to what one reads in Euclid (Heath tr., *loc. cit.*).

3. Euclid's definition reads: An even-times even number is that which is measured by an even number according to an even number."(Heath tr., *loc. cit.*). Jābir's example of 8 certainly satisfies this definition, for $8 = 2 \times 4$, or 4×2. But, then, to say that it arises also out of a pairing of 6 is to violate Euclid's definition.

Therefore it seems that Jābir views an even-even number as that which arises when an even number pairs with itself, or with another even number. Thus,

$8 = 4 + 4$, $6 + 2$, $2 + 2 + 2 + 2$ (double pairing).

Obviously this is a worthless concept, for all even numbers except 2 satisfy this definition.

(It is now clear why it is not appropriate to translate Jābir's "*zawj al-zawj*" as "even-*times* even," unlike the case with Euclid).

4. Jābir's example of 6 will certainly satisfy Euclid's Def. 9, namely, "an even-times odd number is that which is measured by an even number according to an odd number." (Heath tr., p. 278). For

odd, it is the number 1 contained in 3, 5, 7, 9, and in numbers like these.[5] The odd-even numbers are the opposite of the even-odd: they are [the odd numbers contained in even numbers], such as the numbers 7, 5, 3, and 1 which are contained in the even number 8.[6]

[*10*]

From all this arise the four musical modes,[1] being the final result of all the above numerical considerations, namely: the [rhythmic] modes called the "first heavy,"[2] the "second heavy,"[3] the *ramal*,[4] and the *hazaj*.[5] then, from each of these, four

---

6 = 2 × 3, and (given that the unit is considered an odd number by our author) also 6 × 1. However, it is not clear what Jābir means when he says that "6 is contained in 9," etc.

5. According to Euclid, "an odd-times odd number is that which is measured by an odd number according to an odd number." (Heath tr., *loc. cit.*). Jābir's examples all satisfy this definition, since

$3 = 1 \times 3$
$5 = 1 \times 5$
$7 = 1 \times 7$
$9 = 1 \times 9, 3 \times 3.$

But, assuming that our translation is accurate, what does he mean by saying that it is "the number 1 contained in 3, 5, 7, 9, and in numbers like these?" If he did not have 9 in his list, one would clearly see that he is talking about prime numbers.

6. Odd-even (or rather, "odd-times even") numbers are not mentioned in Nicomachus' *Introduction* (and hence not in the *Rasāʾil* of the Ikhwān), nor are they found in all MSS of the *Elements*. Heath tells us (*op. cit.*, p. 283) that in the manuscript in which such numbers are introduced, they are stated to be the ones which, when divided by an odd number, give an even number as a quotient. This would mean that any "even-times odd" number is also "odd-times even" number, since 6 = 2 × 3 = 3 × 2, making the definition superfluous. Thus Heath considers this to be an interpolation.

Jābir's definition is obscure. He gives as examples, 7, 5, 3 and 1: is he talking about prime numbers?

---

1. Here Jabir is talking about rhythmic modes.

2. One of the "famous rhythmic modes" (*al-Īqāʿāt al-Mashhūra*) which are described, among others, by al-Fārābī in his *Kitāb al-mūsīqā al-kabīr* ([1967], p. 1022 ff.). According to the classical accounts, the "first heavy" has three long percussions, sometimes equal in duration, but more often the third one being longer than the other two, e.g. 4 beat - 4 beat - 8 beat cycle in al-Fārābī [1967], p. 1045 ff. (see Lois al Faruqi [1981], p. 369).

3. According to al-Fārābī (*op. cit.*, pp. 1038–1041), it had three slow percussions, forming an arithmetic progression: 4 - 6 - 8.

4. The invention of this mode is credited to Ibn Muḥriz (Lois al Faruqi [1981], p. 276). Al-Fārābī tells us that it consisted of a three-percussion cycle beginning with one long percussion, followed by two short ones ([1967], pp. 1033–1037). Similar descriptions are found in al-Kindī and Ibn Sīnā (Lois al Faruqi, *loc. cit.*). *Ramal* is also a poetic meter.

5. Hazaj is a pre-Islamic Arabic term applied to one of the three kinds of singing in ancient Arabia (see al-ʿIqd al-Farīd of Ibn ʿAbd Rabbihi (d. 329/940) [1887], p. 186; Farmer [1941], p. 25). But the term also designates a conjunct rhythmic mode of moderate tempo, i.e., one in which all percussions are of equal duration and follow one another at regular intervals. According to Ibn Sīnā, *hazaj* designates *any* conjunct (*muttaṣil*) rhythmic mode ([1930], p. 92). But al-Fārābī restricts the

light modes are generated, giving altogether eight [rhythmic] modes. These latter are the "first light heavy,"[6] the "second light heavy,"[7] the rapid *ramal*,[8] and the rapid *hazaj*.[9] Finally, a relationship is established between each one of these and [the melodic modes called] the *asābiʿ*.[10] The variations in these [melodic] modes, which are produced by fingers, bear a parallel in the variations produced [in speech] by the throat, tongue, and lips: for just as these *asābiʿ* give rise to motion and rest, we obtain motion and rest in letters too.[11] So they call [these combined modes]: the "first heavy freed,"[12] the "first heavy tightened,"[13] the "first heavy middle,[14] and the "first heavy carried"[15] (while this "carried" is also called "restricted," perhaps the two [are not quite the same but] separated by a short percussion). In this way, each of the eight [rhythmic modes] is combined with each of the four [melodic modes], and this makes a total of 32 modes.

All this is yielded by their doctrine that [music is] governed by numbers, that is, it is a composition of numbers. . . .

---

application of this term only to the conjunct (*mutawaṣṣil*) modes of moderate tempo ([1967], p. 453). Like *ramal*, *hazaj* is also a poetic meter.

Lois al Faruqi adds that *hazaj* "was thought to have been the first rhythmic mode introduced in the new genre of song of the [1st/]7th century known as *ghināʾ al-mutqan*." ([1981], p. 94).

6. A three percussion cycle, two short followed by one longer (O.O.O. . . : 2 - 2 - 4). (See al-Fārābī [1967], p. 1048).

7. This rhythmic mode is described by Fārābī as a fast version of *thaqīl al-thānī* (OO.O. . . : 1 - 2 - 3) (al-Fārābī [1967], p. 1042 ff. Cf. Farmer [1943], p. 82).

8. The "rapid *ramal*" is described variously by authorities. Thus al-Kindī says that it designates a rhythmic mode of either two or three percussions (OO. . : 1 - 2 or OOO. . . : 1 - 1 - 1) (see Farmer [1943], p. 85). But according to al-Fārābī, the term was used for a rhythmic mode with two percussions, the first short, the second long (O.O. . . : 2 - 8) (al-Fārābī [1967], p. 1029; p. 1033). In contrast, Ibn Sīnā tells us that it is made of three percussions of two different lengths (O.OO. . . : 2 - 1 - 2) (Ibn Sīnā [1935], p. 209). Cf. Lois al Faruqi [1974], pp. 134–135.

9. A conjunt rhythmic mode comprising a sequence of equal percussions performed at a tempo which allows only one percussion to be fitted between any two percussions (al-Fārābī [1967], p. 451. See al Faruqi [1981] p. 143).

10. "*Asābiʿ*" literally means "fingers," a term which designates the melodic modes known to have been organized into a system by the late 1st/7th century musician Ibn Misjaḥ (described by Ibn al-Munajjim (d. 300/912) in his *Risāla fiʾl-mūsīqa* [1976], pp. 853, 868 ff.). See Lois al Faruqi [1981] p. 20; Farmer [1957], p. 448; Wright [1978], p. 41. For Ibn Misjaḥ see above.

These modes are called "fingers" because they are named after the finger or fret position used for producing their starting tones (see notes below). Wright ([1978], pp. 250–251) tells us that at one stage these molodic modes were, indeed, allied to rhythmic modes to produce a corpus of 36 *Ṭuruq*. This essentially verifies Jābir's claim.

11. See Chapter 3 above (for the phonetic terms 'motion' and 'rest' see n. 16 of that chapter).

12. *Muṭlaq*, according to al-Fārābī, designates the open string of a chordophone ([1967], p. 500). Jābir mentions it as one of the octave modes which were systematically described by later musical theorists such as ʿAbd al-Qādir ibn Ghaybī (d. 839/1435) (Lois al Faruqi [1981], p. 216).

13. Again, *mazmūm* is described by Ibn Ghaybī as one of the six octave modes known collectively as the *aṣābiʿ* (Lois al Faruqi [1981], p. 180).

14. The term *wusṭā* signifies the use of the middle finger for producing the starting tone. (For a detailed account see Lois al Faruqi, [1981], p. 389).

15. *Maḥmūl* is mentioned by Ibn Ghaybī as one of the *asābiʿ*, i.e. one of the six octave modes (Lois al Faruqi [1981], p. 164).

[*II*]

Concerning the Balances of those bodies which are mixed together:

[A]

Take, for example, glass[1] mixed with mercury in some proportion of weight known to nobody except you, and you give it to the practitioner of Balance. [You will find that] this expert has the capability of determining for you precisely how much of glass the mixture contains, and how much of mercury. The same is true of mixtures of silver and gold, or of copper and silver, or mixtures of three, four, ten, or even a thousand bodies if such a thing is in practice possible.

So we say: The determination of the quantitative composition of mixed bodies is [carried out by means of] a technique which closely approximates the Balance, and it is a splendid technique! Nay, if you were to say that it serves as a demonstration of the faultlessness of this Science, I mean the Science of Balances, you would be speaking the truth, for indeed such is the case. Now, if you wish to know this technique and become an expert of Balance yourself so that when you are given a mixture of bodies and other [solid] substances, you are able to say what substances in what quantities this mixture contains, then in the name of God—

[B]

Make use of a balance constructed in the manner of the diagrams. This balance is set up by means of three strings going upwards [to the steel beam]: attach two scales to these strings in the usual manner of balance construction, I mean by tying the strings and doing whatever else is needed. Ensure that the middle steel carriage which contains the tongue[1] is located with utmost precision at the centre of the beam, so that prior to the tying of the strings the tongue lowers in neither direction even by a single *ḥabba*. Similarly, ensure that the weights of the two scales are equal, that they have equal capacity, and that the quantities of the liquids they hold are likewise equal.

Once you have accomplished all this according to the specified conditions, not much remains to be done. Suspend this balance like ordinary balances. Next, take two vessels with a small depth of the order of a single hand-measure, or less, or more, or however much you wish. Now fill these vessels with water which has already been distilled for several days so that all its impurities and dirt have been removed, the [container] in which this water is kept should have been washed as thoroughly as one washes drinking cups.[2] Having done this, get hold of an ingot of

1. It has already been pointed out that in some parts of his corpus, our author includes "glass" in his list of metals. Von Lipmann identifies this substance as yellow amber (see Chapter 1 above).

---

1. The term 'tongue' designates the needle which functions as the pointer of an equal-arm balance. It is fixed at the centre of gravity of the steel beam and divides it into two equal arms. This tongue moves with respect to a carriage which is attached at right angles to the beam.

2. *bankān* = *finjān*. the word is of Persian origin (see Kraus ed. [1935], p. 142, n. 12).

pure, clean, fine gold weighing 1 *dirham*, and an ingot of white, unadulterated, pure silver weighting also 1 *dirham* so that both ingots are equal in weight. Place the gold in one of the scales of the balance, and the silver in the other. Next, immerse the scales in the above-mentioned water until they are totally dipped and submerged.

Now, note the balance: you will find that the scale carrying the gold has lowered as compared to the one carrying the silver, and this is due to the smallness of the volume of gold and the largeness of that of silver. This [relative heaviness of gold] results from nothing but the nature dry which it contains. Finally, using counterpoise find out the difference of weight between them, and work out that it is 1½ *dānaqs*. Note that when you mix to this weight of pure gold roughly 1 *qīrāṭ* or 1 *dānaq* of silver the former will drop in weight in the ratio of *ḥabbas* to *qīrāṭs*, since there are 12 *ḥabbas* to each *qīrāṭ*.[3]

So know this, for it is, by my Master, a fountainhead of the knowledge of philosophers! It is in this manner that you determine each one of any two mixed substances, or of any three, four, or five, or however many you will.

For instance, you familiarize yourself with the ratio that exits between gold and copper, silver and copper, gold and lead, silver and lead, and copper, silver, gold and lead. Likewise, you find out the ratio which exists between gold, silver and copper when they are mixed together or between silver, copper and lead. But you can do this by taking one body at a time, or two bodies at a time, or three, or however many you will. . . .

[*12*]

We have pointed out to you in several books, if you have read them at all, that if a letter is duplicated in a word, one of them is to be dropped. [Thus], if in some drug a degree of one of the natures is found—be this degree in the First [Degree of intensity], in the Second, in the Third, or in the Fourth—there are in this drug no degrees other than this. And if this degree is in the First [Degree of intensity], then it is the First; if it is in the Second, then it is the Second; if it is in the Third, then it is the Third; if it is in the Fourth, then it is the Fourth. In order that you learn all this, I shall give you several examples of drugs so that you see it for yourself. But such a thing is not admissible in the case of units lower than the degree, I mean grades, minutes, seconds, thirds, fourths and fifths. . . .

[*13*]

The form in everything is [the number] 17.

If you find in any animal, plant or stone only 5 [parts], you are left with 12. Now, in the [deficient] drug there will always be only one nature, two natures, or three, or [all] four. There is no other [possible outcome of the analysis of letters]. Now, if the drug has only one nature, you distribute the 12 [parts] among the re-

3. Jābir seems to be stating an empirical law that in a silver-gold alloy, the weight of the silver in the alloy : loss of weight of the alloy in water = 1 : 1/12.

maining three; and if it [is one of those drugs which] possess two natures, distribute the 12 [parts] among the other two. But if has three natures, compensate for the 12 [missing parts] by means of the one remaining nature, after having deduced that it serves to supply the deficiency of the other natures of the drug.

So know that! . . .

The Second Part of the Book of Stones According to the Opinion of Balīnās

[*14*]

In the Name of God, the Compassionate, the Merciful

Praise be to God Who chose Muḥammad as Prophet and selected ʿAlī as his Trustee. God's blessings be upon those whom he has chosen, and upon their families. May God grant them salvation!

[*15*]

Now we turn to our main point.

Prior to this book of ours we have written numerous others on the subject of the Science of Balance, and in each one of these books we have provided a lucid and rigorous explication of the various aspects of this Science. Now, since Balīnās disagreed with us in some fundamental principles as well as in some matters of detail, it would be wrong not to specify these disagreements.

[Among] the matter[s] in which he disagreed with us is the question of the effective weights [of the natures]. We mentioned these weights in the first part of this book. We also promised in several books that we shall present an account of stones, and of the forms which the natures take in the Balance, so that nothing concerning these matters remains hidden from the earnest seeker. . . .

We have thoroughly explicated to you those letters on which language entirely depends, specifying instances, from degrees to fifths, when these letters are excessive or deficient.[1] Likewise, we have given you an account of the [effective] weights of all letters as we have them and as Balīnās has them. In addition, we have mentioned to you that in the exact sciences, and in dealing with subtle natural processes, we stand in grave need of [a knowledge of] effective Balances as it is expounded by Balīnās, and that our need for this kind of knowledge is not so great when we deal with locomotion of bodies and their decompositions.[2]

[*16*]

As for us, we say: Animals have a Balance to which we assign a weight of 10 *dirhams* in the First Degree [of intensity]. For the higher Degrees we increase this

1. That is, when the weights they signify do not exactly add up to 17 or its multiple.

2. It is not altogether clear what, in this context, the author means by decomposition of bodies.

value, just as for the subdivisions of a Degree we decrease it. Next, we assign to plants a weight of 7 *dirhams* [in the corresponding Degree], and, again, increase it for the higher Degrees and give smaller values to the subdivisions. [Finally], to stones we assign a [corresponding] weight of 5 *dirhams*, increasing it for the higher Degrees and decreasing it for the subdivisions according to the need. This is our view and belief concerning the manifest aspects of the Art. It does not violate the principles of true judgment, like the work of Balīnās.

As for Balīnās, he made the governing rules identical for all three kingdoms of nature and invoked the authority of Socrates in support, saying, "if all three kingdoms of nature arise out of the natures, then it is clear that, consequently, there is no difference between them with respect to Balance—these are the words of Socrates." So Balīnās assigned a weight of 777,600,000 *dirhams*[1] to [the degree in] the First Degree [of intensity]. And since this man, I mean Balīnās, needed the fifth as the [smallest] subdivision [of a Degree], he assigned to it a weight of 1 *ʿashīr*.[2] He then increased this weight [for the] higher [subdivisions] till it reached where it reached. These quantities have been specified in our account of Balīnās in the first part of this book. . . .

[*17*]

Now listen to what Socrates had to say! . . .

He said: "We make [the degree in] the First Degree [of intensity] 1 *dirham* and 1 *dānaq*, [in] the Second Degree 3½ *dirhams*, [in] the Third 5 *dirhams* and 5 *dānaqs*,[1] and [in] the Fourth 9 *dirhams* and 2 *dānaqs*. We make the grade in the First Degree [of intensity] ½ *dirham*, in the Second Degree 1½ *dirhams*, in the Third 2½ *dirhams*, and in the Fourth 4 *dirhams*.

"We make the minute in the First Degree [of intensity] 2½ *dānaqs*, in the Second Degree 1¼ *dirhams*, in the Third 2 *dirhams* and 1 *qīrāṭ*, and in the Fourth 31/3 *dirham*. We make the second in the First Degree 2 *dānaqs*, in the Second 1 *dirham*, in the Third 1 dirham and 4 *dānaqs*, and in the Fourth 2 *dirhams* and 4 *dānaqs*.

"We make the third in the First Degree 1½ *dānaqs*, in the Second 4½ *dānaqs*, in the Third 1¼ *dirhams*, and in the Fourth 2 *dirhams*. We make the fourth in the First Degree 1 *dānaq*, in the Second ½ *dirham*, in the Third 5 *dānaqs*, and in the Fourth 1 *dirham* and 2 *dānaqs*. Finally, we make the fifth in the First Degree 1 *qīrāṭ*, in the Second 1½ *dānaqs*, in the Third 2½ *dānaqs*, and in the Fourth 4 *dānaqs*."

1. One notes that all three manuscripts contain a numerical error here. But more surprising is the fact that Kraus too reproduces this mistake in his text (Kraus ed. [1935], 159:12–13). See critical notes to Edited Text, 15:8–9 above where this error has been specified. Indeed, according to [3] above, the weight of the degree in the First Degree of intensity is 777,600,000 *dirhams*.

2. See [3] above.

---

1. Again, all three manuscripts, as well the text of Kraus (ed. [1935], 160:7), contain an error. See critical notes to Edited Text, 15:14.

[*18*]

May God protect you, just look at the erudition of this man, his stature in science, and the quality of his judgments! Note, likewise, that he discarded the sexagesimal system [adopted by Balīnās], and the reason for this is his view that it is only a convention to say that one degree equals 60 grades, [and one grade equals 60 minutes, and one minute equals 60 seconds, etc]. And if we had wanted to place one or more steps higher everything that is above a given thing, or if we had wanted to place likewise everything that is below a given thing, then we would have been in no other position than to adopt the sexagesimal system.[1] But the sexagesimal system is used only because it makes calculations easy and gives rise to fewer fractions. . . .

We have already presented above an illustrative model of the weights [which follow a sexagesimal geometric progression], a model according to which all concrete cases are worked out. In this book of mine, however, I shall set forth the pattern of weights according to the doctrine of Socrates as we have reported it. Now if you wish to follow the doctrine of Socrates, go ahead; and if you wish to follow the ideas of Balīnās, do so, for both of them are the same. But if you wish to follow our opinion, then follow us. Our opinion is different from both of them, for it is a closer approximation [of the truth].

[*19*]

	Ist Deg.		IInd Deg.		IIIrd Deg.		IVth Deg.	Hot	Cold	Dry	Moist
	1	:	3	:	5	:	8				
	dān.		*dān.*		*dān.*		*dān.*				
Degree	7		21		35		56	*alif*	*bāʾ*	*jīm*	*dāl*
Grade	3		9		15		24	*hāʾ*	*wāw*	*zāʾ*	*ḥāʾ*
Minute	2½		7½		12½		20	*ṭāʾ*	*yaʾ*	*kāf*	*lām*
Second	2		6		10		16	*mīm*	*nūn*	*sīn*	*ʿayn*
Third	1½		4½		7½		12	*fāʾ*	*ṣād*	*qāf*	*rāʾ*
Fourth	1		3		5		8	*shīn*	*tāʾ*	*thāʾ*	*khāʾ*
Fifth	½		1½		2½		4	*dhāl*	*ḍād*	*ẓāʾ*	*ghayn*

[*20*]

At this point we need to show you by means of tables the Balances of fusible stones.[1] These fusible stones which constitute the first and foremost need of the Art are gold, silver, copper, iron, lead, and tin. [We are presenting these illustrations] so that you learn the reality of the letters [occurring in the names] of all

1. In this paragraph, Jābir's expressions are exceedingly convoluted. Evidently, all he intends to say is that in developing a system of units, one has no choice but to adopt a sexagesimal progression. The reason? He explains immediately below that the sexagesimal system simplifies calculations.

1. He does give the tables at the end of this second part of his book.

these bodies. So you ought to know first that all of these stones have 17 powers. Now, these stones are either red or white. If they are white, they possess hot in the First Degree [of intensity]. They possess 3 times as much cold, 5 times as much dry, and 8 times as much moist.[2]

It is the opposite if they are red, possessing cold in the First Degree [of intensity], with 3 times as much hot, 8 times as much dry, and 5 times as much moist.

[*21*]

The quantitative magnitudes obtained (in the present context, these are the measured weights, I mean those which make up the total of 17:

In the First Degree [of intensity] exists either hot or cold (and these two are [signified by] the letters *alif* or *bāʾ*) weighing 1 *dirham* and 1 *dānaq*, as we have already said at the very outset. Now, 3 times the value of the First Degree (and here we reach the Second degree which is likewise signified by *alif* or *bāʾ*) is 3½ *dirhams*. [This can be viewed] either as 3 times the value of the First Degree or as the value of the Second Degree in its own right. Thus, the total weight of the two active natures is [{1 *dir.* = 1 *dān.*} = {3½ *dir.* = 3 *dir.* = 3 *dān.*}=] 4 *dirhams* and 4 *dānaqs*.

The eight-times weight of dry or moist [in the Fourth Degree], being [signified by] the letters *jīm* or *dāl* respectively, is 9 *dirhams* and 2 *dānaqs*. [This can be viewed] either as 8 times the value of the First Degree or as an independent value of the Fourth Degree itself. As for the five-times weight of dry or moist [in the Third Degree], and these are likewise [signified by] the letters *jīm* or *dāl* respectively, it is 5 *dirhams* and 5 *dānaqs*. [Again, this can be viewed] either as 5 times the value of the First Degree or as an independent value of the Third Degree itself . . .

In this way, among all objects belonging the three kingdoms of nature, from the smallest to the largest, when these are considered according to the precise Balance, and among all the celestial bodies and among all the other wonders of the natural world, the total weight of 17 in red [bodies] is [represented by] 19 *dirhams* and 5 *dānaqs* [= 17 × 7 *dān.*]. This is the figure arrived at according to the precise Balance as it exists in incorporeal objects, in the material objects belonging to the three kingdoms of nature, and in the higher bodies. Similar is the case with white [bodies]. It behooves you to know this!

As for the difference between the white and the red, it lies in the excess of cold and shortage of hot in the white, the case of the red being the opposite; and in the excess of dry and shortage of moist in the red, the case of the white being the opposite. So understand that!

When you desire the weight of a given thing, you ought to find out, [first], what its letters necessitate; next, work out what it adds up to. [Finally], adjust your result so that it reaches a value which is related to 17.[1]

2. Note that throughout Jābir makes the natures conform to the proportion 1 : 3 : 5 : 8.

1. Like Aristotle, Jābir believes that hot and cold were active qualities, whereas dry and moist were passive (see *Meteor.*, 4.1, 378b; *Gen. et Corr.*, 1.6–7, 322b–324a; *ibid.*, 2.2, 329b–330a).

[*22*]

When in a natural object the nature hot is on the opposite side of moist, then we have an instance of the color red. Had this not been the case, the dry due to its preponderance would have torn the moist apart, since [in red bodies] the quantity of dry is enormously greater than that of moist. Reverse is the case with the white, for if [in white bodies] dry had not been on the opposite side of cold, the moist would have overpowered the dry. The meaning of spatial opposition between the natures is that they exist in mutual proximity; but they do not stand against each other in conflict, I mean in being face-to-face. Nor [are these natures separated from each other] by distance such as that which exists between the circumference of a circle and its center. To be sure, had spatial opposition not existed between the natures (and, consequently, the hot in the red had overpowered [the cold], as is inevitable, and similarly the dry had overpowered [the moist]), then the body in question would have exploded. The same is true of all things which are artificially produced.

[*23*]

When a thing in equilibrium exists in an integral state, just as when it is not a [flowing] liquid, then among all things it necessarily occupies the medial position. An example of this among stones is the case of the three bodies, gold, silver, and copper, when viewed in terms of the quantities of their softness and hardness. As for the things other than stones, they are in some manner placed in equilibrium likewise. But this matter warrants further examination and research.

This is so because, [for example], the parts of all animals exist in an integral solid state, in which case being in equilibrium would mean being in an integral solid state. But if all of these parts happened to be fusible, then being in equilibrium would have meant being fusible; and if they happened to be soft, the characterization of equilibrium would have changed likewise. Indeed, if [the parts of animals] happened to have attributes other than these, they would have been considered to be in equilibrium in a similar manner. . . . Since all parts of animals have their own proper constitution, in themselves they are all equally in equilibrium.

It is now abundantly clear that gold is not the most equilibrated metal: if the practitioners of the Art make it such, it is only because they derive worldly benefits out of it. Were they in a position to derive a similar benefit out of copper or lead, they would have made these latter the most equilibrated ones, and to these they would have directed their operations. So one reaches the inescapable conclusion that gold is distinguished only from the point of view of its utility.

You ought to follow what we are saying, for you might need to transform an equilibrated object into one which is [allegedly] unequilibrated. This situation can arise if we were utterly to run out of copper, while facing a glut of silver and gold, and a need for copper. If gold were to be in equilibrium and copper were to be, in comparison, unstable, then we would need to transform the equilibrated gold into the unequilibrated copper, for this would be demanded by necessity.

But here we likewise say: The fruit of a tree is no more in equilibrium than its leaves even though the fruit yields more benefit than the leaves. Nay, one ought to give all things their due weight, for they interchange,[1] God willing! . . .

[*24*]

Let us now consider those matters which concern the Balance of Letters in the elixir, just as we did in the *Book of the Arena of the Intellect*, God willing! So we proceed, seeking support from God.

Some of our earlier discourses have already rendered it unnecessary to define the elixir, for it is now known that the fundamental governing principle of the elixir is 17 and that it is divided into two kinds: red and white. If the elixir is red, it has a preponderance of hot and dry; if it is white, it has a preponderance of cold and moist. And, according to the opinion that is sound and free from corruption, the total effective weight of the elixir is [a multiple of 17, namely] 19 *dirhams* and 5 *dānaqs*. Indeed, all our examples signify the number 17 [even] if [in practice] we arrive at a number which is higher or lower. Thus, it behooves you to know that in all of them [sc. In all natural objects] the governing principle is 17, for the nature hot remains hot no matter where it happens to be, and the nature cold, wherever it exists, remains cold, and the same applies to moist and dry.

[*25*]

This is so because the appellation applied to one nature is not applied to any other. For example, the appellation "*alif*" is applied to no other letter, be it *bāʾ*, *jīm*, or *dāl*. Similarly, the appellation "*bāʾ*" is applied to none of the other three letters, *alif*, *jīm*, or *dāl*; and the appellation "*jīm*" is applied to none of the letters from among *alif*, *bāʾ*, and *dāl*; and finally, the appellation "*dāl*" is likewise applied to no other letter from among *alif*, *bāʾ*, and *jīm*.

If you intend to make a given "*alif*" degenerate into a "*bāʾ*," or into a "*jīm*" or a *dāl*," [you can achieve this] provided you derive these letters from the Second Elements, namely, Fire, Air, Water, and Earth.[1] Upon my life! Some of these compounds undergo transmutation. All this we have meticulously explicated in the *Book of Morphology*; thus, the method has already been clarified: Pursue it! God the Most High willing!

[*26*]

[A]

Let us now return to what we began to say concerning the Balance of metals. So we say, our success depending on God: You ought to know, may God protect you, that metals differ from one another, for otherwise all of them would have been

1. That is, elements pass into one another—this is an assertion of Jābir's belief in transmutation.

one and the same thing. Indeed, it seems proper [that they are diverse]. And among these metals there are those which [in their Balance] exceed 17, others which fall short of it, yet others [whose Balance] equals 17.

If, when analyzing a thing, you find that it equals 17, don't add anything, and don't subtract anything. However, this is an exceedingly rare case. If you find a thing whose [Balance] is greater than 17, subtract it in proportion till it reaches 17. Proportionalized and regularized, it will correspond to that thing which is so rare as to be practically non-existent. So know that, and proceed accordingly!

If, on the other hand, you find a thing which in its Balance falls short of 17, complete it so that it becomes like that rare thing which is, as we said, practically non-existent. Proceed in this manner, for this is the way! God willing. . . .

So, God protect you, [in practice] everything either exceeds [17] or falls short [of it]—this is inevitable. Thus, one obtains the result that gold is among the excessive ones. Indeed, it behooves you to know the meaning of excessive and deficient, even though we have so far spoken of that which [is neither excessive nor deficient, namely that which] precisely conforms to 17; and, God protect you, such can only be the case of the elixir. . . .

[B]

So when a seeker desires to transform gold into elixir, he reduces [the weight of] each of its natures in such a way that this gold is left only with 17, whence the total weight of the natures becomes 19 *dirhams* and 5 *dānaqs* [= 17 × 7 *dān.*]; the rest is discarded.

Similarly, if the seeker desires to transform gold so that it acquires the properties of copper, he finds out, first, the total weight of [the natures in] copper; then, he finds out the weight [of the natures in] gold. Next, he compares the two weights to know which one is greater. If [the weight obtained from] gold turns out to be the greater of the two, the adept reduces it till it drops to the value [obtained from] copper. If, on the other hand, copper exceeds gold, he augments [the weights of the natures] in gold till it conforms to the definition of copper. However, gold necessarily exceeds copper . . . I wish I knew how you will accomplish all this if you are not familiar with the *Ḥudūd*, and if you have not pondered over it! . . .

[27]

People are seriously divided over the question of the weight of tin. Thus, some of them say, "we determine its weight according to its name *ʿal-qalaʿī*'." But the Stoics say, "no, its name is, rather "*al-raṣāṣ*' since its sibling is called '*al-usrub*'." "No," say the followers of Empedocles, "we determine its weight, rather, according to the appellation '*zāwus*' for its nature is most equilibrated, and that is what the word means." But the followers of Pythagoras say, "its name is, in fact, '*al-mushtarī*,[1] for it has the nature of this celestial body. We determine its weight in accordance

1. The planet Jupiter.

with no appellation except '*al-mushtarī*,' for it is *al-mushtarī* which governs it, guides it, and brings it forth. Nay, this is its only name." As for Socrates, he judged in favor of '*zāwus*,' and he is close to the truth. Balīnās said, "its name is '*qaṣdīr*' in which lies its weight; it has no other name." The Peripatetics say, "we determine its weight according to our description "hot and moist,' for it has no name signifying its nature."

From among these differing models, none merits our choice the way '*zāwus*' does; and if we were to substitute for it, we would opt for the description 'hot and moist.' Thus, that which we have illustrated in the figure[2] is worked out according to the name '*zāwus*,' for '*al-qalaʿī*' signifies something other than the name [of the metal in question]. Indeed, the name '*qaṣdīr*' is also an accurate one, and this is so because all [correct] names, while being different in different languages, seek to express a unique language—for what is [ultimately] sought is only the *meaning* of these differing names.

The Third Part of the Book of Stones According to the Opinion of Balīnās

[*28*]

In the Name of God, the Compassionate, the Merciful.

Praise the Creator and the Raiser of the Dead, the One Who subjects to His Acts whatever he chooses. He Who is Powerful over everything, and is the Subjugator of all subjugators. The One Who causes the acts of all things, without a parallel and without a teacher; He acts not out of passion, nor under compulsion: nay, He acts as He wills! He is Magnanimous, Kind, Mighty, Wise!

So praise be to God, the Best of Creators!

God's blessings be upon Muḥammad, the Lord of all messengers, the *Imām* of the first ones and the last ones. All prayers be for him, according to what he merits, and for his noble family.

May God grant them all salvation!

[*29*]

Two books have preceded this one, dealing with the understanding of the Balances of stones. According to the commitment we made in these two books (I mean the first book and the second book), we shall specify in the present book, proceeding in a natural way, the forms which stones, plants and animal [substances] take upon combining with one another. Furthermore, we shall talk about the procedure for the ceration of these substances. So we say . . .

The things from which the elixir derives are [of seven possible kinds]: [i] pure stones, [ii] animal [substances] exclusively, [iii] plants only, [iv] animal [sub-

2. At the end of this part of our text, the author does produce a table of calculation of the weights of the natures in tin: indeed, this has been worked out according to the appellation "*Zāwus*."

stances] *and* plants, [v] stones *and* plants, [vi] stones *and* animal [substances], and [vii] animals [substances] *and* plants *and* stones. This makes a total of seven patterns occurring in the pharmaceutical composition of the elixir, with each one of them having its own governing principles.

[A]

And if in response to an operation, some of them happen to differ from the others, [we know the reason why] for it is known that *alif* is for hot, *bāʾ* is for cold, *jīm* is for dry, and *dāl* is for moist. And, of course, the possibility remains for *alif* to exist in four different positions in the [name of a] compounded thing, since the Degrees [of intensity] are four. The same applies to *bāʾ*, *jīm* and *dāl*. And as we taught you in the beginning, the weights of these four positions of *alif* have correspondingly four different values, namely: 1 *dirham* and 1 *dānaq* [= 7 *dān.*], 3½ *dirhams* [= 21 *dān.*], 5 *dirhams* and 5 *dānaqs* [= 35 *dān.*], or 7 *dirhams* and 2 *dānaqs* [= 56 *dān.*]. . . .

[B]

So turn to the stone you wish to operate upon, and [whose natures] you want to augment by means of an appropriate method of ceration. You find out its weight. If it happens to be an elixir, its weight will be [exactly] 19 *dirhams* and 5 *dānaqs* [= 17 × 7 *dān.*]. But if it is something other than elixir, it will weigh either more or less, depending upon the quantity of the natures in the stone under consideration. So know that!

Augmentation, I mean ceration, is carried out in the same manner [in all stones]. Thus, if the stone possesses hot in the First Degree, add a fifth in the First Degree; if it possesses hot in the Second Degree, add a fifth in the Second Degree; if it possesses hot in the Third Degree, add a fifth in the Third Degree; [finally], if it possesses hot in the Fourth Degree, add a fifth in the Fourth Degree. The weight of the fifth in the First Degree is 1 *qīrāṭ* [= ½ *dān.*], in the Second Degree 1½ *dānaqs*, in the Third Degree 2½ *dānaqs*, and in the Fourth Degree 4 *dānaqs*.

So in the case of things composed of stones only, this is what is necessary for carrying out ceration by means of hot-augmentation.

As for the procedure of cold-augmentation, the rules for this are exactly the same as those of hot which we have just described. The same applies to the procedures of the augmentation of moist and dry. . . . In other words, you find out which from among hot, cold, dry and moist is preponderant in the thing you want to operate upon. Then, you add a fifth to the most dominant nature in these stones. As we have said, a thing is not cerated except by means of [an augmentation of] its characteristically predominant nature. So know this procedure, and follow it in the operations you need to perform on drugs made out of stones only.

[C]

Concerning the elixir made out of animal [substances] only. If you wish either to cerate it, or to transform it from one thing to another, you add a fourth to that nature which is likewise the predominant of the four. If this nature is in the First Degree [of intensity], you add a fourth in the First Degree, in which case the weight of the fourth is 1 *dānaq*; if the predominant nature is in the Second Degree, you add a fourth in the Second Degree; here the fourth reaches a weight of ½ *dirham* [= 3 *dān.*]; if this nature is in the Third Degree, add a fourth in the Third degree, the weight of the fourth here being 5 *dānaqs*; and, finally, if this predominant nature is in the fourth degree, you add a fourth in the Fourth Degree, where the fourth attains a weight of 2 *dirhams* and 2 *dānaqs* [= 8 *dān.*].

So know that!

[D]

And if the elixir which you want to cerate or transform . . . Happens to be made exclusively out of plants, you find out likewise the most dominant of its four natures and add to it a third. If its most dominant nature is in the First Degree of intensity, you add a third in the First Degree, the weight of the third in this case being 1½ *dānaqs*; if this nature is in the Second Degree, you add a third in the Second Degree; here the weight of the third is 4½ *dānaqs*; if this nature is in the Third Degree, you add a third in the Third Degree; and, finally, if it happens to be in the Fourth Degree, you add a third in the Fourth Degree. The weight of the third in the Third Degree is 1¼ *dirhams* [= 7½ *dān.*], and in the Fourth Degree it is 2 *dirhams* [= 12 *dān.*]. . . .

[*30*] [*On Quality*]

Quality is a certain condition of the qualified thing, I mean the condition by virtue of which the thing is qualified. Among these conditions are those which exist in actuality, such as the walking of ʿAbdAllāh when he is, in fact, walking. Further, among such actually existing conditions are either those which change or disappear quickly, for example standing, sitting, being in a state of embarrassment or anger, and the like—such actually existing conditions do not last long; or those which [are more stable and] do not change or disappear quickly, such as [the knowledge of] geometry, medicine, or music when [such knowledge] is actually present in an individual.

And among the conditions are those which exist in potentiality, as walking is to ʿAbd Allāh (thus, animals are plants in potentiality, in actuality they are not, and the same applies to stones in relation to plants and animals). Similar is the case of the acquisition of [the knowledge] of geometry when it is unacquired [in actuality]. Further, potential conditions exist either [a] as a capacity in a thing, such as our saying that ʿAbd Allāh is [in a state of being] fallen to the ground when he has the capacity to do so; or [b] as a natural affection, such as our saying that a given stone is hard, meaning that it cannot be divided easily, or that a given piece of wood is soft, meaning that it can be broken apart without difficulty.

Things are rarely said in discourse to be qualified—I mean characterized—by those conditions which change or disappear quickly. Thus, we do not call pallid the one who turns yellow out of fright, nor swarthy the one who turns black due to a journey [in the heat of the sun]. And as for the conditions which last longer, things might be said to be qualified by them. Thus we call yellow (or, say, black) that which acquires this color as part of its natural make-up (likewise, if it acquires some other condition which is not easily removed, [it is called accordingly]). And these, I mean the conditions which do not disappear easily, are the ones which ought necessarily to be called qualities, since the essential nature of a thing is qualified by them.

Similarly there might be in the soul either [a] easily disappearing conditions, such as sadness or happiness arising out of a certain specific reason and passing away quickly, or [b] longer lasting conditions, such as sadness or happiness arising out of one's innate disposition for it. Obviously the latter is identical [in appearance] to the former. However, we do not characterize as sad one who is sad for a short period of time for some reason, nor happy one who is happy briefly. Rather, we do so when these are part of someone's essential nature, whence permanent or preponderant.

Shape, external form, straightness, curvedness, and the like are also qualities, for each one of these is said to qualify things. Thus, we might say of a thing that it is a triangle or a square, or that it is straight or curved. Rareness, denseness, roughness, smoothness and the like might be thought of as qualities; they seem however not to belong to qualities. This is so because, to be precise, a thing is dense when its parts are close together; rare when they are separated from one another; smooth because its parts lie uniformly on a straight line—none being above or below another; and rough when they are otherwise.

Qualities are possibly of other kinds too. Among these other kinds which we shall mention are [a] those which are perceived by the eye, like shapes and colors; [b] those which are perceived by the sense of smell, like perfumes; [c] those which are perceived by the sense of taste, like the savour of food; [d] those which are perceived by the sense of touch, like hot or cold; [e] those which exist in the intellect, like knowledge and ignorance; [f] which lie in the capacity of things, like the ability or inability to do something—and these exist either actually or potentially; [g] those which are stable; [h] those which are unstable; [i] those which are active; and [j] those which are passive.

Qualified things are named after their quality. Thus in most cases things are named paronymously—such as *kātib* from *kitāba*, *tājir* from *tijāra*, *jāʾir* from *jawr*, *ʿādil* from *ʿadl*. Yet this may not be so in all cases, either because the quality in question exists in potentiality, or due to the fact that language lacks a name for it.

There is contrariety in regard to qualification. For example, justice is contrary to injustice and whiteness to blackness, and so on. Similarly, there is contrariety in regard to qualified things. For example, just is contrary to unjust and white to black. But, [on the other hand], there is no contrary to red or yellow or such colors. Likewise, there is no contrary to triangle and circle.

Further, when one of a pair of contraries is a qualification, the other too will be a qualification. This is clear if one examines the other categories. For example, justice is contrary to injustice and justice is a qualification, then injustice too is a qualification. For none of the other categories fits injustice, neither quantity, for example, nor relation, place, time, nor any other category except qualification.

Qualifications admit of a more and a less; for it may be said that this whiteness is more than that, or that this thing is whiter than that—not in all cases though, but in most. Thus it might be questioned whether it is permissible to call one justice more a justice than another, or one health more a health than another. Some people say that it is not permissible, yet they say that one person has health less than another, justice less than another, and similarly with writing and other conditions. So, as for things spoken of in virtue of these, they unquestionably admit of a more and a less, for it may well be said that this man is more eloquent than that, this man is more just than that, or that this man is better with regard to justice and health.

However, not all things spoken of in virtue of a quality admit of a more and a less. For example, the triangle is spoken of in virtue of the quality of triangularity, and the square in virtue of the quality of squareness: these two do not admit of a more and a less. For one triangle does not exceed another in respect of triangularity, and one square does not possess more squareness than another. All triangles are equally said to be triangles, and the same applies to circles and squares.

Things which are equally said to be triangles [and thus] equally said to fall under the definition [of triangularity] are not called more or less with respect to that definition; the same holds for circles and squares. Conversely, when two things are not said to fall under one definition, the definition of one is not applied to the other. In general, all things which are equally said to fall under a given definition, as well as two things which are not said to fall under one definition, such things do not admit of a more and a less.

One speaks of a more and a less only in cases where the [quality to whose] definition a thing conforms sustains increase and decrease; for example a white thing which conforms to the definition of being white can very well be more or less with respect to whiteness.

It is in virtue of a universally defined quality only that things are said to be similar or dissimilar; for a thing is not similar to another except in virtue of its quality. For example, this triangle is not similar to that triangle except in virtue of the triangle which has already been universally defined.

It may be said that though we only proposed to discuss qualities we have frequently mentioned relatives since we have spoken of knowledge and the like, and knowledge exists in virtue of the known. Indeed, the genera comprehending these things, I mean the universals, are spoken of in virtue of something else, such as knowledge which is spoken of in virtue of the known. But none of the individuals [of a given genus], that is, none of the particular cases [of a given universal], is spoken of in virtue of something else. For example, knowledge, [a genus], is called knowledge of something, but grammar, [a particular case], is not called grammar of something. This is so unless the particular case is set forth as the genus, that is, given the name of the universal, which in this case is knowledge—then, grammar would be called knowledge of something. Thus the particular cases are not relatives and there is nothing absurd in a thing's falling under two different genera.

The Fourth Part of the Book of Stones According to the Opinion of Balīnās

[31]

In the Name of God, the Compassionate, the Merciful

Praise be to God, the Lord of the worlds! May God's blessings be upon our Master Muḥammad and all his family.

The one who recalls what we said in the first, second and third parts of this book would know that we have promised to explicate in this [final] part of the Balances of spirits, those substances which function as spirits. We shall accomplish this by means of illustrative figures following the pattern on which we constructed in the second part the figures for bodies.[1] We have also promised that in this part we shall spell out how one goes about augmenting what is deficient, and suppressing what is excessive.[2]

At this point in time we turn at once to operations involving spirits. Immediately following this, we shall familiarize ourselves with augmentation and suppression, and this will mark the end of these four books.

So we say: In fire, spirits are unlike bodies—but not with respect to color, hardness or casting. For all spirits, or [at least] most of them, may have the same colors as those of bodies—red, white, black, etc.; and, in terms of casting, spirits may be similar to bodies, since all spirits undergo casting in fire the way bodies do, behaving in the same manner. Finally, in terms of hardness some spirits may function like bodies, just as in terms of softness certain bodies may function as some spirits. We are setting forth a specific account of the spirits and the bodies, to the exclusion of others, since it behooves us to know that the Art does not exist except due to spirits and bodies; [that is to say], there is no Art except in virtue of the three kingdoms of nature since [in the real world] nothing else exists.

As for animal [substances], when distilled they yield two spirits and two bodies: the oil and the water which come out of them are spirits, whereas the tincture and the earth which they yield are bodies. . . . The same applies to plants. Concerning stones, the situation depends on whether or not they lend themselves to distillation. If they do, then the same applies to them too.

But if they do not lend themselves to distillation, they are divided into two types: those which vaporize, and those which do not. Those which do vaporize yield two kinds of substances: what vaporizes from them is spirit, and what is left as residue is body. And those which do not evaporate divide likewise into two kinds: the aqueous kind, and the calcined kind. The former is spirit, the latter body. The aqueous kind, in its turn, divides further into two kinds: the kind that flees, and the kind that does not. As for the one that flees from fire, it is spirit; and that which does not, even though it is water, is body.

1. At the end of the book Jābir does give illustrative calculations of the weights of the natures in spirits.

2. The point is repeated that if upon analysis of the name of the spirit the total weight of the natures is not found to be exactly 17 or its multiple, one augments/suppresses the natures.

So this is the complete alchemical classification of the matters relating to all natures, and this is exactly what we have already mentioned in the *Book of the Complete*[3] belonging to the *CXII Books*.

[*32*]

As for the transformation of bodies from one state into another higher or lower state, it is according to our doctrine [an interchange between] the exterior and the interior, for in reality this is what exterior and interior are. The reason is that all the constituents of all things follow a circular pattern of change.

The exterior of a body is manifest, whereas its interior is latent, and it is the latter in which lies the benefit. For example, lead in its exterior is foul-smelling lead, and it is manifest to all people. But in its interior it is gold, and this is hidden. However, if this latter is extracted out, then both the interior and the exterior of lead will become manifest.

[*33*]

Thus there is the Balance of Fire, and the Balance of the rest of the bodies. There are Balances of the natures of stars, their distances, acts and movements. There is also the Balance by means of which one knows the Sphere, just as one learns through the Balance that the essential characteristics of things arise out of the natures. Those who have read our book known as *The End Attained*[1] and our *Book of the Sun*[2] are acquainted with most of these Balances, even with the Balance of the Soul and the Balance of the Intelligence, after which there is no end. And since all of these are intangible, it would not be difficult for such readers to measure the Balance of animals, plants and animals, for these exist in nature and are tangible. . . .

Chapter on the Curriculum for the Training of the Disciple

[*34*]

[A]

First you ought to understand a simple thing concerning the Art. That is, you familiarize yourself with the substances which are reddened, whitened, coagulated, dissolved, softened, and dehydrated.[1] Further, you ought to know that all these

3. Kr 71–73.

1. Kr 373. This work belongs to the Books of Balances.

2. Kr. 51. This is the title of a lost treatise which is part of the *CXII* collection. There is also a *Kitāb al-mirrīkh wa'l-shams* (Book of Mars and the Sun) in the *LXX* collection (Kr 189).

1. For a detailed account of these chemical processes see Stapleton, Azo and Ḥusain [1927].

processes are carried out by the method of Balance. This has been explained to you in the lucid accounts given in many books of ours: [for example], we have thoroughly explicated this already in the *Result*, the *Book of Morphology*, the *Balance*,[2] and in a book belonging to the *CXII* known as the *Book of Tinctures*.

Then, you ought to know the First, Second, Third and the Fourth Elements, [their] accidents and their qualities.[3] For example, [you ought to know that] Fire and its sisters are the Second Elements,[4] durations of time are the Third, and black and yellow compounds are the Fourth Elements.

You see how your personal nature accepts all this, how you handle this, and how the results suit your natural disposition. If you already see that your mind has rejected one specific thing while you are [comfortably] handling several others, you ought first to persist in reading. You should particularly read the *Commentary on the Book of the Elements of Foundation*, if it has reached you. But if you have already moved beyond this stage, congratulations!

Having accomplished this, move up to the sayings of philosophers and their doctrines concerning the natures and their combinations. Pick up a modicum of *kalām*, logic, arithmetic and geometry. To some extent this will render your conceptual grasp of problems easy when they exercise you. But if you are already somewhat trained in these disciplines, the task will be simpler for you, and this would be a more favorable situation.

Next, depending on your choice, you handle the science of the natures, or some other discipline. If you prefer the science of the natures, you study aspects of the natures of stones and the [science of the] specific properties of things.

Then you move in a single leap to the Balances. Thus, you familiarize yourself step by step with all aspects of various kinds of Balances, such as the Balance of Fire, of music, and the Balances of metals. Some of these we have already mentioned in several books, particularly in the *Book of the Elite*.

And if along with the science of the natures you are inclined toward the knowledge of the craft, you study the *Book of Trickeries*[5] so that you can be on your guard against the occurrence of calamities, loss of wealth, and frauds.

The next step now is to become skilled in [matters presented in] the *Book of the Balance*.[6] You should know in what manner and for what reason these things are combined. Now, we have already told you that by this time you ought to have become accomplished and quick-witted.

If [the disciple] does not finish my book, the *Seven*,[7] he will remain deficient in his [knowledge of] the Balances. If, on the contrary, he is trained in it, he will be in a position to construct whatever he wishes.

2. See note 6 below.

3. Note the distinction Jābir maintains between *ṭabʿ* and *kayfiyya*.

4. See Chapter 3 above.

5. Kr 1063. This work is not extant.

6. There are two works in the Jābirian corpus with this title, Kr 197 and Kr 366. Both are lost.

7. A *Book of the Seven* is part of the *LXX* (Kr 132). Also found in the corpus is a collection of seven books, one on each of the seven metals (gold, silver, copper, iron, tin, lead, and *khārṣīnī*), and this is likewise referred to by the author as the *Sabʿa* (Kr 947–953).

All that the disciple needs now is the [skill for the] handling of alchemical operations. Restituted from accounts scattered in [a large body of alchemical] writings, these are operations such as ceration, waterings, pulverization, dissolutions, and coagulations.[8] Another example is that [of the elixir] about which people have been talking since ancient times. But the ancients have wrapped in ever deeper mysteries the method of operations relating to the Supreme Thing. Now, as we have already told you, this difficulty is overcome by nothing other than the [method of] the Balances. So know this method if you intend to achieve a close approximation [of the ideal elixir], or whatever you intend according to your desire.

Proceed with the understanding that this is an art which demands special skills; nay, it is the greatest of all arts for it [concerns] an ideal entity which exists only in the mind.[9] Thus the more one occupies oneself with prolonged studies, the quicker it will be to achieve a synthesis [of the elixir]. But the one who makes only a brief study, his achievement will be [slower] in the same proportion. Know that the fruit of the Balances are the higher operations performed on the products of syntheses and elixirs.

[B]

The Balance comes about only after the mixing of bodies with bodies, spirits with bodies, metals with bodies, spirits with spirits, stones with spirits, or stones with bodies and spirits: the Balance comes about after these substances are mixed [in these specified ways].

Even if spirits, bodies, and metals are in an impure state, weigh them after they are mixed together. Familiarize yourself with all of their constituent natures and know their equilibrium. The Canon of Equilibrium is known to you—if they conform to it, they are perfect. But if they are [quantitatively] higher or lower [than 17], suppress or augment the natures accordingly whence one would obtain from them exactly 17 parts. . . .

[*35*]

People hold diverse views concerning these [sc. Cosmological] issues. Among them are those who give due consideration to the Balances and proceed with the assumption that the principle of everything is the natures. And among them are those who say that in the natural world one thing was created before another. So, a group of Ṣābians and their followers believe that some fundamental building blocks of the natural would have, over others, a priority in existence. But this priority, [they say], is not with regard to arrangement or organization, rather it is a temporal and qualitative priority. Thus I have seen one of them claiming that the first thing which was created in matter is the three dimensions—length, breadth and depth—whence matter became a three-dimensional primitive body. Next,

8. A fuller discussion of these operations is in Stapleton, Azo and Ḥusain [1927].

9. Note the categorical statement that elixirs are only ideal substances and do not actually exist.

[according to this claim], the four qualities—namely, hot, cold, moist and dry—were created in it, and from this arose the natures of things and the elements of creation. Finally, [so the claim goes], the four natures mixed with one another to form compounds, and out of these arose all individuals and all undifferentiated forms existing in this world.

To those [holding such views] it ought to be said: You have introduced several unknowable stages [in your account of the creation of the natural world]—none of them makes sense! You even go so far as to explain the existence of the world [in terms of these stages], whatever they may be. . . .

[A]

So we say [to them], our success depending on God:

[According to you], the first of these stages [of creation] is *ṭīna* which is indestructible. [You believe that] it is not a body, nor is it predicated of anything that is predicated of a body. It is, you claim, the undifferentiated form of things and the element of created objects. The picture of this *ṭīna* [you tell us], exists [only] in the imagination, and it is impossible to visualize it as a defined entity.

You say that the second stage arrives when the three dimensions come to pass in this *ṭīna* whence it becomes a body. This body, [you claim], is not predicated of any of [the four natures], hot, cold, moist and dry, nor is it predicated of any color, taste, smell, or of motion or rest. For, [according to you], all these are qualities, and at this stage qualities do not come to pass in it.

Now [all] this is nonsense!

Then you claim that after this second stage the four qualities[1] come to pass in this body, namely the qualities hot, cold, moist and dry. From these arise the four [elementary bodies], Fire, Air, Water and Earth. But quite obviously it makes no sense to suppose that these four natures exist in any state or condition not defined by the organization and arrangement in which they are now found in the natural world. Thus, Earth is in the middle of the Sphere, Water is above Earth, Air above Water, and Fire above Air. Further, each of the four natures tends to overpower its contrary, with the subdued transforming into the triumphant. Plants and animals exist along with these natures, deriving from them, and transforming [back] into them. Now the afore-described stages [of creation] proffered by you are all intangible. But, as compared to what you describe, it is easier and less demanding on one's imagination to visualize that things arise but not out of a single [abstract] entity.

[B]

Or [let us ask them that] they tell us if it is possible for Water to be created from the same prime matter as the one from which Fire is created. If they say yes, they lapse into inconsistencies. For a given thing which gives rise to something else is the prime matter of the latter. As they say, the sperm of man is the prime matter of

1. Note the very rare application of the term *kayfiyyāt* to primary qualities.

man, and the sperm of donkey the prime matter of donkey. Thus they deem it absurd to suppose that the sperm of man admits the form of a donkey, since the former is not the prime matter of the latter, just as it is equally absurd to suppose that the sperm of donkey admits the form of a man. It is therefore necessary according to this reasoning that the thing which admits the form of Fire is the prime matter of Fire, and being such it cannot possibly admit the form of Water.

[C]

If they say:

We see Water undergoing transformation and thus turning into Fire. [In this process], the substance which was the carrier first of the qualities and characteristics of Water is the carrier now of the qualities and characteristics of Fire. Thus whatever is essentially true of the former is essentially true also of the latter: it is only the accidents of the substance which have changed. Therefore, the eternal prime matter is one and the same—it is the carrier of the qualities and dispositions of Water if they come to pass in it, and those of Fire if these latter come to pass in it.

Then in reply we say:

Water does not transform in a single stroke into Fire. Rather it transforms first into vapors and then becomes Air. Next, Air undergoes transformation and, [finally], turns into Fire. If someone says that Water transforms, first, into Air and, then, transforms into Fire, he is indeed speaking of a transformation [process] which makes [perfect] sense.

Further, your doctrine concerning the simple, indestructible prime matter is not consistent with this, for you do not say that it is only by way of the aforementioned transmutations that Fire is created out of the thing from which, in the first instance, Water is created. Rather you say, "it is possible that the prime matter which is overtaken by the nature and characteristics of Water is subsequently overtaken instead by the natures and characteristics of Fire." And, according to you, this takes place without the intermediary of the transformation that lies between Water and Fire. This makes no sense!

They claim that prior to acquiring forms and before the occurrence in it of the natures, the eternal prime matter is endowed with the potentiality only of accepting in the first instance the characteristics and qualities of Fire. But that there is a kind of prime matter which is endowed with the potentiality of accepting the characteristics and qualities of Water, and that the same goes for Earth and Air. It is through this doctrine that they demonstrate the creation of the four eternally indestructible elements which possess different potentialities. But, then, this refutes their affirmation that the First Element is unique and does not admit of diversity.

[D]

They are asked: "Is it admissible that things return to the eternal prime matter the way they arose out of it?" If they say, "no, it is not admissible," one might ask, "but why not?" If they say, "this is annihilation of things, for then things will be returning to something which is simple, not admitting of combination," then we respond, "and what harm do you see in saying that things will return to that which happens to be indestructible on account of its being an eternal cause. And, further, what harm do you see in saying that while prime matter is simple and it possesses no combinations, it will annihilate the world?"

[E]

It [ought to be] said to them: A majority of philosophers believe that the four natures, which are the fundamental principles of creation and are the elements of the things (I mean [the elements of the primary bodies] Fire, Air, Water and Earth), potentially exist in one another. Thus those people lapse in inconsistencies who say that the four natures exist in something other than themselves, and that they exist in something other than what arises out of them. Such people declare it inconceivable that things can exist in any other way.

So if someone alleges that these four natures are only to be found existing potentially in something other than themselves, and in something other than what arises out of them, let him bring a proof of his hypothesis. [Indeed], he will never be able to do so, for it is irrational [to espouse a hypothesis] which stands in disagreement with this doctrine [sc. the doctrine of the philosophers] and which contravenes the organization and arrangement [of which we have spoken]!

[F]

The incorrectness of their affirmation is deduced from what the philosophers consider as an indubitable premise and an item of necessary knowledge, namely: It is absurd to suppose that a substance can exist without any natural or fabricated acts, so that this substance has no act either in itself or in anything else.

[Yet] this is [precisely] the nature which these people declare as eternal, claiming that it is the element of things, and that the prime matter which arises out of it is indestructible and is devoid of all natural and fabricated acts. And this is the theory which is dismissed by the philosophers who deny the existence of such an entity. To support [their idea of] a substance devoid of all acts, they [sc. The upholders of this theory] have been able neither to offer a proof of what they claim, nor to establish it by an indirect demonstration.

[G]

Since the case is other than all this, the natures are [to be understood] according to what we elucidated for you in all the preceding books, namely that the natures are the fundamental principle [of the real world], and that they are subject to the acts of the Creator, may His praise be exalted! And from this you become familiar with the method of attaining [the knowledge of] the Natural Balance, nay, you even become an expert of all compounds that are constituted out of the natures, able to distinguish goodness from corruption.

[36]

After accomplishing all this, the disciple moves to the task of verbal and written discourse so that his skills reach perfection. If, [following this], his insight in the Art matches his insight in the Science, and if in applications he possesses a refinement of quality, he is to be called a perfect philosopher!

This ultimately brings us to an end, being the final stage required in the training of the disciple whence the disciple meets our definition and description of him. At this time he is among those people who are closest to us!

Now, without delay, we shall present the figures which illustrate Balances, followed by a figure [illustrating] augmentation and suppression. This is the conclusion of the book, God the Most High willing! . . .

—*Seyed Nomanul Haq, translator*

References

Biographical Sources

Khwansārī M. Bāqir. *Rawḍāt al-jannāt*. Ed. by S. Maʾīnī. Tehran: 1933.

Khwārazmī M. b. Aḥmad. *Mafātiḥ al-ʿulūm*. Leiden: Lugduni-Satavourm, E. S. Brill, 1895.

Primary Sources

Jābir, ibn Ḥayyān. *Dix Traités d'alchimie*. Paris: Sindbad, 1983.

———. (*Textes*) *Mukhtār rasāʾil Jābir ibn Ḥayyān*. Textes choisis et éd. par. P. Kraus. Paris-Le Caire: G. P. Maisonaeuve et El-Khandgi, 1935.

———. *The Arabic Works of Jābir ibn Ḥayyān*. Éd. de textes ar. par. E. J. Holmyard. Paris: P. Geuthner, 1928.

Secondary Sources

Berthelot, M. (*CMA*) *La chimie au Moyen Āge*. Vol. I. *Essai sur la transmission de la science antique au Moyen Âge*. Vol. II: *L'alchimie syriaque*, en collaboration avec R. Duval. Vol. III: *L'alchimie arabe*, textes et trad. avec. la coll. de O. Houdas. Paris: Imprimerie Nationale, 1893.

Burckhardt, T. *Alchemy: Science of the Cosmos, Science of the Soul*. Trans. W. Stoddart, Baltimore: Penguin Books, 1972.

Corbin, H. *Cylical Time and Ismāʿīlī Gnosis*. London: Kegan Paul International, 1983.

———. *En Islam iranien*. 4 vol. Paris: Gallimard, 1971–72.

———. *L'alchimie comme art hiératique*. Paris: Editions de L'Herne, 1986.

Darmstaedter E., *A Liber Misericordiae Geber*. Eine Lateinische übersetzung des grösseren *Kitāb al-rahma*. *Archiv für der Geschichte der Medizin* 17 (1925).

Evola, G. *The Hermetic Tradition*. Trans. by E. E. Rehmus. Rochester: Inner Traditions, 1995.

Fahd. T., "Jaʿfar al-Ṣādiq et la tradition scientifique arabe," in *Le shiʿisme imāmite*. Paris: P. Geuthner, 1970.

Fück, W. "The Arabic literature on alchemy according to Ibn al-Nadim." *Arabica*, 4 (1951): 3–4, 81.

Halm, H. *Kosmologie und Heilslehre der frühen Ismāʾīliyya*. Wiesbaden: Deutsche Morgenländische Gesellschaft, 1978.

Haq, S. N. *Names, Natures and Things*. Dordrecht-Boston: Kluwer Academic Publishers, 1994.

Holmyard, E. *The Arabic Works of Jābir ibn Ḥayyān*. Éd. de textes arabes. Paris: P. Geuthner, 1928.

———. "An Essay on Jābir ibn Ḥayyān," in *Studien zur Geshiche der Chimie*. Berlin: J. Springer Verlag, 1927.

———. *Kitāb al-ʿilm al-muktasab fī ixīrat al-dhahab* by *Abū al-Qāsim* . . . Ed. al-ʿIrāqī du texte arabe et trad. angl. Paris: P. Geuthner, 1923.

Ivanow, W. *Studies in Early Persia Ismāʿīlīsm*, 2nd ed. Bombay: Ismāʿīlī Society, 1955.

———. *L'Elaboration de l'Elixir Suprème quatorze traités de Gābir Ibn Ḥayyān sur le grande oeuvre alchimique*. Damascus: 1988.

Kraus, P. (*SG*). "Jābir et al science grecque," in *Mém. prés. é l'Institut d'Egypte*, 1.44. Le Caire: Impr. de l'I.F.A.O., 1942.

———, *Jābir ibn Ḥayyān*. 2 vols. Cairo: Imprimerie de l'Institut français d'archéologie orientale, 1943.

———. (*Corpus*) *Le Corpus des écrits jābiriens. Le Caire, Mém. Prés. à l'Institut d'Egypte*, t. 45. Impr. de. ı'I.F.A.O., 1943.

———. (*Textes*) *Mukhtār rasāʾil Jābir ibn Ḥayyān*. Textes arabes choisis et. Éd. Paris-Le Caire: G. P. Maisonneuve et. El-Khandgi éd., 1935,

———. "Dschābir ibn Ḥayyān und die Ismīʿilijja." *Drit. Jahresber. d. Forsch-Inst. f. Gesch. D. Naturwiss, in Berlin*. Berlin: 1930.

———. *Jābir ibn Ḥayyān. Contribution à l'histoire des idées scientifiques dans l'Islam*. Paris: Les Belles Lettres, 1986.

Lippmann, E. O. von (*Entstehung*). *Entstehung und Ausbreitung der Alchemie*. Vol. I et II, Berlin: J. Springer, 1919–1931; Vol. III. Weinheim, Verlag: Chemie, 1954.

Madelung, W. *Religious Sects and Schools in Islam*. London: Variorum, 1985.

Marquet, Y., *La Philosophie des alchimistes et l'alchimie des philosophes: Jābir ibn Ḥayyān et les "Frères de la Pureté."* Paris: Maisonneuve et Larose, 1988.

Massignon. L., "Inventaire de la littérature hermétiste arabe." *Opera Minora*, t. l. Paris: P.U.F. éd., 1969.

———. "Salmān Pāk et les prémices spirituelles de l'Islam iranien." *Parole donée*. Paris: Le Seuil, 1983.

Nasr, S. H. *Islamic Science. An Illustrated Study*. Westerham: World of Islam Festival Publishing, 1976, and Chicago: Kazi Publications, 1996 (?)

———, "From The Alchemy of Jābir to The Chemistry of Rāzī" in *Islamic Life and Thought* NY: SUNY Press, 1981, pp. 120–123.

———. "Islamic Alchemy and the Birth of Chemistry." *Journal for the History of Arabic Science*, III, I (1979). Vol. 3, No. 1, pp. 40–45.

———. *Science and Civilization in Islam*. New York: Barnes & Noble, 1995.

Ruska, J. "Die siebzig Bucher des Jābir ibn Ḥayyān." *Studien zur Geschichte der Chemie*. Berlin: J. Springer Verlag, 1927.

———. "Über das Schriftenverseichnis des Gābir ibn Ḥayyān und die Unechtheit einiger ihm Zugeschreibener Abhandinngen." *Archiv für der Geschichte der Medizin*, 15 (1923).

———. "Die bisherige versuche, das Dschābir-Problem zu losen." *N. Jahresber. der Forsch-Inst. für Geschichte der Naturwiss. in Berlin*. Berlin: 1930.

———. *Arabische Alchemisten*, t. I. *Chālid ibn Wālid ibn Muʿāwiya, t.* II. *Gaʿfar al-Ṣādiq, der Sechste Imām.* Heidelberg: C. Winter ed., 1924.

Sezgin, F., "Das Problem des Gābir ibn Ḥayyān im Lichte neu gefundener Handschriften." *Zeitschr. d. Deutsch. Morgeni. Geschichte* 115 (1964).

———. *Geschichte des arabischen Schrifttums*, IV. Leiden: E. J. Brill, 1971.

Saʿid, H. M. "Jābir ibn Ḥayyān." *Proceedings of the First International Symposium for the History of Arabic Science*, II. Alep., 1978, pp. 138–144.

Silvestre de Sacy, A. I. "Kitāb Sirr al-Khaliqua li-Balinus al-Ḥakīm. Le livre du secret de la créature, par le sage Bélinous." *Notices et éxtraits des manuscrits de la Bibliothèque du Roi*, 4 (1799): 107.

Stapelton, H. E., Hidāyat Ḥusain, Chemistry in Iraq and Persia in the Tenth Century A.D. in, *Memories of the Asiatic Society of Bengal*, VIII (1927), pp. 25–42.

Ullmann, M. *Die Natur- und Geheimwissenschaften im Islam*. Leiden-Köln: 1972.

Wiedamann, E. *Aufsätzen zur arabischen Wissenschaftgeschichte*. Ed. W. Fisher. New York: George Olm Verlag, 1970.

3

ABŪ YAʿQŪB SIJISTĀNĪ

Abū Yaʿqūb Ishāq ibn Aḥmad Sijistānī was a central figure in the early period of Ismāʿīlī thought in Persia. Some scholars have even identified him as the leading philosopher of the "Persian School" of Ismāʿīlī intellectual thought. Reports regarding his life are sketchy at best. While the date of his birth is not known, it is said that Amīr Khalaf ibn Aḥmad of the Saffarid dynasty executed him between 361/971 and 393/1002. The only evidence concerning the date of his death is found with Rashīd al-Dīn Faḍl Allāh's *Jāmiʿ al-tawārikh.* He has been referred to with a variety of names, such as Yaʿqūb, Abū Yaʿqūb Isḥāq, al-Sijzī and Khayshafūj. He was a contemporary of Fārābī and Ibn Sīnā and may have succeeded Abū Ḥātim Rāzī as the *dāʿī* in Rayy and Muḥammad Nasafī as the person in charge of *daʿwah* in Khurasan.

Sijistānī appears to have been well versed in the available body of Islamic thought at the time, as well as in Greek philosophy and Neoplatonism. While philosophically he makes use of the ideas of Abū Ḥatim Rāzī and Muḥammad Nasafī, except in a few minor cases he does not acknowledge their contributions. Sijistānī did not compose any work on the notion of the *Imāmat* nor did he emphasize the direct and personal authority of the living Imām, as so many Ismāʿīlīs have done. In fact, he did not even use the name Imām to refer to Muḥammad ibn Ismāʿīl to whom Ismāʿīlīs trace their origin. Instead, he emphasized prophecy and the necessity for using philosophical arguments.

In the translations we have included here, several sections of Sijistānī's major works *Kashf al-maḥjūb* (The Unveiling of the Hidden) and *Kitāb al-yanābīʿ* (The Book of Wellsprings). The *Kashf al-maḥjūb*, which is perhaps Sijistānī's *magnum opus*, appears here almost in its entirety. (For further information on the text refer to the introduction that the translator, Hermann Landolt, has included with the translation.) This introduction is essential to the understanding of the text, its intellectual significance as well as the historical context of the text in question. This work represents an important source book for the Ismāʿīlī thought of the Fāṭimid *daʿwah.*

The *Kitāb al-yanābīʿ* consists of forty wellsprings (*yanābīʿ*). It begins with the meaning of "wellspring," the rigorous affirmation of divine unity, and absolute purity of God who stands above all the attributes of being and nonbeing. The central thesis in this treatise is the problem of the Intellect and epistemology, and covers such themes as the Intellect's imperishability, its tranquility and quiescence, its position as the first originated being prior to which nothing can be conceived, its immateriality, how it communicates with the soul, and several categories of its properties. In short, the Intellect, according to him, is the sum of existent beings to which Sijistānī refers to as *al-sābiq* (the Preceder), a standard term in the Ismāʿīlī *daʿwah* literature. The soul emanates from the Intellect and is regulated and directed by the Intellect. Through the persisting influence in the soul, the Intellect comes into the beings engendered by the soul. Thus nature, which has an effect on the soul, preserves in itself rational qualities and man obtains the benefits of the Intellect through the part of the soul in him that "contains" the Intellect. When guided exclusively by the Intellect, the soul returns to an intelligible or spiritual world; therefore knowledge for Sijistānī comprises more than instinctual and learned apprehension of intelligible matter. Besides these two categories of knowledge there exists a special category of inspired or revealed truth granted exclusively to the *muʾayyadūn* (divinely guided, or inspired—i.e., the prophets) so that they can guide human souls to come closer to the intelligible or spiritual world.

Concerning the significance of this book, it suffices to say that Nāṣir-i Khusraw either translated fully or paraphrased all forty chapters of *al-Yanābīʿ* in Persian and incorporated them within his own work *Kitāb khwān al-ikhwān*. The chapters translated here address three central themes: (1) *Tawḥīd*; (2) On Intellect and soul; and (3) esoteric hermeneutics of the symbolism of the cross. Relying on *taʾwīl* (spiritual hermeneutics), Sijistānī attempts to show the essential unity between Islam and Christianity. The critical edition of the text, together with a partial French translation, was published by Henry Corbin in his *Trilogie ismaélienne*, (Paris-Tehran, 1961). The present translation is based on Corbin's edition. The numbers in the round brackets in the body of the text refer to the pagination of Corbin's edition. The content in the square brackets is from the translator.

—*M. Aminrazavi*

Kashf al-maḥjūb

UNVEILING OF THE HIDDEN

Introduction to the Translation

That Abū Yaʿqūb Sijistānī, one of the pillars of the so-called Persian school of fourth/tenth-century Ismāʿīlism,[1] wrote a major work titled *Kashf al-maḥjūb* or *The Unveiling of the Hidden*, and that some of its contents were from the start subject to considerable doctrinal controversy inside and outside Ismāʿīlism, are well-attested facts thanks to early references made to this work by three independent writers, the anti-Ismāʿīlī Zaydī polemicist Abu'l-Qāsim al–Bustī (d. 420/1030), the great scholar al–Bīrūnī in his *India* (written in 421/1030), and the Ismāʿīlī theologian Nāṣir-i Khusraw (5th/11th century), as will be discussed below. Although very little is certain about Sijistānī's life—he is said to have been executed under the governorship of the Ṣaffārid Amīr of Khurāsān, Khalaf b. Aḥmad, which could mean any time between 353/964–965 and 393/1002–1003—it would appear that the *Kashf al-maḥjūb* belongs to the later period of his career and was probably written after the *Kitāb al-iftikhār*—that is, during the very last years of the reign of the Fāṭimid caliph al–Muʿizz li-Dīn Allāh (341/953–365/975), or perhaps even later.[2] Unfortunately, however, no manuscript of the original version, which was presumably written in Arabic, has been found. What we have instead is a Persian translation or paraphrase by an anonymous writer, which has been dated for linguistic reasons to the fifth/eleventh century and might therefore be in reality the work of Nāṣir-i Khusraw or, more likely, another Ismāʿīlī author of that period, such as the equally anonymous commentator of the *Qaṣīdah* of Abu'l-Haytham-i Jurjānī.[3] Preserved in a unique manuscript copied sometime before 804/1402 that

---

1. Several important studies by Paul E. Walker on Sijistānī and his thought are available, notably his *Early Philosophical Shiism: The Ismaili Neoplatonism of Abū Yaʿqūb al-Sijistānī* (Cambridge, 1993) and *Abū Yaʿqūb al-Sijistānī: Intellectual Missionary* (London/New York, 1996). See also Paul E. Walker, *The Wellsprings of Wisdom: A Study of Abū Yaʿqūb al-Sijistānī's* Kitāb al-Yanābīʿ *including a complete English translation with commentary and notes on the Arabic text* (Salt Lake City, 1994) The Arabic text of the *Kitāb al-yanābīʿ* had previously been edited, with a French introduction and an annotated partial translation, by Henry Corbin, in *Trilogie Ismaélienne*, Bibliothèque Iranienne vol. 9 (Tehran/Paris, 1961). In the present introduction, *Wellsprings* refers to the Paras of this Arabic text unless otherwise specified. The Paras can easily be identified in either translation.

2. The *Kitāb al-iftikhār*, in which Sijistānī shows great pride in the achievements of the Fāṭimids, was written "more than 350 years" after the death of the Prophet, ed. Muṣṭafā Ghālib, (Beirut, 1980), 82, i.e., after 360/970–71, at a time at which "God fulfils His promise by manifesting the banner of [the] *qāʾim* on the head of one of his [i.e., the latter's] representatives (*khulafāʾih*) . . . in an unprecedented way" (ibid., 83)—evidently a reference to al-Muʿizz. Although our text does not name al-Muʿizz or any other "representative" of the *qāʾim*, it clearly refers in the prologue to a Fāṭimid "Friend of God on this Earth of Convocation" and implies (VI. 7. 4.) that the "Lord of the Final Rising" comes as seventh after *seven* (not six!) prophetic "Enunciators": and al-Muʿizz is regarded as the "seventh" after the seventh Imam. Moreover, the allusion to the "courage of the Berbers" in V. 5. 3. probably refers to the role played by Berber support of the Fāṭimid cause in Egypt. If we can trust the Persian translation, the allusion in VII. 1. 1. to the "second Intellect" would suggest an even later date since this notion, though famous in philosophy since Fārābī (d. 339/950), does not appear in Sijistānī's other works and belongs properly in Ismāʿīlism to the doctrine of Ḥamīd al-Dīn al-Kirmānī (d. after 411/1021). Indeed it is the latter who, in his *Kitāb al-riyāḍ*, identifies the Neoplatonic Soul with his "second Intellect," thereby criticizing Sijistānī for having given it too low a status in his *al-Nuṣrah*. Cf. Daniel de Smet, *La quiétude de l'intellect: Néoplatonisme et gnose ismaélienne dans l'œuvre de Ḥamīd ad-Dīn al-Kirmānī* (*X*e*/XI*e *s.*) (Leuven, 1995), 229–34. Note, however, that the Soul enjoys a relatively elevated status even in the *Wellsprings* (e.g., Para. 122), which was certainly written before the *Kitāb al–iftikhār*.

3. For a linguistic analysis of our Persian text, see Gilbert Lazard, *La langue des plus anciens monuments de la prose persane* (Paris, 1963), 87. Given that Nāṣir-i Khusraw translated much of

belonged to the library of the late Nasrollah Taqavi, this Persian version was edited and published with an introduction for the first time in 1949 by Henry Corbin as volume 1 of the series *Bibliothèque Iranienne*.[4] One year earlier, Corbin had also completed his own French translation of the Persian text; but this was published only in 1988 in a posthumous edition under the title *Le Dévoilement des choses cachées: Recherches de philosophie ismaélienne*.[5] It goes without saying that the English translation offered here for the first time has greatly benefited from Corbin's work, although it is of course based on my own reading of the Persian text. In addition, I have consulted the two other manuscripts of the Persian text known to exist, even though both of these are in fact no more than independent modern transcripts of the Taqavi *unicum*.[6] The present location of the latter is not known to me.

Space being limited in an anthology, roughly two thirds of the Persian text has been selected here for translation. Each of the seven chapters or "discourses" (sg. *maqālat*) of which it is composed is represented with more or less extensive extracts. The epilogue has been omitted, but the prologue has been translated in full. As is clear from the latter, the seven "discourses" are to be regarded as the most important Sources (*aṣlhā*) of divine Knowledge (*ʿilm*)—or *Gnosis*—which this book proposes to "unveil." The first discourse or Source, then, on *tawḥīd*, is essentially theological; it presents the radically apophatic or negative theology of classical Ismāʿīlism, as opposed to any attempt by the "Lords of Perdition"—that is, ordinary theologians—to define and thereby to reify the absolutely transcendent, unknowable God. By contrast, the remaining six chapters are on what is said to be knowable in the introduction, that is to say, the angelic beings—meaning, most probably, the spiritual "Ranks" (*ḥudūd*) repeatedly mentioned in our text,

---

Sijistānī's *Wellsprings*, he remains a possible candidate, although a rather unlikely one, as was already pointed out by Henry Corbin (see following note) in his introduction to our text, 14. In fact, the commentator of the *Qaṣīdah* of Abū 'l-Haytham Jurjānī (tentatively identified by H. Corbin and Moh. Moʿin in their edition of his *Sharḥ-i Qaṣīda-yi Abū 'l-Haytham-i Jurjānī*, Bibliothèque Iranienne, 6 (Tehran/Paris, 1334/1955), with one Muḥammad-i Surkh of Nayshāpūr) seems a more likely candidate because this text has more than one point in common with ours (cf. *infra*, nn. 7, 68, 73, 83, and especially 86).

4. *Abū Yaʿqūb Sejesṭānī: Kashf al-Maḥjūb* (*Le Dévoilement des choses cachées*). *Traité ismaélien du IVme siècle de l'Hégire. Texte persan publié avec une introduction par* Henry Corbin (Tehran/Paris, 1327/1949); 2nd edition, with additional corrections (Tehran, 1358/1979).

5. Lagrasse, 1988, Editions Verdier, ed. Christian Jambet.

6. MS. Tehran = Tehran, Adabiyyāt 194 j, copy from the Taqavi manuscript, completed 9 Muḥarram 1359 / 27 Bahman 1318 [February, 1940], by Muḥammad ʿAlī Muṣāḥibī Nā'īnī, known as "ʿIbrat". See Aḥmad Munzawī, *Fihrist-i nuskhahā-yi khaṭṭī* (Tehran, 1348 AHS ff., II, 1). p. 829.

MS. Cairo = Dār al-Kutub 1792, incomplete photocopy made in 1935 of a MS. transcribed from the Taqavi manuscript in Ṣafar, 1350 [June-July, 1931] by Ibrāhīm Zanjānī in Tehran. See Munzawī, ibid., and Ismail K. Poonawala, *Biobibliography of Ismāʿīlī Literature* (Malibu, Calif., 1977), 88. This photocopy contains both the *Kashf al-maḥjūb* and Nāṣir-i Khusraw's *Gushāyish wa rahāyish*, but with a substantial lacuna in the middle, cutting 18 pages from the end of the former (in the Corbin edition) and 64 pages from the beginning of the latter (in the Nafisi edition), although the pagination is continuous.

including Intellect, Soul, Prophets, Imams, and "Proofs" (*ḥujjatān*)[7]—and the "degrees of creation." These six "discourses" (i.e., chapters II. to VII.) constitute by themselves a kind of a hexaemeron, from the First Creation to the Sixth Creation. The first three Creations—or, better, stages of one creative process—are, respectively, Intellect, Soul, and Nature, thus following the standard Neoplatonic model, whereas the three remaining stages of the same process lead us again upwards, as it were. Thus, chapter five, concerning the Fourth Creation, deals with the obvious element of regularity in Nature: the species. Not unlike Suhrawardī in his "oriental" philosophy, our text insists particularly on the species being for ever preserved, because they are the earthly manifestations of celestial Forms—that is, the stars. This leads quite naturally to the discussion of a very special "species" in chapter six, namely, the Prophets, who thus constitute the Fifth Creation. As is well known, the classical Ismāʿīlī conception of sacred history is based on a pattern of six prophetic Enunciators (*nāṭiq*) each of whom is the inaugurator of a new Cycle (*dawr*), each Cycle being introduced in turn by a Legatee (*waṣī*) or "Foundation" (*asās*, i.e., ʿAlī b. Abī Ṭālib in the case of the sixth prophetic Cycle) and brought to completion by seven Imāms; and the seventh Imam of each Cycle is understood to be or to become the next *nāṭiq*. This means that the seventh Imam of the sixth prophetic Cycle, concretely: Muḥammad b. Ismāʿīl b. Jaʿfar al-Ṣādiq, should be identical with the seventh *nāṭiq*, and as such should actually be identical with the *qāʾim*, called in our text the "Lord of the Final Rising" (*khudāwand-i qiyāmat* or *khudāwand-i rastakhīz*), the one who inaugurates the ultimate Cycle of Unveiling (*dawr-i kashf*). But this original conception evidently had to be adjusted in the course of time, so that the *parousia* (*ẓuhūr*) of this messianic figure—not necessarily the "return" of the same historical Imam—could still be expected; and our text (VI. 7. 4.) seems indeed to reflect such an adjustment since it makes it very clear that the great "Cycle of Concealment" (*dawr-i satr*) before the Cycle of Unveiling consists itself of seven, not six, Cycles (*haft dawr*).[8] Nevertheless, it is hardly a matter of mere coincidence that this topic has been dealt with exclusively in the seventh subchapter—the final one—of chapter six. Indeed it should be noted that each of the seven chapters of the *Unveiling of the Hidden* is itself composed of exactly seven subchapters, titled each time by what I read as *jastār* rather than *justār* and have, accordingly, translated as "Issue" rather than

7. According to *Wellsprings* Para. 185, "Angels" designates the "spiritual support" (*taʾyīd*) received by Prophets from Intellect, while "Fairies" (*al-jinn*) refers to the benefits they receive from Soul. However, according to the *Sharḥ-i Qaṣīda-yi Abuʾl Haytham-i Jurjānī*, Persian text p. 35, "Angels" (*firishta*) means Prophets, Legatees, and Imāms, i.e., "all those who receive Knowledge through spiritual support (*taʾyīd*) and pass it on to others through spiritual support", whereas "Fairies" (*parī*) means the "Proofs" (*ḥujjatān*), i.e. "all those who receive Knowledge through spiritual support but can only pass it on to others through teaching (*taʿlīm*)"; and ordinary humans (*ādamī*) are "all those who receive it and pass it on through teaching". Our text frequently mentions the same hierarchy, from the Prophets to the "Proofs"; the latter rank is identical with *dāʿī* and *maʾdhūn* according to the *Kitāb al-iftikhār*, 105. Like their "Adversaries", these receivers of *taʾyīd* are "called to arise" in every "Cycle". Cf. III. 6.3.; V. 5. 4. and especially VII. 5. 2. On *taʾyīd* or "spiritual support" cf. II. 4. 2.; III. 6. 3.; III. 7. 4.; VI. 1. 3.; VI. 7. 1.

8. See above, note 2, and below, the note *ad loc.*

"Inquiry." In other words, each of the Seven Sources emerges itself in seven Issues or " outpourings," just as according to Sijistānī's *Wellsprings*,[9] the seven Imāms are said to emerge or to "arise" (*inbiʿāth*) each time from the six prophetic Enunciators prior to the *qāʾim*. This reading of *jastār* not only goes well with Sijistānī's general concept of "sources," which is the basic notion of his *Wellsprings*; it also seems to be confirmed by the occurrence of what can in my view only be read as *jastār* in our text itself (II. 6.1.), as well as by the frequent usage of verbs like *firū-chakīdan* or *firū-rīkhtan* as applied to the "outpourings" of the Light of the Prime Intellect on everything in existence.

It is, perhaps, not so surprising, then, that chapter seven, concerning the Sixth Creation, should be devoted exclusively to a particular notion of what is usually translated as "resurrection" (*baʿth*), a term which is consistently rendered in our Persian version by the verbal form *bar-angīkhtan* (to rouse, stir, kindle) and translated here, depending on the context, as "calling to arise," or "resuscitation," and the like. As was shown by Wilferd Madelung,[10] *baʿth* in Sijistānī's usage of the term is neither identical with *qiyāmah*, which refers specifically to the final Rising of the *qāʾim*, nor does it convey the idea of resurrection of the dead bodies in the sense in which the term is normally understood in Islamic theology. Rather, it constitutes a radical critique of the latter, referring instead, as it clearly does in at least three of Sijistānī's works—the *Kitāb al-iftikhār*, the *Risālat al-bāhirah*, and the *Kashf al-maḥjūb*, to a peculiar notion of transmigration of the soul. According to our text this is to be understood as a continuous re-creation both within various stages of one and the same life (VII. 4.) and over many Cycles to come (VII. 5.–7.), until this process converges with the final Rising of the *qāʾim*. Right from the beginning of chapter seven, *baʿth* or *bar-angīkhtan* is defined as being the equivalent of "calling into existence" (*būdan kardan*) and explained as a process which originates from the very first arising or awakening, namely, the arising of Soul due to Intellect's contemplating Itself, and propagates itself to everything that thereby *exists*—most notably the individual soul or life itself (VII. 2.–3.), but also the Knowledge (or *Gnosis*) that is "called to arise" in the soul of the right kind of student through the right kind of teacher (VII. 4.–6.). The process of *baʿth* or *bar-angīkhtan* of individual souls and their gnostic potential runs parallel to the major "historical" process this book is all about: the "Coming down of Soul in the Form of Man (*ṣūrat-i mardum*)" (III. 1.),[11] which is enacted in stages over the seven Cycles, or brought from the stage of potentiality to the stage of actuality, through the mission (also called *baʿth* in Arabic!) of the prophetic Enunciators from Adam to the *qāʾim* (chapter VI.).

9. Para. 158.

10. Abū Yaʿqūb al-Sijistānī and Metempsychosis". *Iranica Varia: Papers in Honor of Professor Ehsan Yarshater*. Textes et Mémoires vol. XVI (Leiden 1990). 131–43.

11. Cf. *al-ṣūrat al-insāniyyah, Kitāb al-iftikhār*, 96, line 2. Ibid., 78, Sijistānī argues against the "Philosophers" that "resurrection" cannot possibly take place "in a substance whose parts are stripped of the human form". Note that a tradition from the Imām Jaʿfar al-Ṣādiq has it that "The human form (*al-ṣūrat al-insāniyyah*) is the greatest Proof of God to His creatures" (quoted by Ḥaydar Āmulī, *Jāmiʿ al-asrār* eds. H. Corbin and O. Yahya, Bibliothèque Iranienne 16 [Tehran/Paris, 1969], Arabic text Para. 765).

This recurrent prophetic figure is an extraordinary "Sage of such penetrating Knowledge and Wisdom that nobody can rival him" (V. 5. 4.; cf. V. 5. 1.). Yet, while the ultimate Teacher is evidently the *qāʾim* or the "Lord of the final Rising," and identical with the *mahdī* who "guides the humans to that which is in their own inner reality (*ḥaqīqat-i īshān*) . . . and opens the way for the souls to know the spiritual dominion of God, so that the souls become one with the True Realities (*ḥaqāyiq*) and the Spiritual Support (*taʾyīd*)" (VI. 7. 1.), it seems nevertheless that the "learning process" of certain individual souls may anticipate this Final Rising in a "moving onward in the stages of Soul . . . so that Soul will have come down in perfect completeness" (III. 1. 2.; cf. VII. 4. 1.). In fact, even ordinary sense-perception, imagination, and rational knowledge are seen as part of a spiritual and eschatological process leading up to the highest stage (cf. II. 4.; III. 4.; III. 5.; III. 6.)—a most interesting aspect of our text, which calls to mind the kind of dynamic eschatology that was systematically elaborated much later by the great Shīʿī philosopher Mullā Ṣadrā Shīrāzī on the basis of his concept of "substantial motion." Perhaps, then, *bar-angīkhtan* means indeed some sort of an "alchemical" process, as was suggested by Corbin,[12]—but an individual as well as universal process which is, moreover, never "stripped of the human form."[13] Sijistānī may well have thought this process to condition or even to cause the Rising of the *qāʾim* as the Pure Soul (*al-nafs al-zakiyyah*) in the most perfect human body. Although this conclusion is not explicitly stated in our text, it can certainly be supported on the basis of other extant Sijistanian works, notably the *Risālah al-bāhirah*,[14] as well as from a crucial passage in the *Kitāb al-iftikhār*, where the individual souls that are 'adjoined" (read *tujāwiru*) to many individual bodies over long periods of time are said to be the "vessels" (*marākib*) of the Pure Soul (*al-nafs al-zakiyyah*), and indeed the "means" (*sabab*) for its powerful appearance in a "harmonious individual" (*shakhṣ muʿtadil*) at the final stage of the universal process of prophetic mission (*amr al-risālah*).[15] It is to be noted, however, that Sijistānī seems to have been somewhat hesitant as to whether this eschatological scene is to be envisioned as taking place on this earth exclusively, albeit on a spiritually empowered Earth which is the Land of the divine promise of Justice, as is strongly suggested by our text (cf. IV. 4. 1.–2.), or whether it is as purely" spiritual forms" (*ṣuwar khafiyyah*) that the individual souls are "called to arise" through the appearance of the *qāʾim*, as is dearly stated in the *Wellsprings*.[16] Quite generally speaking, there is a marked difference in outlook between the *Wellsprings* with its emphasis on a separate, independent existence of Intellect and the spiritual world,[17] and the *Kashf al-maḥjūb* which stresses, on the contrary, a direct involvement of Intellect in the world as it exists (e.g. II. 3. 1.–2.).

12. *Kashf al-maḥjūb*, introd. 17f.

13. See above, note 11.

14. Ed. with an introduction by Boustan Hirji, "Taṣḥīḥ-i intiqādī-i al-Risālat al-bāhirah", *Taḥqīqāt-i Islāmī 7, 2 (1992)*, 21–50, where the use of the notion *istishfāf*, "rendering transparent," is particularly noteworthy.

15. *Kitāb al-iftikhār* ed. M. Ghālib, 64: MS. Tübingen Ma VI 294, p. 106.

16. Para. 165.

17. Eg. Paras 24: 53–56.

Given the *horror transmigrationis* characteristic of monotheistic "orthodoxies" in general, including that of the official Fāṭimid *daʿwa*, and no doubt also in view of the latter's sustained efforts under al-Ḥākim bi-Amr Allāh (reg. 386/996–411/1021) to stay clear of their own *ghulāt*,[18] it is hardly surprising that Nāṣir-i Khusraw, although generally an admirer of the works of our author, should have condemned the *Kashf al-maḥjūb* (as well as the *Risāla al-bāhirah* and the nonextant *Sūs al-baqāʾ*) for advocating the by now completely unacceptable doctrine of *tanāsukh*.[19] It is true that our text itself condemns *tanāsukh* explicitly in two passages (V. 3. 3. and VII. 3. 2.). However, this warning concerns specifically a "vulgar" kind of transmigrationism, in particular the one implying a change of species, which is totally ruled out because of our thinker's insistence on the "preservation of the species." But the same argument also implies that transmigration within the same species is, precisely, *not* ruled out. As was already noted by S. Pines,[20] this fine point did not escape the sharp eye of Bīrūnī, who mentions in his *India* that "in a book of his which he called *Kashf al-maḥjūb*, Abū Yaʿqūb al-Sijzī . . . propounded a doctrine according to which the species are preserved and *tanāsukh* proceeds within each species only, without passing to any other."[21] It should also be noted that such a peculiar form of "transmigrationism" within the same species only was by no means a thing unheard of in the Islamic world of the time around 400/1000. Ibn Sīnā in his *Risāla al-aḍḥawiyyah*[22] as well as Ibn Ḥazm in his *Fiṣal*[23] distinguish among the "transmigrationists" a special group whose distinctive mark was that they did not accept the transfer of the human soul to any species other than human (as Ibn Sīnā puts it) or, more generally, the transfer of a soul to any species other than the one it left (as Ibn Ḥazm puts it). Nāṣir-i Khusraw, too, was not only aware of this distinct "group" among the "transmigrationists"; he in fact identified it correctly as a Neoplatonic tradition, as distinct from the generalized transmigration across the species, attributed to Plato. For in chapter 43 of his *Khʷān al-ikhwān*, after giving us a brief description of "Platonic transmigrationism," Nāṣir adds the following, most revealing quotation from the *De Natura Hominis* of Nemesios of Emesa, which he apparently attributes to Porphyry: "It is related from Porphyry that in the book *Ṭabīʿat al-insān*, regarding the Greeks, he said that they say that the soul is of many species (*gūnahā*), just as the body (*shakhṣ*) is of many species, and every species of souls goes into

18. Cf. Daniel Peterson, "Cosmogony and the Ten Separated Intellects" in the *Rāḥat al-ʿAql* of Ḥamīd al-Dīn al-Kirmānī, unpublished Ph.D. dissertation, University of California Los Angeles, 1990, chapter four.

19. *Khʷān al-ikhwān* ed. Qawīm, Tehran 1338 AHS, 131ff.. 135, 139 (chapters 42 and 43); *Zād al-musāfirīn* ed. Badhl al-Raḥmān, Berlin, 1341/1923, 421f.

20. "La longue récension de la théologie d'Aristote dans ses rapports avec la doctrine ismaélienne". *REI 22 (1954)*, 16.

21. *Kitāb al-Bīrūnī fī taḥqīq mā lil-Hind min maqūlah maqbūlah fi'l-ʿaql aw mardhūlah* (Hyderabad, 1377/1958), 49. *Alberuni's India* (transl. Sachau) I, 64f.

22. Ed. Ḥasan ʿĀṣī, Beirut 1404/1984, 95. Moreover, Ibn Sīnā (ibid., 120) points out that those who hold this special kind of limited transmigrationism argue on the basis of Aristole's *De Anima*, from which he also quotes the relevant passage (cf. *De Anima* 407b, 22 and 414a, 22).

23. *Al–Fiṣal fī'l-milal wa'l-ahwāʾ wa'l-niḥal* (Cairo 1321 A.H.), 91.

the species of its own bodies. Thus, the soul of man goes only into human bodies, and that of horses only into horses, and by analogy, every soul goes [only] into a body which is suitable for it."[24] What is somewhat surprising, then, about Nāṣir-i Khusraw's reports on the *Kashf al-maḥjūb* is not the fact that he judged it to be transmigrationist, which it is obviously enough, but that he failed to draw our attention to the above distinction when speaking about this work, and in effect blurred it by ranging Sijistānī among the Platonists in chapter 42 of his *Khʷān al-ikhwān*,[25] even though he must have known better.

In any case, Nāṣir-i Khusraw's somewhat confusing condemnation of the *Kashf al-maḥjūb* constitutes rather good evidence for the authenticity of our Persian version, which amounts to virtual certainty when combined with Bīrūnī's clarification. Unfortunately, the same cannot be said about the two references found in an extract from Abū'l-Qāsim al-Bustī's *Kashf asrār al-bāṭiniyyah wa ghawār madhhabihim*, which has been the subject of a substantial article by S. M. Stern.[26] This Arabic text contains a theological critique of two propositions that Sijistānī allegedly made in his *Kashf al-maḥjūb*, but which are not found in our Persian version. For Stern, this was sufficient evidence to conclude that the latter "must therefore be assumed not to reproduce the original text in full."[27] Now, while this remains, of course, a possibility, it would seem at least equally legitimate *a priori* to assume on the contrary that it was Bustī who did not reproduce in full whatever original text he referred to, especially as his "quotations" are clearly adduced with the sole intention of having Sijistānī contradict himself. Moreover, it may be ventured here that Bustī (or his informer, or his transcriber) simply confused the titles of the two Sijistānīan works he had some knowledge of: *Kashf al-maḥjūb* and *Kitāb al-yanābīʿ*; for there are a number of indications pointing to the conclusion that this is precisely what has happened in fact. To begin with, even the title of the *Kitāb al-yanābīʿ* is quoted in garbled form in this text (see Stern, ibid.), and Bustī's claim that in this book, Sijistānī maintained "that the *ajrām* are the cause of the *mufradāt*" (as cited by P. Walker[28]) hardly fits anything in the extant *Kitāb al-yanābīʿ*, not even Para. 56—pace Walker—but could easily be under-

24. *Khʷān al-ikhwān*, 138. This corresponds (with a few omissions) to Nemesius Emesenus, *De Natura Hominis Graece et Latine* (Hildesheim. 1967), 115, line 4 to 116, line 2. The doctrine under discussion was held in particular by Iamblichus, who was therefore praised by Nemesius, as Porphyry was praised by Augustinus for similar reasons: both distinguished themselves thereby from "Platonic" (and Plotinian) generalised transmigration of the human soul to animals. Cf. Heinrich Dorrie, "Kontroversen um die Seelenwanderung im kaiserzeitlichen Platonismus," *Hermes* (*Zeitschrift für klassische Philologie*) *85* (*1957*), 414–35, esp. 422–29. What remains unclear, however, is Nāṣir-i Khusraw's direct source. The known Arabic version of *De Natura Hominis* attributes it neither to Nemesius nor to Porphyry, but to Gregory of Nyssa. Cf. Moreno Morani, *La tradizione manoscritta del "De natura hominis" di Nemesio* (Milan, 1981), 90–100.

25. *Khʷān al-ikhwān*, 135. Note, however, that in *Zād*, 421, he associates him vaguely with Indian transmigrationism.

26. "Abu'l-Qāsim al-Bustī and his Refutation of Ismāʿīlism". *JRAS 1961–62*, 14–35 (reprinted in *Studies in Early Ismāʿīlism* ed. D. Bryer [Jerusalem/Leiden, 1983] 299–320).

27. Stern, ibid., 22 [reprint, 307], where the relevant Arabic passage is given in full.

28. *Wellsprings*, p. 143 (commentary ad Para. 56).

stood as a reference to the doctrine that the celestial bodies preserve the species, which is indeed strongly maintained in our text in several places of chapter five (cf. V. 1.–.3.; V. 3. 4.). More important, what seems not to have been noticed is the fact that the two critical points allegedly made in the original *Kashf al-maḥjūb*, namely, (1) that Intellect, Joy (*surūr*), Sadness (*ghamm, sic*), and "Bliss" (*ghibṭah, sic*) were "actualised simultaneously" (*kulluhā maʿan ḥaṣalat*), while Intellect is "according to him the first of all things, nothing prior to it being knowable," and (2) that "all we can know is the First and the Second [i.e., Intellect and Soul] . . . because we cannot pass beyond our world," are recognizable if incomplete and rather distorted references to parts of what Sijistānī explains in great detail in a coherent block ranging over Sources 14, 15, and 16 of the *Wellsprings*![29] This being the case, it would seem rather unnecessary for Sijistānī to repeat these details again in his *Kashf al-maḥjūb*, although it is true that one might expect him to enumerate some of the "powers of the Intellect" mentioned in III. 1. 3. or to explain the "attributes" of the Intellect which are only globally referred to in I. 3. 1. and I. 3. 2. Nor would the Persian translator—whoever he was—have had any reason to be "prudent" about the two issues criticized by Bustī had they really been discussed in any detail in the original *Kashf al-maḥjūb*, for all these *theologoumena* are reproduced in full by Nāṣir-i Khusraw in his Persian paraphrase of the *Wellsprings*,[30] and the "seven powers of the Intellect" are also discussed, as is well known, in his *Jāmiʿ al-ḥikmatayn* and in the *Sharḥ-i qaṣīda-yi Abu'l-Haytham-i Jurjānī*. Finally, had Bustī really seen a copy of the original *Kashf al-maḥjūb* and read all of it, it would be more than surprising that he did not take the author to task for transmigrationism, whereas if what he quoted, perhaps from memory, was in reality the *Wellsprings*, this omission on his part is perfectly explainable since that work seems indeed free from this particular "heresy."

To conclude, the Persian version of the *Kashf al-maḥjūb* is certainly not an arbitrary compilation of selected thoughts, but a well-structured book that follows a clear plan. While it cannot be ruled out that the anonymous Persian translator of the fifth/eleventh century may occasionally have imposed his own understanding, or that the compiler of the unique Taqavi manuscript simply made a mistake here and there, as will be discussed in the notes to the translation,[31] this work is in all likelihood a complete and, in substance, a faithful rendering of the lost original.

29. Paras 70–84. For the "seven powers of the Intellect," see the discussions in Corbin and Walker, *ad loc*. Also see now the recent article by W. Madelung. "Abū Yaʿqūb al-Sijistānī and the seven faculties of the Intellect," *Mediaeval Ismāʿīlī History and Thought* ed. F. Daftary (Cambridge, 1996), 85–89. Note that by mentioning *ghibṭah*, Bustī adds another candidate to the controversial *ghaybah/ghunyah*!

30. *Wellsprings* Source 14 = *Khwān al-Ikhwān* chapter 12: *W*. S. 15 = *Kh*. ch. 82: *W*. S. 16 = *Kh*. ch. 60.

31. Specifically, the notes *ad* II. 2. 1.; II. 4. 3.; III. 1. 2.; III. 1. 3.; III. 7. 3.; V. 1. 3.; V. 5. 1.; VI. 6. 1.; VII. 3. 1. If in these cases no MS. variant is mentioned, it means that both MS. Cairo and MS. Tehran agree with the edited text. This translation is based on Abū Yaʿqūb Sijistānī's *Kashf al-maḥjūb*, ed. H. Corbin.

[Prologue]

In the Name of God, the Compassionate, the Merciful; from Him we seek Help!

Be aware that the realities of True Knowledge (*ḥaqāyiq-i ʿilm*) are hidden from Iblīs and his progeny, while they are manifest with God's Friends (*awliyāʾ-i khudāy*) and His Chosen ones (*guzīdagān-i ū*). For that is the secret of God, which He makes known to whom He wishes among His Friends. True[1] Knowledge is in His treasure-house, [access] to which He grants to whomever He wants among His Servants. Those debarred from it stray in perdition and wander in blindness. On their hearts are locks which cannot be opened, and on their intellects are chains which cannot be lifted. The Friends of God graze in the pastures of Paradise, picking fruits from its trees without being ever sated and swimming in its rivers without ever tiring. They have recognized the One whom they worship, holding Him separate and pure from the traits of the creatures and keeping Him aloof from all their attributes. The Lords of Perdition have likened the Creator to the creatures, confined Him within definition, and pictured Him with attributes to the point of numbering them! Indeed they have become incapable of recognizing the angels (*firishtagān*)[2] and the degrees of creation, ignoring established knowledge and believing in unfounded assertions; whereas the Lords of the True Realities are cognizant of God's angels and possessed of the science of the degrees of creation. They do not recognize the unknowable but they know the knowable, and place their hope in that which may come to be, [namely], that the angels will descend upon them. For the Friends of God there is no pain in preserving True Knowledge in such a way that the sciences of the True Reading (*ʿulūm-i ta'wīl*)[3] become patterns engraved on their spiritual souls and will be of the essence of the substance of their Soul. Indeed, whatever belongs to the essence of a substance is never severed from it, as with the motion of fire which is not separable from fire.

May God preserve us and you from the yokes and fetters of non-cognition and ignorance, and may He allow us and you apprehension of the true realities and search for the growth of True Knowledge, which is the 'Heaven of Refuge'[4] and the 'Highest Paradise'! May He keep us on the 'Straight Path'![5] Indeed He is ever-generous and noble, the Possessor of abundant grace.

This translation is based on Abū Yaʿqūb Sijislānī's *Kashf al-maḥjūb*, ed. H. Corbin, Paris-Tehran: Institut Français de Recherche en Iran, 1949, pp. 2–96.

1. The adjective "True" has sometimes been added to "Knowledge" in this translation. As often in Ismāʿīlī texts, *ʿilm* means definitely more than just "knowledge"; it corresponds to the special kind of salvatory "Knowledge" which is known as *Gnosis*. It does not, however, imply—at least not in our text—the rejection of the material world generally associated with gnosticism.

2. Perhaps meaning the *imāms*. See Introd., note 7.

3. Much has been written about *taʾwīl*, one of the cornerstones of Ismāʿīlism and Shiʿism in general. For Sijistānī in particular, see Anton M. Heinen, "The Notion of Ta'wīl in Abū Yaʿqūb al-Sijistānī's *Book of the Sources* (*Kitāb al-yanābīʿ*)", *Hamdard Islamicus 2, 1 (1979)* 35–45; and Jean-François Gagnon, *Gnose et philosophie:une étude du* ta'wīl *ismaélien d'après le* Livre des Sources *d'al-Sijistānī*. Unpublished thesis, McGill University, 1995.

4. Cf. Qur'ān 32:19.

5. Cf. Qur'ān 1:6.

Now, by virtue of the shining Light and the great Power coming from the Friend of God[6] on this 'Earth of Convocation' (*zamīn-i daʿwat*),[7] which is the home of the spiritual souls, and by the blessing of my obedience to him and of his kindness to me, I shall undertake to unveil those secrets which were sealed, symbols which were kept in the treasure-house. No one has transcribed this [heavenly] Word into [earthly] script. These are verbal expressions and spiritual symbols which should work as a cure for the people of our time and adequately provide that for which there is a need. I shall unveil [them] in this book based on seven principal sources (*aṣl*), which are the most important of all:

I. On assertion of the One
II. On the First Originated
III. On the Second Creation
IV. On the Third Creation
V. On the Fourth Creation
VI. On the Fifth Creation
VII. On the Sixth Creation

Discourse One: On Assertion of the One

Issue One: On Eliminating Thingness[8] from the Creator

I. 1. 1.

The notion of being a 'thing' should be eliminated from the Creator, as this is properly that by which creatures are designated and through which they can be distinguished from each other. For every thing preserves the form of its respective species in order for the soul to be enabled to tell the colours[9] of the spiritual [lit. 'subtle'] world. Now, which thing, whose [specific] form would be neither of Soul, nor of Nature, nor of Art, would be suitable for God? Such is far from Him by virtue of the majesty (*buzurgwārī*) of His power and the pervasiveness (*rawāʾī*) of His sovereignty. Indeed, God's majesty is beyond taking the name

6. Perhaps meaning the Fāṭimid Caliph al-Muʿizz (reg. 341/953–365/975). Cf. Introd.

7. On the significance of the 'Earth of Convocation' see below, IV. 4. 1.–2.

8. *Chīzī*, the abstract form of *chīz*, is the Persian equivalent of the Arabic *shayʾiyyah*, "thingness," a technical term of *Kalām*, which is sometimes also used for the philosophical notion of "essence" or "quiddity" (see Jean Jolivet, "Aux origines de l'ontologie d'Ibn Sīnā," *Etudes sur Avicenne* eds. Jean Jolivet and Rushdi Rashed (Paris 1984), 11–28), as indeed it is used later in our own text (see II. 2. 1. and the note ad loc.). In the present *Kalām* context, however, I have preferred to translate *chīzī* literally as "thingness," as does De Smet (*Quiétude*, 90). A "thing," according to Nāṣir-i Khusraw, is a knowable entity (*Jāmiʿ al-ḥikmatayn* eds. H. Corbin and M. Moʿin, Bibliothèque Iranienne 3 [Tehran/Paris. 1332/1953], Persian text Para. 89). The position of our author, namely, that God is neither "thing" nor "not-thing" (cf. 1. 7. 1.–2.) is exactly what distinguishes Ismāʿīlī doctrine according to a well-informed Zaydī doxographer of the 6th/12th century, Nashwān b. Saʿīd al-Ḥimyārī, *Sharḥ risālat al-ḥūr al-ʿīyn* ed. Kamāl Muṣṭafā (Cairo 1367/1947), 148.

9. The "colours" of the spiritual world are a frequent theme with Sijistānī; cf. IV. 6. 1. and VI. 6. 1.; also *Wellsprings* Para. 14.

of a thing, whatever thing that may be; and it is improper to attribute thingness to Him or to link him with thingness—except by establishing His transcendent Essence (*dhāt-i buzurgwār-i ū*) beyond all the things by which creatures are designated.

I. 1 2.

Further, all men believe that "God was while no thing was,"[10] and they have commonly agreed that God is not like[11] His own deed [i.e., The Creation]. But a 'thing' cannot escape being either a substance or a body or an accident or motion or rest, whereas God is beyond coming under any of these divisions, so that [it can truly be said that] neither is creature like the Creator, nor the Creator like creature. If God were a 'thing', and had brought forth 'things', He would [himself] be a [thing] 'come forth' since 'things' come forth by way of generation (*bi-nawʿ-i tawlīd*). Therefore, since you have ruled that "No one was generated from Him, nor He from any one,"[12] now [you also must accept that] 'thing' and 'thingness' are eliminated from God, and that 'thingness' is attributed to creature. Understand this!

I. 1. 3.

Further, if attribution of 'thingness' to God were admissible, it would become necessary to say that 'one thing is the Creator' and 'one thing is the creature'. But these 'things' are either substance or accident, and substance is either body or spirit, and body is either animate or inanimate, and animate is either vegetal or animal. Now, coming back to the division of [the thing supposed to refer to] the Creator, what shall we say? Which one among these divisions would apply to the Creator? Clearly the Creator does not come under these divisions, nor does any non-divided [i.e., not subsumed] division apply to Him. No, He is [absolutely] alone, and beyond being susceptible of our attributing to Him things either spiritual or corporeal, [all of] which are multiple. Since we have from the start asserted His being beyond, it necessarily follows that God does not come under the division of the creatures, which may well be thought to be many or few; and since this is so, they are divisible, and every divisible is de-fined, and every de-fined is finite, and every finite is created; and for every created there is the necessity of the Creator. Thus, God is the Creator, and there is for us the necessity to recognize His absolute sovereignty (*kibriyāʾī wa ʿaẓamat-i ū*) so that the assertion of His Oneness be far beyond [implying] the attributes of the creatures whether corporeal or spiritual. Understand this!

10. Persian translation of well-known ḥadīth (*kāna Allāhu wa lam yakun maʿahu shayʾ*), which Sijistānī evidently quotes here because of the word "thing."

11. Reading *namānad* p. 4, line 14 (with both MSS. Cairo and Tehran).

12. Cf. Qurʾān 112:3.

Issue Three: On Eliminating Attributes from the Creator

I. 3. 1.

All attributes are found to exist either in substances or as adjoined to bodies or souls. As for those [attributes] that exist in the absolute substance (*jawhar-i muṭlaq*), that is, in the Intellect, they are, like the latter, directly originated through origination (*ibdāʿ*) from the Originator, and caused through causation from a causing agent (*ʿāll*).[13] And causedness and originatedness (*mubdaʿī*) are the attribute of the Prime Intellect, who is the one created primarily, not out of a thing. And whatever attribute qualifies the primarily created or all other creatures, is far removed from the Creator.

As for those [attributes] that exist in bodies, they are external qualifications such as the colours, the odours, the savours, warmth and coldness, softness and hardness.

As for those that exist in the soul, they are internal qualifications such as knowledge and ignorance, courage and cowardice, generosity and meanness, gentleness and intemperance. Now the Creator is far beyond whatever attribute qualifies the First Substance [i.e., Intellect] and the Second Substance [i.e., Soul] and the composed bodies and the [individual] souls; [He transcends all this] in every respect and by all means. Understand this!

I. 3. 2.

Further, the attributes qualifying a thing result from something other than that thing. For, the beings pertaining to the realm of natural generation (*mawālīd*) take their attributes from the elements, under active influence of the celestial bodies; the elements and the [celestial] bodies receive their attributes from Nature; Nature from Soul; Soul from Intellect; and Intellect from the [creative] Word (*kalimah*) and the Origination by the Originator, who has no attribute whatsoever. For example, sweetness, the attribute of anything sweet, is adjoined to a sweet thing because of the right proportion of warmth; bitterness, the attribute of anything bitter, is adjoined to a bitter thing because of excessive warmth; acidity, the attribute of anything sour, is adjoined to a sour thing because of a lack of warmth. Similarly, the attributes of Soul, which are invisible and internal, are adjoined to the Soul due to its receiving instruction from the Intellect, and they leave it [again] due to its compliance with Nature—but this concerns [only] the individual souls.[14] Also consider the intellectual attributes, which are adjoined to the First-Originated

13. Strictly speaking, the causing agent is not God or "the Originator" himself, but "the Origination" (*ibdāʿ = hast kardan = amr*); see II. 2. 2. and II. 5. 2.; also *Wellsprings* Paras 24–25 and 40 (*al-ʿillat al-ūlā = al-amr=al-kalimah*). This ultimate Cause is also identical with 'Oneness' (II. 2. 1.–3.). As for Intellect as "absolute Substance," see also I. 6. 2. and II. 7. 1.; cf. *Wellsprings*, Para. 55. See also Shigeru Kamada, "The First Being: Intellect (*ʿaql/khiradh*) as the link between God's Command and Creation according to Abū Yaʿqūb al-Sijistānī". *The Memoirs of the Institute of Oriental Culture No. 106* (University of Tokyo, 1988), 1–33.

14. Cf. I. 6. 1. and II. 7. 3. (not translated here).

(*mubdaʿ-i awwal*) due to the Origination and the [creative] Word.[15] And the Creator is far beyond the attributes of Intellect, Soul and Body. . . .

Issue Five: On Eliminating Time From the Creator

I. 5. 4.

Further, time is caused by the motion of the sphere, and the motion of the sphere is the cause of time. Whatever is a necessary concomitant of the motion of the sphere—which is the cause of time—is also a necessary concomitant of every moving object, [whether it be moving] in terms of generation or corruption, increase or decrease, or transportation from one place to another; and [all this] is not in God. For these are attributes of natural things, and God is alone and far from being susceptible of being linked with attributes, whether corporeal or spiritual. As for the time that you attribute to God, [it is to be understood] in the sense that He is the Originator (*mubdiʿ*) of time and the Originator of things both non-composed and composed. As for the imaginal time (*zamān-i wahmī*) from which the natural motions keep coming forth, this is the [lower] limit of the activity of the Soul; for it is through its [respective] imaginal motion (*ḥarakat-i wahmī*) that the universal Soul receives the light of the oneness of God (*nūr-i waḥdat-i īzad*), and it is through it [i.e., the imaginal motion of the universal Soul] that natural time and motion subsist [or: 'arise', *badū qāʾim ast*).[16] Therefore, since imaginal motion, which is the cause of all motions, is related to Soul, and [since] universal Intellect, which is the Prime Originated (*mubdaʿ-i awwal*), is far beyond that motion, how could it be admissible to attribute motion—which is the cause of time—or time—which is caused by motion—to the Creator? Thus, time cannot be attributed to the Creator in any way whatsoever. Understand this!

Issue Six: On Eliminating 'Being' from the Creator

I. 6. 1.

'Being' is attributed to beings either because [their domain] can be conceived as not-being, or because one thinks of a thing above it, which has dominated it.

As for the things which it is possible to conceive as not-being, they are those below Intellect, that is to say, those beings which turn into not-being and are under Nature.

15. This is probably an allusion to the "seven powers of Intellect." Sijistānī discusses in the *Wellsprings*. See Introd., note 29 and *infra*, note 70.

16. Cf. *Wellsprings* Para. 122, where imaginal motion (*al-ḥarakat al-wahmiyyah*), produced by the activity of the Soul, causes the manifestation of matter combined with form (or Nature). The Soul itself originates in no time as a result of Intellect's contemplation, and is as such capable of receiving its benefits from the Intellect. Also see Nāṣir-i Khusraw, *Khʷān al-ikhwān* chapters 21 and 62 (ed. Qawīm, 67, 70, 185). The Neoplatonic tradition (Iamblichus, Proclus] has an "intelligible time" between eternity and physical time.

As for that which is above things, dominating them by the Command of God, it is the Prime Intellect. And that Form which is deposited in it, is the Form of Man (*ṣūrat-i mardum*), which is stable in its own state, [although] it may happen that it inclines to Nature, worships it and becomes submissive to it.[17]

I. 6. 2.

Be aware that the division here is into three categories:

[a] One is a substance, which is neither being dominated nor becoming not-being. That is the Prime Intellect, which due to the Command of God is the noblest of all creatures.

[b] One is both being dominated and becoming not-being. That is the form of the natural beings pertaining to the realm of generation (*mawālīd-i ṭabī'ī*), and the external form of the religious laws (*ẓāhir-i sharī'athā*).

[c] One is being dominated but not becoming not-being. That is the noble Form of Man, which came forth from the permanent substance, that is, the light of the world of Intellect. These [three categories of] beings are remote from the Creator, because He is the Maker-of-Being of the beings, as all beings came forth by virtue of His Command. Therefore, since 'being' is applicable to that which may be imagined as not-being, or to that which is dominated and forced by one dominant and powerful [i.e., the Intellect] above it, it is necessary to eliminate 'being' from God in every respect. Thus, it has been verified that to attribute 'being' to God is impudent, because the beings all became 'being' through His Command.

I. 6. 3.

Further, he who criticizes us for eliminating 'absolute being' (*hastī-i muṭlaq*) from God, while he himself eliminates the differentiated beings from God, [should consider this]: Once you subsume the differentiated beings [under a class], the result is 'absolute being'. Indeed our adversary eliminates from God the being of the celestial spheres and the being of the stars and the being of the elements and the being of the realm of generation and the being of the bodies, substances and accidents, and the being of motions and rest, and every being that you may find among the creatures, all of them our adversary eliminates from God. Now, since [all this] differentiated 'being' may be subsumed under 'absolute being', it is necessary to eliminate both 'absolute being' and differentiated being from the Creator, so that God is far beyond both being and not-being, in every respect. Understand this!

I. 6. 4.

Know that the attribution of 'being" to God is bound to come under one of two alternatives: Either He has no need for 'being,' [in which case] it is redundant.

17. Cf. I. 3.2.

And if 'being' is redundant because the Maker-of-Being has no need for it, then why blame us for eliminating that which He does not need? Or, [on the contrary] it is the case that the Maker-of-Being has Himself no existence except through being. [But in that case,] what difference[18] would there be between the Maker-of-Being and the Made-to-Be? On what grounds would it then not be admissible that the Maker-of-Being equals the Made-to-Be and the Made-to-Be, likewise, the Maker-of-Being? As a result, there would be ambiguity in our knowledge of the Maker-of-Being, the Creator, whereas we must be able to know the Maker-of-Being [as distinct] from the Made-to-Be. Thus, it is necessary to eliminate 'being' from the Maker-of-Being, the Creator, and to attribute it to the Made-to-Be, the humble servant; for it is the latter who is in need of 'being'. Thus it has been verified that 'being' is not in any way whatsoever a necessary concomitant of the Creator. Understand this!

Issue Seven: On Eliminating Anything Antithetical to the Above By-names from the Creator

I. 7. 1.

If in this issue we have emphasized that the correct assertion of the [idea of the] Creator consists in eliminating the above states of being and attributes from Him, thus saying that He is neither thing nor subject to definition nor subject to qualification nor in place nor in time nor being, and then say that we have correctly asserted it on the grounds that the first elimination (*dūr kardan-i awwal*)—that is to say, of corporeal attributes—from the Creator amounts to correct assertion of transcendent Oneness (*tawḥīd-i mujarrad*), this is not necessarily so. Rather, the correct assertion is that which follows [this prior] elimination. The prior elimination (*dūr kardan-i pīshīn*) entails [only] separation from that which marks creatures, while the [subsequent] elimination is the mark of correct assertion of the Creator in such a way that the claim about Him does not amount to [sheer] 'divestment' (*taʿṭīl*). Nevertheless, we say as follows: The Creator is not 'thing' and not 'not-thing'; not subject to definition and not not-subject-to definition; not subject to qualification and not not-subject-to-qualification; not in place and not not-in-place; not in time and not not-in-time; not being and not not-being. As a result, we will have gotten rid of both 'likening' [Him to creatures, *tashbīh*] and 'divestment' [of existence, *taʿṭīl*]. We get rid of 'likening' through the prior elimination (*dūr kardan-i nakhust*), and of 'divestment' through the subsequent elimination (*dūr kardan-i ākharīn*). Thus it has been verified that [true assertion of] the transcendence of the Creator will not be achieved except by elimination of that which comes in as opposite of these eliminations, that is to say, through both the prior elimination in order to get away from likening and through the subsequent elimination in order to eliminate divestment. Understand this!

18. Reading *faṣl* (Persian text p. 13, line 19), in accordance with MS. Tehran.

I. 7. 2.

On the other hand, if we set the correct assertion of [the idea of] the Creator on one elimination of those things which we have [already] eliminated from Him [i.e., the second elimination only], thus saying that He is not 'not-thing' and not 'not-being', it follows necessarily that He becomes linked with that thing which is 'thing' and 'being'. And if we say that He is not 'not-subject-to-definition' and not 'not-subject-to qualification' and not 'not-in-time' and not 'not -in-place', this amounts to likening and is no assertion of pure transcendent Oneness, because it implies that He is subject to qualification and subject to definition and in place and in time. Therefore, both the prior elimination [of 'things'] and the subsequent elimination [of 'not-things'] from the Creator are necessary for the assertion of pure transcendent Oneness to be [real] and absolute Singleness (*fardāniyyat-i maḥḍ*) to remain. Understand this![19]

Discourse Two: On Bringing to Mind the First Creation [i.e. Intellect][20]

Issue One: In What Sense Intellect Is the Centre of the Two Worlds[21]

II. 1. 3.

Further, the centre is that point which is the remotest from all those points that turn around it, as well as the closest of all points to that motion from which the circle becomes manifest. Likewise, Intellect is the closest of all the beings to the Command of God, while the Command of God has reached Nature, the circle. Therefore, Intellect is the remotest thing to have become manifest, because all the species, genera, specific differences, properties, accidents and individuals, had preceded it in this world, with the trace of Intellect becoming manifest as a result. Thus it has been verified that Intellect is the centre of the two worlds. Understand this!

II. 1. 4.

Considered from another point of view, Intellect has been likened to the centre because the centre is at rest. For if the centre were not resting securely, none of

19. For this theme of the "double negation," central to Sijistānī's theology, see, e.g., *Wellsprings* Para. 22.

20. "Creation" (*khalq, āfarīnish*) is used ambiguously in our text as well as in other works of Sijistānī. In the present context, as also, e.g., in *Kitāb al-iftikhār*, 35 (*al-khalq al-awwal*), it refers to what is normally called *ibdāʿ*, i.e., the direct "origination" of the Intellect beyond time. Also note that the title of the present chapter is *Dar Mubdaʿ-i Awwal* according to the table of contents as given in the Prologue.

21. For this theme, cf. *Wellsprings* Para. 84; *Kitāb ithbāt al-nubwwāt* ed. ʿĀrif Tāmir (Beirut, 1966), 47.

the motions would be secure, and the trouble would be unending. In like manner, Intellect is at rest; and it is on account of its rest that the spiritual souls (*nafs-hā-yi laṭīf*) are moving, thereby coming from the limit of potentiality to the limit of actuality. The coming-into-being (*kawn*) of the souls, their being caused to 'arise' (*baʿth*),[22] the motions of the spheres, the composition of the things pertaining to the realm of natural generation (*mawālīd*), [all this] is on account of the fact that Intellect is at rest, like the centre. Understand this!

Issue Two: That Intellect Becomes One with the Command of God When Command Is Expressed as Oneness

II. 2. 1.

Intellect becomes one with Oneness in recognizing the Creator by virtue of the fact that, whenever it is about to seize something external to its own essence through the ordinary method of knowing things—that is, by considering *whetherness*,[23] or the 'isness' of things; *quiddity*, or the '[what-]thingness' of things; *quality*, or the 'howness' of things; *quantity*, or the 'howmuchness' [of things]; *cause*, or the 'whyness' of things—in short, whenever the intellect is about to make these divisions, the light of God keeps it from doing so and makes it necessary for it to confirm pure transcendent Oneness which in no way whatsoever multiplies nor is susceptible of alteration. As a result, the Prime Intellect's confirmation of the Creator is far beyond whatever marks the creatures; it is confirmation of One, not of many. Accordingly, just as Oneness does not undergo alteration from its state of being one and remains perpetually in one and the same state, so the apprehension of the Prime Intellect does not undergo alteration from one and the same state. Moreover, just as the Oneness of God has no parallel among the causes, so the First Caused [= the Intellect] has no parallel among the caused. Therefore, the Preceder's[24] [=the Intellect's] apprehension has no parallel among the apprehensions. And just as every [secondary] cause is in need of the superiority of this Cause [i.e., Oneness], so every caused is in need of the superiority of this Caused [ie., the Intellect]; and every apprehension and confirmation asserting the Oneness of

22. See chapter VII.

23. Replace *māhiyyat* (Persian text p. 17, line 7) with *haliyyat*. *Māhiyyat* in this place is probably due to a simple error (*pace* Soheil M. Afnan, *Philosophical Terminology in Arabic and Persian* [Leiden 1964], 120), for the following reasons: 1. It would make little sense for the author in this context to discuss two supposedly different kinds of quiddity and to translate one of them by *hastī* while omitting "whetherness" (=*hal al-shayʾ* or *hal huwa*; see, e.g., Fārābī in Muhsin Mahdi, *Alfarabi's Philosophy of Plato and Aristotle* [Ithaca 1969], 15ff.), i.e., existence, which corresponds well to the Persian *hastī*. 2. In fact, it is generally *haliyyah* which comes before *māʾiyyah* in Sijistānī's own works, (see especially *Wellsprings* Para. 161; *Kitāb ithbāt al-nubūʾāt*, 8 and 13–20), 3. Nāṣir-i Khusraw gives the same catalogue of categories in Arabic and Persian, with *haliyyat* = *hastī* in the first place, followed by *māʾiyyat* = *chi-chīzī*, *kayfiyyat* = *chigūnagī*, *limiyyat* = *chirāʾī* (*Khwān al-ikhwān* chapter 82, ed. Qawīm, 232f; cf. *Jāmiʿ al-ḥikmatayn*, para. 263).

24. The "Preceder" (*sābiq*) is the standard "mythological" equivalent of the Intellect in classical Ismāʿīlism, the "Follower" (*tālī*) being the Soul.

the Creator is in need of that apprehension and confirmation which belongs exclusively to the Prime Intellect. This is how Intellect becomes one with the Command of God when Command is expressed as Oneness. Understand this!

II. 2. 2.

Intellect becomes one with the Oneness of God in still another way, and that is by apprehending itself. The Oneness of God is a cause which is unique among all the causes since it eliminates from itself whatever would qualify it as a thing or a being; indeed, Oneness is itself the cause of beings and things. Now, as Intellect looks at things, it sees every thing as manifest in itself and sees nothing beneath itself. Although there are things that are substantially removed from it, and its judgments [regarding them] vary, when Intellect looks at itself from the point of view of Oneness, it sees things not as multiple and diverse; no, it sees pure origination (*ibdāʿ-i maḥḍ*) and nothing but the sheer act of making-to-be (*hast kardan-i mujarrad*), without any difference. It becomes, then, one with Oneness in the manner just explained. Understand this!

II. 2. 3.

There is still another way for Intellect to become one with Oneness, and that is by apprehending Oneness. It [does so by] knowing that the Command of God reached the things altogether to bring them into being. It is impossible that there be another Command, by which [second] Command another thing would turn into being from not-being, because the Command of God right from the beginning passed over no useful thing without bringing it from not-being into being. Another Command cannot possibly be found because the beings altogether occupied the space of Creation completely and permanently, so that no space at all was left for any occurrence of not being. Thus, Intellect became one with Oneness and recognized Oneness at this stage because [of its knowledge that] to find any other being is excluded, just as [there is no way that] not-being would ever appear. Understand this![25]

Issue Three: That Intellect Becomes One with the Command of God when Command Is Expressed as the Word

II. 3. 1.

In the terminology of the dialectical theologians, it is understood that a single utterance (*sukhan-i mufrad*) when referring to a substance is called 'word' (*kalimah*).[26] For example, you can say 'healthy' and 'sick' when these two utterances refer to Muḥammad and Khālid, [respectively]. That is to say, "Muḥammad

25. For this theme cf. *Wellsprings* Paras 66–69.

26. This terminology seems somewhat peculiar. Sijistānī evidently intends to show the applicability of the creative word *kun* (Be!), or the *logos*, to everything that is."

is healthy" and "Khālid is sick." Therefore, with regard to the 'Word', Intellect became one with the Command of God in the sense that it links all Being with God by virtue of the Creative Act (*āfarīnish*), and makes the creatures cognizant of the fact that every particle and every drop has come to be there (*ẓāhir shud*) through the Command of God. And the Command of God is inseparable from it; for if it were separable, that thing would be divested [of its very existence, *muʿaṭṭal*]. Thus, Intellect becomes one with the Word in the sense that it necessitates that every particle of the Creation has a share of the Command of God, because every creature shares a part of the Command of God through which it has come to be there and by virtue of which it remains in being (*pāyanda buwad*) and the light of the Command of God shines in it. Understand this!

II. 3. 2.

Another meaning of Intellect's becoming one with the Word is this:

It is the [creative] Word which brought forth the single utterance, although the utterance did not come into being-there [initially] at Creation's transition from the stage of Origination (*gāh-i ibdāʿ*) to the stage of generation (*gāh-i tawlīd*). You should know that as long as things did not come from the limit of Origination (*ḥadd-i ibdāʿ*) to the limit of existentiation (*takwīn*) and generational (*tawlīd*), neither Intellect came into being-there, nor that Seed [i.e., the 'Form of Man'] which was found to be in Intellect. And Intellect was not [even] aware of its own existence (*inniyyat* or *anniyyat-i khʷīsh*)[27] before that, as long as that thing [the 'seed'] had not come from the limit of Origination to the limit of existentiation and generation. Therefore, at the time which the Command of God which is the Origination, reached the human being (*mardum*), the human being became [what it is, i.e.] a 'word-speaker' [*sukhan-gūy*, =*nāṭiq*=rational] and one capable of discernment,[28] and Intellect became one with it. As a result, whatever utterances the human beings bring forth, such as naming things and differentiating between names and attributes and between judgments and between the outcome of these judgments, [all this] belongs to it [i.e., the Intellect]. In view of this [also], Intellect's becoming one with the Word of God is conceivable. Understand this!

Issue Four: That Intellect Becomes One with the Command of God When Command Is Expressed as Knowledge[29]

II. 4. 1.

You should know that oneness of Intellect with Knowledge, and of Knowledge with Intellect, is a necessity. Be aware that many understand it in this way that knowledge is intelligence and intelligence is knowledge, and for this reason they

27. Cf. De Smet; *Quiétude*, 91.

28. Read *mumayyiz* (Persian text p. 19, line 14).

29. On the relationship between *ʿaql* and *ʿilm* see especially Nāṣir-i Khusraw, *Jāmiʿ al-ḥikmatayn*, Paras 274–80.

consider it correct to say that every knower is intelligent and every intelligent being is a knower, even though the coming into being of the two worlds, the wonders of the heavenly spheres and bodies and of the elements and of the things pertaining to natural generation, [all this] is the Knowledge of God. Now since the intelligence acquired by us gives us the benefit of knowing what great benefits are in the power of Intellect while, [at the same time] being incapable of giving us the full benefit thereof, we learn from this that those acts of intelligence acquired by us are outpourings of the universal Intellect upon the particular souls (*firū-rīkhtan-i 'aql-i kull ast bar nufūs-i juzwī*), while [Intellect] is one in knowing all things and all knowables. But Intellect did not become one with the Command except after it became one with Pure Knowledge (*'ilm-i maḥḍ*), which latter is the Command of God. This is the meaning of Intellect's becoming one with the Command of God when Command is expressed as Knowledge.

II. 4. 2.

Further, Intellect has yet another [way of] becoming one with the Knowledge which is the Command of God, and that is the outpouring of [the light of] spiritual support (*ta'yīd*) upon the hearts of God's chosen ones and His servants. This is the Pure Knowledge which belongs exclusively to the Prophets, the Legatees and the Imāms. It is the Knowledge of things found with many Prophets, namely, of future events and turns which cannot be perceived through the knowledge of the motions of the planets and the signs of the zodiac, and the knowledge which they need for the administration of the affairs of the Community, which cannot be perceived through the knowledge of the [worldly] administration of kings. These kinds of knowledge, which are needed for these realities, are called 'Pure Knowledge'. This Knowledge is not contaminated with anything like seeking proofs, which is, of course, the [ordinary] scientific method; it is not the kind of knowledge arrived at by the scholars of this world through one [or another] among the proofs. Now, the Pure Knowledge which is not contaminated by anything else is the one appropriate exclusively to God. Therefore, of necessity, the Prime Intellect became one with the Knowledge of God and then poured out the light of pure spiritual support upon the hearts of the chosen ones among the Prophets, so that they, thanks to that knowledge [obtained through] spiritual support, revealed for humans the way to live [in this world] and to 'return' [to their ultimate home]. Understand this!

II. 4. 3.

Further, Intellect has yet another [way of] becoming one with the Knowledge of God, and that is that which is exclusively with God and was not poured out on any Spiritual Rank (*ḥadd*),[30] neither on the Universal Soul, nor on the Speaker-Prophets, the Legatees and the Imāms. As a result, desire for this was permanently

30. Technical term of Ismā'īlism, referring to "persons" of the superior spiritual world (such as Intellect, Soul) and those of the "world of Religion" (i.e., Prophets, Imams, etc.).

in the intellect[31] and remained with the Prophets throughout the Cycles (*dawrhā*)[32] so that each one [among them] would be seeking his share. Thus, to none among the Spiritual Ranks belongs that which is present with the Intellect, and there is no one who can grasp this. And it is on account of this that Intellect thereby realised complete-perfection, became self-sufficient and became the Lord for whatever is beneath Itself. Understand this!

Issue Five: On the Meaning of Intellect's Becoming One with the Command of God When Command Is Expressed as Command in Itself

II. 5. 1.

This kind of [Intellect's becoming one with the Command] is such as you realise when you look at the religious Laws of the Prophets and apply some of them in blind obedience (*taqlīd*): your soul has a distaste for this and indeed fancies it to be idle sport and vexatious; but once it knows the True Reading (*taʾwīl*) and inner Reality (*ḥaqīqat*) of it, it is no longer repelled. It knows, then, [the rule] from which escaping is beyond reach, becomes familiar with it, sanctions it and acquiesces in it. Just as the universal Intellect acquiesces in the Command of God, so the particular intellect acquiesces in the Command of the Prophets whenever it knows its inner Reality. And if Intellect had not been one with the Command as understood in Itself, the commands of the religious Laws would have no common ground and likeness (*mushākilat*) with intellect. Understand this!

II. 5. 2.

Moreover, the Command of God is the act of making-to-be, and making-to-be has no subsistence except in Intellect—which is to say that were it not for Intellect, there would be no being at all. The proof for this statement is this: Were it not for intellect, no artisan in the world would produce any work. Furthermore, the First Being, i.e., Intellect, is the result of perfect generosity,[33] and perfect generosity is that for which Intellect became the medium by virtue of excellence. Now, nothing can become a medium except at a time when it is itself in being. Therefore, the Prime Intellect was not posterior in being to the act of making-to-be, nor did the act-of-making-to be occur prior to the Prime Intellect. These two have no priority over one another. Thus we say: The Command of the transcendent Originator is the act of making-to-be, and Intellect is the first made-

31. *Sic* (*ʿaql*, Persian text p. 21, line 14). If this is correct, then the particular intellect should be understood. But perhaps the word should be replaced by "Soul" (*nafs*). For the "desire" of Soul, cf. *Wellsprings* Para. 61.

32. I.e. the periods of 'hiero-history' inaugurated each time by a Prophet; specifically, the great 'Cycle of Concealment' (see below, VI. 7. 4.)

33. *rādhī-i tāmm* = Ar. *jūd*, "generosity"; see N. Khusraw, *Khʷān ul-ikhwān* chap. lxxix, ed. Qawīm p. 228, 4–5, translation of Sijistānī's *Yanābīʿ*, Para. 66.

to-be. Therefore, the Command, which is the act of making-to-be, and Intellect, which is the first made-to-be, have no priority over one another. Understand this!

Issue Six: On How the Seed of Both Worlds Is in Intellect

II. 6. 1.

Should you think of Intellect as a substance having subsisted by itself at a time when things did not exist, neither body nor spirit nor anything [else], and that things came subsequently from that [state of non-existence] into existence, this would be a major delusion, an idea far from any reasonable argument and one close to wicked thoughts that induce men into error.

If, [by contrast], you think of Intellect as being the "Mercy of God" (*raḥmat-i khudāy*)[34] which was poured out upon the creatures in such a way that every thing had a glitter from the light of the Prime Intellect in accordance with its own "measure" (*miqdār*), be this a corporeal or a spiritual being, or a naturally generated composite—or let it be a Perfect Form (*ṣūratī tamām*), from which the forms become manifest[35] (for it is by virtue of that 'Form' that one can claim Intellect to be the source for all beings to be (*būdanīhā*), and bring to evidence its issuing-forth (*jastār-i ū*) by pointing to the fact that its light is shining in [all] things)—if it is in this way that you think of the substance of Intellect, then your thinking is right. Thus, Intellect is a light poured forth upon creation, shining in every thing, and its luminosity is in accordance with the measure of the substance of [each] thing, depending on the wide or narrow range of that substance. [What happens], then, [is this:] if the recipient of the light of Intellect is a single spiritual being, then Intellect's impact on it turns out as love; if the recipient of Intellect's light is the [elemental] composites, then Intellect's impact on them turns into the seed of generation and corruption deposited therein, i.e., what occurs due to the motion of the composites [i.e., the minerals];[36] if, however, the recipient of Intellect's light is the beings pertaining to natural generation, then Intellect's impact is translated into [sheer] benefits, because of the [special] seeds deposited in them; and if the recipient of Intellect's light is the human being, then Intellect's impact on it turns out to be the fact that it desires permanence and longs for eternal life. From this point of view, it was necessary to plant the seed of both worlds into Intellect. Understand this!

34. Perhaps an allusion to the Prophet as divine *raḥma*; cf. Qur'an 21:107. The *raḥma*-theme is equally important for Ghazālī (cf. *Mishkāt al-anwār* ed. ʿAfīfī, Cairo 1964, p. 71), and fundamental for Ibn ʿArabī (*Fuṣūṣ al-ḥikam* chapter 16).

35. Instead of "from which the forms become manifest" (*kaz ān ṣūrathā ẓāhir shawad*), one could also translate "which [Perfect Form] becomes manifest from [through] these forms". In this case, the "Perfect Form" (of Man?) could be a reference to the expected *Qā'im* or the "Lord of the Final Rising". In any case, the passage is highly ambiguous.

36. Cf. V. 1. 3.

Discourse Three: On the Second Creation [i.e., Soul]

Issue One: That It Is in the Form of Man that Soul Has Come Down

III. I. I.

Know that it is in the Form of Man, from among all things of the world, that Soul has come down, because the soul is joined to life and makes its abode in harmony (*iʿtidāl*); and in the natural world, nothing beneath the human being is capable of complete harmony. Things in the world fall into three categories: inanimate, vegetal, and animal. Now there is for Soul no descending to and joining those [first] two categories, because the soul joins the life of the senses and the harmony of the intellect, and these two are in Man. Indeed, life is the core of Nature, or its quintessence (*maghz*), while harmony is the core of Intellect.[37] Thus, in view of the fact that the soul borders on one side on intellect and on the other side on nature, and that it has no abode except in between these two, i.e. the life of nature and the harmony of intellect, we have said that it is in the Form of Man that Soul has come down. Understand this!

III. I. 2.

As for the manner in which Soul comes down in the Form of Man, it is this: at the first stage, [humans] recognize the name of things and the attributes of things from the teaching of mother and father and the verbal instruction (*talqīn*) of the people among whom they are being brought up. In this regard, humans are of three groups: The first are those who are satisfied with those names and attributes which they have learned through verbal instruction. The second group are those who, having learned names and attributes from the learned, know what legal matters (*kārhā-ʾyi sharʿī*) are obligatory for them. They are cognizant of jurisprudence, dialectical theology, traditions, poetry, parables and whatever is connected to the exoteric (*ẓāhir*). Now the third group are those who not being satisfied with the knowledge of names, attributes and parables, have searched the true meanings and realities from the Lords of Religion (*khudāwandān-i dīn*). Once they have perceived and understood, their soul is made to master those esoteric Sciences (*ʿilmhā-yi bāṭin*) and noble Mysteries (*sirrhā-yi nīkū*). Then, moving onward on the stages of Soul, they will reach the most beautiful of all dwellings, so that Soul will have come down in the Form of Man in perfect-completeness, for they remain eternally with this True Knowledge and noble status in everlasting paradise.[38] Understand this!

III. I. 3.

Further, [consider] that Intellect is not for one moment [lit.:hour] separated from Soul. For Soul is under the supervision of Intellect while it is through Soul that

37. Cf. *Sharḥ-i qaṣīda-yi Abuʾl-Haytham-i Jurjānī*, Persian text p. 54, line 6.

38. The space between brackets (Persian text p. 28, line 18) reads *dar bihisht* in MS. Cairo (MS. Tehran omits both *dar bihisht* and *bāqī*).

the powers of Intellect, which are joined to it, come into being manifest. And the Command[39] and Intellect are not found in anything other than Man. Were it the case that Soul existed [ie., settled down] in something beneath Man, then Intellect's coming down would have become manifest in that [other] thing. But since it is Man who is properly qualified by Intellect, at the exclusion of everything else, we know that it is because of Soul's coming down [in the Form of Man] that Intellect has become manifest in the world of Nature. In this way, [too,] Soul's coming down in the Form of Man has been verified. Understand this!

Issue Four: On Recognizing the Share of Animals in Soul

III. 4. 1.

Know that between Intellect and Soul, there are two other powers, namely, love (*maḥabbat*) and domination (*ghalabah*).[40] Through love, Intellect gives benefit to Soul; through domination, Soul receives benefit from Intellect. These two powers were issued from Soul to the animals in addition to the two powers that had already been issued to them, namely, giving and taking. You will not see an animal that would not love its partner and its child with natural love, and that would not love to dominate another. And it is obvious that the animals take benefit from the plants; and that they give benefits [to humans] is evident from the existence of such useful things as milk, meat, butter, wool, and hair. These are obvious facts, because, [while] the power of the animals is limited to the five senses, love and domination are found in all five. Thus, love in relation to eye-sight is manifest in such things as the eye's delight in beautiful colours and beautiful faces, and domination in relation to eye-sight consists in the soul's seizing the forms that it desires to create.[41] Love in relation to hearing is found, for example, in the experience of delight from agreeable sounds and nice tales, and domination in relation to hearing in the production of melodies from the pipe. Love in relation to smell is seen, for example, in the experience of delight from fragrance, and domination in relation to smell, for example, in the inhalation of fresh air. Love in relation to taste is at work in such things as the experience of delight from sweet agreeable tastes, and domination in relation to taste in preparing food for consumption. Love in relation to touch is obvious, for example, in the delight one experiences from soft objects and fine clothes, and domination in relation to touch in the act of

39. This translates the Persian text (p. 29, line 2) as it is. However, a comparison with I. 3. 2. would suggest that *wa amr* should perhaps be read as *bi-amr* or *az jihat-i amr* and attached to the preceding phrase. The translation, then, would run as follows: "while it is through Soul that the powers of Intellect, which are joined to it thanks to the Command, come into being manifest. And Intellect is not found in anything other than Man."

40. For this "Neo-Empedocles" theme, cf. Suhrawardī, *Ḥikmat al-ishrāq* ed. Henry Corbin (Bibliothèque Iranienne 2, Tehran/Paris, 1952), Arabic text Paras 147f.

41. MS. Cairo reads *nafs nigāh khʷāhad kardan*, which is probably no more than a conjecture by the transcriber; MS. Tehran is identical with the printed text (p. 33, lines 1–2).

embracing and transmitting semen. This is the share of animals in Soul. Understand this!

III. 4. 2.

Animals still have another share in Soul, and that is the following: some among the animals are capable of learning civilized human behavior (*adab-i mardum*). For example, horses train for warfare and games, the oxen learn draught, the elephants warfare. Similarly, the hawk, the falcon and the cheetah learn hunting, parrots talking. So, if animals had no share in Soul, namely, love and domination, these kinds of civilized behavior would not be found among them.[42]

There is still another share, more noble than these, that animals have in Soul, namely, their desire to stay alive (*baqā*) and their shying away from death (*fanā*). For there is no animal that would not out of its own proper being fear death and try to stay alive. And it is for this reason that one does not destroy animals unless this carries benefit. Understand this!

Issue Five: On How Sensation Is Accessed by the One Capable of Sensation, Namely, the Soul

III. 5. 1.

This may be likened to the reception of the imprint of a seal. Receiving the imprint of a seal is something in between the artisan's work and natural generation of beings about to exist. It is incorrect to assimilate the accession of sensation to [natural generation of] beings about to exist, because the latter requires that there be a state of existence which was not before, whereas through accession of sensation nothing comes to exist in the one capable of sensation that did not exist before. Nor should accession of sensation be assimilated to the artisan's work, because the latter implies acquisition [of new forms],[43] whereas this is not the case in the accession of sensation by the one capable of sensation. Now that both these assimilations have been invalidated, what remains is the reception of an imprint, such as the imprint of a seal. This means that sensation is accessed by the one capable of it neither in the way of generation nor in the manner of art work, but in the way the imprint occurs from the ring to the wax, . . . for the wax receives from the ring nothing that would change either its weight or its shape (*shakl*). This is how sensation is accessed by the one capable of sensation. Understand this![44]

III. 5. 3.

Accession of sensation by the one capable of sensation has yet another modality, which is the noblest of all: the fact that the soul is able to take what sensation transmits from

42. Cf. *Sharḥ-i qaṣīda-yi Abū'l-Haytham-i Jurjāni*, Persian text p. 56f.

43. Cf. below, IV. 3. 1.

44. The image of the "imprint" can be traced to Aristotle (*Deanima*, II, 424a 17–21) and can be seen in Fārābī (*Risālah fī l-ʿaql*, ed. M. Bouyges (Beirut, 1983), Paras 15–16, although Sijistānī's point is not the same. Cf. below, IV. 6. 1.–3, on the spiritual beauty of Nature and Art.

visible objects to the one capable of sensation as proof of what sensation has no access to and is more beautiful and perfect. For example, whenever visual sensation transmits the form of a person to the one capable of sensation, the latter can produce in its inner space a form more perfect, more beautiful and more luminous, and this imagined form, then, becomes an imprint in the substance of the soul, just as what appeared first through sensation became an imprint. Similarly, whenever it hears a charming melody, it can imagine a more beautiful melody, which then becomes an imprint in the soul, just as what it heard first through sensation became an imprint. The same applies to any fragrance or flavour that it can imagine, and every touch: all this transmits to the soul something greater and nobler than what sensation perceives. This is how sensation is accessed by the one capable of sensation. Understand this!

Issue Six: On How Speech Is Accessed by the One Capable of Speech, Namely, the Soul

III. 6. I.

Know that speech is accessed by the one capable of speech with [three conditions]: nature, intention, and convention. As for intention, it is as in the phrase "Leave the house!" As for nature, it concerns the organs of enunciation that are made for speaking, such as the pharynx, the tongue and the lips. As for convention, it means that every group must know its own language and its vocabulary. So, whenever [the three conditions of] intention, nature and convention are met, speech is accessed by the one capable of speech (*nāṭiq*), which means by the soul, so that the soul will master the purpose of the enunciation. But whenever one of these [three conditions] fails, the speech is not accessed by the one capable of speech and the enunciation is invalid. An example of this is the following: Suppose someone wants to say to another person "Leave the house!" but says to the other person "Enter the house!", the speech is not accessed by the one capable of speech, because the enunciation is beside the aim. Similarly, if the intention is right but the natural disposition and the organ of the enunciation are not, the utterance will be beside the purpose, as when somebody who has difficulty pronouncing the letter L and instead pronounces R, thus saying "Reave!", the speech will not be accessed by the one capable of speech. Again, if he gets the intention right and the organ is perfect but convention is not correctly observed and the person speaks in a different way than what is commonly known among the people, as when somebody says, "*Sors*!" to an Anglophone or "Leave!" to a Francophone,[45] the enunciation will not be accessed by the recipient. But when all three aspects are met—correct intention, perfect organ, and commonly known convention—then the enunciation will be accessed by the recipient so the latter can master the intention of the sounds of the utterance. Understand this!

45. Adapted from the original, which uses *ukhruj* with *ʿajamī* and *bīrūn shaw* with *tāz-zabān*, respectively.

III. 6. 2.

Further, speech is accessed by the one capable of speech with an additional [benefit hidden] under the spoken word; in fact, this [hidden benefit] is the well-spring of enunciation, its very source, and [it explains] its multiple emergence occurring in the form of judgments. Thus, whenever an enunciation is accessed and linked with two judgments, [the conditions of] correct intention, harmonious organ and commonly-known convention [being met in the first place], the enunciation is accessed by the recipient with an additional [benefit] which is [hidden] under the enunciation. An example of this is the following: Suppose somebody says "Every human being is living, and every living being is a substance." Now, if the intention in knowing every human being [to be living] and every living being to be a substance is correct, and if the organs used for his words in which two judgments have been made are harmonious, and if he is familiar with the conventional meaning of these sounds, then, an additional [benefit] appears for the one capable of speech. Thus, speech is accessed by the one capable of speech just as it is in the case of a single judgment; but it happens that an enunciation with two joined judgments is accessed by the recipient with additional [benefit hidden] under the enunciation, and that is the conclusion [of the syllogism]. Understand this!

III. 6. 3.

There is still another way for accession of speech by the one capable of speech, and a different meaning, indeed the noblest of all meanings of enunciation, and that is the fact that God bestows upon the Prophets and the Chosen ones the capacity to enunciate through their tongues subtle utterances in which subtle meanings are inbuilt. In the case of Muhammad, for example, it was [his] producing a set of testimonies to the Purity [of the One, *ikhlāṣ*] and those noble meanings that were hidden therein. Nobody is able to perceive these noble meanings except those spiritually supported (*muʾayyadān*).[46] As a result [of their perception of these noble meanings, these] became a balance (*mīzān*) by which they measured the skies and the earth and the souls and the Ranks (*ḥudūd*) of [all] this and its creation. And it cannot [yet] be known how many things they may [still] measure with this [balance], and how many noble meanings they will bring forth from there! This is what is meant by accession of speech by the one capable of speech. Understand this!

Issue Seven: On How Thought Is Accessed by the One Capable of Thought, Namely, the Soul

III. 7. 1.

Know that the wellspring of thought (*fikrat*) is the idea (*khāṭir*) and the mount of thought is the intellectual power (*dhihn*), that is, the mind (*hūsh*). Whenever the

46. I.e. Prophets, Imams and "Proofs". See *Prologue*, and II. 4. 2., III. 7. 4., VI. 1. 3., and VI. 7. 1.

well-springs of the idea are flowing forth upon thought, and the mind is made malleable so that thought can mount it, thought is accessed by the one capable of thought so the latter can master the hidden. But whenever the wellsprings of the idea are blocked, thought has no sustaining power; no, it is weak, short, of no impact or importance; and whenever the wellsprings of the idea are flowing forth but the mind is not made malleable for thought to mount it, what appears is wicked thoughts, so that intellectually absurd ideas get mixed together with [claims of] deeds that are obviously impossible for humans to perform, and incorrect thoughts are brought forth, as with fools and the mentally deficient.

III. 7. 2.

Know that the blockage of the wellsprings of the idea is due to the domination by nature, that surplus which is there in the body without being necessary to [sustain] life, while at the same time the outpouring of the wellsprings of the idea is due to the healthy state of nature. Harmonious temperance here lies in careful upbringing of the body and in restricting oneself to that which sustains life, so that the mind is made malleable for thought and thought can mount it. And this will happen [only] when the one capable of thought no [longer] covets the matters of this world and is no [longer] deluded by the reasons of this world, when all he covets is gathering wisdom and knowledge and his inner being is pure, when he searches the true realities of things. [Once his] certitude and mind are righted through contentment of the one capable of thought, and [the latter, i.e., the soul] places its delight in the gathering of wisdom, then the mind is made malleable for thought to mount it; and it will carry thought to the ultimate high stages and grades and sublime realities. But whenever certitude and mind are not right, because the one capable of thought is coveting this world and gathers the reasons of this world, the mind is balky and keeps itself removed from thought. As a result, thought remains perplexed, has no success in [undertaking] any good work, and is removed from the right course, so that the one capable of thought has [cause for] great concern. [In short, then,] thought is accessed by the one capable of thought by virtue of two things: the flowing forth of the wellsprings of the idea and the malleability of the mind. Understand this!

III. 7. 3.

Further, thought may be accessed by the one capable of thought by way of teaching, that is, if one who knows teaches one capable of learning. By taking the trouble of teaching the student piece by piece, the teacher awakens (*mī-angīzad*) intellectual benefits caused by the flowing forth of the wellsprings of the idea and the malleability of the mind, and there is no need for the student [to do anything] but[47] to retain what he learns thanks to the overflow of the idea, that is to say, due to the flowing forth of the wellsprings of the idea and the malleability of the mind. Indeed this is rather like a prepared meal that the cook brings before the customer,

47. Conjecturing *magar* for *dar* (Persian text p. 39, line 11).

and the latter does not have to take the trouble of cooking. Quite similarly, it is not for the student in his learning to go to the trouble of gathering it all together, he only has the trouble of learning, so that thought may be accessed by the one capable of learning as it is accessed by the one capable of thought. Understand this!

III. 7. 4.

Further, thought may be accessed by the one capable of thought all of a sudden, that is, easily, as is the case with those favours that God bestowed upon Prophets, Legatees, Imāms and "Proofs" (*ḥujjatān*), enabling them to master unseen things that are not realised in the heart of anyone else nor have been heard by any ear,[48] and by virtue of which the life of the souls in Cycles following one another will be abundant. And if the person who is given this favour by God is aware that it is indeed a favour from God and then tries through hard work and acquisition [of learning, *iktisāb*] to produce something similar, he will not be able to do so. As much as his ideas may be flowing forth and his mind may have become malleable, he will not be empowered to produce similar benefits. Moreover, the fact that it is God who bestows this favour upon this person [ensures that] it will settle more deeply in the hearts, that the ears will be more eager to listen to it and that the souls will be more attached to it. It is in these ways, then, that thought may be accessed by the one capable of thought. Understand this!

Discourse Four: On the Third Creation, Which Is Nature

Issue Three: That the Forms of Nature Are Not Posterior to Their Source Material

IV. 3. 1.

Although the Second Creation [i.e., Soul] is the form of the First Creation [i.e., Intellect], it did not fall behind it, not even by the twinkling of an eye. Indeed if it had been removed from it only by the twinkling of an eye, the First Creation [itself] would not have come into existence. Accordingly, it is normal that the forms of Nature should not be posterior to their source material (*aṣlhā*), their prime matter (*hayūlāhā-yi khʷīsh*). To be sure, manufactured forms, i.e., the forms produced by craftsmen, are posterior to their source material, because these forms are acquired,[49] whereas the natural forms come all in sequence. And whenever a naturally generated being comes forth, its form comes with its matter (*māddah*), whether it be small or big. For example, consider the sperm, which is the source material for the birth of a being to be born. The form of the sperm exists in con-

48. Allusion to a famous *ḥadīth qudsī* frequently quoted by Sijistānī (e.g. *Wellsprings* Paras 99, 131, 133). Cf. I Corinthians 2, 9.

49. Cf. III. 5. 1. and IV. 6. 1.

comitance with its source material. Then, when it changes from the state of being a sperm, it becomes a blood clot,[50] having extracted for itself a surplus from its source material, which surplus did not exist in the sperm. Again, the form of the blood clot exists in proportion with its source material, until it becomes an embryo, and the [form of the] embryo is consolidated proportionately to what it will have acquired from its source material, up to the moment it becomes a born being, a living being capable of perception and motion, when again it consolidates its form in proportion to [the matter] it will have acquired from its source. This is why we have said that the natural forms are not posterior to their source material in appearing, unlike the forms produced by craftsmen, which are indeed posterior to their source material in appearing.

IV. 3. 3.

Further: The natural forms in the true sense (*bi-ḥaqīqat*), those which are not susceptible to any change in their fundamental being (*nihād*), are the "forms" of the celestial spheres [ie., the stars], which are imprinted in the orbits of the Sphere. To suppose that either the [body of] the sphere or the forms imprinted in it are inactive [*muʿaṭṭal*, i.e., without voluntary motion of their own] would be impossible, for the following reason: If their rising were due to the motion of Nature, then these forms, that is, the stars, would be rising while their motion would not be due to the motion of the sphere. Rather, their motion would be due to something else, and natural motion would then require that the forms which are the stars have their motion from the [natural upward] motion of fire. But in that case, why is it that the journey of the stars is circular, just like the orbit of the sphere? By virtue of this proof [i.e., since circular motion could not then be explained], we know that the motions of the stars are caused by the spheres, which demonstrates that the forms of the spheres, i.e. the stars, do not fall behind the motions of the sphere. Understand this!

Issue Four: That the Centre of Nature Is More Worthy than the Horizons to Enjoy Contiguity with the Spiritual Beings

IV. 4. 1.

Know that for each among the natural beings, there is a power in which it participates; and the spiritual beings participate in many powers beyond measure. Having realised that the Centre (*markaz*), which is to say, the Earth, participates in its own [specific] power, which God has given it; that it [also] participates in the power of water, which moves on its surface; participates in the power of the air, which is drawn upon it; participates in the power of fire, which is hidden in it; participates in the power of the spheres and the stars—as can be known from the fact that the disc of the sun because of its great size warms the earth and makes the plants grow, whereas in the case of the stars, their allowing the earth to participate is hidden

50. Cf. Qurʾān 22:5 and 23:14.

due to their small size—; having thus seen all the powers being at work in Nature, and that the Earth is their recipient which participates in all of them together, and that all of them converge with it, we know that the Earth is more worthy than the horizons to enjoy contiguity with the spiritual beings. Do you not see that Man (*mardum*), in whom the subtle essence of both worlds is altogether present to the utmost degree, exists on the Earth? that his life is on Earth, and that his Return (*maʿād*) and coming back (*bāz-gasht*) is to the Earth? that he is called to arise (*bar-angīkhtan-i ū*)[51] from the Earth? Thus it necessarily follows, from the premises that we have pointed out, that the earth is no less worthy of being a dwelling place for the angels than the sky, because so many powers that are in harmony with the spiritual beings reach the earth. Understand this!

IV. 4. 2.

Further, there is the fact that it is on the Centre that Prophets, Legatees, and Imāms have appeared, and that it is on earth that the Books known as the Word of God have come down, in the languages of humans who exist on earth. All these are spiritual powers, effecting in anticipation this promise of God: "I shall spread justice on Earth and re-assemble the humans on Earth and give the Earth to the humans of good as inheritance!"[52] If there were anything more noble in existence than the Centre, these [spiritual powers] would have been linked to that other thing. But concerning this link, the fact that the Books and the Angels [are said to] 'come down from the sky' does not mean that they come down from the physical sky: what is meant is the 'Heaven of Religion' (*āsmān-i dīn*), which is elevated in terms of excellence and rank above the humans living at a certain epoch. These subtle realities descend upon the heart of him over whose tongue they are made easily understandable [i.e., the Prophets, Imams, and "Proofs"].[53] That is why we have said that the Centre is more worthy than the skies to enjoy contiguity with the spiritual beings. Understand this!

Issue Six: That the Beauty or Adornment of Nature Is Spiritual

IV. 6. 1.

Having noticed a certain resemblance between the natural forms and the forms produced by craftsmen with regard to figure and shape, and having perceived that the embellishment found in the forms produced by craftsmen must be spiritual, because they are traces of the soul [of the craftsman] and acquired from some-

51. Chapter VII.

52. Cf. Qur'ān 21:104–105, which itself evidently refers to Psalm 37:29: "The righteous shall inherit the land, and dwell therein for ever." The theme is eminently Shīʿite; cf. Henry Corbin, *En Islam iranien* I (Paris, 1971), 57. Cf. also here, VI. 7. 2–3. The reference to Qur'ān 21:105 is also found in the *Sharḥ-i qaṣīda-yi Abū'l-Haytham-i Jurjānī*, Persian text p. 48.

53. On this hierarchy, see Introd., n. 7.

thing other [than their immediate source material][54] you should realise that natural beauty and its forms must be spiritual, too, not natural. Indeed if the beauty of Nature were itself from Nature, it would have to be attributed to one among the natural elements (*ṭabʿī az ṭabʿhā*). But the beauty of Nature does not come from such an element which provides the matter of Nature, and from which its potentiality may be known. Rather, it consists of spiritual "colours" (*ranghā-yi rūḥānī*). Just as the colours imbue the stuff prepared or made to receive the colours of the craftsmen, so the beauty of Nature consists of spiritual colours which imbued the beings to be generated naturally with the traces of Soul, which encompasses Nature. Thus it has been verified that the adornment of Nature is spiritual. Understand this!

IV. 6. 2.

Further, if corporeal things come to exist in corporeal things, they constitute for the latter an increase and an addition, and if they are separated from them, there is a decrease and their quantity diminishes. But if a spiritual thing enters or leaves a material thing, its quantity remains as it is. Now, having thought about the adornment of Nature and the adornment of Art, we realise that it joins another thing and leaves it again without there being any increase or decrease in the thing joined. Take, for example, the brocade weaver: the beauty appearing in the brocade is in the being (*nihād*) of the brocade weaver, for, if the brocade is torn apart or if its threads are pulled out one by one, the quantity of the brocade is neither diminished nor increased. The same applies to the silk used for the weaving of the brocade: if the brocade weaver makes many figurations (*andīshahā*) appear in the silk, the quantity of the silk does not increase. This will make you aware that whatever beauty was joined to the brocade came from the brocade weaver; and the beauty that left the brocade when the latter was torn apart, was spiritual, not corporeal. Or take the narcissus flower. When we contemplate it, and people turn it from hand to hand, smell at it and look at its beauty, the quantity of the flower does not thereby become less. So we learn from the narcissus flower that its beauty was spiritual, not natural. Understand this![55]

54. See above, IV. 3. 1. Instead of *az ū* (Persian text p. 49, line 18), I read *ū az* (with both MSS. Cairo and Tehran) and understand *juzwīst* (line 19) to mean *juz* [*az*] *way ast*.

55. The argument of this passage is almost identical with the one found in the *Sharḥ-i qaṣīda-yi Abū'l-Haytham-i Jurjānī*, Persian text p. 58, where the commentator attributes this idea (*qawl*) to the 'great Master' (*ustād-i buzurg*) and says that he himself has "translated" or "commented upon" it (*tarjuma kardastīm*) elsewhere. It remains unclear whether this 'great Master' is Abū l-Haytham, as was assumed by Corbin in the French introduction to this work (pp. 38–40); but it seems more likely that Sijistānī is meant, because the title *ustād-i buzurg* occurs only in this passage whereas Abū'l-Haytham is generally referred to as *khʷāja-yi mā* in this text. Thus, if Abū'l-Haytham's commentator is indicating here that he "translated elsewhere" the *qawl* of Sijistānī on the spiritual beauty of Nature, then this might well mean that he is, in fact, to be identified with our anonymous translator of the original *Kashf al-maḥjūb*! However, the mysterious *ustād-i buzurg* might of course still be someone else.

IV. 6. 3.

If a soul becomes an expert in the art of painting, it can imitate (*ḥikāyat kardan*) the beauty of this or the colours of that, until it can bring into appearance, if it so desires, the form of whatever it wishes: the form of the animals, or the form of the seat and the house, or the form of the human being. That it can thus imitate [the forms] is due to their being spiritual and in accordance with the spiritual substance. Do you not see that nobody can create a thing of nature, whether animal, vegetable or mineral? But one can bring into appearance whatever he wishes from the beauty of Nature; and one can do so because that [beauty] is spiritual. Understand this!

Discourse Five: On the Fourth Creation [i.e. The Species]

Issue One: That the Species Are Preserved in their Being

V. 1. 1.

If it were conceivable for one species not to be included in preservation, so that it would decay, then the same would be conceivable for all species; and if this were the case, then corruption would abolish all of them. And if corruption would abolish all of them, then what is under the species, that is, the individuals, would also be abolished; and what is above the species, that is, the genera, would also be abolished, because the genera unite the species and the species unite the individuals. And the abolition of the individuals would entail the abolition of the lower world, and the abolition of the genera would entail the abolition of the higher world. But these two worlds are not abolished. Therefore, since the permanence of both the genera and the individuals is a necessity, the permanence of the species, which is what preserves both, is also necessary. Thus it has been verified that the species are preserved in their being and not one is abolished. Understand this!

V. 1. 2.

Further: the species are the radiations of those "forms" which are fixed (*murakkaz*?) in those celestial spheres which are the upper limit of the upward motion of Nature.[56] None of these realities is ever abolished; on the contrary, they are preserved in the celestial bodies, and there is no obstacle between them and the Centre [of Nature, *markaz*, i.e., the Earth] which [obstacle] would keep the species in that abode. Therefore, the permanence of the forms of the sphere is a necessity, and there cannot be any obstacle between the stars and the species. Necessarily, therefore, the species must be preserved in their being.

56. Not entirely clear. The "forms" are the stars (cf. IV. 3. 3.); but the "upper limit" of Nature should normally be the lunar sphere (cf. *Wellsprings* Para. 13).

V. 1. 3.

If somebody holds that the species are greater in number than the forms of the sphere, this is incorrect. In fact, this is based on an erroneous assumption on his part in the matter under discussion, for this person assumes that a multitude of things equals a multitude of species when they constitute one and the same species, such as sulphur, vitriol, gold, and silver. Despite their differences, these are of one species, and their differences are [only] due to the different mixtures (*mizāj*) of the respective places from which they come forth by way of generation (*tawallud*). The plants, too, are all of one species, despite the great differences that exist among them. The same goes for the multitude of the animals, such as the ant, the gnat, the horse, or the camel: although they are all different in form, they are one species. And if God lets the forms of the sphere take charge[57] of the creatures [i.e., the species preserved in their being], he can also have them take charge of the forms of those [individual beings] that are generated and born one after the other. Understand this!

Issue Three: That the Species Do not Mix with Each Other, Neither at the Time of Composition, Nor After Composition

V. 3. 1.

This is because the species are linked to the individuals. So, if it were admissible that the species mix with each other, one would have to admit that individuals [of different species] mix with each other, and find a man who is half donkey half man, or a donkey who is half bird half donkey. But such a thing does not exist and cannot exist. It does not exist because all its benefits would become void; and God does nothing void. And the mixing of species with one another cannot possibly exist because the species are linked to the individuals. Thus it has been verified that the species do not mix with each other. Understand this!

V. 3. 2.

Further: something that exists *in potentia* and comes to exist *in actu* will bring forth from itself into actual existence what was in it potentially. If it were admissible that the sperm of the donkey which is in potentia a donkey, be a horse, or that the sperm of the horse which is *in potentia* a horse, be a donkey, the wisdom of God would be void. But this does not exist. Understand this!

V. 3. 3.

As for the mixing after the separation from the body, a group among the ignoramuses fancied that one species becomes another species. That group is the one to whom the doctrine of transmigration (*tanāsukh*) is attributed, in such a way that the soul (*rūḥ*) of man goes into the body of a dog or a donkey, and the soul of a

57. Reading *bigumāshad* instead of *bigushāyad* (Persian text p. 56, line 10).

dog or a donkey comes into the body of a man. Among all of the nonsense they profess, this is the worst, because it amounts to an enormous slander. For we can see that the form of a dog is determined ["measured"] in the sperm of a dog, that it came from a dog and entered a dog, and that everything needed for it to become capable of sense perception, movement, etc., was existent in that sperm. Having seen whatever increase and decrease it goes through until it is completely formed in its womb, at which moment should we imagine, and would it be permissible to say, that the soul of man has entered that dog? You must realise that such a judgment would be invalid. And then, what could be the benefit of such mixing of the species with one another after [the soul] has left the body? If they say: "God punishes the sinners in the bodies of animals", we reply that if that claim is true, then human bodies are quite sufficient for the punishment of sinners. Indeed there are many in human bodies who are more stinking and dirty than the dog, the wolf and the swine!

V. 3. 4.

Further, each species has a share and a determined measure from its own source, from which it comes forth. These [sources] are the spheres that transmit their influx onto them in such a way that no [species] can ever be separated [from its respective source] with regard to its form. Indeed, to each species in creation belongs respectively one form of the sphere, and it is that [form] which preserves the species in its being.[58] Thus it has been verified that the species do not mix with each other, neither at the time of composition, nor after composition. Understand this!

Issue Five: That the Greater or Smaller Number of Individuals Does not Entail Increase or Decrease in the Virtues

V. 5. 1.

Know that the virtues are [spiritual] matters (*aṣlhā*), that is, basic resources (*māyahā*), and that they have forms which are their recipients.[59] Now think of the following: Regardless of whether a particular virtue is being received by one individual (*shakhṣ*) or many, [the value of that] virtue neither decreases nor increases through the smaller or greater number of individual [recipients]. Consider courage, which is one of the virtues proper to the soul. Whether one individual or many have courage, courage remains exactly of the same quality (*ḥāl*) in the one individual as it is in the many. Indeed, one individual may bring forth such an amount of miracles of courage as [even] a multitude will not be able to do, because, while each among the many individuals has a share of courage, the whole is in that unique person, and the part does not have as much power as the whole![60] Similarly, knowledge is one among the

58. Cf. V. 1. 2. and Suhrawardī's "Lords of the species" (*arbāb al-anwāʿ*).

59. The Persian text (p. 63, lines 11–12) seems somewhat garbled here. What seems clear, however, is that the "forms" in this case are not Aristotelian "forms" but rather material receptacles or moulds, i.e., individual bodies receiving the spiritual matter of "virtue."

60. Probably a reference to ʿAlī b. Abī Ṭālib.

virtues of the soul, which is proper to man. It may well happen that in one individual there is so much knowledge as is not [even] in the totality of all of them, and that what appears in that unique man is more wonderful than what appears in the multitude of men. It is for this reason that it is said traditionally that Adam had so much intelligence and understanding as is not[61] [even found] in all his children together. Thus, what is meant by "Adam" is a unique individual in which virtue is altogether there, and what is meant by "his children" is the multitude of individuals in which virtue is scattered. And one among the *mirabilia* of Adam is precisely that the [human] creatures claim descent from him as his offspring, and that paternity is attributed to him. It is for this reason that we have said that from the greater or lesser number of individuals, it does not follow that virtue becomes less or more.

V. 5. 2.

Further, the virtues being received by individuals may be likened to craftsmanship with regard to [the question under discussion, namely,] increase or decrease. For, with every craft that you may think of, such as woodworking or the art of the goldsmith, you must realise that to receive more gold and silver does not mean for the goldsmith that his art is thereby increased, nor does his receiving less gold and silver imply a decrease in his art. In the same way, we say that the virtues do not become more or less on account of the greater or smaller number of individuals. Understand this!

V. 5. 3.

Another proof for what we have established is this: it is evident that virtues move in the world from one people to another. For it is established that at one time, knowledge was with the Greeks. They were famous for this virtue, and they had sharp discernment and a penetrating mind. Later, this virtue moved and came to the Muslims. And prior to these two peoples, [this] virtue was in the land of Iran, and at some time among the people of India; and each of these nations has many books about this. But they could not act in such a way that the virtue of knowledge would remain in Greece, or with the Iranians, or the Indians; for it had to come to the Muslims, because there can be no increase or decrease in the virtues. The same applies to courage, as mentioned earlier: it appears in any given nation but then leaves it and moves to another. Thus, at one time, courage was with the Turks, at another time with the Iranians, at another time with the Byzantines, at another time with the Arabs, at another time with the Indians. Right now, it is with the Berbers, and courage is obvious in them. If increase and decrease [of the number of bodies] were applicable to virtue, courage would have remained with every people and would not have been annulled [there] by its appearance in another people. That is why we have said that the virtues do not increase or decrease on account of the greater or smaller number of individuals. Understand this!

61. Adding *nabāshad* (Persian text p. 64, line 6).

V. 5. 4.

The proof for the accuracy of what we have said is the following: there exists a Sage of such penetrating Knowledge and Wisdom that nobody can rival him, of such eminence and virtue as is seen in nobody [else] before he leaves that world. And when he leaves this world, his Knowledge and virtue is scattered among the humans. At the time when his Knowledge appears [again] among the humans, they know that it is his Knowledge that reached them. That is why the Knowledge of the Prophet is passed on as inheritance to the Legatee, and from the Legatee to the Imām, and from the Imām to the "Proof." Thus it has been verified that the virtues do not increase or decrease on account of the smaller or greater number of individuals. Understand this!

Discourse Six: On the Fifth Creation [i.e., Prophethood]

Issue One: On How Prophethood of Prophets Is Facilitated

VI. 1. 1.

Everything in creation has a quintessence, which is indispensable for that thing to be in existence and to manifest its benefits—those benefits which are vested in it. We have already said that the quintessence of "animal" is man, the [rational] living being capable of speech (*mardum-i nāṭiq-i zindah*). The benefits of man are manifest. They are the amazing crafts that man invented with his intellect, his subtle intelligence and his sheer skill. The whole purpose of creation ended up with man, and after man, no form appeared in creation that [would have] surpassed man in nobility. Necessarily, [therefore] the quintessence of man lies in uttered thoughts (*sukhan*). However, all the thoughts uttered by humans during one Cycle are like milk which, once milked, is beaten in a skin so that butter is formed as a result. The result of the utterances of humans during one Cycle, being of the subtle nature [of the quintessence], is, then, difficult to comprehend for one man; but [its enunciation] is facilitated for the tongue of him who thereby is capable of accepting the task of a Prophet; and because this is so, that enunciation will settle in the hearts of his people. For this enunciation is the quintessence of those thoughts uttered by them in their own gatherings. As a result, to hear it is agreeable for the ear, because they are familiar with those tones. This is how prophethood of Prophets is facilitated. Understand this![62]

VI. 1. 2.

There is still another meaning to this. The Creator knows what is to the advantage of his servants, and what they need in view of an auspicious administration of this world. For this purpose, he made manifest firmly tied knots in the celestial bodies, each knot facing a specific individual, so that, whenever it was the right time

62. Cf. *Wellsprings* Para. 164.

for a noble [human] to be born, He would open one of those knots. As a result, noble powers coupled with auspiciousness and virtues would continuously reach the person so fortunate. [This] possessor of charisma (*khudāwand-i karāmat*) would, then, at all times contemplate in himself something of the luminosity of the spiritual world (*ʿālam-i malakūt*) and of the overwhelming power of the divine (*jabarūt*), becoming thereby capable of receiving the word of God and of being acquainted with that divine Law (*sharīʿat*) which contains both the colours of the spiritual [world] and the dispositions pertaining to administrative laws, so that those accepting it will be of blessed destiny just as those rejecting it will be of cursed destiny. Understand this!

VI. 1. 3.

There is still another way to see how prophethood is facilitated for Prophets, namely, by way of the manifestation of the activity of Intellect. For everything, from the beginning of Creation to its end, has its [proper] activities.[63] Thus, the elements and the celestial bodies manifest their activities in the beings pertaining to the realm of natural generation; Soul's intention is active in the plants and the animals, and Soul's proper activity is manifest in Man, in view of the spoken Word (*sukhan*). In sum, then, nothing in creation had an unfulfilled desire to deploy its activity, except for Intellect's desire [to exercise] lordship and glory. Among all possible activities, nothing indeed would befit Intellect except manifestation of domination and deployment of glory; and this lordship, glory and domination must be such as to dominate the most eminent of all things, which is Man. Thus, lights were pouring forth from Intellect, and then, an individual body (*shakhṣ*) having the most complete harmony, the most subtle natural constitution and the most perfect disposition was fashioned from Nature and Soul in such a way that [this individual] was capable of receiving the spiritual support of Intellect (*taʾyīd-i ʿaql*). As a result, these blessings reached Soul and Nature, and [the manifestation of] their good and sacred qualities was facilitated, and many things appeared from there. This is how prophethood of Prophets is facilitated. Understand this!

Issue Two: That Prophethood Overpowers Discourse and the Professionals of Discourse

VI. 2. 1.

Prophethood overpowers [mere discourse] because it is single and without equal in its time, whereas discourse occurs among men who are equals. Therefore, the person endowed with prophethood is confident of the message that reaches him, and he knows that it does not reach anyone other than himself so there might be dispute and contradiction between himself and that other person. [By contrast], the professionals of discourse are many in the world, and there is much contradiction and dispute because of their multitude. One group, then, wishes to approach

63. Read *kār-kardan-hāʾist* (Persian text p. 70, line 19).

Prophets, seeking to contradict them and [presuming] by virtue of that speech to be their equals, while another group is incapacitated before the Prophet due to the inimitable quality of the prophetic message. Those [presuming] to be his equals by virtue of discourse cannot dominate him because the prophetic message he has is more than speech; rather, it is he who dominates them. Understand this!

Issue Three: Why the Later Prophet Confirms the Truthfulness of the Earlier Prophet[64]

VI. 3. 1.

Should a later Prophet disown an earlier Prophet, claiming that prophethood belongs to him [alone], that no Prophet will come after him and that there was no Prophet before him, people will disown him even more. His work will turn out to be more difficult, and people will have stronger arguments against him. But if he confirms the truthfulness of the earlier Prophet, he will be strong in accomplishing his prophetic task, because he will say, "Before me, there was one who proclaimed the same Call that I am proclaiming." He will have a proof against those who disown him, saying [to them], "Why do you disown my prophethood when I am proclaiming the same Call that was proclaimed by him who was before me and when I am following the same Path he was following?" For this reason, it is necessary that the later Prophet confirm the truthfulness of the earlier Prophet. Understand this!

VI. 3. 2.

Furthermore, Prophets are like the members of [one body, i.e.] prophethood; for prophethood will not stand good unless its members and limbs are a perfect whole. Whenever a deficiency appears in one member, this deficiency will affect most of the other members, for prophethood has no firm standing unless that member is [also] perfect. And if a later Prophet does not confirm the truthfulness of an earlier Prophet, he will have made inoperative a member of his own [body] and introduced a weakness. Understand this!

VI. 3. 3.

Further, there is a common ground and likeness (*mushākilat*) between two Prophets that succeed one another. Both have truth by virtue of [their] spiritual essence being one and the same (*bi-yikī-i ḥaqīqat*), for the rank of the preceding prophetic messenger is like the stage of potentiality, and the rank of the succeeding prophetic messenger is like the stage of actuality; and nothing comes ever to the stage of actuality unless it has been in the stage of potentiality. Therefore, it is necessary for that prophetic messenger who comes next, since he is at the stage of actuality, to confirm the truthfulness of the one who is at the stage of potentiality. For if he

64. For this theme, cf. *Kitāb ithbāt al-nūbuwwāt*, 162–66.

disowns him, he disowns his own potentiality from which he evolved to the stage of actuality; and if he disowns his own potential, his effectiveness will be weakened; and if his effectiveness is weakened, his words will not settle in the hearts of the people of his community. But if the later prophetic messenger confirms the truthfulness of the one before him, it will be necessary for the Prophet who comes next to confirm his truthfulness as well. Thus, it is necessary for that Prophet who comes last to confirm the truthfulness of all the Prophets prior to him. Understand this!

VI. 3. 5.

There is yet another major and subtle reason for the later Prophet to confirm the truthfulness of the earlier Prophet, which is the following: Many later Prophets lived under the Law of earlier Prophets and acted for some time under that Law, and [then] reached prophethood [themselves]. If [such a Prophet] would give the lie to the one under whose Law he had himself been acting, he would be weakening his own person and would debase himself, since he had accepted the truthfulness of that [earlier] person as long as prophethood did not [yet] belong to him. He would become suspect in his own prophethood, and bad thoughts would come up regarding himself, since he [would have to admit that he] accepted the truthfulness of someone without having knowledge of his truthfulness and was deluded by someone who cheated him. Indeed [the later Prophet] must not allow any doubt to come up in himself with regard to the noble quality he saw in himself while living in obedience of [the earlier Prophet,] having then accepted his truthfulness by acting under his Law and worshipped God under that religion. This way, he will be safe from bad thoughts and will eliminate the talk of the adversaries (*sukhanān-i ḍiddān*) from his person. Therefore, it is necessary for the later prophetic messenger to confirm the truthfulness of the earlier prophetic messenger. Understand this!

Issue Four: Why the Preceding Prophet Announces the Following Prophet

VI. 4. 1.

By announcing the prophetic messenger following him, the preceding prophetic messenger [in effect] announces himself. This is so because the preceding Spiritual Rank (*ḥadd*) is in comparison to the subsequent one like something that exists *in potentia*, while the subsequent prophetic messenger is like something that exists *in actu*, as we have already said; and something that exists potentially desires to attain the rank of actuality. Thus it is in view of the desire of the possessor of potentiality to evolve in actuality that he announces the Prophet after him. Understand this!

VI. 4. 2.

Moreover, if the preceding prophetic messenger disowned the prophetic messenger coming after him, [this would mean that] the preceding prophetic messenger would be for ever more excellent and more eminent, and that the particular Law and the Book which he brings would be [for ever] more perfect and more luminous. Also, if he did not announce the one after him, the willingness of the people to embrace his religion would be weak. Therefore, if he does announce the coming of that Spiritual Rank (*ḥadd*)[65] after himself, they are willing to embrace his own religion most warmly, and they will expect the advent of that Spiritual Rank after him, for the latter is to have far more lights of the spiritual domain (*anwār-i malakūt*) than he has. Consider for example someone inviting people to a feast, preparing food and drink of many kinds, and saying to them: "If you are eager to come to my feast and willingly consume my food, I shall give you another feast, better than this!", they will be eager to come for the sake of the other feast. Understand this!

Issue Five: That the Proof of God Is Not Established With One Prophet Alone

VI. 5. 1.

God most exalted made it imperative to pay attention to [His] proof (*ḥujjat*) and to send Prophets; but you must know that he did not privilege any one Prophet. The reason for this is that time does not remain unchanged, rather, it rotates and causes the [human] creatures to change accordingly, due to the motion of the stars in the skies and the fact that in their rotation they travel through the signs of the zodiac and the degrees [of the Sphere]. In sending the Prophets, God has no purpose other than the benefit [of the humans]. He does it not in order to remove any disadvantage from Himself but for the sake of that rule (*siyāsat*) which will be best for the humans so they will have a permanent standing (*pāyandagī*) in this world and the other. Now, if what we have established is true and time does not remain unchanged, it follows that the rules must vary just like time; and [since] the world is in rotation and the moral norms (*khūyhā*) of the people in this changing world turn in various ways, it follows that there must be a ruler for each rule specifically since each rule is different. And it is not possible that different rules have one and the same ruler; for if one and the same person were to manage all the rules, he would be unable to lead the affairs of everybody to their achievement and could not take care of all. In effect this would amount to approving of lawlessness and giving up the choice of the best option. It is for this reason that the proof of God is not established with one Prophet alone. Understand this!

VI. 5. 2.

Another point: Had God sent no more than one Prophet, it would be inconceivable that [this] one Prophet alone would have come with all the Laws and would have realised all the spiritual Realities (*ḥaqīqatuhā*) that He deposited at the top of

65. Probably an allusion to the coming of the *qāʾim*, or the "Lord of the Final Rising" (cf. VI. 7 .1.–4.).

the Laws, and that he would have grasped the meanings alluded to in the Books [that came] over the tongue of the subsequent Prophets. For that which was allotted to the prior Prophets is only a little of the lights from the spiritual dominion of God, the rules of administration [of this world], the Books and the Laws of the later Prophets, who were privileged to find the way to the spiritual dominion of God. And the word of God is the proof of God for the servants of God. If this were not so, this would amount to invalidation of the proof of God—but God does not invalidate his own proof. Rather, he keeps his own proof valid and manifests it so as to reduce the invalid to nothing. Thus it has been verified that the proof of God is not established with one Prophet alone. Understand this!

VI. 5. 3.

On the other hand: Had God not brought forth Prophets, and had He postponed [this] until the Seal of the Prophets came forth, whom He would [then] have graced with the clearly-spoken Qur'an and the Law of the true religion (*sharīʿat-i ḥanīfī*), the people of the earlier periods would have been in want of the proof of God, and God would have rendered invalid his own proof for a long time. Therefore, since it is inconceivable that God would render his own proof invalid for ever or for a long time, sending out Prophets was a necessity [for Him] in the past times, and is so, likewise, in the remaining times. Thus it has been verified that the proof of God is not established with one Prophet alone. Understand this!

Issue Six: Why Descent [*From Heaven*] *Is Kindred to Jesus, Among All the Prophets*

VI. 6. 1.

The meaning of the kinship [indicated] in Jesus' descent from Heaven to Earth is this: In Christ (*masīḥ*), the image (*mithāl*) of Adam became a visible event (*dīdār*);[66] for he gave[67] from that tree from which [Adam] had been debarred. Indeed, while spreading the True Knowledge and the Wisdom, which was transmitted among his disciples, Jesus did not alter the Law of Moses except that he changed the Sabbath to Sunday. His constant concern was to give his disciples [the capacity to see] 'colour'—that is, the colours of the spiritual [world], up to the moment when he left this world. But the preestablished 'measuring' (*taqdīr*) of God was such that the previous Law should be abrogated and a new Law should appear. Thus, after Jesus, one heptad among the [successive] heptads passed by and the preestablished 'measuring' came true from among the people living during the Cycle inaugurated by him, that is, the codification of the Law attributed to Jesus, which is the one that is now in the hands of the Christians. Yet God has [also] given an account of Christ to the effect that he is the sign of

66. Cf. Qur'an 3:59.

67. MS. Cairo reads *bi-chashīd* for *bakhshīd* of the edited Persian text (p. 79, line 15); MS. Tehran could be read either way.

the Final Rising of Liberation (*nishān-i rastākhīz*), which means that whatever Knowledge and Wisdom Christ revealed to his disciples, that Knowledge belongs [properly] to the Lord of the Final Rising of Liberation (*khudāwand-i rastḵhīz*). [Therefore,] the descent of Jesus from Heaven signifies that the Knowledge and Wisdom re- vealed by Jesus will be manifest to the Lord of the Final Rising (*khudāwand-i qiyāmat*). Indeed in some traditions it is said that the Mahdī will be Jesus son of Mary (ʿĪsā-yi Maryam), which means that that which Jesus imagined about himself, the preestablished 'measuring' of that will come true with the Mahdī. This is why the descent [from Heaven] is kindred to Jesus, among all the Prophets.[68]

VI. 6. 2.

Another possible meaning of this is the following: Each one among the Prophets was granted triumph over his enemies so that his rule could stand, except Jesus, who indeed experienced hardship from his enemies and left this world without having received any help against his enemies. So God promised the Final Rising (*qiyāmat*) to grant him triumph, and He will call him to arise (*bar angīzad ūrā*) with victory and in triumph. Understand this!

VI. 6. 3.

Furthermore, Christ is kindred to the Spirit of God and the Word of God, for it was blown into Mary so he would grow and be born. You should know that all the religious Laws are like bodies for the Word of God, and the Word of God is like the Spirit animating all the religious Laws. Now God promised that the Final Rising will be close to the descent of Jesus, that is to say, the descent of the Word of God, so that the religious Laws shall be alive and their benefits will appear, and that whatever inner realities and secrets are hidden in the religious Laws come out into the open. This is what is meant by the descent of Jesus from Heaven. Understand this!

Issue Seven: Why the Lord of The Final Rising Is Kindred to the Mahdī

VI. 7. 1.

The Mahdī is the one who shows humans the Path. All the Prophets before him guided humans to the Path of God; but their words were veiled, and their Sciences were hidden, because the times required this. But once the process has reached its end and the lifting of the veils has come near and the Cycle of Unveiling (*dawr-i kashf*) has arrived, clear proofs will come out into the open, and well-ordered signs of that will appear. The person who will appear then will guide the humans without [having recourse to] veils and symbols, and he will

68. Cf. *Wellsprings* Paras 143–46.

unveil to them all of the [True] Knowledge that had been in the religious Laws and the [prophetic] Books, and every Wisdom and Mystery that had been hidden. The name of that person [i.e., Mahdī] is derived from [the root] HDY [to guide], which implies that there is no way for anyone to avoid him and his Call (*daʿwat*), or to escape from his arguments and proofs, because he guides the humans to that which is in their own inner reality (*ḥaqīqat-i īshān*) and shows the way to those sciences to which 'the Horizons and the Souls'[69] bear witness and opens the way for the souls to know the spiritual dominion of God, so that the souls become one with the True Realities (*ḥaqāyiq*) and the Spiritual Support [of the 'chosen ones', *taʾyīd*]. Then all will be peace and joy, and all the stubborn will join the religion of God out of their own choice, eagerly and truly, and offer their obedience. This is why the Lord of The Final Rising is kindred to the Mahdī. Understand this!

VI. 7. 2.

It is said that when the Mahdī comes, wolf and sheep will drink water in one and the same place. 'Wolf' means the adversary (*ḍidd*), those who harm the friends of God (*awliyāʾ-i khudāy*) and confront them with hostility, while 'sheep' means a person with whom [they,—or people generally] feel confident and in whose goodness they place their hope. In this sense, then, there will be agreement between the adversary and the friend [of God] due to the power of the Lord of the Final Rising. That they 'drink water' [in the same place] means that there will be agreement between them in Knowledge, Wisdom, and Unveiling of the True Realities.[70]

VI. 7. 3.

Further, it is said that the Mahdī will kill Gog and Magog. This means that during the time and Cycle of the Lord of the Final Rising those who strayed from the Path and stuck to corrupt creeds will be put to death. The "spilling of their blood" [means that] the doubt will be removed from their hearts and souls. After that, "justice will be spread and tyranny will be abolished", that is, the justice which is Knowledge will be spread and the tyranny which is Ignorance will be abolished.[71]

VI. 7. 4.

Further, The souls during the Cycle of Concealment (*dawr-i satr*) may be likened to a serious illness affecting the body, and the Cycle of Unveiling (*dawr-i kashf*) may be likened to the state of health that one hopes for when leaving the illness behind. The Lords of the Cycles of Concealment may be likened to the physi-

69. Cf. Qurʾan 41:53.
70. Cf. *Kitāb ithbāt al-nubūʾāt*, 168f.
71. For the "spreading of justice" see above, IV. 4. 2.

cians who cure the sick. Now by God's preestablished 'measuring', the period of time appointed for these sick ones was a total of seven Cycles, and at the completion of these seven Cycles the illness was to leave these afflicted ones. The Lord of the First Cycle [*khudāwand-i dawr-i pīshīn*, i.e. Adam] may be likened to the kind of physician who prevents the sick from eating anything, as do the physicians of India. The Lord of the Second Cycle is rather like the physician who prescribes drugs, and the Third and the Fourth, up to the Seventh, may be compared to those physicians who prescribe, each in his turn, an appropriate medical treatment. When it comes to the Lord of the Final Rising, he liberates them from the fetters of illness altogether, introduces them to his own norm, his own food and drink, and brings them to the state of health. And that is the sign of the Mahdī, while those [medical treatments] are the benefits [derived from] the sciences and wisdoms of him who guides mankind towards the Mahdī and Lord of the Cycle of Unveiling. It is in this sense that the Lord of the Final Rising is kindred to the Mahdī. Understand this![72]

Discourse Seven: On Bringing to Mind the Sixth Creation [i.e., the 'Call to Arise']

Issue One: That Calling to Arise Is Coupled with Existing

VII. I. I.

Be aware that it has been transmitted from among the sayings of the wise of [all] religions that Soul is a Form arisen (*bar-angīkhta*) from the First Intellect; indeed it is named 'the Second Intellect' for this reason. You also should know that in the language of the Arabs, 'calling to arise' (*bar angīkhtan*) means 'calling into existence' (*būdan kardan*). As Abū Yaʿqūb [i.e., Sijistānī, presumably in the Arabic original text] puts it, *al-inbiʿāth* (arising, originating, emanation) is the *infiʿāl* (passive or reflexive form) of *al-baʿth* (arousing, awakening, resuscitation, resurrection); *al-munbaʿith* (the one arising) is *al-munfaʿil* (present participle active), and *al-mabʿūth* (the one made to arise, awakened, resuscitated, resurrected) is *al-mafʿūl* (past participle passive). Therefore, since Soul is a Form arisen (*bar angīkhtah*) from Intellect—for it is due to the reflection of Intellect that it came into being-there—, it follows that the dead must be called to arise; indeed Intellect's self-reflection rests on this point. It further follows from there, for those of fine understanding, that Calling to Arise (*bar angīkhtan*) is forever coupled with Existing (*būdan*), which means that Becoming (*kawn*) is always coupled with the Awakening (*baʿth*).

72. Cf. *Kitāb ithbāt al-nubuwwāt*, 181–93; Wilferd Madelung, "Das Imamat in der fruhen ismailitischen Lehre," *Der Islam 37 (1961)*, 43–135, esp. 109. The cyclical theory outlined in our text is peculiar since it implies that the "cycle of unveiling", i.e., the cycle inaugurated by the "Lord of the Rising" or the *qāʾim*, is no longer identical with the seventh (as is classical Ismāʿīlī doctrine, including Sijistānī's own in most of his works), but comes after it (cf. Introd.). Note, however, the "preventive medicine" of Adam; this may reflect Sijistānī's (and Nasafī's) "radical" doctrine that Adam did not bring a *sharīʿah*.

In sum, then, from the reflection of Intellect, Soul is called to arise; the latter causes the continuance (*baqāʾ*) of Nature; and from this in turn the beings generated by it (*mutawallidāt-i ū*) exist. Thus it has been verified that Becoming is coupled with the Awakening, which means that Calling to Arise is coupled with Existing. Understand this!

VII. I. 2.

Further, Things are primordially 'measured' in Creation, so they will not depart from that formation (*khilqat*) under which they came into being-there, due to the preestablished 'measuring' (*taqdīr*) of their Creator and Existentiator; and no thing is ever separated from its own likeness (*shakl*), nor from its opposite. All like things are linked with each other, and so are the opposites, in view of the intermediaries which share a likeness with every two opposites. Now, the Call to Arise has either the likeness of Death, or is its opposite. If it has the likeness of Death, it is inseparable from it and will not be removed from it. If, on the other hand, it is the opposite of Death, there must be an intermediary between them which shares a likeness with both sides, with Death and with Calling to Arise. But the Call to Arise is indeed the opposite of Death, so there must be an intermediary; and there is no common ground that would be an intermediary encompassing both sides, Calling to Arise and Death, except the living beings who are bound to die. Thus, Calling to Arise is inseparable from Existing, which means that the Awakening is inseparable from Becoming. Put in a better way, it means that if there is Existing, then there is Calling to Arise, and if there is Calling to Arise, then there is Existing. Thus it has been verified that Calling to Arise is coupled with Existing, which means that Becoming is coupled with the Awakening. Understand this!

VII. I. 3.

Another way: To exist is to find again the life which had disappeared from the living person, just as being called to arise is to find again the life which had disappeared from the dead person. This way, death is [paired] with life, and being called to arise with being dead. Put another way, there is a Call to Arise for the living as there is a Call to Arise for the dead. Understand this!

VII. I. 4.

Further, the Call to Arise is based on a fundamental point: that reward reach the humans of good, and that punishment get hold of the humans of evil. Likewise, Existing is based on a fundamental point: that fortunate destiny reach the well-fated, and that unfortunate destiny get hold of the ill-fated. Now, since in view of 'reaching' and 'getting hold of' happiness or misery, the two—Becoming and the Awakening—have been assimilated, we know that they are coupled together and are inseparable. From this point of view, [too], it has been verified that the Awakening is coupled with Becoming, which means that Calling to Arise is coupled with Existing. Understand this!

Issue Two: That to Think that the Multitude Will Be Resuscitated Is Contrary to the Truth

VII. 2. 1.

Thinking about [the number of] those humans that lived during one Cycle, according to common understanding, how long would it take to arrive at the [correct] number for the Cycle of Adam?—and that by itself lasted for seven thousand years! And after Adam, the world is seen to be filled with humans at each period. So, when any of these populations reaches the end, the world is again filled to replace them with creatures after them. If these creatures are added up by counting seven thousand years [per period], the [total] number of these humans will be beyond counting—not to mention those populations that existed prior to Adam!—and this calculation will end up in sheer nonsense and ignorance. Under these assumptions, if such a multitude would have to be resuscitated, the part allotted to each individual from that which had been flowing forth upon them from the Intellect would appear to be small, and the benefits would be little indeed! Thus, to think that the multitude will be resuscitated is contrary to the truth. Understand this!

VII. 2. 2.

In other ways, too, resuscitation of the multitude would imply much iniquity. For there were among the peoples of the past unweaned children and fools deprived of reason, who cannot be held responsible for retribution. And what about those people who live in the outermost regions of the earth, such as the Africans, the Turks and the people of Sind? If they were resuscitated while having acquired no [merit] from knowledge and action, how could they gain eternal reward? And if they were punished, this would not befit the mercy of the Creator. For the mercy of the Creator is not an idle matter. The mercy of the Creator is great; it is Wisdom, and it has reached every thing. Thus it has been verified that they would not be included in a resuscitation [supposed to] take place at the gathering of the multitude. Therefore, they and those before them are called to arise in such a way as is necessary and befitting. Understand this!

VII. 2. 3.

Moreover, to assume that the multitude will be resuscitated [entails another problem]. It is beyond dispute that all individuals are called to arise with the body. There is indeed no disputing this; for to invent spirits without bodies, and to rule that this must be so, is a major imposture. Now if we assume, with regard to the [people of the] preceding Cycles, that all these will be assembled in one place, the four elements will not be enough to make up their bodies, so that a surplus will be needed for them in God's creation; but a surplus in God's creation is something inconceivable. And even supposing one element to be sufficient for their bodies, what thing would there be for them to stand on? All of the earth would then be used up for the bodies, but this material would have to be of such proportions that a surplus would be left for the bodies [to stand on]! Thus, to think that the multitude will be resuscitated is contrary to the truth. Understand this!

Issue Three: That Information about the Call to Arise Is Hidden from the Soul

VII. 3. 1.

Know that the soul does not by itself or alone possess that experience (*maʿrifat*) that would enable it to grasp its own substance. Knowledge and experience is in man at that time at which [the soul] is adjoined to a natural body whose senses are free from deficiencies. Once the soul leaves one among the human bodies, this knowledge of experience goes into hiding: it is deposited in a place where human experience cannot establish itself. Now for every period of time and every moment there are sources of theological discourse in appropriate order, that is, continuously and appropriate to each, [those sources, i.e., Prophets and Imāms, being each time] the entrance to fundamental and derived sciences. If the information (*maʿrifat*) of the former [or: gained from the first source] were mixed up with the information of the latter [or: gained from the last source], then there would be adding up[73] of those informations which should be held in isolation. To this end, information about the Call to Arise is hidden from the soul. Understand this!

VII. 3. 2.

Whoever knows the substance of his own soul, knows it by virtue of its experiences (*bi-ḥaqq-i maʿrifathāyash*) and the noble status of its inner realities. Having disentangled his soul from extension in material space and measurable bodies, he knows that the soul is a luminous substance which has been coloured by spiritual colours such as those words passed on which had once been composed [by Prophets, *taʾlīf karda*],[74] chants proffered, harmonies sensed. He is aware of the fact that the soul comes down, leaves, moves onward and [again] enters the path; but he does not search for information about the Call to Arise, for this is hidden behind veils, and only God knows it. And whoever thinks of the soul as a substance extended in matter or as a measurable body, is searching the soul for what is not in its substance, and [therefore] remains in error and brings about his own perdition. Such a person has only the choice between the following [useless] options: either he will think that Soul is dispersed and scattered through the life of the bodies, or [he will think of] a materially extended and measurable substance in which it inheres, or that it survives without a body. But he will find no proof for such a doctrine except rhetorical persuasion, that is, the kind of satisfaction gained from blind imitation, as is the custom of our adversaries. Or he will opt for the transmigration (*tanāsukh*) of the souls in the bodies in such manner as is believed by the feeble and ignorant ones. But God in his transcendent Power and subtle Knowledge is far beyond any feebleness and ignorance. Therefore, information about the Call to Arise is hidden from the soul.

73. Translation of *bā maʿrifat* (Persian text p. 87, line 13) uncertain. Corbin seems to have conjectured the reading *nā-maʿrifat* in his translation (*Le Dévoilement*, p. 181).

74. For *taʾlīf* see *Wellsprings* Para. 10.

VII. 3. 3.

Further, [were this information not hidden,] hope and fear of humans, on which the spiritual health of both worlds depends, would be annulled. For there is a Call to Arise which carries an individual to a higher degree, as there is one which carries a person to a lower degree. If the person knows that God makes him reach a higher level at the time of the Call to Arise, he will lose his chance to acquire [merit] and thus miss that noble rank and his own elevation. Therefore, not to be informed about the Call to Arise is necessary for this reason, [too,] so that hope and fear remain constant and, as a result, God may enact justice on the souls in a manner suited to them and appropriate to their actions. To this end, information about the Call to Arise is hidden from the soul. Understand this!

Issue Four: That the Call to Arise Implies Discipline of the Soul

VII. 4. 1.

Inasmuch as acquisition of Knowledge implies spiritual discipline (*riyāḍat*) of the souls, it means for them to get rid of evil disposition in order to apprehend their own substance, and to be purified from every vileness. And Knowledge is Called to Arise in the soul through the learning process by which a disciple learns from a teacher. Through this learning, which means discipline for the soul, the latter receives the power to ascend in order to apprehend the Mysteries and to realise the Sciences it learned from its teacher, until, due to that Knowledge, it reaches a point such that someone having seen that person before would believe he is another person. Because of the magnificent, pure and subtle nature [of that Knowledge], this person will have reached in his own substance so much power and eminence that it is beyond measure. He will know, then, that this eminence and excellence did not come to him from Nature, but from the fact that his substance had been attracting the quintessences of the souls which [already] had pure essence and subtleness of Knowledge. Thus it has been verified that the Call to Arise implies discipline of the soul. Understand this!

VII. 4. 3.

Further, association with the wise and those who know implies discipline of the soul for a man, so he can benefit from them thanks to a purified substance. He will educate himself in their ways, follow the path which is theirs, and accord his life with theirs, so that his soul acquires the discipline to shun vice and to desire virtue. This process of his acquiring a refined soul may happen in the very same body that was there at the beginning. But, if it happens that his soul is adjoined to a more harmonious body, further removed from evil and closer to good, his discipline will have been more vigorous, his acquisition of refinement more obvious. Understand this!

May God facilitate the discipline for the Call to Arise to the people of Truth, by His grace!

Issue Five: That in View of the Call to Arise, Ill-Fated May Turn Well-Fated and Well-Fated May Become Ill-Fated

VII. 5. 1.

Be aware that it often happens that ill-fatedness is induced when the student falls into the hands of a teacher who is in error and gone astray, who presents his own error as attractive to the student and influences him with ignorance, so that, after having known the way, he gets disoriented and, having had Knowledge, he becomes an ignorant person. But it also happens frequently that an ill-fated person finds a wise and pure man of Knowledge who guides him to the path of religion and of the other world, so that, after having been in error, he finds the right path and, after ignorance, becomes wise. Therefore, the one to whom God grants association with good guides must thank God and must strive, with good action and good doctrine, for that which elevates him. For, inasmuch as he endeavours to do good deeds and to acquire uncontaminated doctrine, what he thus gains from the men of Knowledge and the Wise will be inseparable from him, after he leaves the body, at the time of the Call to Arise. He will meet great felicity as counterpart (*mushākil*) of his own soul due to the struggle for good he had undertaken, for that is indeed the cause for his meeting great reward, as he had been promised.

VII. 5. 2.

On the other hand, he who neglected to observe those matters of Knowledge that had been given him and of which he had been made aware, and who allowed himself to be deluded by errors and by what he was induced to by that teacher gone astray, will meet, after he leaves the body, those ills which are the counterpart of his own soul. And this is due to his negligence and carelessness, for that is indeed the cause for his meeting punishment. So, well-fated may become ill-fated, and ill-fated may turn well-fated, in view of the Call to Arise. Understand this!

Issue Six: That the Call to Arise May Be Extended Over a Long or a Short Period

VII. 6. 1.

Be aware that long or short periods of time apply to the Call to Arise, since it may happen that a disciple willing to follow the path finds the [right] master to guide him, as it may happen that a master gone astray captures an ill-fated ignorant disciple. Indeed, a disciple willing to follow the path may not find a master during his lifetime, as it also may happen that he finds many masters every year and every month. Or it may happen that an already lost disciple will not find anyone to assist him in his state of perdition, as it also may happen that he finds at every moment many persons in whose presence he could forsake his error. It even happens that during a whole age, plenty of good masters are available and yet the ill-disposed who are in disorientation are also present in abundance. Inevitably, therefore, for the beneficial and corrupt sciences to be made to arise, there are long and short periods of time. Since this was a necessity, and may well [continue to] be so, as it now is, it is admissible that there is a shorter and a longer Calling to Arise. But the Knowledge of this is with the One Powerful [i.e., God].

VII. 6. 2.

Moreover, it may happen that a master of those subtle esoteric sciences keeps them for himself and does not transmit them to anyone he finds unworthy. That he cannot find anyone worthy to receive the Knowledge will give him deep sorrow. If he finds a worthy person—be it an Abyssinian slave or a servant from Sind, he will disclose this subtle Knowledge and impart it to him; but if he cannot find anyone worthy to receive it, he will keep it secret even from his own children and family. Similarly, the Calling to Arise causes Prophets, Legatees, Imāms, and "Proofs" to arise in an order proportionate to the time of the Word and the degree (*ḥadd*) of appropriateness (*mushākilat*) and worthiness, and likewise it makes arise Pharaohs, Tyrants, and Adversaries. For this reason, the Call to Arise may be long or short. Understand this!

VII. 6. 3.

Further, it sometimes happens that when a master of Wisdom guides people and imparts his Knowledge to a person of understanding and intelligence, this Knowledge does not, then, stay with the latter but rather leaves him quickly, as it also happens that, having passed through the ear of that person, it stays within his heart. For with regard to the Call to Arise, God has secrets that are hidden behind a veil from the creatures of this world. The design in this secret is His. It is to Him that they return, and through Him that there is retribution and punishment. Understand this!

Issue Seven: That Noble Action Is of Greatest Benefit in View of the Call to Arise

VII. 7. 1.

You should know that the action of the noble has two parts: one is based on reason, the other on the religious law. The one based on reason is that you keep your hostility from humans, who are of your kind and share with you the conditions of a human being. Noble behaviour towards them, just as towards yourself, is an obligation for you on that journey on which your spiritual health (*ṣalāḥ*) depends, as well as that of humanity at large; it means that you have a keen desire for God and thank Him for those benefits that He made clear to you. As for the action based on the religious law, it means that a man be aware that the fulfillment of the religious duties enjoined on mankind is an obligation that applies to himself and his wishes, and that in his dealings with humans he respect the obligations laid down in the religion of God as revealed through the Lords of the Cycles. And these two kinds of action—the one based on reason and the one based on the religious law—are of benefit in view of the Call to Arise, and keep harm from affecting the souls after death. We shall clarify this point with clear argument.

VII. 7.2.

Thus we say that the spiritual health of this world, its subsistence and the subsistence of those in it, depend on actions based on reason. If all men in the world behave in a manner opposite to this, corruption will be in the world, the civilisation of mankind will be destroyed and the cosmic order, on which everything that is noble, beautiful and pleasant in the world depends, will be abolished. In this case, harm will affect those persons who will be called to arise during the remaining Cycles, just as the benefit resulting from noble action, on which the subsistence of the world depends, will affect those persons who will be called to arise during the remaining Cycles. From this, it necessarily follows that noble action is of benefit in view of the Call to Arise. Understand this!

VII. 7. 3.

As for the noble action in terms of the religious law, it is connected with prosperity, evidence of blessing, and removal of ill-fatedness and misfortune. Therefore, once the humans settle on noble action in terms of the religious law, there will be plenty of good, evidence of blessing will be forthcoming, good fortune and divine favour will be constant, so that spiritual health in the world will be strong, and much good will reach those persons who will be called to arise during the last Cycles, for this will have been caused by the noble actions adhered to. But in the same way, if they decide to neglect action in terms of the religious law, disregard the pillars of religion and are disposed to engage in vile action, there will be little evidence of blessing, lasting corruption and much adversity and evil. The corruption of the world will, then, become an enormous burden for the humans in the world, and abundant evil and harm will result from this for those persons who will be called to arise during the remaining Cycles. Thus it has been verified that noble action is of greatest benefit in view of the Call to Arise. Understand this!

VII. 7. 4.

Further, [the works] of the noble enhance each other and form a whole of which each is an integral part and becomes one with the other, whether they are based on reason or on the religious law. For, if the intelligent and pious person engages in action regarding both the reasonable and the ordained, such as doing what is good, keeping one's hostility from humans and wishing them well, prosperity will adhere to him, his soul will become pure, and his intellect a source of luminosity, so that the soul is strengthened for the learning process, eagerly desires its Return (*ma'ād*) and renounces pleasure in worldly things (*zāhid shawad dar īn jahān*). Moreover, a person engaging in one ordained work will be keen on engaging in others as well, as he who frequently performs acts of purification and ablution will also do the prayer frequently, or he who spends his fortune for alms will also be eager to perform the pilgrimage personally. Therefore, given that the noble actions work in such a way that they give humans the power to seek virtue, and that a person having undertaken one part will be eager to engage in the other, and that there is no doubt that the desire for virtue benefits the soul, it has been verified that noble action is of benefit in view of the Call to Arise. Understand this!

VII. 7. 5.

Finally, he who engages in noble actions and refrains from vile things is in his own estimation more praiseworthy and more at peace with himself, and his sorrow and grief are diminished. By the same token, he who refrains from noble actions and does vile things is in his own estimation more blameworthy, is haunted by misgivings, and his sorrow and grief are more severe. Clearly, the cause of his scant knowledge and of his severe sorrow is not this world; for if it were so, the opposite would be the case: the sorrow and grief of bad people would be light, for they are the ones who have taken a big share from this world, and the sorrow and grief of the good people would be severe, for they are the ones who have taken a small share from this world. Indeed that sorrow and that grief of the [former] are in view of the other world; and the other world is the promise of the Call to Arise. Understand this!

—Hermann Landolt, translator

Kitāb al-yanābīʿ

THE BOOK OF WELLSPRINGS

Tawḥīd

Second Wellspring: On the Pure Being of the Mubdiʿ

(22) The pure being related to the *Mubdiʿ* (the Principle of origination) that transcends being and not-being, is indeed the act of being of the *Sābiq* [the First Intellect] derived from the act of being of the divine origination (*ibdāʿ*) which it bestows on it. In other words, the *Mubdiʿ* whom the *Sābiq* knows by the act of its being, its knowledge by the act of its being of the one who originated it becomes the being of the *Mubdiʿ* and not that a certain being is existent out there or a certain not-being is nonexistent outside of what manifested itself for the *Sābiq* from its act of being. That is because the *Mubdiʿ* is neither a "being" like the beings of the originated things, nor a "non-being" like the non-beings of the ipseities (*aysiyyāt*). Rather, His being [as He qua He] is to express the negation of beings and non-beings from the *Mubdiʿ*, may He be glorified.[1]

This translation is based on Abū Yaʿqub Sijistānī's *Kitāb al-yanābīʿ*, edited by H. Corbin (Paris-Tehran: Institut français de Recherche en Iran, 1961), pp. 18–28, 41–43, and 94–96.

1. On al-Sijistānī's concept of *Mubdiʿ*, cf. P. E. Walker, *Early Philosophical Shiism: The Ismaili Neoplatonism of Abū Yaʿqūb al-Sijistānī* (Cambridge, 1993), pp. 72–80.

(23) If a being for the *Mubdiʿ* the Sublime is affirmed by the Intellect, then negating the beings and non-beings [from Him] would be beyond it. By what thing does the [First] originated being [or the Intellect] proves that? By its act of being which is the Intellect, or by its act of non-being which is the divine [act of] origination? If by its act of being it proves the being of the *Mubdiʿ*, whereas its act of being is the Intellect, then the *Mubdiʿ* would be the Intellect and the Intellect would be the *Mubdiʿ*. Its conclusion would be: the [First] originated being is the *Mubdiʿ*, and this is evidently absurd. If it proves the act of non-being of the [divine] Command, then how can the being be proved by the non-being? This is more absurd than the former.

(24) So beware of seeking a being beyond the *Sābiq* [Intellect] after the manifestation of the *Sābiq*. The Logos is its cause; it is also the first cause for the manifestation of the *Sābiq*, so when the *Sābiq* manifested itself, it united with it and became like the being of the *Sābiq*. It is this by which the *Sābiq* is singled out, and it has not effused it on its 'caused one' (*maʿlūl*), which is the Second [being, i.e., the Soul]. Whereas what is other than the pure being—the latter is united with its being—it has effused it on its 'caused one'. God is more sublime than all the caused ones, both being and not-beings, and most exalted above them.

(25) Indeed we have negated all beings from the *Mubdiʿ*, the Real, because every being requires a cause [for its existence], as we found [in the case of] the Intellect, the most noble of essences of beings. Its being also requires a cause, which is the Command of God, sublime be His glory. Whereas He, the *Mubdiʿ*, the Real, does not have any cause, He is exalted above that so He does not require a being. If He does not require a being, then it is not requisite to negate that He is non-being. Therefore, beyond the non-beings there is no affirmation [or proof] of a thing that "it is." So He is exalted above everything, and is sanctified beyond that which the heretics relate to Him.

Intellect and Soul

Fourth Wellspring: The Realm of Intellect and the Realm of Soul and Their Respective Qualities

(32) We find that the Natural World is similar to all the natural things of which it consists, and what the natural things consists of being similar to the Natural World, this entails that the realm of Intellect and the realm of Soul also resemble each other. [In turn] these two, I mean, the Intellect and the Soul, are also similar to their respective realms. Then we find that both the [human] intellect and soul are part [of the Universal Intellect and Universal Soul respectively]. Now, it cannot be said with respect to each of them that they enter into [or are inside] (*dākhil*) the Natural World in the sense that a thing set up in it [is said to do]. Nor could it be said that they are outside (*khārij*) the Natural World in the sense of a substance encompassing the Natural World in a bodily sense.

The same is the case, we say, with the Universal Intellect and Universal Soul. It cannot be said with respect to them that they are inside or outside the world in the sense of an encompassing thing. Rather, they enter it in the sense of an exit, [or, a leaving] and are outside it in the sense of an entry. We will explain to you this [matter] more thoroughly to make you understand.

(33) The knowledge of [the above matter] will be in respect of the [human] soul (*nafs*). You observe that [the *nafs*] enters the object of its knowledge in the moment of conception, [and] when it is through with that, it is outside that [thing]. In the same manner, you see the Intellect and the Soul are as if inside the Natural World, in a sense, at the moment of conceiving (*taṣwīr*) it and representing (*tashkīl*) it. On the other hand, they are outside of them, in a sense, when they are through with them at the completion [of the act of conception and representation].

It is impossible to conceive that outside the Sphere of spheres there is something that has distance (*masāfah*), because distances are in the spheres. If you imagine that outside the Sphere [of spheres] there is distance which pertains to the Soul and Intellect, then your imagination is false, unsound and corrupted. Rather, at times the distance between the purified particular soul and the Universal Soul is effaced. When the soul is not weary of its wayfaring (*sulūk*), then all kinds of happiness, joy, strength and continuous blessings accrue to it. This happens when it forgets the physical world, and engages in the wayfaring toward its spiritual realm.

(34) The eminence of [the spiritual substance lies in that,] that nothing can cause its substance to cease unlike the other [nonspiritual substantial] things which eliminate each other, because a spiritual thing is not localized in a place which could subject it to elimination. So it is possible, in this respect, that the Natural World in its totality, including all its parts, is inside the realm of the Intellect and the realm of the Soul, without these two being eliminated [by it] in any way or, without any change or transformation entering into these two. That is because when the Originator (*Mubdiʿ*) originated the First One [i.e., the Intellect], He did not leave anything outside of it, because He originated it as perfect without having any imperfection [in it]. If something had been left outside the Intellect, then the Intellect would have been imperfect according to the measure of its being veiled from the forms of things.

(35) Now if the [divine] act of origination (*ibdāʿ*) could not have left anything outside the First Originated [i.e., Universal Intellect], then the Natural World would also be inside it without either eliminating it, or vieing with it, or causing any discomfort, calamity or loss to it by being inside it, because this Natural World has no worth (*miqdār*) before the spiritual world. Although the relationship between the individual soul and Universal Soul is extremely tenuous during [its] wayfaring to that luminous realm, in spite of that thin [relationship], it is able to forget this world. Since it can forget it, it has learnt that it does not possess any worth in spite of [the extremely] tenuous [relation of the individual soul with Universal Soul], and has no relationship with the spiritual world to be taken into consideration. So you should know this.

(36) One of the characteristics of the realm of Intellect and Soul is that, it is possible for it to imagine the greatest intellectual and imaginative distance. It is possible that its intellectual and imaginative [imagination] be a point of imagination (*tawahhum*). [A situation of this sort would] correspond to [the geometrical

case of] an infinite circle. This is so because an infinite circle is but a mere point [with an infinite radius].

Its other characteristic is that it is contrary to the Natural World from the point of potentiality and actuality, for the Natural World conserves the forms of the things born [i.e., the three kingdoms of mineral, plant and animal] in potentiality. When [a potential form] emerges to actualization, it is corrupted and made to return to its state of potentiality. However, the realm of Intellect preserves the forms which pertain to soul which have emerged to actualization. It holds them in their structure and in their substantiality. So you should know this.[2]

Fifth Wellspring: The First Intellect is the First Originated Thing

(37) Every encompassing thing is inevitably more eminent than [its] object of encompassing and precedes in existence; otherwise it would not be possible for it to encompass. Supposing the object of encompassing is anterior in existence to the encompassing thing, and the encompassing thing comes into existence posterior to the object of encompassing, then there will be a moment when the object of encompassing due to its anteriority would not be an object of encompassing, and there would be a moment when the object of encompassing due to the existence of the encompassing thing will be posterior to it.

(38) When I reflected on the Intellect, I found it perceiving [encompassing] the universality of things; therefore I ruled that it precedes in existence [and] is anterior to everything encompassed [by it]. If certain intellectual perceptions had been anterior to it [in existence], then those perceptions prior to the existence of the Intellect would not have been outside the perception of the Intellect. For it is impossible to suppose (*tawahhum*) that at times the Intellect perceives a certain thing and at times it does not because that supposition would imply that either that thing is intelligible, or that it is not intelligible. If it is intelligible, then the Intellect perceives it, if it is not intelligible [then] it is baseless [to assume] that an object of hypothesis is perceived but not by the Intellect. So no existing thing precedes the Intellect because it perceives [encompasses] everything. It is the perceiver and the object of perception, [whether it be] intelligible, imaginable or sensible. But God is more sublime and mighty than every act of perception, perceiver, and the object of perception. He is the most exalted beyond all things.

(39) Moreover, the Intellect resembles the number one which is first in numbers; no number, neither odd nor even, precedes it. Rather, all the numbers multiply [and proceed] from one and by one. In the same way, the Intellect is one and is the essence for all intelligibles. The intelligibles multiply [and proceed] from the Intellect and by the Intellect. Just as numerical multiplicity returns to [number] one which integrates all its parts, for one is found in [in every number whether it be] one thousand or ten thousand or any number after it or before it, and in every

2. Compare *Khwān al-ikhwān* of Nāṣir-i Khusraw, ed. Yaḥyā Khashshāb (Cairo, 1940), chapt. 14, 35–38.

number there is number one, and [vice versa] multiplicity is present in one. In the same way, all intelligibles in their totality return to the one intellectual knowledge. So the Intellect resembles one in these respects. Rather the numerical unity's effusion is on the numbers [due to which they multiply]. Then I found that one is the cause of [all] numbers and prior to all of them, that no number precedes it, [so I ruled that] for sure the Intellect is prior to all caused things (*maʿlūlāt*). It is [their] cause and nothing from among them precedes it. So you should know this.

(40) Also, God, exalted be His remembrance, has mentioned that His one command that originated the primordial things (*mubdaʿāt*), was [the order] '*kun*' (Be). It is an address to an addressee. It entails that the addressee is the one who comprehends it [in this form] otherwise it is absurd that God addresses in the form of 'Be' to one who does not understand it. Since that is absurd, [then] it is admitted that He addresses one who comprehends it and that cannot be other than the substance of the Intellect for which it is possible to comprehend the address of the Creator, the Glorious and the Mighty. When the [divine] command proceeded to manifest the lower world, He expressed it as 'creation' (*khalq*) and 'bringing forth' (*tafṭīr*). For He said, "He has created (*khalaqa*) the heavens and the earth and made darknesses and light" [Qurʾān, 6:1], and the Exalted one said, "He has brought forth (*fāṭir*) the heavens and the earth" [Qurʾān, 6:14]. [He has addressed in this form] because the command addressed [in the form] of '*kun*' (Be) to the one who has no measure to receive it is absurd and impossible.

(41) In the same way, for the creation of our souls He used [the term] 'creation' (*takhlīq*), when He said in one of his *āyāt*, "Verily We have created (*khalaqnā*) everyone from the dust" [Qurʾān, 20:5], and not the command in the form of 'Be' (*al-ʿamr al-kunī*). [That will be the state] till we reach the level of the "intellectuals," and have the intelligence of perceiving [the matters concerning] God and [the matters pertaining] to His Messenger, peace of God be upon him and his progeny. Then [only] such an address will be incumbent upon us, for His address is not imperative for the children who have no intelligence, just as [His address in the form of '*kun*' (Be) was imperative for the First Intellect. This is an indication that by the command of God, the Glorious and Mighty, there was the manifestation of the *Sābiq* (Preceder)[3] which is the First Intellect, and that nothing precedes it in the primordial origination (*ibdāʿ*), rather it is [anterior] to every thing. But Sublime is the One Who transcends all the attributes and relations. He is the most Exalted and Great.[4]

Sixth Wellspring: One Cannot Conceive of Anything Prior to the First Intellect

(42) How can one conceive of a thingness (*shayʾiyyah*, or reality) prior to the Intellect when the Intellect is the thingness of all things, and the thingness of all

3. For al-Sijistānī's concept of Intellect (*Sābiq*) cf. P. E. Walker, op. cit., pp. 87–94.
4. Compare *Khʷān al-ikhwān*, chapt. 28, pp. 76–80.

things is the Intellect? If it is permitted to assume that a certain thingness is prior to the Intellect when the Intellect is the thingness of all things, then the Intellect would be prior to itself (*dhāt*); but a thing is not prior to itself. Therefore, to assume a thingness to be prior to the Intellect is an impossibility. Further, how can the primordial origination (*ibdāʿ*) be a thing prior to the Originated-thing (*mubdaʿ*, i.e., the Intellect) and not a thing along with the Originated-thing? If it is admitted that with the Originated-thing prior to its manifestation, there is a thing but not the originated-thing, then it is admitted that a thing is originated and a thing is not originated in the sense of thingness. If that were to be the case, then the Creator has originated what is permitted to be other than the originated-thing in the sense of the thingness. If the primordial origination of the Originator is not the originated-thing, and the meaning of the thingness is existent in it, then the thingness has manifested along with the manifestation of the originated-thing and after it. So you should know this.

(43) Further, the meaning of thingness is the affirmation of a certain essence. Now, the essences are found to be either sensory or intelligible. As for the thingness of the objects of the sense, their affirmation is through the senses, and what the senses do not affirm, is affirmed conceptually by the Intellect. In the same way, the thingness of the intelligibles is [affirmed] by the Intellect. If the Intellect does not admit it then it is not affirmed, neither as an object of sense nor as an object of sensory intuition (*mawhūm*). And that which is not affirmed neither as an object of sense, nor as an object of sensory intuition, then its thingness also does not exist. So you should know this.

Eighth Wellspring: That Intellect is Quiescent

(47) Any moving thing manifests its movement for [attaining] a thing that is quiescent. Nothing is anterior to the Intellect to make one imagine that there is motion in its substance to attain something quiescent which precedes it. Since nothing is anterior to the Intellect, then the Intellect is quiescent and motionless so that its quiescence perceives the motion of every physical and spiritual thing in motion.

(48) Also, the motion is for seeking something: either for seeking a place, or for seeking what the moving thing needs. But the Intellect has no need for anything that could move it for its search; nor is it displaced from its 'place' so that its displacement moves it to seek its own place. Because all the 'places' through the substantiality of Intellect are one place, and its inclining is equal toward all places. So to assume its movement for seeking a 'place' is absurd and impossible.

(49) If someone says, "[The Intellect] moves to seek its Originator (*Mubdiʿ*); it needs to perceive It and encompass [or comprehend] It, and if the need is affirmed in it then the motion for it is [also] affirmed. Therefore we say the needy is in motion, and its motion is possible." We say: If the Intellect imagines that it can perceive its Originator and is needy of that [perception] then it will not be the Intellect. That is because the Intellect makes it incumbent to repel the imagination of perceiving [its] Originator, and the Intellect cannot contradict [what is

ingrained] in its substance. Therefore, the Intellect cannot imagine perceiving who originated it because of its knowledge by its unity (*waḥdat*).[5]

Eleventh Wellspring: On the Manner by Which the Intellect Addresses the Soul

(57) The Intellect addresses the Soul in two addresses, one superior and one inferior. The inferior address concerns the physical things because of the attachment of the Soul to them and the compassion of the Intellect for [the Soul]. For if the Intellect abandons addressing it while it is still attached to the physical things, then an animated form which is a product of the Natural World cannot attain the completion of the form [requisite of the divine] wisdom. So when the Intellect addresses it after its attachment to the physical things, an animated form attains its perfection and is ordered according to its species under different genres attributed to it. The essence of its address to it is like what is manifested from its 'caused ones' (*maʿlūlāt*) which is Nature and what is below it: the natural things. That is because, on investigation, you will find that none of them transgresses what the innate Intellect [within it] makes requisite for its mold and apparition (*shibh*). So it is understood that the Intellect addresses the Soul at first at the birth of matter and form then about how things should be ordered so that the eminence of [divine] wisdom is manifested. The effect of the address remains in the natural things (*ṭabīʿiyyāt*) eternally and forever.

(58) [This address] is also indicated by the Soul when it receives benefit from the Intellect. For it knows that when it creates order in Nature, it is due to the benefit [given] to it by the address of the Intellect when it is attached to [Nature]. If the Intellect does not give physical address to the Soul, the Soul cannot indicate any intellectual benefit. When the Soul employs [Nature for its activity] to attain the benefits of the Intellect, it is learnt that it is able to bring order in [Nature] due to the address of the Intellect to it; otherwise doing so would not have been possible for it. So this is the [nature of the] address of the Intellect to the Soul regarding physical things.

(59) The Intellect [gives] another address to the Soul regarding the physical things: it makes it aware of the insignificance of the natural physical things, and their mutual differences and contradictions. It also indicates to it that the benefits from its [Soul's] world, which it has forgotten, are better and more eminent than these physical things of contradictory and contrary nature to which it is attached. It manifests itself to it to struggle in this world and to forget it, and long to rejoin its world and seek pure intellectual benefits by which it will attain its deliverance [from the bonds of physical things], accomplishment and contentment.

(60) As for the address of the Intellect to the Soul with respect to spiritual things, the foremost is the constant eternal yearning (*shawq*) which it effuses on it so that you see it perpetually yearning and being nostalgic for its Cause [from which it has emanated]. When it becomes conscious (*taṣawwur*) of the yearning

5. Ibid., chapt. 71, pp. 183–84.

effused upon it by the Intellect in order to turn toward it, you will see it cheerful, happy [and] oblivious to its attachment to Nature, nay, as if the traces of natural things had separated and withdrawn from it. [In such a state] it continues to attain [intellectual] benefits according to its capacity and comprehension. But when the difficulty of wayfaring makes it feeble, then the exhaustion of fatigue drops from it with regard to the descent and not the ascent.

(61) The Intellect has another spiritual address to the Soul, and that is, the effusion of incapacity (*ʿajz*) on it for obtaining all the benefits of the Intellect. So it, I mean the Soul, is [suspended] between [acquiring] yearning and incapacity from the effusion of Intellect due to its spiritual address to it. Therefore it continues to acquire yearning, and is halted by incapacity to wayfaring beyond its measure and degree. If it had effused only yearning on it without incapacity, then its essence (*dhāt*) would have been paralyzed (*baṭalat*), because it cannot encompass what it desires and the incapacity has not been effused on it from its Cause [to prevent it from transcending its limit]. Likewise, if only incapacity had been effused on it without yearning, [the Soul] would have remained imperfect, and would not have attained any benefits [from the Intellect], nor would it have known that both yearning and incapacity effused on it were deemed necessary [in the Intellect itself] for the purpose of negation and affirmation of the Originator. The negation is like incapacity and affirmation like yearning.

(62) When the Intellect desires to affirm its Originator, the 'negation' prevents it from conceptualizing 'how' (*kayf*, the Divine is), or any allusion [to Him] or [His] locatedness (*ayniyyah*). When it desires to negate [His existence], the 'affirmation' restrains it from conceptualizing His nonexistence (*taʿṭīl*) and denial. In this way motion and repose are manifested from it in the Soul: motion corresponds to yearning and repose to incapacity. From motion and repose there are manifested matter and form. Matter corresponds to yearning and form to incapacity, because matter perpetually yearns to receive a new form one after the other, whereas form restrains it from receiving another form simultaneously with it.

So this in brief is the mode of the address of the Intellect to the Soul, and [the manner by which] the Soul receives [benefits] from the Intellect.[6]

Twelfth Wellspring: On the Manner of Imagining the Conjoining of Benefits from the Intellect to the Soul

(63) When the natural benefits inherent in the substance and nature of the spheres and stars rotating around the center [of the earth] by the perpetual motions are conjoined to the "offsprings" (*mawālīd*, i.e., the three kingdoms: mineral, plant, animal), then due to that motion the natural forms possessing individuals are configured which are subject to generation and corruption, while they, I mean the spheres and stars, persist in their state, whereas the benefits from the Intellect to the Soul are by the perpetual quietude (*sukūn*) by which the Soul benefits from the Intellect so that by the conjoined benefits from the Intellect to the Soul, the

6. Ibid., chapt. 75, pp. 188–91.

eternal, enduring spiritual form [of the Soul] is configured. If the Soul does not benefit from complete quietude (*al-sukūn al-tāmm*) from the Intellect before receiving its benefits, then the benefits conjoined to it will be adulterated by the natural physical things which are subject to decline and mutation. Such benefits which are subject to decline according to the measure of their resemblance to the natural things possessing motion are not reliable.

(64) There has occurred difference in the views of those who possess Intellects and those who do inference due to [the measure of their quietude]. Each one of them infers and extracts [knowledge] according to the measure of quietude in his Soul benefited from the Intellect. If anyone from among them increases the receptivity for the quietude, he receives the Intellectual benefits [more], [and] his benefits would be more stable and less subject to decline. He whose receptivity to its quietude is least, his benefits are more subject to decline and least stable. He who attains complete quietude, his receptivity to its benefits are perfect, not subject to change and there is no decline in it. They are the *muʾayyadūn* from God, the Mighty and Sublime.

(65) Let us return to what we intended to discuss in this Wellspring. We say: By the creation of the Intellectual quietude in the Soul, a number of Intellectual benefits are 'opened' in it which do not 'close' until the quietude is interrupted by its inclination toward transient natural things though that inclination may be very insignificant and the Soul does not reckon it. This [matter] will be clear to you during [your] reflection [on it]. Sometimes the 'opening' of the matters concerning Intellectual benefits are prolonged for you, and you 'ascend' to encompass them [or comprehend them], by an ascent which is spiritual and of the nature of light. But you find your Soul to be weak without [elapsing] any time and without [traversing] in space. You will know that it is with regard to it. The quietude which is a mount for the Soul for [its] inquiry has subverted from its hand due to its inclination toward natural things possessing transient contradictory motions. Sometimes a reflective person begins reflecting again on what was lost to him in encompassing what he was contemplating on, so [once again] he 'ascends' as he had done before according to the measure of help from Intellectual quietude. Again he finds his self (or soul) weak, as in the previous state because of non-quietude (*ʿadam al-sukūn*) due to his inclination toward perpetually moving natural things. So according to this similitude the benefits from the Intellect conjoin with the Soul.[7]

Sixteenth Wellspring: On the Origination (*ibdāʿ*) *of the Intellect and the Origination of a Number of Powers* (*quwwah*)

(76) One can imagine those powers [lit. things, coming into existence] along with the substantiality of the Intellect all at once, because in the substance of the [divine act] of origination (*ibdāʿ*) there is no retardation. They are divided into seven categories.

7. Ibid., chapt. 76, pp. 191–92.

The first one is 'eternal duration' (*al-dahr*) which is an extension [of the Intellect] and can never separate from it. Every acquired intellect [i.e., human intellect, *al-ʿaql al-muktasab*], in order to perceive an intelligible, integrates with the eternal duration of that intelligible for its perception. So from this it is learnt that the absolute eternal duration is an extension of the *Sābiq* [i.e., the Intellect] at [its] origination and will be with it forever.

(77) The second is 'truth' (*al-ḥaqq*) which is its extension and never separates from it. The acquired intellect [of man] which perceives intelligibles, contains the reality (*ḥaqīqah*) of that thing, and its false conjecture [about anything] is contrary to it and futile for it. So it is learnt that the absolute truth was originated with the *Sābiq* at [its] origination and will be with it forever.

(78) The third is 'happiness' (*al-surūr*) which is its extension and never separates from it. Happiness exists in the acquired intellect when it encompasses an intelligible. So it is learnt that absolute happiness has been the extension of the Intellect at [its] origination and will be with it forever.

(79) The fourth is 'demonstration' (*al-burhān*) which is never delayed by the acquired intellect during its encompassing an intelligible. So from this it is learnt that demonstration has been an extension of the Intellect at [its] origination and will be with it forever.

(80) The fifth is 'life' (*al-ḥayāh*) which is found to exist simultaneously with the acquired intellect during the movement to encompass intelligibles. So it is learnt that the absolute life is an extension of the *Sābiq* at its origination without retardation from it and will be with it forever.

(81) The sixth is 'perfection' (*al-kamāl*). Perfection is not retarded from the particular acquired intellect [or human intellect] when it encompasses an intelligible, for it does not conjecture the intelligible to be imperfect but perfect during encompassing [it]. So it is learnt that perfection has been an extension of the *Sābiq* at its origination and will be with it forever.

(82) The seventh is 'self-subsistency' (*ghunyah*). Self-subsistency in the acquired particular intellect is actually existent when it encompasses certain intelligibles. So it is learnt that self-subsistency is an extension of the *Sābiq* at its origination, and will be with it forever. Among the powers of the Intellect that originated with it simultaneously, self-subsistency is most excellent and most eminent. If the *Sābiq* effuses self-subsistency from its powers on anyone, then that effusion is the most excellent and most exalted [of all the effusions].

(83) Among the most inferior in degree of the intellectual effusions is the effusion of eternity. Nevertheless, regarding the natural realities, it is most eminent because of its eternal duration. That is why God made it the treasurer of the motions pertaining to time.

(84) Under these powers multiple symbols are hidden but this is not the place to explain; otherwise we would have elucidated them. Each one of these powers has many ramifications which are innumerable and endless. Above these Intellectual powers that originated simultaneously with [the Intellect], it has other [powers] which can neither be described by the logical discourse nor by the [human] imagination because these are the powers [lit. things] which only the *Sābiq* possesses. We do not know when it will effuse by discharging on its 'caused one'

(*maʿlūl*, i.e., the Soul) so that it would be possible for it to [manifest] them through expression, imagery, and stipulation. These are [the things] which are manifested in the course of cycles and periods about which only (the Intellect) knows, because all [these matters] in their totality are contained in it in a point which is the center of the worlds. Blessed is He Who is most powerful to manifest a substance such as [the Intellect] which is eminent and perfect. But God is exalted and more lofty than all the relations and allusions.[8]

Fortieth Wellspring: The Manner by which Taʾyīd (*Divine Guidance or Inspiration*) *Conjoins the* Muʾayyadūn *in the Physical World*

(186) The conjoining (*ittiṣāl*) of *taʾyīd*[9] to the *muʾayyadūn*, in our physical world is nobler and subtler [in quality] than the conjoining of higher celestial powers (*quwwah*) to the lower "offsprings" [*mawālīd*, i.e., the three kingdoms of mineral, plant and animal]. That is because, we find the powers from the spheres and stars are persistent in the natural born things without the born things being conscious of the mode of their conjoining. Then we find every member [of these three kingdoms] receives from the traces of their [celestial and astral] motions according to the measure of subtlety and density inherent in it, and accordingly produces certain forms from the natural properties and powers latent in it. In the same way the divine assistance flashes (*lāmiʿ*) from the spiritual world.[10]

(187) We find that among living beings, man is the only one for whom it is possible to extract benefits from arts and crafts due to the aptitude inherent in him for that, give justice to everything, and produce admirable arts by which there is the perfection of the worlds and the manifestation of their beauty (*zīnah*).

Also, only in the human species do we find the messenger [of God] for whom it is possible to employ the spiritual world and extract benefits from it due to the [spiritual] aptitude inherent in him, give justice to everything, and produce admirable policies (*siyāsāt*) by which there is the perfection of the spiritual world and manifestation of its beauty.

(188) The [sign for the] beginning of *taʾyīd* in the *muʾayyad* is, that he becomes capable of discovering things (but not through the senses) which are the principles for deducing hidden meaning in the sensibles. Rather, [the *muʾayyad*] finds himself existing amidst the sensibles, [but] detached from them, [and] craving for intelligibles (*maʿqūlāt*) which have no connection with material things. The difference between a scholar (*ʿālim*) and *muʾayyad* is, that the man of knowledge is always anxious to protect his sciences (*ʿulūm*), and his ruling (*ḥukm*) is on sensibles which are material in nature, whereas a *muʾayyad* is independent of these [methods].

8. Ibid., chapt. 60, pp. 150–52.

9. The term *taʾyīd* is a verbal noun derived from the verb *ayyada*. The notion of *taʾyīd* conveys the idea of divine assistance and inspiration which is a source of supernatural wisdom. This notion is derived from the two verses of the Qurʾān (2:87 and 253) in which God says about Jesus, "We inspired him, *ayyadnāhu*, with the Holy Spirit."

10. Compare *Khwān al-ikhwān*, chapt. 91, pp. 217–19.

He [spontaneously] conceptualizes in his mind (*khāṭir*), whereas a scholar is incapable of doing that, and infers it through reasoning and by sensible proofs.

Sometimes something spiritual crosses their mind [i.e., *muʾayyadūn*] which is not defined; so they interpret it by sensible expressions by which it is possible for the people to witness what they were interpreting for them. That concrete image of the sensible becomes strongly rooted in their mind. At times they see what they report to them is contrary [to their empirical knowledge], but they abandon their empirical knowledge (*ʿiyān*) and accept their report. [Now] if the conjoining of *taʾyīd* was from the dimension of the senses, then their reports would not have such an eminence of surpassing sensible, empirical knowledge.

(189) It is said, 'The only [true] report is that which is concretely seen', but the conjoining of *taʾyīd* with them is not from the dimension of the senses. It [*taʾyīd*] is 'pure logos' (*nuṭq maḥḍ*), free from any linguistic forms and compositions, by means of which they are victorious (*qahr*) over the people who have access [to knowledge] by their senses, and they perceive it through language and linguistic compositions. At times the *muʾayyad* receives *taʾyīd* by being attentive to a member of a species, for instance, an animal, or a tree or anything other than these two. By [his attention] the realities from the various [forms of] hidden knowledge are 'opened' (*fatḥ*) to him and many secrets from the hidden [realities] dawn upon him. [When he reaches this station], the *taʾyīd* becomes firm in that form.

(190) At times when a person speaks about something whose 'meanings' [or content] he does not know in the presence of the *muʾayyad*, then *taʾyīd* of an astonishing category 'opens' for the *muʾayyad* from the speech of that [person]. Whatever is 'opened' for him becomes the primary Divine Law (*nāmūs*), the implementation of which becomes obligatory for the people of the period of his cycle. So in this manner *taʾyīd* conjoins with the *muʾayyad* in the physical world. All success is due to God.

Spiritual Hermeneutics: Symbolism of the Cross

Thirty-first Wellspring: The Meaning of the Cross for the Community of Jesus, Peace be upon Him

(143) Cross is a name for a piece of wood on which a man is crucified in such a manner that all the people [collected] can see him. The crucified is the dead body. Jesus, peace be upon him, reported to his Community that when the Lord of Resurrection (Qāʾim), whose symbol was he himself, will unveil the realities (*ḥaqāʾiq*) hidden in the forms of *Sharāʾiʿ* the people will know them and they will not deny them.[11] Just as when all the people see a crucified person, they come to know him and notify his form although until then the majority may not have known him.

11. The notion of cycle refers to the concept of Ismāʿīlī sacred history of religion, which is divided into seven cycles, each cycle founded by a speaker-prophet, *Nāṭiq*. The seven *Nāṭiq*s are: Adam, Noah, Abraham, Moses, Jesus, Muḥammad, and Qāʾim (or Messiah). The first six are the

Because of this [deeper] meaning his Day [i.e., the Qāʾim's] is called "the Day of unveiling", as He said, "On the Day when matters will be completely unveiled and they will be called to prostrate" [Qurʾān, 68:42]. So the crucified on the wood will be unveiled, although before that he was hidden under the veil.

(144) The other indication: He [Jesus] informed his Community that the Lord of Resurrection would facilitate his and his deputies' [task] in extracting the explication (*bayān*) of everything. So the religion will be without any assumption; there will be explication [of many levels of the religion], just as [various] limits (*ḥudūd*) are combined in this dead [piece] of wood.

(145) It is narrated in some reports that on the 'Night of Destiny' (*laylat al-qadr*), the light will radiate, and all the bodies, trees and fishes will prostrate to that light. That is a parable struck for the potency of the Resurrector, peace be upon him, and his deputies and their power over extracting explication from everything. They will be able to report about things in their intellects from the dimension of primordial nature (*fiṭrah*), discretion and deduction.

(146) The piece of wood on which [Jesus] was crucified was brought by other than his people who crucified him openly and manifestly. [This is a parable implying that] the explication which the Resurrector and his deputies, peace be upon them, will unveil will be of the *Sharāʾiʿ* of the messengers who were anterior to him. So the [Cross] becomes a sign, a clear explication for all the limits [*ḥudūd*, of initiatic hierarcy of the Resurrector], and the veneration of it becomes a requisite thing for them [i.e., the Community of Jesus] as our veneration of the *Shahādah*.

Thirty-second Wellspring: On the Correspondence Between the Cross and the Shahādah.

(147) The *Shahādah* is based on negation and affirmation. It begins with negation and ends with affirmation. Similarly, the Cross is [constituted] of two pieces of wood, one piece is firm [or stable] by itself, and the other has no firmness but is firm by the firmness of the other.

The *Shahādah* is composed of four words; similarly the Cross has four parts. One part is firm in the earth; its way station (*manzil*) is [homologous to] the way station of the 'master of *taʾwīl* (esoteric hermeneutic)' upon whom the souls of the aspirants are firmly established. The part opposite to it which is high up in the air, its way station is [homologous to] the way station of the 'master of *taʾyīd*' upon whom the *muayyadūn* are firmly established. The other two parts which are in the middle, one on the right and one on the left, [are homologous] respectively to the *Tālī* (the Follower, i.e., Soul) and *Nāṭiq* (the speaker-prophet); one is the master of composition [of the natural structures, *tarkīb*], and the other is the master of the codification [of religious ordinances, *taʾlīf*]. They face each other. [This]

---

revealers of the divine *Sharāʾiʿ*; the last one would unveil the inner truths or realities of all the *Sharāʾiʿ* revealed to the speaker-prophets. He will not reveal any new Law. Cf. H. Corbin, *Cyclical Time and Ismāʿīlī Gnosis*, trans. by R. Manheim and J. W. Morris (London, 1983), pp. 84–99.

part is established on the Preceder [*Sābiq*, Intellect, the verticle part] which extends to all the letters.

(148) The *Shahādah* is composed of seven syllables. Similarly the Cross has four angles and three extremities. The four angles and three extremities indicate the seven Imāms [lit. completers, *atimmāʾ*] of his [Jesus's] cycle as the seven syllables in the *Shahādah* indicate the Imāms of the cycle of our *Nāṭiq* [Muḥammad], peace be upon him. Each one of [of the four parts of the Cross] has three dimensions, so the aggregate is twelve, similarly, the *Shahādah* is composed of twelve letters. Also its combination is from three letters not repeated: similarly the composition of the Cross is from the surfaces, lines and angles. The lines correspond to the letter *alīf*, the surfaces to the letter *lām*, and the angles to the letter *hāʾ*. Just as the *Shahādah* is completed by its association with Muḥammad—peace be upon him and upon his progeny—similarly the Cross acquires eminence after the master of the cycle has brought it into existence.

—Latimah Parvin Peerwani, translator

References

Classical and Modern Biographical Sources

Abū Rayḥān Bīrūnī. *Kitāb taḥqīq mā li'l-Hind*, rev. ed. Hyderabad: 1958.

Alberuni's India. Trans. E. C. Sachau. Delhi: 1964, p. 49.

Kāshānī, A. Q. *Zubdat al-tawārīkh, tārīkh-i Ismāʿīliyyah*. Ed. by M. T. Dānesh-Pazhūh, in *Revue de la Faculté des Letteres*. Tabriz: 1965, pp. 1–218.

Rashīd al-Dīn Faḍlallāh. *Jāmiʿ al-tawārīkh*. Ed. by M. T. Dānesh-Pazhūh and M. Modarresī. Tehran: 1960.

al-Rasūl al-Majd, I. A. *Fihrist al-kutub waʾl-rasāʾil*. Ed. by A. Munzawī. Tehran: 1966, pp. 140–44, 183, 193, 196.

Primary Sources

Kitāb al-yanābīʿ. Ed. and partially trans. French by H. Corbin. In *Trilogie ismaélienne*. Tehran-Paris: 1961.

Kashf al-maḥjūb. *Le Dévoilement des choses cachées*. Ed. by H. Corbin. Tehran: 1949. Reprinted as *Abū Yaʿqūb Sejestānī*, *Le Dévoilement des choses cachées* (*Kashf al-Maḥjūb*): *Recherches de philosophie ismaélienne*. Trans. from Persian with introduction by H. Corbin. Paris: Lagrasse: 1988. This work is a Persian translation or paraphrase, quite possibly by Nāṣir-i Khusraw. The Arabic original has not been found.

Secondary Sources

Alibhai, M. A. *Abū Yaʿqūb al-Sijistānī and Kitāb sullam al-najāt: A Study in Islamic Neoplatonism*. Ph.D. diss., Harvard University, 1983.

Altmann, A., and Stern, S. M. *Isaac Israeli: A Neoplatonic Philosopher of the Early Tenth Century*. Oxford: 1958.

Al-ʿĀmirī, A. H. *A Muslim Philosopher on the Soul and Its Fate: al-ʿĀmirī's Kitāb al-amad ʿalaʾl-abad*. Edition and trans. with commentary by E. K. Rowson. New Haven: 1988.

Ammonius (pseudo). *Kitāb Ammuniyūs fī ārā' al-falāsifah bi-ikhtilāf al-aqāwīl fi'l-mabādi'.* Ms. Istanbul, Aya Sofya 2450. German translation, and commentary by U. Rudolph. Stuttgart: 1989.

Daftary, F. The *Ismāʿīlīs: Their History and Doctrines.* Cambridge: 1990.

Ivanow, W. *The Alleged Founder of Ismāʿīlism.* Leiden: 1952.

———. *Studies in Early Persian Ismāʿīlism.* Bombay: 1955.

———. "Early Shiʿite Movements." *Journal of the Bombay Branch of the Royal Asiatic Society,* 17, 1 (1941): 1–23.

———. *Studies in Early Ismāʿīlism.* Leiden: 1983, pp. 220–33.

———. "The Early Ismāʿīlī Missionaries in North-West Persia in Khurasan and Transoxania." *Bulletin of the School of Oriental and African Studies,* 23 (1960): 56–90.

Kamada, Sh. "The First Being: Intellect (*ʿaql/khiradh*) As the Link Between God's Command and Creation According to Abū Yaʿqūb al-Sijistānī." *The Memoirs of the Institute of Oriental Culture.* Tokyo: 1988, no. 106, pp. 1–33.

"Ḳarmati." *Encyclopedia of Islam,* v. 4, 2nd. ed. Leiden-London: 1960–pp. 660–665.

Madelung, W. "Aspects of Ismāʿīlī Theology: The Prophetic Chain and the God Beyond Being." *Ismāʿīlī Contributions to Islamic Culture.* Ed. S. H. Nasr. Tehran: 1977, pp. 51–65.

———. "Abū Yaʿqūb al-Sijistānī and Metempsychosis." *Iranica Varia: Papers in Honor of Professor Ehsan Yarshater* (*Textes et Memoires Volume XVI*). Leiden: 1990, pp. 131–43.

Poonawala, I. *Biobibliography of Ismāʿīlī Literature.* California: 1977.

———. "Al-Sijistānī and his *Kitāb al-maqālīd.*" In *Essays on Islamic Civilization Presented to Niyazi Berkes,* ed. by D. P. Little. Leiden: 1970, pp. 274–83.

Stern, S. M. "Arabo-Persia: Abū Yaʿqūb al-Sijzī's nickname *panba-dāna* 'cotton-seed.'" In *W. B. Henning Memorial Volume,* ed. by M. Boyce and I. Gershevitch. London: 1970, pp. 415–16.

Walker, P. *Early Philosophical Shiʿism: The Ismāʿīlī Neoplatonism of Abū Yaʿqūb al-Sijistānī,* Cambridge: Cambridge Univ. Press, 1993.

———. "Abū Yaʿqūb al-Sejestānī." *Encyclopedia Iranica.* Ed. E. Yarshater (London-Boston: 1982–1998). Vol. I: 396–98.

———. "The Doctrine of Metempsychosis in Islam." In *Islamic Studies Presented to Charles Adams.* Eds. W. Hallaq and D. P. Little. Leiden: 1991, pp. 215–34.

———. "An Early Ismāʿīlī Interpretation of Man, History and Salvation." *Ohio Journal of Religious Studies* 3 (1975): 29–35.

———. "Cosmic Hierarchies in Early Ismāʿīlī Thought: The View of Abū Yaʿqūb al-Sijistānī." *The Muslim World,* 66 (1976): 14–28.

4

ABŪ ḤĀTIM RĀZĪ

Abū Ḥātim Aḥmad ibn Hamdān Rāzī (d. 322/934) was the chief *dāʿī* (missionary) of Rayy and the leader of the *dāʿwā* in the Jibal. He greatly expanded Ismāʿīlī activities in Iran, only to go into hiding in Tabaristan after the conquest of Rayy by the Sunni Samanids in 313/925. It was in Daylam where Abū Ḥātim succeeded in converting a number of rulers, among whom one can mention the governor of Rayy, Aḥmad ibn ʿAlī, Ashraf ibn Shīrwayh, and Mahdī ibn Khusraw Fīrūz.

His correspondence with other figures, who were also expecting the appearance of the Mahdī, such as Abū Ṭāhir al-Jannābī, is an indication of his keen interest in the occultation of the Mahdī. In fact, it was his false prediction of the date of the Mahdī's return that aroused the anger of his patron Mardāwīj, who may even have claimed to have been the representative of the hidden Imām himself. Kirmānī tells us of the account of the famous debate between Abū Ḥātim Rāzī and Zakariyyāʾ Rāzī that took place in Mardāwīj's presence.

Along with a number of other Ismāʿīlī thinkers such as Nasafī and Sijistānī, Rāzī belonged to the Persian school of Ismāʿīlism, which did not accept the Imāmate of ʿUbayd Allāh. These figures were deeply engaged in philosophical speculations offering rational defense for such concepts as the Imamate, prophecy, cosmology, and metaphysics. It was in this period and because of such figures as Rāzī that Neoplatonism entered systematically into Ismāʿīlī doctrine, in particular the concept of the unknowable God, emanation, and the hierarchical chain of Being, leaving aside those aspects of Neoplatonism that were inconsistent with the Islamic credo. In this regard, Rāzī's doctrines were elaborated originally by Nasafī. Rāzī discusses the central Neoplatonic propositions of Nasafī concerning creation in his *al-Iṣlāḥ*. Among the central ideas of Rāzī is how he applied the concepts of emanation to the cosmological notions of *kun* and *qdr*, holding the view that the three letters of *qdr* are issued from the first three letters of the word *kun*, identifying the former with the soul and the latter with the Intellect. The human soul, Rāzī says, is a trace of the higher soul that is perfect, like the Intellect.

In this chapter we have included a portion of Rāzī's major work *Aʿlām al-nubuwwah.* The first section, entitled "The Prophets are the Origin of Scientific Learning and Bequeathed It to the Sages," deals with the question of prophecy, the nature of a prophet's knowledge of the world, and the nature of revelation in respect to the prophet's intellect. This treatise explores the subject of epistemology with emphasis on *a priori* knowledge as the basis upon which philosophical inquries are made. In the second section, entitled "The Origin of Astronomical Observation," Rāzī continues with the theme of revelation in the context of the philosophy of science, arguing that had it not been for divine guidance, man could not have attained knowledge to the extent that he has. In the third section, "The Origin of the Known Drugs," Rāzī continues to argue that without the element of prophecy and revelation and divine providence, it would have been impossible for man to have acquired such a vast knowledge of drugs, both herbal and chemical. In the fourth section, "All Knowledge Goes Back to the First Sage," Rāzī concludes his discussion that knowledge has been possible by virtue of a "gate" (meaning the Imām) through whom the gift of knowledge has been bestowed.

—*M. Aminrazavi*

Aʿlām al-nubuwwah

SCIENCE OF PROPHECY

Chapter VII

Section I: The Prophets Are the Origin of Scientific Learning and Bequeathed It to the Sages

Now that we have completed our discussion of the miracle of Muḥammad, that is, the glorious Qurʾān, and shown how there remains in the world an ongoing and paramount indicator of its miraculous quality, returning to this point repeatedly in order to clarify its various aspects and reveal its full force,[1] we now turn to our reply to another of the apostate's claims:

He has stated that the philosophers have acquired their knowledge by formulating their own opinions and discovered it by means of their own careful

This Translation is based on Abū Ḥātam Rāzī *Aʿlām al-nubuwwah*, edited by Ṣalāḥ al-Ṣāwī and Gh. R. Aʿwānī (Tehran: Imperial Iranian Academy of Philosophy, 1977), chapter VII, pp. 271–318.

1. In the previous chapter Abū Ḥātim has argued at length that the progressive success of the Islamic polity in the world, and Islam's role in producing and maintaining social order, is the most eloquent argument for the miraculous nature (*iʿjāz*) of the Qurʾān, a dogma universally accepted but variously interpreted; see *Encyclopedia of Islam* 2 s. v. *iʿdjāz.*

inquiries, relying therein on innate inspiration[2] resulting from the acuity of their natural faculties.[3] By this knowledge I am referring to the information found in medical books about the natures of drugs and their specific characteristics, the information in Ptolemy's *Almagest*[4] about the motions of the celestial sphere and the planets, the calculations about the stars and the various subtleties and astrological implications connected with this, the science of geometry and mensuration as found in Euclid, information about the latitudinal and longitudinal dimensions of the earth and the distances between the different heavens, and other such information contained in these books. Now the apostate claimed that all of this information was arrived at by independent discovery and innate inspiration, the philosophers having no need therein for our leaders,[5] that is, the prophets.

Then he went further, boasting that "the benefit and harm to be derived from these books are greater than the benefit and harm to be derived from the books of the adherents of religious traditions."[6] In his pride, he said, "Tell us where your leaders have pointed out the difference between poisons and nutriments, and the effects of drugs! Show us a single page treating such a thing, comparable to the pages—not just a few, but thousands—which have been transmitted from Hippocrates and Galen, to the benefit of human beings! Show us any knowledge about the motions and causes of the celestial sphere which has been transmitted from any one of your leaders, or anything about the wonderful subtle natures of things, such as geometry or, for that matter, language,[7] which was unknown until your leaders came up with it!"

He went on, "If you say that the origin[8] of all this was taken from your leaders, we reply that your claim is invalid and cannot be granted you; for we know what it is that you are claiming comes from your leaders, and it is the silly fool-

2. *Ilhām*, "inspiration," refers to an innate ability to learn or do something without outside instruction. It is used of animals for instinctive behavior; for human beings, Abū Ḥātim opposes it throughout this chapter to *waḥy*, often also translated "inspiration" but here rendered "revelation," which is specific knowledge bestowed by God on an individual in one of several ways, all transcending natural processes.

3. Literally, "their nature (*ṭabʿ*)"; *biʾl-ṭabʿ*, translated "by nature" in the following discussion, refers to one's natural faculties, unaided by outside revelation.

4. Literally, "the *Almagest* and Ptolemy"; Abū Ḥātim seems to be unclear on the relation between author and work, just as he refers regularly to Euclid's *Elements* simply as "Euclid," as if this were a title.

5. *Aʾimmah*, plural of *imām*, a complex term with rich religious connotations, particularly in Shīʿite Islam, used regularly by Abū Ḥātim for the founders and authority figures of both religious and intellectual traditions.

6. *Ahl al-sharāʾiʿ*, literally, "the people of religious legal systems," the *sharīʿah* of Islam being the totality of its legal and ethical tenets and essentially identified with the religion itself, and the other revealed religions, Judaism and Christianity, being here regarded from the same point of view.

7. *Min amr al-lughāt*, "the matter of languages"; the text seems questionable here, but the problem of the origin of language is in fact a third major topic, besides the origins of astronomy and medicine, treated in the following discussion.

8. *Aṣl*, "origin, root, foundation, first principle" combining the ideas of temporal priority and fundamental basis, and necessarily translated variously in the following discussion.

ishness which is bandied about among both common people and the elite."[9] He went on, "And if you ask whence comes people's knowledge of the effects of drugs on bodies, and of the motion of the celestial sphere, and in what language people were summoned to invent languages,[10] we have things to say which require no resort to your leaders. Some of these things have been derived on the basis of standard principles[11] recognized by the appropriate experts, such as observation of the stars and knowledge of the effects of drugs on bodies and the knowledge of how they inhere in foods and scents; others have been passed on from generation to generation ever since the beginning[12] of time; others again are known by nature, just as a goose knows how to swim without being taught by your leaders. Thus is the argument which you advance refuted."

This is the apostate's statement, which we have reproduced just as he made it. And here is our reply:

As for his claim about the benefit and harm derived from such books, that they are superior therein to the glorious Qurʾān and the other revealed books, we have already given an explanation about that which suffices for anyone who judges fairly without obstinacy or self-deception.[13] "As for him who rebels and chooses the life of this world, hell will be his home; but as for him who fears to stand before his Lord and restrains his soul from lust, the Garden will be his home."[14]

As for the books he mentions, saying that they come from the philosophers' leaders, we say that they in fact go back to[15] the veracious Sages who were supported[16] by God, and that the names of their leaders which now appear in them are simply pseudonyms. That is, the names which are cited as being the authors of these books, like Galen, Hippocrates, Euclid, Ptolemy, and the like, are aliases for the names of the Sages who originally composed them, and the books themselves are based on valid wisdom and organized first principles. I engaged in a

9. The text here is uncertain; "silly foolishness" is *al-ḍaʿf al-raqīʿ*, reading *raqīʿ* for the MSS' *waqīḥ* or *rāʿ* (?). Without wider context, it is unclear what Abū Bakr is referring to, although it may include the medical lore preserved in prophetic tradition and known as "prophetic medicine" (*al-ṭibb al-nabawī*), and perhaps the pre-Islamic Arabian *anwāʾ*, a system correlating star risings and settings with meteorological phenomena.

10. Text uncertain: *bi-ayyi lughah tudʿā ʾl-nās ilā ikhtirāʿ al-lughāt.*

11. *Rusūm*, "traces, traditions, prescriptive pronouncements preserved as authoritative and recognized by later followers," variously translated in what follows; Abū Ḥātim often uses this term as a near-synonym of *aṣl*.

12. *Nihāyah*, literally, "end," but the reference here and in the discussion below is to tracing a chain *back* through time.

13. In the previous chapter, Abū Ḥātim has argued that the social and ethical norms laid down by the Qurʾān are absolutely essential to man's welfare, unlike the insights afforded by the sciences, which are known and pursued only by a few specialists, and which the vast majority of people both can and do live perfectly well without.

14. Qurʾān 79:37–41.

15. *Rusūm.*

16. Singular *muʾayyad*; in Shiʿite and especially Ismāʿīlī writing, this term implies some sort of revelation by God.

debate with the apostate about things found in the Book of Balīnās;[17] we had been told that the author of this book was a man of our own era, and of our own religious tradition, who adopted that name and composed that book, and we mentioned something of what he had to say and the examples he presented in his book. I brought this up to the apostate, and he said, "That is true, and we already knew it; this man's name was So-and-so, he lived during the time of al-Maʾmūn, and he was a sage who philosophized." We had also heard the same thing from others.[18] So this man followed the same path as those ancient sages, adopting a name of the same type as those names,[19] and speaking in the same way. But he spoke explicitly about the Unity of God, refuting the Dualists and other apostates, and asserted the createdness of the world, supporting this with many powerful arguments; he then spoke about how the world was generated and about the causes of things, employing many examples, some of which were simple and whose point could be grasped easily, while others were more abstruse. This is the same way those other sages, who adopted those names, proceeded.

I also read in the *Book of Daniel* that when Nebuchadnezzar conquered Jerusalem and took its people captive, he chose some young men from among those captives to serve him, one of them being Daniel. These men served him until he saw his vision and inquired of the magicians, enchanters, Magians, Chaldeans, astrologers, and seers about it, seeking its interpretation; they were unable to tell him what it was or interpret it, but Daniel did both. Nebuchadnezzar said to Daniel, "No one in all my kingdom was able to tell me my vision or interpret it, but you were able to do so, because the pure spirit of God is in you; your name shall be Belteshazzar." Subsequently, he had another vision, and said "Summon to me Daniel, the greatest of the sages, whom I have named Belteshazzar, after the name of my God." Daniel was summoned to him, and interpreted his vision for him after telling him what it was. He said that "Belteshazzar" means "Image of Bāl," Bāl being the idol which they used to worship.[20]

The reason we mention all this is with reference to our statement that the names to which these books are attributed are aliases for the sages who composed them. These aliases have meanings which are known to those who know the relevant language. Those sages initially adopted those names as aliases for their own names. But then they were imitated by these erring liars, who looked into these transmit-

17. This is the work of natural philosophy and alchemy known as *Kitāb sirr al-khalīqah* or *Kitāb al-ʿilal* and attributed to Balīnās (pseudo-Apollonius of Tyana), the putative author of numerous other occult works in Arabic as well. See the introductions by U. Weisser to her edition (Aleppo, 1979) and translation (*Das "Buch über das Geheimnis der Schöpfung" von Pseudo-Apollonios von Tyana*, Berlin, 1980). Abū Ḥātim has already cited the introductory paragraphs of this work in chapter three, where he refutes Abū Bakr's claim that the religious traditions are full of contradictions by suggesting that apparently contradictory accounts must be understood symbolically or allegorically, and points to the same use of symbolism and allegory among the philosophers, including Proclus and Democritus (citing material from ps.-Ammonius), Plato, and Balīnās.

18. For a discussion of the historicity of this claim, see Weisser, translation, p. 54.

19. That is, as becomes clear below, a name ending in "s"; Galen, Ptolemy, and Euclid appear in Arabic as Jālīnūs, Baṭlamiyūs, and Iqlīdus.

20. See Daniel 1–4, especially 4:9. The true etymology of "Belteshazzar" is obscure.

ted works[21] and relied on them, without holding to what is transmitted from the founders of the religious traditions. They made the opinions of the former their base, and went deeply into them, and came up with these dreadful babblings which they claim as wisdom and philosophy, purporting to follow the ways of the sages. They spoke of the Creator—be He exalted and glorified—and of the principles of things, displaying utter confusion about them, and claimed that they had derived through their own cleverness and natural faculties what the sages who preceded them were unmindful of. Thus they came up with these babblings of which we have already given an account, and in which we have shown how they disagreed, illustrating their controversies, confusions, and contradictions, and their headlong pursuit of these erroneous paths.[22] In just this way the apostate claimed that he had attained through his own cleverness what those who preceded him were not clever enough to realize, coming up with his own silly doctrine and claiming to be the equal of Hippocrates in medicine and of Socrates in deriving subtleties. For this is the same way followed by those liars who preceded him, imitating the philosophers and adopting their names, choosing apostasy as their religion[23] and tradition,[24] and holding to a doctrine which strips God of all His essential qualities.[25] I personally have met someone who followed this path and adopted the name Nasṭūlus, and another who called himself Nasṭūs.

Such was the way followed by these liars. But as for the true ancient sages who composed these valid works[26] on astronomy, medicine, geometry, and other natural sciences, they were the sages among the people of their eras, the leaders of their ages, and God's proofs to His creatures in their times, whom God supported with revelation[27] coming from Him and whom He taught this wisdom. Thus each of them contributed a particular kind of wisdom. One contributed the science of medicine, while others contributed other mathematical and natural sciences. They presented them to the people, who took them from them, since God wanted to make His creatures aware of the wisdom in these principles,[28] to manifest the ranks of these prophets in their times, and to display God's proofs to His creatures by means of their tongues. So, for example, it has been handed down that the principles of astronomy come from the prophet Idrīs. Some people have

21. *Rusūm.*

22. In chapter IV of this work Abū Ḥātim reproduces a doxography of Greek philosophers, both pre- and post-Socratic, illustrating their contradictions on various topics. This doxography, which bears little relationship to reality and betrays considerable Neoplatonic influence throughout, is very closely related to a work attributed in manuscript to "Ammonius"; see U. Rudolph, ed., *Die Doxographie des Pseudo-Ammonios: Ein Beitrag zur neuplatonischen Überlieferung im Islam*, Stuttgart, 1989.

23. *Sharīʿah.*

24. *Rasm.*

25. *Taʿṭīl*, "stripping" God of his attributes, an accusation commonly hurled at the Muʿtazilites, as well as the Neoplatonic philosophers, and virtually equivalent in the eyes of religious conservatives to atheism.

26. *Rusūm.*

27. *Waḥy.*

28. *Uṣūl.*

interpreted God's words in the story of Idrīs that "We raised him to a high place"[29] as meaning that God raised him up to the mountain which is at the navel of the world, and sent him an angel to teach him the things connected with the celestial sphere, its terms[30] and zodiacal signs, the planets and the periods of their orbits, and other aspects of the science of astronomy.

Furthermore, they say that the Hermes mentioned by the philosophers is Idrīs, his name among the philosophers being Hermes but in the Qur'ān Idrīs—both these names resemble those names like Galenos, Aristoteles, and so forth, which end in "s"—and in the other revealed books Enoch.[31] This, then, is an indication that such men used to have these names as aliases. The same pattern can be seen, among the names of prophets mentioned in the Qur'ān, in Elias as well as Idrīs. Among those prophets and sages mentioned by the People of the Book there are Simon, the disciple of the Messiah, who was called Petros; his brother, one of the twelve, whose name was Andreios; among the twelve apostles, Philippos; Marcos, one of the four; and Malghūs, the apostle who was obeyed among them.[32] Among the prophets they mention are Sarāqsīs, Agabos, Lucios, Paulus, and Philadelphius.[33] So there are many such names among the prophets and sages, which resemble the names of the ancient philosophers who composed the books of medicine, astronomy, and geometry, using such names as aliases—as we mentioned with regard to Idrīs, saying that he was the first to teach people the science of astronomy, and that he is the same as Hermes, being known among the philosophers by that name.

If someone should ask, "Why, then, did Muḥammad prohibit investigation into astronomy, if it is one of the sciences of the prophets?" We reply: Because this is abrogated, in the same way as the rest of the prophets' works are abrogated and prohibited.[34] God has ordered people not to occupy themselves with such

29. Qur'ān 19:57.

30. *Ḥudūd*, Greek *horia*, sections of the zodiacal signs assigned to individual planets; see al-Bīrūnī, *The Book of Instruction in the Elements of the Art of Astrology*, trans. R. R. Wright (London, 1934), section 453; Ptolemy, *Tetrabiblos*, trans. W. G. Waddel and F. E. Robbins (Cambridge, Mass., 1940), section I.20–21.

31. On the identification of the Qur'ānic Idrīs with both the Biblical Enoch (whose "ascension" comes ultimately from Genesis 5:24 and is described in several Jewish apocalypses) and the Greek Hermes, see *Encyclopedia of Islam* 2 s. vv. Hirmis, Idrīs. Numerous sources report that Hermes ascended to Saturn and was thus able to observe the motions of the celestial spheres; see E. K. Rowson, *A Muslim Philosopher on the Soul* and *Its Fate: al-ʿĀmirī's Kitāb al-Amad ʿalā l-abad* (New Haven, 1988), 241f. I have not, however, seen the more terrestrial variant of this ascent offered here. The "navel of the earth" is apparently equivalent to what is usually termed the "dome of the earth," its assumed "center," at the intersection of the equator and the prime meridian. It was usually placed at, or on the meridian of, the Indian city of Ujjayn, but sometimes on Ceylon or elsewhere; see *Encyclopedia of Islam* 2, s. v. al-Ḳubba.

32. I do not know who is being referred to here.

33. Agabos (MSS Āghāyūnus) is mentioned at Acts 11:27f., 21:10, and Lucios at Acts 13:1. I have not been able to identify the other names, possibly garbled in the MSS.

34. "Abrogation," *naskh*, is a Qur'ānic term, referring there to the supersession of the earlier Jewish and Christian revealed books by the Qur'ān, but was much elaborated and more widely applied in later Islamic legal theory.

things at the expense of investigation into the religious ordinances[35] of Islam, while not forbidding these things categorically.[36] His prohibition is meant to discourage such investigation, because if a man goes into such things too deeply, without focusing careful attention on the religious ordinances, the Unity of God, and the subtleties of the true (religious) sciences, he will become confused and led to apostasy, ending up in the same position as those errant ones who call themselves philosophers; thus he prohibited going deeply into such things. Another reason is that someone who investigates these things takes on a task which he cannot carry out properly, tells untruths, acts like a soothsayer,[37] makes extravagant statements, and multiplies false claims about the judgments of the stars; as has been transmitted from the prophet's statement, "Beware of investigating astronomy, for it leads to soothsaying," thus discouraging Muslims from telling untruths, making false claims, and falling into the intellectual confusion feared for them if they do not look carefully into their religion.[38] This, then, is the reason for the prohibition of astronomy and the investigation of it. He did not simply forbid it, for if he had, it would not be permissible for any Muslim to investigate it at all, and astronomy would be treated like the other forbidden things, such as wine, carrion, blood, and pork. In short, the origin of the science of astronomy is from Idrīs; Hermes is Idrīs; he was a prophet, and a member of our community, not the community of the apostates; there were five generations between him and Adam.

As for knowledge of the natures[39] of things, when God created Adam with a body composed of the natures which come from the earth, and provided him with nourishment produced by the earth, the various natures being in some cases opposed and in others similar, some harmful and some beneficial, "He taught Adam all the names."[40] For Adam's body and the bodies of his offspring could only be maintained with nourishment, but some nourishment is harmful and some beneficial; and since their bodies were subject to disease, and every disease must have some remedy, He taught him which things generate diseases, and what the proper remedy is for every disease. For he could not do without that, and God's Mercy would not permit him and his offspring to fall ill without knowing of remedies for their diseases. So it was that God taught Adam about all these natures, and Adam then passed this knowledge on to his offspring, some of whom retained it and some of whom forgot it, and so it was passed down from generation to generation. Thus God has said in the glorious Qur'ān, "And he taught Adam all the

35. *Sharāʾiʿ*.

36. Abū Ḥātim distinguishes between qualified prohibition (*nahy*) and categorical forbidding (*taḥrīm*).

37. *Kāhin*, a pre-Islamic Arabian oracular figure, suppressed by Islam; see *Encyclopedia of Islam* 2 s. v.

38. The only *ḥadīth* resembling this recorded in Wensinck's concordance of the standard collections is in Ibn Ḥanbal, *Musnad* Cairo, 1313), I, 78, where a series of prohibitions includes "*wa-lā tujālis aṣḥāb al-nujūm*," "do not sit with the astrologers."

39. *Ṭabāʾiʿ*, referring to the properties of physical, particularly organic, substances, and often, as here, connoting pharmacological and medical knowledge.

40. Qur'ān 2:31.

names," and thus He taught him all that he needed for his religion and for the life of this world. Nothing other than this was possible, in God's wisdom, since mankind could not do without the worship of God, and knowledge of Him, for a single moment, and it was not possible for them to live in this world a single day without knowing what was good and bad, harmful and beneficial, for their bodies.

This is the "beginning" for the knowledge of the natures of things which the apostate mentioned, saying "from generation to generation since the beginning of time." Here he spoke truly; but the "beginning" is not what he maintained—that is, the beginning is not reached with Hippocrates and Galen, from whom he says "not just a few, but thousands" of pages have been transmitted on medicine and the knowledge of drugs. What about the peoples before Hippocrates and Galen? Were they in no need of the knowledge of drugs? Certainly those who preceded them shared the same natures as those who came after them, right down to today. But if there were those before Hippocrates and Galen who knew of the natures of drugs, then these two must have taken their knowledge from those who preceded them, and the process ends up back at the beginning of creation, namely, Adam. It is he who is the "beginning." And if Hippocrates and Galen were able to add something to this knowledge, then the way they did so was as we have said, namely, that they were able to do so with support and revelation from God. But he who follows this way is in fact a prophet supported by God; and the prophets are *our* leaders, not the leaders of the apostates. And it cannot be denied that God does reveal to prophets things which people need but have forgotten, and in that way renews the teaching for them. For example, they say that the Messiah would not pass by a stone or a tree without its speaking to him.[41] "Speaking" here does not mean "addressing" in the conventional sense, but rather "serving as an indication and object of consideration." For when someone considers something and becomes aware of its potential benefit and harm, that thing has "spoken" to him; this is something well known among people of knowledge and discrimination. So it was with the Messiah: he would not pass by something without becoming aware of its nature, by means of revelation from God. And this was also the way of the sages who composed those works; they were unable to do so except by means of revelation and support from God, and thus they were prophets. No one can become aware of the nature of a thing by means of his own intellect and cleverness; that is simply not valid for intellects.

The apostate was offering an absurdity when he claimed that such knowledge has been attained by deduction, inspiration, inquiry, experimentation with taste and odors, and the other things that he mentioned, and when he claimed that these sages were inspired with this by their own natural faculties, without instruction, and that God made them free of any need for our leaders, just as He inspired the goose to swim by nature and made it free of any need for our leaders. I say, Glory to God! as I marvel at the apostate. How was he led to this argument, which befits the blindness of his heart and deficiency of his intellect, when he claimed that the sages were inspired to derive these subtleties without support from God

41. I have not found parallels to this statement.

and instruction from the leaders, but rather by their natural faculties, just as the goose swims by its nature, and that they were not in need of our leaders, just as the goose is not in need of our leaders? Does the fool not realize that, even if it were as he claims—that is, that the sages derived these things by nature—this would not necessitate that this inspiration and nature be comparable to the inspiration and nature of the goose? For the goose is naturally created able to swim, having no need in that for reflection or discovery, just as all animals are naturally created able to do something—birds naturally fly in the air, aquatic animals swim in the water—and no species is able to go against what it has been naturally created for, because it does that by compulsion, not choice. Some animals both fly and swim, such as geese; some swim but do not fly, such as fish; others fly but do not swim, such as pigeons. Geese are naturally created to swim and fly, both young and old are naturally created to do that. One sees that goslings swim as soon as they hatch from their eggs, and among all geese there is not a single one which goes against this nature. So it is with all animals; there is not a species of which any single member goes against what it is naturally created for, precisely because it was naturally created for that.

But the rule for human beings with regard to deriving and discovering knowledge is not like that. For out of a thousand men or more, only one will be able to derive these subtleties, even if we grant the validity of the apostate's claim about nature and inspiration. Those who have expert knowledge of arithmetic, geometry, astronomy, and medicine are very few in number amidst the large total number of human beings. But if their deriving these subtleties by nature were comparable to the goose's swimming by nature, then all people would necessarily be arithmeticians, geometers, astronomers, and physicians, and the experts in geometry, the physicians, and the astronomers could not possibly be exceptional in their knowledge compared to the rest of people. For all geese swim, both young and old. Furthermore, one would have to deny any role to instruction in their knowledge, just as one denies any role to instruction in the swimming of geese. Then, indeed, they would be in no need of our leaders, just as geese have no need of our leaders.

But suppose someone were to claim that if all people turned their attention to these matters, they would all be geometers, arithmeticians, astronomers, and physicians, just as the apostate argued when he claimed that if people turned their attention to learning and inquiring into philosophy they would attain what the philosophers have attained.[42] In reply, we ask: Have you ever seen a philosopher who inquired into philosophy by nature, before learning the first principles of philosophy and looking into the procedural rules of the philosophers, and before beginning by being instructed in these first principles, and only then inquiring and

42. In his account of his debate with Abū Bakr in the first chapter of his book, Abū Ḥātim has Abū Bakr argue that a God Who was truly wise would not single out certain individuals as prophets, but would inspire (*alhama*) all people with knowledge of what would benefit and harm them; asked whether God in His wisdom has actually done so, he replies that all people are in fact potentially philosophers, but most fail to turn their attention to what is most important.

drawing analogies, after being instructed? If this person says yes, he is simply trying to get the better of us by flagrantly lying. If he says no, then instruction is the first step, only after which comes inquiry and analogizing. But the goose is in no need of instruction, even at the beginning; he needs neither someone to make him swim nor some one to teach him how to swim; rather, all geese, young and old, swim by nature, as we have said. But man absolutely requires instruction at the beginning; if he does not receive instruction at the beginning, he achieves nothing by his nature. This is not in his capacity, he is not naturally created for it, nor compelled to it. Therefore he must necessarily have recourse to a leader to teach him; without one, his nature will be of absolutely no benefit to him or free him of any need, as the goose is free of the need for instruction from our leaders and of having recourse to them.

By his nature man only does things which his nature cannot go against, such as his sensory acts—seeing, hearing, smelling, tasting, touching—for these he is compelled to do. If he looks at something, he sees it; if the sound of something reaches his ears, he hears it; and if an odor enters his nostrils he smells it—assuming his senses are in sound order. He is also naturally created to walk on his two legs, and to grasp things with his two hands. All people are naturally created to do these things, just as geese are naturally created to swim, and they are equal in them, just as all geese are equal in swimming. It is *this* nature in people which resembles the goose's nature in swimming.

Every species of animals is naturally created to do its own act, and does not go against what it is naturally created to do. Man, however, is both naturally created for things, and given choice in things; he shares the former with animals, but is distinguished by the latter. Among the things in which he is given choice is learning the sciences, in which there are both specialists and laymen, and some who are incapable of learning even a single letter. So there must necessarily be among them both leader and led, both knowledgeable and ignorant. This is something that is obvious to even the common people, so how could the people of knowledge and discrimination not be aware of it? Have you ever seen someone blinder in his heart and more deficient in his intellect than the one who would compare the swimming of geese by nature to the deriving of the science of philosophy and knowledge of the motions of the celestial sphere, the natures of drugs, and other subtle sciences such as geometery and so forth? And have you ever seen anyone more ignorant than one who would claim that people have derived these subtleties, without need for our leaders, just as geese have no need for our leaders when they swim, and then go on to claim that he is the greatest philosopher in the world in his own time and the greatest sage among the people of his era? By my life! This claim, with this analogy and this comparison, is not farfetched enough for him; he then goes on to defame the Muslims, saying, "I grant that they labor under the affliction of befogged intellects and overpowering passions." What befogging of intellect and overpowering of passion, I ask, could be more severe than the befogging of the intellect and overpowering of passion in someone who draws an analogy like this? We say: We grant that, in this analogy and this philosophy of his, God has blinded his heart and befogged his intellect!

Then he asks us to tell him by what language the first of our leaders became familiar with languages, and whether this does not necessarily require inspiration,[43] claiming further that if a leader knew a language and then wished to teach it to people he would be unable to do so unless they already possessed it, so that one must absolutely appeal in the end to inspiration. Thus the claim of the apostate.

We reply: Let the apostate maintain either the eternity of the world or its beginning in time. If he claims that it is eternal, this puts an end to our argument with him about languages, since they will be coeternal with the world, granting the claim of those who do maintain the eternity of the world, and there is nothing more to be said about inspiration or learning. If, on the other hand, he concedes the beginning of the world in time,[44] we would say that He who originated the world, when He created this humankind, taught him languages, as we do in fact say that He—be He honored and glorified—"taught Adam all the names." It may be that God taught Adam all the languages, and that he in turn taught them to his children; or it may be that God taught him only some of them, and that He—be He honored and glorified—then taught the rest of them to those of Adam's progeny who were in a similar position of prophethood. Thus it has been said that Adam knew the Syriac language,[45] and that once he began to have offspring, his progeny learned his language in the same way as we see children following their fathers in their languages in all climes and islands; so also then would it be that for each prophet, when God had taught him a language, his community followed his model and learned his language.

For instance, we can observe directly that in former times only a very small number among the Persians were acquainted with the language of the Arabs, but once they received the religion of Islam they undertook to learn Arabic, to the point that most of them have achieved proficiency in it—but by learning, not by inspiration. Have you ever seen a Persian who was inspired with the language of the Arabs without having to learn it, in accordance with the apostate's claim that "if a leader wished to teach a language to people he would be unable to do so unless they already possessed it, so that one must absolutely appeal in the end to inspiration"? The Persians have learned Arabic, without already possessing it, but they have not acquired the ability to speak it by inspiration, but by learning.[46]

43. Apparently Abū Bakr is arguing that a language cannot be externally taught without prior knowledge of another language, so that some sort of internal inspiration is necessary to explain the beginning of the process; but the argument is not entirely clear. "Became familiar with" is *waqafa ʿalā*; the causative form of this verb, *waqqafa*, with its verbal noun *tawqīf* (translated below as "instilling") is the standard term employed by those, such as Abū Ḥātim, who see the origin of language in a revelatory act by God to a single individual.

44. As Abū Bakr in fact did, maintaining that the world itself, unlike the five eternal entities (Creator, Soul, Space, Time, and Matter), was created by the Creator after the failure of the Soul's attempt to create on its own. His view is summarized by Abū Ḥātim in the first chapter of this work.

45. This view, which was ultimately Rabbinic, was predominant among Muslim scholars, although a minority held that Adam spoke Arabic; see *Encyclopedia of Islam* 2, s. v. Adam.

46. In his *Kitāb al-zīnah*, I, 64, Abū Ḥātim mentions that he is a native speaker of Persian; this remark occurs in the course of a disquisition on the superiority of Arabic to other languages, illustrated by the deficiencies of Persian.

So in general the way one learns a language one is unaccustomed to is in fact to acquire it by learning, not by inspiration. And for every language there must necessarily be a leader to whom God taught it, and who then taught it to people. It is said, for instance, that the first to speak Arabic was Ishmael son of Abraham, whose tongue God loosed for it and to whom He taught it, because he was a prophet;[47] then Ishmael taught it to his progeny, who acquired it from him by learning, not inspiration, in the same way as one can observe directly how the Persians have acquired it from the Arabs, by learning, not by inspiration. This is quite clear and indubitable. But if the argument is clear by direct observation in the case of this language, then that is an indicator that the same holds for the other languages and that each of them began with a single man, to whom God taught a given language, which he in turn taught to those who followed his model. And if it is clear that the secondary case is one of learning, not inspiration, then it is a valid conclusion that the original case is also one of learning, not inspiration. And if it is valid that that original case is from a single man who learned the language, and we find no one else prior to him, then it is valid to conclude that that first man learned it from the Creator of languages, just as that first man was himself created by the Creator of languages and Creator of the entire creation, and that God taught him by means of revelation. If that is inspiration, then it is from God—be He honored and glorified—and is a sort of revelation.[48]

Thus the apostate must necessarily fall back on what the adherents of the religious traditions say, namely, that the beginning of the learning of all things comes from God—glorified be His name—by His granting revelation to His prophets, who have then taught them to people. Thus it is said that Babylon was called Babylon on account of the babble of tongues that arose (*tabalbalat*) in it after Noah emerged from the ark; for the children of Noah and those who were with him in the ark dispersed into different lands, each of them speaking a different language, so that their progeny acquired their languages from them, the original one in each land having been taught his language by God. If this was a case of "inspiration," then it is in fact revelation from God—be He honored and glorified—and learning from Him; if, on the other hand, each first speaker learned from an angel, that is still revelation from God—be He honored and glorified—and learning from Him. For the prophets have occupied various ranks, God favoring some to various de-

47. Abū Ḥātim repeats this assertion in his *Kitāb al-zīnah*, 141–46, where a number of different views by earlier scholars are cited.

48. Abū Ḥātim's view of the origin of language, summed up in the term *tawqīf*, "instilling (by God)," seems to have been the dominant one among Muslims up to his time, and was represented by, among others, al-Ashʿarī (who also, however, uses the term *ilhām*). In Abū Ḥātim's lifetime it was challenged by the Muʿtazilite Abū Hāshim, who argued for a purely conventional origin for language (*iṣṭilāḥ*), the members of a society agreeing to assign a given vocable to a given entity. (It is not clear whether this latter theory is compatible with Abū Bakr's view.) On this entire question, see B. G. Weiss, "Medieval Muslim Discussions of the Origin of Language," *Zeitschrift der deutschen morgenländischen Gesellschaft* 124 (1974), 33–41; Abū Ḥātim's views on language, as expounded in the *Kitāb al-zīnah*, are discussed by G. Vajda, "Les lettres et les sons de la langue arabe d'après Abū Ḥātim al-Rāzī," *Arabica* 8 (1961), 113–30.

grees over others. To some the angel came with revelation and appeared before them so that they saw him with their eyes. Others saw the angels only with their spirit. Thus Gabriel used sometimes to come to Muḥammad in the form of a man, while at other times he would go into a trance when revelation came to him and then regain consciousness and recite what God had revealed. Others have something cast into their hearts, that being inspiration and support from God—be He honored and glorified—and revelation from Him. Others receive revelation in dreams. Others look at something and take a lesson from it, God casting this into their spirits and teaching them the benefits and harms inherent in that thing, as we have mentioned in the story of Jesus, saying that he used not to pass by a stone or a tree without its speaking to him. The revelation by God—be He honored and glorified—to His prophets occurs in all these ways—He grants them revelation however He pleases, in accordance with their degrees.

Now if someone should object, saying, "People are inspired with various things, and see various things in dreams," we reply: There are three sorts of inspiration. First, there is that which is revealed by God—be He honored and glorified; in this case, that which is uttered by him whom God inspires turns out to be valid, and the truth and wisdom in what he says becomes apparent in what he utters from that inspiration; and if it is valid, then we know that it is from God. For instance, God—be he honored and glorified—has mentioned "And we revealed to the mother of Moses, (saying,) 'Suckle him! But if you fear for him, then cast him into the river'" and then said "We shall bring him back to you and make him one of Our messengers";[49] this turned out to be valid, since God did indeed bring Moses back to her and made him one of the messengers. Second, there is that which is instilling by God—be He honored and glorified—in those who act rightly among His servants, in that which they undertake or leave alone among matters both secular and religious. And third, there is inspiration which comes from the babblings of the soul, like the speech of those babblers in which there is neither order nor truth; this comes from nature, lightness of the brain, and the seductions of Satan. So much for inspiration.

Similarly, visions are of various sorts. That which the prophets see in their dreams can never in any way be invalid, nor does it require elucidation;[50] if they see something, that very thing occurs. This sort of vision is particular to them. But they also share another sort of vision with other people; for sometimes they see something in their dreams which does require interpretation, and in this case their dreams are just like the dreams other people see, which contain truth once they are elucidated. This is a sort of vision which the prophets share with other people in having, while being singled out for the other kind which we mentioned first. Other kinds of vision are those that come from nature and from residual thoughts. These two kinds contain no truth, and the prophets are free of this sort of vision; they are what are called "confused dreams"[51] and have no interpreta-

49. Qurʾān 28:7.

50. *ʿIbārah*, usually translated "interpretation"; the present translation distinguishes it from *taʾwīl*, (exegetical) "interpretation."

51. *Aḍghāth aḥlām*; the phrase comes from Qurʾān 12:44, 21:5.

tion and cannot be validly elucidated. This is in contrast to the validity of the elucidation of valid visions which are of the secrets of the upper world and are seen by the right-acting person; these are of the same sort as the visions seen by the prophets, and are thus valid when interpreted, although they are not as lucid as the latter; as the Prophet said, "A good vision from a good man is one-fortieth of prophecy."[52]

Such, then, is the nature of visions which are revelations to prophets, they being as we have described them, not requiring any elucidation or interpretation, and seen only by the prophets to the exclusion of other people. Such also are the ranks and degrees of the prophets; of all of these ranks Muḥammad was granted an Abundant share, and God favored him over those who were not of his degree in that. And the inspiration which is revelation from God is as we have stated.

Now the inspiration of him who is inspired with languages is revelation from God—be He honored and glorified—and instilling and learning; it is thus prophecy. This is not the same as that inspiration which is the babblings of the apostates, who claim that it is general among people, in accordance with whatever speech they come forth with; rather, it is reserved for the prophets alone, to the exclusion of other people. And of languages, some are superior to others, just among the prophets some are of a higher degree than others. The best of languages are four: Arabic, Syriac, Hebrew, and Persian; for God—be He honored and glorified—sent down His books to His prophets in these languages. Then the books were translated into the other languages for various communities, except for the glorious Qurʾān; for the Qurʾān is in the Arabic language, which is the best of the four, and it is unamenable to translation for reasons which it would take to long to go into here in this book but which we have explained elsewhere.[53]

Thus the origin of all languages, according to what we have said, is instilling from God—be He honored and glorified—in His prophets, who then taught them to the people. It is not the case, as stated by the apostate, that they were derived by people with no revelation from God, and that it is possible for all people to be inspired with that. If such were the case, no language would be coherent, but would be subject to so much variation as to have no structure; for anything which is derived from differing people and on which views diverge will itself be inconsistent and incoherent—just like the inconsistency we have mentioned in the tenets of those so-called philosophers who contradict one another. But since we find every language to be coherent and agreed upon by a community of people, we know that the origin of every language must be from a single man supported by revelation from God—be He honored and glorified—and thus it is valid to conclude that all languages come from the prophets.

Again, if the case were as claimed by the apostate, the people of every age would necessarily be inspired by some language which they initiated and which

52. This *ḥadīth is* widely reproduced, with numerous variations, particularly in the fraction cited; see, for instance, Muslim, *Ṣaḥīḥ* (Cairo, 1930), XV, 20f.; Ibn Ḥanbal, *Musnad* (*Cairo*, 1313), I, 315, II, 219, etc.

53. This probably refers to the fuller discussion in the author's *Kitāb al-zīnah*, I, 61f.

they speak;[54] but then how is it that this inspiration has now been cut off, this aptitude submerged, and this nature not continued, so that no one can mention any group who have invented a language that people have acquired from them and perpetuated over a long period without cessation, except for what is reported about the languages mentioned above? If this were a general phenomenon, our opponents would necessarily be able to mention to us some originated language; but they will never come up with such a thing, since the origin of languages is in fact from the prophets, as we have said.

Therefore, once prophecy was sealed, so were languages—as were all other things connected in their origins with the prophets and sages, by revelation from God—be He honored and glorified—and there remain in the world only what has been instituted[55] by them. Thus we do not find in the world anything other than their institutions or what has been derived from their institutions and built on their foundations. Among such originated institutions which belong to the category of the wisdom of the sages, we may point to what has been originated in our own community and derived from the Arabic language, namely grammar and prosody, which are gauges for the correctness of the speech of the Arabs. The foundations of these two sciences were acquired from the sages of the community and the leaders of right guidance. For grammar was instituted by the Commander of the Faithful ʿAlī for Abu'l-Aswad al-Duʾalī,[56] and the Commander of the Faithful was the sage of his age, or rather the chief of the sages after the messenger of God in this community. God—be He honored and glorified—inspired him with the derivation of that. ʿAlī was not a prophet, but rather one granted sagacity and divinely addressed;[57] but those granted sagacity and divinely addressed in this community correspond to the prophets in other communities, and their wisdom is derived from Muḥammad. ʿAlī was singled out for this grace among the members of the community, and the prophet consigned to him secrets with which he favored him over others. Then ʿAlī taught these secrets to those in the community who were worthy; some of them he restricted to certain members of the elite, concealing them from the masses, while others he bestowed freely upon both elite and masses.[58] Now grammar belongs to the category of the wisdom of the sages, although it is not directly connected with religion. ʿAlī derived it from the language of the Arabs and passed it on to Abu'l-Aswad al-Duʾalī, who acquired it from him and then analogized from it; then other people acquired it in turn from him, and expanded the process of analogizing in it. Similarly, the foundation of prosody was taken by al-Khalīl b. Aḥmad[59] from one of the companions of

54. Reading *yatakallamūn* for the text's *yastakmilūn.*

55. *Rusūm.*

56. On this famous partisan of ʿAlī see *Encyclopedia of Islam*, New ed. s. v. His legendary role as the founder of Arabic grammar, at the instigation of ʿAlī, is widely reproduced in the sources.

57. *Murawwaʿ muḥaddath,* Shiʿite terms distinguishing the mode of supernatural cognition granted the Imams from the direct Qurʾānic revelation to the Prophet.

58. Abū Ḥātim alludes obliquely to Ismāʿīlī imamology, distinguishing the esoteric knowledge of the Imams ("the elite") from the secular wisdom he also traces back to them.

59. Died ca. 170/786, the founder of Arabic lexicography as well as prosody. See *Encyclopedia of Islam*, New ed. s. vv. al-Khalīl b. Aḥmad, ʿArūḍ.

ʿAlī b. al-Ḥusayn b. ʿAlī b. Abī Ṭālib,[60] who was also the sage of his age and the imām of his time. Then al-Khalīl b. Aḥmad analogized from it and made it available to the people. Thus these two foundations were originated in this community, both coming from the sages of the religion and the leaders of right guidance.

It is the same with every sort of wisdom in the world, whether of minor or major importance: in each case its origin goes back to the prophets, who bequeathed it to the sages and the learned after them, and it subsequently became the object of instruction among the people. And the situation with languages is the same. For if the matter were as claimed by the apostate, that is, that people were equal in wisdom, all people being inspired with it and acquiring it by nature rather than by revelation from God—be He honored and glorified—and instruction, and that languages also functioned in this way, then none of them would have a coherent foundation or a proper structure, contrary to the coherence and structure that we actually observe in languages. The same applies to every book composed in the fields of wisdom, such as the *Almagest*, or Euclid, or other similar works. For these have a coherence and structure which indicates that in each case the foundation goes back to a single man, no one else sharing with him in its composition. But if this is established, one may validly conclude that it is a result of instilling by God—be He honored and glorified—and revelation from Him, rather than of derivation by nature. For it is not possible for a single man to be singled out from among all people who have arisen over many ages, and for that one man to be uniquely accorded such a capacity, when he has the same nature as the rest of them, unless there is in him some divine power granted him by the Creator of all creation—be He glorified and exalted. This power is the revelation which earns its receiver the title of prophet, in accordance with what we have explained about the ranks of prophets. This will not remain hidden to anyone who considers what we have said and regards it with an unbiased eye. God does not keep distant anyone except those who are obstinate and do injustice to themselves.

Section II: The Origin of Astronomy and Astronomical Observation

The apostate has asked: "Where have your leaders pointed out the difference between poisons and nutriments, and the effect of drugs? Show us a single page treating such a thing, comparable to the pages—not just a few, but thousands—which have been transmitted from Hippocrates and Galen, to the benefit of human beings! Show us any knowledge about the motions and causes of the celestial sphere which has been transmitted from any one of your leaders, or anything about the wonderful subtle natures of things, such as geometry and other things." He has gone on to say: "And if you ask whence comes people's knowledge of the

60. ʿAlī Zayn al-ʿĀbidīn, the third imam of the Ismāʿīlīs (and fourth imam of the Twelvers), died 94–95/712–13. In contrast to the connection commonly made between Abu'l-Aswad and ʿAlī in founding Arabic grammar, I know of no other sources linking al-Khalīl's work on prosody with a companion of Zayn al-ʿĀbidīn.

effects of drugs on bodies. . . ," and made claims in this matter which we have already reproduced in his own words. We have now treated the subject of how the goose is inspired to swim, and the subject of languages, in a convincing manner, God willing; and we have stated our views on the sages who used aliases in place of their names and who laid these foundations, maintaining that they were prophets and in fact our leaders.

Those sages are not, then, to be counted among the leaders of the apostates who studied those books and foundations after them, calling themselves by their names, but rejected the religious ordinances and spoke about the Creator—be He glorified and exalted—and the first principles of things with that self-contradictory twaddle which they have made up and which shows their confusion and testifies to their error. The apostate thus has no right to glory in those veracious sages who founded these sciences, for they are our leaders, not the leaders of the apostates. By glorying in them and boasting himself of these foundations the apostate is like nothing so much as the shaykh who stood at the finish line of a race course when the horses had been set to race and one of them had come in first. When the shaykh saw that horse he could not contain his delight and began to clap his hands, jump about, and go into ecstasies; but when someone asked him whether the horse was his, he replied, "No, but his bridle is!" Such is the apostate's boasting of those sages and their foundations. And his relation to them is no different than that of the carpenter's neighbor in the well-known proverb.[61] For the apostate denies prophecy, while these sages were prophets, as we have stated regarding Idrīs and others. The apostate has looked at their foundations and learned from them, while being ignorant of their merit and their ranks, demoting them from those ranks with which God favored them to the base level which he has chosen for himself, in his ignorance and error.

Yet were he to consider their situation justly, he would realize that it is beyond human capacity even to determine the exact distance between two cities which are relatively close together, being separated by less than a hundred miles, without first surveying it with carefully measured, straightened, and calibrated cords and rods, and observing and performing the surveying operation himself; for were two or three men to survey it, they would inevitably produce different results. How, then, can one possibly claim that someone is able to determine the distances between the celestial spheres, which are far beyond the grasp of human imagination? By direct observation? And how could they possibly make positive determinations of their magnitudes and then record these in their books, as they in fact have transmitted to us, saying that the latitude (?) of the sphere is 100,000 *farsakhs*[62] and that the distance between the nearest sphere and the surface (?) of the earth is 100,900 *farsakhs*?[63]

61. I have been unable to identify this proverb.

62. A *farsakh* is approximately six kilometers. The term for "latitude" is *ʿarḍ*; it is quite unclear what Abū Ḥātim is referring to, and the figure given is likely corrupt.

63. The term translated "surface" is *qabāla*; although the wording is odd, the meaning is fairly certain. But the expected figure would be 47,300 *farsakhs*; see W. Hartner, "Mediaeval Views on Cosmic Dimensions and Ptolemy's Kitāb al-Manshūrāt," *Mélanges Alexandre Koyré* (Paris, 1964),

And they go on in the same way to mention the distances between every pair of spheres, giving figures which we omit for the sake of brevity.

Furthermore, they have said that the total distance from the highest sphere to the boundary between the heavens and the earth is 1,000,980 *farsakhs*;[64] that the circumference of the earth is 24,000[65] *mīls*;[66] that its diameter is 7,030 *mīls*; that the latitude of the earth, from the South Pole, around which revolves Canopus, and the North Pole, around which revolves the Great Bear, [is 180 degrees, and its longitude, (?)][67] along the equator, is 360 degrees, the degree being 25 *farsakhs*,[68] the *farsakh* 12,000 cubits, the cubit 24 fingers, and the finger six *ḥabbas*; that there are 90 degrees between the equator and each of the poles, and that twenty-four of those degrees proceeding latitudinally along the circumference from the equator are land, the rest being covered by the Great Sea; that each region to the north and south consists of seven climes; that there are a total of 4,200 cities on earth; and that the total length of the sea from al-Qulzum[69] to the eastern regions of China, the land of al-Wāq Wāq,[70] is 4,500 *farsakhs*.

Moreover, they have spoken about the volumes of the planets, stating that the volume of the sun is 164 3/8 times that of the Earth,[71] and going on in the same way to speak about the volumes of the rest of the planets. Now these are matters which send intellects reeling just to hear about, and which weary tongues just to describe, much less to express judgment on. Who could possibly attain this by his nature, derive it by his cleverness, and reach such conclusions by his powers of discovery? Who would be capable of coming up with the *Almagest*, with all it has to say about observational astronomy, the structures and causes of the spheres, astronomical instruments such as the astrolabe,[72] the zodiacal armillary,[73] and other instruments and measuring devices which are in the hands of people, having been handed down from the sages, and whose use has been learned by both elite and masses? And who would be capable of coming up with Euclid, with its figures and its information about spheres, sides, hypotenuses, and centers, with their arithmetical[74] and geometrical magnitudes?

256f., and B. R. Goldstein, *The Arabic Version of Ptolemy's* Planetary Hypotheses (Philadelphia, 1967), 7–12.

64. The expected figure, based on Ptolemy's figures as given by Goldstein (previous note), would be 28,425,700 *farsakhs*.

65. Reading *arbaʿa wa-ʿishrūn alf* for *arbaʿumiʾa wa-ʿishrūn alf*.

66. A *mīl* is a third of a *farsakh*.

67. The text is apparently defective here, and something like this must be supplied.

68. This figure yields a total for the circumference of the earth of 9000 *farsakhs* or 27,000 *mīls*, in contrast to the figure of 24,000 *mīls* given above.

69. Classical Klysma, near modern Suez; see *Encyclopedia of Islam*, new ed. s. v. al-Ḳulzum.

70. A fabūlous island, potentially identifiable with Japan (as here), Madagascar, and other places; see *Encyclopedia of Islam*, new ed., s. v. Baḥr al-Hind.

71. Ptolemy's figure (Goldstein, op. cit., 11) is 166 1/3.

72. *Dhāt al-ṣafāʾiḥ*; see *Encyclopedia of Islam*, new ed. s. v. Asṭurlāb.

73. *Dhāt al-ḥalaq*; see G. Celentano, *L'Epistola di al-Kindī sulla sfera armillare* [*Risāla fī dhāt al-ḥalaq*], Naples, 1982.

74. Reading *al-ʿadadiyyah* for text *al-ḍarūriyyah*, "necessary" (?).

Could any sensible person possibly maintain that all these matters are attainable by human cleverness, that these sages discovered them by nature, that their intellects could reach so far, that they ascended into the heavens and looked out over the celestial spheres? Is that how they knew the number of the spheres and the number of the planets, and were able to distinguish between planets and the fixed stars which determine ascendants and descendants, and knew the mansions of the moon, and divided the sphere into twelve zodiacal signs, the signs into degrees, the degrees into minutes, the minutes into seconds, and the seconds into thirds, attaining such precision in their calculations? Moreover, they knew the place of each planet in its sphere, and could calculate the motions of the five planets, both direct and retrograde, as well as the motions of the two luminaries, with all their variation; for some take more than thirty years to traverse the sphere, while others do so in less than a month. In addition, there are the places of their auspicious and inauspicious aspects, and their exaltations and falls. All this has been set down by the sages in their books, their calculations being correct and well-ordered, with no more disagreement than the minor differences we find between different almanacs. These calculations are coherent and consistent, correlated with the passing of the years and the activity of the planets, so that one can determine the place of every planet, according to sign, degree, and minute, at any year, day, or hour.

And yet more, there is all they have to say about the judgments derived from the sciences of the heavens, the occurrence of individual phenomena high in the air, events and occurrences among the structures which encompass the climes,[75] and in general all the secrets of the Lord of the Worlds from beneath the earth to the highest heaven, as well as prosperity and hard times,[76] low prices and high, periods of good health and of plague, when to expect rain and dew, when the winds will blow, and when it will be light and dark—[. . .][77] one receives training in these things and spends one's life learning them from those learned in them, having them instilled in him by them, studying their books, and diligently inquiring into the rules they have laid down.

How, then, can anyone claim that all this became known through individual discovery and cleverness, without instruction, the prior existence of a foundation, and inquiry into the foundations which the sages set down in these books? Can anyone actually maintain that any creature on earth has the capacity to attain knowledge of these matters through his own cleverness and by his own nature, with no teacher to learn from, or that anyone could possibly have composed these books on his own initiative as an act of pure originality? Can the chain of knowledge and learning in these things be traced backed to anything other than a celestial teacher, linked to God, the Creator of these things, Whose knowledge encompasses them so that nothing is hidden from Him? Surely it is He who taught the people of this earth, by means of His revelation to His prophets, and it is He who instilled in

75. It is not clear to me what Abū Ḥātim refers to here.

76. Reading *al-shiqqah* for text *al-saʿah.*

77. Something has apparently fallen out of the text at this point.

them these calculations. If these foundations, all so coherent and consistent, did not have a single source, they would surely be subject to differences and contradictions; for when anything is a matter of cooperative human effort in this world, with several individuals observing and dealing with it directly, they always differ, and how could this fail to be the case with celestial matters, which are, as we have explained, so well structured? How utterly absurd! Anyone who would deny that the origin of all this is from the prophets, through revelation from God, the Deity of the heavens, claiming rather that it has been derived by human cleverness and is a product of human nature, is hopelessly blind, unspeakably ignorant, and lacking in any shred of intellect. As for what the apostate has said and the claims he has made in the blindness of his heart, that that is derived from astronomical observation, as well as from the foundations that have been handed down[78] in such works as the *Almagest*, Euclid, Ptolemy, and other books known by specialists in their fields, and that some of it is known by nature—we have spent a good deal of this chapter dealing with it.

But we will say yet more. Were one to bring together people from different communities—selecting those with fine intellects and perfectly balanced powers of understanding and discrimination, those with unquestionably solid judgment, refined nature, and sound talent, none of them having any prior knowledge of astronomy or having ever look into the works that have been handed down on this subject and its calculations, and were they then to inquire with their own powers of judgment, consider with their own intellects, and ratiocinate[79] with their own understanding, spending their entire lives at the task and striving to attain one iota of the calculations of astronomy, or even to distinguish between the planets and the fixed stars—they would be incapable even of telling the difference between Venus and Jupiter, much less anything more. How then could they come up with all the different calculations for the celestial spheres as has been done, or specify the ordering of the planets as we find it specified? Indeed, suppose one were to collect them around any of the astronomical instruments that have been devised, such as the plates of the astrolabe, or the zodiacal armillary, and then ask them how they work or what one does with them, while they turn them over in their hands, looking at both sides and seeing the incised terms, signs, degrees, hours, arcs, locations of the fixed stars, and so forth; and suppose one were then to ask them to set the diurnal arc for that day and determine the present hour and the elapsed daylight time, or to check the ascendant and the sun's altitude, or to see which sign the sun or another planets is in, without any teacher to instruct or inform them, they could spend their entire lives working on it, striving to derive it with their own intellects and natures, but as the days elapsed they would gain nothing but increased blindness and decreased guidance.

Such would be the situation with a single one of these instruments, which they could manipulate with their hands and perceive directly with their senses, using their own eyes to see what it was like and look it over thoroughly. How

78. Reading *al-marsūmah* for text *al-mawsūmah.*

79. *Qāsū*, literally, "draw analogies."

then could they deduce with their own natures the motions of the sphere, being unable to learn in this way what it is like? And how could they achieve the calculations of the planets, their orbital motions both direct and retrograde, and the other abstruse matters which we have already spoken of? And how could their imaginations deal with such matters that they do not observe and could not conceive of? This is crystal clear and no one can reject it, except through lying and sheer obstinacy.

The same argument applies also to astronomical observation. Suppose one were to ask people from various communities to undertake astronomical observation, all of them having the qualities of intellect, judgment, consideration, and balanced temperament that we have described above, and to have them meet in the desert of Sinjār[80] and give them the task of observing the two luminaries—whose risings and settings could not be missed even by children and the dimmest of people, unlike the other five planets, which they would not be able to identify by sight—their task being to observe the motions of the sphere and thereby learn about the rising and settings; they would have no prior knowledge of the subject, nor would they have any observational instruments with them—no almanacs or astrolabes. No matter how long they spent at this, they would get nothing more out of it than staring at the planets and watching the two luminaries rise and set, and the knowledge they gleaned from regarding these things would be no more than the knowledge brute beasts have—unless, that is, they had acquired some prior knowledge and solid acquaintance with the matter, or until they were brought some observational instruments, such as almanacs, astrolabes, and the like, all this presupposing, again, some prior advanced knowledge and training with the learned. This being the case, we have refuted the apostate's argument in which he claimed that they could attain some knowledge of these sciences by observation. But if it is impossible to make any progress by observation without these instruments which we have specified, then what could it be that they came up with by means of their own cleverness, without instruction or training and with no prior foundation?

Now someone may raise an objection, pointing out that al-Maʾmūn requested a group of people to carry out observations, and that they managed to progress beyond certain discrepancies among the almanacs which already existed and thereby originate the *Mumtaḥan* almanac, this being something created afresh and representing progress through observation.[81] But in fact those responsible for this progress were only able to achieve it after being provided with the appropriate instruments and consulting existing almanacs; and in any case they had prior acquaintance with this matter, being dependent upon instruction, training, and advanced knowledge. Thus this was no independent discovery on their part, nor was it derivation by nature; rather, it came about by going back to the foundations, and depended on prior acquaintance and knowledge.

80. So MS A, for text Sabkhāʾ, but the reading is doubtful. Sinjār is some seventy miles west of Mosul.

81. On *al-Zīj al-mumtaḥan*, "the tested almanac," see J. Vernet, "Las 'tabulae probatae,' *Homenaje a Millás-Vallicrosa* (1956), II, 501–22.

On the basis of this parallel, we see that astronomical observation is another instance of the general point we have been making. The apostate thus cannot argue from observation and nature, and this leaves no alternative but to concede that all of this is derived from the established sources, well known among specialists, with no role for observation or nature; and thus there can be no valid independent discovery in these matters, except by way of instruction and recourse to the rules laid down by the sages, with support and revelation from God. Without this, independent discovery is impossible for people. But if this is true, then we may validly conclude that those sages were unable to discover anything by means of their own cleverness and nature, and that the origin of all that must be revelation, as we have stated. They were not able to ascend to the heavens and thereby become aware of these hidden things; rather, God disclosed them to them by means of a revelation coming from Him. For He—be He exalted and glorified—"knows the unseen and does not disclose His unseen to anyone, except for a messenger with whom He is well pleased."[82] Glorified be He above permitting anyone to share in the knowledge of these unseen things without Himself granting this to him, and far exalted be He beyond such a thing!

Section III: The Origin of the Knowledge of Drugs

In the section on astronomy we have dealt sufficiently with that subject, God willing. We have also had something to say about medicine; but we will now return to that topic in order to treat it comprehensively. The apostate has claimed that "People became acquainted with the effects of drugs on bodies, and learned how they are constituted, by means of tasting and smelling, achieving this progress by means of nature." He also included this claim in what he mentioned about the goose swimming by nature.

In reply, we say: Learning about drugs by nature is the same as learning about the stars. Now someone might object, saying that this is a subject which is more accessible than astronomy, since drugs are here on earth and can be perceived directly by the senses—and the apostate has claimed that they have become known by means of tasting and smelling—while the stars are in the heavens and the sphere cannot be sensed or touched, and therefore the case of drugs is not the same as that of something that those interested cannot reach out and grasp. But to this we say: It is true that drugs are directly accessible to the senses, and that one can taste and smell them. But we would like to point out that these drugs are found in different lands, widely separated from one another. Some are imported from the East, others from the West, and yet others from the South and the North. For instance, myrobalan is imported from India, mastic from Byzantium, musk from Tibet, cinnamon from China, silkstone (?)[83] from the land of the Turks, opium from Egypt, aloe from Yemen, borax from Armenia, and so forth for all the various drugs which come from east and west. Some have offensive odors, others smell pleasant; some

82. Qur'ān 72:26f.

83. *Ḥaṣā' l-khazz*, not listed in the pharmacopeiae I have consulted.

are bitter, some sweet, some pungent, some spicy, differing in taste in these ways. Some consist of the bark of trees, others of their roots, their leaves, their fruits, their flowers, or their sap. Some are stones, and various sorts of minerals from the earth, such as the different kinds and colors of alum and nitre coming from a wide variety of lands, including Armenia, Byzantium, and Kirmān, and other mineral salts and stones from the earth. Then there are the galls of birds, wild beasts, and other land and sea animals, as well as their brains, lungs, and other organs; the flesh of lethally poisonous snakes, used as antidotes and in other ways; and different kinds of collyrium[84] from birds, beasts, reptiles, and insects. For example, scorpions are dried and used in an electuary to treat gout, or burned and their ashes used in an infusion for the sufferer from kidney stones, or macerated into an ointment good against gross tumors; flies are used in an ointment with which one dresses scorpion stings; frogs are useful in removing aching teeth; and hornets and Spanish flies are effective in making hair grow. There is also animal urine and excrement, from both domestic and wild beasts, bird droppings, and even human feces and urine; for example, camel manure is used in a electuary against quartenary fever, the urine of Arabian camels is used as a medicament for crippling rheumatism, various drugs are macerated in human urine for dandruff, human feces is ground dry and blown into the throat of someone attacked by diphtheria or used wet as a compress, dove droppings are put into an electuary taken to increase sexual potency, and bat guano is used in several drugs. Beyond these, there are many other drugs we have not mentioned, imported from various lands and having various names in the different languages of the people of those lands, who constitute different communities in rivalry and conflict with one another.

Where, then, are those sages, whose opinions were in agreement, who all possessed fine intellects and perfect natures, with strong bodies and long lives, who spoke with one voice, cooperating and helping one another, who roamed through the climes of the world and travelled around its lands and islands, associating with every community and living in every land, and learning the language of the people of every land and island, so that they knew the names of the drugs to be found in every place, and experimented with them, becoming acquainted with their trees and herbs, discovering their qualities, and learning by taste and smell the specific effects of all the drugs with their various uses and natures? For some of them affect the brain, some the liver, some the spleen, and some the bladder; some loose and others bind; each one has its specific effect on one of the organs in either the upper or the lower parts of the body. Some are such lethal poisons that one who tastes them finds himself given the taste of death within an hour, and they can used as medications only by smelling, not tasting. Where is the one who could become acquainted with specific effects like these in such drugs by tasting and smelling, and learn the proper weights and quantities to be administered, down to the *qīrāṭ* and the *mithqāl*,[85] by means of nature and inspiration?

84. *Kuḥl*, perhaps a corruption in the text.

85. The *mithqāl* varied regionally from about three to five grams. There are twenty-four *qīrāṭs* (carats) in a *mithqāl*.

For some of these are administered in a dosage of a single *qīrāṭ* or less, while others are administered in a dosage of twenty *mithqāls* or more, and if the quantity is too much or too little more harm than good results; there are poisons, in particular, for which an overdose is fatal and an underdose ineffective. There are also cases where a compound potion consists of fifty different kinds of drugs or more, each in a different weight or proportion that one must not go over or under.

Where, then, are those sages who have made a thorough study of all these drugs, tasting of tree after tree and fruit after fruit, learning how they grow, becoming familiar with their qualities, and determining their ratios, equivalents, and quantities; and who have also made a thorough study of all the birds, wild beasts, and domestic animals in the world, one animal after another, tasting their gall, and one bird after another, as well as plunging into the seas and bringing forth their animals, and tasting the flesh, brains, urine, and dung of all of these, including even human urine and feces; and who have thus become acquainted with all this through taste and smell, and have learned by nature and progressive discovery the effect of every single thing in each of these categories and how it flows through the blood vessels, each medicament bringing to bear its own action on the malady for which it was concocted, in the upper or lower part of the body, in its interior or on its exterior, after it has reached the stomach and mixed with the blood to form a single thing, and then been dispersed from the stomach into the various organs and blood vessels, that is, the circulatory system? Is it possible to maintain that a group of people actually cooperated, having strong bodies and long lives and travelling around the world until they came to know these things, after gathering them all and testing them by means of their taste and smell, and thus determined their natures, all this by means of their own nature and inspiration, as the apostate claims, and that, moreover, they all agreed, having no differences of opinion about any of this? For, surely, if all this came from a group engaged in cooperative effort, some disagreement would necessarily arise in something of it; and then there would be none of this consistency that we in fact observe in the field of pharmacology, with general agreement among physicians and experts on the natures of such substances. This would hold true even if we spoke only of a group convening in a single land and gathering the drugs to be found there; how, then, can we imagine such a thing given the vast distances between the various lands, and the difficulties involved in gathering and testing these drugs, without some prior acquaintance with them on the part of those testing them and some foundation to which they can have recourse?

Someone might claim that it was the people of each land who tested and became acquainted with what was to be found there in their own land first, and then these things were subsequently transferred from land to land and gathered in that way. But we reply that this is not possible, since their effect appears only after they have been gathered together and mixed. How could the people of each land know about what exists there in their land in isolation, before this gathering together and mixing? How could they know the proper quantity of each thing in their own land in isolation, without knowing the quantity of the corresponding components from another land, which they were unacquainted with and had not tested?

We maintain that the knowledge of the natures of these drugs must necessarily originate either from a single man, or from a group; but if from a group, then it could only have occurred in the way we have just described. But if someone maintains that such a group did meet together at a single time and thus reached this agreement and arrived at this knowledge, he has put forth a view that no intellect can accept. For it is impossible to imagine a group dispersing through all these lands from the east to the west, each one arriving at the knowledge of something of the substances to be found in his own land, in the way we have described, and then all of them meeting together, gathering all these substances together and agreeing about them, without any of them being overtaken by death or any of the world's misfortunes before they could achieve this. This flatly contradicts good sense.

If, on the other hand, one should maintain that one group after another became acquainted with these things by means of their nature in different times and various ages, and then subsequently gathered them all together, this is even more absurd. For if we have one medicament which is a mixture of fifty sorts of drugs, it is not possible that the views of different people scattered over various times and diverse places could be combined to produce knowledge of it, one man having arrived at the knowledge of one thing at one time and another coming along at another time and attaining the knowledge of something else, and then these views being combined with regard to that single mixture composed of fifty sorts of drugs, without there occurring some sort of disagreement. This is even more objectionable than the previous proposal.

Finally, if one should claim that a single man became acquainted with these natures, living a sufficiently long time so as to travel around the world and discover them, in their variety as we have described it, this is even more remote from what intellect can accept. Could anyone test all these drugs without examining all trees and plants, their fruits, leaves, roots, and so forth, and all animals, including predators and other wild beasts, domestic animals, birds, sea life, reptiles, and the rest, so as to know what is harmful and what beneficial, what useful and what useless, of their flesh, gall, and other parts, as well as their urine and dung, and to know the specific characteristics in each? What intellect would not reject this, and what intellect would hearken to it and accept it?

Was it a group, then, who arrived at the knowledge of the natures of these drugs, or was it a single person? If a group, was it at one time, or at various times? And suppose them to have had the fortitude to taste these filthy things we have mentioned, such as urine and dung, despite their putridity and foul smell and taste; how could they survive their lethal poisons? For among them are things so poisonous they kill instantaneously. We have ourselves seen an herb that grows in the deserts of our region and that, if eaten by someone who does not know it, kills him on the spot; and there are many others like that as well. Where in the world is there the one who could discover the natures of these things by taste and smell, and by his own nature and inspiration? Where in our own time is there someone who has discovered anything of the sort so as to use the known to render judgment on the unknown?[86]

86. *Yaḥkum biʾl-shāhid ʿalāʾl-ghāʾib*; this is standard terminology in theological argumentation.

Is it not the case that anyone who makes such a claim is wanting in intellect and bereft of understanding? And is it not the case that anyone who hearkens to such a thing and does not reject it is even blinder in his heart and further astray?

By my life! There is a group among those who style themselves "philosophers" who have made ridiculous claims like these, making up lies about the ancient sages and associating them with silly fables unworthy of them. They say, for instance, that Plato travelled into a mountainous region in the far north, where the sun does not shine and plants do not grow, and stayed there for a time looking for a way to conquer death through experimentation and medicaments, seeking mixtures that would prolong life, and that he had with him a thousand men, whom he sent out across the earth, east, west, north, and south, to taste what they found and seek drugs.[87] They also say that Aristotle sent out some people with Alexander[88] to find out about the ends of the earth and what they were like, which places were more salubrious and which less so, which more wholesome and which more polluted, how many climes there are in the world and how many *farsakhs* is the extent of each, and to bring back drugs and try them out. Those who travelled east reached a place where they suffered from the heat of the sun and feared that they would be burned up, and dug underground chambers and entered them. Those who travelled west continued on to a place where they were unable to go further, because of the quantity and intensity of the vapor there; they reported that they saw the sun enter the sea, while others said that it entered the heavens, and yet others said it went behind the vapor. Those who travelled northward were stopped by the cold and ice; they fell ill and then returned. And those who travelled southward reached a land in which there are drugs, medicaments, and minerals unknown in our lands.[89] Such are the claims they make about Plato and Aristotle. As for Pythagoras, they claim that he ascended into the air, attaining successively to the worlds of Nature, Soul, and Intellect, and observed all the forms to be seen there, the beauty and splendor, and the lights.[90] It was Pythagoras who had as a pupil Filānus, who travelled to India and from whom Brakhmas acquired philosophy, as has been described in a previous chapter.[91]

Then to these ridiculous claims they add their claims that the origins of all things go back to these men, and that everything from which the human race derives benefit and whose knowledge has come to people, including astronomy, medicine, and other things, was derived by them. They are supposed to have disseminated this knowledge to the horizons, composing eighty books of medicine for

87. I have not found parallels to this account.

88. *Dhū'l-Qarnayn*; "the Two-Horned"; for the standard identification of this Qur'ānic figure with Alexander the Great, see *Encyclopedia of Islam*, new ed., s. v. al-Iskandar.

89. I have not found parallels to this account.

90. Abū Ḥātim has already mentioned this purported ascension in chapter IV of this work, where he attributes the statement to Pythagoras' pupil Filānus. The passage is borrowed from ps.Ammonius; see next note.

91. "Brakhmas" is certainly Brahma; "Filānus" is unidentified. Abū Ḥātim has given further details about Pythagoras' Iranian and Indian pupils in chapter IV of this work. His source is the ps.-Ammonius; see Rudolph, op. cit., 166–85.

the Persians and thirteen books of medicine, wisdom, and aphorisms for the Indians, and composing all these books out of their own opinions and putting them together with their own intellects, all on the basis of their own inspiration and nature, without any support from God—be He exalted and glorified. They even go so far as to claim that they invented the urn of unquenchable fire in Persia, which is worshipped by the Magians, as well as other suchlike fabricated claims unacceptable to the intellect.

How is it that the apostate did not mention these fables, claimed by these errant liars, along with what he mentioned of the claims of the Magians and Manichaeans, and the fables he retailed from those who made them up about them, such as the story that Mani used to be snatched from among them and ascend into the air to the height of the sun, where sometimes he would remain for hours and other times for days before redescending, and that he elevated Shapur—for whom he had written the *Shāpūrakān*—into the atmosphere and made him disappear there for a time?[92] Surely these claims are no different from the claims of those liars that Pythagoras ascended into the air, reaching the worlds of Nature, Soul, and Intellect, until he was able to attain this knowledge by direct observation. Is not this exactly what the Manichaeans claim about Mani, as like as like can be? Why is it then that the apostate has no word of criticism against the self-styled philosophers of his own party for these claims, when he criticizes and lambastes the Muslims for what the Manichaeans claim about Mani? Why does he not hang these bells on his own neck and those of the adherents of his own party? Surely he is more worthy of them, belonging as he does to the same party as those who makes these claims for Pythagoras, and circulate these lies about Plato and Aristotle.

As for claiming some close relationship between Muslims on the one hand and Magians and Manichaeans on the other, that is like making the elephant the offspring of the she-ass. Should he justify this by the fact that Manichaeans and Magians affirm prophecy as the Muslims do, we reply that not everyone who affirms prophecy is to be believed in all his claims, nor does such a person speak truly and correctly when affirming the heretical notions they have concocted. We confirm what he says when he affirms prophecy, but reject as lies the absurdities they concoct. But if the apostate claims to reject as false the claims made about Pythagoras, Plato, and Aristotle, maintaining that they[93] disagreed on these matters, just as they disagreed on first principles—as we have mentioned, showing how they contradicted one another in their statements and called one another liars—then why does he raise internal disagreement as a argument against the adherents of religious confessions, given that the disagreement to be found among his own leaders is so hideously blatant as to be unexceedable?

92. Mānī's ascent to the sun is reported in several sources, but I have not seen parallels to his levitation of Shapur. The *Shāpūrakān* was Mānī's sole book composed in Pahlavi. See G. Monnot, *Penseurs musulmans et religions iraniennes: ʿAbd al-Jabbār et ses devanciers* (Paris, 1974), 162, 281.

93. That is, the philosophers, including those who make these claims about their predecessors. Here, as throughout his discussion, Abū Ḥātim treats the philosophers as a distinct dogmatic sect.

But perhaps he would have recourse to an argument which I have in fact heard from him, when we once debated on this topic. At that time I challenged him, saying, "The disagreements among your people are worse and more blatant than those you claim against the adherents of religious traditions," and he replied, "On this point you and we are like two men who have fallen out, of whom one says to the other, 'Isn't your sister a notorious slut?' and the other replies, 'Perhaps, but your sister is also an infamous trollop.'" That is how he answered, falling back on such coarseness, his literal meaning being "Perhaps, but if we have disagreed so have the founders of religious traditions." I then said to him, "If that is the way things are, then it is best to adhere to the religious tradition[94] of Muḥammad, and more beneficial in both this world and the next. In this world, one thereby avoids bloodshed, keeps one's property and family inviolate, preserves standards of decency, and protects lines of descent through proper birth after legitimate marriage, and this is more befitting the sense of honor, even among those who do not believe in Islam, than granting complete sexual liberty to mothers, daughters, and sisters—aside from all the other benefits which we have already discussed. In the next world, there is the promise of the great and glorious reward which is beyond all comparison, and the threat of the punishment painful beyond all other pain. It shows a higher resolve to put one's trust in this than to become enmeshed in a doctrine stripping God of His essential qualities and to fall into apostasy, a position which does nothing to avoid bloodshed, keep one's property and family inviolate, preserve standards of decency, or protect lines of descent, and which leads in the next world to a painful punishment."

As for the one who accepts this claim about Plato and Galen,[95] to him we say: Did Plato, with all his wisdom and well-grounded knowledge, not realize that if there is no way to conquer death in these populated areas of the earth where the sun shines and all sorts of plants grow—and those mixtures by which one treats every malady come from such populated areas—if, I say, there is not be found here any medicament that will ward off death, then how would he find such a thing in desolate regions and among the mountains where the sun does not shine and where there are no plants to be found? How could he have so deceived himself, being taken in by his desires, after having observed and become aware that no one in the universe escapes death? Could he not draw the lesson from that? With all his wisdom, did he not have the intellect to realize this basic condition? Is this, then, anything other than a lie on the part of those misguided souls, who, wanting to magnify Plato, managed to defame him with the very thing by which they thought to dignify him?

As for those who make the further claims that Plato sent out a thousand men to the east and west of the earth, and that Aristotle sent out some people with Alexander to find out about the ends of the earth and the various climes and islands, and to bring back drugs and try them out, what we have already said about drugs and about those who claim to have discovered them by nature and cleverness should

94. *Sharīʿah.*

95. This mention of Galen is anomalous; perhaps the text is corrupt here.

suffice. Our reply is applicable to both this group and the other, since they essentially follow the same way, and it should be convincing for anyone who is fair-minded, God willing. To that we will only add that if those who were sent out learned anything about drugs in the lands they visited of which Plato and Galen were unaware, then they were a model for Plato and Galen to follow; and in that case, where are the names of those who were more assiduous in this field than those two, and who endured more trouble in pursuing it than they did? And where are those drugs which they brought back from those lands? And why are they not credited with them the way Plato and Aristotle are credited with their books?

What these claims amount to in the end is lies and fabrications which are of a piece with the silly false claims of the apostates. The only reason we have brought them up is that the apostate, ignoring such claims as these, blamed the Muslims for the concocted absurdities that the Magians and Manichaeans claim for Zoroaster and Mani, out of a spirit of sheer apostasy and intense hostility to Islam. The only comparison to him possible is that in the old line: "Like the mountain goat that butted a stone one day, trying to split it; it did no damage to the stone but hurt its horns."[96]

Section IV: All Knowledge Goes Back to the First Sage

In our chapter on drugs we have given some idea of the difficulties they raise, despite the fact that they are on the earth and can be perceived directly by the senses, specifically by taste and smell. These difficulties are similar to those raised by the stars, although the latter are in the heavens, and the situation in learning about drugs by means of nature and cleverness is the same as that in learning about the stars. We have shown that pursuing such knowledge is in fact an arduous task, that one must rely in it on the foundations laid down by the sages, and that there is no way to attain such knowledge except by instruction, training, and following the rules they have set. Any claims other than this, about achieving anything by nature and cleverness, are false, and anyone claiming such a thing is a sinful liar guilty of terrible mendacity. These drugs can be known by taste and smell only by someone who has some prior knowledge of them, and can then taste and smell what he knows will not harm him when he does taste and smell it, having no fear of its deleterious effects, and can thus distinguish the better from the worse, the unadulterated from the adulterated, and the pure from the mixed. In this respect they can be known by smell and taste; but that a person could learn their actual nature by smell and taste, and discover the particular properties inherent in them without any prior knowledge of them, is the utmost in absurdity. The accomplished physician with pretensions to philosophy, who knows his drugs, and the man totally experienced in this field and having no knowledge of anything about it are in exactly the same position when it comes to learning the nature of something with no prior knowledge of it. Anyone claiming anything else is simply saying what is not true.

96. Although this is set out in the printed edition as verse, it does not scan; the text is probably disturbed, or, less likely, the expression is proverbial but not poetical.

When I made this point to the apostate, he persisted in his false claims. I then asked him whether he had himself, by his nature and cleverness, discovered anything unknown to his predecessors, as an example confirming his claim. He replied, "Yes, I can tell you about an extraordinary instance of this. I had a remarkable experience with Aḥmad b. Ismāʿīl[97] during the time I was living in Bukhara. He went out one day for a pleasure excursion, with me in his retinue. He led us to a pleasant spot, very green and full of flowers, and dismounted, as did we all. Examining a nearby herb, he asked me, "What is this herb good for?" Without stopping to consider, I answered spontaneously, "It is a diuretic." He ordered the herb picked. Then food was brought out and a table set up, and the herb was placed on one side of it. We sat down with the amir, and he invited one of his attendants, who was accustomed to dining with him, to sit on the side of the table where the herb was placed. We began to eat, and the attendant took the herb, just as one would take any green, not knowing anything about it or what had transpired. But before finishing his meal he rose from the table and went off to urinate. As he was going, his master asked him what was the matter and why he was leaving the table. He replied, 'I have an uncontrollable urge to urinate.' The amir and everyone else were amazed at this."

I asked him, "Did you know about this herb prior to this time?" He replied, "No, by God, I had never seen it before and did not recognize it." I asked, "Is this herb to be found in our land, and are you acquainted with it now?" He replied, "No, by God, I am not acquainted with it and I do not know whether it is to be found here or not." I asked, "Are you not familiar with those charlatans[98] who sit along the road and dupe the commons with their chicanery?" He replied, "Is there anyone more familiar with them than I?" I then said, "This story of yours falls under the category of such chicanery, not that of knowledge of the natures of drugs gained by nature, cleverness, and experience." He replied, "What could be more clever than this?" I retorted, "How can this be considered cleverness at all? How can you compare this to the cleverness of those sages, who according to what you claim discovered the knowledge of the nature of things by their cleverness and derived it by tasting and smelling, not, you say, having any knowledge of that except by cogitation, consideration, analogizing, experiment, smelling, and tasting? Then, you say, they recorded in their books the knowledge they had attained, so that it became a foundation that could be relied on. But then, while maintaining that these foundations were laid down in this fashion, you state that you yourself spoke about this herb spontaneously, without reflection, deliberation, or experimentation; and you say that you had no prior knowledge of this herb and had never tasted or smelled it, and that even now you are not acquainted with it and do not know whether it is to be found in these lands or not. Is not what you say here simply chicanery, and is not your claim closer to chicanery than to the

97. Ruler of the Samanid dynasty in Bukhara, 295–301/907–914. It was his first cousin, Manṣūr b. Isḥāq, to whom al-Rāzī dedicated his celebrated medical work the *Kitāb al-manṣūrī*.

98. *Zarrāqūn*, or possibly to be read *razzāqūn*; "chicanery" below is *zarq* or *razq*. For a discussion of this term, referring specifically to roadside astrologers and fortune-tellers, see C. E. Bosworth, *The Mediaeval Islamic Underworld* (Leiden, 1976), 257f.

cleverness and experimentation of the sages? Is not this in fact the very essence of chicanery? You claim that you are the best acquainted of people with charlatans; again, is this not the very essence of chicanery? And is not chicanery simply deception and hoodwinking? And if this was the way those sages acquired knowledge of the natures of drugs, then they too were charlatans who deceived and hoodwinked people. But if that were so, then nothing they handed down would be valid, and people would gain no benefit from their books, since chicanery is false and deceptive, having no basis and no coherence. And while you may have foisted your chicanery successfully on that man, we will not be taken in by you. This is the weakest argument you have come up with yet." At this point he gave up the debate.

I ask God's forgiveness for anything I have added to or left out of this account; while the wording may have some additions and omissions, this was the gist of it. The only reason I have told this story is that, when I asked the apostate what knowledge of the natures of drugs he had discovered in his entire life through his own nature and cleverness, what we have mentioned is the only thing he could come up with to confirm his claim—and this despite his claim to be the equal of Hippocrates and Galen in medicine, and of Socrates and Aristotle in the other philosophical sciences and the knowledge of natures. And such is what all the claims of the apostates regarding knowledge of things by means of cleverness and nature amount to—self-contradictory foolishness. If this story which he told is true, you can see what a fool he is; if he was lying, that is just what we would expect.

As for what the apostate mentioned about this subject in his book, saying that "some of these things have been passed on from generation to generation ever since the beginning of time," if by "the beginning of time" he means the "absolute time" which he believes to be eternal, making it part of the very basis of his system and claiming a distinction between it and "relative time," then he has made an absurd claim and contradicted himself.[99] For he maintains that "absolute time" is eternal and infinite; but he has not claimed that medicine is eternal along with this time. If, on the other hand, he means the "relative time" corresponding to the motions of the celestial sphere, he is still guilty of absurdity. For medicine and astronomical calculation were only taken up after the appearance of mankind, and mankind is the last of the generated beings to appear in the world, according to both the adherents of religious traditions and the philosophers, while the celestial sphere, its motions, and other things connected with it are prior to all generated beings; therefore, the beginning of knowledge of these subjects does not correspond to the beginning of time from this perspective, either. But we say, rather, that the science of medicine, the knowledge of the natures of drugs, and other sorts of knowledge, including astronomy and philosophy, have been acquired by each later generation from an earlier, in a chain whose beginning is a sage who was the

99. Abū Bakr's distinction between "absolute time," one of his five eternal entities, and the "relative time" measured by and dependent on celestial motions, has been discussed in the first chapter of this work.

first to possess them, and that that sage became acquainted with these complexities by means of support and revelation from God—be He exalted and glorified—and is to be counted among the prophets. For no one has the capability to attain to the knowledge of these things in any other way.

The argumentation we have presented will suffice as an indication and proof of our position. We will conclude by stating that if the sages to whom these foundations are attributed really were their starting point, then this occurred in the way we have stated. If not, then they took them, piece by piece, from those who preceded them, each of them, like their predecessors in turn, depending on support from God—be He exalted and glorified—until one finally reaches someone who really was the first and whom God initiated by teaching him these things. For God—be He exalted and glorified—sent His prophets and taught them, from every sort of thing, that which people need in their affairs, both secular and religious; and that is what makes the world function properly. If God—be He exalted and glorified—had not taught them they would not have known. For He created all creatures, He knows all that is apparent and hidden, and He does not give a share of His knowledge of these things to any of His creatures except the prophet. He is "the Knower of the Unseen, and does not reveal His Unseen to anyone except whom He approves as a Messenger";[100] He "knows best where to place His message";[101] "and He gives no one a share in His governance."[102]

—Everett K. Rowson, translator

References

Abū Sulaymān al-Sijistānī. *Kitāb al-iftikhār*. Ed. M. Ghalib. Beirut: 1980: 43–56.

Corbin, H. "De la gnose antique à la gnose ismaélienn." In *Oriente et Occidente nel medioevo: Atti del XII convegno Volta*. Rome: 1957, pp. 138–43; Reprinted in his *Temps cyclique*, pp. 203–208; English translation, "From the Gnosis of Antiquity to Ismāʿīlī Gnosis." Trans. by J. W. Morris, in Corbin, *Cyclical Time and Ismāʿīlī Gnosis*, London: 1983, pp. 187–93.

Ghalib, M. *Aʿlām al-ismāʿīliyyah*. Beirut: 1964, pp. 97–98.

Goriawala, M. *A Descriptive Catalogue of the Fyzee Collection of Ismāʿīlī Manuscripts*. Bombay: 1965, p. 8.

Halm, H. "Abū Ḥātim Rāzī." In *Encyclopedia Iranica*. Ed. E. Yarshater. Vol. I: 315. Extracts from Abū Ḥātim's *Kitāb al-iṣlāḥ* and from other Ismāʿīlī works on the subject are to be found in Halm, *Kosmologie*. Wiesbaden: 1978, pp. 206–27. Hamadānī's introductory comments in his incomplete edition of Abū Ḥātim's *Kitāb al-zīnah*. Cairo: 1957–58. Vol. I: 14ff.; also, "Some Unknown Ismāʿīlī Authors and Their Works." *Journal of the Royal Asiatic Society* (1933), pp. 359–78.

Ivanow, W. *The Alleged Founder of Ismāʿīlism*. Leiden: 1952, pp. 87–89. Also his *Studies in Early Ismāʿīlī Treatises*. Leiden: 1983, pp. 30–46 and 116ff.; also representing

100. Qur'ān 72:26f.
101. Qur'ān 6:124.
102. Qur'ān 18:26.

some misinterpretations of Abū Ḥātim's views in his *A Guide to Ismāʿīlī Literature*. London: 1933, pp. 24–26.

Poonawala, I. K. *Bibliography of Ismāʿīlī Literature*. California: 1977, pp. 36–39.

Sezgin, F. *Geschichte der arabischen Schrifttums*. Leiden: 1984, Vol. I: p. 573.

Stern, S. M. "Abū Ḥātim al-Rāzī." In *The Encyclopedia of Islam*. Leiden-London: 1960 on. Vol. I: 125.

5

ḤAMĪD AL-DĪN KIRMĀNĪ

Ḥamīd al-Dīn Kirmāni ibn ʿAbd Allāh was a prominent Ismāʿīlī philosopher and a prolific author who lived during the reign of Ḥākim bi-Amr Allāh, the Fāṭimid caliph. Kirmānī, who has been called by some the "Ismāʿīlī Ibn Sīnā," died some time after 411/1021. He spent a major part of his life as a *dāʿī* missionary in Iraq and later Egypt and was given the title *ḥujjat al-ʿIrāqayn* ("Proof of the two Iraqs"), the Arab and the Persian. Not much is known about his activities in that region, but based on the title of his book *Kitāb al-majālis al-baghdādiyyah wa'l-baṣriyyah*, which has not survived, he must have had extensive discussions with the learned circles in Baghdad and Basra. In the early part of the fifth/eleventh century, Ḥākim bi-Amr Allāh had been pronounced by some as "divine". Kirmānī went to Cairo to settle a dispute that had erupted concerning the nature of the Imāmat and the "divinity" of the caliph. Kirmānī wrote a treatise entitled *al-Risālat al-wāʿiẓah* refuting the "divinity of Ḥākim and arguing for the absolute transcendence of God. He also wrote a major work (408/1017) entitled *al-Wāʿiẓah fī nafy daʿwat ulūhiyyāt al-Ḥākim bi-amr Allāh*, as a response to the supporters of the "divinity" of Ḥākim.

Intellectually, one can consider Kirmānī as a link between Abū Ḥātim Rāzī and Nāṣir-i Khusraw, and some of his work, such as *al-Aqwāl al-dhahabiyyah*, which is a direct descendent of Rāzī's *Aʿlām al-nubuwwah*, attests to this intellectual lineage.

While it does not appear that later Ismāʿīlī thinkers have been influenced by Kirmānī, he had been a voice of moderation arguing against certain extreme positions of Ismāʿīlīs as well as other Shiʿite sects who practiced antinomianism and argued concerning the observance of the *Sharīʿah*. In his arguments against the deification of the Imams, Kirmānī quotes Jewish and Christian sources, often in Hebrew and Syriac. He had a vast knowledge of Islamic metaphysics and made an attempt to treat a wide range of philosophical topics in his work *Kitāb al-riyāḍ fiʾl-ḥikam bayn al-saʿdayn ṣāḥibay al-iṣlāḥ waʾl-nuṣrah.* The discussions contained in this work are indicative of the sort of issues that were of concern to Persian philosophical circles.

The first translation we have included in this chapter is from *Rāḥat al-ʿaql*, a treatise that is generally regarded to be the most important work of Kirmānī. This book, which is comparable to the *Najāh* or *Shifāʾ* of Ibn Sīnā in its rigor and intellectual profoundity, traces the development of Ismāʿīlī thought from its beginning with the "proto-Ismāʿīlī" works of the second/eighth century, such as *Umm al-kitāb* and the Jābirean *Corpus*, and reaches its zenith with the work of Kirmānī. *Rāḥat al-ʿaql* is a *summa* of philosophical and theological issues pertinent to Ismāʿīlī thought, a work that is indicative of earliest attempts to systematize Ismāʿīlī philosophy and to bring about an understanding of the truth based on two precepts: first, one has to have lived a morally virtuous life by upholding tenets of the faith; and second, the adept must have prepared himself philosophically. *Rāḥat al-ʿaql* is an allegorical work that has been arranged in chapters and paragraphs. Chapters are called *aswār* (walls) and paragraphs, *mashāriʿ* (paths). The novice has to travel through fifty-six paths within seven walls in order for the soul to gain the knowledge of reality. Reality, Kirmānī argues, is divided into four different realities, first the world of Divine creation or the incorporeal world (*ʿalām al-ibdāʿ*); second, the realm of nature (*ʿalām al-jism*); third, the domain of religion (*ʿalām al-dīn*), which corresponds to the hierarchy of the Ismāʿīlī *daʿwah*; and finally, the return of the world to its original oneness with God. The consciousness of this metaphysical process is attainable through philosophical knowledge, and in this regard, Kirmānī's metaphysical scheme shows the extent of influence of the Neoplatonic concept of emanation (*inbiʿāth*).

In the first section of this chapter, Kirmānī offers an argument for the existence of God using a version of the cosmological argument. In the second section, he speaks of the way the Unmoved Mover moves all things; then questions concerning the Divine Intellect and Nature are discussed. The third section offers a discourse on the question of emanation. The manner in which emanation is issued forth from the First Intellect and the necessary and unintentional nature of it are among issues discussed here.

The second part includes the entire translation *of al-Risālah al-durriyah* (The Brilliant Epistle), which deals with God's unity (*tawḥīd*) from a philosophical point of view. Kirmānī begins by praising God and the Prophet Muḥammad and then explains the reason for writing this treatise. A discussion concerning the nature of unity and the unified is presented and different connotations of the concept of unity are investigated both conceptually and linguistically. The relationship between unity and a person who stands in a unified relationship is elaborated upon as well as such topics as multiplicity and necessity.

—M. Aminrazavi

Rāḥat al-ʿaql

REPOSE OF THE INTELLECT

To establish the creation, which is the first existent, that its existence is not by virtue of its own nature, and that it is a cause in which all the other existents culminate, and that it is neither a body, nor a potentiality in a body, but that it transcends the corporeal world.

[59] We affirm that, because of the Most High's exaltation above all degrees of rank, whether of perfection and deficiency or of unity and multiplicity, and because the privative particle *lā* denies of Him all attributes and all descriptions which are the mark of originated things and, as we have previously indicated, places Him beyond what intellects can reach by their light and their thoughts, it is hopeless to find a way to comprehend Him by means of any attribute. Thus, there must be other than the Most High, something of which attributes may be predicated, an existent, which is within the capability of intellects to attain and of discourse to discuss. Since that thing other than the Most High, whose existence is by the Most High's originating it, is that of which intellects are able to attain discursive knowledge and about which they can give information derived from attributes present in the created cosmos, we affirm that that which ranks first in existence is conceived to have not been, and then to have come to be, by way of creation and origination, from nothing, on the basis of nothing, in nothing, by means of nothing, for nothing, with nothing. It is the first thing. Thus, its existence is, in terms of ranking, an enduring existence and a first existence, by reason of its being a first end and a first cause on which the existence of all other existents depends, heading toward the second end. An analogy to this is found in the number one, in its relationship to the existence of numbers generally. It is ranked first and established by its being a first end and a first cause on which depends the existence of all other numbers, heading toward the second end. This establishes it with regard to the ranking of the existents. With regard to actuality, and its necessary emergence into existence, if the existence of the first were not established there would be no way for the second to attain unto existence, and if the existence of the second were not established, there would be no way for the third to attain unto existence. Thus there can be no existence for the second and the third except by establishment of the existence of that which precedes them, and is a cause of their existence.

[60] From the existence of the third and the fourth and other existents the existence of a first is established. It is a cause, the absence of which would entail the nonexistence of subsequent members of the series. Thus, by their very exis-

This translation is based on Ḥamīd al-Dīn Kirmānī's *Rāḥat al-ʿaql*, edited by M. K. Ḥusayn and M. M. Ḥilmī (Cairo: Dār al-fikr al-ʿArabī Press 1952), pp. 59–68.

tence, existent things establish that there is a first principle from which they descend, in their ranks, in existence. That first principle we call the First Intellect and the First Existent. Its existence is not by Its own nature, but by the creative act of the Exalted One, blessed be He.

Moreover, we affirm, on the contrary, that, since the existents are dependent for their existence on causes prior to them, and since every existent thing, in its nature, is the act of that which precedes it in the chain, being its object in terms of matter and an agent in that which is lower than it in terms of matter, the existence of existent things indicates necessarily that all existents terminate in a cause which is the certain terminus of all causes. This ultimate cause, in its nature, is an act proceeding from the One of Whom it is inappropriate to say that He is an Agent. It is an object, but not material. It is, furthermore, an agent, but not in a matter that is other than itself. That is to say that the existence of the existent thing is dependent upon the establishment of its cause that precedes it, whose nonexistence would entail its own nonexistence. Take the number nine as an example, which is a cause for the existence of ten. When its existence is not established, the existence of ten is impossible. Thus, if the existence of the existent things is established, so too are the various causes established—as is the fact that they continue to ascend from multiplicity toward that which is prior to them, growing fewer until they culminate in a single established thing, a cause which terminates all causes—like the number nine, whose existence indicates the existence of eight, and the existence of eight which points to the existence of seven. Thus, the process of ascent from multiplicity does not conclude until it resolves itself in that from which they come to exist, culminating in an established number one. This is the cause of all of them, and it is by it that they exist. Thus, that number one is prior in rank and its existence is not by its own nature. Rather, it is, in its nature, an act proceeding from the One of Whom it is inappropriate to say that He is an agent. It is an object, but not material. It is, furthermore, an agent, but not in a matter that is other than itself. Rather, we say that it is an act in its nature, by reason of its being a first existent according to what we said afterward about Him of Whom it is inappropriate to say that He is an Agent. Thus, by reason of its being an agent and an act, its being an act necessarily implies its quiddity. This leads to what does not end, according to what we made clear in our treatise known as "The Meadow," bearing witness to what we said about the establishment of a first, on whose existence depends the existence of all else, and resolving the existents into their causes and their ending in one whose existence is not [61] by its own nature, but by reason of another. That is to say that we find the human being, which is the last of existents and their second end, to resolve into many things which are objects, like the matter from which he was made, are all of them, the realm of nature. Many things are agents, for which the realm of nature becomes a matter and in which they act in order to bring to existence that which is supposed to exist, like the human being and other things. These are, all of them, active. These are the angels to whom the world is entrusted. He—that is, the human being—is an agent acting in matters other than himself when creating artificial forms, and an object of the realm of nature, and an act of the angels who are actual, and His activity comes by reason of his being the act of another who undertook his actualization, that is, his creation. We found the realm of nature and the agents in it divisible into things that are not, in multiplicity, like the realm of nature in what unites it and the actors in it, but fewer in number. These are prime matter and form, together, and that to which prime matter and form become matter in the creation of the celestial spheres and the elements. These are the angels, by which I mean the active element. The realm of nature and the agents in it are agents to the human being and various others of the existents, but are also an object to that from which they spring. As for the realm of nature, it is composed of prime matter and form, and as for the agents there is that which is, like them, an agent, but is prior to them, and an act to the active angel who is prior to all. And their actuality comes from their being an act to that which actualized them.

We found that prime matter and form and the agent that acts in them resolve into one thing, from whom their existence derives, because analysis comes to an end with the principle of multiplicity by natures who admit of nothing behind their principle, which is two, except one. What forbids their resolution into two things, playing the role of mothers and fathers or of the human beings and prime matter that act upon them is that it would lead to an infinite regress, which would cause the nonexistence of the existents. Thus, it has been established by the culmination of analysis in one, upon which depends the existence of all that is other than it, that this one is the established cause, and it is an act in its nature, and an agent in its nature, and an object of action by its nature. Then we affirm, since the potential is deficient, and since its emergence to actuality (which is the degree of perfection) cannot occur except by reason of that upon which it depends and that which is completely actual in its nature and its act, and the souls of men in the realm of nature are potential and, hence, deficient, and their emergence to actuality cannot occur therefore except by reason of something else which is actual, complete in its nature and its act, and since there are those among the souls of men [62] who do emerge to actuality, like the prophets and the legatees[1] and the Imāms, upon whom be peace, and their successors in attaining the two perfections and the two happinesses and becoming a focal point of the virtues and completely free of vices, it is the fully actual in his nature and act by whom they attain their perfection and ascend to the degree of actuality, and it is by their dependence upon him that they exist as complete. Were it not for him, their emergence to actuality could not have occurred. For it is by something completely actual in its nature and acts that potentially actual beings embark upon their emergence to actuality.

Its nature must inevitably be either a body or a potentiality in a body, or else neither a body nor a potentiality in a body, but transcendent to the world of corporeality. For he transcends the world of corporeality. It is not true that he is a body or a potentiality in a body, since all that is comprised within the world of

1. In the Ismā'īlī view of sacred history, each "speaking prophet" or "enunciator" (*nāṭiq*) is followed by an immediate successor known as a *waṣī* (the Arabic term means "legatee" or "executor of a will) or an *asās* ("foundation"). The prophet brings a revelation or a religious law, the true interpretation of which is entrusted to his immediate heir. Thus, for instance, 'Alī ibn Abī Ṭālib was the *waṣī* or *asās* to the Prophet Muḥammad. The legatee was also the first of the Imāms.

corporeality, both bodies and potentialities in bodies, is matter which is acted upon and which, thanks to its deficiencies, receives emanation in order to achieve perfection. It is incapable of acting to grant everything what is appropriate to it, and it is unable to bring it to the end that represents its perfecting, except by means of another that is actual. That is like the higher bodies, which do not attain to actuality by themselves except in the presence of lower bodies which receive their act and are affected by them, and it is like the lower bodies which do not attain to actuality by themselves except by reason of the higher bodies which affect them. They are, all of them—both those that act and those that are acted upon—incapable, by reason of their being the kind of thing that is an object, deficient in their activity from creating many things, except with the help and assistance of another. This is like glass, which nature is unable to bring into being in the same way it produces gold and other such things. The most that it is able to do is to produce that which is then treated by human beings and made into glass. Or, again, this is like iron, which nature is unable to bring into existence in the same way it brings silver into existence, and its existence is dependent upon its management by human beings, and their treatment of it, and their extraction of it from that which is itself incapable of bringing it to the degree of an existent. Or it is like women, whose nature is to be adorned with jewelry and clothing, and an artistic representation on the cheek and dye in the hand, all of which is a perfection to them. [63] It can only produce them, and that which makes an adornment for them is accomplished and completed by human beings. Like the souls of men who are incapable of extracting it/them completely, not needing others in their actuality, and their becoming is an object, needing another to project its act and to perfect it, deficient in its nature and its act by reason of its nature being composed of two things, each one of them distinct from the other. Like the human being, whose nature is composed of two things—body and soul, each one needs the other in its existence. What is deficient by the precedence to the perfect, is complete in nature and in act.

We have postulated that it is complete and perfect in its nature and complete in its action. Now, if it is perfect and complete in both nature and action, the proposition that it is deficient in its nature and action is nullified, and if the notion is nullified that it is deficient, so too is the proposition that it is a body or a potency in a body, since bodies and whatever things are in bodies need other things and are deficient. So it is neither a body nor a potency in a body, and if it is neither a body nor a potency in a body, the proposition is established, as soon as its existence is granted, that it transcends the corporeal world. Now if it is established that it transcends the corporeal world, we assert its being also in need of another in its act. Like the souls that receive its act, undertaking to emerge from potentiality to actuality necessitates its being deficient in its act even if it is complete in its nature. But that which is deficient in its act and complete in its nature is preceded by that which is complete in both its nature and its act, which is higher in rank and priority. From this, it has been established that that which precedes in existence, which is higher in rank, this is the actual by which the potential emerges to actuality. This is the first existent, whose nature is fully sufficient for its act, needing no other.

Since that has been established, along with the fact that the perfect prior which is the first existent is sufficient in its nature and in need of no other in its act, we ask,

Is it possible that this first existent is the Most High, praised be He, Who is exalted above all attributes connected with the existence of existent things, or is it not? This is a quest whose search leads the soul to what is believed in that regard. We declare, it is not possible at all. For it is inevitable that that existent is either that from which creation appears, or it is itself the first created thing. It is absurd that it is that from which creation appears, since that which comes into existence from it is deficient in its act, and the judgment is inevitable that, if it were that from which creation originates, that which comes into existence from it would be perfect, not needing any other in its act. Now, since it is absurd that it is that from which creation appears, it is established that it is the first created thing, perfect in its act, in need of no other, the existent from it, the deficient, that which is in need of an other in its act, which is the first in existence, and the prior in existence, and the perfect in existence, and the perfection in existence, and the First Intellect and the first limit and the first created thing and the thing [64] ranked first in existence. This is the thing of which it is conceived that it was not, but then came to be by way of an act of creation, becoming perfect and eternal. It is the angel brought near to the throne, the greatest of names, and there is no God except that God Who created it.

What we have said about analysis and its culmination in an established thing in which all things culminate also holds true with regard to the realm of religious legislation, which is the prophetic work, and its witness to us is by means of balanced guardianship. It is in keeping with the divine work. That is to say that we analyze that wherein consists the perfection of the human soul, and its life, and its actualization, and we arrive at that from which its existence derives, and we find that it resolves into many things, which are brought together by two things: one of them is the law, which unites its principles, which include the edicts governing the two worships, that of knowledge and that of practical action. In one of them is the shaping of the soul, and in the other consists its establishment as one that, by reason of the perfection of the human soul, plays the part of the macrocosmos, consisting of the celestial spheres and the elements and the stars and their natural powers from the human body and his soul, which are manifold. They are equivalent to the prophetic work, and correspond to it. The other is the Imām, who unites the dignitaries of the religious hierarchy[2] who preserve the religious law and establish its characteristics and promulgate its prominent points and summon to knowledge and practical action according to it, who, by their place and their teaching, allow the existence of the human being *qua* human being, and who, with regard to the perfection of the human soul by affecting it through teaching and guidance and bringing it to the degree of perfection and the abode of the intellects, tread the path of the angels who are entrusted with the world, who are actual with regard to the world, influencing its bodies and its natural powers in order to extract that which is supposed to exist in terms of animals and plants and minerals to bring it to existence and whose existence in the divine work is like their

2. The phrase "dignitaries of the religious hierarchy" points to the important Ismāʿīlī notion of the *ḥudūd al-dīn*, who were the variously ranked officials of the complex organization presided over by the Imām.

existence in the prophetic work and corresponding to it. Just as the elements and their powers, by themselves, have no power to extract their offspring except by things that act upon them, and not from things acting by themselves except by the elements and their powers which affect them. Similarly, the sciences of the law and its principles are not extracted except by the religious dignitaries entrusted with the spread of their sciences and the revelation of that which is hidden in it. It is not, however, true of the dignitaries that they can act upon the soul by itself, except by means of legal precedents and the law's stipulations and its sciences. This is part of the balance and the equivalence between . . . [gap in the text?]

Then we resolved the law with its principles and its characteristics and the dignitaries [65] which have been undertaken to that from which the totality takes its existence, that it might be a trustworthy witness of that to which we resolved the world and the agents in it. We found them resolving themselves into two things, not into many, like the principles of the law, its sciences and its actions, but less than that. One of them is the scripture, with its inimitability. That is equivalent to, and in keeping with, that to which the world resolves itself, in all its basic elements and its celestial spheres and its stars—namely prime matter, which with its form is one thing. The other is the "foundation," who is entrusted with the preservation of the scripture, from which the law comes. It is like the matter to the "foundation." He works in it and extracts its hidden knowledge and expounds it and confirms the religious law and assists it. That is equivalent to the angel who works in prime matter and form, from which comes the corporeal world and nature. We analyze the scripture and the "foundation," resolving them to that from which they take their existence, and we find that their existence is from the speaking prophet, who is one thing. The entire realm of divine legislation culminates, thus, in one end, beyond which there is nothing of the same genus. That is equivalent to that to which prime matter and form resolve themselves, along with that which acts upon them, it being one thing by reason of the fact that the existents culminate in something beyond which there is nothing except that which is not of the same genus as the existents.

It cannot be that the existence of the "foundation" and the scripture is from two things unless from one, since there is no mediator between the speaking prophet and the "foundation" and the scripture which is the source of the religious law and its establishment. Just as it cannot be that prime matter and form and the agent in them resolve themselves into two things by the culmination of analysis in the first of the existents which, if it is not one, leads to an infinite regress, and the existence of that which leads to an infinite regress is impossible. We have found that learners in the realm of divine legislation cannot ascend to the degree of knowledge, and to reaching perfection, except through the existence of a teacher and a guide who has been established to teach them and to guide and raise them. That is equivalent to what we concluded about the necessity of the existence of someone upon whom a potential being depends for his emergence into actuality. Moreover, we found the dignitaries of religion, who undertake instruction and guidance, all of them, high and low, are incapable in and of themselves of extracting the sciences and grasping them, and are in need of someone who will make those sciences clear to them. This corresponds to what we have determined about the incapacity of the existents of the world, both those that act and those that are acted upon, to bring things to their perfection. We have also found whoever cannot extract the sciences on his own to be lacking in both his nature and his act. In his nature, by reason of his being [66] unable to undertake the judgment of the law or in his act by reason of his being not formed to religious and divine knowledge. That corresponds to what we have determined about the path of that which is acted upon and is in need of another for its own act, thus being deficient in its nature and its act, whether in its nature by reason of its being of two things (each distinct from the other), or else in its act, needing another in it.

We found that, with regard to someone who is deficient with regard to his nature and his act, there arises to him someone else, perfect in his nature and deficient in his act, like the "foundation" who is complete in his nature by reason of being perfect, but is deficient in his act, by reason of his being in need, in it, of scripture and religious law in order to be able to work upon souls, and to summon to allegorical understanding and knowledge, corresponding to the "worlds" in the prophetic work, confirming the external meaning that is connected with practical action. That accords with what we determined with regard to the being of him who raises potential beings to actuality, who transcends the corporeal realm, complete and perfect in his nature, deficient in his act by virtue of his need, for the completion of his act, of receptacles which are on the level of matter, on which he acts.

We found the being of the "foundation," as a "foundation," dependent upon the speaking prophet, who is perfect in nature and in act, by whom is his existence and to whom is his return. That corresponds to what we determined about the existence of something prior to that which is complete in its nature and deficient in its act, which is that by which the potential emerges to actuality, complete in both nature and act together. It is the first of all existents, and the first end of the existents. We found the speaking prophet in the world of divine legislation a root, in which culminate all the dignitaries. There is nothing above him except that being who causes him to attain this high degree, he being complete in his nature by his attainment of perfection, complete in his act by reason of his being not in need of what he stipulates and makes plain, and what he brings from the clear scripture to another who is helped by it, except that by which is his support and his completeness from Him Who is above him. That corresponds to what we have determined about the existence of the First Existent as a root, in which everything that exists culminates, and that there is nothing above him except Him Who created him, may He be praised. He is complete in his nature and complete in his act.

From the speaking prophet's being a cause in which all religious things, whether potential or actual culminate, and the equivalence of the existents from him to the divine creation, arises the demonstration that the first thing is a cause in which all causes culminate, just as the speaking prophet becomes a first root from whom exist both the scripture and the "foundation." The first thing becomes a first root from which exist prime matter and the separate form, just as [67] the speaking prophet's being a speaking prophet is not because of who is of his genus among humankind. The first thing's existence is not from whoever is of its genus. Just as the speaking prophet comes into being from another by whom he exists, the first exists by virtue of another. That is the interpretation of the saying of God, "The likeness of a good word is as a good tree" (14:24).

From what we have presented, the establishment of the existence of the First Existent has become clear, and that his existence is not by his own nature, and that he is an act and an agent and something acted upon in his nature, and an end in which all the existents culminate, and that he is not a body and not a power in a body, and that he transcends the corporeal world.

This [Figures 1 and 2] is a picture of these existents in their correspondences and equivalents, that you may see with your own eyes. Blessed be God, the Lord of the worlds. There is no God but He, blessed be He, the Most High, and greatly exalted above that which the wrongdoers say. I take refuge in God, and ask him for assistance, and commit all my affairs unto Him, for truly he watches over his servants.

Figure 1: The Structure of the World of Unity

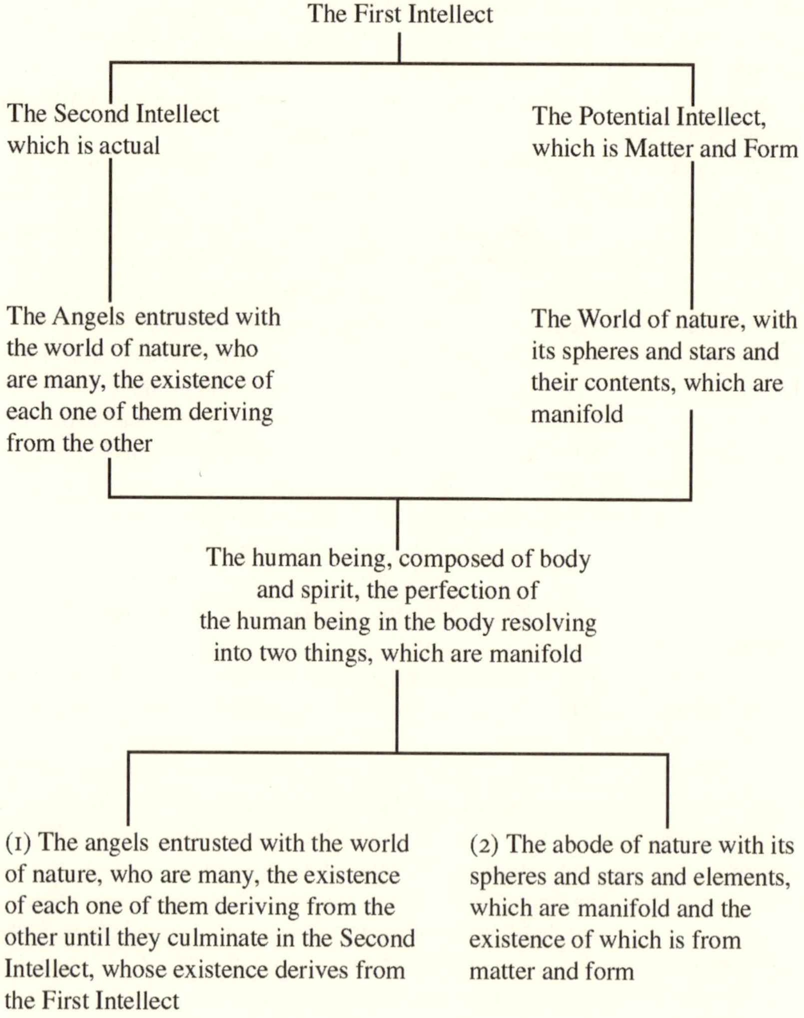

Figure 2: The Structure of the World of Religion

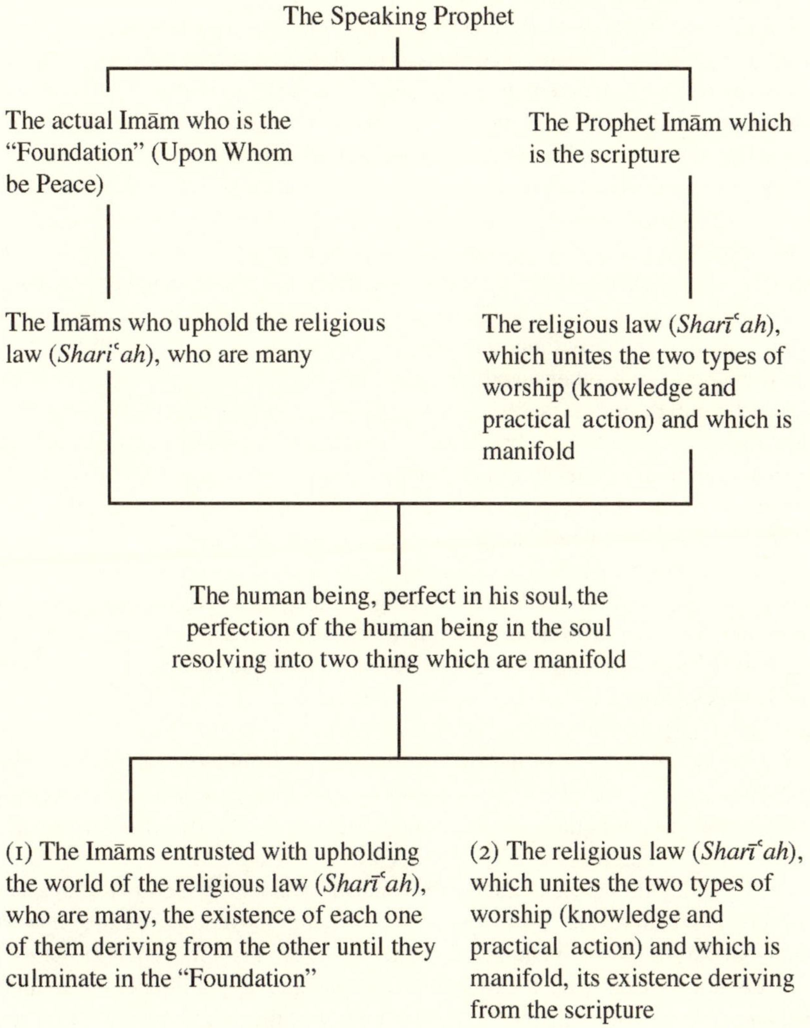

The Speaking Prophet
The actual Imām who is the "Foundation" (Upon Whom be Peace)
The Prophet Imām which is the scripture
The Imāms who uphold the religious law (*Shariʿah*), who are many
The religious law (*Sharīʿah*), which unites the two types of worship (knowledge and practical action) and which is manifold
The human being, perfect in his soul, the perfection of the human being in the soul resolving into two thing which are manifold
(1) The Imāms entrusted with upholding the world of the religious law (*Sharīʿah*), who are many, the existence of each one of them deriving from the other until they culminate in the "Foundation"
(2) The religious law (*Sharīʿah*), which unites the two types of worship (knowledge and practical action) and which is manifold, its existence deriving from the scripture

On his being the prime mover of all moving things, and in what way he moves them, and that he is the cause of the existence of all that is other than himself, and that he does not need anything other than his own nature in his act, and that he is intellect in his nature and a thinker of his nature and an object of thought by his nature (section 3:7, pp. 89–94).

We affirm that motion, since it is a kind of act, and since it is of the nature of acts that they do not exist except by reason of a principle, whether they are in matter or occur in their nature, has a principle from which its existence springs. Since motion is present in the world, it follows that motion has a principle, and since it is established that it has a principle, investigation discloses that this is divided into a principle which is both a mover and a first moved—like the life that emanates from the world of unity and perfection, which is the world of intellect, into the world of body, which is termed nature. This is the mover of bodies according to what is appropriate to them, according to the divine economy. It is that which is moved by its own movement, because it is within the corporeal world. It is moved toward a principle which is a mover and a second moved, like the second perfection in the world of intellect, and perfection in the souls of those who corroborate, which is sometimes called prophecy and at other times is called apostleship, which is the mover of the souls of the human race toward deification, worship, desiring the best and happiness, by its summoning them to practical action. It is also the moved by its awakening a desire and its inspiring fear and its being among them. The movement of the two together is not from their nature but from another, an extraneous movement without purpose accompanying the mover with his intention to move what is other than himself, without the purpose of moving himself. As for the mover of bodies, by reason of his being among them when he moves them that he might obtain what had not been his to obtain of sanctification and glorification and happiness in continuation and everlastingness except by his moving of them. This is a moving which is like what happens to a sailor, who moves his boat, which he himself is in. Or it is like what happens to the soul, in terms of movement, when it moves the parts of its body in order to change location. As for the mover of souls, by his being of the human species when he begins the summons to deification and worship and instruction and inspiring desire and fear in order that he attain what had not been his to attain in terms of station, except by his summoning and his instruction and his deification his worship, then he is necessarily moved, even if it had not been his purpose to move his nature. And since the movement of the two of them is not from their nature, but rather [90] from another, their being set in motion cannot be except for their need for their motion, which is their act of contact with something by which came their motion by their natures.

For, if they do not need another for their movement (which is for a certain purpose) in which resides the purpose of their being moved, nor do they need to reach that purpose by their natures, then they are not in movement, just as the soul, if it were not in need, when seeking vengeance on another, of direct movement of the hand, which is other than itself, for striking, and the tongue for invective, and the person as he is for boldness, movement would not have been necessary in the first place. And since their movement would not occur except because of their need in action for another which functions, with regard to them, as that which receives their action (like relationship of the body to nature, or of learning souls to helping souls), so that it attains, by them together, perfection, and since, with regard to station, the deficient thing which lacks is beneath the perfect which has no need, this necessitates, from the perspective of divine organization, that there be in existence that which precedes the moved mover needing another in its act, such that it does not need in its action any other that would imply a lack in it. So it possesses a perfection by which it can dispense with help in bringing action to existence by another; and the existence of such a being is necessary.

There is nothing that precedes the moved movers and has perfection, power, glory, abundance, splendor, radiance and lights, and that dispenses by its nature with need of another, other than the Creation, which is the first created being and the First Existent. It is the Creation, which is the first created being, and the First Existent, which is the prime mover, which does not move, and its movement of another is like the movement that a beloved brings out of its lover, or like the movement of the magnet stone moving iron toward it. The matter in this is that the first moved mover, which is one of the emanated things, is its limit and its second perfection, on which depends its undertaking sanctification and glorification and praise, and in which is its joy, its happiness, its continuation and its endurance in its thinking of what precedes itself in existence, the prime mover, which is the Creation and the First Existent. Its thinking of it is a form in its nature, undertaking for it by that the actualization of which is perfection in sanctification, glorification, praise and joy in what he has of perfection and continuation and joy. The form always is an agent in what is to it a form, moving it to what it has to be moved to, and this form, which is its mover, moves it to the doing of what its perfection necessitates, by which it attains to it, and necessitates sanctification and glorification and joy in continuation and eternal existence.

[91] Thus he does not find any alternative at his preparation to this action to using the body, in which he is, for his perfection in his existence is not by his nature, but by the two of them together. For this reason it is said, since the perfection of the body, which is the first perfection by what moves it, makes this a boundary to the soul, it is the perfection of a high natural body to a limit which it reaches, and when the body is used for an action the movement which is the most lasting of motions and the most perfect of them takes place. It becomes by that a mover of corporeal things and a moved thing by their motion, and by the continuation of its act is what perfection necessitates by way of sanctification, glorification, praise, joy, happiness and splendor, the extension of the movement to continuation and eternity.

Thus, the cause of the movement of the moved is this intelligible form from the creation, which is the First Existent. That form is the First Existent's perfection, and reception of the emanation which flows through all of the existents, giving them existence and continuation, demands it. By this form, the prime mover becomes a prime mover to all that is other than it, and the moved becomes a first moved by its nature. If we believe there to be motion in it, it is but the grasping of its nature by its nature, and its joy in its nature by reason of its sublimity and glory and its acknowledgement of incapacity to comprehend what comes into existence from it.

The way of this first moved mover is not the way of the intellects that emerge from it, which are free of receptive matter or of what is, to them, like an object; for that which emerges from the intellects whose natures are intellects, and thinkers, and objects of thought, and the nature of the first moved mover is not altogether intellect, since there is in its nature that which is not intellect. This is the body, which is like matter to it, and like the object in which it works, and its intellect is thought not by its subject but rather by its form, the perfection of which consists in the thinking of that which emerges from it. Then that it is a cause for the existence of what is other than itself, meaning that the existents are the caused effects of their causes, and their causes are prior to them in rank, in terms of existence, and they are the limits to them. There is nothing among the existents which is the limit of all limit and prior to every prior, except the creation, which is the first created thing and the First Existent, and it is thus the cause of the existence of everything other than itself. Since the creation, which is the created thing that precedes everything, is in everything, if it were not, the cause for the existence of everything other than itself, there would be no existence of existent things. But since the existents do, in fact, exist, it is necessary that there be that in which the existents culminate, which, if you go beyond it searching for something else behind it, you go beyond to that which has the existence of a cause on which depends the existence of the totality. There is not that in which the existents culminate, nor a thing behind it, except the creation, which is the created thing, and the first created thing is the cause of the existence [92] of the existents in the same manner as the number one is the first of the numbers.

There follows the impossibility of a thing's being the cause of the existence of another thing, which does not occur except by reason of an obstacle which hinders its causation, either an obstacle in its own nature or an obstacle external to its nature and different from it. And since there is no obstacle to the first created being which prevents its acting with the totality of its power—neither externally, from a thing which precedes it, nor from its own nature, in terms of a matter which hinders it—the first created thing, which is the creation, is the cause of the existence of the existents. Furthermore, the existence of a thing from another thing does not come about except by the first thing's being in the utmost of perfection and the extreme of completeness, excellent in its nature, having richness and power and possessing the generous offers of its nature that allow the existence of things from it—like the knowledgeable man, possessing the sciences, who helps the student. If he were not knowledgeable, it would be impossible for a knowledgeable person to arise from contact with him. Or it is like the jar which, when it is filled with water, is able to overflow. But if the jar contained only a small amount of water, it would stand in need of water from another jar, and would be unable, on its own, to overflow. But since the creation, which is the first created thing, is at the peak of perfection and the extreme of completeness and richness and excellence, it is the cause of the existence of that which is other than it.

Now, since the first created thing is the first living thing, and since it would not be living if it did not act, the first created thing is necessarily an agent. And since it is an agent, and the agent is the cause of the existence of its effect, it follows that the first created being is cause to the existence of that which is other than itself. Thus, it is the prime mover and the first cause.

Furthermore, since it does not need others for the production of its actions, owing to its perfection, for its action is upon its own nature, and its nature is the matter for its nature, upon which it works, and its nature is the form for its nature, by which it works. That which has an existence of this kind does not need another for its act, and thus it is not permitted that that which comes into existence from

Him need an other in its act, for it is not permitted that there be two distinct things coming into existence except from two things necessitating their existence. What combines two things is composite, and whatever is composite is preceded in the order of existence and has something that is prior to it. Since God, be He praised, is exalted above being composite, and above an attribute being attached to Him, it is impossible that two distinct things take their existence directly from Him. And since it is impossible that two distinct things take their existence directly from Him, it must be that that which comes into existence from Him is one. And since it is one, and an agent not needing any other for [93] its act, the first created being, by virtue of its being first in existence and cause of the existence of that which is other than itself, does not need any other for its act.

For this reason, we affirm that [human] souls, when they need the help of the senses, which are distinct from them, for their act, are like the souls of animals, which do not survive death. And every soul rises in action to the highest degree, preserving it, and in knowledge to the summit of the existents, and it comprehends them in what diffuses in its nature from the light of unity, arising with that which is other than itself, needing the senses in its actions. The light of unity demands it and maintains close connection with it and helps it, after it had been the one demanding the light and being the connection to it. Thereupon, the first created being is intellect, and thinker, and object of thought. Thus, its being intellect is by virtue of its being the pure intellect, coming into existence directly from God Most High, and its being a thinker comes by virtue of its act in its own nature, and its comprehension of it, which is its thinking of it. It does not need, in its thinking of its nature, which is its act, any other, as we need it in our comprehension of our own natures, in terms of knowledge and thinking, things other than ourselves which help us. But, rather, the nature of that intellect is that it thinks its own nature. And its being an object of thought comes by virtue of its nature being intelligible to it, and it does not need a thing other than itself in order to be an object of intellection. Rather, its nature is intelligible by nature. The thinker is the object of thought, and the object of thought is the thinker. It is one nature, like the situation of the intellects in nature, at their comprehension of their essence and their knowledge of their nature, that it is a living essence grasping the forms which precede it in existence. That which comprehends its essence and knows its nature to be a living essence is nothing other than it. Indeed, it is the comprehender and the knower of its nature, and that which is comprehended by it and known by it is nothing other than itself, but is it itself. It is that which knows its nature and is known by reason of its nature, and the known is the knower, and the knower is the known. It is one nature.

Thereupon, the intellects in nature rather think these intellects which transcend them, by reason of their being like them, such that they are intellect by their ascent to the realm of perfection and the existents which have perfection, and they are thinker by its thinking of its nature, and they are the object of thought by its nature's being an object of thought by reason of its intellect, which is the thinker. Thus the first created being does not need for its act that which plays the role played by matter for agents. For if its act could not be brought to completion except in some receptive matter, it would not deserve to be first in existence. Instead, it would be necessary that something precede it, something which caused that from which it took its existence. And since the Most High is exalted and glorified beyond His being something that can have something prior to it, it is necessary that that which exists from Him be exalted above being [94] associated with something else. So, if there is not anything else with it, and if it is cause to all else, it does not need anything other than itself. God Most High made this clear when He said, "O ye people, reverence your Lord who created you from one soul, and created from it its partner."[3]

He makes clear in what He created in terms of horizons and souls, which are the balance scales of religion and the measure by which the realities of things are known in their balance and their congruence, and He indicates this, may He be praised, in His saying "We shall show them our signs in the horizons and in their own souls until it becomes clear to them that it is the truth."[4]

This testifies of the speaking prophet's being first among the dignitaries in his age, and a preacher to all of what moves them to worship of their Lord, and a worker in their souls of the forms of unity, by reason of the first being a mover to all moved things to what will cause them to praise their maker, and from the perfection which pertains to the speaking prophet being in his fulfillment to the end, which draws by its perfect actions and its polished utterances the people to its summoning. He is the cause of the multitude's following him, and their obedience to him and their separation from relatives in allegiance to the love they have for him. For the existence of the perfection which is in the first in its most extreme form is the cause which moves others. That occurs in the manner in which the beloved moves the lover. From the speaking prophet's being comes the cause for the existence of all the existents in the realm of religion in his age, of which he is the first, and the principle of its wealth and its ordinances and its dignitaries. The first being the cause of the existence of what is other than itself, and from the speaking prophet's being comes his perfection in laying down laws of worship and establishing the rules of unity which are the source of happiness, from any helper, i.e. the First does not need another than himself in his act. And from the speaking prophet's being an intellect in his nature, and a thinker in his nature, and a thinker of his nature by reason of his nature, and intelligible in his nature by reason of his nature.

If he has finally reached perfection, that the first is like that—intellect, thinker, and object of thought—then let Him be praised, Who is exalted above the imagination and the thought, for He is veiled by the splendor of His creation from being comprehended by an attribute. There is no god but He, and there is no change and no power except by the aid of God, the Exalted and the Great.

I take refuge in God and seek His help, and I commit all my affairs unto His care, for He is watchful over His servants. God is sufficient for us, best of guardians, best of masters, best of helpers.

3. Qur'ān 4:1.
4. Qur'ān 41:53.

On the Manner of Emanation

[97] We said in what preceded that each of the existents, since they are many, is distinguished by a name appropriate to it and indicative of it. The first intellect, which is the first created being, was created from nothing, and is distinguished by the name of "Creation," by reason of its being of the essence of an act proceeding to existence from the Exalted One, praised be He, not from a thing playing the role of matter among the essences of the existents. We made it clear that a knowledge of the manner of the creation is veiled, and that the intellects despair of a way to lift that veil and to attain to such knowledge, this is because He is such that He is not grasped by their essences and because, when seeking to grasp Him, they need to emerge from being intellects.

But in the emergence of the intellect from its being an intellect is the negation of its essence, and the indication that the manner of creation is not like the manner of emanation, which luminous intellects have grasped and of which they have given account. For, if it were like them, creation would be emanation, and emanation would be creation. So the notion that creation is to be grasped in the same way that emanation may be grasped is refuted, according to what we have made clear in what has preceded.

Emanation is an effect that does not proceed from primary intention, and it is an existence from which emanates an essence that combines two things: by one of them it grasps or comprehends, and by the other it is grasped or comprehended. Thus, this essence—at its perception of its nature and its joy in it—radiates. Accordingly, there emanates from the midst of the two things emerging from it something that is established with the very establishment of the essence. This means is that the creation, which is the first created thing, since it is living by its essence, and powerful by its essence, knowing by its essence, perfect, eternal, an intellect, an intelligizer, and much more, according to what we have explained in the foregoing, by reason of its being at the summit of the virtues. Its essence comprehends its nature by means of its power, by virtue of its power, and perceives and thinks it. Furthermore, its essence, which is that of an intellect, becomes an intelligizer of itself, and its self or essence, in turn, is an object of intellection for its essence as an intellect. No obstacle hinders it, neither an external one nor one in its essence, from what its perfect power necessitates. And it sees what it loves of its essence—for instance, that it is first in existence, that nothing precedes it, that it is a cause on which depends the existence of the existents, and that it is the ultimate in brilliance, light, luminosity, glory, exaltedness, greatness, pride, immensity, power and splendor, and that it is pure act that emanates into existence without an intermediary in existence between it and the Exalted One [98], may He be praised. It rejoices in its essence, in its state at that glance, with a rejoicing that exceeds all rejoicing, and it is delighted with a delight that has no analogy to the existents in ourselves, because of their deficiency in perceiving the desired and attaining to the beloved. For it is greater and mightier.

From that pleasure at the radiation of its essence—at its comprehension of its essence and its intelligizing of it and its glance at it in its essence, rejoicing in it—

there occurs, from it, a radiance of light. It is like what happens to the blood when happiness arises in the soul upon the meeting of its sweetheart, viewing its beloved. The interior color red permeates to the exterior of the body, to the cheeks, and appears in the skin of the face. However, owing to the existence of obstacles appearing in its nature and to its incapacity, this redness does not go further and does not penetrate the extremities of the body beyond its appearance in the skin of the face. And what emerges from that light at its radiating—since the essence that radiates from it is free of obstacles, and owing to the completeness of its power—arises outside it, established, standing stable in accordance with its cause. The situation resembles what comes from the sun when it shines upon the face of the water, or upon the surface of a polished mirror. It is an emanation of light emerging from it and standing by its own essence. And its existence is by the existence of the sun and its shining, such that if we were to assume the sun to be eternally established in the sky, shining upon a mirror or upon the surface of water remaining eternally, the light emanating from them would be an eternal existent. For, with regard to the illumination which is appropriate to it, the essence of the Creation (which is the First Intellect) is not like the sun, but greater, and the purity of its essence is not like the surface of the water or a mirror, but more clear, and the beauty and splendor of its nature is more glorious and splendid than any beauty and any splendor. So the glance of the first created being, which is the First Intellect, at its nature, and its intelligizing of it, and its comprehension of it, is like the sun's contemplation of the surface of a mirror and its illumination of it, and the essence's being intelligible and illuminated is like the mirror that is illuminated by the light of the sun, and the existence of the emanation emerging from the First Intellect is like the existence of the light emerging from the mirror by its reflecting the light of the sun that shines upon its exterior. The fact that the intellect and the object of intellection are one nature and one thing is like the fact that the sun and the mirror, from the corporeal perspective, are one nature and one thing. Furthermore, the essence of the First Intellect, by reason of its being both an intelligizer and an intellect, is nobler than they are by being only intelligible or objects of intellection. [99] And if the nature of thc First Intellect, because it is a single creation, is like the being of the sun—i.e., better than the illuminated mirror and nobler than it—and if the two are, from the perspective of their two bodily natures one thing, so the emanation as a shining of light from the nature of the Creation, which is the First Intellect, is established, according to what we have mentioned.

There may emanate from the intellects that are in the realm of nature and that emerge to actuality and attain their second perfection with the passage of time what goes as follows: That is to say that the souls of the speaking prophets, may the blessings of God be upon them, which have become pure intellects, nonetheless continue at the beginning to seek knowledge of what is external to them by means of the senses, which serve as their instruments. They acquire it until, by means of that which shines upon them from the realm of sanctity, they are able to dispense with sensory props. The soul, after having been served by the senses which imparted knowledge to it, becomes a servant to them by reason of its power and its connection with the sources of illumination and light and by its looking to what it conceives as its essence, in that it shows it its power and its capacity, and it leads what it realizes in its essence. The powers of the soul increase in their conceptualization of what is external to them, and they make the common power, which is the imaginative power, which had received from the senses the forms of the perceptibles. It pays its service to it; it is the thing most close to it, formed in its shape.

The imaginative faculty extends itself by increasing the power of the thinking essence, just as it used to receive the forms from outside and lead them to it so that the air was formed from the imaginative power. So there arises for the senses an image which it sees, and this image is an emanation from the soul which has risen to the degree of the intellects and attained its second perfection. Its existence is the opposite of what exists in the essence of the forms by way of the senses.

This seeking for the interior functions as a forming of the soul, and the emanation from the interior to the exterior is a realization of the sense from the intellects of the speaking prophets, upon whom be peace. It is like what we do when we seek certainty of the limit or definition of something, comprehending its reality from reversing the definition of which—whenever it is reversed and its meaning established—the knowledge that it is what we wanted becomes valid. An example is our saying, "Physical objects are long and wide and deep," and our reversal of this, seeking for certainty and knowledge in its reality, by our saying, "Everything that has depth and width and length is a physical object." When the first meaning is established at the reversal, and when nothing has been nullified from it, we attain certainty and knowledge of its reality, that it is its limit or definition and its essence.

Or it is like our saying, "Man is living, articulate, a second emanation," coupled with our reversal [100] of this statement, seeking certainty and knowledge in its reality, by our saying, "Every second emanation that is articulate and living is a man." When the first meaning is established and when nothing is nullified from it at its reversal, certainty is established, as well as the knowledge of its reality and that it is its limit, or definition, and its essence. That means that whatever does not have its definition reversed by attachment of the word "all" to it—and the meaning of the desired differs in its reality—does not correspond and does not take a definition. An instance of this occurs in our statement, "Every human being is an animal," and our reversal of this statement upon seeking and contemplation, that that is a definition to it, by which it is distinguished and which points to its nature, by our saying, "Every animal is a human being," the meaning of which does not correspond to what the first statement mandates by reason of the fact that it introduces into humanity something that does not pertain to a human being. So its falsehood is known, and it is not taken as a definition, but is discarded.

Similarly, the speaking prophets, may peace be upon them, do not comprehend God by knowledge, and there shines out in their holy souls His form, from the world of unity, and they seek Him by the matter which is outstretched toward them from the lights of knowledge from illuminations of the divine realm. And it is reversed from interior to exterior—I mean to say, from the nature of the soul—and is conveyed to the sense which is external to them, and it is represented to them. This is the certain truth, in which there is no doubt.

What is not reversed and does not arise in the senses,—even if they have trust in it—they do not make an unequivocal judgment about it, and they await what will come to be from the divine power of emanation in their natures, for it is not represented to them except by reason of an increase of that power, and that enters into the question of revelation. We will speak at length on that subject in its place, by the power of God and the blessing of his saint which has been emanated upon us.

The exalted religious dignitaries by way of creation, and it is the first emanation, combine all the perfections, not in time, and it is the ultimate of degrees of intellects in their perfection.

By this the human being that emerges from potentiality to actuality in the realm of nature is separated from the human being who is the angel brought near, whose existence is by way of the first emanation in the realm of Creation.

Praise be to God, who guides us. We would not be guided were it not for God's guidance, along with his saint (may God's blessings be upon him). I appeal for pardon to God, and I ask Him for help, and I commit my affairs to Him, for He truly watches over His servants.

—Daniel C. Peterson, translator

al-Risālat al-durriyyah

(THE BRILLIANT EPISTLE)

On the meaning of *tawḥīd* (unification), *muwaḥḥid* (the unifier) and *muwaḥḥad* (the unified)

In the Name of Allah, the Beneficent, the Merciful.

Praise be to Allah, Who is too mighty to have an equal and too sublime to be described by speech in any way. The intellects are perplexed about Him, therefore they barely begin to search for a path to attain something to name Him therewith, but the incapability of reaching Him surrounds them. And the insights (*albāb*) are baffled (about Him), therefore they barely think of something, intending to make it an attribute of Him, but the ignorance of how to judge Him with it seizes them.

I praise Him with the praise of the one who affirms only that which is comprehended of itself by His essence. And there is none among His originated things that is a deity, and there is none among His originated creatures but a supplicant

Translated by Faquir Muhammad Hunzai, from *al-Risālat al-durriyyah fī maʿnā al-tawḥīd,* ed. M. Kāmil Ḥusayn, Cairo, 1952, and the reading of ms. Tubingen DC 1258.

to Him through glorification. And I truly bear witness according to my creation, and thereby I hope to attain salvation and success when there will be no longer time to escape, that divinity is not among the things that can be comprehended by an intellect or a soul, nor is it among those that can be judged by an imagination or a sense, except that while affirming Him they are compelled to say that He is Allah, other than Whom there is no deity. Nor is there anyone worthy of worship (*maʿbūd*) other than Him.

And I bear witness that Muḥammad, the one crowned with the lights of *taʾyīd* (divine help) and holiness and honoured with the leadership of (all of) mankind, the former and the latter, His servant and messenger, invited to the principles of faith (*aḥkām al-īmān*) and to the attainment of mercy in the neighborhood of God, through a law (*sharīʿah*) that he spread and introduced, and practices (*sunan*) that he established and laid down, and obedience that he urged as beneficial and disobedience that he abstained from and prohibited, and pillars of truth that he raised high, and motives of falsehood that he eradicated as something repelled, and a trust that he conveyed yet prevented its assumption. May God bless him with ever-increasing and pure (*zākiyah*) blessing so long as a night becomes dark and a morning shines. And may the peace (of God) continue eternally and multiply sempiternally upon the one who is (divinely) helped (*muʾayyad*) with the comprehensive lights and is rich with the blessed and reverent Imāms from his progeny, his legatee, inheritor of his knowledge, his successor and protector of his authority, ʿAlī ibn Abī Ṭālib, the guardian of the religion and its crown and the custodian of the straight path and its course. And may the best of blessings and salutations of God be upon the pure Imāms, the forefathers of Imām al-Ḥākim bi-Amr Allāh, the Commander of the Faithful, and upon him and those who are waiting to come till the Day of Resurrection.

Now then, when the trial pervaded the people of the guiding mission (*al-daʿwah al-hādiyah*), may God spread its lights, due to the withholding by the sky of the rain, and the perplexity seized them due to the stopping by the earth of the nurturing of the seeds, and the distress surrounded them due to the domination of the famine, and the causes of insanity alternated among them, and the teeth of test bit them, and the vicissitudes of time snubbed them, the wisest of them was flabbergasted and the most clement of them was dismayed. Their hope and expectation diminished. They gave up all hopes and thought that they were doomed to perdition. Then by the favor of the friend (*bi-naẓar walī*) of God (i. e., the Imām) and the son of His Prophet . . . His succour came to them as a mercy. He illuminated for them what was dark and elucidated what was obscure. And that was his chosen, . . . the one who was the most truthful in speaking, the most trustworthy in executing the duty, the most steadfast in the religion, the most firm in obedience and the most long-standing in migrating among them, namely, Khatgīn al-Ḍayf, may God guard him in the best obedience. He appointed him as the gate (*bāb*) of his mercy and the chief *dāʿī* (*dāʿī al- duʿāt*), with the title of *al-ṣādiq al-maʾmūn* (the truthful and trustworthy), so that he may reunite them and preserve their order.

On this renewal of the gift for them, they rejoiced. For (his) favor for them became greater by his gift (read *minḥah*). And (for this) they thanked God, may

He be exalted, and His friend in the earth, may peace be upon him. They used to attend his circle (*majlis*) and converse with one another. Some of the people of *daʿwah* (mission), may God protect its lights, put some questions to make them a means of testing and a way of spreading discord. I thought it appropriate to answer each of the questions according to what has been extended from the blessings of the friends of God on the earth . . . and devote a separate epistle to what I am going to write, so that thereby the pillars of intimacy, by confidential conversation between me and my brethren, may become strong and the soul may be prepared with training to encounter the antagonists and the hypocrites. Thus I decided and wrote this epistle answering the first of the questions and named it *al-Risālat al-durriyyah* (The Brilliant Epistle). For it is a light in its meanings and a pearl in its contents. The rest of them will follow it. I ask God for help to complete them, by His strength and power.

The actual question: A questioner asked and said, What is *tawḥīd*? It is known in our saying that it means "making *muwaḥḥad* (unified, one) (*fiʿl al-muwaḥḥad*)" and the *muwaḥḥad* is the object of the *muwaḥḥids*. But it is not permissible for us to say that God is the object of the *muwaḥḥids*. Further, he said that *tawḥīd* is not possible without the imagination of a multiplicity; it is applicable only to what is made *wāḥid* (one) of the entire multiplicity. But in the divinity there is no multiplicity to make *wāḥid* out of it. Explain this for us.

First, we say that the *Mubdiʿ* (Originator) . . . having no similitude, does not depend on the unification of the unifiers (*tawḥīd al-muwaḥḥidīn*), nor on the purification of the purifiers (*tajrīd al-mujarridīn*), so that He would leave His having no similitude if the unifiers do not unify Him, or that He would leave His transcendence (*min ʿuluwwihi*) from the characteristics of His originated things if the purifiers do not purify Him. But He . . . has no similitude whether the unifiers unify Him or not, whether the purifiers purify Him or not.

And it is the element (*ʿunṣur*) and nature of speech that, when someone intends to inform about the traces and essences that transcend the comprehension of the senses, its meanings become too narrow and too subtle (to convey them), let alone that which (even) the propositions of the intelligence and the soul cannot comprehend. Thus speech is unable to denote that which is not like it. Thus there is nothing in that which is composed of letters, such as a word or speech, which can denote the reality sought in *tawḥīd*. For what is intended to be comprehended about the *Mubdiʿ*. . . through a description, is beyond the most noble meanings that the composed letters can convey.

Since this is the case and it is inevitable to speak and affirm what the rudiments of the intellect neccessitate, namely, an agent from whom the existing actions came forth, nor is it possible to dispense with the expression of the subtleties of the imaginary thoughts that flash in the mind, and (since) the simple letters to which recourse is taken in expression and whence the speech and demonstration come forth, due to their limitation in bearing the subtle meanings, are unable to convey what is not from their element and incapable of informing about what is not from their substance, the speaker is compelled to speak with the most noble, most sublime and most subtle meanings that the letters can convey from their cognation (*sunkh*) and origin. When there is compulsion (to speak) then there is no more noble and more subtle meaning in the speech than *wāḥidiyyah* (being one) and no more exalted than the meaning of our saying "*fard*" (single), owing to the fact that, to that which has no similitude, *fard* may be applied more appropriately, from among that which is composed of letters to Him than *Mubdiʿ* even if it does not befit Him. Since the name referring to His being *Mubdiʿ* (Originator) is due to Him (only) by virtue of His *ibdāʿ* (origination) and He was there while there was no *ibdāʿ*, and He is not He without being *fard*. But He is *fard* forever. And He, as such, is *fard* due to the impossibility of the existence of His similitude.

Again, when the field of thinking is extended in attaining the most appropriate of the meanings which the composite letters convey to be said about the *Mubdiʿ* in bewilderment and compulsion, it is the *fard* which can be applied to Him—even though the meaning (of *fard*) is applicable to some of His originated things (*mukhtaraʿāt*), the field of thinking remaining confined to what the intellect comprehends through its light and to that which its propositions may comprehend of what is beyond it (i.e., the field of the intellect), namely, the meaning conveyed by our saying *"fard"*. For the meaning of *fardiyyah* (being single) in *wāḥidiyyah* (being one) exceeds the meaning of *wāḥid* (one), *aḥad* (unique), and *waḥīd* (alone), in *wāḥidiyyah* by virtue of its being *ṣamad* (One to whom people resort to in their needs, that which has no emptiness, i.e., is self-sufficient). And the meaning of *fard* in *wāḥidiyyah* is not, upon careful examination, to be distinguished from the meaning of *wāḥid* by virtue of its having an additional meaning in *wāḥidiyyah*, except by virtue of its being the cause of *wāḥid*. And that which is the cause always precedes the effect, about which we have spoken in our book known as *Rāḥat al-ʿaql*, with which the darkness of ignorance disappears and through which the light of justice speaks. We have written it as a preface and have extended the field of definition so that it may be helpful for what we want to speak about.

Tawḥīd does not mean—as we have said about the meaning of *fard*, the careful examination of the meaning in communicating about God—that He is *fard*, so that the one who carefully examines (the meaning) may be a *muwaḥḥid*. Nor is it the case that God is restricted to one particular meaning so that by virtue of that meaning, it may be established that He is *fard*. For the glory of His grandeur is in a veil making it impossible for the letters to render it by any means. And how can it be possible for the letters to render it while they barely erect a lighthouse in their composition to guide? But the water of His power overflows, and they barely announce any information to speak with a meaning, small or great, but the incapability (of that) establishes itself and spreads. God, the Existentiator, the Worthy of worship, thus, transcends the rational propositions and the physical qualifications.

Tawḥīd, indeed, is an infinitive on the (grammatical) measure of *tafʿīl*. The philologists do not use this kind of quadrilateral verb-forms except for the one whose action is abundant. For instance, if someone massacres, it is said: "*qattala fulānun yuqattilu taqtīlan fa-huwa muqattil*". The one who kills only once is called *qātil*, but the one who massacres many times, *qattāl*. *Tawḥīd*, with respect to its meaning, has two aspects: One is related to the *ibdāʿ* of the *Mubdiʿ* . . . and the other to the act of the *muʾmin* (believer) who is a *muwaḥḥid* (unifier). With respect to the aspect related to the *ibdāʿ* of the *Mubdiʿ*, *tawḥīd* necessitates a *muwaḥḥid* who is the agent of *wāḥid* (*al-fāʿil li'l-wāḥid*) and a *muwaḥḥad* (unified), which is the object (of the *muwaḥḥid*) in the sense of *wāḥid* (one). And *wāḥid* is used in many ways, such as:

(i) A *wāḥid* is *wāḥid* by virtue of the finiteness of its essence (*dhāt*) toward the sides by which it separates itself from others, such as the bodies of sensible things. In this respect, it deserves to be called *wāḥid*. And its limitation toward the sides and the comprehension of its limits, all this shows that this *wāḥid* is contingent.

(ii) A *wāḥid* is *wāḥid* in the sense that it is given a specific meaning that is not found in others, such as the property of the magnet in attracting iron. In this respect, it deserves to be called *wāḥid*. And its specification with this meaning, with the exclusion of the others, necessitates it to be contingent.

(iii) A *wāḥid* is *wāḥid* in the sense of essence (*ʿayn*), such as the essence of whiteness, the essence of blackness, the essence of a substance, and the essence of a thing. In this respect, all of them deserve to be called *wāḥid*. And the fact that this *wāḥid*, in its existence, depends on the existence of someone other than who precedes it, and that its existence does not detach itself from its essence, being always with it, as long as it has an essence within existence, necessitates its being contingent.

(iv) And the *wāḥid* is *wāḥid* in an absolute sense. The absolute *wāḥid* betrays its essential "pairedness (*izdiwāj*)", which consists of the *waḥdah* (oneness, unity) and its receptacle.

All these aspects (of *wāḥid*) necessitate that *wāḥid* be absolutely contingent. When it is established that *wāḥid* is absolutely necessarily contingent, then it necessitates that *tawḥīd*, which means "making one (*fiʿl al–wāḥid*)," which latter pronounces the contingency of its (own) essence, does not befit the glory of the *Mubdiʿ*. . . . Thus the *Mubdiʿ*, may He be sanctified, is *muwaḥḥid* in the sense that He is the *Mubdiʿ* of *wāḥid* and *aḥad*.

As to (the aspect of) *tawḥīd* related to the *muʾmin* who is a *muwaḥḥid*, it does not mean that he "makes one (*yafʿalu al-wāḥid*)"; rather, it changes from its previous meaning that is "making one (*filʿal-wāḥid*)" to another one. As when the particle "*ʿan*" is used with the verb "*raghiba*" its meaning changes (from the previous one). For instance, when it is said, "*raghiba fulānun ʿan al-shay*'", it means "so-and-so disliked the thing," but the "*raghiba*" alone means contrary to it (i.e., to like). Thus the meaning of *tawḥīd* of the *muwaḥḥid* (in the case of the *muʾmin*) is to divest the *muwaḥḥad* from a certain meaning. As in the sense of isolating (*tajrīd*) or separating (*ifrād*) a thing from another thing, it is said, "*waḥḥadtu al-shayʾa ʿan al-shayʾ* (I isolated a thing from another thing)."

When *tawḥīd* (in this case) means divesting the *muwaḥḥad* from a certain meaning, as we mentioned, and divinity is a necessity whose existence cannot be repudiated and the fact of the agency (*fāʿiliyyah*) is a power that cannot be negated, and from among the things falling under existentiation, from the Originated Intellect (*al-ʿaql al–ibdāʿī*) to the Emanated Intellect (*al-ʿaql al-inbiʿāthī*)—there is that which possesses the highest degree of knowledge, beauty, power, light, might, grandeur, nobility, and sublimity, such as the Intellect, the Precursor (*sābiq*) in existence; and there is that which is below it in rank, such as the Successor (*tālī*) in existence, and so on till what is below them from the world of nature, and what it contains till the human intellect at the end—it is not impossible for an ignorant to think that the divinity lies in some of them. Each of these things (under existentiation) because of the subsistence of the traces (of creaturehood) in it, bears witness against itself that it is not God, then from that proposition it follows that the *tawḥīd*, which means to divest the *muwaḥḥad* (unified)—which because of the subsistence of the traces in it bears witness against itself that it is not God—from divinity and to negate it from it and to isolate it from it and sustainership (*rubūbiyyah*) and what is related to it, is the act of the *muʾmin* who is a *muwaḥḥid*, so that by that *tawḥīd* it may be established that the divinity belongs to someone else. As it is known from the things that fall under existence, there are things that have no intermediaries opposite to those that have intermediaries, such as blackness and whiteness that have intermediaries, such as redness, yellowness, and so on. The things that have no intermediaries, they as such, have two sides, two states and two aspects. That is to say, when one of the two sides is negated by that negation, the other side is established, such as eternal and contingent. They do not have intermediaries between them; when eternity is negated from a thing, contingency becomes inseparable from it. And like substance and accident that have no intermediaries between them; when the characteristic of substance (*jawhariyyah*) is negated from a thing, the characteristic of accident (*sifat al-ʿaraḍ*) becomes inseparable from it. Then it is not imaginable that there is an intermediary between the Lord (*rabb*) and the vessel (*marbūb*), or between the *Mubdiʿ* (Originator) and the *mubdaʿ* (originated) as we have explained the meaning of our sayings, "the *ibdāʿ* (origination) is the essence of the *ibdāʿ*", in the book *Rāḥat al-ʿaql*. Then the *muʾmin* is a *muwaḥḥid* (unifier) in the sense that he divests the *muwaḥḥad* (unified), who is the *mubdaʿ*, from divinity, as he finds the trace of *ibdāʿ* and the subjects and predicates in itself. Thus the Prophet . . . said: "*Al-muʾmin muwaḥḥid wa-Allāh muwaḥḥid* (The believer is a *muwaḥḥid* and God is *muwaḥḥid*)."

Again the meaning of the multiplicity that is necessitated by our saying that "*tawḥīd* stands in two aspects", is either with respect to the *fard* (Single), may He be exalted, . . . that is the *ibdāʿ* of multiplicity, that is multiple singles (*afrād*) and units (*āḥād*), or with respect to the *muʾmin*, who is divesting all these numbers and singles from the divinity, one by one.

And then, first we will tersely show the truth contained in our saying that "the *fard* is the cause of *wāḥid*," according to the capacity of the epistle, even though we have explained it in our books. We say that the existence of all those things that are the essence of the first effect (*al-maʿlūl al-awwal*) is from the essence of the cause, which is the effect and the effect is the cause (*hiya huwa wa-huwa hiya*) by virtue of the effect in its existence being from the element of the cause. And it is the nature of the effect that nothing is granted to and nothing exists in it except what its cause itself has poured forth over it, for what exists in the effect exists in the cause out of which the effect came into existence. For if the existence of what exists in the effect were not in the cause, it would have been impossible to grant the effect that which did not exist in its cause. For instance, fire that is the cause of heating in what adjoins it, had the heat not been existing and subsisting in the essence of the fire, it would not have been found in what adjoins it. And how can a thing grant a thing from itself while the field of its element is empty of it? Or how can it bestow a thing while the bones of its existence are worn out?

When this is the case, we thought to investigate whether the *fard*, which is the cause of numbers, can from its essence indicate the ranks of countable things or not. We found it by virtue of what is hidden in it, such as the letters, their conjunction, their disjunction, their signs, their kinds, their multiplication, their calculation, that it comprises and indicates the entire ranks which God has originated. And the ranks in arithmetic are twelve, even though in form they are nine, vis-á-vis existents. This is the form of twelve ranks hidden in the *fard* . . .

And corresponding to those kinds are the letters of *"lā ilāha illaʾLlāh,"* which show the *ḥudūd* (ranks), over whom the light of oneness pours forth, and upon whom are based the heavens and the earth and what they contain. . . .

The brilliant proof of what we have said in this regard is the existence of the seven letters vis-á-vis the lords of the cycles, through whom and through what is poured forth over the souls from them, the purpose of the spiritual form that is created in their cycles becomes complete. If you calculate the numerical values (of the letters) according to the calculation of the *jummal*, they stand vis-á-vis the days of the sun in one revolution, which are three hundred sixty-five days; the result of the multiplication of the rank four into rank seven stands vis-á-vis the mansions of the moon in one revolution, which are twenty-eight mansions; the result of the values of the letters of the fourth rank according to the calculation of the *jummal* stands vis-á-vis the numbers of the lords of *taʾyīd* (divine help) from the *ḥudūd* (ranks) of every cycle, which are fifty-one; and the result of the multiplication of the letters of the seventh rank into itself, together with the number of the *ḥudūd* of every cycle, except the supreme of them which is one, stands vis-á-vis the Names of God . . . which he who counts them enters paradise, and which are ninety-nine names.

Had we not chosen brevity and decided that prolixity does not befit the epistles, we would have similarly expounded these ranks and numbers with which the abundance of the oceans of the friends of God, may peace be upon them, in sciences and the subtlety of the deduction of their followers from them, specifically and generally, would have been conceived. But this we have left so that the one who thinks about it may have happiness in every moment and the one who reflects on it may renew for him a good deed in every instant from what shines to him from the wonders of wisdom.

Thus it is evident that in the *fard*, by virtue of its being the cause of the *wāḥid*, are contained the ranks of all the countable (lit. that which fall under the number) existents, and that *tawḥīd* with respect to God is the *ibdāʿ* of the *wāḥid* and units (*āḥād*), and with respect to the *muʾmin* is to divest the divinity from the units.

We say that the community, due to its deviation from the lords of guidance and due to relinquishing the injunctions of obedience, does not reach (even) the remotest end of the ways of *tawḥīd*, except a few who follow the friends of God, the Exalted, on His earth, may peace be upon them. Therefore, the one whom they worship with their descriptions of and belief in Him, is not searched for except (in) the one who exists and falls under origination (*ikhtirāʿ*) and His Essence is comprehended by the power of *ibdaʿ*. When the One Whom they worship is originated and over-powered, then their *tawḥīd* is short of that by which they would deserve the garden of paradise and its felicity and falls short of that by which they can enter the garden of eternity and dwell in it.

And how can they reach the eternal blessings while the prerequisite of attaining them is to reach their source? It is unimaginable that a traveler may reach peace, pleasures, bounty and blessings in a desired abode while he is miles away from it. Nay, "Verily, the wicked will be in hell" (82:14). And indeed the negligent are in excruciating punishment. "Say, Shall We inform you who will be the greatest losers by their works? Those whose effort goes astray in the life of the world, and yet they reckon that they do good work. Those are they who disbelieve in the signs of their Lord and in the meeting with Him. Therefore their works are vain, and on the Day of Resurrection We assign no weight to them" (18:103–5). God has refused to pour forth His light except over one who surrenders to His friends and enters the house of His worship through its gate; one who made his *tawḥīd* to divest His originated things from (divinity) and his worship is surrendering to His friends; Whose obedience is his purpose and Whose disobedience his object of fear. And he knows that this world is the abode of tribulation whose star never falls and it is a dwelling of humiliation whose screw never turns. Its delights have to come to an end and what is loved from it is going to perish; its children are bound to extinction and mankind among them to resurrection (lit, gathering and dispersing). We ask God . . . for help to attain peace from its ruses and to take a share from its benefits. May God make us and the community of the believers among the righteous and sincere servants and unite us with our pure lords in paradise (*ḥaẓīrat al-quds*) and in the vicinity of the Lord of the worlds.

I completed this epistle with the praise of God, the High, and with the blessing and peace upon the pure Prophet Muḥammad, the revered and righteous, and with the peace upon the one who is true to his word, ʿAlī, the legatee, and the Imāms from their progeny, the intercessors of their followers and the genera of their species. May the peace of God be upon all of them and the best of peace and greetings upon the *qāʾim* (Resurrector) among us, al-Manṣūr Abū ʿAlī Imām al-Ḥākim bi-Amr Allāh, the Commander of the Faithful. With the praise of God and His help the *Brilliant Epistle* is completed.

—*Faquir M. Hunzai, translator*

References

Baumstark, A. "Zu den Schriftzitaten al-Kirmānīs." In *Der Islam*, 20. (1932): 308–13.
Brockelmann, C. *Geschichte der Arabischen Litteratur*. Leiden: 1943. Vol. I: 325–26.
Corbin, H. *Trilogie ismaélienne*. Tehran-Paris: 1961: passim.
———. *Historie de la philosophie islamique*. Paris: 1964, pp. 130–31.
Goriwala, M. *A Descriptive Catalogue of the Fyzee Collection of Ismāʿīlī Manuscripts*. Bombay: 1965, pp. 37–57, nos. 51–65.

Griffini, E. In *Zeitschrift der Deutschen Morgenländischen Gesellschaft*, lxix (1915): 87.

Hunzai, F. M. *The Concept of Tawḥīd in the Thought of Ḥamīd al-Dīn al-Kirmānī*, Ph.D. diss., McGill University, 1986.

Ivanow, W. *An Early Controversy in Ismailism*. Leiden: 1948, pp. 115–59; 2nd ed., Bombay: 1955, pp. 87–122.

———. *A Guide to Ismailism Literature*, 2nd ed. London: 1933, pp. 43–46.

———. *Ismaili Literature*. Tehran: 1963, pp. 40–45.

———. *A Creed of the Fatimids*. Bombay: 1936, pp. 10–12.

———. *Nāṣir-i Khusraw and Ismailism*. Bombay: 1948, pp. 44.

Kraus. P. "Hebräische und syrische Zitate in ismaʿilitischen Schriften" *Der Islam*, 19 (1930): 243–63.

Madelung, W., and Strothmann, R. *Gnosis-Texte der lsmaʿiliten*. Göttingen: 1943. Also in *Der Islam*, 37 (1961): 119–27.

Nasr, S. H. "Philosophy and Cosmology." In *Cambridge History of Iran*. Cambridge: 1975. Vol. iv: 436–440.

Sezgin, F. *Geschichte der arabischen Schrifttums*. Leiden: 1967. Vol. I: 580–82.

6

RASĀʾIL IKHWĀN AL-ṢAFĀʾ

Treatises of the Brethren of Purity

The *Rasāʾil Ikhwān al-Ṣafāʾ* (*Epistles* or *Treatises* of the Brethren of Purity) were written around the middle of the fourth/tenth century by a group of philosophers from Basra who called themselves the Ikhwān al-Ṣafāʾ (Brethren of Purity). The authorship of the *Rasāʾil* has been the subject of controversy in modern scholarship, but their Ismāʿīlī affiliation cannot be doubted if one reads their *al-Risālat al-jāmiʿah*, a summary, as well as the esoteric interpretation of the *Rasāʾil*, which has been wrongly attributed to Maslamah al-Majrīṭī (d.ca. 398/1007). The *Rasāʾil* comprise fifty-two epistles that are the result of an integration of divine laws revealed to the prophets with Pythagoreanism, Neoplatonism, Hermeticism, and Ismāʿīlī/Shīʿī theosophy. They are arranged in four sections: (1) the Mathematical Sciences, which consist of fourteen treatises; (2) the Physical and Natural Sciences, which consist of seventeen treatises; (3) the Psychological and Rational Sciences, which consist of ten treatises and (4) the Divine Sciences, which consists of eleven treatises.

The central ideas in the *Rasāʾil* are the purification of the human soul, attainment of knowledge and human brotherhood. The emphasis throughout the *Rasāʾil* is to turn from the sleep of negligence and the slumber of ignorance to the awakening of the soul to knowledge and its purification by actions according to true knowledge before entering Paradise. The knowledge that they emphasized embraced all divinely revealed knowledge, and all the branches of traditional knowledge available to them. These different branches of knowledge and different revealed laws, according to them, were medicines and potions for the treatment of sick souls suffering from ignorance, and their means for the salvation from the "sea of matter and bondage of nature" and regaining the best form in which man had been created by God.

At the heart of the *Rasāʾil* is the symbolic significance of numbers and Pythagorean mathematics, which these treatises reflect more fully than practically any other work of Islamic thought. In a sense the *Rasāʾil* are a synthesis of the more esoteric currents of early Islamic thought associated especially with Shiʿism, with both Hermeticism and Neopythagoreanism all integrated into an Islamic esoteric perspective.

In this chapter we have included three treatises. The first section consists of two epistles concerned with the Ikhwān's concept of man. The idea presented by the Ikhwān is that man is the microcosm that epitomizes all the qualities found in the universe, which they called the macrocosm. Man's wholeness is shown by drawing parallels to many of the created phenomena in the universe. The description in these epistles, the use of symbols and analogies, the poetic beauty, and a mystical quality they render, are unlike the other epistles. These two epistles in a sense summarize the whole corpus of the *Rasāʾil.*

In the second section, the first treatise of the division of mathematical sciences of the *Rasāʾil Ikhwān al-Ṣafāʾ* has been included. Following a discussion concerning divisions of abstract sciences into four sections, abstract, logical, natural and theological, further subdivisions are made such as arithmetic, geometry, music, astronomy, etc. The treatise then discusses the nature of numbers, their natural order, special properties, friendly numbers and different categories of them. After an extensive and highly analytical discussion, the treatise is brought to a conclusion with a brief discussion regarding the goal of the sciences.

The third selection is concerned with ecological and environmental crisis. The treatise is based on a fable in which animals charge man with environmental degradation and disregard for others, and they complain to the king of jinns. The translation is a selection from *The Case of The Animals Versus Man Before the King of the Jinn.*

The *Rasāʾil* occupy a unique position in the history of Islamic thought and have exercised a great influence on the Muslim intellectual elite. The complete text of the *Rasāʾil* was first published in 1305–1306/1887–1889 in Bombay, then in 1928 in Cairo (ed. by K. Ziriklī), and then in 1957 in Beirut.

—*S. H. Nasr*

Microcosm and Macrocosm

Twenty-sixth Epistle

On the Maxim of the Sages that "The Man is a Microcosm"

[3] In the Name of God, the Most Compassionate, the Most Merciful.

Praise be to God, and peace be upon His servants whom He has chosen. "God is better than what they associate [with Him]."

This translation is based on *Rasāʾil Ikhwān al-Ṣafāʾ*, edited by Kh. A. Kullī, The epistles are drawn from the Ziriklī edition. The numbers in the brackets in the body of the text refer to the pagination of that edition. (Cairo: Al-Maktab Press 1957), pp. 3–24 and 73–81.

Know, O brother—may God inspire (or assist) you and us with a spirit from Him— . . . we would like to mention in this epistle the meaning of the maxim of the sages that "the man is a microcosm."

Then we say, know that the first sages observed this corporeal world with the vision of their eyes and witnessed the manifest dimensions of affairs with [the perception of] their senses. Then they reflected upon its states with their intellects, scrutinized the characteristics of its universal individuals with [their] insights, and considered the varieties of its individual things with their deliberation. They did not find a single part [of the cosmos] more complete in structure, more perfect in form, and more corresponding in its totality to the cosmos than man. [4] For verily man is a totality brought together from a corporeal body and a spiritual soul. [The sages] found likenesses for all the existent things of the corporeal world in the structure of his body's constitution, such as the astonishing composition of [the world's] celestial spheres, its different kinds of constellations, the motions of its planets, the composition of its pillars and "mothers" (*ummahāt*, i.e., four elements), the diversity of its mineral substances, the various kinds of plants, and the astonishing bodily frames (*hayākil*) of its animals.

Moreover, they also found different kinds of spiritual creatures, such as the angels, the jinn, the human beings, the satans, the souls of other animals, and the activity of their states similar to the human soul with its powers permeating in the structure of the body.

When these affairs became clear to them in the human form, they named [this form] a "microcosm." Here we want to mention a few of these likenesses and similarities so that they give an evidence of the soundness of their view about him, and an explanation of their description of [man] so that it is nearer to the understanding of the learners and easy for the seekers [of knowledge] to contemplate upon them.

On Considering the States of Man with Respect to the States of Existent Things According to our Explanation Here

We say, all the existent things are substances and accidents brought together from matter and forms, and composed from the twain, as we explained in the epistle on "Matter".[1] All the accidents are either corporeal or spiritual, as we explained in the epistle on "The Intellect and The Intelligible."[2] Man in his totality is brought together from two substances connected [to each other]; one of the twain is this corporeal body which has height, breadth, and depth, and is perceptive by means of the senses, the other is this spiritual soul, [capable of] vast knowledge and perception by means of the intellect.

The corporeal body [of man] is a structure which is a combination of the organs of different shapes, such as hands, arms, head, neck, spinal chord, hips, knees, legs, and feet. Each one of them is also composed of the parts which are of different forms,

1. *Rasā'il Ikhwān al-Ṣafā'*, Vol. 2, fifteenth epistle, pp. 3–19.
2. Ibid. Vol. 3, thirty-fifth epistle, pp. 227–42.

ambiguous (*mutashābih*) in parts, such as: bone, nerve, blood vessels, flesh, skin, etc., as we explained in the epistle on "The Composition of the Body."[3] The [above parts] [5] are also engendered from the four humors: blood, phlegm, yellow bile and black bile, and they are also born from the chyme. The chyme is produced from the food, the food from the plants, and the plants from the four pillars [or elements], as we explained in the epistle on "Plants."[4] Each one of [these four elements] is constituted of two natures out of the four known natures, as we explained in the epistle on "Generation and Corruption."[5] Each one [of these four natures] is a form which completes the body and at the same time is a base for the other thing in the natural bodies, as we explained in the epistle on "Matter and Form."

Matter and form are also two substances which are simple, spiritual, intelligible, created and originated as willed by their Creator, exalted be His glory, for activity and passivity, and to be receptive [to His will] without the instrumentality of any mode, time, or space but through His saying, "Be, and it becomes" [Qurʾān, 2:117 etc.], as we explained in the epistle on "Intellectual Principles."[6]

As for man, his state is what you observe. He is, as we reported, a totality brought together from a dark body and a spiritual soul. If one takes into account the state of his body and what it contains, such as the astonishing composition of its organs, and the diverse formation of its articulations, [one finds that] it resembles a house [prepared] for its dweller. But when one takes into account the state of his soul, the wonders of its controlling powers in the structure of the bodily frame, and the permeation of [its] powers in the various parts of its body, [one finds the soul] resembles a dweller in his house along with his servants, wife, and children.

If one considers [the man] in another respect, one finds that the structure of his body with diversity of the shapes of its organs and the variety of the composition of its articulations is similar to the shop of an artisan. In the same way his soul in respect of the permeation of its powers [or faculties] in the structure of his bodily frame, its marvelous acts in the organs of his body, and the various movements in the articulations of his body, is similar to an artisan in his shop with his disciples and apprentices, as we explained in the epistle on "The Practical Crafts."[7]

In another respect, if one considers the structure of his body in respect of the multiplicity of the combinations of the strata of his bodily frame, the wonders of the composition of the articulations of his body, the many diverse organs, the branching and division of his blood vessels and their extension into the regions of the organs, the disparity in the [blood] vessels in the depths of his body, and the activity of the faculties of the soul, [the man] resembles a city full of bazaars with various crafts, as we explained in the epistle on "The Composition of the Body."[8]

3. Ibid. Vol. 2, twenty-third epistle, pp. 318–333.
4. Ibid. Vol. 2, twenty-first epistle, pp. 128–51.
5. Ibid. Vol. 2, seventeenth epistle, pp. 45–53.
6. Ibid. Vol. 3, thirty-third epistle, pp. 200–10.
7. Ibid. Vol. 1, eighth epistle, pp. 210–226.
8. Op. cit. note 3.

[6] In another respect, if [man] is considered from the point of view of the soul's governing control over the states of the body, its good management, and the permeation of its powers and activities in the structure of this body, then [man] resembles a king in a city with his soldiers, servants, and retinue, as we discussed in the epistle on "The Intellect and Intelligible."[9]

In another respect, if one considers the state of the [human] body and its being engendered along with the state of the soul and its configuration with the body, the body resembles the womb and the soul resembles the embryo, as we explained in the epistle on "The Configuration of the Particular Soul and its Emergence from Potentiality into Actuality."[10]

In another respect, if one considers one finds the body like a ship, the soul like the captain, works like the goods of traders, this world like the ocean, death like the shore, the next world like the city of merchants, and God the Exalted like the king who gives recompense there.

In another respect, if one considers one finds the body to be like a horse, the soul like the rider, the world like a racecourse, and works like the race.

In another respect, if one considers one finds the soul to be like a farmer, the body like a farm, works like seeds and produce, death like the reaping, and the next world like the threshing floor, as we explained in the epistle on "The Wisdom in Death."[11]

In another respect, if one considers one finds the marvelous frame of the body, as we explained in the works on anatomy, and the numerous ways the soul benefits from the sciences due to its association with the body, [the body] resembles a school of sciences and the soul resembles a pupil in the school, as we explained in the epistle on "Sense and the Sensible."[12]

In another respect, if one considers the composition of the body, the permeation of the powers of the soul in [the body], and controlling the states of man, [one finds the man] resembles a record full of sciences. It is [also] said that [man] is the epitome of the 'Guarded Tablet'. The sages have constructed many similes [in that context]. We desire to mention briefly some secrets [of those similes] according to what is befitting us.

Man is the Epitome of the 'Guarded Tablet'

It is mentioned that there was a king who was a sage and a chieftain. He had small children [7] who loved him dearly and revered him. He wanted to teach them good manners, cultivate them, and discipline them so that they became fit for joining his court, for it was not befitting for any one to come to the assemblies of the kings except those who were cultivated by courtesy, disciplined in sciences, molded by beautiful character-traits, and purified of the blemishes. He thoughtfully and pru-

9. Op. Cit. note 2.
10. *Rasāʾil*, Vol. 3, twenty-seventh epistle, pp. 25–36.
11. Ibid. Vol. 3, twenty-ninth epistle, pp. 52–67.
12. Ibid. Vol. 2, thirty-fourth epistle, pp. 334–52.

dently arrived at an idea that he should build for them a castle which should be one of the most fortified of buildings, and each one of them should be given a separate seat in it. All around the assembly-hall [in the castle] there should be written every kind of science which he desired them to learn, and to make the forms of everything he desired by means of which to cultivate them.

[When the castle was ready, he brought them] in the castle and seated every one of them in the place allocated for each one, and at their service were placed the attendants, [both] the maidservants and male-servants. Then he said to those sons, "Observe around you what I have sketched before you; study what I have written in it for you; meditate upon what I have explained in it for you, and reflect on them in order to know their meanings whereby you will become outstanding philosophers (*ḥūkamāʾ*) and righteous learned men. Then I will receive you in my assembly. You will become my favorite, eminent confidants. You will always be in comfort so long as I am there and you are with me."

Now what he had written in that assembly-hall for them was something from [each] science. On the highest dome of the assembly-chamber he had sketched the form of spheres, explained their mode of circular motion; the constellations and their apogee, the planets and their motions. Besides, he had clearly given their proofs and laws.

In the courtyard of the assembly-hall he had sketched the form of the earth, the division of climes, the terrain of mountains, oceans, lands, and rivers, and explained the borders of towns, cities, highways, and countries.

In front of the assembly-hall he had written the science of medicine and the science of natures; the forms of plants, animals, minerals with their species, genres, and individuals, and explained their characteristics, their advantages and disadvantages.

On the other side [of the assembly-hall] he had written the science pertaining to artisans and merchants and explained the mode of cultivating [land] and breeding [animals]. He had sketched cities and markets and explained the rules pertaining to buying and selling, interest, and commerce.

On another side of [the assembly-hall] he had written about the science of religion, communities, *sharāʾiʿ* [revealed divine laws] and customs (*sunnan*); and explained what was lawful and prohibited and penal laws and ordinances.

On another side [of the assembly-hall] he had written about politics (*siyāsah*) and governance of the country, and explained the mode of levying tax, [8] and the method of keeping records and accounts. He had [also] explained the sustenance of the army, the protection of the subjects, and the separation of the armed forces from the bodyguards.

Those were the six genres of sciences by which the princes were trained. But this is a parable struck by the sages. The wise king signifies God the Exalted; the small children mean mankind; the castle edifice implies the sphere in its entirety; the allocated seats symbolize the human form; the pictorial cultural presentations (*ādāb*) imply the astonishing composition of the [human] body; and the sciences written in it signify the faculties of the soul and its knowledge (*maʿārif*). We will explain this briefly later on in different chapters.

On the Eminence of the Substance of Soul

We say, know that the substances of the [human] souls have a 'dwelling place' (*manzilah*) and esteem before God which the substances of physical bodies do not have. That is because of their proximate relation to Him, and the distant relation of the corporeal bodies to Him. The reason for this is that the substances of the souls are living in themselves, knowing and active, whereas the substances of the corporeal bodies are dead and passive, so they are unlike them. We have already explained in the epistle on "The Intellectual Principles"[13] that the relation of the existent things to the Exalted Creator is like the relation of numbers to [the number] one. The Intellect corresponds to two, the Soul to three, the Primal Matter to four, Nature to five, the Body to six, the sphere to seven, the pillars [or elements] to eight, and the "offsprings" (*mawlūdāt*, i.e., the three kingdoms: minerals, plants, and animals) to nine.

In another respect, the relation of the soul to the intellect is like the relation of the light-ray of the moon to the light of the sun. The relation of the intellect to God is like the relation of the light of the sun [effusing] from the sun. Just as when the moon becomes full from the light of the sun its light becomes an imitation of the light of the [sun], in the same way when the soul receives the effusion from the intellect its virtues become perfect and its acts imitate the acts of the intellect. When its virtues become perfect, then it knows its essence [or self] and the reality of its substance. When the virtues of its substance become clear to it, then it comes to know the states of its realm which is the human form. For God the Exalted has created man in the best stature, and shaped him in the most perfect form, and made his form a mirror for Himself in order to see the form of the macrocosm in it. [9] That is because when God, exalted be His sublimity, desires to inform the human soul about the treasures of His knowledge, and make it witness the cosmos in its totality, He knows that the cosmos is too vast, and it is not in the capacity of man to go around the cosmos so that he witnesses the whole of it because his life is too short and the cosmos is too big. So out of His wisdom He decided to create for it a small condensed world from the big world. He fashioned in the microcosm everything that was there in the macrocosm and modeled it in its presence and made it witness it, as He the Mighty said, "He made them bear witness on their souls: Am I not your Lord? All of them said: Yes" [Qur'ān, 7:72]. Now among them whoever was a learned witness, and knew its reality, his witnessing it was true, but whosoever was ignorant, his witnessing was rejected, because He, the Mighty and Sublime, said, "Except for the one who bears witness by truth, such are the ones who have knowledge" [Qur'ān, 43:86]. Don't you see that He does not accept the witnessing of anyone except of the people of knowledge?

Then know that the 'opening' to all kinds of sciences lies in man's knowledge of his self [or soul]. Man attains knowledge by three ways: [1] by considering the states of his body, the composition of its structure, and the attributes related to it without [considering] the soul; [2] by considering the states of his soul

13. Op. cit. note 10.

and the attributes pertaining to them without [considering] the body; [3] by considering the states of both [the soul and body] as connected to each other and the attributes related to the totality [of the two]. We have already explained some of these considerations in our epistle on "The Composition of the [human] Body."[14] In this epistle we would like to mention another aspect of it. So we say:

On Considering the States of Man with Respect to the States of the Spheres

Know that God the Exalted has made similes and allusions in the composition of the human body pointing to the composition of the spheres, the constellations, the heavens (skies) and their levels. He has made the permeation of the powers of the soul in articulations of his body and in its different organs like the permeation of the powers of the genera of angels, the tribes of jinn, man, and satans in [various] levels of the heavens and the earth, from the highest of the high to the lowest of the low.

There is a likeness between the composition of the human body and the composition of the spheres. The spheres have seven levels which lie within the cavity of each, as we explained in the epistle on "Introduction to Astronomy."[15] [10] In the same way nine substances are found in the composition of the human body which lie within the cavity of each other, enveloping [each other] in the likeness of [the spheres]. They are: the bones, marrow, flesh, blood vessel, blood, nerves, hair, nails and skin. The marrow is in the cavity of bones, stored for the time when needed. The bundles of nerves are on the articulations so that they are held together and do not sever. The cavity in them is filled with flesh for their protection. In the cavity of the flesh there are arteries, veins, and capillaries for its protection and well-being, and everything is covered by the skin, which is a covering as well as beauty for them. The hair and nails grow due to the skin [lit. matter] for the purpose [of beautifying the body]. So the body altogether becomes similar to the composition of the spheres in quantity and quality. That is because [spheres] have seven levels. The former are seven substances, and the latter lie within the cavity of each other. The former are the similitude of the latter.

The celestial sphere is divided into twelve constellations. It is found that in the structure of the [human] body there are twelve openings resembling it. They are: the eyes, ears, nostrils, nipples of the breast, mouth, naval, and the channels of excretion.

Among the constellations six are southerly and six are northerly, in the same way six openings are found in the [human] body on the right side and six on the left which resemble the [spheres] both in quantity and quality.

In the celestial sphere there are seven moving planets through which the laws of the celestial sphere and generated things are regulated. In the same way there are seven active powers in the body through which there is the well-being of the [human] body.

14. Ibid. Vol. 1, third epistle, pp. 73–109.
15. Op. cit. note 10.

These planets (*kawākib*) have souls and bodies. They perform physical acts in the bodies, and spiritual acts in the souls. In the same way seven physical faculties are found in the [human] body. They are: the faculties of attraction, fixation, digestion, repulsion, feeding, growth, and formation; and seven other faculties which are spiritual. They are the [five] sensible faculties: [the faculties of] sight, hearing, taste, smell, touch, speech and intellect. The sensible faculties correspond to the five moving planets, the faculty of speech corresponds to the moon, and the faculty of intellect corresponds to the sun. Each one of the five planets has two domiciles in the celestial sphere, one in the domain of [11] the sun and one in the domain of the moon, whereas the sun and the moon have one domicile, as we explained in the epistle on "Astronomy." In the same way, it is found that in the structure of the [human] body' each one of the sensible faculties has two channels, one on the right side and one on the left. The channel of the power of sight is in the eyes, that of hearing is in the ears, that of smell is in the nostrils, that of touch is in the hands, and that of the concupiscent taste is in the mouth which is more toward the right side [of the body], and in the genitals which is more toward the left side [of the body].

As for the power of speech, its channel is from the throat to the tongue, whereas the power of the intellect is at the center of the brain. The relation of the power of speech to that of the intellect is like that of the moon to the sun. The moon derives its light from the sun in the course of traversing twenty-eight mansions of the moon. In the same way the faculty of speech derives the meaning of the words from the intellect in the course of traversing the throat and interpreting it through the medium of the twenty-eight letters of the [Arabic] alphabet. The relation of the twenty-eight letters of the alphabet to the power of speech is like the relation of the twenty-eight mansions to the moon.

In the celestial sphere there are two constellations, the head and tail. Their essence (or self, *dhāt*) is hidden but their acts are manifest. Through them the stars bear fortune and misfortune. In the same way it is found that in the [human] body there are matters which are hidden in themselves but their acts are manifest. Through them there is the well-being of the body and the health of the acts of the soul. They are the healthy and unhealthy temperaments. That is because, if the temperament of the humors of the body is sound, then its parts are healthy, the acts of the soul are harmonious and they run a natural course. But if the temperament gets corrupted, then the physical structure [of the body] is disturbed, and the acts of the soul are hindered and blocked in their course. The misfortune of the two constellations has harmful effect on the sun and the moon, because they become the compelling causes of their eclipse. In the same way unhealthy temperament has harmful effect on the rational and intellectual powers because it greatly and severely obstructs their activities.

The eyes in the [human] body correspond to the two domiciles of Jupiter in the celestial sphere, the ears to that of Mercury, the nostrils and nipples of the breast [12] to that of Venus, the channels of excretions to that of Saturn, the mouth to the domicile of the sun, and the naval to the domicile of the moon. The naval is the gate to the nourishment in the womb before the birth [of man], the mouth is the gate to the nourishment whilst [man] in this world is the channels of excretion are juxtaposed to [the naval and mouth] just as the two domiciles of Saturn are juxtaposed to the two domiciles of the sun and the moon.

Just as in the sphere there are constellations in which there are limits, dimensions, and degrees, and they have different qualities, in the same way in the [human] body there are organs, articulations, blood vessels, nerves, and different kinds of bones which correspond to the limits of the spheres. However, the explanation [of all this] will take too long so we abandon mentioning that.

On the Similarity of the Human Body to the Four Elements

We say, Know that below the sphere of the moon there are four pillars (or elements). These are the mothers (*ummahāt*) through whom the offsprings—the animals, plants, and minerals—subsist. In the same way, within the structure of [human] body are found four parts which make up the whole of the body: the head, the breast, the belly, and the area from the abdomen to the bottom of the feet. These four correspond to those [four]. The head corresponds to the element fire in respect of the visual rays and sensory motions. The breast corresponds to the element air because of the breath and the breathing of air. The belly corresponds to the element water in respect of the moistures within it. The area from abdomen to the bottom of the feet corresponds to the element earth because it is established upon [the earth], just as the other three [elements] are established above and around the earth.

These four pillars give rise to vapors from which winds, clouds, rain, animals, plants, and minerals are engendered. In the same way the four members give rise to vapors in the human body, like mucous from the nostrils, tears from the eyes, and saliva from the mouth, the winds born in the belly, and the liquids that come out, like urine, excrement, and others.

The structure of the [human] body is like the earth. Its bones are like mountains, its bones' marrow like the minerals, its abdomen like the ocean, its intestine like rivers, its veins like streams, its flesh is like the land, its hairs are like the plants, the places where hair grows [13] like good soil, the places where it does not grow like briny earth, the face down to the feet like a flourishing city, the back like some ruins, the front of the face like the east, behind the back like the west, the right like the south, the left like the north, the breathing like the winds, [the person's] speech like the thunder, his shouts like lightning, his laughter like daylight, his weeping like rain, his despair and sorrow like the darkness of night, his sleep like death, his wakefulness like life, the days of his youth like the days of spring, the days of his young manhood like the days of summer, the days of his maturity like the days of autumn, the days of his old age like the days of winter.

His motions and acts are like the motions and rotations of the planets, his birth and his presence like the ascendant stars, his death and his absence like [the stars] that have set, the regularity in his affairs and states like the regularity of the stars, his retreat and retardation like their retreat, his sicknesses and maladies like their combustion, his pause and perplexity in some matters like their pause, his ascending to a position and exaltation like their rise to a positions and illumination, his decline from a position and fall like their decline and fall to their perigee, his union [with his spouse] like their union, his conjugation like their conjunction, his separation like their dispersion, his gesture like their appearance.

Just as the sun is at the head of the planets in the celestial sphere, so also among men there are kings and leaders. Just as the planets are connected to the sun and to each other, so are people connected to kings and to each other. Just as the planets turn away from the sun through strength and increase of light, so also people turn away from kings through power [to rule], robes of honor, and [high] degrees.

Just as Mars is related to the sun, so is the head of the army to the king. Just as Mercury is related to the sun, so are scribes and viziers to the kings. Just as Jupiter is related to the sun, so are the judges and possessors of knowledge related to the king. Just as Saturn is related to the sun, so are the treasurers and lawyers related to the kings. Just as Venus is related to the sun, so are the members of the harem and singers related to the kings. Just as the moon is related to the sun, so are the rebels related to the kings. Just as the moon takes light [from the sun] at the beginning of the month until it stands face to face with it and resembles it in light, becoming familiar to it in its condition, in the same way, rebels follow the command of kings, then they refuse to obey them and struggle against them in the kingdom.

[14] In addition, the states of the moon are similar to the states of the things of this world, that is, animals, plants, etc., since the moon begins to increase in light and perfection at the beginning of the month until it becomes complete in the middle [of the month]. Then it starts to decrease and dissolve and is effaced by the end of the month. In the same way, the states of the inhabitants of this world increase in the beginning. They never cease growing and being configured until they are complete and perfect. Then they begin to decline and decrease until they dissolve and come to nothing.

On the Numerous Faculties of the Soul

We say, this body with its numerous astonishing things, the order of its organs and the diverse ways of the formations of its articulations is similar to a city. The soul is like the king of that city, its numerous faculties like the soldiers and helpers, its acts and motions in it like the subjects and servants. That is because the human soul has many powers [or faculties] which can only be enumerated by God the Exalted. Each of these faculties has a passage in one of the organs of the body which is other than another faculty, and each faculty has a relation with the soul which is different from the relation of other [faculty]. We desire to mention something about it so that it gives some indication about the rest [of the faculties].

The [soul] has five powers of sensation which are like the masters of information. The soul appoints each one of them to a region in its kingdom in order to bring information of that region without any other power associating with it. Its explanation: the hearing power's channel is through the ears. The soul has appointed it to perceive only the audible things which are sounds. The sounds are of two species: animal and nonanimal. The nonanimal [sounds] are like the sound of drum, thunder, stone, tree, wind instrument, string instrument, and whatever resembles these [sounds]. The animal [sounds] are of two species: sounds [which express] rational speech, and sounds [which do not express] rational speech. The sounds which do not [express rational speech] are like the neighing of horse, the braying of a donkey, the mooing of an ox. In short, the sounds of the nonrational and rational animals are of two species: indicative (*dāllah*) and nonindicative. The nonindicative [15] are, for instance, tunes, melodies, laughter, weeping, scream, groan, etc. The indicative [sounds] are those which are expressed through language. They indicate the meanings in the thoughts of the souls, as we discussed in the epistle on "Logic."[16]

Each species [of sounds] is [further divided into] other species and individuals whose number is known only to God, the One and Victorious. The audible power is appointed [by the soul] to perceive [the sounds] [and] is responsible for bringing their reports to the faculty of imagination whose dwelling place is the frontal lobe of the brain. This power, in perceiving these sounds and bringing their reports, is similar to the master of reports of the king who brings reports to him from one of the regions of his kingdom.

As for the power of sight, its passage is in the eyes. The soul has appointed it to perceive the objects of sight which are divided into many species. Among them are: lights and darkness, colors which are black, white, red, and yellow and the rest of the colors born through the combination [of these four]. In addition, among the objects of sight there are measures which possess depths, shapes, forms, motions, and repose. Each species [of visual things] has below it other species, which in turn have individuals below them. All of them are under the perception of the power of sight which controls and discriminates them and brings their reports to the faculty of imagination whose dwelling place is the frontal lobe of the brain. The relation of this power to the soul is like the relation of the guard and postman to the king who bring reports to him from every region of his kingdom.

As for the power of smell, its channel is through the nostrils. The soul has appointed it to perceive odors, and control and discriminate them. They are of two species: pleasant and unpleasant. The pleasant [odors] are called good [odors], and the unpleasant ones are called stinking. Below each species [of odors] there are other species which do not have individual names as the rest of the sensations have. But the rational faculty ascribes [name] to each odor when it is conveyed to it through inhaling. Hence it is said, the smell of musk, the smell of camphor, the smell of aloes, the smell of narcissus, etc. From the point of what is being inhaled, [the odors] are plenty whose number can only be enumerated by God the Exalted. The power of smell is appointed [by the soul] to perceive [the odors] and control them by bringing their reports to the faculty of [16] imagination. Its relation to the soul is like one of the information officers to the king, as we explained in the context of the powers of vision and hearing.

As for the power of taste, its channel is through the tongue. The soul has appointed it in connection with tastes, to perceive them, to control them and discriminate them from each other. They are of nine species. The first one is sweet

16. *Rasāʾil,* Vol. 1, tenth epistle, pp. 309–21.

[taste], which is agreeable to the nature of man. The second one is bitter [taste], which is disagreeable to the nature of man. Then there are intermediary [tastes]: sour, saline, greasy, pungent, acrid, strong, and fresh. Each one of them has many species, and each species has individuals, whose number is not known to any one but God, the One, the Victorious.

The power of taste, which is in the tongue, has been appointed for the purpose of attaining tastes by perceiving them, controlling them, discriminating them from each other, and bringing their reports to the faculty of imagination. Its relation to the soul is like the relation of the information officer to the king, analogous in the affair as [the powers] of hearing, sight, and smell.

As for the power of touch, its channel is through the hands. The soul has appointed them for the affair of the tangible objects. They are of ten species: hot, cold, moist, dry, smooth, coarse, hard, soft, heavy, and light. Each one of these has under it many species, and each species has individuals whose [number] is known only to God, the Sovereign, the Overpowering Ruler, the Invincible, the Victorious. The power of touch which [manifests] through the hands is appointed for the purpose of tangible objects, for perceiving and controlling them, for discriminating them from each other, and bringing their reports to the faculty of imagination. Its relation to the soul is like the relation of one of its sisters mentioned above.

The soul with these five powers, the different sensations, and whatever is under every genus [of sensation], species, and individuals of different forms, various shapes, and different structures, resembles the five great messengers among the prophets. Their sender is One, but their *sharā'i'* are different. Each *sharī'ah* consists of various obligatory acts, different laws, and variegated customs. Under the [jurisdiction of those] laws there are many communities whose number can only be enumerated [17] by [God] the Necessary Being, the One in every respect. Just as those communities refer to God to separate them from what they differ, the same is the case with all the sensibles. Their reference [point] is the rational soul for discriminating them from each other and making each one know its realities. It arbitrates over them and grants them their waystations (*manāzil*).

Know, O my brother, that to the human soul has been ascribed five other faculties. Their relation to the soul is other than the relation of the five [powers] mentioned above. Their permeation in the organs of the body is different from the permeation of those, and their acts do not resemble their acts. That is because, these five powers are like assistant associates for attaining the forms of information. The relation of the three of them to the soul is like the relation of the king's confidants [to the king] who are always present in his assembly, informed about his secrets, and helping him in some special tasks. These are: the faculty of imagination (*al-quwwat al-mutakhayyilah*) whose channel is the frontal lobe of the brain; the faculty of reflection (*al-quwwat al-mufakkirah*) whose channel is the middle of the brain, and the faculty of memory (*al-quwwat al-ḥāfiẓah*) whose channel is the back part of the brain. The relation of one of them to the soul is like the relation of the chamberlain and interpreter to the king. And it is the rational faculty which informs [the soul] about the meanings of reflection on the sciences and [their] needs. Its channel is the throat [stretching] till the tongue. The relation of one of them to the soul is like the relation of the minister to the king who is designated by him for the administration of his kingdom and governance of his subjects. This is the faculty through which the soul manifests writing and all kinds of arts. Its channel is the hands and fingers. These five faculties for attaining [various] forms of information [for the soul] are like a corporation.

Its explanation: When the faculty of imagination obtains the sense impressions from the [five] senses perceived by them and transmitted to it, it collects all [this information] and passes them to the faculty of reflection whose channel is the central lobe of the brain. [This faculty] isolates [the information], and realizes right from wrong, truth from error, benefit from loss, and then transmits that [information] to the faculty of memory, whose channel is the back part of the brain, to preserve it for the time when needed and recalled. [18] The rational faculty obtains those preserved impressions, interprets that [information] whilst explaining to the faculty of hearing of those present at the time.

The sounds stay in the air until the ears take their share, then they fade. But the divine wisdom and divine providence have decreed, and nature has striven to register those sounds in the art of writing. That is, if the power of art [of writing] wishes to fix them, it molds them with the pen in the forms of letters in different colors and retains them in scrolls so that the knowledge of the past remains beneficial to those passing by, and there remains the trace of the earlier [generations] for the latter generations, and a discourse from those who are already gone to those who are present. This is the most significant favor of God the Exalted to man about which He mentions in His Scripture. For He said, "Recite: And thy Lord is the Most Generous, who taught by the pen, taught man what he knew not" [Qurʾān, 96:3–5].

Know, O my brother, if an intelligent and understanding person reflects on this power mentioned above, and on the mode of its permeation in the organs of the body, on its control in perceiving the sensibles, on its conceptualizing the patterns of information, and on informing the soul about everything in all circumstances, then this will be a witness to him from itself for itself, and an indication from himself that the Universal Soul has many powers dispersed in the atmosphere of the spheres, in the various levels of the heavens, in the "pillars of the mothers" [i.e., the elements], in the animals and plants; that they are charged with protecting the creation, and are set up for the well-being of the universe. They are the angels of God, sublime be His name, who are the most sincere and pure among His worshipers in realizing Him [from all created attributes]. They do not disobey God in what He commands them. They do what He commands them to do without any address to transcendence or word. In the same way these powers fulfill the needs of the soul without [uttering] a word or address to it.

It will also become clear to him that God, sublime be His laudation, is cognizant of the secrets of all the worlds as well as their conditions. Nothing escapes Him from their affairs, not even an atom's weight [of a thing]; similarly man's soul is cognizant of all the sense impressions of its senses and the reports of its faculties. They follow its command in what should be brought to it from the reports of their sense impressions without a word or address.

On Considering the States of Man with Respect to Existent Things Below the Sphere of the Moon

[19] As for considering [the states] of man with respect to existent things below the sphere of the moon, know that existent things below the sphere of the moon are of two kinds: simple and compound. The simple [things] are the four pillars: fire, air, water, and earth. The compound [things] are the things that are born from them, the engendered, corruptible things, I mean, animal, plant, and mineral.

The mineral is the first to be engendered, then plant, then the animal, then man. Each kind possesses a characteristic that it is the first to acquire. The characteristic of the four pillars [i.e., elements] is the four natures—heat, cold, wetness, and dryness—and the transmutation of some of them into others. The characteristic of a plant is to take nourishment and to grow. The characteristic of an animal is sensation and movement. The characteristic of man is rational speech (*nuṭq*), reflection, (*fikr*) and deducing logical proofs (*barāhīn*). The characteristic of angels is that they never die.

Man may share the characteristics of all these kinds. Man has four natures, which accept transmutation and change like the four pillars. He undergoes generation and corruption like a mineral. He takes nourishment and grows like plant. He senses and moves like an animal. And it is possible that he will never die, like the angels, as we explained in the epistle on "Resurrection."[17]

Know, O my brother, the animals are of many species. Each species has a characteristic different from the others. Man shares with them in all their characteristics. But [animals] have two characteristics that embrace all the others: seeking benefits and fleeing from harmful things. [However], some [animals] seek benefits through severity and domination, such as predators. Some seek benefits by barking, such as, dogs and by mewing, such as, cats. Some seek them through artifice, like spiders. And all this is found in man. Kings and sultans seek benefits through domination, beggars through asking and humility, artisans and merchants through artifice and friendliness.

All [animals] flee from harmful things and enemies, but some repel the enemy from themselves by killing, severity, and domination, like predators, and some through fleeing, like rabbits and deers. Some [animals repel] through weapons and armor, like hedgehogs and turtles, and some through fortifying themselves [20] in the earth, like mice, vermin, and serpents. And all of this is found in man: he repels enemies through severity and domination. If he fears for himself, he wears weapons. If he cannot master [the enemy], he flees from him. If he cannot flee, he defends himself through fortifications. Sometimes man repels his enemy by artifice, just as the crow overcame the owl in the book *Kalīlah wa Dimnah*.

As for man's sharing with the engendered things their characteristics, you should know O my brother—may God assist you, and us, with a spirit from Him—that every species of the animal has a special characteristic imprinted within its nature, and all of these are found in man. Man is brave like the lion, timid like the

17. Ibid. Vol. 3, thirty-seventh epistle, pp. 276–304.

rabbit, generous like the rooster, stingy like the dog, chaste like the fish, proud like the crow, wild like the tiger, sociable like the dove, clever like the fox, gentle like the cow, swift like the gazelle, slow like the bear, mighty like the elephant, servile like the camel, thieving like the magpie, haughty like the peacock, guiding like the sand grouse, astray like the ostrich, skillful like the bee, strong like the dragon, dreadful like the spider, mild like the lamb, spiteful like the donkey, hard working like the bull, headstrong like the mule, dumb like the whale, a great talker like the nightingale and the parrot, usurping like the wolf, auspicious like the sandpiper, harmful like the rat, ignorant like the pig, sinister like the owl, and full of benefit like the bee.

In short, there is no animal, mineral, plant, pillar, celestial sphere, planet, constellation, or existent thing possessing an element without that [characteristic] or its likenesses being found in man, as we have already discussed about everything in short. These matters which we have mentioned in the case of man are not found in any species of existent things in this cosmos except in man.

This explains why the sages have said that man alone stands after multiplicity, just as God, sublime be His laudation, alone stands before all multiplicity. On the basis of what we have enumerated, the astonishing composition of the human body, the wonderful controls of his soul, and what manifests from his total structure: the arts, sciences, character traits, opinions, systems (*ṭarāʾiq*), schools of law (*madhāhib*), works, acts, utterances, and physical and spiritual effects, he is named 'microcosm'.

[21] Therefore, O brother, meditate on this [human] frame [or body] which is based on wisdom, ponder on this 'Book' which is full of knowledge, and reflect on this 'straight path' which is stretched between paradise and hell so that you succeed in [doing] good deeds (*khayrāt*) through it, and are able to cross on the straight path. Meditate on this 'scale' whose axiom is 'equity', so that you know the weight of your good and evil deeds. Do the reckoning of your [deeds] before the capital [of your time] finishes, for indeed paradise is beyond all these [matters].

Remember what God has warned you against, and mentioned it to you in His words, "Thy soul sufficeth as reckoner against thee this day" [Qurʾān, 17:14], and "This Our scripture pronounceth against you with truth. Lo! We have caused (all) that ye did to be recorded" [Qurʾān, 45:29], and He said, "This is My straight path, so follow it" [Qurʾān, 6:153].

If you are not good at how to recite this Book, or how you should reckon this 'reckoning', or how you should weigh this 'scale', or how you should cross this ['straight] path', then come to [our] '*Majlis*' (*assembly*) of the Brethren. There will be advisors for you, or sincere noble-hearted friends for you who are distinguished, best scholars. They will love you, and will be affectionate to you. They will make you know about that which you will not refuse; they will teach you that about which you will become certain and will have no doubt in it by witnesses from your self [or soul], and logical proofs from your essence, and denotations from your substance. If your soul awakens from the sleep of heedlessness, and slumber of ignorance, and you observe things with your insight as they observe, and follow their just conduct as they follow, and practice according to their good custom, and gain an understanding of their intellectual *sharīʿah*, then you will enter their spiritual city. You will assume their angelic character-traits; you will know their sound opinions, and learn about their true information. Then you will be confirmed with the post-eternal spirit of life, and live the life of the fortunate ones which is blessed, everlasting, post-eternal by your pure eternal soul, not by your body which is subject to decay and annihilation.

Know that Divine wisdom and providence has made the organ of every member of the animal [kingdom] correspond to the whole of its body, about which we have already explained in the epistle on "The Merit of Relation."[18] We desire to mention an aspect of it in this epistle in order to elucidate the comparison between microcosm and macrocosm.

[22] Man is the most perfect among existent things, and most complete among engendered things below the sphere of the moon. His body is one of the parts of the whole cosmos, and this part is similar to things in [their] totality. Also, the human soul is more similar to the Universal Soul—the Soul of the whole cosmos—than [the other] particular souls. Hence the powers and acts of his soul which permeate the structure of his body are similar to the powers of the Universal Soul which permeate the whole cosmos.

Its explanation: In the structure of the Universal Soul's Body which is the whole cosmos, there are seven eminent beings constantly in motion which govern [the course of events] by the permission of the Sovereign, the absolute Ruler, the Mighty and Sublime. Each one of them has a body in which there is spirit called soul. Each one of them does certain acts in the world which are specific to it alone, which are mentioned in the works on the laws of astronomy. In the same way, God the Exalted has placed in the structure of the human body organs whose structures correspond to the whole of his body. He has created for every organ [of the body] a power which is specific to it in order to manifest by it its acts in the structure of the body and all around it. He has also made its acts correspond to the acts of the spiritual powers of the seven planets.

Its explanation: [The relation of] the mass of [heart] to the body is like the relation of the sun to the whole cosmos. That is to say, its mass lies at the center of the spheres, about which we have explained in the epistle on "The Heavens and the Universe." In the same way, God the Exalted has placed the mass of the heart in the center of the body. Just as from the mass of the sun the light and rays disseminate to the whole cosmos, and its spiritual powers permeate all parts of the cosmos, through which there is life of the cosmos and its well-being, in the same way the heat disseminates from the mass of the heart. It permeates the arteries and [and through them] to all parts of the body, by which there is life of the body and its well-being.

Also the relation of the [mass of the] spleen to the body is like that of Saturn to the cosmos. That is, the mass of Saturn disseminates its spiritual powers with its rays which permeate all parts of the cosmos, and through these powers there is the attachment of forms to matter and their persistence by the permission of God.

18. This is a chapter from the sixth epistle of the *Rasāʾil*, Vol. 1, pp. 189–94.

In the same way, from the mass of the spleen there disseminates black bile which is cold and humid. It permeates the blood in the arteries [and spreads] to all parts of the body, by which the wetness [23] in the blood remains constant and the parts [of the body] remain attached to it. The reality of what we have said and the validity of what we have described are known to the group proficient in the art of medicine and those who are well-grounded in the philosophical sciences.

Also, the relation of the mass of the liver to the body is like that of the mass of Jupiter to the cosmos. That is [to say] from its mass there disseminates rays with its spiritual powers which permeate [various] parts of the cosmos, through which there is the order of its parts, balance of its pillars, the proportion of its existent things in the cosmos in excellent states and most perfect qualities. The reality of what we have said is known to the sages, the prophets and their vicegerents—the Imāms—who are the treasurers of Divine knowledge and the trusties of His mysteries.

Also, the relation of the mass of the gall bladder to the body is like that of Mars to the cosmos. That is, from its mass there disseminates its spiritual powers with its rays which permeate all parts of the cosmos, by which the existent things attain stability and reach the utmost degree of [their] ends. In the same way, from the mass of the gall bladder there is disseminated yellow bile which permeates the blood [and spreads] to all parts of the body. It is the attenuant for the humors, returning them to their ultimate goals and final ends.

Also, the relation of the mass of intestines to the body is like that of Venus to the cosmos. That is, from its mass there disseminates with its rays its spiritual powers which permeate all parts of the cosmos. [These powers] create joy, pleasure, and cheerfulness in all physical and spiritual creations in the cosmos. Through them there is embellishment of existent beings and beauty in engendered things of the cosmos, by which I mean, both the world of celestial spheres and the world of mothers [or elements]. In the same way, from the mass of the intestines, there disseminates concupiscent power which seeks nutrition which is the mass for the body, and matter for the humors, and through it there is life in the body, the pleasure of living and physical subsistence in the human and natural bodies.

Also, the relation of the mass of the brain [to the body] is like that of Mercury to the cosmos, that is, because from its mass there disseminates along with its rays its spiritual powers which permeate all parts of the cosmos. Through them there is sensation (*ḥiss*), consciousness and cognition (*ʿirfān*) in all the creatures of all the worlds—the angels, mankind, jinn, satans, and all the animals. In the same way, from the center of the brain there disseminates a power by which [man has] sensation, consciousness, mind (*dhihn*), reflection, vision (*ruʾyat*), and all kinds of knowledge.

[24] Also, the relation of the mass of the lungs [to the body] is like that of moon to the cosmos, that is, from its matter there disseminates with its rays its spiritual powers which at times permeate the world of the pillars [i.e., of the elements], and at times the world of celestial spheres. [The moon] is between [the two states of] being manifest [and being hidden]. That is, one half of the mass of the moon is always full of light, and one half of it is always dark. [For instance,] at the beginning of the [lunar] month it faces the world of pillars [i.e., of the ele-

ments] with its face full of light, but toward the end of the month it faces the world of the celestial spheres. The reality of what we have said, and the soundness of what we have explained is known to the scholars of the science of *Almajest* and astronomy. In the same way, from the mass of the lungs there disseminates power which at one time attracts the air from outside the body and sends it to the heart, and from there it blows in the arteries, and from the arteries to all parts of the body. It is called the pulse. By it [i.e., the air] the body has life. At another time it exhales the air from inside [the body] as a result of which there are respiration, sounds and all [kinds of] speech.

So, O brother, wake up from the sleep of heedlessness and the slumber of ignorance. May God give you and us and all our brothers success in doing the right thing, and may He guide you and us and all our brothers on the rightly guided path. Indeed He is kind to all His servants.

Forty-third Epistle

The Nature of the Way Leading to God, the Almighty and Glorious In the Name of God the Most Compassionate, the Most Merciful

[73] Praise be to God, and peace be upon His servants whom He has chosen. "God is better than what they associate [with Him]?" [Qur'ān, 7:9]

Know, O brothers—may God inspire (or assist) you and us with a spirit from Him—that God the Blessed and Exalted created the creation and regulated it; He ordered its affairs and made them run their course. "Then He established Himself upon the Throne" [Qur'ān, 10:4], and exalted Himself.

It was from the grace of His mercy, extreme generosity, and complete beneficence that He selected a group of His servants, He chose them and drew them near Him, He intimately conversed with them, and unveiled to them the hidden content of His knowledge and His unseen mysteries. Then He sent them to His servants in order to invite them toward Him and to His vicinity, and report to them about the hidden content of His mysteries so that they [could] arise from the sleep of ignorance and awaken from the slumber of heedlessness, and live the life of men of learning; live the life of the fortunate ones and reach the perfection of existence in the realm of eternity as it has been mentioned in His Scriptures and described in the languages of His messengers, may the peace of God be upon them. For He said, "He created the heavens and the earth in six days, then He mounted the Throne" [Qur'ān, 7:54]; and, "Lo! God chose Adam and Noah, the family of Abraham, and the family of 'Imrān above all people" [Qur'ān, 3:33]; and, "God sent the messengers as bearers of glad tidings and warners, and with them He sent the Book" [Qur'ān, 2:213]; and "God doth call to the Home of Peace: He doth guide whom He pleaseth to a Way that is straight" [Qur'ān, 10:26].

Know, O brothers—may God assist you and us with a spirit from Him—that it is not possible to arrive there except by two traits. One is the purity of the soul (*nafs*), and the other is the straight way.

As for the purity of the soul, that is because it is the essence of man's substance. Verily, the name 'man' applies to soul and body. The body is this visible corpse which is composed of flesh, blood, bones, blood-vessels, nerves, skin, etc. All these are earthly masses which are dark, heavy, mutable, and corruptible. Whereas the soul is a substance, which is celestial, spiritual, living, luminous, subtle, dynamic, incorruptible, cognizant, and perceptive to forms of things. Its likeness in perceiving the forms of existent things which are sensible and intelligibles is that of a mirror. If the mirror is proper in shape, and its surface is polished, then you see the forms of physical things in their reality, but if the mirror is crooked in shape, then the forms of physical things are seen other than what they actually are. Also, if the surface of the mirror is rusty, then nothing at all will be seen in it.

So is the state of soul. If it is learned and ignorance is not accumulated in it, if it is pure in substance not defiled by evil deed, if it is clear in its essence [or self] not turbid by vicious character-traits, if its aspiration is sound and has not swerved by corrupted opinions, then it will see in itself the spiritual forms of things which are in its realm. Then it will perceive them by their realities and will witness the matters hidden from its senses by its intellect and purity of its substance, as it witnesses the physical things by its senses if the senses are sound and wholesome.

On the other hand, if the soul is ignorant, impure in [its] substance, defiled by evil acts, or stained by evil character traits, crooked due to base opinions, and persists in that state, then it will remain veiled from perceiving the truths of spiritual things and will be incapable of reaching God the Exalted. [As a consequence,] the blessings of the other world will be missed by it, as God the Exalted said, "Nay! Most surely they will be veiled from their Lord on that Day" [Qur'ān, 83:15].

Know O brothers—may God assist you and us with a spirit from Him—that the veil [of the soul] from its Lord is its ignorance about its substance, its realm, its origin and return. Its ignorance is due to the stain which has accumulated on its essence from its evil actions and ugly deeds, as the Blessed and Exalted said, "Nay! Rather, what they used to do has taken possession of their hearts" [Qur'ān, 83:14]. [75] As for its crookedness, that is due to its corrupted opinions and evil character-traits, as God the Exalted said, "When they deviated, God made their hearts deviate" [Qur'ān, 61:5].

Know O brothers—may God assist you with a spirit from Him—that as long as the soul continues to have these [evil] qualities, it can neither see itself, nor see those beautiful, eminent, delectable, and pleasant things in its essence [or self] which are in its realm as described by God when He said, "Therein will be what the souls desire and [wherein] the eyes will delight, and you will abide in it forever" [Qur'ān, 43:71], and "No soul knows what is hidden for them of that which will refresh the eyes, a reward for what they did" [Qur'ān, 32:17].

Know O brothers—may God assist you with His Spirit—that so long as the souls do not witness those things, they will not aspire for them, nor will they seek nor yearn for them, and so will remain as if they were blind, as God the Exalted said, "For surely it is not the eyes that are blind, but blind are the hearts which are in the chests" [Qur'ān, 22:46].

Know O brothers—may God assist you with His Spirit—that if the soul remains blind to matters of its realm, and imagines that its only existence is in this state in which it is at present in this world, then it would be greedy to remain in this world and desire to be here forever. It will be pleased and satisfied [here]. As a consequence, it would forgo the next world and forget everything concerning the Return as God the Exalted mentioned, "They are pleased and satisfied with the life of the world" [Qur'ān, 10:7]; and "They are in despair of the next world as the unbelievers are in despair of those in the graves" [Qur'ān, 60:13]. Then if it is reminded of the divine statement which came through the tongues of His messengers, peace be upon them, nothing is remembered by it, as God the Exalted said, "And when they are reminded, they remember not" [Qur'ān, 37:13]. So it would remain in its blindness, ignorance, and transgression till death, and would be persistent in arrogance as if it did not hear [God's guidance]. And when there comes the inebriety of death, which is the separation of soul from body and abandoning its use, then its separation from it would be with reluctance. It will remain in that state deprived of the use of the body and perception of sensibles. Then it would return to itself in order to advance, but the advancement would not be possible for it due to the weight of the heavy load of its evil deeds and abominable habits, as God the Exalted said, "They will bear their burdens on their back" [Qur'ān, 6:31]. Then it would be clear to it that the pleasures of the sensible which it enjoyed by means of the body were lost to it, and the pleasures [76] of the intelligibles which were in its realm were not obtained by it. Then it would be clear to it that "it had lost both this world and the next world, and that is a manifest loss" [Qur'ān, 22:11] which had happened [to it].

The Cultivation of the Soul and Reformation of Character Traits: A Resumé

As for the other trait, it is the 'straight way'. Anyone intending to attain a goal in earthly matters will investigate for his purpose to attain his goal the shortest [possible] way and easiest method. That is because he has learnt that if he does not have the easiest method, then he could be delayed in attaining it, or he could become weary in his method. Now the shortest way is the one which goes straight, and the easiest method is the one in which there are no obstacles.

Similarly, it is also requisite for those whose goal is God the Exalted after purifying their soul, [those] who are craving for the blessings of the next world in the House of Peace and who desire to ascend toward the kingdom of heaven and enter in the company of the angels, that they should investigate the shortest possible way [to attain] their objectives, as God the Exalted said, "Such have investigated the right guidance" [Qur'ān, 72:14]. And He the Sublime also said, "This is My straight way, so follow it. Follow not other paths, lest you be parted from His path. This is His directive for you" [Qur'ān, 6:153]. The Exalted one [also] said, "Say, what if I bring you better guidance than that you found your fathers' following?" [Qur'ān, 43:24].

So we would like to clarify what the 'straight way' is that about which He has given His directive through the tongues of His prophets, may peace of God be upon them, and commanded us to follow it. We will also explain how we should tred on it so that we attain what our Lord has promised, as God the Exalted said, "We have found that which our Lord promised us to be true. Have you found that which your Lord promised you to be true?" [Qur'ān, 7:44]. However, it is not possible to explain this [matter] effectively except by means of well-measured words, appropriate analogies, and clear proofs like the method of explanation of God the Exalted, and the wont (*sunnah*) of His messengers, may the peace of God be upon them, given in eloquent description of all the signs (*āyāt*) of God on the horizons and in our souls "until it is evident to them that He is the Real" [Qurʾān, 41:53], as God the Exalted said, "And in the earth are the signs [of God] for those who have certitude, and in your selves as well. Can you not perceive that?" [51:20–21]. When we have done that, the thresholds of treasured knowledge and hidden mysteries will be opened "which none will touch but those who are pure" [Qurʾān, 56:79].

Know O brothers—may God the Exalted assist you and us with a spirit from Him—that one should not discuss [77] the essence of the Exalted Creator, or His Attributes by the way of speculation and conjecture nor dispute about these [matters] until after the soul has attained purity. Otherwise [such discussions] will lead to doubts, perplexity, and an erroneous [path], as God the Exalted said, "And among mankind is the one who disputes concerning God without knowledge, without guidance, and without an enlightening Scripture" [Qurʾān, 31:20].

So before anything else, we will begin and explain how we should purify the soul from the evil character traits to which we have become habituated from childhood. For explaining that we shall compose many chapters on the 'discipline' [of the soul], and mention in each chapter many similitudes, so that it becomes most clear in explanation, is understood better, and is more intense in admonition. After that, we shall describe in these epistles other matters in which we shall explain what is the straight way leading toward God the Almighty and Majestic, and how one should follow orderly discourse and clear proofs so that it becomes a direction for those who seek [this] goal, and guidance for those who desire it. Then after these modes we shall begin with unveiling the divine matters which are living and hidden mysteries that we have known by intuition from God the Exalted, through what we have deduced from the exegesis of the Books of His friends, [through] the Revelations of His prophets, peace be upon them, and through what has come from the tongues of the sages in their allusions and symbols.

[These divine matters deal with] the cause of the genesis of the universe from nothing (lit. after it was not), the plight of the soul and its vanity, the creation of the first Adam and his disobedience, the account of the angels and their prostration to Adam, the tree of [paradise] Khuld, the Kingdom which never crumbles, the reason why [God] took the covenant from the progeny of Adam, the reports about the resurrection, the blowing of the trumpet, the awakening and rising [of the dead from the graves], the 'reckoning', the discharging of the Judgment, the crossing over the 'path' (*ṣirāṭ*), liberation from the [hell-]fire, the entrance into paradise, the visit of the Lord, the Blessed and Exalted, and similar reports which are mentioned in the Books of the prophets, may peace of God be upon them, as well as the realities of their meanings. For among mankind there are some who are intelligent, discerning and philosophical. When they reflect on these matters and draw analogous conclusion by their reasoning, they [still] cannot conceive their real meanings, and if they take what the literal word of the Revelation indicates, their minds cannot accept that. So they remain in doubt and perplexity, and when the perplexity continues with them for a long time, they deny them by their hearts, though they do not articulate that for fear of being killed.

[78] Also among mankind there are people who are below them in knowledge and discrimination; they believe and know that [those reports] are true. There are others who accept them out of [blind] imitation without reflecting on them, and also there are people who when they hear issues like these, their minds avert them and they feel disgusted at their mention, and they accuse the speaker or the inquirer of them of disbelieving (*kufr*) [in the revelation], heresy (*al-zindiqah*) and burdening [oneself with something] not requisite. Those are the people whose souls have been immersed in the slumber of ignorance. So it is incumbent upon the reminder (*mutadhakkir*) that he should become like a gentle physician to them, charming in treating them by being most friendly, [and] according to his capacity give them the reminders through the signs from the Divine Books, the reports of their prophets available to them, and the laws from their *sharāʾiʿ* such as penal laws, prescriptions, and parables. All these are allusions to the soul by means of reminding [it of] what has been neglected by it in the matter pertaining to its origin and return, [they include] the specific number and amount of duties, the prophetic laws according to their known conditions, [and] their execution at the stipulated time, facing toward different directions [in worship], and worshiping in different ways.

If they are the followers of *Tawrāt*, or *Injīl*, or the Qurʾān and if their attachment is to the external precepts of their *sharāʾiʿ*, and their craving and interest is in the recitation of the Books of their prophets, and they affirm the truth of what is in them from the prescriptions for the Religion and this world, then this is a proof for the reminders of what they have ignored concerning their world [of the soul], and what they have forgotten concerning their Origin and Return. It is also an evidence against them that they had resisted against the meaning of these issues which we have mentioned.

Now, if those people who refuse to know the meanings of these issues are the worshipers of graven images, idols, fire, the sun, stars, and their like, [the reminders should find out if any instruction resembling the *sharāʾiʿ* is available in their traditions] for surely in their Books of laws, the forms of their temples, prescriptions of their traditions there must be similitudes to those [issues] and allusions to something similar in the *sharāʾiʿ* and the religions of the prophets. But the reminders need to know them.

Among people there are some who when they hear the issues like these, the courage of their souls breaks forth to give their responses and they desire to know their meanings. When they hear the response to them, they accept without proof and demonstration, but on the basis of imitation. These are the people whose souls are healthy souls which have not been distorted by corrupted opinions and are not sunk deep in the sleep of ignorance. So the reminder is required to proceed with them gradually in teaching, [79] as we described in the first two epistles which we composed for the students and aspirants. When their souls become cultivated and their minds purified, and their reflections powerful, then they should be given the answers to these issues with demonstrations, as we explained in five epistles which we patterned on the human form, and elucidated their proofs by similitudes which are in the human form.

Among people there are some who are learned. They have inquired into some sciences; they affirm some books of the sages [or philosophers], or they listen to the theologians, and the philosophers and jurists at large in their debates. [They observe that] they speak on similar issues but answer them differently, and do not agree on any one thing, nor is any one opinion correct for them. Rather, disputes and contradictions occur among them [on issues]. Now that is because they do not have one correct principle, nor one straight standard by which to answer all these issues, rather their principles are contradictory and their standards are different and not straight.

Know O brothers—may God assist you and us with a spirit from Him—the answer based on contradictory principles, and judgment based on different standards will be contradictory and incorrect. We have answered all these issues, most of which resemble these issues, on the basis of one principle and one standard, and that is the human form. For the human form is the greatest proof of God for His creation, for it is most near to them. Its proofs are most clear. Its demonstrations are most correct. It is the book which He wrote by His hand; it is the temple which He constructed by His wisdom; it is the scale which He has placed among His creatures; it is the measure by which He will measure them on the Day of Religion [and will recompense them for] what they deserve from Him from reward and retribution; it is the totality in which the forms of both worlds are brought together; it is the sum total of sciences which are in the Guarded Tablet; it is the witness against anyone who struggles [in denying God]; it is the way toward everything good; it is the path stretched between heaven and hell.

So for him who claims leadership in the real sciences and says that it is good to answer these issues mentioned above, it is necessary that the answer sought from him should be based on one principle and one standard. It will not be possible for him [to answer those issues] unless he [chooses] the human form from among the forms of all existent things from the spheres, stars, elements, animal, plant, etc., and make it [his] principle. If he makes his principle things other than the human form, then it will not be possible for him to measure the rest of existent things with them and answer these issues as we measure and answer them. If he follows [our way], then everyone will agree upon one opinion, one Religion, one way, and the contradictions will be removed, the truth will become clear to all and that will become a cause for the deliverance of all [from mutual disagreements].

We do not permit anyone to inquire into things of this nature, nor question about them except after the cultivation of his soul, about which we have spoken and [which we have] described in these works, [and in that we] have followed the tradition (*sunnah*) of God, the Blessed and Exalted, about which He gave the report and said, "And We appointed for Moses thirty nights, and added to them ten" [Qurʾān, 7:142]. That is: Moses, peace be upon him, used to get up [for worship] during the night time, and fast during the day time until his soul (*nafs*) was purified. Then God the Exalted liberated him [from the impurities] during that [period] and spoke to him.

It is reported that the Prophet, peace be upon him and on his progeny, and benediction, said, "Whoever is pure in serving [or worshiping] God for forty days, God opens his heart, expands his breast and loosens his tongue [to speak] by wisdom though he may be tongue-tied and illiterate (lit. covered, *ghulf*)."

That is why it is incumbent upon the sages who desire to open the gate of wisdom to the students and unveil the secrets [of wisdom] to the aspirants that first and foremost they should discipline them, and cultivate their souls by good manners so that their souls become cleansed and their character-traits (*akhlāq*) purified. For wisdom like the bride desires the 'meeting-place' to be empty because it is from the treasures of the next world. If the sage does not do what is requisite of the wisdom such as disciplining the students prior to unveiling the secrets of wisdom, then his similitude will be like the chamberlain of the king who allows ill-mannered people to go in the presence of the king without [teaching them] good manners and order. If he does so, then surely he would deserve chastisement. But if he does what is requisite in teaching them courtesy, and they do not observe it or accept [its teaching] from him, then the sage is not subject to reproach; rather they should be blamed. That is because if you take the food and drink to the hungry [and thirsty] it would satisfy him. But if he does not eat until he dies of hunger, then he has forcefully taken his life, and "whoever kills a believer intentionally his recompense is hell, to abide therein [forever], and the wrath of God is upon him" [Qur'ān, 4:93].

[81] May God give you success, O pious and compassionate brother, and us right guidance. May He guide you and us and all our brothers in whatever country they live. Indeed, He is most kind to His servants!

—Latimah Parvin Peerwani, translator

A Theory on Numbers

The First Treatise of the Division of Abstract Sciences

Praise to God and peace upon His worshipers whom He has chosen!

Know that it is the method of our noble brothers to study all the sciences of the things which are in this world, be they substances or accidents, tangible or abstract, simple or compound; and to inquire into their principles and the numbers of their species, kinds, and properties, and into their arrangement and order as well as into the process of their originating and growing out of one cause and

This translation is based on the first treatise of the division of the *Rasā'il ikhwān al-ṣafā', On Numbers*, translated by Bernard Goldstein, (Cairo, Dar al-fikr Press 1347). Reprinted from *Centaurus* 10 (1964): 135–60.

one origin by one Creator; and to rely, in demonstrating them, on numerical analogies and geometric proofs, similar to what the Pythagoreans used to do. Therefore, we had to put this treatise before all the others, and in it we will mention interesting things belonging to the science of numbers and their properties which is called *Arithmetic*, by way of preface or introduction so that the way may be easier for students to acquire the wisdom which is called philosophy, and its acquisition may be simpler for novices in the study of abstract sciences.

So we say: the beginning of philosophy is the love of the sciences and the middle of it is the knowledge of the true nature of the universe by virtue of human ability, and its end is speech and action which is in accord with knowledge.

The philosophical sciences are of four kinds: the first kind is the abstract sciences, the second is the logical sciences, the third is the natural sciences, and the fourth is the theological sciences. The abstract sciences are of four kinds: the first kind is Arithmetic, the second is Geometry, the third is Astronomy, and the fourth is Music.[1] Music is the knowledge of the composition of sounds and the principles of melodies are derived from it. Astronomy is the science of the stars by means of proofs which are recorded in the book, *Almagest*. Geometry is the science of mensuration by means of proofs which are recorded in the book of Euclid. Arithmetic is the study of the properties of numbers and the qualities of the universe which conform to it, which Pythagoras and Nicomachus recorded. One begins the study of the philosophical sciences with the abstract sciences, and the first of the abstract sciences is the study of the properties of numbers because it is the easiest science to acquire;[2] then mensuration, (musical) composition, astronomy, the logical sciences, the natural sciences, and finally the theological sciences.

The first thing about which we will speak in the science of numbers is in the nature of an introduction or a preface.

Expressions point to certain meanings, the meanings are the objects of names and the expressions are the names. The most general expression or name is "thing", and a "thing" may be one or more than one. *One* is used in two ways: in its proper usage, and in metaphor. In its proper usage it is a thing which can not be partitioned or divided, and everything which can not be divided is one when looked upon from the aspect by which it can not be divided. If you wish, you may say: one is that in which there is nothing but itself, by which it is one.

As for one in metaphor, it is every aggregate which is considered a unity, so for example, ten is called a unit, and a hundred is called a unit and a thousand is called a unit. One is the epitome of oneness as black is the epitome of blackness; and oneness is the quality of being one as blackness is the quality of being black. Plurality is an aggregate of ones, and the first of the plural numbers is two, then three, four, five, and so on, ad infinitum. Plurality is of two kinds, numbers and that which is numbered. The difference between them is that a number is the quan-

1. Nicomachus, *The Introduction to Arithmetic*, I iii. English translation in D'Ooge, Robbins, Karpinski, *Nicomachuas of Gerasa* (London, 1926).

2. Nicomachus I iv.

tity of forms (*ṣuwar*) of things in the mind of the counter, while that which is numbered are the things themselves.[3]

Reckoning is the putting of numbers together and their separation. Numbers are of two kinds, whole numbers and fractions. One, which precedes two, is the source and principle of all numbers, and from it all the numbers are generated both whole and fractional, and they may be reduced to it again.

The whole numbers are generated by argumentation and the fractional numbers by division as follows: when another one is adjoined to one, it is said that they are two; and when another one is adjoined to the two of them, the aggregate is called three; and when another one is adjoined to them, it is called four; and when one is adjoined to them, it is called five. Similarly the whole numbers are generated by increasing them one by one ad infinitum, and this is their table:

1 2 3 4 5 6 7 8 9.

Numbers are reduced to one as follows: if one is taken from ten, nine remains; and if one is taken from nine, eight remains; and when one is taken from eight seven remains; and similarly ones are taken away until only one remains. But nothing can be removed from one because (by definition) a part can not be taken from it. So now you understand how the whole numbers are generated from one and how they are reduced to it.

Fractional numbers are obtained from one as follows: the whole numbers are put in their natural order, namely, one, two, three, four, five, six, seven, eight, nine, ten; and one is pointed out from every aggregate. It will be clear how fractions are obtained from one. If one is pointed out from two, it is called a half; and if one is pointed out from three, it is called a third; and if one is pointed out from four, it is called a fourth; and if one is pointed out from five, it is called a fifth; and similarly for a sixth, seventh, eighth, ninth, and tenth. Moreover, if one is pointed out from eleven, it is called one part in eleven;[4] and from twelve, a half of a sixth; and from thirteen, one part in thirteen; and from fourteen, a half of a seventh; and from fifteen, a third of a fifth; and according to this pattern one may regard the rest of the fractions. So now you understand how the fractional numbers as well as the whole numbers are generated from one and how one is the origin of both of them, and this is their table:

2	3	4	5	6	7	8	9
half	third	fourth	fifth	sixth	seventh	eighth	ninth

10	11	12	13	14	15
tenth	eleventh	twelfth	thirteenth	fourteenth	fifteenth

3. D'Ooge, Robbins, Karpinski, p. 113.

4. There are no ordinals in Arabic higher than a tenth. In order to compensate for this deficiency, an eleventh is called "one part in eleven" and a twelfth is called "a half of a sixth". In general, if a number has no factors, a fraction of that rank must be called one part in it. If the number does have factors, then one uses a compound name for a fraction of that rank.

Whole numbers are fixed in four ranks: units, tens, hundreds, and thousands. The units are the numbers from one to nine, the tens from ten to ninety, the hundreds from one hundred to nine hundred, and the thousands from one thousand to nine thousand. Twelve single words (in Arabic) suffice for all the numbers, namely, (the numbers) from one to ten, ten words; and one word, hundred; and one word, thousand; so there are twelve single words in all. The other words are derived from these or combined from them or they are a repetition of them. For example, twenty is derived from ten, thirty from three, forty from four, and so on. Combinations such as two hundred, three hundred, four hundred, five hundred, are combinations of a hundred with the unit numbers. And similarly, two thousand, three thousand, and four thousand are combinations of the word thousand with the words for the unit numbers, the tens and the hundreds, so one says: five thousand, seven thousand, twenty thousand, a hundred thousand, etc., and this is their table:

1 2 3 4 5 6 7 8 9 10
20 30 40 50 60 70 80 90
100 200 300 400 500 600 700 800 900 1,000
2,000 3,000 4,000 5,000 6,000 7,000 8,000 9,000 10,000
20,000 30,000 40,000 50,000 60,000 70,000 80,00.0 90,000 100,000
200,000 300,000 400,000 500,000 600,000 700,000 800,000 900,000

The units are 1 2 3 4 5 6 7 8 9 10; the tens are 20 30 40 50 60 70 80 90; the hundreds are 100 200 300 400 500 600 700 800 900; the thousands are 1,000 2,000 3,000 4,000 5,000 6,000 7,000 8,000 9,000 10,000.

The existence of numbers on four ranks, i.e., units, tens, hundreds, and thousands, is not a thing which follows necessarily from the nature of numbers as the existence of even and odd numbers, whole and fractional numbers. But it is a conventional matter which the philosophers have laid down by their own will. They did this so that numbers would conform to the arrangement of natural things, for most natural things were established by the Creator in four orders. For example, there four natures, heat, cold, dampness, and dryness; four elements, fire, air, water, and earth;[5] four humours, blood, phlegm, and the two biles, yellow bile and black bile; four seasons, spring, summer, autumn, and winter; four directions and four winds, the east wind, the west wind, the south wind, and the north wind; four cardines, the first house, the seventh house, the tenth house, and the fourth house;[6] and four sublunar existents, metals, vegetables, animals, and man. Hence one finds that most natural things come in fours.

These natural things come in fours by the intention of the Creator and the exigencies of His wisdom. The categories of natural things conform the spiritual things which are above natural things and are not corporeal; for things which are

5. Nicomachus II i.

6. The four cardines are the rising and setting points of the zodiac, and the upper and lower culminating points of the zodiac.

Cf. Al-Bīrūnī, *The Book of Instruction in the Elements of the Art of Astrology*, ed. and transl. R. Ramsay Wright (London, 1934), para. 247.

above the natural are (also) set in four ranks. The first of them is the Creator; then under Him, Active Universal Reason;[7] then under it, the Universal Soul; and under it, Primary Matter;[8] and all these are not corporeal.

The relation of the Creator to the universe is like the relationship of the number one (to the other numbers);[9] and the relation of Universal Reason to the universe is like the relation of the number two; and the relation of the Soul to the universe is like the relation of the number three; and the relation of Primary Matter to the universe is like the relation of the number four.

Every number has its units, its tens, its hundreds, and its thousands or what exceeds them, ad infinitum, and the source of all of them are the numbers from one to four: 1 2 3 4. The rest of the numbers are composed and generated from them, and they are the source of all the numbers. You see this when you add one to four, the total is five; and when you add two to four, the total is six; and when you add three to four, the total is seven; and when you add one and three to four, the total is eight; and when you add two and three to four, the total is nine; and when you add one and two and three to four, the total is ten. This is the rule for the rest of the numbers, the tens, the hundreds, and the thousands and what exceeds them, ad infinitum. And similarly the elements of writing are four and the rest of the letters are compounded from them, and words are composed from the letters as we will explain later. Consider it, and you will find what we say true and correct. Let those who wish to know how God invented things in (Universal) Reason and how He brought things into existence in the Soul and how He formed them in the Primary Matter, consider what we have discussed in this chapter.

The first thing which the Creator invented and innovated from the light of His unity was an extensive substance called Active Reason, as He made two arise from one, by repetition. Then He made the Universal Soul arise from the light of (Universal) Reason, as He made three from the adding of one to two. Then He made Primary Matter from the movement of the Soul, as He made four by adding one to three. He then made the rest of the created world from Primary Matter and He arranged it by the intermediary of Reason and Soul, as He made the rest of the numbers from four by adjoining what precedes it as in the examples above.

When you think about what we have said concerning the composition and the generation of numbers from the number one, you will find it one of the clearest

7. Cf. Plotinus, *Ennead* V vii. "We call Intelligence the image of the One. Let us explain this. It is its image because that which is begotten by the One must possess many of its characteristics and resemble it, as light resembles the sun. But the One is not Intelligence. How then can it produce Intelligence? By its turning towards itself the One has vision. It is this vision which constitutes Intelligence." *Ennead* V vi. "The Soul is the Word and a phase of the activity of Intelligence just as Intelligence is the word and a phase of the activity of the One." According to van den Bergh, "the Intellect and World Soul stand in Plotinus' system in the relation of Aristotle's active and passive intellect (*De Anima* III v)." *Averroes' Tahāfut al-tahāfut*: (London, 1954), II 13.

8. Primary Matter refers to the Platonic forms and hence is spiritual and not corporeal Cf. F. Dietenci, *Die Philosophic der Araber* (Leipzig, 1875), I 164.

9. In the arithmology of Nicomachus, as well as other Greeks, the monad was identified with God. D'Ooge, Robbins, Karpinski, p. 104.

proofs of the uniqueness of the Creator, and the process of His creation and invention of things. For although the existence of numbers, and their composition can be conceived from the number one, as we explained above, nothing essential to it is changed, i. e., that the number one is indivisible. Similarly, although God is the one who created all things from the light of His unity, and made their beginning and made them grow, and they have their existence, duration, completeness, and perfection through Him, nothing essential to Him is changed, i.e., His unity before His act of creation, as we will explain in the treatise concerning the Principles of Reason. We already informed you that the relation of the Creator to the universe is analogous to the relation of the number one to the numbers; as one is the origin of the numbers and that which generates them, their beginning and their end, similarly God is the cause of all things and their Creator, their beginning and their end; and as one can not be divided, nor can it be compared to any other number, so God can not be compared or likened to anything in His creation; and as one encompasses and accounts for all the numbers. so God knows all things and their natures. Hence God is exalted over what the unjust say in grandeur and magnificence.

The orders of the numbers are four according to most people, as we mentioned already, but the Pythagoreans put them in sixteen ranks and this is their table to:[10]

Ones	1
Tens	10
Hundreds	100
Thousands	1,000
Ten thousands	10,000
Hundred thousands	100,000
Millions	1,000,000
Ten millions	10,000,000
Hundred millions	100,000,000
Billions	1,000,000,000
Ten billions	10,000,000,000
Hundred billions	100,000,000,000
Trillions	1,000,000,000,000
Ten trillions	10,000,000,000,000
Hundred trillions	100,000,000,000,000
Quadrillions	1,000,000,000,000,000

The fractions have many ranks, bemuse every whole number has one part, two parts, and a number of parts. For example, twelve has a half, a third, a fourth, a sixth, and a twelfth, and similarly twenty-eight, etc. But although the ranks and divisions of fractions are numerous, their scheme is in descending order, each rank is smaller than the previous one. All of them are included in ten words, one word

10. The numbers beginning with 10^5 are given names which I was unable to identify: *nawʿāt, ghayāt, sūrāt, ḥalbāt, al-baṭṭāt, haniyāt, daʿūāt, wahuwāt, majwāt, wamūr, mārū.*

which is general and ambiguous and nine words which are special and fixed. Among the nine words is one word without (etymological) derivation (from its whole number), and that is a *half*, and eight words which are derived: a third (from three), a fourth (from four), a fifth (from five), a sixth (from six), a seventh (from seven), an eighth (from eight), a ninth (from nine), and a tenth (from ten). The word which is general and ambiguous is a "part" because one in eleven is called a "part" in eleven, and similarly for thirteen, seventeen, etc. The rest of the expressions for fractions are formed by combining these ten words. For example, one in twelve is called a half of a sixth, and one in fifteen is called a fifth of a third, and one in twenty is called a half of a tenth. The rest of the significations of the fractions are similarly understood as the adjoining of one of them to another.

These two kinds of numbers continue in quantity ad infinitum. Whole numbers start with the smallest quantity, two, and continue to increase without limit. Fractions begin with the largest quantity, a half, and diminish without limit. So both of them begin at a fixed point, but have no end point to limit them.

Chapter Concerning the Special Properties of Numbers

Every number has one or more special properties meaning the particular qualities of the described object which nothing shares with it. The special property of one is that it is the source of all the numbers as we explained above and it generates[11] all the numbers both odd and even. A special property of two is that it is the first whole number and it generates half of the numbers, the even numbers as opposed to the odd numbers. A special property of three is that it is the first odd number and it generates a third of the numbers, some odd, some even. A special property of four is that it is the first perfect square. A special property of five is that it is the first recurrent number, also called spherical. A special property of six is that it is the first perfect (*tāmm*) number. A special property of seven is that it is the first complete (*kāmil*) number. A special property of eight is that it is the first perfect cube. A special property of nine is that it is the first odd perfect square and it is the last of the rank of units. A special property of ten is that it is the first number of the rank of tens. A special property of eleven is that it is the first deaf number [cf. p. (34)]. A special property of twelve is that it is the first excessive number. And in general, a special property of any number is that it is half the sum of its adjacent number, and if its adjacent numbers are added together, their sum will be twice the given number.[12] For example, one of the numbers adjacent to five is four and the other is six, their sum is ten and five is half of it, and similarly with the rest of the numbers. And this is their table:

1 2 3 4 –5– 6 7 8 9.

One has only one adjacent number, two; and one is half of it, and it is twice one. We say that one is the source and generator of the numbers because when one is

11. A number is said to *generate* all its multiples, and they are *generated* by it.

12. Nicomachus I viii.

removed from existence all the numbers are removed with it, but when the numbers are removed from existence, one is not removed. We say that two is the first whole number because numbers are a plurality of ones, and the first plurality is two. We say that three is the first odd number because two is the first number and it is even and three being adjacent to it, is odd. We say that it generates a third of the numbers, some odd and some even because it comes after two numbers and can be counted the third from them.[13] This third number will sometimes be even and sometimes odd.

We say that four is the first perfect square because it is the product of two multiplied by itself, and any number which is multiplied by itself is a (square) root and the product is a perfect square. We say that five is the first recurrent number because when it is multiplied by itself it returns to itself, and if that number is multiplied by itself, it again returns to its essence and so on forever.[14] So, for example, five times five is twenty-five, and if this number is multiplied by itself, the product is six hundred and twenty-five, and if this number is again multiplied by itself, the product is 390.625, and if this number is multiplied by itself, the product is another number ending in twenty-five. Do you not see how five conserves itself and whatever derives from it eternally, whatever it may reach? And this is their table:

5 25 625 390,625.

As for six, it is similar to five in this sense, but it is not self-continuing as five is. Its prolongation is 6 36 1296. Six times six is thirty-six; six returns to itself, and thirty appears. When thirty-six is multiplied by itself, the product is 1296, six again appears, but not thirty. So it is evident that six conserves itself but not what is derived from it. But five conserves itself and what derives from it eternally and forever.

It was said that a special property of the number six is that it is the first perfect number, i.e., if the divisors of a number add up to itself, it is called a perfect number, and six is the first of them. Six has a half which is three, and a third which is two, and a sixth which is one, and if these divisors are added up, the sum is equal to six. No number before six has this property, but after it twenty-eight, four hundred and ninety-six, and eight thousand one hundred and twenty-eight are all perfect numbers.

And this is their table:

6 28 496 8,128.

It was said that seven is the first complete number because seven combines in itself the meanings of all the (preceding) numbers. For all the numbers are even or odd, two is the first even number, and four is the second; three is the first odd number and five is the second. If the first odd number is added to the second even

13. Three generates all its multiples, i.e., 3 6 9 12 15 18, etc. One sees that they alternate between odd and even numbers.

14. Nicomachus II xvii.

number, or the first even number is added to the second odd number, the sum is seven. So, if you add two, the first even number, to five, the second odd number, the sum is seven; similarly, if you add three which is the first odd number to four which is the second even number, the sum is seven. And if one, which is the source of all numbers, is taken with six which is a perfect number, the sum is seven which is a complete number. This is their table: 1 2 3 4 5 6 7. This is a special property of seven which no other number before seven possesses, and it has other special properties which we will discuss when we discuss the fact that the universe is constructed in accordance with the nature of numbers.

It was said that eight is the first perfect cube because of the following argument. If any number is multiplied by itself, it is called a (square) root and the product of two of them is a perfect square as we explained before. But if the perfect square is multiplied by its (square) root, the product is called a perfect cube. Two is the first number, and if it is multiplied by itself the product is four, which is the first perfect square, then the perfect square is multiplied by its (square) root which is two and the product is eight. Hence eight is the first perfect cube.

Eight is the first *solid* number because there can not be a solid body without interlocked surfaces and there can not be a surface without mutually adjoining lines and there can not be a line without ordered points as we will explain in the treatise on *Geometry*. The shortest line consists of two points and the narrowest surface consists of two lines, and the smallest solid body consists of two surfaces, so the conclusion from these premises is that the smallest solid body has eight parts. One of them is a line which has two parts. If a line is multiplied by itself, they form a surface which has four parts, and if the surface is multiplied by one of its lengths, it will have depth from it, so then there will be eight parts in all, two of length, two of width, and two of depth.

It was said that nine is the first odd perfect square because three times three is nine and neither seven nor five nor three is a perfect square.

Ten is clearly the first number of the tens' rank as one is the first number of the units' rank, and this is clear without the necessity of commentary. It has another special property similar to a property of the number one, namely, that it only has one number adjacent to it, twenty, and ten is half of it as we explained in the case of one which is half of two.

It was said that eleven is the first *deaf* number because it has no fractional part with a name of its own, but a part is called one part in eleven or two parts in eleven. All of the following numbers are called deaf:

11 13 17 23 29 31 37 41 43 47 53 59 61 67 71 73 79 83 89 91.

It was said that twelve is the first *excessive* number, because if the sum of all the divisors of a number are added and are greater than it, it is called an excessive number, and twelve is the first such number. It has a half which is six, and a third which is four, and a fourth which is three, and a sixth which is two, and a twelfth which is one. If these divisors are added up, the total is sixteen which exceeds twelve by four.

So, in general, every whole number has a special property peculiar to itself but we omit their mention as both easy and superfluous.

Numbers are divided into two divisions, whole numbers and fractions as we explained above, and whole numbers are divided into two subdivisions, even numbers, and odd numbers. An even number is any number which can be divided into two halves which are whole numbers, while an odd number is any number which exceeds an even number by one or which falls short of an even number by one. The generation of even numbers begins from the number two, continuing by repetition without end as is seen:

2 4 6 8 10 12 14 16 18 20.

The generation of odd numbers begins from the number one, to which two is adjoined continually, ad infinitum:

3 5 7 9 11 13 15 17 19.

Even numbers are divided into three kinds: powers of two, pairs of odd numbers, and pairs of pairs of odd numbers.[15] Powers of two are all numbers which may be divided into two equal halves of whole numbers which in turn may be so divided, continuing until the process of dividing reaches one. For example, sixty-four: half of it is thirty-two, and half of that is sixteen, and half of that is eight, and half of that is four, and half of that is two, and half of that is one.[16] And the generation of these numbers begins with two, which is multiplied by two, and the product is multiplied by two, etc., continuing ad infinitum.

Whoever wishes to understand this thoroughly, ought to double the squares of the chess-board, because he will always remain within the powers of two, and these numbers have other special properties which Nicomachus explained in his book at length, and we will quote a part of it, He says:[17]

Let these numbers be set in their natural order, which is one, two, four, eight, sixteen, thirty-two, sixty-four, and so on, ad infinitum. One of their special properties is that if one multiplies the two extreme terms, the product will be equal to the mean term multiplied by itself, if there is only one mean term; or if there are two mean terms, the product of the extreme terms is equal to the product of the two mean terms. For example, let 64 be the last term of the series and one the first. This series has one mean term which is eight, so I say: if one is multiplied by sixty-four, or two times thirty-two, or four times sixteen, the product is equal to eight times eight, and this their table:

1 2 4 8 16 32 64.

And if one adds to it another rank so that there will be two mean terms, then I say: if one multiplies the two extreme terms, it will be equal to the product of the two mean terms.[18] For example: if 128 is multiplied by one, or sixty-four by two, or

15. Nicomachus I viii.
16. Ibid. This example is used by Nicomachus.
17. Ibid.
18. Ibid.

thirty-two by four, the product will be equal to the product of sixteen times eight. And this is their table:

1 2 4 8 16 32 64 128.

These numbers have another special property. If one adds the numbers of the series starting with one and ending arbitrarily, the sum will be one less than the next number of the series. For example, take one, two, and four, the sum is smaller than eight by one. And if eight is added to it, the sum is smaller than sixteen by one. And if sixteen is added to it, the sum is smaller than thirty-two by one. Similarly, you discover the ranks of these numbers, however great, and this is their table:

1 2 4 8 16 32 64 128 256.

Pairs of odd numbers are all numbers which can be divided in half once, but do not lead to one by division, such as six, ten, fourteen, twenty-two, twenty-six.[19] All of these examples are numbers which can be divided once, but do not lead to one. These numbers are obtained by multiplying every odd number by two, and this is their table:

6 10 14 18 22 26 30 34 38 42 46.

Pairs of pairs of odd numbers[20] include all numbers which may be divided in half more than once, but do not lead to one by divison, such as twelve, twenty, twenty-four, twenty-eight, and similar numbers, and this is their table:[21]

12 20 24 28 36 44 52 60 68.

These numbers are generated by multiplying a pair of odd numbers by two, once or many times. And these numbers have other special properties whose mention we will omit fearing to be redundant.

Odd numbers are divided into subdivisions: prime numbers and composite numbers. Composite numbers are of two kinds, those which are associated with one another, and those which are relatively prime.[22] The distinction is this: the prime numbers include all numbers, together with one, which are not generated by another number, such as: three, five, seven, eleven, thirteen, seventeen, nineteen, twenty-three. etc. The special property of these numbers is that they have no fractional part other than the one named from them.[23] So, three has no fractional part except a third; five has no fractional part except a fifth, and similarly has no fractional part except a seventh; and so on for eleven, thirteen, and seventeen. In general all the deaf numbers can not be generated except by one, and the name of their fractional parts is derived from them.

19. Nicomachus I ix.
20. Read *al-fard* instead of *wa'l-fard* in the Arabic text.
21. Nicomachus I x.
22. Nicomachus I xi.
23. A prime number is a number which has no divisors other than itself and one.

The composite numbers include all the numbers which are generated by another number, excluding one, such as nine, twenty-five, forty-nine, eighty-one. etc. And this is their table:

9 25 49 81 121 169.

Two numbers are *associated* with one another if both of them are generated by the same number, excluding one. For example, nine, fifteen, and twenty-one are associated because three generates all of them. Similarly, fifteen, twenty-five, and thirty are all generated by five. These numbers and those like them are said to be *associated* by the number which generates them. And this is their table:

9 15 21 25 35.

Two numbers are *relatively prime* if two different numbers other than one generate them, but what generates one of them does not generate the other, such as nine and twenty-five. Three generates nine but does not generate twenty-five, whereas five generates twenty-five, but does not generate nine. So these numbers and others like them are called relatively prime.

Chapter Concerning Perfect, Defective, and Excessive Numbers

Every odd number has the special property that if it is divided into two parts, in any way, one of the parts will be even and the other will be odd; and every even number has the special property that if it is divided in any way, the parts will be either both odd or both even, and this is their table:[24]

Odd	*Even*	[*Even*][25]
10 11 1	4 10 4	[9 10 1
9 11 2	7 10 7	8 10 2
8 11 3	2 10 2	7 10 3
7 11 4	1 10 1	6 10 4
6 11 5	5 10 5	5 10 5]

Numbers may be divided into three kinds by considering them from another point of view: perfect, excessive, and defective.[26] A *perfect* number is any number whose divisors add up to itself, such as six, twenty-eight, four hundred and ninety-six, and eight thousand one hundred and twenty-eight. If the divisors of each of these numbers are added up, the sum will be equal to itself. There is only one perfect number in each rank of the numbers: six in the units, twenty-eight in

24. Nicomachus I viii.

25. Square brackets are used here to emend the text. The even column in our edition makes no sense. Square brackets will also be used to indicate mathematical equations in modern notation.

26. Nicomachus I xiv. ff.

the tens, four hundred and ninety-six in the hundreds, and eight thousand one hundred and twenty-eight in the thousands. This is their table:

6 28 496 8128.

An *excessive* number is any number whose divisors add up to more than itself, such as twelve, twenty, etc. Half of twelve is six, and a third of it is four, and a fourth of it is three, and a sixth of it is two, and a twelfth of it is one: all these divisors add up to sixteen which is more than twelve. A *defective* number is any number whose divisors add up to less than itself, such as four, eight, ten, etc. Half of eight is four, and a fourth of it is two, and an eighth of it is one: the sum of them equals seven which is less than eight. The rest of the defective numbers are of the same kind.

Chapter Concerning Friendly Numbers

From another point of view the numbers may be divided into two subdivisions, one of them called *friendly* numbers. This means any two numbers, one excessive, and one defective such that the sum of the divisors of the excessive number is equal to the defective number and the sum of the divisors of the defective number is equal to the excessive number. For example consider two hundred and twenty which is an excessive number, and two hundred and eighty-four which is a defective number. The sum of the divisors of two hundred and twenty is equal to two hundred and eighty-four, and the sum of the divisors of the latter number is equal to two hundred and twenty. So these numbers and others like them are called *friendly* and there are (only) a few of them. This is their table:

excessive number	220
half of it	110
fourth of it	55
fifth of it	44
tenth of it	22
twentieth of it	11
eleventh of it	20
twenty-second of it	10
forty-fourth of it	5
fifty-fifth of it	4
hundred tenth of it	2
two hundred twentieth of it	1
Total	284

defective number	284
half of it	142
fourth of it	71
seventy-first of it	4
hundred forty-second of it	2
two hundred eighty-fourth of it	1
Total	220

Multiplication of Numbers

One of the special properties of numbers is that numbers increase by multiplication and addition without limit. That happens in five ways. Firstly in the natural order: 1 2 3 4 5 6 7 8 9 10 11 12, and so on, ad infinitum. Secondly, in the order of even numbers: 2 4 6 8 10 12 14 and so on, ad infinitum. Thirdly, in the order of odd numbers: 1 3 5 7 9 11 13 15 17, and so on, ad infinitum. Fourthly, by subtraction by any of the preceding methods. And fifthly, by multiplication which we will explain later.

Chapter Concerning the Special Properties of the Subdivisions

Each subdivision of the numbers has many properties which have been recorded in the Book of Arithmetic in detail, but we will restate part of it in this chapter.

One of the special properties of the natural order of numbers is that the sum from one to any arbitrary number is equal to the product of one more than the last number multiplied by half of the last number

[i.e., $S = \frac{n}{2}(n + 1)$]. For example, when we say: what is the sum of the numbers from on to ten; we add one to ten and multiply it by half of ten and we get fifty-five; or multiply five by itself which is twenty-five. Then we multiply five by the other "half" which is six [i.e., $11 - 5 = 6$] and we get thirty; the sum is fifty-five, and this is its solution and the pattern which was sought.

The order of even numbers is one, two, four, six, eight, ten, twelve, etc. ad infinitum. One of the properties of this order is that the sum is always odd. Moreover, the sum of one to any arbitrary number is equal to the product of [half of][27] this times one more than the other half of this number, adding one to the total. For example, when we say to you: what is the sum of the numbers from one to ten according to the even order; you take half of ten and add one to it, then you multiply it by the other "half" and add one to the total and that is thirty-one, and similarly for the rest of the numbers.

The order of odd numbers is one, three, five, seven, nine, eleven, etc. ad infinitum. One of its properties is that when these numbers are added according to their natural order, there are two (kinds of) sums, one even, and the other odd, one following after the other, continuing ad infinitum,[28] and all of the sums will be perfect squares. Moreover, when they are added according to their natural order from one to any arbitrary number, the sum is equal to half of the last number rounded off to the next whole number and then squared. For example, when we say: what is the sum from one to eleven; its solution is that you take half of the number which is five and a half and round it off to six, then multiply it by itself which equals thirty-six, and that is its solution, so take it as a pattern.

27. Emendation based on the example which follows in the text, "you take *half* of ten and add one to it, then you multiply it by the other *half*. . . ."

28. The sums are: 1; $1 + 3 = 4$; $1 + 3 + 5 = 9$; $1 + 3 + 5 + 7 = 16$; $1 + 3 + 5 + 7 + 9 = 25$; etc. These sums are all perfect squares and are alternatingly odd and even.

The meaning of multiplication is the duplication of one of the numbers by the number of ones in the other number, as for example, when we say: how much is three times four; its meaning is how much is the sum of three taken four times.

Numbers are of two kinds, whole numbers and fractions as we explained before, and moreover, the multiplication of numbers is of two kinds, simple and compound. Simple multiplication is of three kind, a whole number by a whole number, like two times three, or three times four, etc. a fraction by a fraction like a half times a third or a third times a fourth, etc. and a whole number times a fraction, like two times a third, or a third times four, etc. Compound multiplication is also of three kinds: a fraction and a whole number times a whole number like two and a third times five, etc.; a whole number and a fraction times a whole number and a fraction like two and a third times three and a fourth etc.; and a whole number and a fraction times a fraction like two and a third times a seventh.

Chapter Concerning Whole Numbers

The Multiplication of whole numbers is of four kinds and there are ten categories for the multiplication of all of them. The four ranks of numbers are units, tens, hundreds, and thousands. The ten categories are: units times units, one of them is one and ten of them are ten; units times tens, one of them is ten and ten of them are a hundred; units times hundreds, one of them is a hundred and ten of them are a thousand; units times thousands, one of them is a thousand and ten of them are ten thousand; and these are four categories. As for tens times tens, one of them is a hundred and ten of them are a thousand; and tens by hundreds, one of them is a thousand and ten of them are ten thousand; and tens by thousands, one of them is ten thousand and ten of them are a hundred thousand; and these are three categories. And as for hundreds times hundreds, one of them is ten thousand and ten of them are a hundred thousand; and hundreds times thousands; one of them is a hundred thousand and ten of them are a million; and these are two categories. As for thousands times thousands, one of them is a million and ten of them are ten million, and this is one category, so there are ten categories in all and this is their table:

units times units; units times tens; units times hundreds;
units times thousands; tens times tens; tens times hundreds;
tens times thousands; hundreds times hundreds, hundreds times
thousands; thousands times thousands.

Chapter Concerning Multiplication, Square Roots, and Perfect Cubes

The words which algebraists and geometers employ and their meanings.

So we say: for any two numbers whatever, if one of them is multiplied by the other, the product is called a rectangular number. But if the two numbers are equal the product is called a perfect square and the two numbers are called square roots of this number. For example, if two is multiplied by two, the product is four, or three times three is nine, or four times four is sixteen. Four, nine and sixteen, and similar numbers are all called perfect squares; while two, three, and four are called square roots, so two is the square root of four, three is the square root of nine, and four is the square root of sixteen, and one considers the rest of the perfect squares according to this pattern. The square roots are as follows:

2	3	4	5	6	7	8	9
4	9	16	25	36	49	64	81.

If one multiplies any number by any other number, then the product of them is called a rectangular number which is not a perfect square, and the two different numbers are called its factors and they are called sides of this rectangle, which is the geometric term. For example, two times three, or three times four, or four times five, etc. The product of these numbers which are multiplied is called a rectangle which is not a square

Chapter Concerning Rectangular Number[29]

When any rectangular number, whether a perfect square or not, is multiplied by any number whatever, the product is called a *solid* number, but if the number was a perfect square and it was multiplied by its square root, then the product is called a perfect cube, as for example, if four which is a perfect square is multiplied by two which is its square root, the product is eight; and similarly if nine which is also a perfect square is multiplied by three which is its square root, the product is twenty-seven. And similarly if sixteen which is a perfect square is multiplied by four which is its square root, the product is sixty-four. Hence, eight, twenty-seven, and sixty-four, and similar numbers are called perfect cubes. A *prefect cube* is a solid such that its length, its width, and its depth are equal, and it has six rectangular faces whose sides are equal and perpendicular (to each other); and it has twelve edges, eight solid angles, and twenty-four plane angles.

If a perfect square is multiplied by a number less than its square root, the product is called a *diminished solid number*[30] which is a solid whose length and width are equal but whose height is less than they are. It has six rectangular faces whose sides are perpendicular; but it has only one pair of opposite faces which are rectangular whose sides are equal and perpendicular and four faces which are elongated [i.e., whose sides are unequal]; twelve edges, every pair of which are parallel; eight solid angles; and twenty-four plane angles. If a perfect square is multiplied by a number greater than its root, the product is called an *augmented solid number*, such as if four which is a perfect square is multiplied by three which is greater than its square root, the product is twelve; similarly, if nine is multiplied by four which is greater than its square root, the product is thirty-six. Hence, twelve, thirty-six, and similar numbers are augmented solid numbers and an augmented solid is one whose height is greater than its length and width. It has six

29. Plane and solid numbers are much more extensively treated in Nicomachus Bk. II.
30. Literally a brick. Cf. Nicomachus II xvii.

rectangular faces, one pair of opposite faces are rectangles whose sides are equal and perpendicular, and four oblong faces whose sides are parallel and perpendicular. It has twelve edges, every pair of which are equal and parallel; eight solid angles; and twenty-four plane angles.

If any rectangular number which is not a perfect square is multiplied by its shorter side, the product is called a diminished solid; and if it is multiplied by its longer side, the product is called an augmented solid; and if it is multiplied by a number smaller than both of them or greater than both of them, the product is called a *free solid*, as for example if twelve which is a rectangular number not a perfect square, one of its sides being three and the other four, is multiplied by three, the product is thirty-six, which is a diminished solid number; and if it is multiplied by four, the product is forty-eight which is an augmented solid number; and if it is multiplied by a number less than three or more than four it is called a free solid. A free solid is one whose length is greater than its width, and its width is greater than its height. It has six faces, every pair of which are equal and parallel; twelve edges, every pair of which are parallel; eight solid angles and twenty-four plane angles.

Chapter Concerning the Properties of Perfect Squares

We say: if one more than twice its square root is added to a perfect square the sum is a perfect square [i.e.,

$$x^2 + 2x + 1 = (x + 1)^2].$$

If a perfect square is diminished by one more than twice its square root, the remainder is a square [i.e.,

$$x^2 - 2x + 1 = (x - 1)^2].$$

For every two perfect squares which follow each other: if the square root of one of them is multiplied by the square root of the other and a fourth is added to it the total will be a perfect square. For example: if the square root of four which is two is multiplied by the square root of nine which is three, the product is six, to which is added a fourth, totaling six and a fourth, and its square root two and a half. The product of two and a half times itself is six and a fourth whose square root is two and a half. For every two perfect squares which follow each other: if the square root of one of them is multiplied by the square root of the other, the product is the geometric mean between them and the three numbers are in one proportion. For example, four and nine are perfect squares whose roots are two and three: two times three is six, and four is to six as six is to nine. The other cases follow the same pattern.

Chapter Concerning Problems from the Second Book of Euclid's Elements

Given any two numbers, if one of them is divided into any number of parts, then the product of the two numbers is equal to the product of the one which was not divided, times all the parts of the number which was divided, one part after the other. For example, given ten and fifteen, and let fifteen be divided into three parts: seven, three, and five, then we say:

1. The product of ten times fifteen is equal to the product ten times seven plus ten times three plus ten times five [i. e., the law of distributivity (Euclid, II, 1):

$$a(b + c + d) = ab + ac + ad].$$

2. Let any number be divided in parts arbitrarily, then the product of this number by itself is equal to the product of this number times all its parts (Euclid, II 2). For example, let ten be divided into two parts: seven and three, then I say: the product of ten times itself is equal to the product of ten times seven plus ten times three [i. e.,

$$(a + b)(a + b) = (a + b)a + (a + b)b;$$
$$\text{or } (3 + 7)(3 + 7) = (3 + 7)3 + (3 + 7)7].$$

3. Let any number be divided into two parts, then we say: the product of this number times one of its parts is equal to the product of this part times itself plus the product of the two parts (Euclid II, 3). For example, let ten be divided into two parts; three and seven, then we say: the product of ten times seven is equal to the product of seven times itself plus three times seven [i. e.,

$$(a + b)b = ab + b^2;$$
$$\text{or } (3 + 7)7 = 3 \cdot 7 + 7^2].$$

4. Let any number be divided into two parts, then we say: the product of this number times itself is equal to the product of each part times itself plus twice the product of the two Parts (Euclid II, 4). For example, let ten divided into two parts: seven and three, then we say: the product of ten times itself is equal to the product of seven times itself plus three times itself plus twice seven times three [i. e.,

$$(a + b)^2 = a^2 + b^2 + 2ab;$$
$$\text{or } (7 + 3)^2 = 7^2 + 3^2 + 2 \cdot 3 \cdot 7].$$

5. Let any number be divided in two halves, then in two different parts; the product of one of the different parts times the other, plus half the difference between them multiplied by itself is equal to the product of half of the number times itself (Euclid II, 5). For example, let ten be divided in two halves, then into two unequal parts: three and seven. Now we say: the product of seven times three plus half the difference between them, which is two, times itself is equal to the product of five times itself [i. e.,

$$[(a + b)/2]^2 = ab + [(a - b)/2]^2;$$
$$\text{or } [(3 + 7)/2]^2 = 3 \cdot 7 + [(7 - 3)/2]^2;$$
$$\text{or } 25 = 21 + 4].$$

6. Let any number be divided into two halves, then add something to it. We say: the product of this number together with its increment times that increment plus half of the number times itself is equal to the product of half of that number together with the increment times itself (Euclid II, 6). For example, let ten be divided in two halves, then add two to it. We say: the product of twelve times two plus five times itself is equal to the product of two plus five together times itself [i.e.,

$$(x + a)a + (x/2)^2 = [(x/2) + a]^2;$$
$$\text{or } (10 + 2)2 + 5^2 = (5 + 2)^2;$$
$$\text{or } 24 + 25 = 49].$$

7. Let any number be divided into two parts, then we say: the product of that number times itself plus the product of one of its parts times itself is equal to twice the product of that number times that part plus the product of the other number times itself (Euclid II, 7). For example, let ten be divided into two parts: seven and three. Then we say: the product of ten times itself plus seven times itself is equal to the product of twice ten times seven plus three times itself [i.e.,

$$(a + b)^2 + b^2 = 2(a + b)b + a^2;$$
$$\text{or } (3 + 7)^2 + 7^2 = 2(3 + 7)7 + 3^2;$$
$$\text{or } 100 + 49 = 140 + 9].$$

8. Let any number be divided into two parts, then add one of the parts to the original number. We say that the product of all that (the number plus the part) times itself is equal to four times the product of that number times the part plus the other part times itself (Euclid II, 8). For example let ten be divided into two parts: seven and three, then add three to it. Now we say: the product of thirteen times itself is equal to the product of ten times three taken four times plus the product of seven times itself [i.e.,

$$(2a + b)^2 = 4(a + b) + b^2;$$
$$\text{or } (10 + 3)^2 = 4 \cdot 3(10) + 7^2$$
$$\text{or } 169 = 120 + 49].$$

9. Let any number be divided into two unequal parts, then the sum of the product of each of them times itself is double the product of half of that number times itself plus the product of half the difference of what is between the two numbers times itself (Euclid II, 9). For example, let ten be divided into two halves, then into two unequal parts: three and seven. We say that the product of seven times itself plus three times itself is twice the product of five times itself together with the product of two (which is half the difference between the two parts) times itself [i.e.,

$$a^2 + b^2 = 2[(a + b)/2]^2 + 2[(a - b)/2]^2$$
$$7^2 + 3^2 = 2[(7 + 3)/2]^2 + 2[(7 - 3)/2]^2$$
$$49 + 9 = 2 \cdot 25 + 2 \cdot 4$$
$$49 + 9 = 58].$$

10. Let any number be divided into two halves, then add some increment to it. Now the product of that number with its increment times itself plus the product of the increment times itself is twice the product of half the number with the increment times itself together with the product of half the number times itself (Euclid II, 10). For example, let ten be divided in half, then add two to it. We say: the product of twelve times itself plus the product of two times itself is twice the product of seven times itself together with the product of five times itself [i.e.,

$$(a + x)^2 + x^2 = 2[(a/2 + x)^2 + (a/2)^2]$$
$$(10 + 2)^2 + 2^2 = 2[(5 + 2)^2 + 5^2]$$
$$144 + 4 = 2(49 + 25)$$
$$148 = 2 \cdot 74].$$

Chapter Concerning the Science of Numbers and its Nature

The philosophers have put the study of the science of numbers before the study of the rest of the abstract sciences, because this science is potentially embedded in everyone and a man ought to reflect (on it) with his reasoning power alone without taking examples from another science, but from it one takes examples for everything else that can be known.

The examples which we expressed in figures in this treatise are for the beginner students whose mental powers are weak, but for those who are sharp-witted, these examples are not necessary.

One of our goals (in writing) this treatise is what we explained in the beginning, and the other goal is to bring attention to the *Science of the Soul* and incitement to the knowledge of its essence. For when the understanding intelligent man studies the science of numbers and reflects upon the quantity of its species, the divisions of its several branches, and the special properties of these several branches, he knows that all of them are accidental and have their being and existence in the soul. So the soul is an essence, because accidents do not have existence other than in essence, and can not exist except through it.

The Goal of the Sciences

The goal of philosophers is the study of the abstract sciences and the training of their students in it. Indeed, it is the path to the natural sciences; the goal of studying the natural sciences is the ascent from it to the theological sciences which are the highest goal of the philosopher and the aim to which they are ascending with true knowledge. The first step of the study of the theological sciences is the knowledge of the essence of the soul, and the search for its source, where it was before its fastening to the body; and inquiry into its life to come, where it will be after its separation from the body, which is called death; and inquiry into the manner of reward for the good people, and how it will be in the world of spirits; and inquiry into the lot of evil doers and how it will be in the other place. Moreover, another quality which men are recommended to acquire is the knowledge of their Lord, and there can be no means of knowing Him except after knowing oneself as God, the Exalted, has said: "Who forsakes the religion of Abraham but he who is ignorant of himself" (2:124) meaning be is ignorant of the soul. And as it is said, if one knows himself, be knows his Lord. And it has been said, if he informs you of himself he informs you of his Lord. It is binding on every scholar to study the science of the soul and the knowledge of its essence and its arrangement. God has said: "And by the soul, and He who fashioned it, and who taught it its sin and its piety, he who keeps it pure will be happy, and he who corrupts it will be disappointed" (91: 7–10). And God said in the story of the beloved woman in the narrative of Joseph: "The soul is inclined to evil unless my Lord has had mercy"(12: 53). And God has said: "As for Him who fears to stand in the presence of his Lord and forbids his soul from low desires, surely Paradise will be (his) abode" (79: 40–41). And God has said: "On the Day (of Judgment) every soul will plead for itself" (16: 112). And God has said: "Oh soul that art at rest: Return to your Lord completely satisfied" (89: 27–28). And God has said: "God takes the souls at the time of their death and as for those that die not, (he takes them) during their sleep" (39: 43).

Thus there are many verses and proofs in the Qur'ān on the existence of the soul and on its changeable conditions and they are decisive against anyone who denies the existence of the soul.

When those philosophers, who used to discuss the science of the soul before the descent of the Qur'ān, the New Testament, and the Torah, inquired into the science of the soul with the natural talents of their minds, they deduced the knowledge of its essence by the conclusions of their reasoning. This induced them to compose philosophical books which were mentioned previously in this first treatise. But because of extensive discourse in them and their transmission from language to language, one can not understand their meaning or know the goal of their authors. The understanding of the meaning of these books is closed to those who inspect them and the goals of their authors trouble those who examine them. We have taken the core of their meaning and the highest goals of their authors and we have presented them as briefly as possible in fifty-two treatises, of which this is the first. The others follow it and you find them according to the order of the numbers.

The treatise is completed, praise to God, Lord of the universe, and may God bless his apostle, Muḥammnd the prophet, and his family who are righteous, and may He surely grant them peace.

—Bernard R. Goldstein, translator

Man and the Animals

Chapter 1

It is said that when the race of Adam began to reproduce and multiply they spread out over the earth, land and sea, mountain and plain, everywhere freely seeking their own ends in security. At first, when they were few, they had lived in fear, hiding from the many wild animals and beasts of prey. They had taken refuge in the mountaintops and hills, sheltering in caves and eating fruit from trees, vegetables from the ground, and the seeds of plants.[1] They had clothed themselves in tree leaves against the heat and cold and spent the winter where it was warm and summer where it was cool. But then they built cities and villages on the plains and settled there.[2]

They enslaved such cattle as cows, sheep, and camels, and such beasts as horses, asses, and mules. They hobbled and bridled them and used them for their own purposes—riding, hauling, plowing, and threshing—wore them out in service, imposing work beyond their powers, and checked them from seeking their own ends,[3] where

This translation is based on *Rasāʾil Ikhwān al-Ṣafāʾ*, translated by Lenn E. Goodman as *The Case of the Animals Versus Man Before the King of the Jinn* (Boston: Twayne Press, 1978), pp. 51–77 and 198–202.

1. The primal vegetarianism of man is a widespread motif, suggested as early as Genesis. For in Eden, Adam is given to eat "of every tree," except of course the tree of knowledge of good and evil. (Gen. 2:16–17); and even after his expulsion his provender is construed as "thorns and thistles" and "the herb of the field" (Gen. 3:18). But Noah is told that animals may serve as his food (Gen. 9:3). To the ascetically inclined interpreter a collocation of these passages would naturally suggest that human meat eating postdated a vegetarian epoch, and that is what the Ikhwān profess. Taken in context however, the first reference permits fruits of all trees by way of excluding the one forbidden tree. The second refers to conditions of hardship and toil but does not exclude a nonvegetarian diet. The third permits meat eating provided that living flesh not be consumed, thus presupposing that flesh had been consumed hitherto.

The notion that man's first diet was vegetarian harks back to mythic roots. (For one extended statement, which, like that of the Ikhwān, turns mythlike materials to account as elements in an ethical argument, see Porphyry, *On Abstinence from Animal Food*, II, 5ff.) Levi-Strauss explains the significance of myths regarding human carnivorism in *The Raw and the Cooked* (trans. John and Doreen Weightmann [New York, 1970]) as relating to the contrast of man's civilized with his hypothetically precivilized state.

2. Natural man presumably was not as vulnerable as civilized man, but also not as dominant. Like other beasts he kept to his own turf and shunned creatures which were likely to be dangerous to him. His efforts at self-protection, however, from the elements and the other species led to enclosure which made him capable of flexibility with regard to habitat. So began human dominance of nature, by man's expropriation of habitats beyond that in which he first was placed on being thrust into nature. Nomadic life is here construed as closer to nature and, as in Ibn Khaldūn, "closer to being good," than settled life (see *Muqaddimah*, II, 4 (trans. F. Rosenthal [New York, 1958], vol. I, p. 253); and gathering here seems "better" and more natural than agriculture. But, unlike Ibn Khaldūn, the Ikhwān al-Ṣafāʾ do not explore here the social and economic conditions requisite to the maintenance of any such *modus vivendi*, although such exploration would not be irrelevant to their question regarding man's relations with other species.

3. Like contemporary defenders of animal rights the Ikhwān note the frustration of animals' innate natures and desires as a prime abuse of domestication. Peter Singer notes the inability of

hitherto they had roamed unhindered in the woodlands and wilds, going about as they wished in search of pasture, water, and whatever was beneficial to them.

Other animals escaped such as she wild asses, gazelles, beasts of prey, and wild creatures and birds which once had been tame and lived in peace and quietude in their ancestral lands. They fled the realms of men for far-off wastes, forests, mountain peaks, and glens. But the Adamites set after them with various devices of hunting, trapping and snaring, for mankind firmly believed that the animals were their runaway or rebellious slaves.

Time years went by, and Muḥammad[4] was sent, God bless and keep him and all his House. He called men and jinn to God and to Islam. One party of jinn answered his call and became good Muslims.[5] In the course of time a king arose over the jinn, Bīwarāsp the Wise, known as King Heroic.[6] The seat of his kingdom was an island called Balāsāghūn in the midst of the Green Sea, which lies near the equator.[7] There the air and soil were good. There were sweet rivers, bubbling springs, ample fields, and sheltered resting places, varieties of trees and fruit, lush meadows, herbs, and flowers.[8]

---

hens to form a pecking order in crowded, battery conditions and the unnatural confinement of calves intended for veal (lest grazing and muscular activity impart sinew and iron to their muscle) in stalls too small to allow turning of the head for grooming by the calf's tongue (see "Down on the Factory Farm," in Peter Singer, ed., *Animal Liberation* [New York, 1975]).

Here the fundamental Liberal assumption is placed on its naturalistic basis—that all creatures should be left to do what comes naturally to them, since the natural inclinations naturally lead to what is most wholesome and advantageous for a creature, and thus a life according to unhampered natural inclination is assumed (romantically) to be the best kind of life. See Epicurus, *Principal Doctrines*, 8, 15, 25 and *Vatican Fragments*, 21. 52; Lucretius. *De Reruin Natura*, I, 10 ff.

4. It is relevant to the case the animals will present that the Ikhwān begin from the beginning, that is, like the Arabic universal histories and Washington Irving's history of New Amsterdam (which was facetiously modeled on them), from creation, to establish, for example, the aboriginal natural relations of humans and other animals. But then again, the Ikhwān are anxious to begin their story, and there will be ample opportunities to till in the relevant historical matter. Hence, from Creation to Muḥammad. The founder of Islam (Ca. 570–632), the Messenger in the Qur'ān, who was born and died in Arabia.

5. The existence of the jinn, the demons anti sprites of Arabic parlance *(cf.* Latin *genii)* was taken for granted by popular and traditional Islam; and, according to Islamic doctrine, jinn were included in the Muḥammadan dispensation. The Qur'ān (Surah 72) tells of a party of jinn listening intently to Muḥammad as he received Qur'ānic revelations (which he recited aloud) and then, acknowledging their former error, professing sincere conversion to his faith. According to tradition these then became emissaries to other jinn, and so there were many Muslim jinn, just as there were both good and evil jinn, according to the account the Jinn give of themselves: Qur'ān 72:11. (All references to the Qur'ān in this book will be in this form, the Sura number followed by the verse number according to the edition of Fluegel [Leipzig, 1883].)

6. Biwarâsp, the name is Persian.

7. The historic Balāsāghūn was a Soghdian town which figured in the military history of the Qārā-Khāns, et al., but the Ikhwân place their jinni realm in a fanciful island in the Green Sea, that is, in the Indian Ocean.

8. The Ikhwān mention carefully the natural resources which made this island a favored spot for animal or human habitation. They observe the same practice with regard to other lands as well. No habitat is regarded unfavorably; even most extreme environments contain features which are beneficial or necessary to their denizens.

Once upon a time in those days storm winds cast up a seagoing ship on the shore of that island. Aboard were men of commerce, industry, and learning as well as others of the human kind. They went out and explored the island, finding it rich in trees and fruit, fresh water, wholesome air, fine soil, vegetables, herbs and plants, all kinds of cereals and grains which the rainfall from heaven made grow. They saw all sorts of animals—beasts, cattle, birds, and beasts of prey—all living in peace and harmony with one another, demure and unafraid.[9]

These folk liked the place and undertook to settle there. They built structures to live in. Soon they began to interfere with the beasts and cattle, forcing them into service, riding them, and loading them with burdens as in their former lands. But these beasts and cattle balked and fled. The men pursued and hunted them, using all manner of devices to take them, firmly convinced that the animals were their runaway and recalcitrant slaves. When the cattle and beasts learned that this was their belief, their spokesmen and leaders gathered and came to set their complaint before Bīwarāsp the Wise, King of the jinn. The King, accordingly sent a messenger to summon those persons to his court.

A group from the ship, about seventy men of diverse lands, answered the summons. When their arrival was announced, the King ordered that they be welcomed with decorum and shown to their lodgings. After three days he brought them into his council chamber. Bīwarāsp was a wise, just, and noble king, open-handed and open-minded, hospitable to guests, and a refuge to strangers. He had mercy for the afflicted and did not allow injustice. He ordained what was good and would not tolerate what was evil but interdicted all wrong doing. His sole hope in all this was to please God and enjoy His favor.[10] When the men came before him and saw him on his royal throne, they hailed him with wishes of long life and well-being. Then the King asked through his interpreter, "What brought you to our island? Why did you come uninvited to our land?"

One of the humans answered, "We were drawn here by all we have heard of the merit of the king, his many virtues—goodness, nobility of character, justice, and impartiality in judgment. We have come before him that he might hear our arguments and the proofs we shall present, and judge between us and these escaped slaves of ours who deny our authority, for God upholds the righteous cause and will render right triumphant."

"Speak as you wish," said the King, "only make clear what you say."

9. The Ikhwān propose that predation and even competition among animals are attributable either directly or indirectly to the acts of humans.

10. Biwarāsp is painted as a model king—a princely mirror of the sort whom Muslim jurists held up to actual kings as an ideal. He combines the Platonic kingly virtue of justice with the traditional Middle Eastern virtues of magnanimity, liberality, and compassion. The obligation to command what is decent and interdict what is indecent is Qurʾānic (see 9:68), and serves as the thematic basis for all Islamic public policy, since it is taken to mean that there is a general (that is, societal, hence specifically leader-directed) obligation to institute what is right and good and to restrict institutionally what is wrong or bad—thus, in effect, to legislate moral standards through public policy and juridical practice.

"I shall, your Majesty," the human spokesman answered. "These cattle, beasts of prey, and wild creatures—all animals in fact—are our slaves, and we are their masters. Some have revolted and escaped, while others obey with reluctance and scorn servitude."

The King replied to the human, "What evidence and proof have you to substantiate your claims?"

"Your Majesty," said the human, "we have both traditional religious evidence and rational proofs for what I have said."

"Let us have them," said the King.

Then a spokesman of the humans, an orator, descended from ʿAbbās,[11] God's grace upon him, rose, mounted the witness stand, and said, "Praise be to God, Sovereign of the universe, hope of those who fear Him and foe to none but the unjust. God bless Muḥammad, seal of the prophets,[12] chief of God's messengers and intercessor on the Day of Judgment. God bless the cherubim, His upright servants, all who live in heaven and earth who are faithful, and all Muslims. May He in His mercy place you and us among them, for He is the Most Merciful.

"Praised be God who formed man from water and his mate from man, multiplied their race and lineage, mankind and womankind, gave honor to their seed and dominion over land and sea, and gave them all good things for their sustenance, saying, 'Cattle He created for you, whence you have warmth and many benefits. You eat of them and find them fair when you bring them home to rest or drive them out to pasture.'[13] He also said, 'You are carried upon them and upon ships,'[14] and,

11. ʿAbbās b. ʿAbd al-Muṭṭalib b. Hāshim was the uncle of Muḥammad. Since the prophet of Islam was not survived by any male issue, ʿAbbāsid or Hāshimite descent figured prominently in the legitimist claims which continued to be made throughout the centuries after his death. And the dynasty which established itself in 750, founded Baghdad, and continued to rule (or reign) over much of the Middle East (including the Basra of the Ikhwān) until 1258, traced their descent to ʿAbbās.

The Būyid dynasty, exercising hegemony over Iraq from their Persian capital in Shirâz (945–1053) relegated the ʿAbbāsid khalifs to a titular/ritual role, to the extent that they were able. This division of authority gave scope to the Ikhwān for harsh criticism of the ʿAbbāsids in the present *risāla* but nowhere in its pages (10 the) explicitly propagandize in behalf of the (Shīʿite) Buyids.

12. Popularly understood, "seal of the prophets," as an epithet of Muḥammad is thought to designate the finality of the Muḥammadan dispensation. But as Ilse Lichtenstadter points out, the Qur'ān itself refers to Muḥammad simply by name or as Gods messenger; the term 'seal of the prophets' (33:40), she writes, expressed "only his conviction that he affirmed, through his revelation the veracity of earlier 'messages' brought by his prophetic predecessors; he joined their ranks, carrying on their work and projecting it into the future by confirming, as the seal does for a document, the eternal truth it conveys." This original and insightful gloss, Lichtenstadter hastens to add, sheds light Aḥmadiyyah sect, a modernist movement born in the Indian subcontinent. See Ilse Lichtenstadter, *Introduction to Classical Arabic Literature* (New York, 1974), pp. 47, 52.

13. Qur'ān 16:5–6. The warmth referred to is the fabric made of the cattle's hair, whence clothing and shelters may be made. Verse 7 continues: "They bear your loads to lands you could not reach without great hardships. Indeed your Lord is clement and compassionate."

14. Qur'ān 23:22; *cf.* verse 21, "In truth there is a lesson for you in the cattle. We (namely, God) give you sup from what is in their bellies, and you have many benefits front them, and of them you eat."

'horses, mules, and asses for riding and for splendor.'[15] He also said, 'so that you might be mounted upon their backs and remember the goodness of your Lord.'[16] And there are many other verses in the Qur'ān and in the Torah and Gospels which show that they were created for us, for our sake and are our slaves and we their masters. God grant pardon to you and to myself."

"Cattle and beasts," said the King, "you have heard the verses of Qur'ān this human has cited as evidence for his claims. What say you to this?"

At that the spokesman for the beasts, a mule, got up and said,[17] "Praise be to God, One, Unique and Alone, Changeless, Ever-abiding and Eternal, who was before all beings, beyond time and space and then said, 'BE!'—at which there was a burst of light He made shine forth from His hidden Fastness. From this light He created a blazing fire and a surging sea of waves. From fire and water He created spheres studded with stars and constellations, and the blazing lamp of the heavens. He built the sky, made wide the earth and firm the mountains. He made the many storeyed heavens, dwelling place of the archangels; the spaces between the spheres, dwellings of the cherubim. The earth he gave to living things, ani-

15. Qur'ān 16:8; *cf.* the sequel, verses 10–16. "He it is who sends down water front the sky for you, from Him, as drink, whence there are trees on which your flocks may feed. And with it He causes crops to grow for you—olive and date trees, and grape vines, each with its fruit. Truly in that there is a sign for thoughtful folk. He put the night and day in your service, the sun, moon, and stars, subservient to His command. In this truly there are signs for discerning folk. . . . He it is who subjected the sea to you, that you might eat moist flesh from it and bring forth ornaments from it to wear, and that you may see ships cleaving it . . . and pitched towering mountains on the earth that it may hold fast by you; rivers and passages that you might perhaps find your way, and landmarks—and by the stars are they guided. . . ." The syntax of this inspirational passage may be somewhat sprung, but the meaning is clear, that God's grace is manifest in the adaptation of nature to human needs. This may be read as presuming that nature was designed to serve man's needs or more strongly, that sun, moon, stars, sea, rivers, mountains, passes, night, and day exist solely for man's sake. But neither anthropocentric reading strictly is implied. As in Biblical usage, the Qur'ān may be expressing a result as a purpose (since all results are regarded as foreseen), and the "subordination" of nature to man may express simply the fact that he benefits from it, not necessarily that he is its lord. The central import remains undisturbed, for even a casual beneficiary of God's grace in nature ought to feel the gratitude and the sense of a planned order which Muḥammad calls for from the "discerning." Thus the anthropocentric overtones of the passages the human cites are not essential to the Qur'ānic message, and the Ikhwān can confidently abstract from them and not feel bound by them in their inquiry.

16. Qur'ān 43:12. Ships, it is true, are man-made, not an aboriginal feature of nature. But the presence on earth of seas and navigable waterways is regarded by Muḥammad (as in the passage cited in note 15) as an act of grace, in part because it makes possible the ease of water-borne transport.

17. Like any proper formal discourse the mule's remarks open with the *khuṭbah* or preface in praise of God. The *khuṭbahs* found in writings where thematic exposition plays a major role are actual introductions which set the tone and foreshadow the themes of what will follow. Since the mule intends to deal with the rights and wrongs of animal-human relations, his *khuṭbah* harks back to the creation at which the divine law was first imposed upon nature. This forms a groundwork for claims as to the divine intention regarding the relations of the species, and many of the subsequent speakers, animal and human, follow the mule's example. The manner in which the Biblical conception of cosmic time and universal history casts its spell over Islamic imagination is very evident in these little introductions.

mals, and plants. He created the jinn out of the fiery simoom and humans out of clay. He gave man posterity "from vile water in a vessel sure,"[18] allowed man's seed to succeed one another on earth, to inhabit it, not to lay it waste, to care for the animals and profit by them, but not to mistreat or oppress them. God grant pardon to you and to myself.

"Your Majesty," the mule continued, "there is nothing in the verses this human has cited to substantiate his claims that they are masters and we slaves. These verses point only to the kindness and blessings which God vouchsafed to mankind, for God said that He made them your servants just as he made the sun, the moon, the wind and clouds your servants. Are we to think, your Majesty, that these too are their slaves and chattels and that men are their masters? No! God created all His creatures on heaven and earth. He let some serve others either to do them some good or to prevent some evil. God's subordination of animals to man is solely to help men and keep them from harm (as we shall show in another chapter) not, as they deludedly suppose and calumniously claim, in order that they should be our masters and we their slaves.[19]

"Your Majesty," the spokesman of the beasts continued, "we and our fathers were inhabitants of the earth before the creation of Adam, forefather of the human race. We lived in the countryside and roamed the country trails. Our bands went to and fro in God's country seeking sustenance and caring for themselves. Each one of us tended to his own affairs, kept to the place best suited to his needs—moor, forest, mountain, or plain. Each kind saw to its own. We were fully occupied in caring for our broods and rearing our young with all the good food and water God had allotted us, secure and unmolested in our own lands. Night and day we praised and sanctified God, and God alone.[20]

"Ages passed and God created Adam, father of mankind, and made him His viceregent on earth. His offspring reproduced, and his seed multiplied. They spread

18. See 23:13, 77:20–21, 32:7, etc. Note that even the heavens for the Ikhwān are divided into diverse habitats each with its own proper denizens.

19. God has blessed mankind through the animals, it is conceded. But the scriptural passages imply no more—not that man is sovereign over nature nor that it was created for his sake. For the same usages are applied to the heavenly bodies, which in medieval usage were regarded as superior to man in the "great chain of being" and, therefore, could not rationally be spoken of as subordinate to human use in any sense, which implied an inferior rank or ontic dignity.

20. The animals observed the laws of nature, and this constituted their constant "praise" of God. Each kept to its own habitat and followed the pattern of life which God had laid out For it. The laissez-faire ideal of each (species) caring for its own and not molesting others is here directed pointedly at the humans, who are familiar with this ideal but whose very existence upon earth is predicated on breaching that ideal. The romantic ideal of peace assumes this kind of absolute noninterference—which Isaiah uses to symbolize universal peace among nations—but, as commonly happens with expressions of romantic dissatisfaction and other rhetorical forms of protest, a relative distinction (in this case that between man's widespread exploitative activities and the more confined and limited exploitativeness of the animals) is painted as an absolute distinction, as though humans alone exploited nature and other species and the animals did no such thing.

The animal spokesman pleads the priority of animals to humans as legitimating the independence and self-direction of the beasts. He does not then presuppose the "dogma of simultaneous creation."

over the earth—land and sea, mountain and plain. Men encroached on our ancestral lands. They captured sheep, cows, horses, mules, and asses from among us and enslaved them, subjecting them to the exhausting toil and drudgery of hauling, being ridden, plowing, drawing water, and turning mills. They forced us to these things under duress, with beatings, bludgeonings, and every kind of torture and chastisement our whole lives long. Some of us fled to deserts, wastelands, or mountaintops, but the Adamites pressed after us, hunting us with every kind of wile and device. Whoever fell into their hands was yoked, haltered, and fettered. They slaughtered and flayed him, ripped open his belly, cut off his limbs and broke his bones, tore out his eyes; plucked his feathers or sheared his hair or fleece, and put him onto the fire to be cooked, or on the spit to be roasted, or subjected him to even more dire tortures, whose full extent is beyond description.[21] Despite these cruelties, these sons of Adam are not through with us but must claim that this is their inviolable right, that they are our masters and we are their slaves, deeming any of us who escapes a fugitive, rebel, shirker of duty—all with no proof or explanation beyond main force."[22]

Chapter 2

When the King heard this, he ordered a herald to carry the news throughout the kingdom and summon vassals and followers from all tribes of the jinn—judges, justices, and jurisconsults. Then he sat down to judge between the spokesmen for the animals and the advocates of men. First he addressed the leaders of the humans: "What have you to say of the injustice, oppression and usurpation with which you are charged by these beasts and cattle?"

"They are our slaves," said the human representative, "we are their owners. It is for us as their lords to judge them, for to obey us is to obey God, and he who rebels against us is transgressing against God."[23]

The King replied, "Only claims which are grounded in definite proof are acceptable before this court. What proof base you of your claims?"

"We have philosophical arguments and rational proofs[24] in support of the soundness of our claims," said the human.

21. The animals make full use of graphic description of their abuse at the hands of men for the sake of the emotive response elicited by the *frisson* these descriptions evoke.

22. A moral outrage is added to the physical outrage of the violation of animals' liberties and lives by the claimed legitimacy of these procedures, although force is the only legitimating factor, since it is manifest that no element of choice could be invoked on the part of the beasts, were choice to be accorded them. Here the Ikhwān rely upon the notion of virtual subjecthood to secure this conclusion, as they do in their emotive passages to secure empathy. There is a further irony in the human claim of an inviolable right over the animals. For, to the Ikhwān, no natural state is permanent and thus, no claimed right is inviolable.

23. A similar claim was made by Muslim rulers, and the satiric impact of this parallel would not have been lost on the audience of the Ikhwān.

24. The traditional/religious arguments have already been shown to be unavailing to the human claim. The reader should bear in mind, however, the distinction between religion, which is an

"What are they? Will you present them?" asked the King.

"Certainly," the man said. "Our beautiful form, the erect construction of our bodies, our upright carriage, our keen senses, the subtlety of our discrimination, our keen minds and superior intellects all indicate that we are masters and they slaves to us."

The King turned to the spokesman of the beasts. "What have you to say to the evidence he has introduced?"

"There is nothing in what he says to prove what the human claims."

"Are not standing upright and sitting straight the qualities of kings and bent backs and lowered heads the attributes of slaves?" asked the King.

"God assist your Majesty to the truth," the animal spokesman replied. "Heed what I say and you shall know that God did not create them in this form or shape them in this way to show that they are masters. Nor did He create us in the form we have to show that we are slaves. Rather He knew and wisely ordained that their form is better for them and ours for us. Since God created Adam and his children naked and unshod, without feathers, fleece, or wool on their skin to protect them against heat and cold, since He gave them fruit from trees as their food and leaves of trees for their clothing, and since the trees stood upright, spreading up into the air, He made man stand erect so it would be easy for him to reach the fruit and leaves. By the same token, since He gave us the grass on the ground for our food, He made us face downward so it would be easy for us to reach it.[25] This, not what he alleged, is the reason God made them erect and us bent downward."

"What then do you say of God's worth, 'We formed man at the fairest height'?"[26] asked the King.

The spokesman replied, "The heavenly books have interpretations which go beyond the literal and are known by those whose knowledge is deep.[27] Let the King inquire of scholars who know and understand the Qur'ān."

---

institution, and theology, which is a branch of thought. Theological claims may still be adduced, but they must be based on reason, that is, they must represent natural (as opposed to scriptural) theology. Scripture, as has been shown already, assigns no absolute ascendency to man over the animals and thus, no traditional religious argument can be created in behalf of such a claim. The task devolves on reason.

Reason and religion (that is, the traditional elaboration of revelation as preserved in scripture) are here accorded parallel roles. "Orthodox" thinkers in Islamic jurisprudence were to argue that reliance upon "reason" as a means of interpreting the divine law leads inevitably to the introduction of subjective notions with the interpretation. But such orthodoxy did not exist in the earliest phases of the development of Islamic jurisprudence but arose as a developed school of traditionalism in response to what were felt to be the freewheeling tendencies of earlier, more rationalistic speculation. The Ikhwān, in any case, not being orthodox and indeed belonging to a period at which traditionalistic orthodoxy had by no means come to maturity, felt no compunction in not subordinating rational arguments to tradition, as later and more orthodox thinkers were expected to do.

25. Ecological considerations, specifically the adaptation of each species to its eco-niche, not any inherent beauty or intrinsic merit are the basis of human form, as of the forms of all species.

26. Qur'ān 95:4.

27. The Qur'ān itself (3:5) alludes to those whose knowledge is deep *(al-rāsikhūn fi 'l-'ilm)*: "He it is who has sent down to you this Book in which are sure verses, which are the substance of

So the King asked the learned sage, "What is the meaning of 'the fairest height'?"

"The day God created Adam," he replied, "the stars were at their zeniths, the points of the signs of the zodiac were solid and square, the season was equable and matter was prepared to receive form. Thus his body was given the finest form and the most perfect constitution."

"This would suffice to give a ground for their boasts of honor and excellence," said the King.

The wise jinni said, "'At the fairest height' has another meaning in the light of God's words, 'who created, fashioned, and proportioned you as He pleased.'[28] This means, He made you neither tall and thin nor short and squat but at a mean."

The spokesman for the animals said, "He did the same for us. He did not make us tall and thin, nor short and squat, but in due proportion. So we share equally with them in this."

"How is it that animals are so well proportioned and so evenly formed?" the human asked. "We see that the camel has a massive body, long neck, small ears, and a short tail; the elephant, an enormous bulk, great tusks, broad ears, and tiny eyes. The cow and buffalo have long tails and thick horns, but no tusks. Rams have two big horns and a thick tail, but no beard; goats have a fine beard, but no fat tail, so their private parts are exposed. Rabbits have a small body but big ears, and so it goes. Most animals—wild beasts, beasts of prey, birds, and crawling creatures—are irregularly built and misproportioned."

"On the contrary, O human," said the animal spokesman, "you have missed the beauty and wisdom of their creation. Do you not realize that a slight to the work is a slight to its Maker? You must start with the knowledge that all animals are the work of the wise Creator, who made them as He did with reason and purpose, for their own good and protection from harm.[29] But this is understood only by Him and by those whose knowledge is deep."

---

the book, and others which are unclear. Those who have unsteadiness in their hearts pursue its uncertainties, eager for strife and eager to explain them. But none but God knows the interpretations. And those who are deeply rooted in understanding [*al-rāsikhūn fi'l-ʿilm*] say 'We believe in it. All is from our Lord.' Yet none can heed it but those with hearts to understand." While this passage seems directly to admonish Muḥammad's hearers not to endeavor to interpret the Qur'ān, the internal admission that the Muslim scripture contains problematic verses was taken as an invitation to allegorical interpretation by subsequent generations, and "those whose knowledge was deep" became the designation of the class of investigators who were likely to interpret these correctly in view of the Qur'ānic grouping of persons so described with the faithful among those destined for a divine reward (4:160).

28. Qur'ān 82:7–8. These verses were a subject for speculation perhaps because they seem to suggest (if taken literally) that God physically handled Adam's clay. The great Muslim theologian al-Ghazzālī (1058–1111) wrote a commentary on these words, and Ibn Ṭufayl (d. 1185) returned to them" as well in his *Ḥayy ibn Yaqẓān* (trans. L. E. Goodman [New York, 1972])—in view of the possibility they afforded for a discussion of the interaction of matter and spirit. But the Ikhwān read the passage as referring to the modulation of form to function in all animal species.

29. The investigator must work on the assumption of the wisdom of creation. Just as scientists assume the universal operation of efficient causality and seek causes when they do not find them, not stopping at each juncture to inquire, where evidence fails, whether here the rule of causality

"Tell us and inform us then," said the human, "if you are the scholar and speaker of the beasts, why does the camel have such a long neck?"

"To match his long legs," he replied, "so that he can reach the grass on the ground, to help himself rise with a load, and so that he can reach all parts of his body with his lip to scratch and rub them. The elephant's trunk takes the place of a long neck. His large ears serve to shoo flies and gnats from the corners of his eyes and mouth—for his mouth is always open, he cannot close it fully because of his protruding tusks. But his tusks are his defense against predators. The rabbit's large ears provide cover, a blanket in winter and a shade in summer; for his skin is tender and his body, delicate. And so we find that God made the parts, limbs, and organs of every species adapted to its needs in seeking the beneficial and shunning the harmful. This is the idea to which Moses alluded (peace be upon him) when he said, 'Our Lord who gave its nature to every thing and guided all things.'[30]

"As for your boasts of the beauty of your own form, there is nothing in that to support your claim that you are masters and we slaves. For beauty of form is only what is desired in the male and female of each species that attracts them to one another to mate, copulate, and produce offspring and progeny for the survival of the species. Thus beauty of form is different in every species. Our males are not aroused by the beauty of your females, nor our females by the charms of your males, just as blacks are not attracted by the charms of whites nor whites by those of blacks, and just as boy-lovers have no passion for the charms of girls and wenchers have no desire for boys.[31] So, Mr. Human Being, you have no grounds for boasting of superior beauty.

---

has petered out, so biologists must presume the universality of functional causality, that is, of teleology, that form serves function. The assumption is not arbitrary but educated by experience and rewarded as a heuristic device—but it does go beyond whatever evidence we have, as it must if it is to be used heuristically. The *a priori* assumption of causality being universal has, of course, been called into question in some interpretations of the findings associated with quantum phenomena, and the relevancy of teleology in biology has also been questioned. In both cases the critique, like the assumption which it criticizes, stands on metaphysical ground. There is no evidence for the rejection of universal causality (or teleology) just as there can be no evidence in its behalf. But its heuristic value, or, as Kant would have it, its role as a regulative idea, remains intact. Nature would be unintelligible without the assumption of universal causality, and biology would be impossible without teleology.

30. Qurʾān 20:52. Here both form and (ethological) function are ascribed to the act of God. The former is the product of creation; the latter, the object of divine guidance.

31. Since form is relative to function, physical beauty must be a subjective matter accountable only to the adaptive needs of the species and not expressive of any objective status in the ontic chain. This is a corollary of the (Qurʾānic, not Darwinian) principle of adaptation which the Ikhwān apply. They offer evidence for the subjectivity of the sense of beauty from the alleged variations in standards of attractiveness from people to people and within peoples among individuals of divergent sexual orientations. This does not imply that the animal spokesman believes blacks and whites to be of different species. Any variation of taste would have served in his argument. He might have argued that males in general are attracted to females and vice versa, but the example of homosexual versus heterosexual orientation apparently seemed a clearer cut case, and the alleged racial difference of tastes was intended to heighten the sense of subjectivity in regard to this area of valuation. For a discussion of Islamic views on race, see Bernard Lewis, *Race and Color in Islam* (New York, 1971).

Chapter 3

"Your vaunted powers of perception and fine discrimination are not unique, for there are animals with finer senses and more precise discrimination. The camel, for example, despite his long legs and neck and the elevation of his head in the air, finds his footing along the most arduous and treacherous pathways in the dark of night, which you could not make out and not one of you could see without a lantern, torch, or candle. The horse too sees in the dark, or at least he hears distant footsteps in the dead of night and often wakes his master from sleep by nudging him with a foot to warn him of an enemy or beast of prey. An ass or cow is frequently observed to return to its familiar home when its master has led it away on a path it did not know and left it. Yet there are men who may travel the same road any number of times and still stray from it and lose themselves. In a flock of sheep and ewes a great number may give birth in a single night and then be driven out to pasture early in the morning not to return until nightfall. Even so it is observed that when the young, a hundred or more, are released each goes to its dam, without any doubt on the part of the mother or confusion on the part of the young. With humans a month or two or more must pass before they can distinguish their own mother from their sister, or their father from their brother. Where then are the superior senses and fine discrimination which you boast of against us?

"As for the alleged superiority of your intellects—why we find not the slightest trace or sign of it, for if you had such overwhelming minds you would not have boasted against us of things which are neither your own doing nor acquired by your own efforts, but are among the manifold gifts of God, to be recognized and given thanks for as acts of grace. The intelligent take pride only in things which are their own doing, sound arts and industries, sound views, true sciences, upright conduct, just practices, ways pleasing to God.[32] As far as we can see you have no superiority to boast of, but only unfounded claims, unwarranted allegations, and groundless contentiousness."

Chapter 4

The King then said to the human, "You have heard their reply. Do you have anything to add?"

32. The animals here adopt the Stoic axiom that one is accountable only for that over which one has control. For the Stoics the realm of guaranteed control extended only to the inclination of the will, and they therefore argued that only in regard to intentions could a person be praised or blamed. Kant similarly held that the only thing which is unqualifiedly good is a good will. The animal spokesman here, however, proposes a wider possible sphere of moral accountability and hence of moral pride. There are arts, industries, sciences and views, actions and practices for which an individual may claim responsibility. This voluntarism may seem incompatible with the general doctrine of God's responsibility for all things including arts and industries and even the inclination of the will itself, but the Ikhwān do not seem to be preoccupied with the possibility of such a contradiction. They do not seem to regard the notion that arts, sciences, and even the inclination of the will are gifts of God as incompatible with the assignment of human responsibility for these.

"Yes, your Majesty," he said. "There is further evidence that we are their masters and they our slaves. We buy and sell them, give them their feed and water, clothe and shelter them from heat and cold. We protect them from beasts of prey which would tear them to pieces, treat their illnesses and care for them when they are sick or diseased, teach them when they know nothing, put up with them when they are mad, put them out to pasture when they are spent. All this we do out of kindness and compassion for them, but these are things masters do for their servants and owners for their property."

"You have heard his assertion," said the King, "answer as you see fit."

The spokesman of the beasts replied, "He argues that they buy and sell us. The same is done by Persians to Greeks and Greeks to Persians when they conquer one another. Which is the slave and which the master? The Indians treat the Sindians the same way, and the Sindians the Indians; the Abyssinians, the Nubians, and the Nubians, the Abyssinians. The Arabs, Turks, and Kurds behave the same way toward one another. Which of them, pray, are really the slaves and which the masters? Are these not, O just King, simply the turns of human fortune with the changing influence of the stars and conjunctions of the constellations? As God Himself said, 'These are but the days whose revolutions I bring about among men'—and no one understands this but the learned.[33]

"As for his statement that they feed and water us, and all the rest he mentioned that they do for us, these things are done not out of kindness or compassion as he claims but out of fear that we might die and they lose their investment in us and the benefits they derive from us, the opportunity to drink our milk, wear our fleece or wool or fur, ride on our backs, and have us carry their burdens."

Then the ass spoke up and said, "Your Majesty, had you seen us as prisoners of the sons of Adam, our backs laden with rocks, bricks, earth, wood, iron, and other heavy loads, struggling and striving to carry them while they stood over us with sticks in their hands to beat us brutally about the face and back in anger, you would have pitied us and shed tears of sorrow for us, merciful King. Where then are their mercy and compassion?"

The ram said, "You would have pitied us, your Majesty, if you had seen us as their prisoners, when they seized the smallest kids and lambs and separated them from their dams to preempt our milk, cook our young and bound them hand and

33. Qur'ān 3:134. The verse in full reads: "If ye are stricken with a wound, so too are the enemy stricken with a wound. These are but the days whose revolution I bring about among men—that God may know who is faithful and take martyrs from among you. For God loves not the iniquitous." Muḥammad here comforts his followers after a defeat. But the Ikhwân, read the passage allegorically—hence their remark that no one understands it but the learned. The "days" referred to are the battle days of pre-Islamic discourse—hence, the fortunes of war, whose "revolutions" God is said to bring about. Since the verb refers to the causing of revolutions in human fortunes, the animals take it as an allusion to the revolutions of the heavens, whose rising and falling constellations the learned (that is, the astrologers) can read as visible indications of the divine plan and destiny in regard to sublunary nature. Here the ecological idea of succession is merged with the concept of dynastic/imperial succession and with the astrological notion of the order and succession of astral events. Human—and animal—fortunes may rise or fall. The divine plan remains. Hence a position of dominance is no argument for human primacy in the divine scheme of things.

foot to be slaughtered and skinned, hungry, thirsty, bleating for mercy but not pitied, screaming for help with no one to aid them. We saw them slaughtered, skinned, dismembered, their entrails torn out, their heads, marrow bones, and livers on the butchers' blocks, to be cut up with great knives and boiled in cauldrons or roasted on a spit in an oven while we kept silent, not weeping or complaining, for even if we had wept they would not have pitied us. Where then is their mercy?"

The camel joined in, "Also had you seen us, your Majesty, as prisoners in the hands of the Adamites, our noses bound up with rope and our halters in the hands of drivers who forced us to carry heavy loads and make our way in the dead of night through dark defiles and waterless plains over a rocky track, bumping into boulders and stumbling with our tender pads over rocks and rough and broken ground, hungry and thirsty, our sides and backs ulcerated and sore from the rubbing of the saddles, you would have pitied us and wept for us. Where then is their pity?"

The elephant said, "Had you seen us, your Majesty, as prisoners in the hands of the sons of Adam with chains on our feet and cables about our necks while they handled iron goads to drive us, forcing us to the right or left in spite of our enormous bulk, mighty frames, long trunks, and tremendous strength, you would have pitied us and wept for us, your Majesty. Where then are the compassion and pity which this human claims they feel for us?"

Then the horse spoke, "Your Majesty, had you seen us as their prisoners on the battlefields, with bits in our mouths, saddles on our backs, and girths about our midparts, an armored rider on our backs charging at full tilt, plunging into clouds of dust, hungry and thirsty, swords at our faces, lances to our chests, and arrows in our throats, swimming in blood and advancing toward death, you would have had pity on us, O King."

The mule said, "Had you seen us, your Majesty, as their captives, our feet hobbled, our mouths bridled, our cheeks snaffled, and locks across our crotches to prevent our satisfying our natural desires, laden with pack saddles, atop which rode those low and foul-mouthed men who were our keepers and drivers and who insulted us with the vilest words at their command, whipping us about the face and hindquarters in such rage that often they were carried away and reviled themselves and their human sisters saying, 'This ass' prick up the ass of the dealer's wife!' or the buyer's or the owner's—meaning their own fellows. All these abuses turn back upon them, since they are most suited to them.

"Your Majesty, if you consider their stupidity, uncouth behavior and foul speech, you will be amazed at how little is their discerning of their own abominable ways, ugly attributes, vicious characters, and wicked actions, their manifold barbarities, corrupt notions, and conflicting dogmas. They do not repent or take stock of what they do. They do not heed the warnings of their prophets or respect the commandments of their Lord, who said, 'Let them show compassion and indulgence. Would you not wish that God show compassion to you?[34] 'Tell

34. Qur'ān 24:22. "Let not those who have affluence and ease among you shun to share with kin and with the poor and with those who have emigrated in the cause of God. Let them show com-

the faithful to forgive those who have no hope in the days of God.[35] For He also says, 'There is no creature that walks the earth or flies on wings which is not a nation like you.'[36] And He said, 'So that you may sit firmly on their backs and remember the grace of your Lord and say, praised be He who subjected them to us, for we could not have done it. And to our Lord we shall return.'"[37]

When the mule had finished speaking, the camel turned to the much maligned pig and said, "Stand up and speak, tell of the Adamites' oppression of the swine, set your complaint before the merciful King. Perhaps he will feel compassion for us and free us from our enslavement to them, for you too belong to the cattle."

But one of the jinni scholars said, "No indeed, the pig is not of the cattle. On the contrary, he is a beast of prey. Do you not see that he has tusks and eats carrion?"

But another jinni said, "On the contrary, he belongs among the cattle. Do you not see that he has hooves and eats grass and hay?"

Another said, "He is a cross between cattle and beasts, like the giraffe who is a cross between cow, leopard, and camel, or like the ostrich, whose form resembles not only that of a bird but also that of a camel."

Then said the pig to the camel, "Good Lord! What am I to say, and of whom shall I complain with all the conflicting things that are said of me. You have heard the opinions of the wisest of the jinn, and men differ even more about us; their doctrines and sects are even farther apart in our regard. Muslims say we are accursed and grotesque. They abominate the sight of us and find our smell revolting and our meat disgusting. They are loath even to pronounce our name, The Romans, on the other hand, eat our meat with gusto in their sacrifices and believe that it makes them blessed before God. The Jews detest, revile, and curse us although we have done them no wrong or injury, but only because of the enmity between them and the Romans and Christians.[38] The Armenians treat us the same

---

passion and indulgence. Would you not wish that God show compassion to you—for God is most compassionate and merciful," Once again the Ikhwān give a universal significance to remarks which were first applied in a very specific historical juncture. In the animals' plea, the unfortunate become the beasts, and the humans are identified with the affluent who should show indulgence. The notion of kinship is not in the portion of the verse quoted and is not relied upon in the appeal of the beasts.

35. Qurʾān 45:13. Those who have no hope in the days of God—that is in resurrection and redemption—here become the animals, in accordance with the eschatology adopted at the close of the *risâla.*

36. Qurʾān 6:38. The connection of this verse to its context in the Qurʾān is somewhat disjointed. The passage continues: "We have omitted nothing in the Book. Then to their Lord they will be gathered." The Book here is taken traditionally to be the Book of Destiny, and the passage seems to suggest the (Muʿtazilite) doctrine that animals will be requited in the hereafter. But the Ikhwān seem to reject such a doctrine at the close of this *risālah.*

37. Qurʾān 43:13,

38. The Beirut editor adds in a note: "This again is a chimerical notion on the part of the Ikhwān. since the Jews' detestation of swine antedates Christianity." It is Biblical, of course (Lev. 11:7). The whole passage is somewhat anachronistic. For by the Romans (*abnāʾ al-Rūm*) is usually meant the Greeks of Byzantium, that is, the Eastern Roman empire. But they did not eat pork with gusto

as others treat sheep or cows and regard our fat bodies, rich meat, and abundant offspring as special blessings. Greek doctors use lard in their treatments and prescribe it in their medicines and cures. Animal keepers mingle us with their beasts and feed us in the same stalls because they believe an animal's condition to be improved by contact with us and even by scenting our smell. Magicians and sorcerers use our skins for their books, spells, amulets, and magic devices; saddlers and shoemakers prize our bristles and vie for the pluckings from our snouts, so great is their need for them. That is why we are confused. We have no idea whom to thank and against whom to complain of injustice."

When the pig had finished speaking, the ass turned to the rabbit, who was standing between the camel's forelegs, and said, "Tell of the mistreatment rabbits have suffered at the hands of man. Make your complaint before the King. Perhaps he will look into our case in his mercy, take pity on us, and set us free."

But the rabbit said, "We are already free from the tribe of Adam. We no longer venture into their dwelling places but have withdrawn into forests and glens where we are safe from their wrongs. Nonetheless, we are harassed by dogs, hunting birds and horses, who are men's abettors against us. They bear men to us and search us out for them along with our brethren the gazelles, wild asses, wild cattle, mountain sheep, and mountain goats.

"In dogs and birds of prey it is excusable that they aid man against us," the rabbit went on, "for they have a reason to eat our meat, as they do not belong to our kind but are carnivores. But the horse is a beast, and our meat is not for him, so he should take no part in aiding men against us, unless out of ignorance and little understanding and discernment of the true nature of things."

Chapter 5

"Stop right there," the human interrupted. "This censure of horses has gone too far! If you knew that they are the finest animals in man's service you would not have spoken in this way."

"Tell us," said the King, "what great good you find in horses,"

"Their merits are many, both in their praiseworthy nature and in their marvelous character," the man replied. "They are beautifully formed, their bodies and parts in proportion, their frames well built, their colors pure and coats glossy; they

---

in their sacrifices. The pagan Romans and Greeks did, but they (did not suppose this made them blessed before (the monotheistic) God. I suspect the Ikhwān may have in mind the sacrifices of swine which Antiochus Epiphanes (r. 175–163 B.C.) ordained in his own honor, for this foe of the Hasmoneans was a monarch of Syria whose ardent Hellenism would allow him to be thought of as a "Rūmī" in the Arabo-Islamic frame of reference. Muslim abhorrence of swine, which are forbidden as food in Islam, seems to stem from Muḥammad's early Jewish contacts. The Jerusalem Talmud, *Berakhot*, 2, treats swine as a symbol of filth, and the Babylonian Talmud, *Menuḥot*, 64b, regards one who raises swine as accursed. But for the Christians' "sacrifices" see the jinni rejoinder to the Christian in chapter 19.

are swift and responsive, taking whatever direction their rider may give them, left, right, forward, back, pursuing or fleeing, charging or retreating. Besides, horses are sharp witted. They have keen senses and are well mannered. Often they refrain from staling or dropping while a rider is mounted; and, if their tails are wetted, they hold them still so as not to spatter their master. A horse must have the strength of an elephant to carry its rider with his weapons, helmet, and armor along with its own saddle, bridle, and coat of mail. The iron equipage alone must weigh nearly half a ton as he runs. And he must have the fortitude of an ass to endure the thrust of spears at his chest and throat in battle. Yet he lopes like a ravening wolf, walks like a proud bull, trots like a fox, leaps like a great rock torn loose by a torrent, bounds like a wildcat. In a race for stakes he runs as though the victory would be his own."

"True," the rabbit answered, "but in spite of all these praiseworthy qualities and fine traits of character, horses have one great flaw which casts a shadow over all their virtues."

"What is that?" asked the King. "Can you explain?"

"It is lack of insight," said the rabbit. "A horse will as readily run inflight with his master's enemy, whom he has never seen before, as with the master at whose home he was born and raised. He will as readily carry an enemy to his master as he carries the master in pursuit of an enemy. In this case he can be compared only to a sword which has no awareness, sense, or spirit. For it cuts off the head of the owner who burnishes it as readily as it does that of one who desires to break it or render it useless, seeing no difference between the two.

"A similar fault," the rabbit continued, "is found among men. Often one of them turns on his parents, brothers, or kin, works against them, and treats them as meanly as he would his worst enemy, who never gave him any kindness or cause for gratitude.[39] And in just this way these humans drink the milk of cattle as they drank their mother's milk and ride upon the shoulders of beasts as they rode upon their father's shoulders when they were small. They use animals' wool and fleece for coats, carpets, and upholstery, but in the end they slaughter, flay, disembowel, and dismember them and set them to boil or roast, unfeeling and unremembering all the good, all the blessings, so generously received of them."

When the rabbit had finished his censure of men and horses, the ass said, "You should not be overly reproachful. No one creature has been granted so many gifts and virtues that it does not lack something greater, and none is so deprived that it does not have at least some gift which no other has. God's gifts are many. No one individual can compass them all. Nor does any single species or genus have a monopoly on God's goodness. Rather God's generosity is parted among all creatures at large in greater or lesser shares. Indeed, the more clearly divinity shines

39. See Plato *Statesman*, 298ff.: the ambiguity of power. Just as the sword cuts friend and foe alike, the physician may cure or kill. The blindness of an artifact or natural object is its retention of the same nature and behavior regardless of circumstances. Human moral blindness, by contrast, is changeability. The possibility of choice (and hence of moral fallibility) renders humans capable of turning against their friends. The fatal human blindness, however, does arise from the possibility of choice—and that is to be pled in mankind's favor.

through in a being, the plainer is its servitude.[40] The two celestial luminaries, for example, the sun and moon, received from God so generous a share of light, magnificence, splendor, and majesty that people often succumbed to the delusion that they were lords or gods, so clearly do the marks of divinity show in them. For this reason they were made subject to the insecurity of eclipses, providing a sign to the discerning that if they were gods they would not be darkened. The same holds true for the rest of the stars. They may be granted brilliant light, revolving spheres, and long lives, but they are not immune from flickering, or retrogression, or even falling, to show that they too are subordinate.[41] The same holds true with all the rest of creation, whether angels, men, or jinn. No one of these is given all the fair virtues and estimable gifts, but each lacks something greater. Perfection belongs to God alone, one and triumphant."[42]

When the ass had finished speaking, the ox added, "But whoever has received a rich share in God's gifts ought to show his gratitude by giving of the surplus to those less fortunate beings who are deprived of the same gifts. Observe how the sun pours out light unstintingly on all creatures from the generous share it has been allotted. In the same way the moon and stars shed their influence, each according to its capabilities. This, then, is the course men ought to take as well,

40. Here the Platonic notion of participation is applied to the explanation of the divergent levels of perfection possible for diverse kinds. No finite creature can exhaust divine perfection, but all partake of a share in it, each in its own way manifesting some partial and relative expression of God's absolute perfection. God's gifts need not be shared out equally, and in a sense they cannot be, for species express divine grace in diverse ways, and creation as a whole is the richer for its diversity, the presence in it of all kinds and levels of things. But none has so low a place as not to have some unique perfection of its own, an expression of grace vital to its sustenance in its adaptive niche. And even the loftiest members of the celestial hierarchy are in some ways the lowest, for they are plainly the most manifestly subservient. The Ikhwān may have in mind the Qur'ānic passage regarding the obeissance of the celestial bodies before God, which Kindī as well as the Muʿtazilite *mutakallimūm* interpreted as expressing the subordination of celestial nature before God. See Qur'ān 55:5 and Kindī's *Rasā'il,* ed. Abū Ridah (Cairo, 1950–1953), vol. 1, no. 8, and the discussion by R. Walzer, "New Studies on Al-Kindī," in *Greek into Arabic* (Oxford, 1962), pp. 196ff.

41. The sixth-century Christian philosopher and controversialist John Philoponus argued (against Aristotle) that the stars were not uncompounded substances (and, therefore, immutable, indestructible, and uncreated). Their diverse colors suggested that they were composed of diverse materials; and their flickering, that they were undergoing some process. Philoponus argued that as terrestrial fires glare and glow with diverse hues depending on what fuels them, the stars might be undergoing diverse processes of combustion. He thereby became the founder of astrospectroscopy, as Shmuel Sambursky has pointed out. See Philoponus' *De Caelo*, apud Simplicius *De Caelo*, ed. J. L. Heiberg (Berlin, 1894), p. 89 and *De Opificio Mundi*, ed. G. Reichardt (Leipzig, 1897), p. 102, and the discussion by Sambursky in *The Physical World of Late Antiquity* (London, 1962), pp. 158ff. The thrust of Philoponus' argument is identical to that of the Ikhwān: Nothing in nature is perfect or absolute (Aristotle to the contrary notwithstanding, since he held the heavens and the cosmos at large to be divine, eternal, and immutable)—only God, who transcends nature and change, can be so regarded.

42. See Qur'ān 14:49, 40:16; 12:39, 13:17, 38:65, 39:6—all verses which allude to God as "one and triumphant." The Ikhwān, pacifically, here gloss the paired epithets as referring to God's unique, transcendent perfection, which individuals and species represent or express in diverse ways but which none engrosses.

since they are granted divine gifts of which other animals are deprived. They ought to share these gifts ungrudgingly."[43]

When the ox had finished speaking, the cattle and beasts all cried out together, "Have mercy on us, just and noble King, and free us from the oppression of the tyrannous sons of men."

The King of the jinn then turned to the body of jinni scholars and sages who were present and said, "Have you heard the complaint of the cattle and beasts and their description of the injustice, oppression, and ruthless trespass they have borne at the hands of men?"

"We have heard all that has been said, and it is true and correct and everywhere to be seen," they replied, "night and day. It is by no means obscure to the aware. It was for this very reason that the race of jinn too fled from among men to deserts, wastelands and moors, mountaintops, hills, valleys, or seashores. We too saw their evil ways and vicious mores and shunned the lands in which they dwelt. Yet despite our circumspection, men never rid themselves of prejudice against us. They still believe that the jinn are tempters of men, causes of their aches and pains. Thus we become bogies of women, children, and the ignorant. They seek protection from us by wearing talismans, amulets, charms, and such. Still no one has ever seen a jinni harm or kill a human, snatch his clothes, steal his belongings, break into his house, pick his pocket, cut his sleeve, slip his lock, or lie in wait for a traveler, revolt against a ruler, mount a raid or a kidnapping. On the contrary, all these are the special distinctions of men in their behavior toward one another night and day, heedless and unrepentent."

43. The ox here makes an ethical obligation of what he regards as a natural law, in keeping with Plato's fusion of *nomos* (law) and *physis* (nature) in the concept of natural law developed in the *Timaeus*. There the cosmic order is treated as a divinely imposed rule, and human ethical standards are derivable from the maxim to live in accordance with nature. Kant preserves the Platonic rationalistic awe at the twofold natural law, which he expresses in his famous remark, "Two things fill the mind with ever new and increasing admiration and awe, the oftener and more steadily we reflect on them: the starry heavens above me and the moral law within me" (*Critique of Practical Reason*, Conclusion.) The fusion of the moral with the cosmic law was the central principle or insight not only of the Platonists but also of all three of the monotheistic religions from their inceptions; and the monotheists welcomed Neoplatonism particularly because it regarded the cosmos from the perspective of the procession (*prohodos*) or emanation of being/goodness/grace from the One, God, to all particulars. It is to this concept of emanation, the work of Plotinus (205–270) that the Ikhwān here cause the ox to allude—a distancing which involves some prudence on their part, since emanationism was regarded as a somewhat heterodox doctrine especially in the early period of Islām, since it was read by the Neoplatonists as an alternative to creation. But emanation is an insistently recurrent theme in the cosmology (and politics) of the Ikhwān—as it is to become a persistent preoccupation of Muslim thought at large.

Regarding emanation as the source of inspiration Maimonides writes, "Emanation to a thinker may be sufficient to make him a seeker, a person of discernment and understanding. although he is not moved to teach other than himself or to write, finding no such desires in himself, or no such abilities. Or it might be sufficient to move him necessarily to write or teach . . ." (*Moreh Nevukhim*, II, 37, trans. L. E. Goodman, in *Rambam, Readings in the Philosophy of Moses Maimonides* (New York, 1976), p. 387. Maimonides compares emanation to wealth: it may be sufficient to its possessor or sufficient to enable him to make others wealthy as well. Such superabundance, he argues, creates a sense of compulsion on the part of the bestower; the Ikhwān express it as a matter of obligation.

When this speaker had finished, a herald announced, "Honored participants of this assembly, night has come. Return to your lodgings in honor; and, God willing, return safe in the morning."

Chapter 6

Having recessed the court, the King was left alone with his counselor, Bīdār, a distinguished and intelligent person and a philosopher. Said the King, "You have observed the session and heard the arguments on both sides. You understand what they came for. What then do you think is right, and what do you advise us to do?"

The Wazir said, "God strengthen your Majesty and guide him to the right course. I think it best for the King to command the judges, jurists, scholars, and thinkers of the jinn to assemble in his presence and consult on this matter, for this is a weighty and momentous case involving lengthy contentions, highly problematic, and subject to numerous opinions. Consultation gives insight to the undecided, improved perception to the perplexed, and the assurance of certainty to sound judgment."

"You are right," the King replied, "what you say is good, and your plan is a fine one."

The King then summoned the jinni judges of the family of Birjīs and the jurists of the family of Nāhīd,[44] jinni thinkers of the tribe of Bīrān and scholars of the stock of Luqmān, experienced jinn from the tribe of Hāmān, philosopher jinn of the tribe of Kaywān, and hardheaded, forthright jinn of the house of Bahrām.

When they were assembled before him, he met with them in private and said, "You have learned of these parties who have landed on our shores and entered our country. You have seen them here in our court and have heard their claims and their charges and the complaints of these captive animals against the injustice of men. The animals have sought our aid and protection. What are your views, and what do you recommend be done?"

Then the chief jurist of the house of Nāhīd said, "God strengthen the King's hand and guide him aright. The plan I would suggest is that the King command these beasts to write a brief stating the injuries they have suffered from men and seeking a ruling from the jurists. This will give them a means of gaining their freedom and escaping from this tyranny; for the judge, no doubt, will decide in their favor and rule either that they should be sold or freed or that their tasks should be lightened and they be given better treatment. Then, if the tribe of Adam does not act in accordance with the judgment, no crime can be charged against the animals should they, take flight."[45]

44. Birjīs and Nāhīd are the planets Jupiter and Venus respectively. Consultation was the ideal method of policy formation in Arabic and Islamic culture, and the Ikhwān do not miss the chance of portraying the good jinni king as taking advice from ministers and counselors.

45. The paradox of "oriental depotism" was that while the monarch's authority might in theory be very extensive (never absolute!) particularly with regard to the adjudication of disputes and the

"What do you think of this suggestion?" the King then asked the assembly.

All agreed that it was a fine and sensible idea except the forthright jinni of the house of Bahrām,[46] who said, "Have you considered, who will lay out the price to buy the animals if the Adamites agree that they should be put up for sale?"

"The King," said the jurist.

"With what?" asked the King.

"With the treasury of the Muslim jinn."

"There is not wealth enough in the treasury of the Muslim jinn to meet the cost," said the speculative jinni.[47] "Besides, many human beings will not wish to sell them since they need them so badly, and some do not need the money—kings, nobles, and the well to do, for example. Such a sale could never be accomplished, so do not weary yourselves trying to think of a way to do it."

"What do you think is the right plan?" asked the King.

"I suggest, "said the thinker," that the King should order all the cattle and beasts in captivity to humans to concert a plan to flee, all on the same night, far from the realm of men, as did the wild asses and gazelles. Then when the humans

---

"righting of wrongs," the practical powers of enforcement were very limited outside the confines of the court. The medieval handbooks and "mirrors for princes" like folk literature are filled with accounts of the ruses by which monarchs accomplished their designs, having first determined what was right in their view, an ample illustration, whether the anecdotes are fictive or contain a kernel of truth, of how woefully the executive power of the would-be despot fell short of his theoretical authority. See, for numerous examples, the *Siyāsat-nāmah* of Niẓām al-Mulk (eleventh century) (trans. Hubert Darke [London, 1960]). The anecdotes of military and political ruses retailed by Machiavelli as encouragement and exemplar to the prince of his tutelage are very much a part of this tradition of political maneuvering in which the key to the art of effective rule was the manipulation of small force to maximum effect. Pleas such as Locke's for the limitation of governmental authority could be intelligible only in the modern type of situation in which technological efficiency and national (rather than merely local) military organization made possible the widespread and effective deployment of power on a scale which was inconceivable in the Middle Ages—even for the jinn.

46. Bahrām—the name conjures up the memory of the legendary Persian hero.

47. The jurist is impractical, a common failing of Muslim jurisprudence not overlooked by the satirical eye of the Ikhwān, who enjoy the opportunity to use both animals and jinn as foils against which to display the foibles of their own society.

Despite the "lack of separation between church and state in Islam," the medieval Muslim monarch, like his Christian counterpart was in many ways a secular ruler deriving much of his authority (but not all of his power) from his religious role as defender of the faith. Muslim jurists, as custodians of a vast corpus of religious norms whose theoretical impact on practical life was pervasive, were constantly demanding fuller enforcement of those norms by kings—an enforcement which by the nature of the case could never be more than partial. (Relatively few Muslim rulers, for example, degraded the Jewish and Christian minorities to the satisfaction of the '*ulamā*' or juridical scholars.) From a secular perspective one can say that, as in Christendom, there was some tension over the division of secular authority and power between the "clerks" and the "secular arm" in Islam. Of the three monotheistic faiths, the Jews were in a sense the most fortunate in this regard during the middle ages. For lacking a geographical base or any monarchical or universal secular authority of their own, the rabbis could regard the existing gentile secular authorities with a distance which was impossible for Muslims or Christians to attain toward their own rulers, while the secular authority of the norms of Jewish religious law as a universal institution remained virtual rather than actual in all but the personal/familial and infracommunal spheres.

awoke in the morning they would find none to ride or carry their burdens. They would not be able to pursue the animals because of the great distance and the difficulty of the road. Then the animals would be free."[48]

The King was resolved to follow this plan and asked the others how they viewed the thinker's proposal.

The chief scholar, of the house of Luqmān,[49] said, "In my opinion this will not be brought off. It is too ambitious. Most of these beasts are tied up or stabled at night, so how could they all accomplish a coordinated flight on a single night?"

The hardheaded, outspoken jinni added, "The King might send bands of jinn on that night to open the gates for them and loose their bonds and tethers. We could hold the watchmen until the beasts had gone far enough from human habitation. Your Majesty should know that there would be great reward for him in doing this. I am speaking absolutely candidly because I am touched by their plight. God is aware of the sound and benevolent intent of the King's resolve; His aid will ensure success. To help the oppressed and free the enslaved is the best thanks for God's blessings.[50] In one of the books of the prophets, they say, it is written that God said, 'O King that reigns, I did not give you power that you might gather riches and gratify your lusts and passions but that you in My place might answer the entreaties of the oppressed, for I do not repulse them even if they be unbelievers.'"

At this the King was determined to accept what the speculative jinni had proposed. He said to the assembly around him, "What do you think of what has been said?"

They all agreed it was a generous and high minded plan.

All approved the plan except the philosopher of the house of Kaywān who said, "God give you insight, your Majesty, into the unseen side of things and reveal to you the difficulties latent in tactics. The task proposed is fraught, unavoidably, with tremendous dangers, defects which are not remediable or rectifiable."

"Tell us your view," said the King to the philosopher. "Make clear what you fear and of what you are wary, so that we may be informed and aware."

"I shall, your Majesty," he said. "There was something left out of this proposal for the beasts' escape from the Adamites' hands. When the race of Adam

48. The radicalism of the speculative jinni is portrayed as the result of his rationalism and must be corrected by the experience and learning of the more retrospectively historical jinn; *cf.* Michael Oakeshott, "Rationalism in Politics" in the book by the same title (New York, 1962).

49. Luqmān—a legendary sage referred to in Qurʾān 31:11–19 (the Sura as a whole bearing his name) and thought of by the Arabic historians as a fabulist and author of proverbs, identified by some western authors with Aesop (that is, Aethiops) because of his alleged Ethiopian ancestry and slave origin. In the lore of jinn and sorcery Luqmān is the subject of numerous magical folk tales.

50. The argument is complex: the outspoken jinni does not overlook the possibility of divine reward for the action he advises. But he does not urge simply that the king execute his plan on that ground. Rather, he uses the notion of a divine reward as a means of introducing the concept of divine aid and approval of the plan, in other words, as an occasion for invoking the norms derivable from the highest theistic ideals in behalf of seeking the release of the enslaved and oppressed—an assertion in behalf of an activist political morality placed in the mouth of a jinni counselor and addressed not to the rabble but to the king—hardly an actionable piece of subversion but a plea pregnant with the affirmation of the legitimacy of revolution, should conditions demand it.

awaken in the morning and discover that these beasts are gone, fled from their lands, will they not know with certainty that this was not the work of humans nor devised by the beasts themselves, but surely by the wiles of the jinn?"

"No doubt," said the King.

"Is it not the case," the philosopher continued, "that thereafter, whenever men think of all the benefits and comforts they have lost through the animals' flight, they will be filled with grief, rage, and regret for their loss and rancor, malice, and hatred toward the jinn? They will conceive secret schemes and devices to ensnare us, search for us everywhere, and everywhere lie in wait for us. In place of our once secure life, the race of jinn will know nothing but trouble, enmity, and fear,

"One who is prudent and intelligent," the wise jinni added, "is one who makes peace among enemies and does not draw enmity on himself."

Everyone agreed that the wise philosopher was right.

Then one jinni scholar said, "What harm have we to fear from the enmity of men? You know very well that the race of jinn are light, fiery spirits, which move upward by nature, while the sons of Adam are gross, earthly bodies, which move downward by nature. We see them, but they do not see us. We may flit amongst them unperceived and surround them without their sensing us. What is there for us to fear from them?"

"Alas," the wise jinni replied, "you overlook their strongest point and their most significant advantage. Do you not realize that even though the sons of Adam have earthly bodies, they also have heavenly spirits and angellike rational souls which make them superior to us? You must know that there are lessons to be learned from the events of ancient times and the experience of what passed between men and jinn in ages gone by."

At that the King said, "Tell us, wise one, what was it happened in ancient times, and what events transpired?"

"I shall, your Majesty," said he. "Between men and jinn there is an inborn enmity, an inveterate hostility and mutual aversion which would take long to explain."

"Tell us as much as seems convenient," said the King, "beginning with the origin of this enmity."

Chapter 7

The wise jinni said, "In ancient times, before the creation of Adam, the forefather of the human race, the inhabitants of the earth were jinn. It was they who covered the earth, land and sea, mountain and plain. Their lives were long and filled with blessings in abundance. They had kings, prophets, religious faith and law.[51] But they grew wanton and iniquitous. They ignored the precepts of their prophets and

51. There are two terms for religion in Arabic: *dīn*, a faith or creed and *sharī'ah*, a law or way of life. This twofold conception of religion was common to all three medieval monotheistic religions, but in modern times Protestant theologians, reverting to the quasi-antinomian tendencies of

increased corruption in the earth,[52] until at length the earth and its inhabitants joined in crying out against their iniquity.

"With cite close to that cycle of time and the inauguration of a new age, God sent an army of angels down from Heaven to settle on earth and drive the jinn in flight to the far corners of the world. They took many captives including the accursed Satan Lucifer,[53] the pharaoh of Adam and Eve,[54] who was still an undiscerning lad. As he grew up among the angels, Lucifer acquired their knowledge. Outwardly he looked like them, but his real nature and scamp were different. With the long passage of time he became a chief among them, and for eons his commands and prohibitions were obeyed by them. But then that epoch too came to an end, and a new age began. God made a revelation to those angels who were on earth saying, 'I shall place a viceregent on earth other than you, and you shall I raise to the Heavens.' The angels on earth were loath to leave their familiar homeland and answered, 'Wilt thou place on earth one who will work corruption there and shed blood as did the race of jinn, while we praise and sanctify thee?' God said, 'I know what you know not, for I have sworn an oath upon Myself that in the end, after the era of Adam and his seed I shall not leave a single one—angel, jinn, human, or any other beast—upon the face of the earth except those whom I choose.'[55] (There is a mystery in this oath which we have explained elsewhere.)

"When God had formed Adam, fashioned him, and breathed into him of His spirit, and from him formed Eve, his mate, He commanded the angels who were upon the earth to bow down before the pair and yield to their command. All obeyed except Satan, who was proud and arrogant. A savage, envious frenzy had seized him when he saw that his dominion was at an end and that he must be a follower, and a leader no longer.[56]

Pauline Christianity and reliance upon grace and faith in contradistinction to "works," promulgated the notion that the essence of religion was faith. Enlightenment thinkers, eager to separate morality from theology (and thus to make possible the argument against organized and established religions that what was essential in religion was faith, a matter of conscience, which must inevitably be free, while morality was quite separable from faith and often diametrically opposed to hypocritical faith—all else in religion, being neither morally nor intellectually significant, was "empty forms") accepted the Protestant notion of religion unquestioningly; and, through their influence, the terms 'creed' and 'faith' became widely used synonyms for religion, as though the practical content from which religions derive their only publicly manifest significance, were somehow of no account.

52. The phrase, of course, is Biblical and reflects the Biblical notion that moral corruption (that is decadence and lawlessness) pollute the earth and render it unfit for habitation—at least by those who have dealt corruptly (see Gen. 6:11–12; Deut. 13:13ff., etc.). This tendency, which J. H. Hertz felicitously termed the ethicizing of nature, articulates the Biblical naturalism in the thinking of the Ikhwān, since they regard pollution not merely as effluence but as the direct by-product of aggression and usurpation.

53. Satan Lucifer—Iblīs in Arabic.

54. In the usage of the Ikhwān the term pharaoh is generic and signifies any evil genius, the pejorative sense deriving from the Exodus story as recorded in the Qur'ān 7:102ff, 10:80ff, 20:8ff, etc.

55. See Qur'ān 2:28.

56. See Qur'ān 2:30ff.

"God then commanded the angels to bear Adam, peace be upon him, up to the heavens and into the garden and made a revelation to him saying. 'Adam, thou and thy wife shall dwell in the Paradise and eat amply whatever you will, but do not approach this tree, for if you do you will both be doing wrong.'[57] This Paradise is a garden in the east atop a mountain of hyacinth which no mortal man can climb. Its soil was good; its climate temperate, summer and winter, night and day.[58] It had many rivers, verdant trees and every sort of fruit, meadows, fragrant herbs, and flowers. The many animals did no harm, and the birds sang sweet, melodious songs. Both Adam and Eve had long hair streaming down from their heads, as lovely as ever graced a maiden, reaching their feet and covering their nakedness; this was the clothing in which they wrapped themselves, both cloak and ornament of their beauty. They used to walk along the river banks, among the plants and flowers, eating the many varieties of fruit from the trees and drinking water from the streams, not tiring their bodies or troubling their souls. There was no irksome plowing, planting, irrigating, reaping, threshing, milling, or kneading, no spinning, weaving, or washing, nor any other of the tasks at which their children in our days toil in the struggle to sustain life in this world. They lived in the garden just like any other animal, in contentment, leisure, and delight.

"God inspired Adam with the names of the trees, fruits, plants, and animals in the garden. As soon as Adam could speak, he asked the angels about them, but they gave no answer, so he sat down to teach them their names, benefits, and dangers. Thereafter the angels submitted to his command, for it was plain that he was better than they. When Satan saw this, his envy and malice grew. All through the morning and into the night he planned crafty and treacherous schemes against Adam and Eve. Then he approached them in the guise of one who offers friendly advice and said, 'God has already made you superior by gracing you with clear speech and discernment, but if you ate of this tree, you would grow even wiser and surer and would remain here forever secure, immortal, and ever-abiding.' They were deceived by his words, for he swore that he was, 'a faithful friend.' They were carried away with eagerness and neither could wait to taste the forbidden fruit. But when they had eaten of it, their hair parted and revealed their nakedness. They were left naked, the sun's heat beating down on them, blackening their bodies. The animals, seeing the change in them, shied away from them, and God commanded the angels to expel them from the Garden and cast them at the foot of the mountain.[59]

57. See Qurʾān 2:33ff.

58. The Ikhwān echo their description of Paradise in the favorable descriptions they give of man's terrestrial environment. But they add naturalistic gardenlike features to create the image of an idyllic abode. For the impact of the concept of the enclosed garden see Moses Hadas, *Hellenistic Culture, Fusion and Diffusion*, chap. XVI, "Blessed Landscapes and Havens" (New York, 1959), pp. 212ff.

59. See Qurʾān 7:10ff: "I created you, then formed you, then said to the angels 'Bow down before Adam!' and all prostrated themselves—save only Satan, who was not among those who bowed down. He said 'What prevents thee from bowing down when I have commanded you?' Satan replied 'I am better than he. Thou hast created me from fire and him from clay.'"

"They fell in barren wasteland without plants or fruits, and there they remained for a long time, weeping and grieving over their loss and regretting what had become of them. Finally God's compassion reached out to them. He forgave them and sent an angel to teach them how to plow and sow, reap, thresh, grind, bake, spin, weave, sew, and make clothing. When they had reproduced and their seed had become numerous, some of the jinni race mingled with them and taught them the arts, planting and building, and showed them what was beneficial to them and what was harmful.[60] These jinn befriended mankind and won their affection, and for some time they lived together on the best of terms.

"But each time the race of Adam remembered how the accursed Satan Lucifer had deceived their forefather and defrauded them, their hearts were filled with rage, malice, and rancor toward the race of jinn. When Cain killed Abel, Abel's descendent believed that this was done at the instance of the jinn, and hated them even more. They sought them everywhere and tried to ensnare them by every device of magic, witchcraft, and sorcery they knew, imprisoning some in bottles and afflicting them with all kinds of smoke and vapors which are noxious, noisome, and revolting to the jinni race.

"So things went until God sent the Prophet Idrīs,[61] who improved relations between the men and jinn through community of faith, law, submission,[62] and

---

"Then God said 'Get thee down then from hence. It is not for thee to vaunt thyself here. Get thee gone, thou art made small!' Satan replied 'Spare me till the day when they shall be resurrected.' 'Thou art spared.' 'Now since Thou hast caused me to stray will I lie in wait for them beside the straight path. . . .' 'Get thee gone, disgraced and banished! Whoso follows thee, of them—Hell shall I surely fill with ye all together!'

"'O Adam, dwell thou and thy mate in the Garden, and eat whither ye list, but approach not this tree or ye will be doing wrong.'

"But the devil whispered to them, revealing to them their hidden shame: 'Your Lord forbade this tree to you only lest ye become angels or immortals.' He swore to them that his advice was faithful and sincere. Thus he led them into deception.

"And when they tasted of the tree their shame was revealed to them, and they strove to cover it over with leaves from the garden. But their Lord called to them 'Did I not forbid that tree and say to you that Satan is your avowed enemy?'

"They answered, 'Lord, we have wronged ourselves, and if Thou dost not forgive us and have mercy on us, we are lost!' He answered 'Get you down, each a foe to the other. There is a dwelling place for you upon the earth and a provision for a time. There shall ye live and there shall ye die, and thence shall ye be brought forth."

The stark rhetorical style of Muḥammad's archaic Arabic is reminiscent of a medieval passion play. The humbling of the angels is taken by the Ikhwān to symbolize the subordination to reason of the animal soul.

60. As in many traditional sources, the arts and industries upon which human sustenance depends are regarded as being of superhuman origin. This is in keeping with the general notion of the Ikhwān that human achievements, being adventitious to what might (by logical abstraction) be regarded as man's primitive nature, are not to be accounted to the glory of the human species. The earlier suggestion that arts and sciences might be accounted to human credit is here at least very strongly qualified.

61. Idrīs, the Islamic equivalent of the Enoch or Hermes Trismegistus figure, is the conveyor of occult knowledge to humankind. He is mentioned twice in the Qur'ān, once (19:57) as a saint

religion. The jinn returned to the domains of men and lived in concord with them until the days of Abraham, God's beloved. But when Abraham was cast into the fire men thought knowledge of the ballista had come to Nimrod the Tyrant from the jinn.[63] And when Joseph's brothers cast him into the pit, this too was laid to the deceit of Satan who was of jinni race.[64] When God sent Moses, he reconciled the jinn and Israel through religious faith and law,[65] and many jinn embraced his faith.

---

and prophet whom God had "raised to a lofty place" and once (21:85) along with Ishmael and a third person as steadfast or forebearing, a highly valued virtue in Muḥammad's ethical scheme. According to Islamic tradition, he was a descendant of Seth and ancestor of Noah, and by one account was close friends with an angel who bore him to the fourth heaven—a rather literal gloss on the "high place" of the Qurʾānic reference. While the identity of Idrīs is unclear in some sources (for example, he is sometimes taken to be Elijah or al-Khiḍr) and his name is of obsure origin (sometimes derived from that of Ezra, sometimes from that of the Christian apostle Andrew or the Andrew who was cook to Alexander the Great and becomes glorified in the Alexander romance—cf. J. Horovitz, *Koranische Untersuchungen* (Berlin, 1921], p. 88f. *s.v. Idrīs*), nevertheless Idrīs emerges clearly as a central figure in the thought of hermetically inclined Muslim thinkers. Ibn ʿArabī, the dean of Muslim mystics (1165–1240), calls Idrīs "the prophet of the philosophers," where the term philosopher is to be understood in the hermetic sense as denoting one who seeks and practices the arts and sciences of theosophy—theurgy, astrology, alchemy—the sense connoted in references to the "philosophers'" stone. This would be the natural person to "improve relations" between men and jinn.

62. Submission—the literal meaning of *islām,* that is, the placing of one's life and destiny in the hands of God (see Qurʾān 2:112). The term is used here generically to denote the assumption of an attitude of religious faith and trust, not anachronistically as a reference to the faith of Muḥammad's followers to which that name is assigned. It is a central doctrine of Muḥammad's that his faith was preceded by numerous essays in essentially the same direction,

63. According to the Qurʾān (21:51ff. 26:69ff. 29:15ff, etc.), Abraham was cast into the flames for his iconoclastic rejection of pagan worship. The Qurʾānic account of Abraham is laced with Midrashic accretions and strongly colored by the changing relations of Muḥammad with the Jews of Medina. Common forefather of the Arabs and Jews and founder of monotheism, Muḥammad's Abraham takes on a more peculiarly Islamic coloration as founder of a monotheistic cult centered in the Kaʿbah at Mecca and grantor of preference to Ishmael, after Muḥammad's break with the Medinian Jews and reorientation towards Mecca.

The Ikhwān are painfully aware that Nimrod the Tyrant (as they consistently refer to him) was a monarch of their own Mesopotamian land, and their repeated references to him as a persecutor of freedom of conscience in religion seem to bear overtones of a plea for toleration, especially through the unspoken contrast of Nimrod the Tyrant with Bīwarāsp the Wise, who openly and generously receives all the diverse parties that appear before his court.

64. The story of Joseph is told at length in Qurʾān 12.

65. Moses is conceived of by the philosophically inclined thinkers of Islam in accordance with views articulated by Philo and among Muslim thinkers by Fārābī (d. 950) as not merely a prophet and founder of a religion but a lawgiver along the lines projected by Plato in his conception of the Philosopher-King. Maimonides explains that prior to Moses prophets spoke of their personal spiritual experiences leading to encounter with divinity, addressing themselves to family members and others who came within the sphere of influence of their personalities. Moses by contrast legislates for a nation.

The nexus between law and faith (that is, the spiritual/intellectual side of religion), to which the Ikhwān here allude, was that the law was regarded as the practical interpretation of the truth discovered by spiritual/philosophical insight, just as Plato had said it should be. Through belief and symbol, poetry and rhetoric, the prophetic legislator binds the hearts and imaginations of his

"In the days of Solomon, God strengthened the power of his throne and made jinn and demons subservient to him.[66] Solomon subdued the kings of the earth; and the jinn vaunted themselves over mankind, claiming that Solomon had achieved this through their help. Without the jinn's assistance of Solomon, they said, he would have been like any human king. The jinn led humans to believe that they knew the unknown; but, when Solomon died, and the jinn, still undergoing their humiliating chastisements, knew nothing of his death, mankind realized that if they had had occult knowledge they would not have remained in such degrading torment.[67]

"Also, when the Hoopoe brought his report of Bilqīs,[68] and Solomon said to the throng of jinn and men, 'Which of you will bring me her throne before they

---

hearers to the practices which will lead to the perfection of their characters morally and intellectually, to the extent possible, thus conveying these insights from a high and abstract level to a broad and practical, immediately graspable level. Adherence, such as that of the jinn, is a natural response.

66. The legends of Solomon's intimacy with the jinn are Midrashic, doubtless pegged upon the Biblical ascription (1 Kings 5:9ff) of wisdom to the tenth-century B.C. monarch of Israel—which was understood supernaturally. *Cf.* 1 Kings 3:28—where the popular response is already interpreted as one of awe at Solomon's portentous wisdom. The lore of "Suleiman bin Daoud" and the jinn enters Islam through the Qur'ān and reverts to midrashic and other sources as well as the fertile imagination of the storytellers for constant enlargement of matter and detail, a process which continues down to Kipling's delightful tale of the butterfly who stamped in the *Just So Stories*. For Solomon in the Qur'ān, see 2:96, 4:161, 6:84. 21:78ff. The former passages refer to God's inspiration of Solomon along with other prophets. The last reads as follows: "And [tell of] David and Solomon—how they judged as to the plow land when the strayed sheep grazed in it. We bore witness to their judgment. We gave understanding to Solomon, judgment and learning to them both. And in time with David we set the mountains [see Ps. 114:4, 6] that they might give praise, and the birds—We were the doers. . . . To Solomon the tempest wind to course at his command to the land toward which was Our blessing—and We knew all things—demons to dive for him and do other work besides, under Our superintendence . . ."; *cf.* 38:33ff.

67. See Qur'ān 34:10ff: "We gave David of Our grace: 'O ye mountains and birds echo back his song.' And we made iron soft to him [the Qur'ānic David was skilled in the armorer's craft]. . . . And to Solomon we gave the wind, whose morning course was a month's journey and whose evening course was a month's journey, and caused molten brass to flow for him, and gave him some of the jinn to labor before him by leave of his Lord. . . . They made for him what he would—shrines, images, platters like great troughs, and mountainous kettles. . . . But when We had ordained his death nought showed them he had died but a tiny creature that crept upon the earth, which gnawed away his staff. Then, when he fell, the jinn realized that had they had knowledge of the unseen they would not have remained in such degrading torment."

68. The story of Solomon and the Queen of Sheba (1 Kings 10:1–13) is reported in Qur'ān 27:15–45: "We gave knowledge to David and Solomon and they said 'Praise be to God who preferred us over so many of his faithful servants!' Solomon was heir to David, and he said 'O ye folk, we have been instructed in the discourse of the birds (1 Kings 5:13 states plainly that Solomon discoursed *of* the trees, *of* the beasts, *of* the birds, *of* the creeping creatures and *of* the fish, but that was no hindrance to the makers of legends] and have been granted all things—truly this is a dear act of grace.' Armies of jinn rallied to Solomon, as did humans and birds. They advanced in battle array, until they came to the valley of the ants, and an ant said 'Enter your dwellings, O ye ants, lest Solomon and his forces trample you unaware.' . . . He reviewed the birds and said 'What's this? I do not see the hoopoe? Is he missing? I shall surely chastise him sorely—or kill him unless he gives a good excuse!' The bird arrived not long after" with his report of Sheba; see chapter 12. The story of

arrive?' the jinn boasted, and one sprite, Iḍtar son of Māyān of the house of Kaywān, said, 'I shall have it here before you rise from your place.' That is before court was recessed. Solomon said, 'I want it faster than that.' At that, a man who had knowledge of the Book, Āṣaf son of Barkhiyā, said, 'I shall have it here in the twinkling of an eye.' And when Solomon saw it already standing solid at his side, he knelt in prayer. Man's superiority to the jinn had been made manifest. The court ended, and the jinn retired, their heads hung in shame, followed by the crowd of men who tramped after them clapping their hands and hooting at them.[69]

After the events I have mentioned, a band of jinn escaped from Solomon, and one rebelled against him. Solomon dispatched some of his troops in pursuit and taught them how to snare the jinn with magic spells, mystic words, and revealed verses, and how to confine them by means of sorcery. He also produced a book for this purpose which was found in his treasury after his death. Until he died, Solomon kept the rebel jinn at work with arduous tasks.

"When Christ[70] was sent, he called all creatures, humans and jinn alike, to God. He imbued them with a desire to find Him, showed them the way, and taught them how to mount to the Kingdom of Heaven. A number of bands of jinn embraced his faith. They took to a monkish path and did ascend up to heaven. There they overheard tidings among the supernal throng and relayed reports of them to the soothsayers.

"When God sent Muḥammad, God bless and keep him, jinn were kept from eavesdropping, and they said, 'We do not know whether evil is intended against those who are on earth or whether their Lord desires them to go right.'[71] Some bands of jinn entered Muḥammad's faith and became fine Muslims. Since then jinni relations with Muslims have been peaceable down to our own days.

Solomon and the Queen of Sheba was a favorite of Muḥammad's—perhaps because it brought the Biblical potentate into contact with a people of Arabia—and also apparently a favorite of the Ikhwān; as with the Adam and Eve story, elements of it recur in both texts. The Ikhwān presumably were attracted by the role of the jinn in Solomon's service and the recurrent assertion of God's sovereignty—symbolized by his subjection of the jinn to a mere mortal, paralleling the incongruence between Sheba's earthly (but highly portable) throne and the true might of God's throne. For the naturalistically inclined, the jinn were natural forces, and God's subjection of them to Solomon is an early harbinger of the alchemical *homo faber* or Faustus type, who may govern nature with God's help but is lost (as the Ikhwān repeatedly remind their readers) without reliance on God's aid.

69. The humans are hardly sporting, especially not as perceived by the jinn. But the point of the lesson taught at the jinn's expense was divine sovereignty. Reliance upon natural or magical force inevitably is "slower" than direct appeal to God, since He is source of all such powers. The jinni relied on his own power, which was derived from that of God. The human ("who had knowledge of the Book") appealed directly to God. The weakness of this mode of comparison is that it makes the divine simply another counter in the magical technology—as, for example, the name of God in kabbalistic theurgy becomes simply another (highly potent) magic spell. The object had been to subordinate demonology and magic to theism, but the outcome could easily become making God simply a super demon.

70. Muslims accept the annointedness of Jesus and acknowledge him a prophet but deny his divinity.

71. Qur'ān 72:10.

"Assembly of jinn," the jinni scholar concluded, "do not antagonize them and spoil our relations with them. Do not stir up their dormant hatred or revive that inveterate prejudice toward us which is ingrained in their nature. For that hatred is like the fire that lies hidden in stones[72] and appears when they are struck together and lights up the matches that can burn houses and bazaars. God protect us from the triumph of the wicked and the dominion of the iniquitous, which brings ruin and disgrace!"

When the King had heard this startling account, he lowered his eyes in thought. Then he said, "Tell us, wise one, what in your opinion is the right thing to do with these animals who have come seeking our protection? How shall we let them go satisfied that our decision is just?"

The wise jinni replied, "A sound judgment can be reached only after much deliberation, careful and exhaustive investigation, and consideration of the past. What I suggest is that the King hold a court of inquiry tomorrow in the presence of the disputants and hear their arguments and explanations so as to clarify the merits of the case for those who will undertake to judge it. After that there will be time to formulate a decision."

The outspoken jinni said, "If these beasts are unable to stand up against humans in argument because they lack their powers of clear and eloquent speech and men win out over them with their clever tongues and fine explanations, do you believe that these animals should remain their prisoners, to be tormented by them forever?"

"No," he said, "but the beasts must have patience in captivity until the cycle of the epoch has run its course and a new order is begun. Then God will bring them freedom and deliverance just as he delivered the House of Israel from the oppression of the House of Pharaoh, the House of David from the tyranny of Nebuchadnezzar, the House of Himyar from that of Tubbaʿ,[73] the House of Sāssān from the tyranny of the Greeks, the House of ʿAdnān from the torment of the House of Ardashīr.[74] The days of this nether world run in cycles allocated among its inhabitants, turning at the behest of God and by His foreknowledge and the

72. See Anaxagoras, fragment 17, *apud* Simplicius' commentary on Aristotle's *Physics*, 163.20.

73. The last reference is to the pre-Islamic history of Arabia as alluded to in the Qur'ān (44:30ff and 50: 11ff). Tubbaʿ was a recurrent name among the (tyranpous) kings of the Ḥimyarites.

74. The references are to Persian relations with the Greeks and Arabs. Ardashīr is Artaxerxes. The first king of that name (d. 240) overthrew the Parthians, reunited Persia, founded the Sassanian dynasty, established Zoroastrianism as the state religion, and repulsed the Roman army of Alexander Severus (although with heavy losses). The rise of the Sassanians was out of the ruins of Seleucid power in Persia and was thus the overcomoing of Greek domination which harked back to the conquests of Alexander the Great. ʿAdnān, a descendant of Ishmael, is the eponymous ancestor of the northern Arabians. The reference then is to the cessation of Persian hegemony in and influence on Arabia, decisively marked by the conquest of the Sassanian forces by Muslim armies at the battle of Qādisiyyah in 635.

The Ikhwân express a sympathy for both Persian and Arab nationalistic sentiments as liberating—despite the historic antipathy of the two movements to one another and despite the more catholic viewpoint of the Ikhwān themselves. Nationalism for them cannot be an end in itself. They regard demands for freedom from alien hegemony as just and natural, but council patience until the "epoch" be fulfilled—hardly an unambiguously conservative, pacific, or quietistic counsel.

action of His almighty will, through the influences of the conjunctions of the stars as they revolve each thousand years, or twelve thousand years, or thirty-six thousand years, or three hundred and sixty thousand years, or each day of fifty thousand years."[75]

Chapter 30

When the frog had finished speaking a jinni sage said, "You overlook one thing, O humans, and you animals too, you of the earth with your gross and heavy earthly bodies with their three dimensions, you who dwell on land or sea or mountain, you fail to note the multiplicity of spiritual creatures, luminous wraiths, right spirits, subtle specters, uncompounded souls, and disembodied forms which dwell within the apertures between the tiers of the heavens and travel through the vast expanse of the spirit world and amidst the spheres—all sorts of angels, Cherubs, and Bearers of the Throne, all the luminous spirits in the globe of the aether and all the nations of jinn and troops of demons, the ranks of Satan all together, who dwell in the globe of the Zamharīr.

"If you, the human and the animal kinds, knew how many genera of these creatures there are, which are not bodies composed of the elements nor objects extended in the dimensions, and if you knew how many species and diverse forms of them there are and how diverse are even our individuals, then the multiplicity of corporeal animals' genera and specific forms and particular individuals would seem small indeed to you. For the extent of the globe of the Zamharīr is more than ten times the extent of the earth and sea. And the diameter of the aetherial globe is again more than ten times that of the Zamharīr. And the diameter of the sphere of the moon is ten times greater than the breadth of that entire globe. And in the same proportion is the sphere of Mercury to that of the moon; and so in the same relation with all the concentric spheres up to the highest encompassing sphere. And the whole expanse of all of these is filled throughout with spiritual creatures so that not a single span is left unoccupied by some kind of spiritual beings, as the Prophet told when he was asked about God's words 'None knows His hosts but He,'[76] and he said, peace upon him and all his house, 'There is not in the seven

75. The cosmic rhythms, being invariant, so far as most ancient observations and calculations could determine, were at least from the time of Aristotle *(cf. Metaphysics*, Lambda) paradigms of the divine perfection and naturally became emblems of divine justice once they were invoked by Hellenistic Greek philosophers as symbols if not engines of divine providence, through which nature was governed. The Ikhwān thus naturally expect balance and equilibrium to be struck among moral as well as physical accounts by the completion of the cycles of the heavens. Like the neo-Darwinians, then, they temporalize the chain of being. But just as their natural hierarchy has no apex which is superior to all the rest in every way (although man is superior in one crucial way) so their history has no absolute culmination which obviates all that has gone before (although the Qur'ānic judgment day, beyond history, ends it and breaks the rhythm of the cosmic cycles themselves, since even these were a compromise of eternity with temporality and thus must end once history has served its purpose).

76. Qur'ān 74:34.

heavens a hand's breadth of place without some angel, standing, bowing, or prostrating before God.'[77]

"If you considered what I have said, O you human and animal kinds," the jinni sage continued, "then you would realize that you are the least of creatures in number and the lowest in rank and status. You would understand then that the multiplicity of which you boast, O human, is not a sign of your being masters or of others' being your slaves. Rather all of us are slaves of God, exalted be He, His hosts and subjects, whom He has subordinated one to another according to the determination of His wisdom and the dictate of His sovereignty. And to Him is due the praise for that and for His abundant and manifold bounties."

When the jinni sage had finished speaking the King said, "We have heard what you have stated, O race of humans, and what you have gloried in, and you have heard the reply. If you have anything to add beyond what you have stated, present your proofs if you speak truly, adduce your arguments, and elucidate your claims."

At that the orator from the Ḥījāz, from Mecca and Medina, rose and said, "Yes, your Majesty. We have other virtues and distinctions which show that we are lords and these animals are slaves to us and we are their masters and owners."

"What are they?" asked the King.

"The promises of our Sovereign to us that we of all the animals will be resurrected and raised up, brought out of our graves and dealt our reckoning on the Day of Judgment, admitted by the Straight Path and entered into Paradise, the blessed Garden, the eternal garden, the Garden of Eden, Garden of Refuge, the Abode of Peace, of Rest, of Abiding, Abode of the Trusting, the Tree of Beatitude, the Spring of Salsabīl, rivers of wine, of honey, of milk, and of pure, sweet water, with storeyed citadels and dark-eyed maids to wife, and God close by, All-merciful, All-glorious, All-bountiful, and the scent of the breeze and the verdure, all stated in the Qur'ān in some seven hundred verses and all of which these animals are deprived of.[78] This shows that we are masters and these are slaves to us. And we have further distinctions, which I do not mention. I have said my say. God grant pardon to myself and you."

Then at that point rose the spokesman of the birds, the nightingale, and said, "Yes, it is as you say, O human, but state also the balance of the promise, O humans, the torment of the grave, the interrogation by Nakīr and Munkar, the terrors of the Day of Resurrection, the rigor of the accounting, the threat of entry into the flames and chastisement in Hell and the burning fires of Gehenna, the searing and the blazing, the scorching and the seething of the Abyss, the close shirts of pitch, the drinking of putrescence and purulence, the eating of the Tree of Zaqqūm, the nearness to the Master of Wrath, Gatekeeper of the Fire, propinquity to the demons, the hordes of Satan all together—all that is stated in the Qur'ān, side by side with every

77. The *ḥadīth* is read as signifying the ontic plenitude of the Great Chain of Being, which dwarfs all sublunary creation.

78. I hesitate to cite in full, but chiefly: Qur'ān 7:40ff, 15:45ff, 19:61ff, 36:54ff, 37:42ff, 38:51ff, 43:70ff, 44:51ff, 52:17ff, 55:46ff, 56:12ff, 76:12ff.

verse of promise, by way of threat and admonition.[79] All this applies to you and not to us. We are clear of all of this. Just as we are promised no reward, we are threatened with no retribution. We are content with our Lord's judgment in our case, neither for us nor against us. As He withholds from us the blessing of the promise, so He removes the terror of the threat.

"The evidences, then, cancel each other, and the advantages of your position and of ours are equal. So you have nothing by which you may claim superiority."

"How are the advantages of our position and of yours equal," demanded the Hijāzī, "when we in either case survive eternally and immortally? If we are obedient, then we shall be with the prophets, leaders, saints, and sages, the blessed and the best, the most virtuous and great souled, the pure, abstemious, devout, upright, aware, insightful, sage, understanding, excellent, and elect, who are like the angels, who pursue the highest goods and yearn after their Lord and turn toward Him in all situations and occasions, hearken to Him, look to Him, and contemplate His greatness and magnificence, trust Him in all their affairs, beseech Him alone, seek from Him alone, and hope in Hint alone, for their concern is His dread.

"And if we are rejected, still we shall seek refuge in the intercession of the prophets (peace upon them) and especially in our lord Muḥammad (peace upon him), and then we should remain thereafter in the Garden with the Houris and the youths, addressed by angels saying 'Peace be unto you, pleasance to you, enter among the immortals'[80] But you, the animal kind, are deprived of all this. For after you are departed you do not survive."

Then the animal spokesmen and the jinni sages all said together, "Ah humans, now at last you have come to the truth, you have spoken what is right and answered truly. For such claims as you now make are indeed something to boast of and such deeds as you speak of are indeed something to strive for and such lives and characters, such manners and diverse sciences as you ascribe to these holy persons are indeed something to be sought after and striven for. But tell us, O humans, of the characteristics of these persons, expatiate on their way of life, inform us of their ways, of their insights, of the excellence of their characters and the rectitude of their doings, if you know aught of these and state these things if you are aware of them."

Then the entire body fell silent for a time, thinking over what they had been asked. But no one had an answer.[81]

At length a learned, worthy, keen, pious, and insightful man rose. He was Persian by breeding, Arabian by faith, Hanafite[82] in his Islam, Iraqi in culture, Hebrew in lore, Christian in manner, Damascene in piety, Greek in the sciences, Indian in contemplation, Sufi in intimations, regal in character, masterful in thought, and divine in insight. He said, "Praised be God, Lord of the worlds,

79. See, for example, Qur'ān 11:106ff, 22:19ff, 25:11ff, 38:57ff, 40:46ff, 43:74ff, 56:41ff, 78:21ff.
80. See Qur'ān 16:30ff.
81. The final irony of the many ironies of the *Case of the Animals Versus Man*.
82. An orthodox school of Islamic jurisprudence.

Destiny of the faithful and foe to none but the unjust. God bless the Prophet Muḥammad and all his house together.

"Now then," he commenced, "most just Majesty; since it is now clear and has been made clear in your presence that what the human party claims is true and it is now plain before this court that among this party there are saints of God, the choice flower of His creation, the best, the purest, who are God's elect, and that these folk have noble attributes, fair characters, pious acts, diverse sciences, sovereign insights, royal traits, just and holy lives, and wondrous ways, which tongues weary to recite and description cannot do justice to in their essence, which would take long to describe, and which lengthy sermons cannot adequately reach the core of when seeking to enumerate their ways and the virtues of their noble ways of life and character, though they went on for ages—what does your just Majesty command regarding these human strangers and these animals, who are their slaves?"

The King then ordered that all the animals were to be subject to the commands and prohibitions of the humans and were to be subservient to the humans and accept their direction contentedly and return in peace and security under God's protection.[83]

Here the fable ends.

—Lenn E. Goodman, translator

References

Biographical Sources

Awa, A. *L'Esprit critique des Frères de la Pureté*. Beirut: 1948.

———. "Ikhwān al-Ṣafā'." In *A History of Muslim Philosophy*, ed. by M. M. Sharif. Wiesbaden: 1963–1966. Vol. 1: 289–310.

Bausani, A. "Scientific Elements in Ismāʿīlī Thought. The Epistles of the Brethren of Purity." In *Ismāʿīlī Contributions to Islamic Culture*, ed. by S. H. Nasr. Tehran: 1977, pp. 123–40.

Blumenthal, D. "A Comparative Table of the Bombay, Cairo and Beirut Editions of the Rasā'il Ikhwān al-Ṣafā'." *Arabica*, 21 (1974): 186–203.

Brockelmann, C. *Geschichte der arabischen Litteratur*. Weimar: 1902 and Leiden: 1943–1949. First ed., vol. 1: 213–14, 2nd. ed., vol. 1: 236–38.

Corbin, H. *History of Islamic Philosophy*. London: 1993, pp. 133–36.

Dieterici, F., *Die Abhandlungen der Ichwan es-Sefa in Auswahl zum ersten Mal aus arabischen Handschriften herausgegeben* von Fr. Dieterici, Leipzig: 1886.

Hamdani, A. "An Early Fāṭimid Source on the Time and Authorship of the *Rasāʾil Ikhwān al-Ṣafāʾ*." In *Arabica*, 26 (1979): 62–75.

83. Man then is placed in the end in a role of stewardship over nature—given freedom to use the benefits nature affords, but always under the overseership of God, who remains the animals' protector as well as their provider, to whom man himself will be accountable when his epoch of stewardship is at an end.

———. "ʿAbū Ḥayyān al-Tawḥīdī and the Brethren of Purity." *International Journal of the Middle East Studies*, 9 (1978): 345–53.

———. "The Arrangement of the *Rasā'il Ikhwān al-Ṣafā'* and the Problem of Interpolations." *Journal of Semitic Studies*, 29 (1984): 97–110.

Hamadani, H. F. "Rasā'il Ikhwān al-Ṣafā'." In the Literature of the Ismāʿīlī Ṭaiyibī Daʿwat." *Der Islam*, 20 (1932): 281–300.

Marquet, Y. "Imāmat, résurrection et hiérarchie selon les Ikhwān al-Ṣafā'." *Revue des Études Islamiques*, 30 (1962): 49–142.

———. "Les Cycles de la souveraineté selon les épîtres des Ikhwān al-Ṣafā'", *Studia Islamica*, 36 (1972), pp. 47–69; and "Les épîtres des Ikhwān al-Ṣafā'." *Studia Islamica*, 61 (1985): 57–79.

———. Ikhwān al-Ṣafā'." In *Encyclopaedia of Islam*, new edition. Leiden: 1960.

Nasr, S. H. *An Introduction to Islamic Cosmological Doctrines*. Albany (N.Y.: 1993), pp. 25–104.

———. *History of Islamic Philosophy*, ed. by S. H. Nasr and O. Leaman. London: 1996, pp. 144–154.

Netton, I. *Muslim Neoplatonists: An Introduction to the Thought of the Brethren of Purity*. London: 1982, pp. 95 ff.

Plessner, M. M. "Beiträge zur islamischen Literaturgeschichte IV: Samuel Miklos Stern, die Ikhwān al-Ṣafā' und die Encyclopaedia of Islam," *Israel Oriental Studies*, 2 (1972): 353–361.

Poonawala, I. K. "Ikhwān al-Ṣafā'." In *Encyclopedia of Religion*, ed. by M. Eliade, vol. 7, 92–95. London: 1987.

Stern, S. M. "The Authorship of the Epistles of the Ikhwān al-Ṣafā'." *Islamic Culture*, 20 (1946): 376–72; also *Islamic Culture*, 21 (1947): 403–404.

———. "New Information about the Authors of the Epistles of the Sincere Brethren." *Islamic Studies*, 4 (1964): 405–28.

Tibawi, A. L. Ikhwān al-Ṣafā' and their *Rasā'il*." *Islamic Quarterly*, 2 (1955): 28–46.

———. "Further Studies on Ikhwān al-Ṣafā'." *Islamic Quarterly*, 22 (1978): 57–67.

Widengren, G. "The Pure Brethren and the Philosophical Structure of Their System." In *Islam: Past Influence and Present Challenge*, ed. by A. T. Welch and P. Cachia. Edinburgh: 1979, 57–69.

Primary Sources

There is a partial French translation of the *Rasā'il* in M. Marquet, *La Philosophie des Ikhwān al-Ṣafā'* (Algiers: 1975) and a partial Italian translation is to be found in A. Bausani, *L'Enciclopedia dei Fratelli della Purità* (Naples: 1978). A complete German translation and commentary was being done by S. Diwald, from which one volume appeared as *Arabische Philosophie und Eissenschaft in der Ennzyklopädie Kitāb Ikhwān al-Ṣafā' (III) Die Lehre von Seele und Intellekt* (Wiesbaden: 1975).

Ikhwān aṣ-Ṣafā': Mensch and Tier vor dem König der Dschinnen, Trans. A. Giese, Hamburg: 1990.

7

AL-MU'AYYAD FI'L-DĪN SHĪRĀZĪ

The full name of this central figure and chief *dāʿī*, who throughout the Ismāʿīlī works is referred to as "Sayyidunā al-Muʾayyad fiʾl-Dīn," is Hibat Allāh ibn Mūsā ibn Dāwūd Salmānī. He is believed to have been a direct descendent of Salmān Fārsī. While it is difficult to establish the exact date of his birth, one can say that he was born some time in the middle or end of 390 A.H./999 A.D. in Shiraz and died in 470/1077 in Cairo, where he is buried near al-Azhar University. Not much is known about his early education, but coming from a family of missionaries, he was promoted to be the head of the missionaries of Shiraz and the *ḥujjat* for the whole of Persia.

Shīrāzī was caught between the *khalīfah*, who regarded him as a threat first and then befriended him, and the non-Ismāʿīlīs, in particular the courtiers who feared his popularity among the people. Al-Muʾayyad was engaged in a direct political game with various vazirs and courtiers of his time, which lasted all his life. This is primarily the reason he moved in and out of Shiraz virtually throughout his life, went to Ahwaz, but finally had to leave the country out of fear for his life. He went to Egypt to see the Ismāʿīlī Imām and wrote in great detail of his spiritual experience after coming in contact with the Imām. He then went to Aleppo in 442/1067, and in 450/1058 was elevated to the position of "*dāʿī al-duʿāt*" (missionary of missionaries), a position which he had sought all his life.

Shīrāzī left a legacy as statesman, politician, and missionary, as well as numerous pupils, among whom are Nāṣir-i Khusraw, Ḥasan-i. Ṣabbāḥ, and Lamak ibn Mālik. One of his students, Ḥātim ibn Ibrāhīm al-Ḥāmidī, from Yemen, compiled the bulk of al-Muʾayyad's sermons, entitled *Jāmiʿāt al-ḥaqāʾiq*, which constitutes an encyclopedia of Ismāʿīlism.

Shīrāzī is not a philosopher in the strict sense of the word, but he should be regarded as a theologian and an Ismāʿīlī intellectual. In this chapter we have included parts of his sermons in which he elucidates the esoteric secrets of the Qurʾān. The first lecture, "Potential and Actual *Jannat*," discusses the esoteric symbolism of heaven, while the second lecture, entitled "The Real Names of God," offers an analysis of Divine Names—in particular *al-Raḥman* (mercy). In the third lecture, Shīrāzī explains "the meaning of *al-Salām*, followed by the twelfth lecture, entitled "the walāyat of ʿAlī." The concept of *walāyat* (spiritual guardianship) and the role of Imām ʿAlī as the interpreter of esoteric Islam are emphasized. Shīrāzī continues the same theme in the thirteenth lecture, "True Faith in the Unity of God Cannot be Achieved without the Guidance of the Imāms," as well as in the fourteenth lecture, where "The True Meaning of the Tradition" is brought forth. This chapter ends with a discussion concerning the nineteenth lecture of Shīrāzī, titled after the prophetic hadith "He Who Knows Himself Knows His Lord."

—M. Aminrazavi

Khuṭbah

SERMON

Lecture First: Potential and Actual "Jannat"

May God make you profit by your living a pious life and your submitting to the will of the Imām of the time. You must bear in mind that luckily for you, you are living in the dominion of the descendants of the Prophet whose sovereign power for sometime was usurped by the tyrants. After all God has restored it to its legitimate claimants. By this, He has proved the rightfulness of the cause of the Imāms and the utter falsehood of the pretences of their opponents.

The Holy Qur'ān says, "They intend to put off the light of God by blowing it by their mouths. But God has decided to keep His light burning forever." This refers to the Imāms. Their enemies did their best to put out the Light of God. Thank God for the favour He has done to you by keeping the divine light burning forever for your good. Keep aloof from those who turned their backs to this light and have shown utter ingratitude to Him. They have done no harm to God but to themselves. They have scratched their bodies by their own nails. They have treated with scorn the holy mosques of God and the arches of the mosques. To put it in plain language they have wronged the Imāms, the descendants of the Prophet. The Holy Qur'ān says, "O *mu'mins* [faithful ones], go to the mosque properly dressed". The mosque here stands for the Imām. The enemies of the Imams enjoy peace and prosperity under them and yet they revolt against them. This is the work of traitors. God is with the Imāms. No treachery can succeed with them. He always helps their cause and makes their mission prosper.

This translation is based on Al-Mu'ayyad fi'l-Dīn Shīrāzī's *Khuṭbah*, edited and translated by J. Muscati and A. M. Moulvi (Karachi; Islamic Association Press, 1969), pp. 78–91, 141–53, and 174–78.

Last time I explained to you the meaning of the Verses up to the Verse: "*Jannat* has been kept ready for the pious and it is not far away from them". There are two forms of *Jannat* the potential *Jannat* and the actual *Jannat*. The potential *Jannat* is embodied *in daʿwat al-Ḥaqq i.e.* the teachings of the Imām of the time. The *daʿwat* is the substance of the Qurʾanic teachings and the extract of everything that pertains to religion. When a *muʾmin* is initiated into the mystery of this faith, he is being prepared, stage by stage, by the knowledge acquired through the Imāms and his living a straight life, for the second *jannat*, the actual *jannat*. He cannot enter this *jannat* unless he gets over his animal nature by this process.

Just as an embryo in a womb cannot experience life in this world unless it develops into a full-formed babe, similarly man in this material world which is a sort of a second womb for him, has to develop, through knowledge and practice, the qualities of the inmates of Paradise before he can experience the life in the *jannat*. The life there is as much different from the life of this world as our life from the life in the womb.

I have pointed out to you that every *ḥadd* in his time whether he is a Prophet, a *waṣī* or an Imām, from the point of view of his teaching is a *jannat* who qualifies us for entry into the actual *jannat* and experiencing a new life.[1]

The verse referring to *jannat* is followed by second verse which says "This is what you have been promised for every *awwāb* and *ḥāfiẓ*. The word *awwāb* means one who in all his activities and even non-activities in this life, looks to his Lord for guidance. This is the sum and substance of religion which is a ceaseless chain, link within a link. It has two sides, the celestial and terrestrial. On the terrestrial side of the chain the links are placed one above the other every one of whom derives his authority from his immediate predecessor right upto the Prophet. On the celestial side are the angels, the spiritual beings, on a rising scale upto the "Tablet" and the "Pen" which are the upper head of the celestial chain.

The Prophet says "Between me and my God there are five mediums one above another. They are Jibra'īl Mīkāʿīl, Isrāfīl and the Tablet and the Pen". This is the highest point which an *awwāb* can reach for his authority.

The word ḥāfīz indicates that the different positions of the Imāms are well-defined. Every one of them has a fixed position. It is they who guard the various steps in spiritual progress. God says "We have adorned the firmament of this world with the stars. We have guarded them against every intruding devil. If these devils attempt to listen to what is going on in the celestial world they will not be allowed to hear. They will be thrown away from every direction and will be severely punished." In another passage He says, "*We have brought down the dhikr and we are its preservers.*"

We shall deal with these verses at the next *majlis*. May God help you in deriving the fullest benefit from this knowledge and acting on it. May He guide you to the right path which is the only straight path leading to salvation.

1. The truth of this can become clear by studying the following Tradition: "*Yā ʿAlī anā wa anta abawā hādhihiʾl-ummah i.e.* "O ʿAlī I and you are the parents of this nation."

Lecture Second: The Real Names of God

O *mu'mins* [faithful ones], may God help you in thanking Him for the favour He has done to you by guiding you through the Imāms. Cut short your connections with the wicked world which have been corroding your inner-self. Attach yourselves to the place where you will be free from worries. This is the Abode of Bliss the keys of which are in the hands of the Imāms.

Disown those who have become ungrateful to them. They are like those about whom God says, "Don't you observe those who have denied the favours of God and have become ungrateful and have thus led their people to hell-fire where they will burn forever. It is the worst imaginable place. They maintained that God had associates. They did so to lead people astray. Tell them, (O Muḥammed), enjoy ye this life of short duration. Your ultimate destination is hell."

Last time I dealt at length with the explanation and the inner meaning of a verse from the Holy Qur'ān and now I am going to deal with the verse which follows the previous one. The verse is as follows: "with regard to him who fears the *Raḥmān* in *ghayb* and comes to God with a penitent heart. . . . .'

The commentators say that the word *ghayb* means unseen. Here it stands for the world which is hidden from the people living in this world. The *Raḥmān* according to them is derived from *Raḥmat* and is synonymous with *Raḥīm*. But *Raḥmān* is applicable to none but God and *Raḥīm* is applicable to God as well as man. *Raḥmān* they say means the one who transforms a wicked man into a virtuous one when He wishes to favour him. The word *Raḥīm* does not imply all this. They say when it applies to man, sometimes he does show kindness and sometimes he does not. At times he is able to show it and at times he is not. There is a very subtle difference between these two epithets.

The Holy Qur'ān says: "There are people who disdain from devotion to the *Raḥmān*. There is a tradition to the effect that these people believed in God but did not believe in the *Raḥmān*. If God and *Raḥmān* mean one and the same thing then there is no meaning in saying that they believed in God and did not believe in the *Raḥmān*. This is one of the subtleties of the Holy Qur'ān which needs an elucidation. There is another verse in the holy Qur'ān which says, "*When they were ordered to bow down to the one whom you order us to bow to?*"

We say that God is *Raḥmān*. *Raḥmān* is the most important of all the names of God. The names have forms which can be written down and effaced and the substance which they stand for. They are the symbols of realities. The *Ḥudūd i.e.*, the Imāms, are the spirit of the forms and the realities of the symbol.

The word *Raḥīm* from the point of view of its substance stands for the great *Ḥudūd* some of which are spiritual beings and others are in human form. It is through them that we can attain to the true knowledge of the Unity of God. It is through them that we can reach the Abode of Bliss. It is they about whom God says, "*And He taught Adam all the names and said to the angels, tell me what you know of their names if you think you are right.*"

It was, the names of these *Ḥudūd* (authorities) which were taught to Adam and it was through the knowledge of these names that Adam established his superiority over the angels. Ṭabarī and other commentators like him who float on the surface and do not dive deeper say that these *asmāʾ* stand for horses, camels, donkeys cattle and sheep. They go to the length of mentioning all sorts of things including the wooden plates and utencils under the category of *asmāʾ*. Our *majālis* are above this rude and crude stuff. The asmāʾ stand for nothing else than the living *Nāṭiqs i.e.*, spokesmen of God—the *Ḥudūd;* and Allah and *Raḥmān* also belong to this category. It is blasphemous to say that the asmā' stand for cattle and donkeys.

God has praised the one who fears *Raḥmān* in *ghayb i.e.,* the one who knows the position of the *Ḥudūd* in this world of darkness and appears before Him with a penitent heart. We must bear in mind that the heart is the centre of human activities. It governs the body. The working of the body depends upon it.

Just as the arteries of the human body depend for the supply of blood on the heart, in the same way, in spiritual matters also we depend for guidance on the Imām of the time who is the heart of the *Sharīʿat*. The Holy Qurʾān says, "*We shall show you our signs in the world and among yourselves in order that the truth may become clear to you.*" In short, just as our physical existence depends on our hearts, our spiritual elevation depends on the Imāms. The Holy Qurʾān says, "*There will come the day when we shall call every generation to appear before us with their Imāms*"!

May God make you fear God in *ghayb* and may you approach Him with your hearts directed to Him. This will suffice for this *majlis*. The rest of the verse I shall explain to you at the next meeting.

Lecture Third: The Meaning of al-Salām

O *muʾmins* [faithful ones], may God help you in listening with attention to what you hear from the Imām and in carrying out his orders. I appeal to you to fear God and be devoted to the Imāms. If you are firm in your devotion to the Imāms no harm will occur to you. Do not get frightened at the idea that on your death you will be shifted from bright rooms in your palaces to the dark and dingy tombs. To entertain such fears is a sign of the weakness of your faith. Let not the thought that your beautiful bodies will one day be reduced to dust, worry you in the least. When the precious pearl is out of the shell, there is no importance left for the shell. If it is broken to pieces nobody minds it.

You must bear in mind that it is only the vicious people who will be made to suffer in the grave. It is they who should fear and not you.

Look at the trouble your parents have taken from the days of your childhood in the growth of your bodies and in the improvement of your physical life on earth. But for the interest they took in you, you would not have been what you are. Your souls are a thousand times more important than your bodies. The Imams are your spiritual parents. Avail yourselves of a few days of life which are at your disposal here and look after your spiritual elevation under the care of your spiritual parents. Once you miss this opportunity, you will repent for ever. You will not be given a second chance to set things right.

O *muʾmin*s, last time I explained to you the external and the inner meaning of the verse, "He who fears *Raḥmān* in *ghayb* and approaches Him with the heart bent to Him............" Those of you who were attentive to what I said have profitted by it and have seen for themselves the way leading to salvation. Now I am going to explain to you the rest of this verse. It says, "Enter it with *salām*. This is the day of perpetuity." The word *salām* needs an explanation. The commentators say that it means 'safety'. They further say that *salām* is the greeting which the inmates of the *jannat* offer to one another God says "They will not hear in *jannat* useless or sinful talk. They will hear nothing but *salām*. According to another verse God himself is *salām*. The verse says "He who is the salām, the guardian of faith and the preserver of safety." The *jannat* itself is called *dār al–salām*. The Holy Quran says "*They have for them 'dār-al-salām' with God.*"

When *al-salām* is used as an epithet of God, it means that God is safe from description *i.e.*, He is above description in words and is much above even the subtlest thought which a human being can entertain of Him. All the attributes of God that can be uttered by tongue refer to the angels and the Prophet and the Imāms. God is the Creator of them all. He cannot be described by the epithets which are applicable to His creatures. He is *salām* because of His safety from all this. In short, God is above human description.

The *jannat* is called *dār-al-salām* because its inmates are free from diseases and defects and from changes from one condition into another which are the peculiar characteristics of the inmates of this world. If this definition which is the correct definition of the *jannat*, the Qur'ānic definition is accepted and it cannot but be accepted, then it logically follows that the inmates of the *jannat* have no bodies composed of four humors and exposed to disease and decay.

This gives the lie to those who maintain that the human being will enter hell or heaven along with their bodies. May God give you the courage to follow the real faith and may He keep you away from the influence of those who twist and turn the meaning of the words of God.

Lecture Twelfth: The Walāyat of ʿAlī

O *mu'mins* [faithful ones], may God help you in deriving the fullest benefit from the glories of this day. It was on this day that God conferred on us the highest of His favours. It was on this day that a great ordinance was issued by God which is the terminating point in the revelation of the religious laws. It was on this day that everything was made clear and the path was made smooth for the seekers of truth by the verse, "I have perfected your religion. I have bestowed on you My highest favours. I have chosen for you ISLAM as a religion."

At first the Prophet was reluctant to proclaim the ordinance to the people who he believed were prejudiced against it. A Qur'ānic verse made the matter clear and left no room for hesitation in his mind. The verse is as follows, "O Prophet, deliver the message which has been revealed to you by your Lord. If you fail to do so it will mean that you have not delivered His message to the people. God will guard you against the people".

There is no sect in Islam which believes that the Prophet fell short of delivering the message of God in such matters as the performance of prayers, the payment of *zakāt*, the fasting or going on pilgrimage or taking part in the *jihād.* We know well that he exerted his utmost in making the people offer the prayers which one cannot perform without undergoing some physical discomfort. He preached the people to pay the *zakāt* and the people did pay, although one does not find it easy to part with money. The people were made to fast and we know well that in fasting one has to put up with unbearable heat and thirst. He exhorted the people to go on pilgrimage which one cannot undertake without undergoing all sorts of hardships. He ordered the people to join the *jihād* and they did so at the risk of their lives.

In short, he made no hesitation in the delivering of God's message in these matters. It was only the question of *walāyat* which worried him the most. It was the ordinance pertaining to the *walāyat*, the allegiance to ʿAlī and the Imāms from amongst his descendants that he was not prepared to proclaim. Finding the people burning with hatred and jealousy he hesitated to deliver this ordinance to them and he was waiting for a favourable time when the above verses were revealed to clear his doubts.

If someone were to suggest that the Prophet was not hesitating to deliver this ordinance, this stand will make the revelation of the above verse meaningless and superfluous.

These verses which lay emphasis on the delivery of the ordinance prove to us that faith in the *walāyat* is the corner stone of our religion. If one does not believe in the *walāyat* and discharges all the primary and secondary duties enjoined on us by our religion, the performance of these duties will not help him in the least. His good deeds minus the belief in the *walāyat* will lead him to no other place than hell fire. Belief in the *walāyat* of the Prophet is a pivot. On this hinges the whole system of our religious laws. If one has no faith in the *walāyat*, the duties laid down in our religion will lose the force of application on him. Hence, the performance or non-performance of these duties will make no difference in his case.

It must be borne in mind that after the death of the Prophet the belief in the *walāyat* of the Imāms from his progeny is as important a part of our religion as the belief in the *walāyat* of the Prophet in his life time. This is supported by the Tradition according to which the Prophet is reported to have said at Ghadīr Khumm, "Am I not more precious to you than your own selves." This is an echo of the Quranic verse which says, "The Prophet is more dear to the *muʾmins*' than their own-selves to them." It is said, that in response to this question of the Prophet, when the *muʾmins* said "Yes, you are dearer to us than our own-selves", the Prophet said, "O God, be witness to their admission". After this he said, "ʿAlī is the master of one who acknowledges me to be his master. O God love those who love ʿAlī. Help those who help ʿAlī. Desert those who desert ʿAlī. Let the truth accompany ʿAlī wherever he goes."

NOTE: *Yawm al-ghadīr* is the day on which the Prophet declared Hazrat ʿAlī to be his brother on his return from his last pilgrimage which is known in history as *ḥajjat al-widāʾ*. This took place on the 18th of Dhiʾl-ḥajjah when the Prophet and his followers on their return from the pilgrimage made a halt at *Ghadīr Khumm.*

Aḥmad ibn Ḥanbal, one the four Sunni Imāms, has mentioned this incident in his well-known book Masnad al-kabīr. He quotes Barrah ibn ʿAzīb one of the *aṣḥāb* of the Prophet saying, "We were in the company of the Prophet when he halted at Ghadīr Khumm and led the congregational prayer. After finishing the prayer the Prophet took the hand of ʿAlī and raised it up saying, "Am I not dearer to the *mu'mins* than their own-souls?" They said "Yes". Again he said, "ʿAlī is the master of the one who acknowledges me to be his master. O God, love those who love ʿAlī and hate those who hate ʿAlī." After hearing this ʿUmar ibn al-khaṭṭāb went up to ʿAlī and said, "Congratulations to you, O son of Abū Ṭālib, you have become the master of every male and female *mu'min*."

Lecture Thirteenth: True Faith in the Unity of God Cannot be Achieved Without the Guidance of the Imāms

The Holy Qur'ān says, "There are some people who say, 'we believe in God and in the day of judgement' but in reality they do not believe." This is the characteristic of the hypocrites who do not profess what they believe in and do not believe in what they profess. By the words 'we have faith in God and the day of judgement' they intend to say that all their actions will be judged by God who will reward or punish them on the Day of Judgement. God has belied them by saying that "In reality they do not believe", that is to say they do not speak the truth.

The knowledge of the oneness of God is beyond the acquisition of the human mind by itself. There are some people who maintain that they can acquire this knowledge by themselves without the help of the Prophet or the Book of God. They go a step further and say that if God had not sent the Prophets, in this matter they could have easily dispensed with their teachings. If they think that by means of their intellect they can know the maker by seeing the things made and the Creator by looking at His creation, it is the height of insolence on their part. It is preposterous to imagine that a human being can acquire this knowledge without the help of the proper mediums namely the Prophets and the Imāms. We know by experience that even the power of talking which is inherent in man and which is much easier for him to acquire than the knowledge of the oneness of God, does not develop in him without the help of a teacher. Although it is in his nature to talk and he has been provided by God with the necessary apparatus for it, he does not and cannot talk unless he learns to do it from someone else. If this is the case with his talking how is it possible for him to acquire the complicated knowledge of the oneness of God without the help of a Prophet or an Imām? It is an impossibility.

Those who maintain that they can know the Maker from the things made, forget that even this much knowledge which they claim to be self-acquired is based on their seeing and hearing things from one another. It is because of their hearing things from one another that they are able to say that there must be a builder when they see a house.

If a man were to grow up in a desert where he sees no house and hears nothing of this kind his intellect will not help him in coming to the conclusion that there must be a builder if he sees a house for the first time. This being the case it is as clear as daylight that the divine knowledge cannot be acquired without the help of the proper medium. This leads us to the conclusion that those people about whom the Holy Qurʾān says, "They say we have faith in God and in the Day of Judgement but in reality they are faithless", are the people who do not believe in the mediums *i.e.,* the *waṣī* of the Prophet and the Imāms from his progeny. No correct knowledge of the oneness of God can be acquired without our referring to them. We cannot acquire a correct faith unless we seek the knowledge through them.

The Prophet has given us the outlines of the subjects which are dealt with in the Qurʾān. For the details we have to go to the Imāms who are the masters of the subject. Had the Book been enough for us to teach us everything and solve all our difficulties independently of those divine agents who are the masters of this Book of God it would not have been necessary for God to tell us "If they had referred the matter to the Prophet and to the spiritual heads from amongst them they, who are men of depths, would have explained it to them." The 'men of depths' referred to in the above verse are the Imāms from the progeny of the Prophet who possess the profoundest knowledge of the Book of God and the Tradition of the Prophet.

Lecture Fourteenth: The True Meaning of the Tradition, "I Am the City of Knowledge and ʿAlī is its Gate."

Every knowledge refers to the investigation of a fixed subject matter pursued by a fixed method. This view is supported by the verses of the Qurʾān and the Tradition of the Prophet. The Holy Qurʾān says, "There is no righteousness in your entering the houses by their back doors; but righteousness lies in fearing God and entering the houses by their proper doors." The words houses and doors used in the above verse are used figuratively. They do not stand for ordinary houses and doors. We know well that the doors are meant for entrance. Had the words been used in their ordinary sense, there would have been no necessity for God to admonish us to do a thing which every one of us does in the ordinary course of affairs. The houses and the doors referred to in the verses are quite different from the houses and doors that we are familiar with. This is made clear by the well known Tradition of the Prophet which is as follows: "I am the city of knowledge and Ali is its gate. Let those who want to acquire knowledge approach the city by its proper gate."

After having proved by the verses of the Qurʾān and the Tradition of the Prophet that knowledge always refers to the investigation of a particular subject pursued by a particular method our next step would naturally be to find out the subject matter of the knowledge of which, according to the Tradition, the Prophet is the City and ʿAlī is the Gate. If we maintain that the subject matter is the prayer and how to perform it or the *zakāt* and how to pay it or the fast and how to observe it, then we cannot but admit that ʿAlī's knowledge in this respect was in no way better or higher than that of those who had the opportunities of associating with the Prophet and attending his sermons. But it is not so. The knowledge mentioned in the Tradition refers to the philosophy of *taʾwīl* the reconciliation between traditionalism and rationalism and the knowledge of *ḥudūdallāh*, the spiritual and physical ones. It is this knowledge about which the Prophet says, 'I am the city of knowledge' and about which the Qur'ān says figuratively, "There is no righteousness in your entering the houses by their back doors."

In short, ʿAlī is the person who is well qualified in the knowledge of which the Prophet is the City and ʿAlī the Gate; and all those who have embraced Islam know nothing of this knowledge excepting those who have approached the *waṣī* of the Prophet and entered the city of knowledge by its proper gate. Those Muslims who do not approach this channel have only this advantage that their blood is unlawful for the Muslims to shed and their property is safe with them. The Prophet has divided the Muslims into two classes. He says, "I have been ordered by God to fight on with the people until they say 'there is no God but God and Moḥammed is the Prophet of God.' When they say this their lives and properties are secure with us unless they do something which calls for punishment. They will have to settle their accounts with God." This is the advantage that they will get from their embracing Islam. With regard to the second class of people the Prophet says, "Those who say there is no God but God, with sincerity will enter the 'jannat'." On being asked as to what is meant by sincerity the Prophet replied "It means the knowledge of the *ḥudūd* of God and the discharging of the obligation that one owes to them." This refers to those learned Muslims who enter the city through its gate.

Lecture Nineteenth: He Who Knows Himself Knows His Lord

O *mu'min*s [faithful ones], may God confer His favours on you and may He guide you to the right path. Stick to the principle of reticence. Stick to the Imāms. If you do so, you will never go astray and you will enjoy the shade of the *Ṭayyibah Tree*. Its branches are over-hanging on your heads. Its blessings are always open to you, provided you know this and give serious thought to it. Thank God for the special favour that He has conferred on you by guiding you through the Imāms and fear the day when yon will be brought before God and when every one will be rewarded or punished according to his deeds in this life, the day when no injustice will be done to any one. The month of Rajab is gone and Shaʿbān is come. It is a sacred month. Put on the clean dress of piety. May God show mercy to you. May He help you in keeping your hearts clean. Do not keep your bodies clean and neglect your souls. Let you not be deceived by the health of your bodies if your hearts are diseased. Keep aloof from the filth of idol worship and infidelism. Never tell lies. Seek guidance from those who have been pronounced by the Quran to be pure.

Last time I spoke to you on a philosophical subject and now I am going to speak to you on a similar one. It is said that once the learned divine, namely Imām Jaʿfar al-Ṣādiq, was asked by people to explain to them the meaning of the Tradition of the Prophet, "He who knows himself knows God." The divine said, "You must bear in mind that man by nature belongs both to the physical and to the spiritual world. As far as his body is concerned he is like any other material body in this world. Every particle of it belongs to this world. The heat in his body belongs to the fire in this world. The flexibility of his body is due to the air in it. The humidity of his body is due to the water and the heavy mass of his body belongs to the earth. At the time of the dissolution of the body every particle of it goes back to its physical source to which it belongs. This is what we can perceive by means of our senses.

He has something else which can neither be perceived nor compared to anything that we find in this physical world. His being recognised as the noblest of all the creatures of God is not due to his physical body but to something else which is called the soul.

We know that the component parts of the body such as heat, humidity, flexibility and the mass have originated from the sources such as fire, water, air and earth. We also know that on the dissolution of the body these component parts have to go back to the sources where they have come from. Moreover, we know that the only medium through which the human body can appear on earth is its parents. Besides, it cannot grow unless it is fed on the food belonging to this physical world.

Similar is the case with the soul. It cannot shape itself without the medium of its spiritual parents. It cannot develop unless it is fed on spiritual food. The spiritual parents are the *Ḥudūd* of God on earth. It is they who give a proper shape to the souls and feed them on spiritual knowledge and lift them up to the spiritual world. Their relationship with the souls is just the same as the connection of the human body with the four elements of this world.

Thus, he who reflects on the connection of his body with the physical world and its entire dependence on this world comes to the natural conclusion that the body is the creature of the Universe and the Universe is its Creator. On these lines when he goes a step further and thinks of the relationship of his soul with the *Ḥudūd* and its entire dependence for its development on them and of its final return to the source from where it has come he will naturally know the Lord of his soul and will realise the true position of the *Ḥudūd* of God on earth, namely the Imāms. He will further realise that just as the Universe is the master of his body the *Ḥudūd* are the masters of his soul. When he comes to this stage it is sure to dawn on him that God is unlike the bodies which are made of earth and that He is above being compared to anything in the physical world. It will further dawn on him that God is not only unlike his body but even unlike his soul which is like the spiritual heads of God and which belongs to the spiritual world. In other words he will realise that God is neither the body nor the soul. This is the meaning of the Tradition, "He who knows himself knows God."

O *muʾmins*, may God make you men of insight and confer upon you the last of His favours, the forgiveness of your sins. Praise be to God who is hidden from the knowledge of men and who is above imagination. Greetings be on His apostle, the best of mankind, Muḥammad who dispelled the darkness by the light of Islam and who invited people to the abode of safety. May there be greetings on ʿAlī, his *waṣī* the Lion of God, the Solver of our Difficulties and the dispeller of our grief, ʿAlī ibn Abī Ṭālib, the master of philosophy and may the greetings be on the Imāms from his choice progeny for ever. God is enough for us. He is the best pleader of our cause.

—Javad M. Muscati and A. M. Moulvi, translators

8

NĀṢIR-I KHUSRAW

Abū Muʿīn Nāṣir ibn Khusraw ibn Ḥārith al-Qubādiyānī, better known as Nāṣir-i Khusraw, was a prominent Ismāʿīlī dignitary of the Fāṭimid Caliph-Imām al-Mustanṣir bi'Llāh's time (427–487/1036–1094). He was a *dāʿī*, a philosopher, a traveler, as well as a renowned poet who ranks among the greatest of Persian poets. At the age of forty-two, in 437/1045, while he was in Merv holding an administrative post probably in the court of Chagrī Bayg Dā'ūd, a Seljūq prince, he experienced a drastic spiritual upheaval that resulted in his conversion of faith from probably being a Twelver Shiʿite to an Ismāʿīlī Shiʿite. He came to Cairo, the then Fāṭimid capital, in 439/1047, where he received proper instruction in Ismāʿīlī theosophy and was given the high status of 'Ḥujjat of Khurasan' in the Fāṭimid *daʿwah* organization. In 442/1050, he settled down in the valley of Yumgan (in present-day Afghanistan), which was then ruled by the Amīr of Badakhshan, ʿAlī ibn Asad, an Ismāʿīlī, who had close relations with Nāṣir-i Khusraw. He spent the rest of his life there until his death in 481/1088–89, propagating the Fāṭimid *daʿwah* and composing works on Fāṭimid philosophy. His fame as a great Ismāʿīlī spiritual philosopher has remained undiminished until the present day among the Ismāʿīlīs of Iran, Afghanistan, China, Tajikistan, and the northern area of Pakistan, such as Hunza, Chitral, and Gilgit, where he is revered as *pīr* (Sufi master). In Central Asia, his fame and popularity today are such that not only is his tomb in Yumgan kept as a shrine but also a great number of (most likely spurious) texts are ascribed to his authorship and many people of the local Sunni population claim descent from him.

Nāṣir-i Khusraw composed a number of philosophical and theological works, such as *Wajh-i dīn* (The Face of Religion) and *Gushāyish wa rahāyish* (Expansion and Liberation). But among his extant works that deal with philosophy, the most important is *Kitāb jāmiʿ al-ḥikmatayn* (The Sum of the Two Wisdoms). In the age of Nāṣir-i Khusraw, philosophy of Greek origin was repudiated as being incompatible with revelation by the Muslim jurists, Sunni and Twelver Shiʿite alike. The earlier Muslim thinkers, such as Fārābī, placed philosophy (which for him included the inner reality of religion) at the top, and Avicenna put philosophy and revelation on the same highest plain, whereas Nāṣir-i Khusraw held philosophy to be partial truth, the universal truth being revelation. This is the central idea expounded in the *Jāmiʿ al-ḥikmatayn.*

All of the philosophical works of Nāṣir-i Khusraw, including this book, were composed in Persian. *Jāmiʿ al-ḥikmatayn*, which is his main philosophical testament, was written in 462/1070 at the request of the Amīr of Badakhshan in order to explain to him a philosophical *qaṣīdah* by Abu'l-Haytham Jurjānī, an obscure Ismāʿīlī philosopher-poet (d. fourth/tenth). The poem is composed in eighty-two distiches and contains eighty-one issues pertaining to Ismāʿīlī views on ontology, cosmology, epistemology, theology, hermeneutics of the Qurʾān, and so on. Nāṣir-i Khusraw, who attempts to give the solutions, presents them in two ways—(1) through the philosophy of Greek origin, and (2) through Ismāʿīlī theosophy—thereby trying to harmonize the two wisdoms through the method of *taʾwīl* (hermeneutics of symbols—literally taking a thing back to its origin).

In this chapter we have included three selections of Nāṣir-i Khusraw's works. In the first selection, there is a translation from *Jāmiʿ al-ḥikmatayn* that deals with the reason Nāṣir-i Khusraw composed *Jāmiʿ al-ḥikmatayn.* This is his introduction to this work in which the most important discussion is his theory that there is no conflict between philosophy and revelation. It also deals with his theory of correspondence between the several worlds. In this selection, Nāṣir-i Khusraw attempts to give the dual meaning of the seven lights, one from the point of the philosophers and another from the point of Ismāʿīlī thinkers based on revelation, thereby attempting to demonstrate that essentially there is no dichotomy between the two wisdoms. The selection also discusses the spiritual hermeneutics of angel, *jinn*, and devil. Nāṣir-i Khusraw attempts to give the *taʾwīl* of the Qurʾānic concepts of these three categories of beings, as well as the views of the philosophers, again attempting to harmonize the two wisdoms. Lastly, the selection covers the subject of the intellect and epistemology. There are two themes: one deals with the difference between intellect and knowledge (Nāṣir-i Khusraw agrees with the philosophers that knowledge is an attribute of the intellect thereby demonstrating the superiority of intellect over every created thing) and the other deals with the difference between the perceiver and perception. The central idea is that the human intellect is incapable of comprehending its Originator, but it is capable of comprehending all the originated things by receiving the light of God through its pure affirmation of His unity devoid of sensible and intelligible attributes.

The second selection is from Nāṣir-i Khusraw's *Gushāyish wa rahāyish* (Expansion and Liberation) translated by the translator as *Knowledge and Liberation.* This consists of two parts; cosmology and ontology. In the section on cosmology, such issues as creation and eternity, generation and corruption, and whether God has a body or not are treated. In the section on ontology, different types of existents, the nature of the human soul, and its relation to the body and substance are among the issues discussed.

The third selection consists of several of Nāṣir-i Khusraw's philosophical odes. There is a long tradition of philosophical poetry in Iran, in which profound philosophical issues are discussed in poetic form. In these poems, Nāṣir-i Khusraw, who is one of the most illustrious representatives of the tradition of philosophical poetry in Persia, first discusses Divine unity, time, multiplicity, and creation. Then, the problem of words and speech, and after that, angelology are discussed. The fourth section is devoted to a discussion of free will and determinism, and the final section deals with the question of becoming.

—*S. H. Nasr*

Kitāb jāmiʿ al-ḥikmatayn

THE SUM OF THE TWO WISDOMS

Philosophy and Revelation

On the Reason for Composing this Book and [the Meaning of] its Name

(10) Abū Muʿīn Nāṣir ibn Khusraw ibn al-Ḥārith says: Praise be to God the Exalted, Whose remembrance is requisite for speaking about this book because this is a new book. Anything which is temporally originated (*ḥādith*) has a cause. A temporally originated thing must have five causes: (i) efficient cause, for instance the carpenter who makes the throne; (ii) instrumental cause, such as an axe, a saw, etc., so that the craftsmanship of this carpenter manifests through those [instruments]; (iii) material cause, such as wood which receives the craftsmanship from the carpenter; (iv) formal cause, such as the form of the throne in the soul (*nafs*) of the carpenter; (v) final cause, which is the purpose for making the throne, and that is for making the king sit on it.

(11) The sages of real Religion (*ḥukamā-yi dīn-i ḥaqq*)[1] and philosophy are in agreement that the first cause is effect of the final cause. Because upon reflecting on the purpose of the throne [it is found that], it is for the sitting of the king. It is made by the carpenter through the instruments and the wood by the command of the king so that he would sit on the throne. So the final thing which manifests itself as the created thing should be the first cause of that thing. That is why the sages quote this famous saying, "First reflection then action." Don't you see that first the reflection of the carpenter is that the king should have the throne, and his final act is that the king should sit on the throne. [In the same way the

This translation is based on Nāṣir-i Khusraw's *Jāmiʿ al-ḥikmatayn*, edited by H. Corbin and M. Moʿin (Tehran-Parīs: Institut Franco-Iranien, 1965), pp. 10–21, 104–107, 137–44, and 274–89. Its French translation by Isabelle de Gastines was published in Paris in 1984. The numbers in parentheses refer to the pagination of Corbin-Moʿin's edition, while items in square brackets are the translator's additions.

1. By *ḥukamāʾ-i dīnī* Nāṣir-i Khusraw means the Fāṭimid thinkers.

question,] what is the purpose of the creation of this cosmos? That it finally manifests man and after him nothing is manifested. They said the purpose of the Creator of the cosmos [creating] this creation first was to obtain man, so from its creation finally man was manifested.

(12) In its appropriate place in this book we will explain about this meaning that for any book which is composed these five causes are requisite: (i) the efficient cause which is the author of the book; (ii) the instrumental cause which is the reed-pen and knife; (iii) the material cause, which is the paper and ink; (iv) the formal cause which is the discourse and address; (v) the final cause which is to make the knowledge in that book accessible to the seeker. The cause of all the causes is the final cause, about which we have already mentioned; it is more important than the efficient cause because whatever the composer of the book, the author of the meanings or the editor of the text does it is for the reason that the seeker of that knowledge, who does not know this [knowledge], has access to what he does not know. If justice means disapproval of violence to the oppressed, then making an ignorant gain access to knowledge is a greater justice because ignorance is manifest violence. If giving a share from whatever is accessible to us to a deserving person is a virtue (*iḥsān*), and if giving something from our wealth to our kinsmen is the command of God, then our kinsmen are men amongst all animals, so giving a portion of knowledge to them—which is a real human quality (*insāniyyāt*)—is obedience to God, as He said to His Messenger in this verse in His words, "God commands justice, virtue and giving to kinsmen" [Qurʾān, 16:90]. All these are the qualities of the Messenger. He cautioned us, "I perform these three acts because God has commanded me to do so." That is why the sages have established five causes for the coming into existence of any thing. If at any time one of the causes is missing, then that event does not take place. I mean, if the carpenter has tools, wood, form of the throne [in his mind], but nobody wants the throne, then the carpenter will not make the throne; or if the carpenter is there, has tools, knows how to make the throne, and the king wants the throne but the wood, which is the material cause, is not there, then the throne cannot be made; or if four causes are there, I mean, the carpenter, the wood, the knowledge of the carpenter—the form of the throne—, and the king wants [the throne] but the instruments [for making it] are not there, then this invention which is the throne cannot come into existence.

(13) The sages of real Religion have said there are seven causes for any temporal thing to come into existence. Until all those seven [causes] are there that temporal thing cannot come into existence. [They are:] (i) efficient cause, I mean the artisan; (ii) instrumental cause; (iii) material cause; (iv) formal cause; (v) spatial cause; (vi) temporal cause; and (vii) final cause. [The fifth and sixth causes are also necessary because] an artisan makes his craft in space and time, hence these two are also the causes for the creation of a temporal thing. [Seven causes] are more proper [than five causes] because in the creation of the cosmos, too, it is apparent that the causes of the temporal origin of the existent things [and] the things born [i.e., minerals, plants, and animals] are the seven planets in seven spheres that govern the individual [existents]. They are the [cause] of the temporal existence of mineral, plant and animal [kingdoms] by the decree of the Almighty and All-knowing.

(14) Now we say "It is due to the rational soul that man has superiority over the cosmos, and supremacy over the earth, water, air, fire, as well as land animals, so that he utilizes each one of them for his benefits."

Those who are the leaders in Islam say whoever says 'I know that scammony [soap] soothes the nature of man', or 'I know that oxymel [mixture of honey and vinegar] pacifies bile', is an unbeliever (*kāfir*). How can ignorance be more powerful than this? A group of people is obsessed by *kufr*. It is not in the nature of a physician to say, 'I have created scammony', nor an astronomer would say, 'I cause the eclipse of the sun'. If a physician who according to his knowledge says myrobolan (fruit, *halīlah*) alleviates the pain of fever and bile from the natures is a *kāfir*, then someone who says that water alleviates the pain of thirst, and bread removes the pain of hunger, is also a *kāfir*. This is so because all things, whether they are medicinal [plants], food or water, are created by God. There is no limit to this aberration and *kufr* in which most of the members of the *ummah* (Community) have fallen.

(15) We return to our discourse—the how and why of the things created in the universe by God the Exalted, and His placing the soul in man that is the seeker of how and why [of everything]. [The sages say,] there is a similarity between the eatable things created for the 'sensory soul' (*nafs-i ḥissī*), [and the things possessing quality created for the rational soul]. That is because they saw man deriving taste from eatable things, and meaning from things having quality. The sensory soul does not become strong if it does not derive taste from eatable things, and the rational soul does not become strong if it does not derive meaning from things possessing qualities (*kayfiyyāt*) whether seen or heard. Just as the sensory soul seeks taste from food and drink, in the same way the rational soul seeks meaning in the things which can be seen and heard. The physical universe in its totality, from the rotating spheres and the stars of different magnitude, actions, colors, and motions, is the subject of inquiry (*mukayyif*). The things of the earth, such as, the substances, plants, and animals of different species, shapes, forms, tastes, colors, actions are also all subjects of inquiry and knowing for man.

Every [reflective] human soul desires to know why the heavens [or skies] rotate, while the earth remains stationary; why the sun shines constantly, while the moon is sometimes full, sometimes crescent, sometimes visible, sometimes hidden; why the earth is solid, while water is soft; why dried clay when mixed with water becomes soft, but if a stone and iron are mixed [the stone] does not become soft; why dried clay when mixed with water becomes soft, but when put in the fire becomes hard and turns into brick; why stone and iron remain solid in water but become soft in fire, and other things which he observes but does not know why they are so.

So on the basis of the intellectual analogy and logical proof we say, the creation of these knowable things, and the bringing of this knowledge-seeking soul (*nafs-i dānish-jū'ī*) in man, the soul's insistence and greed for knowledge about those things is in accordance with the way God has created the human soul and said to it. Ask and seek why such a thing is as it is, and do not imagine that this creation is vain. He Himself says this in His Book, this *āyat* in His word, "They reflect on the creation of the heavens and the earth, "Our Lord! Thou hast not created this in vain! Glory be to Thee. Preserve us from the chastisement of the Fire" [Qur'ān, 3:191].

Today, those titled as jurists (*fuqahā' laqabān*) of the Religion of Islam say, "If someone says, 'The day appears by the rising of the sun', or 'I know which star moves and which one is fixed', he is a *kāfir*." They have preferred ignorance to knowledge and say, "we have nothing to do with the how and why of the creation." The Messenger, on him be peace, said, "Reflect on the creation, but do not reflect on the Creator." Since it is not permitted to reflect on the Creator, according to the ruling of this report (*khabar*) which we mentioned, it follows that reflection on the creation is necessary, according to what is mentioned in this report. That is because, if it were not permitted to reflect on the creation, as it has been on the Creator, then the creation and the Creator would have been equal. Speech emanated from the sacred prophetic soul and manifested through [his] thought which is the locus of the descent of the Trustworthy Spirit (*rūḥ al-amīn*), is indeed a veridical, strong, and logical proof [for reflecting on the creation].

(16) Whoever holds a belief that it is incumbent to seek the why and how of the creation, makes his knowledge seeking rational soul powerful over the land animals by the divine power, so much so that he makes everyone subordinate to him. Due to having such a soul, man becomes worthy of the divine Address. It—I mean the rational soul—is charged with the divine mandate to investigate the why of everything that he sees and hears from the things subject to inquiry, to seek for meaning from the categories (*maqūlāt*). Children asking their parents 'what is that' in order to know the names of different things and colors they see shows the soundness of our thesis—the human soul is naturally disposed (*majbūl*) to explore [for knowledge]—and is our evidence.

But since the child is small and [intellectually] immature, he becomes satisfied by hearing the name of that thing, and does not investigate what is the act of that thing, and what is its use, for the meaning of a thing is its real name. Also, the children's asking for the names of things indicates that Adam, on him be peace, was first informed about the names of things through divine teaching. So his descendants seek the names of things in the beginning, as God the Exalted said in His word, "And He taught Adam all the names" [Qur'ān, 2:31].

The *Ḥashwiyān*[2] of the *ummah* (community) said that God the Exalted taught Adam the names of everything He had created, so by knowing those names he attained supremacy over the angels because they did not know the names of things. This explanation is very superficial and meaningless because if someone, for instance, sees [the fruit] myrobolan and knows that its [name is] myrobolan, and another person [sees it who] does not know its [that] name and says its name is not myrobolan but it is called the pear, [in this case] none of the two has superiority over the other because both of them do not know the act of myrobolan, nor the purpose for which it is used, nor how much of it should be eaten. If one of the two knows its action, its usage, and how much of it should be eaten then that knowledgeable person has superiority over that ignorant due to knowing the action of

2. ʿAbd al-Karīm al-Shahrastānī lists this group under the category of Sunnite literalists, c.f., *al-Milal wa'l-iḥal* (Cairo, 1968), vol. 1, pp. 105–106; also, cf., "Ḥashwiyya", by A. S. Halkin in *The Journal of the American Oriental Society*, 54 (1934), pp. 1–28.

myrobolan. So by simply knowing the names of things a person does not attain superiority over others because the same thing is called by an Arab by one name, by a Turk by another name, by an Indian by another name, by a Greek by another name, by an Ethiopian by another name. But the meaning of the action of that thing to which these groups give different names is one meaning.

(17) So we have proved that what the commentators [of the Qurʾān] explained [regarding Adam] that God the Exalted is All-Wise and All-Knowing, [and] He taught His chosen one—who was Adam, peace be upon him—the names of the things so that by [knowing those names] he attained superiority over the angels, is absurd and erroneous.

The sages of the Religion said "The real names of the things are their meanings and actions. God the Exalted taught Adam, on him be peace, those names so that whatever he saw in the universe he knew its action and its benefit for himself and for his descendants.

Every kind of science, such as medicine, astronomy, etc., has been discovered by a prophet through divine teaching (*taʿlīm-i ilāhī*), which that prophet [had learnt] from Adam.[3] And Adam, they said, by [knowing] those names which were not the verbal names, and were taught [to him] by God through inspiration became superior over the angels.

(18) The *ʿulamāʾ* of the real Religion hold the sciences of medicine and astronomy as proofs for affirming prophecy to the philosophers who deny prophecy and revelation. They [i.e., the *ʿulamāʾ* of real Religion] say, "Whoever is the first one to know, for instance, that a certain medicine can be made from [the mixture of] a drug growing in Rome, a drug brought from China, a drug brought from India; that one [drug] should be of the weight of a grain, another of the weight of one drachma, the third one half a grain in weight; that one [drug] should be pounded, one should be melted, and one should be burnt; then all of them should be mixed together and given to a [sick] person for curing such-and-such illness must necessarily be a prophet. For it was God Who 'taught' him where man's benefits lie, and the cure for the diseases through those things in that much measure. Otherwise nobody would have been able to know those drugs, neither through experiment nor through tasting them."

They also say, "The person who was the first one to discover that out of some myriads of stars, which we see in the sky, seven are planets; then he recognized the course of each one as well as its act and nature must be a prophet who by [direct] divine teaching knew this high science." So by the religious argument and the argument from their [philosopher's] science, the affirmation of prophecy becomes requisite.

Today, a group [of philosophers] whom God has created for bringing together the science[s] has declared the divine act of origination [of the Creation] (*ibdāʿ*) futile. Whoever considers the [divine act of the origination of the] creation futile

3. This view prior to Nāṣir-i Khusraw was maintained by the Ismāʿīlī thinker Abū Ḥātim Rāzī (d.c. 322/933–34); cf. his *Kitāb aʿlām al-nubuwwah*, ed. by S. al-Sawy and Gholam-Reza Aavani, English preface by S. H. Nasr (Tehran, 1977), pp. 273–318.

becomes a *kāfir*, as He says in His word, "And We have not created the heaven and the earth and all that is between them in vain. That is the conjecture of those who deny the truth (*kafaru*). And woe unto those who deny the truth, from the Fire!" [Qur'ān, 38:27]. This is the reason for the dominance of ignorance over the majority.

(19) Since those titled as *ʿulamaʾ* (*ʿulamāʾ laqabān*) have denounced the one who knows the science of the created things as *kāfir*, the seekers of how and why [of a thing] have become silent, and the exponents of this science have also remained quiet, so ignorance has gained mastery over the people, especially the inhabitants of our land of Khurasan, the region of east. The prince of Badakhshān, ʿAyn al-Dawlah waʾl-Dīn, Zayn al-Millah, Shams al-Aʿlā, Abuʾl-Maʿālī, ʿAlī ibn Asad[4] says in this context,

Verse:

The pride of the learned is in learning and culture,
The pride of the ignorant is in dress and garment,
The culture and learning of the cultured are now
contemptible; for how many are still cultured!
The worthless are at the helm; the gratifying accomplished
ones kept at distance,
None knows the cause of all these but
the One Who is the Giver of causes.
So says ʿAlī ibn Asad: This world is full of sorrow and trouble.

(20) No one has written a book on the how and why of the creation, because out of the five causes, which we have shown earlier to be necessary for composing any book, the first one, the seeker of this knowledge, who is the final cause, has ceased to exist. Secondly the exponent of this knowledge, who is the efficient cause, has also passed away; and with the disappearance of these two causes from among the people of this land, [the science of Religion] has vanished. None has remained in this land, which we mentioned, who is capable of harmonizing (*jamʿ*) the science of true Religion, which is a product of the holy Spirit, with the science of creation, which is a branch of philosophy. For the philosophers relegate those titled as *ʿulamāʾ* to the rank of beasts, and hold the religion of Islam in contempt on account of their ignorance [of the science of creation]; while those titled as *ʿulamaʾ* declare the philosophers *kāfir*. As a result, neither the true Religion nor true philosophy has remained in this land. As long as a philosopher is not religious [he cannot harmonize the science of creation and the science of true Religion].

When I came to this land [Khurasan] from the sacred presence of Imām Muʿādhdh Abū Tamīm,[5] the true Imam, the descendant of the chosen Messenger, the vicegerent of his ancestor, the treasurer of the wisdom of the All-Wise and All-Knowing, on him and on his pure ancestors and noble descendants be the benediction of God, I had already studied the works of the men of learning in

4. Amīr of Badakhshān, an Ismāʿīlī who had close relations with Nāṣir-i Khusraw; cf. *EIR*: vol. I, p. 848.

5. Fāṭimid Caliph-Imām al-Mustanṣir biʾLlāh (427–487/1036–1094).

philosophy, and was the custodian of the science of true Religion which is the interpretation (*taʾwīl*) and inner meaning (*bāṭin*, or the objective) of the Book of *Sharīʿah*.[6] . . . . In 406 A.H., the Amir of Badakhshān known as ʿAyn al-Dawlah Abuʾl-Maʿalī ʿAlī ibn Asad al-Ḥārith—sent me *a qaṣīdah* in which Khwājah Abuʾl-Haytham Aḥmad ibn al-Ḥasan al–Jurjānī,[7] may God have mercy on him, had questioned about certain things . . . He requested me to resolve those issues raised [in that *qaṣīdah*] . . . I became happy and thanked God the Exalted, because in this period when most of the people have turned away from the real Religion, the market of wisdom is in debt, and the constitution of those upholding the *Sharīʿah* is corrupt, I found a great man who could combine the worldly authority (*wilāyat-i dunyawī*) with the recognition of the stages of religious authority (*wilāyat-i dīn*), and whom worldly power and inheritance—do not keep away from seeking religious knowledge, insights and truths.

(21) Since the efficient cause of this book was ready which was myself, and the formal cause was also ready which was the forms of knowledge imprinted in [my self], then the instrumental and material causes became existent, and the final cause was attained in such a great seeker [of knowledge, the Amir of Badakhsān]. I was in a stable fortified place, so only the need for time remained, [which materialized] when the composition of this book became necessary.

Since this book is based on solving the difficult issues of the Religion and the problems of philosophy, so I named this book *Jāmi ʿal-ḥikmatayn* (The Book Harmonizing the Two Wisdoms). In it I have spoken to the sages of Religion with *āyāt* from the Book of God the Exalted, and reports of His Messenger, on whom be peace, and to the sages of philosophy and accomplished logicians, with intellectual demonstrations and premises resulting in happy conclusion, for wisdom's treasure-house is the 'heart' (*khāṭir*) of the Seal [i.e., Muḥammad], the heir of the prophets, peace be upon them, and a scent of wisdom is also [found] in the books of the ancient [sages].

On the Seven Lights

Distich 9

> Seven lights radiate their lights so that,
> each being accepts the fire from each
> one according to the measure of its subtlety

(104) The opinion of the sages of philosophy on the celestial lights and the subtlety that reaches from them to the 'mothers' (*ummahāt*, i.e., elements) is that any subtle quality that appears in the 'mothers' [i.e., the elements] is manifested

6. For the Ismāʿīlī concept of *taʾwīl* cf., I. K. Poonawala, "Ismāʿīlī *taʾwīl* of the Qurʾān", in *Approaches to the History of the Interpretation of the Qurʾān*, ed. by A. Rippin (Oxford, 1988), pp. 199–222.

7. An obscure Ismāʿīlī philosopher poet, the author of an Ismāʿīlī philosophical poem whose questions were the subject of at least two commentaries by the Ismāʿīlī thinkers, (1) Nāṣir-i Khusraw's *Kitāb jāmiʿ al-ḥikmatayn;* (2) Muḥammad Surkh Nishāpūrī's *Sharḥ-i qaṣīdah-i Abuʾ l-Ḥaytham Jurjānī*. This work has been edited by H. Corbin and M. Moʿin' (Tehran-Paris, 1965).

from the higher world. As for the higher world, they said, it transcends the celestial spheres. They also maintained that these seven governing planets are like the apertures of that world to this world. The light and subtlety flow from that world [to this world] in equal [measure]. However, these bodies from which the light reaches here differ in nature, so the receivers of light and subtlety in this world are also different due to their disposition and the place [they occupy]. This is the reason why every [terrestrial thing] differs in light and subtlety. They said that all the fusible substances aspire to become gold, and all the congealed substances aspire to become a red hyacinth. However, because their dispositions and the places [they occupy] are different, so a disposition that becomes purer and accepts the effects [of the light and subtlety] completely becomes gold and ruby. The one whose disposition is defiled and murky does not reach [the level] of gold and ruby. The substances are of different kinds, such as, copper, lead, iron, etc., and chrysolite, garnet, amber, etc.

They held the same view concerning [the diversity in] plants and animals. The light and subtlety from the higher world do not reach in equal measure to all the things [in the world] because the luminaries are of different magnitude and nature. The dispositions of things [in this world] are different, and the places [they occupy] are different. The motions of the spheres around the mothers [or elements] are also different. So the place of the earth that is below the zone of the sphere, the components of the sphere move very rapidly over there, and that motion is [like that of] a water-wheel. Another place of the earth is below the pole. There the components of the sphere move very slowly. That motion is [like that of] a millstone. This is the reason, they said, why the bodies that have a crystal like disposition in having subtlety, transparency and luminosity, shine. Then there is a disposition that is dark, opaque and obscure [so it does not reflect light]. Some fruits become sour and red like jujube. They gave example of foods such as meat, bread, etc. to show that [although] the subtlety and light come in equal measure [from the luminaries] but become different in the receivers. So when an intelligent man consumes it, his acumen and comprehension increase, but if a mouse consumes it then treachery and plundering become manifested in it. If a dog eats it then evil temper and aggression toward man become manifested from it. So they established that these differences among existent things are in respect of the receivers and not in respect of the difference of the world. For example, by means of fire an egg is cooked, wax is melted, a stone is broken to pieces, and a brick is hardened.

(105) The response of the people of interpretation (*ahl-i taʾwīl*), peace be upon them, concerning the relation of the seven lights to the realm of *ibdāʿ* (origination) is, anything that exists in the sensible world is an effect (*athar*) of something that exists in the higher world. That is because, we see that in the sensible world there are seven lights, and the things born [here, i.e., the three kingdoms] receive light and subtlety from them. These luminous existent things indicate that in the higher world there are seven pre-eternal, primordial lights, that those pre-eternal [lights] are the causes of physical lights.

Those seven pre-eternal lights, they said, are: first, the [primordial] origination (*ibdāʿ*); second, the substance of the Intellect; third, the totality of the Intellect consisting of three dimensions: intellection, intellect and intelligible. No other existent thing has this characteristic but the Intellect. It knows itself, and its essence [or self] is known [to it]. Fourth is the Soul which has emanated from the Intellect; fifth is *Jadd;* sixth is *Fatḥ*; and seventh is *Khayāl*.[8] In the exoteric *Sharīʿah* [the last three degrees] are called Gabriel, Michael and Seraphiel. The seven planets—the sun, the moon, Saturn, Jupiter, Mars, Venus and Mercury—in the physical world are the effects of those subtle things and roots (*uṣūl*) which are the originated things (*mubdaʿāt*). In the microcosm, which is man, the traces of those primordial substances are also seven. They are: life, knowledge, power, perception, act, will, and perpetuity.

(106) Each man receives a share from those seven primordial substances—those seven essences (*maʿnī*) that we mentioned—according to the measure of the receptivity of the substance of his soul, just as each of the seven physical substances of the mine receives a share from the seven planets according to the measure of the receptivity of its physical substance. A soul may be at the level of prophethood, just as a metal may be of the level of gold. A soul may be at the level of being the *waṣī* [legatee of the prophet], just as a metal may be of the level of silver. Just as metals are of seven kinds: gold, silver, iron, copper, tin, lead and mercury, in the same way there are seven levels in the *daʿwah*: Messenger, *Waṣī*, Imām, *Ḥujjat, Dāʿī, Maʾdhūn* and *Mustajīb*.[9] Just as each of the metallic substances receives a share from the light and subtlety of the physical planets according to the measure of the receptivity of its substance and disposition, in the same way the substances of men too, have a share from the primordial pre-eternal lights, according to the measure of the receptivity of the substance of [man's] soul. Though all the metallic substances are not gold, [yet] each one of them receives a share from the lights and the subtlety of the physical planets due to which it separates from the level of the simple [elemental] natures.

8. Nāṣir-i Khusraw does not explain what he means by the three hypostasis *Jadd, Fatḥ* and *Khayāl*. But an early Ismāʿīlī work, *Kitāb al-iftikhār* by the Fāṭimid thinker Abū Yaʿqūb Sijistānī (d. ca., 386/996) furnishes us with some explanation. *Jadd*, according to the concept of Sijistānī, means fortune (*bakht*). When it helps a person at his birth, he continues to ascend from one status to another until he reaches the status of a great king. When it helps a morally pure person, he becomes the lord of the people of his epoch, governing them, holding sway over them and not them over him, he rules over them and not them over him, and he guides them according to the divine Pleasure and Knowledge. *Jadd* becomes a mount for him to ascend to the celestial realm of his Lord, inspiring him with what is needed by him in the divine Law for his Community, making it easy for him to compose it in the language of the people of his time. *Fatḥ* (lit. opening) is another power bestowed upon the fortunate one (*majdūd*) by which he can interpret the ambiguities (*mutashābihāt*) in the revealed divine Law. *Khayāl* (imagination) is the third power bestowed upon the morally pure person, by which he can "imagine" what will happen to his community after his death, and what the Imāms after him should inherit from his purity and subtle qualities so that they can protect the Religion and govern the community according to the revealed divine Law with the help of those powers. Cf. Abū Yaʿqūb al-Sijistānī, *Kitāb al-iftikhār*, ed. by M. Ghalib (Beirut, 1980); for the analyses of these three hypostasis cf. H. Corbin's introduction in French to *Kitāb jāmiʿ al-ḥikmatayn*, pp. 91–112.

9. For the Fāṭimid *daʿwah* hierarchy, cf. H. Corbin, *Cyclical Time and Ismaili Gnosis* (London, 1983), pp. 84–99.

(107) According to man, who is the sovereign of the world, each of these substances [i.e., metals] has a place according to its [metallic] degree, but each one is associated and connected with gold which is the noblest of all the metals receptive to form by receiving a form. In the same way, though all men are not at the level of prophethood, yet each member of the *daʿwat-i hādī*, has received a share from the subtlety of the [primordially] originated lights—the intellectual planets. By receiving that share and subtlety, he has separated from those people who are at the level of simple [elemental] natures and physicality.

Each member of the *daʿwat* has a degree and 'locus' with the Universal Intellect, the sovereign of the higher realm, due to its [Intellect's] affinity and connection with the Messenger—the most eminent in receiving a share from that light which has reached him completely, because the followers of the Messenger are [part] of the Messenger, according to what God the Exalted narrated about Abraham, peace be upon him. He said in his prayer this ā*yat* in His word, "whoever followed me is part of me" [Qurʾān, 14:39].

In short, according to the ruling of this decisive and explicit divine Word, the followers of the chosen Messenger, peace and benediction upon him and [his progeny], who after following him followed his progeny (*ʿitrat*), and did not follow the strangers, and after the [Messenger] did not turn back are part of the Messenger. As the Messenger said to his *waṣī*, peace be upon him, in this report, "ʿAlī is part of me and I am part of ʿAlī."

Just as in the [astronomical] firmament of the world seven lights are famous whose names we have already mentioned, in the same way in the firmament of Religion there are seven famous lights: Adam, Noah, Abraham, Moses, Jesus, Muḥammad, and the Lord of the resurrection [i.e., Qāʾim or Messiah), peace be upon them and upon him. This is a logical demonstration based on the 'contradictory premises' (*muqaddamāt-i khulfī*). According to His word, "Only those who have knowledge will comprehend them." [Qurʾān, 29:42]

On Angel, Pari, and Devil

Distiches 14–15

> Angel, *pari* and devil, I have learnt exist,
> and absolutely they do exist, but repeat what
> and how [are they]. Speak! Fortify your answer
> with logical proof if you wish to extricate
> this topic from its veil

(137) This man says, "I accept the existence of angel, *parī* and devil, but this acceptance without logical proof is not enough." So, [he says], tell me what each one of it is, and how it is, in these words, "Repeat what and how they are. Fortify your answer with logical proof."

The essence (*māhiyyat*) of a thing is the *whatness* of a thing, and that is the investigation about the genus of a thing. Whereas its quality (*kayfiyyat*) means its *howness*, and that is its shape and color if it is a body, and attribute and act if it is not a body. For example, if someone says, ['this is] a tree', and someone else asks,

'What is a tree?' This question pertains to his inquiry about the genus of a tree. Its answer would, be—if some vegetation [of the genre of the tree] has grown there—'The tree is of this genus.' If there is no [vegetation] there, then the answer to him would be, 'The tree is a body that is subject to growth; it transforms soil and water to another form.' If someone asks, 'what is the mode of a tree?' The answer to him would be, 'Its one end is deep in the soil and the other end is in the air, and it has many branches and leaves.' This is the meaning of *what* [and] *how* which he has asked in this distich.

(138) The philosophical, intellectual response [of the sages of philosophy] to someone who asks, 'What is an angel?' is the celestial bodies of the heaven are the angels. They are alive and intelligent, and operate in the universe by the command of God. Thābit ibn Qurrah al-Ḥarrānī,[10] who translated philosophical works out of Greek script and language into Arabic language and Arabic script, was of the opinion that the spheres and the stars were alive and intelligent. Basing [his thesis] on logical proof, he said, "Man has life and rationality because his corporeal body is the noblest [of all the corporal bodies]. In the noblest corporeal body, which is the body of man, the noblest soul has descended and that soul is alive and rational." This is a correct premiss. Then he said, 'The bodies of spheres and stars are noble, subtle and extremely pure.' This is the second correct premiss. The conclusion deduced from these two premises is, the spheres and planets should have very noble souls, since the soul that is very noble is the rational soul. So these spheres and planets have rational souls, therefore they are alive and intelligent. This is the logical proof given by this philosopher that the spheres and stars are angels and they are intelligent.

(139) The philosophers do not accept [the existence] of *parī*, but they accept [the existence] of devil. They say "When the souls of ignorant and wicked people separate from [their] body, they remain in this world. That is because they exit from their body with sensible and concupiscent desires. Those desires attract them [to this world] so they cannot transcend the [world of] natures. Such a soul enters a hideous body; it traverses the world; it lures people; it prompts them to [commit] evils; it leads people astray in the deserts to destruction." This is the substance of what Muḥammad Zakariyyā' Rāzī[11] says in his *'Kitāb-i ʿilm-i ilāhī*. [He states:] "The souls of the evil doers who become devils appear to a person in some form, and order him to go and declare to people that an angel has appeared to me and said, 'God has bestowed prophethood upon you, and I am that angel.' [Such a declaration] creates disagreement among the people, and many are killed due to that soul that has become a devil." We have already refuted the theory of that impudent, disillusioned man in [our] *Bustān al-ʿuqūl*, so we will not take up time

10. Thābit b. Qurrah (d. 289/901) a pseudo-Sabaean astrologer-philosopher from Harran in north Syria who translated many Greek and Syriac works into Arabic. Cf. M. Fakhry, *A History of Islamic Philosophy* (London, 1983), pp. 3, 15, 17.

11. Abū Bakr Muḥammad b. Zakariyya' Rāzī (d. ca. 313/925) the famous Muslim physician and philosopher has been the target of criticism by many Muslim thinkers including the Ismāʿīlī thinkers for his denial of the necessity of prophecy. Cf. Abū Ḥātim Rāzī's *Kitāb aʿlām al-nubuwwah*, op. cit. note 3.

on this occasion to respond to this disillusioned man's [theory]; otherwise we will digress from what we intend to explain. So this is the theory of the philosophers on angels and devils.

(140) The response of the *ahl-i taʾyīd*[12] (People of divine inspiration, or divinely assisted) to this question is, we say on the command of the Treasurer of the knowledge of the Book of God and the *Sharīʿah* of the Messenger, peace be upon him and on his vicegerent, an angel is a separate [immaterial] spirit. It is created by God by His act of origination (*ibdāʿ*) through the intermediary of the Intellect, Soul, *Jadd*, *Fatḥ*, and *Khayāl* which are exoterically known in the Book and the *Sharīʿah* as the Pen, Tablet, Seraphiel, Michael and Gabriel [respectively]. The primordially originated beings (*mubdaʿāt*) have two roots, Intellect and Soul, and three branches, *Jadd, Fatḥ* and *Khayāl*. The created physical existent things [also] have two roots, the "fathers" and the "mothers" (*ābāʾ wa ummahāt*), I mean, the stars and spheres, and the natures [i.e., the four qualities: hot, cold, wet and dry]. Those born from these are also three: mineral, plant and animal. The last [in the animal kingdom] is man. The microcosm of the Religion[13] too, has two roots, Messenger and *Waṣī*, and their three branches, Imām, *Ḥujjat*, and *Dāʿī*, and the branches born of each member are multiple in number.

(141) So the angels are primordially originated, separate [immaterial] beings. Their existence is due to their act. Their act is manifest in the spheres and stars. The light and the power of the spheres and stars who are visible and not audible angels, are from those primordially originated angels. The divine purpose in decreeing these created visible angels is to obtain the angels *in potentia* in man. These potential angels are brought to actuality by the Messenger and his *Waṣī* through the Book and the *Sharīʿah*. Just as the stars, the visible [angels], are intermediary between the actual primordially originated angels and the potential angels who are men so that they bring them to the state of manifestation, in the same way the Prophets, *Awṣiyāʾ* (plu. of *Waṣī*) and Imāms are intermediaries between the potential angels, humankind, and the actual angels, the primordial divinely originated beings, so that through the Book and the *Sharīʿah* they transform people to actual angels. Whoever can transform a potential angel to an actual angel has already reached the level of angelicness, and is the vicegerent of God on the earth. As He said in His word, "And had We willed We could have set among you angels to be vicegerents in the earth" [Qur'ān, 43:60]. That is the reason why God has commanded us that after having faith in Him, the Sublime, we should have faith in His angels, His Books and His messengers, as He said in His word, "Each one of the believers believes in God, and His angels and His Books and His prophets" [Qurʾān, 2:285].

12. The term *taʾyīd* (lit, support, aid) is used by Nāṣir-i Khusraw in a very specific sense to denote divine guidance originating from the divine Logos (*kalimah*). This *taʾyīd* is granted by the *kalīmah* to the Universal Intellect, which then grants it to the Universal Soul to aid the latter to attain its own perfection. The Universal Soul with the aid of *taʾyīd* creates the souls of the real human beings who then become the recipients of *taʾyīd* and are thus called by Nāṣir-i Khusraw *ahl-i taʾyīd;* cf. Nāṣir-i Khusraw, *Shish faṣl*, Persian text, ed. and trans. into English by W. Ivanow (Leiden, 1949), p. 74.

13. The text reads microcosm (*ʿālam-i ṣaghīr*), which may be an error by the copyist.

(142) God the Exalted has mentioned two groups of people from His creation whom He has created for His worship, one is *jinn*, which in Persian language is called *parī*, and the other is *ins*, i.e., humankind. He said in His word, "I created *jinn* and humankind only that they might worship Me" [Qur᾿ān, 51:56]. He did not say, "I created devil (*deva*)." Rather, He said, The devils were *pari[yān]* but they became disobedient so they became devils due to sinning against their God according to this *āyat* in His word, "When We said to the angels 'fall prostrate before Adam,' they fell prostrate, all save Iblīs. He was of the *jinn*, and he rebelled against His Lord's command" [Qur᾿ān, 18:50].

So the reason for the existence of devils, according to the ruling (*ḥukm*) of this *āyat*, is the existence of man, because He says that Iblīs, prior to being commanded to obey Adam, was from the [group of] *parī*. So the created things are of two categories: man and *parī*. *Parī* is divided into two categories: angel and devil, i.e., among the *pari[yān]* whoever remained obedient [to God] became an angel, and whoever was disobedient became a devil. He did not make any distinction between angel and *parī* in the Book. He only said, "since a *parī* became disobedient, it became a devil." So He placed angel and *parī* on the same level according to this ā*yat* in His word, "When We said to angels, fall prostrate before Adam, and they fell prostrate, all save Iblīs. He was from *jinn*", i.e., "We said to the angels to prostrate before Adam. They all prostrated save Iblīs. He was from *parīyan*." From this ā*yat* it is evident that [Iblīs] was [initially] a *parī*. So whoever was obedient [to God] became an angel, and whoever was disobedient [to Him] became a devil. Thus it is quite clear that the cause of a *parī* becoming an angel is obedience [to God], and the cause of a *parī* becoming a devil is disobedience [to Him]. Now the obedience and disobedience to God are through the intermediary of the Messenger according to what He said in the narrative of Adam, 'since Iblīs did not obey Him, he became a devil though he was an angel.'

(143) So it follows that the Messenger is messenger for both *parī* and man as He says in the real Book in His word, "Say, it is revealed unto me that a company of *jinn* gave ear, and they said 'Lo! we have heard a marvelous Qur᾿ān that guideth unto righteousness" [70:1–2]. In another place He said to His Messenger, "We sent toward thee a group of *pariyān* so that they hear the Qur᾿ān. They said, 'Give ear! When they had heard it, they went back to their folks and said 'O our folks! respond to the caller of God.'" This He said in His word, "We sent toward thee a member from the *jinn*, who wished to hear the Qur᾿ān and when they were in its presence, said 'Give ear!' and when it was finished, turned back to their people, warning" [46:29]. In another place He said, "Say 'O mankind! I am a messenger of God unto both (*jamīʿan*) of you," [7:158], i.e., man and *parī*. The word *jamīʿan* includes both *parī* and man. This word also indicates that *parī* is from among mankind because [the Messenger] said, "'O people, I am a messenger of God to you both, i.e., mankind and *parī*.'" In the chapter *al-Raḥmān* also, He addressed [both to mankind and *pariyān*] thirty-one times in the form of reproach, saying, "O mankind and *pariyān*! Which is it, of the favors of your Lord, that you accuse the Messenger of lying?" And, "Which is it, of the favors of your Lord, that you deny?" [55:13 ff.]

From these verses it follows that the Messenger was the messenger [of God] for both mankind and *pariyān*.

(144) It is necessary to know that people are of two kinds in the world of Religion (*ʿālam-i dīn*): *pariyān* and humankind. *Pariyān* are of two categories: whosoever among them remains obedient [to the Messenger's message] exits from this world as an angel, and whosoever turns away from the obedience exits from this world as a devil.

Among the multitude it is known that a *parī* has a beautiful face, and a devil has an ugly face. Since the devil's ugliness is due to [its] disobedience, so it follows that the beauty of the *parī* is due to [its] obedience. However, this beauty and ugliness are due to the "belief" [i.e., obedience or disobedience]. Moreover, the form [of *parī* and devil] is spiritual and not physical.

According to the multitude the *pariyān* are hidden from the people. The Arabic word for *parī* is *jinn*. '*Jinn*' [in the Arabic language] means 'hidden' (*pūshīdah*). Thus it follows that in the *ummah* of the Messenger there is a group which is hidden and another which is manifest. Those who are hidden are potential angels, and whoever [from this group] leaves this world in the state of obedience [to the Messenger's message], will become an actual angel. Whoever is disobedient [to him] is a potential devil, and when he leaves this world he will become an actual devil. Those who are manifest are potential *pariyān*, and until they do not become (actual) *pari[yān]*, they are not potential angels. Whoever is not a potential angel, cannot become an actual angel. Thus, whoever from this manifest group becomes a *parī*, becomes hidden from the others so that by being a *parī* he may become an angel. This we said is a similitude for exotericists (*ahl-i ẓāhir*) and esotericists (*ahl-i bāṭin*). Whoever transcends the exoteric [or the external dimension of the Book of the *Sharīʿah*] and understands [its] inner [meaning or objective] is like a man who becomes a *parī* and becomes beautiful in form.

According to the Messenger, peace be upon him, two classes of people are devils: those who turn away from the hidden dimension [of the Book of the *Sharīʿah*], the *Jinn*-devils belong to this category, and those who turn away from the manifest [i.e., the exoteric dimension of the Book of the *Sharīʿah*] in order to enter its hidden dimension. Human-satans belong to the latter category. God the Exalted said, "Thus We have appointed unto every prophet an adversary—human-satans and *jinn*" [Qurʾān, 6:112].

We say: The rational soul in every person is a potential angel, and a potential angel is a *parī*, as we said above. The concupiscent soul and irascible soul are the two potential devils in each person. The person whose rational soul brings his irascible and concupiscent [souls] under its obedience, becomes an angel, while he whose concupiscent and irascible [souls] bring his rational soul under their obedience, that person becomes an actual devil. The chosen Messenger, upon him be peace, said: every man has [within him] two devils that deceive him. This report is: "In every man there are two satans who tempt him." From this report it becomes evident that a man has a rational soul, which is one, and he has two devils, i.e., the concupiscent soul and the irascible soul. Then they asked [him], "O Messenger, do you also have these two devils?" He replied, "I [also] had two devils (*du dīw*), but God gave me victory over them, so I made them surrender (*musalmān*) [to my rational soul]." The text of the report is, "I had two satans (*shayṭānān*), but God gave me victory over them so I made them surrender (*aslama*)."

So we have made it clear that in man there is an angel and a devil, but he himself is a *parī*. The devil is not created by God. Rather its existence is from its disobedience to Him. The *pariyān* are potential angels and can become actual angels if they persist in the obedience [to Him]. In the same way, the [potential] devils can become actual devils if they persist in disobedience. Human beings are potential angels and potential devils, while that world is replete with actual angels and actual devils.

This is an exhaustive and clear exposition on [angel, *parī*, and devil].

On Intellect and Epistemology

Distiches 50–55

One problem has risen like in the game of chess;
from everyone its answer must be sought.
Is intellect superior or knowledge?
Which one of the two has eminence over the other?

About these two I have heard excess equal to
one hundred ass-loads.
How can a person have knowledge if he has not
learnt it?
A carpenter cannot do carpentry without his tools.
A person who has not suffered humiliation
while learning will not have a
great access to the glory of knowledge.
Because they do not know the definition of
intellect nor of knowledge,
they speak extravagant things about
the two without hesitation and reserve.
From their knowledge they reason
the knowledge of God. Surely they have become
unconcerned about the true course.

(274) This question concerns the difference between the intellect and knowledge, and that out of the two which one is superior. He further says "If a person has not suffered humiliation during instruction and learning, he has not attained the honor of knowledge. He also says that knowledge is that which must be acquired, and criticizes a person who judges God's knowledge from his knowledge. However, none says to him that since you maintain, "knowledge is that which must be acquired," that means you are saying, either that God is not the knower, or that He has learnt the knowledge. But, he has removed himself away from this accusation. These six distiches which we have stated contain one question.

(275) The response of the sages of philosophy to this question is; there are two categories of perception (*idrāk*), either a certain thing is perceived by itself, or it is not perceived by itself. A thing which is perceived by itself is sensible, an object of sight perceived by the sense of sight; an audible object perceived by the sense of hearing; an object of smell perceived by the sense of smell; an object of taste perceived by the sense of taste; and an object of touch perceived by the sense

of touch. However, a thing not perceived by itself is not sensible; rather it is intelligible. The substance of the soul is not sensible because it is perceived through its activity, it moves the body in diverse ways, i.e., either by the motion of speech, or by the motion of walking or working, etc. Since this substance cannot be perceived by itself but by its act which is manifested through the body, [the sages of philosophy] called this substance the object of knowledge (*maʿlūm*). They said that only the intellect which being superior to the soul can perceive it, because it is superior to it, for a thing is perceived by something that is superior to it. Do you not see that only the intellectuals have proved that the soul is eternal, immaterial, and an active substance? By this knowledge the intellectuals have become secure from [the fear] of annihilation of the soul. The ignorant fear death because [they presume] that after the physical death, which is the separation of the soul from the body, they will not have [their] being. [The sages of philosophy] maintain that it has been demonstrated that the soul is the object of knowledge, and is intelligible and not sensible, and we perceive it through [our] intellect. Therefore, we infer [lit, learn] that knowledge is an act and effect of the intellect, and intellect is more eminent than its effect.

(276) Plato's opinion on the knowledge and will of God is, as he said "We do not say that the First Agent has will (*irādat*) or that it does not have will, because it has manifested the will in the soul." It is not admissible to say that God has manifested the will by another will. Because if so, then the other will too must have been manifested by another will, in which case the wills become *ad infinitum* having no final will. Since the soul has will, and it is the object of knowledge, it is inadmissible [to conceive] that the Originator of the soul has the will, because the will pertains to the soul.

(277) He also said, "We do not maintain that whatever He creates, He does so out of knowledge, i.e., He first has the knowledge [of the thing], then He creates it, because Intellect is His intelligible (*maʿqūl*), and our knowledge is from the Intellect." So it is not admissible that God creates knowledge through knowledge; [the very idea] is absurd, because things are made [or created] through knowledge; but knowledge is not made through knowledge. Since we have some knowledge, and our knowledge is from the Intellect, we deduce that Intellect is created by Him. These are the postulates of Plato concerning the will and knowledge of God, and Intellect.

(278) The Iranian [maybe the Greek] philosopher has made a distinction between *maʿrifah* (innate knowledge) and *ʿilm* (science). He says "*maʿrifah* is that which is unvarying in man from the time of his childhood to his old age." For example, the *maʿrifah* of thirst, hunger, fear of something that he does not know, or the *maʿrifah* of shapes, colors and other sensibilia, and the *maʿrifah* of pain and [other] things that man knows by nature (*bi-ṭabʿ*) but the names of those things he must learn from someone. For instance, he does not know this is a piece of paper which they name white [paper], and the lines written on it they name black [lines] etc. Many animals which are completely formed also share *maʿrifah* with man.

(279) He said, "Whatever skills, professions (or crafts) man learns through reflection (*tafakkur*), inspiration (*ilhām*), revelation (*waḥy*) or from others, whether willingly or out of constraints, all this is called *ʿilm*." [It spans the range] from

language to professions, to philosophy. People differ in professions and sciences. Then he says, "*maʿrifah* is the basis of intellect, mind is the basis of remembrance, and possibility (*imkān*) is the basis of power (*qudrat*)."

(280) The response of *ahl-i taʾyīd*, peace be upon them, concerning the distinction between intellect and knowledge is as follows; they say, "The definition of *ʿilm* is, 'the concept of a thing as it is'. The definition of *ʿālim*, i.e., the possessor of knowledge is, 'a person who conceives the thing as it is.'" They say, "The definition of *ʿaql* (intellect) is, 'it is a simple [not composite] substance by which people perceive things.'" They maintain life (*ḥayāt*) is the custodian of the body, the rational soul is the custodian of life, and the intellect is the guardian of the rational soul. [It is the intellect] which gives nobility to the soul to recognize its substance. Knowledge (*ʿilm*) is the act of the intellect. Man perceives things as they are by the intellect. Therefore man is called intelligent (*ʿāqil*) because he has something by which he perceives things as they are. This attribute, i.e., intelligent (*ʿāqil*) is not admissible for God because He is the Originator of the Intellect. This attribute is applied to man when we say, 'so and so is intelligent'. They [i.e., *ahl-i taʾyīd*] qualify God as Knower though *ʿilm* is an attribute of the Intellect, but [according to them] it is an attribute of God metaphorically (*biʾl-mathāl*), as God said about His attribute, "The Knower of the hidden and the manifest" [39:47], but this is an attribute of the Intellect which knows intelligibles and also sensibles. Since the Intellect is a gift of God to us which is denied to other animals, it is not proper to qualify God the Exalted by an attribute which has been given by Him [to man]. Therefore, when anyone among the knowers of real knowledge (*ʿilm-i ḥaqīqat*) qualifies God as the 'Knower', he means, He is the Originator of the Intellect, and knowledge is the act of the Intellect. And [if] he says, 'He is Powerful, he means the power of the powerful men is from Him; likewise the [power of] creativity has been given by Him to the creative. "So blessed be God, the best of creators" [Qurʾān, 23:14].

On the Difference Between the Perceiver and Perception

Distich 56

> Between the perceiver and perception
> a distinction should be made by someone who
> has awakened from the sleep of heedlessness

(281) In this question he inquires about the difference between the perceiver and perception. The third [act] which is the object of perception has not been included in the enquiry.

Perceiver means someone who perceives a thing, perception, i.e., *andar yāftan*, is his act, and the object of perception is something that is perceived. This [query] is like this: if someone says, 'make a distinction between the agent (*fāʿil*) and the act *fiʿl*,' the agent is the one from whom the act is manifested, for instance, a carpenter. His act is carpentry [the knowledge of] which is in his soul; the bed is something in which [his act of] carpentry has become manifested. So the sages have maintained that the act is intermediary between the agent and the object of act (*mafʿūl*). The act is either in the agent itself *in potentia*, or in the object of act itself in actuality. So the act cannot stand by itself, i.e., the [skill of] carpentry is hidden in either the soul of the carpenter, or it has manifested [from the carpenter's soul] in the bed itself [by the carpenter]. In the same way the perception which is the act of the perceiver is hidden in either the perceiver, or it is manifested [in the perceiver by perceiving] the object of perception. The perceiver is the substance of the soul of man and his perception of things is through the five senses: sight, hearing, smell, taste and touch. So the soul has five powers. It perceives five kinds of objects of perception by these powers. Each of these powers has a place underneath that instrument which is [like] a vein.

(282) One of the powers [of the soul] is the sense of sight. Its place is in the center of the pupil of the eye underneath the transparent membrane. Whoever looks into the eye of a person, he sees his own face [in a mini form]; due to this reason it is called 'a small man' (*mardumak*) of the eye. That is because the perception of the objects of sight such as colors, shapes—[imprinted] on the natures—and motions are perceived by the soul through this power which, as mentioned earlier, is underneath that mine. This power accepts physical forms, and transmits them to the universal sense (*ḥass-i kullī*) which is the soul. The soul through the intermediary of this power recognizes them, conceptualizes them, and distinguishes them [from other forms] in order to know to which thing that color and form pertain.

(283) The other power of the soul is hearing. Its place is in the orifice of the ear. It perceives [all kinds of] sounds having sense or no sense. Contrary to the objects of the sense of sight, the form of sound and speech is invisible waves. Whatever this sense perceives from its objects of sense, it transmits to the comprehensive sense, that is the soul, so that it distinguishes them.

(284) The other power [of the soul] is taste. Its place is beneath the skin of the tip of the tongue. It perceives tastes. What the [sense of] taste perceives is different from those two senses mentioned earlier. This sense also transmits its perception to the soul who is the lord of these powers.

(285) The fourth power of the soul is smell. Its place is in the nostrils after the membrane behind which is the brain. This sense perceives smells that neither are the objects of sight, nor hearing nor taste. Whatever this sense perceives from its perceptions, it also transmits to the soul which is the universal sense.

(286) The fifth power of the soul is touch. It is dispersed throughout the body. It is more intense under the skin and on the tip of the fingers. [This sense] perceives things which are soft, rough, in motion and repose, hot and cold. Whatever this sense perceives is different from what the other senses perceive. This sense also transmits its perceptions to the soul who is the universal perceiver.

Thus we have explained that the soul has five powers for [receiving] five kinds of perceptions. The act of each of these powers in its object of perception and sensation is its perception, and whatever is its object of sense (*maḥsūs*) is its object of perception.

(287) We say, "It should be understood that when each of these perceptive powers perceives the object of its perception, then by its act of perception it becomes the object of perception. For example, when the eye looks at a thing which has color and shape its power of sight accepts that color and form separate from matter; it becomes that color and form in order to perceive it. So this sense of sight

which is the active agent (*fā ʿil*) becomes the object of act (*maf ʿūl*) by its own act. That is because that object of sight remains in the same state after the seer has seen it whereas the state of the seer who accepts that color and form is transformed. Thus we have demonstrated that the perceiver, i.e., the subject who perceives, becomes the object of perception through his [act of] perception; his state transforms whereas the object of perception remains in the same state."

(288) The reason this subtle point has been explained is: a group of people maintains that we can perceive (*andar yābim*) the Originator of the Intellect by [our] intellect. [If so] then the Intellect would become the active agent, and its Originator, the Sublime, would become its object [of perception], but that is absurd. We have demonstrated to intelligent people by this rational argument that the Intellect perceives its Originator by pure affirmation [of His unity] without any sensible and intelligible attributes. The Originator, the Real, the Sublime, is not the object of perception of the Intellect. Rather, the Intellect receives the nobility and light [of the Sublime] by the light of perceiving Him by pure affirmation. So the passivity is on the part of the Intellect and not God, the Sublime, the Exalted. This is a categorical response by the intellectual will for this question.

(289) The sages [of real Religion] have said, time is threefold: one is present, such as, today, this hour; the other is past, such as, yesterday, day before yesterday; the third is future, for instance, tomorrow, day after tomorrow. The temporal things are also threefold. They have also said the eye is an instrument for perceiving something that is present today; the ear is an instrument for perceiving something that was yesterday and in the past. Reflection (*fikrat*) is an instrument for perceiving (*idrāk*) a thing that will be tomorrow and the day after tomorrow. They said, "The Intellect is an instrument for perceiving the [primordially] originated things (*mubda ʿāt*) and not [their] Originator. To God belong praise and benevolence."

—Latimah Parvin Peerwani, translator

Gushāyish wa rahāyish

KNOWLEDGE AND LIBERATION

Cosmogony

1 On the Creator and the Created

[4] O brother! You asked about the Creator (*āfarīdigār*) and the created (*āfarīdah*), and you said that it is inevitable for the Creator to be prior to the created. How-

This translation is based on Nāṣir-i Khusraw's *Gushāyish wa rahāyish*, translated by F. M. Hunzai (London: I. B. Tauris and The Institute of Ismāʿīlī Studies, 1998), pp. 24–53.

ever, you wanted to know whether or not there was time between the Creator and the created; 'Was He not Creator and Sovereign prior to what He created? [And] if there was no creation, what was He Creator and Sovereign of? If He became Creator and Sovereign when He created and brought forth His sovereignty, is He now better and greater than when He was neither Creator nor Sovereign? [If that is the case], now that He has originated the creation and is different from what He was before the creation, then the term 'generated' (*muḥdath*) necessarily applies to Him because that whose condition changes is generated. We wish that this subject be explained with demonstration, so that we know what our belief about it should be.' Peace!

[5] O brother! Know that this inquiry is extremely difficult and many people have lost their way in it, because there are treasurers of divine knowledge, and whoever does not have recourse to and seek the truth from them is drowned in the ocean of falsehood. [Such a person] opposes this well-known and famous saying among Muslims of the Holy Prophet: 'Say, *Lā ḥawla wa-lā quwwata illā bi ʾLlāhi ʾl-ʿaliyyiʾl ʿaẓīm* (There is no power and strength except in Allah, the High, the Great).' And he who does not have recourse to the Imām of his time, who does not seek knowledge of the truth from him, and who relies on his own power and strength, is a wrong-doer.

[6] O brother! I will untie this knot for you by the command (*farmān*) of the lord of the time (*khudāwand-i zamān*) and, by his power and strength, I will destroy the ambush of the devil which he has placed on this path and show you the straight path. Just as there is a measure and balance for hidden knowledge which is measured and weighed for me, so I will measure that knowledge [for you] with the measure of justice and will weigh it on the balance of truth. As God has said in this sense, 'Woe to the miserly who, when they receive measure from the people, take full measure, but when they measure or weigh for them, do skimp' (83:1–3).

[7] We say that first it is necessary to know what time is so that this knot can be untied. It should be known that in reality, time is [contained in] the act (*kār-kard*) of an agent (*kār-kun*), because it is [a measure of] the movement of the [celestial] sphere. Thus, when a measure [equal to] a constellation passes from the sphere, we say that two hours from night or day have elapsed, and when half of the sphere passes we say twelve hours of time from day or night have elapsed. [However], if you take away the sphere from [your] imagination, nothing remains of time. When the existence of a thing depends on another thing, then if you remove the latter, the former which had come into existence through the latter [also] disappears. For instance, if we remove the sun from [our] imagination, the day would be removed. From this demonstration it is evident that if from the imagination you remove the sphere, time [too] would be removed. [In reality], since the rotation of the sphere is the act of an agent by the command of the Creator, time is [caused by] the act of the Creator Himself.

[8] In this connection, those in possession of wisdom have also said that time is nothing but [a measure of] change in the conditions of body, one after the other. This view is the same as that of time being [contained in] the act of an agent, because the totality of [the world's] body is within the vault of the spheres, and when the spheres rotate its condition changes as every point of it moves from its

existing place to another place. [Furthermore], the rotation of the spheres does not stop because its time is never-ending.

[9] It is inconceivable for the simple [person] that time can be removed from the imagination. This is because of the fact that since the human soul is linked with a body which is under time, it cannot go beyond [time] without being nurtured with the knowledge of the truth. As God says, 'O assembly of *jinn* and men, if you can penetrate the bounds of the heavens and the earth, do so, but you cannot without the proof' (55:33)—that is, *jinn* and men cannot conceive anything in their souls other than what they see in the heavens and the earth, and they cannot go beyond what is under the heavens and time unless they receive nurture [of true knowledge] from the Imām of the time who is the proof of God (*ḥujjat-i Khudā*) on earth.

[10] Since in reality time is [a measure of] change in the condition of the body which is the heavens, it is [caused by] an act of the Creator of the heavens and the earth. Thus, from whichever aspect you seek the truth about time, you will find that it is [contained in] the act [of an agent]. When you know this, you will realize that it is absurd for someone to ask whether or not there was time between the Creator and the creation. This is because [on the one hand], when he declares that the Creator has to come before the creation, while time itself is in the creation as we explained, it is tantamount to his affirming that the Creator exists before the creation; [on the other hand], when he says that there was time between the Creator and the creation, it is a contradiction because it amounts to saying that there was time before time, which is similar to saying that there was creation before creation, and this is absurd.

[11] As for your assertion regarding the Creator and His sovereignty before the creation, that if He became Creator and Sovereign after [establishing His] creatorship and sovereignty [of the world], then He is different from what He was before the creation, it should be known that both the Creator and the creation in their entirety were in the Command of God (*amr-i bārī*)—purified and exalted is He—and in their state of existentiation nothing was prior or posterior. The Command of God is not a part of Him, but a trace which is like a writer's script, in which there is nothing of his essence. Since God's ipseity [essence] is above matter, instrument, power, form, likeness, and act, His Command is to be understood in the sense that it is self-subsistent, and all existences and existents are contained in it.

[12] Since the soul of the writer dwells in the turbidity of body and the darkness of nature, the writing which is a trace from him cannot come into being by itself and is incapable of existence, unless he seeks help from nature for the provision of paper, ink-pot, pen, place, time, and movement to bring forth his trace. But since God is free from matter and form, all existents came into being together [and] simultaneously from His Command which is a trace from Him. The Creator and the creation, the Sovereign and sovereignty, all of them were in that trace without there being any connection with His ipseity; just as writing has no connection with the soul of the writer who, after having written something, remains intact without increase or decrease. Thus, the Sovereign in a true sense is the First, that is, the First Originated Being (*mubdaʿ-i awwal*) with which the Divine Command immediately became one, and that is the First Intellect (*ʿaql-i awwal*), which

is complete in both actuality and potentiality. The Creator and agent [of creation] in reality is the Universal Soul (*nafs-i kull*) which, in relation to the Universal Intellect (*ʿaql-i kull*), namely the First Intellect, is like a thought of the rational soul.

[13] Thus, the Creator and creation, the Sovereign and sovereignty, are all in the Divine Command which has no connection with God's ipseity. The rational proof of this statement is that whatever appears in this world, such as plants and animals, come into being by the aggregation and mixture of the elements, the support of time, and the concurrence of space. The fact that all these things support one another shows that all of them are originated from one entity, just as multiplicity has originated from the number one. Had all the above-mentioned things, such as the elements, time, and space, not originated from one entity, they would not have supported but opposed one another. Since all of them work with and support one another, they all execute one command. Thus, first there has to be a command, then those who execute the command.

[14] It is evident, therefore, that all existences and existents were gathered together in the Divine Command, all at once from nothing, without there being any priority and posteriority over one another. And the Divine Command—to bring it close to the imagination—is like a date-seed in which appears all at once and in no time what [subsequently] appears on the tree, such as its leaves, branches, roots, wood, filaments, thorns, dates, and so on. If some of these things had not been in the date-seed, then the date-palm would not have [been able to bear] leaves, branches, wood, or filaments. If these essences (*maʿnīhā*) had not been in the date-seed, nothing would have come from it and it would have remained unripe, without growing; but when it ripens, all essences appear in it. This is a proof of the fact that all those essences of the tree came into existence together in that seed all at once and in no time. When such things are perceptible to the senses, then the Divine Command, which does not need the support of anything, is more deserving to have all existents [gathered] in it without time and space. whatever it does. As God says, 'Our Command is but one, as the twinkling of an eye' (54:50)—that is to say, the existentiation or coming into being of time and space is [instantaneous] like the seeing of light by the eye. Thus, just as in a date-seed what comes into being all at once comes forth in time, similarly what has gathered together and come into being in the Divine Command in no time, instantaneously and from nothing, comes forth by the act [of the Creator].

[15] [As for] the generated, in reality it originates from a thing, whereas that which originates from nothing is called the eternal (*qadīm*). In reality the eternal is the Divine Command from which all things come into being. Since we have established that the term 'generated' (*muḥdath*) is not applicable to the Divine Command, then it is more befitting for it not to be applicable to [God] who originated it. [As for] the creature (*makhlūq*), it is that which receives help and power from something else. In reality the [first] created being is the Universal Soul whose help (*māddah*) comes from the Divine Command through the mediation of the [Universal] Intellect. And the generated is this physical world, because the generated is that which is susceptible to generation, that is to say, to states such as movement, rest, increase, and decrease, which are all found in the physical world.

[16] It is therefore evident from the explanation which we have given that the Creator, the creation, and the creature were all in the Divine Command. God's ipseity has no connection or disconnection with them because He is free from [all] association, [because] a thing which is associated with another thing does not befit to be God. The attribution of creatorship and sovereignty made to God is not because He is the Creator and Sovereign, but in the sense that the existence of the Creator and Sovereign is from His Command, and all existents are attributed to Him in order to glorify Him—just as when a man commands others to build a mansion, it is built by carpenters and other workmen, yet it is not said that they made it but that this mansion was built by so-and-so, whereas he did no work except to command. Such should be the belief regarding the creation of the world, the Creator and the created, so that the soul may be liberated.

2 On the Eternal and the Generated

[17] O brother! You asked that of two entities between whose existence there is no time, how can one be prior to its companion? You stated that it follows reason that if there is no time between the existence of two entities, then both are either eternal or generated. The difference between the eternal and the generated is that the former is prior to the latter in time, just as a tree [may be regarded] as eternal and its fruit as generated because the tree is prior to the fruit—all analogies of the eternal are like this. And when time is removed between two entities, priority and posteriority cease to exist between them; both of them are either eternal or generated. [And you said,] 'Since you have already established that there was no time between the existence of the Divine Command and all [other] existents, and whatever God willed came into being in it all at once, then the world and the Divine Command are both eternal. However, no one can deny that first there has to be an agent [worker] and then [follows] the work. It is necessary that you explain how it is possible to be prior and posterior without time so that we believe in it and know the reality of that completely.'

[18] Know, O brother, that the question should be asked according to the right principle (*qānūn*). It is correct to state that if there are two entities of which one does not precede the other [in existence], then both are either eternal or generated. But it is not correct when you say that if one of the two entities does precede the other in existence and there is no time between them, then [both have to be either] eternal or generated. There is no need to apply the status of being eternal or generated to them if, as you have already asserted, one of them precedes the other as a worker precedes his work and there is no time between their existence. This requires a proof (*burhān*). However, if what you mean to say is that in the absence of time between the two entities, one cannot be prior to its companion, this rule (*qāʿidah*) is [also] not correct, because if one were not prior to the other, then both will have to be either eternal or generated—otherwise your statement would have been correct. If one of the two entities does not precede the other in time, it is [still] necessary for one of them to be eternal and the other to be generated; and if one necessarily precedes the other, it is not necessary [to postulate a duration of] time between them; and if time is not necessary, they should not be

judged as eternal or generated, because there are entities among which time is inconceivable.

[19] Take the example of a man who works for an hour and then rests for another hour: there is no [passage of] time between [the end of his] work and [the beginning of his] rest. But everyone knows that one first attends to work and then to rest, and whoever denies this and says that work is not prior to rest, then it is deemed not worthy of discussing with him; or if he says that there is time between work and rest, he would have spoken absurdly. By this explanation we have refuted the assertion of the one who says that if there is no time between the existence of two entities, then both are either eternal or generated, because it is known that work is prior to rest, and the rest comes after it. [In this analogy], to work is to be eternal and to rest is to be generated, even though there is no [passage of] time between these two states.

[20] It becomes clear [therefore] that the Creator of the world is eternal and the world is generated without necessitating any time between them. The benefit of this inquiry for you is to know that time is not necessary between the Creator and the creation, and that the Creator precedes the creation without any time. If the priority or precedence which the Creator has over the creation was due to time, then the last of that time would have been the origination of creation; and if the end of that time were to be known, then the beginning of time would also be necessarily established. The beginning of time would then be the beginning of the existence of the eternal, and if the beginning of the eternal were to be established, then [the Creator's status] of eternity would cease and He would become generated. When the reader of this book throws this question back at his adversary, he should have reflected on what we have said and the importance of this inquiry.

3 On Time before the Creation

[21] O brother! You asked, 'Since you have established that the Creator is eternal and the world generated, and the eternal is that which does not have a beginning, whereas the generated has a beginning, thus affirming that the world has a beginning, tell us why the Creator who is omnipotent delayed in the creation of the world, and why did He not create before He [actually] created it? As it was necessary [for Him] to create in wisdom because God is always wise, why did He not start earlier as there was none to prevent Him [from doing so]? And when God had not yet created the world, what prompted Him to create it, whereas before it there was nothing? According to reason, if someone is able to do a good work but does not do it, this is considered bad on his part; and if he is unable to do a good work, he is either prevented from doing it by someone else or he does not know how to do it—but God is [free] from constraint and ignorance. And if someone does not do a work for a long time and then does it, there is something that has prompted him to do it, whether it be his own thinking or another thing. But God is free from both these states in the creation of the world, because He was there [before the creation] and there was nothing and nobody [other than Him]; and He is independent of thinking, of accepting the plan or seeking the counsel of someone else.

Then what was the delay in the creation of the world till the appointed time or period when He created it, and what was the reason for it? Explain!'

[22] Know, O brother, that a period (*waqt*) means a state between two times. When someone says 'now' (*aknūn*), this 'now' is a period, which means that it gives an indication between what has passed from time and what is going to appear from it in the future. The state of 'now' is intermediary between these two times, and in reality time itself is [a measure of] change in the state of body. You come to know from the creation of the world that time is change in the state of body, and that when there is no body, there is no time. It is evident therefore that when there is no time there will be no period, and there will be neither priority nor posteriority, because first there has to be time for there to be priority and posteriority, period and nonperiod, just as [when] an attribute is predicated of a thing, if the thing does not exist, there will be no attribute as well. Since a period is between two times, that is the past and the future, as morning is a period which is going to come and night is a period which has elapsed, if we remove day and night from the imagination, the period will also be removed.

[23] The period between two times, the past and the future, is like the space (*gushādagī, farākhī*) between two lines, of which each one is a boundary that limits [the space]. But if the line is single, it cannot be a boundary limiting a thing because this space, which is called surface (*saṭḥ*), does not come into existence without two lines or by one line which is brought back from one end to [join] the other. It is not possible to know the measure of what is on both sides of one line, just as [the number] one has no limit, and nobody can describe its features in the same way as two is described as one upon one, that is paired with each other, or three as one united with two.

[24] The answer to this question is implied in our response to the previous inquiry. Since we have made it clear that the world comes after its Creator without there being any time in between, [and] having established that there was no time before the creation of the world. It is absurd for someone to ask why God delayed in the creation of the world until the period He created it, because this period itself came into existence as a result of the creation of the world. If the creation of the world is called prior or posterior, it is called so in a metaphorical sense and not in a real sense—otherwise, the question will continue [*ad infinitum*]. Thus, in reality the period itself is [embedded in] the origination of the world, just as the dimensions of a body are the surfaces of it. This explanation will be grasped quickly by a clear thought, and be comprehended and understood by a bright mind. Peace!

4 On Whether God has a Body

[25] O brother! You asked, 'The anthropomorphists say that God is a body, and [to support this view] they argue that whatever activity we see in the world is all done by bodies, whether these be the diverse works which people do or other things which animals do but man is unable to do. Such [is the work of] the bee which makes a beehive out of mud and honey from flowers, or the craft of silk-worms

which turn mulberry leaves into silk, or oysters which make pearls from rain-water. Likewise is the work of plants, of which each one does a thing which man is unable to do, such as the date-palm which makes dates from dust and water, and every plant produces a thing which is different from its form. All these in their entirety are bodies. When the wise see such craft (*ṣanʿat*), they testify that it is created by a powerful agent, and if someone denies this his argument is not accepted. Since the entire world is a craft based on wisdom, and because all these crafts are produced by bodies, it follows that the Maker of the world is [also] a body. And they say that if the Maker were not a body, these bodies would not have admitted the craft from Him, just as if a carpenter [did not have] a body, the wood would not be able to admit his craft. The same is the case with [all] other crafts. This is a clear and bright demonstration. What proof should we posit before them that the Maker of the world is not a body? Find the answer to this problem and prove it!'

[26] Know, O brother, that in this world there does not exist a [single] body which is a maker, neither animal nor plant, because the maker in reality is the soul, and the body is like its instrument. The soul has three levels: one is the vegetative soul (*rūyandah*), the second is the animal soul (*khwurandah*), and the third is the rational soul (*gūyandah*). [Now, anything] which has species cannot dispense with a genus. There can be many species [under a genus], such as the animal is a genus and its species are birds, reptiles, and wild beasts. When we realize that the soul has three levels, we come to know that it [too] has a genus, which is the source of all the souls [that is, the Universal Soul]. [Since] we find the rational soul to be the most noble of the [three levels of] the soul with good and diverse deeds, we come to know that it is capable of receiving knowledge (*dānish-padhīr*) from the universal soul.

[27] As for the function of plants and animals, it is based not on knowledge but on their [specific] properties. A property is that which belongs to a thing [or species] to the exclusion of other species, such as [the act of] smiling and [the phenomenon of] hair turning grey are the properties of man that no other animal has. Similarly, to make honey or silk are the properties of the bee and the silk-worm respectively. Every plant and tree is characterized by its grain and fruit, without which it cannot produce anything else, such as the growth [of foliage] in plants and trees. Man has [the capacity for] many crafts. All crafts, whether natural [innate] or voluntary—such as the crafts of the bee, the silk-worm, the oyster, and the plant which are natural, and those of man which are voluntary—all of these are sought by the soul and not by the body. When the soul [in a body] wants to produce a craft which it knows on [another] body, it can do so with the help of that body which is compatible with it and admits its craft because of similarity [between the two bodies]. However, if the soul wants to produce the craft within itself, it does not need the mediation of a body and can produce it by itself [in imagination]. For instance, a carpenter who knows how to produce a door, can conceive it within himself without time, instrument, and the mediation of a body; his soul does not need a body to produce it. [Since] we find that the craft belongs to the soul and the world admits its craft, we come to know that the maker of the world is the Universal Soul and that these three [levels of] the soul which we mentioned are its species.

[28] Every maker requires six entities to produce his craft adequately: firstly, his body; secondly, the matter upon which he produces his craft, such as wood for a carpenter and iron for an ironsmith; thirdly, the instrument, like axe and saw for the carpenter, or anvil and hammer for the ironsmith; fourthly, movement—and from his need for movement to produce his craft it becomes evident to the wise that a worker is not free from need, [because] the one without need does not work; fifthly, a place in which to produce his craft: and sixthly, a time in the duration of which to complete his craft. When these six are attained, the craft will be the seventh of them, which is the purpose of the six entities. Thus, the craft of the Universal Soul in this world [consists of] the plant and animal [kingdoms]. The plant is the cause of the animal and the animal is its effect. The cause is that which, if it is removed, the effect too is removed; for instance, if you remove the plant, the animal is removed because the animal depends on the plant for nourishment. But man is not the cause of anything else; rather he is the purpose [of creation], and his goal is the recognition of God so that he may return to the [original] source from where he has come.

[29] Therefore, we say that the primordial maker is the Universal Soul which has attained those [six] entities already mentioned. The first thing it has attained, instead of body, is the great imperishable sphere [of the heavens]; the second, instead of matter, are the four elements, namely earth, water, air, and fire, from which it produces plants and animals; the third, instead of instruments, are the seven planets, through which it makes shapes, colours, and splendours for plants and animals; the fourth, instead of place, is this vast space within which is contained the universal body; the fifth is the endless movement visible in its body which is the sphere—this great motion is also evident to all in its instruments which are the planets, and in the four elements which take the place of matter; the sixth is the moveable time which passes successively until it produces the seventh, which we see [manifest in this] world of diverse ornamentations.

[30] Just as in the case of a carpenter, we see his body, his instruments, and the craft which he produces, but the soul within him which is the maker is invisible, [so in the case of the Universal Soul] we see the sphere which stands for its body and the elements which stand for matter, but the Universal Soul itself is invisible to the eye. When the soul of the carpenter leaves his body, the body stops functioning; therefore we know that if the Universal Soul were to abandon its movement and instruments, no craft will be produced from them, but they will be scattered. And just as we know that when the body of the carpenter scatters after the soul has separated from it, there is a nullification of his craft, so we know that when the Universal Soul, which is the maker of this world, abandons its support for the world, then all the crafts of the world will be ruined. Thus, whatever is found in a constituent part [microcosm] of the world is also true of the whole [macrocosm] of the world. Since man is a part from among the parts of the world, when we observe that his body stands and functions because of his soul, so we know that the body of this world also stands and functions because of its Soul. And just as the soul of man, which is his maker, is not perceptible to our senses whereas his body and instruments are perceptible, so we come to know that whatever we see and find with our senses in this world are the body, instruments, and

matter of [the Universal Soul], which is their maker, but [the Soul] itself is not perceptible to the senses.

[31] Thus, it is established that the maker of the world is the one who is not perceptible to the senses, and since whatever the senses cannot perceive is other than body, it is clear that the maker of this world is not a body. This is a clear proof for you to reflect upon and understand, so that you may be liberated.

5 On the Subtle and the Dense

[32] O brother! You asked about the state of the world: 'From what did the Universal Soul create the world? Since the Universal Soul is subtle, from where did it bring this density [of matter] in such abundance, and how did the dense originate from the subtle? When [the Soul] willed to create the world, what were the six entities which, as you described, are needed by every maker in order to produce his craft, since the world is crafted? Explain so that, God willing, we may know.'

[33] Know, O brother, that for the Universal Soul the spheres are like a body, the stars like instruments, and the four natures [elements] like matter to every maker. All the [six entities] which we mentioned are composite, crafted, and made by the Universal Soul. But its making of the spheres and what they contain is not like the making of plants and animals; it is rather like the human soul making its body. [Just as] we see today that every maker produces the craft which he knows, so we realize that his body is also crafted and made by his soul. But the way the soul of a carpenter has made his body is not like the way he makes a throne or a chair. On the contrary, the substratum from which the soul of a carpenter made his body was a gift whose seed was in the Divine Word [which originated] from nothing.

[34] In the physical world, the gift received by the soul of the carpenter was that water which came from the loins of his father to the womb of his mother. From that substratum which it had received, [the soul] made a body for itself as a receptacle, in such a way that nobody knows [how] it was able to make this body without [the help of] an instrument perceptible to our senses. The instrument [that enabled] the human soul to make its body was that power from which the seven internal organs—that is the heart, liver, gall bladder, spleen, lung, kidney, and brain—were made in the womb. By that power, the human soul fashioned the seven internal organs from what was subtle in the food [consumed by the mother], and from that which was dense it made the bones, flesh, skin, and so on. [In this way, the soul] enfolded a body around itself and made its enclosure in the physical world, thus becoming able to make other bodies.

[35] Furthermore, just as the prime matter from which the [Universal] Soul made this world as its body was a gift from God, but [the knowledge of] how the Soul created the spheres from it is hidden and no intellect is able to know that, so today nobody knows how a particular soul can make the internal organs, such as bones, flesh, and skin, in the womb of the mother from the food which she eats. But everyone knows that [this is due to] that power which is innate in the human soul and that the essence of the soul cannot acquire this power which is a gift from God—may He be purified. And just as the human soul did not need instruments to create its body, the Universal Soul did not require instruments for the making

of its body; rather it was able to make the spheres as its body from the power which was in its essence as prime matter and which it had received as a gift from God. And just as the instrument of the human soul in making its body was that [given] power within itself, the instrument of the Universal Soul in making the spheres was also that given power within itself. And just as the human soul had potentially the seven organs which we mentioned earlier and by which its body was made, the Universal Soul also, in the gift of prime [matter] from which its body came into existence, had those seven powers from which came the seven planets—namely Saturn, Jupiter, Mars, Sun, Venus, Mercury and the Moon—to make the world which is the body of the Universal Soul. And just as the human soul condensed and separated the subtlety (*laṭāfat*) from the food which the mother ate, made the seven internal organs from that which was purer and finer in it, and made bones, flesh, and skin from that which was dense, the Universal Soul also condensed the prime matter which it had received from God as a gift, made the seven active planets from that which was subtle and luminous, and then from what remained made the spheres and the elements, corresponding to what we see in the world, which is weighed according to the balance of intellect.

[36] He who knows the [power of the] creation of the world, knows the power of his own creation, and he can fashion the form of his soul with the same balance according to which the form of his body has been fashioned. For as God says, 'Verily, you have known the first creation, then why do you not reflect?' (56:62). According to this verse, he who does not comprehend the creation and recognize [its true nature] transgresses God's command, and he who transgresses God's command, his place is in the fire.

[37] Now, let us come to our main point which is this: just as the body and instrument of the Universal Soul, with respect to [our] recognition of plants and animals, are visible but incomprehensible [to us], so the instrument from which it made the spheres and stars is comprehensible but invisible. This is because the more the cause of the world [the Universal Soul] comes close to its origin, that is the First Cause [the Universal Intellect], the farther it recedes from finding and knowing it. [When it is not possible for the Universal Soul to reach the First Cause, how can it be possible for man] to reach it, which is his [first] cause [too]? Moreover, whatever man discovers is due to it [the Intellect], but he is unable to comprehend it, because that First Cause is the universal [macrocosm] of which man is a part [microcosm]. But anything other than man is a mere trace of it, and no trace can ever discern the whole, just as a writer's script which is a trace of him cannot recognize him. This knot has now been untied. Attain so that you may know! Recognize so that you may achieve salvation!

Ontology

6 On Different Kinds of Existents

[38] O brother! You asked, 'What [is meant by] the term 'existent' (*hast*), how many kinds of existents are there, what is each one called, and how can it be recognized? In the *tawḥīd* [profession of One God], should God be called existent or

not, for if we do not call Him existent, then He becomes non-existent (*nīst*), which is *taʿṭīl* [negation of God's existence]? Explain this so that we may know.'

[39] Know, O brother, that the existent is of two kinds: one is called necessary (*wājib*) and the other contingent (*mumkin*). The necessary existent is higher than the contingent existent [because] without the necessary existent the contingent cannot exist. For instance, the necessary existent is like a bird and the contingent existent like its egg; it is not possible for the egg to reach the state of a bird without the help of the bird from which it has come into existence and whose position is like that of the necessary existent.

[40] We say that the world in its entirety is the contingent existent, not the necessary existent, because all its parts are contingent existents. The contingent existent is that which is intermediate between the existent and the non-existent. For instance fire, which is one of the constituent parts of the world, is a contingent existent because its heat may be transformed into cold and its dryness into moisture, thus turning fire into water. The cooling of heat and the drying of moisture in this world testify to the correctness of this state. Therefore, fire is water in contingency, and similarly all components of the world are in [a state of] contingency. Likewise, plants and animals are contingent and not necessary, because the plants and animals which exist today may or may not exist tomorrow. All such things are called contingent existents, including the two entities of plant and animal, each of which is a part of a part of the world.

[41] According to this explanation, the entire world is a contingent existent which cannot exist without the necessary existent. Inevitably, the creator of the world [that is, the Universal Intellect] has to be a necessary existent, because if we say that it is a contingent existent, then it should also have a necessary existent. Then let us stop at this point [and say] that the originator of the world is a necessary existent whereas the world itself is a contingent existent, just as a palm-date is like a contingent existent because from it the palm-tree may or may not come into existence. Since, as we mentioned, the existent is of two kinds and both of them are species, and whatsoever is a species must have a genus, it is inevitable for the genus to be superior to both species, the necessary and the contingent, in rank and not in time or anything else. That is the Command of God—may His Name be mighty—which is the Absolute Existent (*hast-i muṭlaq*), the existent which has come into existence from non-existence. Under it there are the necessary existent, which is the [Universal] Intellect, and the contingent existent, that is, the [Universal] Soul which is under the Intellect. The Soul has the potential, through effort, to become one day like its source (*aṣl*), just as it is possible for a date-stone to grow one day into a palm-tree. But it is not befitting for God to be a genus, because the status of genus is given only to that which has species under it. The genus then is like the cause and the species like its effect. It is not befitting for God to be either the cause or the effect, and it is therefore not appropriate to say that God is an existent. It should be known that the Absolute Existent [the Command of God] is originated by Him, and His ipseity transcends existence [and] its opposite which is nonexistence.

[42] It should be known further that whatever has one rank is superior and prior to that which consists of many ranks. The necessary existent has one rank.

The contingent existent, which is intermediate between existence and non-existence, has three ranks: the spatial existent, the temporal existent, and the relative existent. The spatial existent [is exemplified in the statement] 'there are dates in Kirman' or 'there are stars in the sky'; the temporal existent [in] 'there is light in the day'; and the relative existent [in] 'man has speech' or 'a cow has hooves'. All these ranks are included in the contingent existence. [Since] the contingent existent has ranks whereas the necessary existent does not, we come to know that the contingent existent is lower in rank than the necessary existent and is dependent on it for existence. The necessary existent is one, just as the genus of animal, which is like the necessary existent, is one, whereas bird and rational animal [mankind], which are species under it, are contingent existents. The existence of bird, reptile, and man depends on the existence of the [genus] animal; if you remove the animal, all these species would [also] be removed. Thus, if in imagination you remove the necessary existent, the contingent existents would also be removed. Attain so that you may know! Recognize so that you may be liberated!

7 On the Meanings of 'no-thing' and 'is not'

[43] O brother! You asked: 'How should we understand [the word] "no-thing" (*nah-chīz*) and how should we recognize "is not" (*nīst*)? Is there any difference between "no-thing" and "is not", or do they have the same meaning as "thing" (*chīz*) and "is" (*hast*)? Explain so that we may know.'

[44] Know, O brother, that a group of people claim that 'no-thing' and 'is not' are only two names, otherwise they are one [in meaning]; similarly they say that 'thing' and 'is' both have the same meaning. If you have understood [this, know] that the word (*nām*) 'thing' is not applicable except to the meaning (*dhāt*) which is attainable (*yāftanī*), and the word 'is' is applicable only to a thing with respect to the present time in which it is found, not with respect to the past nor with respect to the future. [This is] because time is of three modes: the past which has elapsed, the future which is going to come such as tomorrow or the next year, and the present such as today or this year. The word 'is' is applicable to a thing only with respect to the present time, not with respect to the past or the future. Thus, we should not say 'yesterday is hot' or 'tomorrow is cold'; rather we should say 'today is hot' or 'this year is cold'. It would be absurd to say that 'is' and 'thing' are both one and have the same meaning, or to say that 'no-thing' and 'is not' have the same meaning. If it were possible to say so, then [in the case of 'no-thing' and 'is not'] we would have said 'so and so *no-thing*' means a thing in the sense of 'so and so *does not* have a thing,' or we would say '*is not* belongs to so and so' in the sense of '*no-thing* belongs to so and so'; [likewise], if 'is' and 'thing' were both one and the same thing, it would have been permissible for us to say 'so and so does not have an *is*' [in the sense of] 'so and so does not have a *thing*'.

[45] As for the word 'no-thing', it should be known that it means to nullify a thing by applying the prefix 'no' (*nah*) to a thing which has an attainable meaning; otherwise if 'no-thing' necessarily had a meaning which could be applied to it or to which it was possible to indicate, then it would itself have been a thing. Logically, when the word 'no' is prefixed to anything, that thing should have a

meaning; but this is impossible because when you prefix the word 'no' or 'non' to one of the things or names, [you are negating] that particular thing or name to which you have applied the prefix and not any other thing apart from it. For instance, if someone says 'no-wall', this utterance is not applicable to anything; or if he says 'no-cow' or 'no-man', here a meaning does not become necessary; However, when the word 'no' or 'non' is prefixed to a name or a thing that comes alternately after another thing and between which there is no intermediary [state]—such as day and night, blind and seeing, odd and even—then the name of that [second] which follows [the first] becomes established. Thus, if you say 'no-night', this amounts to saying 'day', or if you say 'non-hearing', this amounts to saying 'deaf', or if you say 'non-blind', this amounts to saying 'seeing'. But if the word 'no' or 'non' is prefixed to the word 'is', then inevitably it is applied either to the past or to the future, and you would have said that something has been or will be. [The expression] 'has been' signifies the past and 'will be' the future; the former is a sign of the past and the latter of the future. [For instance], when you say 'there is no night,' it refers to something which has been in the past or will be in the future, but does not exist at the [present] time which is intermediate between these two times; it is a sign of a thing which has been in the past or will be [in the future].

[46] Thus, we have established that [the meaning of] *nīst* ('is not') is not free from being either time which has passed or time which has not come, but it is not time in the present. For instance, in summer you may say, 'it is not spring, it is Tīr-māh,' in which one [the spring] is past and the other [the first month of summer] is present; but you cannot say [at the same time] 'it is not summer,' because it is the present time and 'is not' does not apply to the present. Thus, it has been explained that the meaning of 'no-thing' is not equal to that of 'is not' because the word 'no-thing' is not applicable to all the three [tenses]—that is, you cannot say that 'no-thing is not,' or 'no-thing has not been' or 'no-thing will not be,' [whereas 'is not' is applicable to both the past and the future]. Attain so that you may know! Recognize so that you may be liberated!

8 On the Nature of the Human Soul

[47] O brother! You asked about the doctrine of a group who say that the human soul is nothing but the equilibrium of elements (*iʿtidāl-i ṭabāyiʿ*), and that when the elements come together appropriately, they reach a point where movement and knowledge are generated. [The group] supports this doctrine by the argument that when the body loses its equilibrium, the soul ceases to exist. Thus, the soul is nothing but the equilibrium of elements, and when they return to their origins, the soul ceases to exist. If this is so, then you have neither reward nor punishment [for the soul in the hereafter]. You wanted a categorical answer to be given in this connection, so that you may refute this doctrine and have a firm belief in the survival of the soul, and so that observance of the Holy Prophet's law (*sharīʿat*) becomes pleasant. You will learn that the soul is not the equilibrium of elements such that when they return to their origins it ceases to survive; rather the soul is something other than the equilibrium of the elements. Peace!

[48] Know, O brother, that had there not been 'how' and 'why', then all people would have been wise, and had there not been someone to answer the questioner, then truth would not have been distinguishable from falsehood. Thus, by divine help, we say in response to that group who say that the soul is nothing but the equilibrium [of elements], that this equilibrium which they claim to be the soul is not free from being either substance or accident. If the soul is a substance [in] equilibrium, then it is [different from] the origins from which it comes into existence, [in which case] it would be the fifth element, not [a mixture of] the four elements. Then let them show us that fifth one which comes forth from these four elements but is not from them, the one which is harmonious whereas these four are [discordant], so that we may see it as we see these four. But they are not able to find that harmonious one which they claim to have come forth from the four elements which are different and not in equilibrium. They are unable to do so because it is absurd for someone to say that a body can produce another body by itself. Thus, it is evident that what they claim [to be the soul] is not a substance. Had it been a substance [composed of the elements], it would have been visible and accessible like they are visible and accessible [to our senses].

[49] Then, inevitably, the equilibrium which they claim to be the soul will be called by them an accident (*ʿaraḍ*). If they say that it is an accident, then they cannot say that it has action, because an accident is that which cannot subsist on its own, and action does not come into being from that which is not self-subsistent. Moreover, since the accident itself is an action [of an agent], it is not possible for that action to produce another action [on its own], just as it is not possible for a body to produce another body or to be originated by itself. And since that which is called equilibrium has no action, then those actions which we find from the soul—such as comprehension of things, discrimination of one thing from another, and so on—these do not belong to the equilibrium which they claim to be the soul. It is evident, therefore, that since equilibrium does not have action, their claim that it is the soul is false.

[50] Another answer we give to the one who says that the soul is the equilibrium of elements is that whereas the elements are hot, cold, wet, and dry, equilibrium is neither hot nor cold, neither wet nor dry. Had it been possible to originate from hot, cold, wet, and dry, something which is neither hot nor cold, neither wet nor dry, then it would also have been possible for fire to produce cold and for snow [to generate] heat. But this is absurd and impossible, [just as] it is equally absurd and impossible to say that something harmonious originates from different elements and which contains within itself nothing of them. If it were possible for the harmonious to originate from opposite elements, then it would also have been possible for something opposite to emerge from the harmonious. Then there would not be any difference between the one who says that these four opposites originate a harmonious thing [which they call the soul], and the one who says that it [the soul] consists of equilibrium and harmony, whose essence is the same without differentiation, and which originates death as well as life, blindness as well as sight, health as well as illness. This argument is absurd and no intelligent person would accept it. And if, according to their claim, one says that the soul is the equilibrium of elements, then opposite actions should not come forth from it because,

as we have already explained, the opposite does not come from the harmonious. [But] the soul is that from which comes both generosity and parsimony, bravery and cowardice, piety and impiety, which makes it clear that it is not the equilibrium of the elements. Similarly, when two white bodies come together, it is not possible to originate something other than white, just as when two black bodies come together, there comes forth nothing but a black thing. [Hence], it is impossible and absurd to originate something harmonious from opposite things when they come together; and since the elements are opposite to one another, it is not possible that from their gathering there should originate something harmonious without any differentiation in it.

[51] Thus, we have established that the soul is not the equilibrium [of elements]. It is a substance which brings opposite elements into harmony and puts them together by the power with which God has endowed it. And great is the wisdom which appears to the soul in its resurrection after [leaving] the body. As God says in the following verse after a detailed description of creation one after the other, 'And certainly We created man from a quintessence of clay, then We placed him as [a drop of] sperm in an unshakeable place, then We made the sperm a clot, then We made the clot a lump of flesh, then We made the lump of flesh bones, then We clothed the bones with flesh, then We made him another creation. So blessed is God, the best of Creators' (23:12–14). Then He has said, 'After that you will most surely die. Then surely on the Day of Resurrection you shall be raised' (23:15–16). If this were not the purpose of creation, then no wisdom would have appeared in this world. But the soul, which brings together these opposite [elements] in the body, leaves them again. If it separates from them with the recognition of the Creator and in obedience and worship, then it will remain in the eternal world in delight, but if it does not acquire knowledge and departs in ignorance and disobedience, then it will remain in hell. Attain so that you may know! Recognize so that you may be liberated!

9 On the Soul's Existence and Self-subsistence

[52] O brother! You asked about the soul, 'Does it exist or not, and is it self-subsistent or does its subsistence depend on the body? Is it from among substances or from accidents? What is the proof that the soul is a substance and self-subsistent when we do not find it without a body, and without a body no action should come forth from it? Demonstrate [the proof] that we may know.'

[53] Know, O brother, that our bodies are alive because of the soul, and the proof of the soundness of this statement is that our bodies are moveable and that whatever is moveable, its movement is [caused] either from outside or from inside. An entity whose movement is [caused] from outside is moved [either] by another entity, as wind moves a tree or water moves a water-wheel and a boat, or another entity pulls it towards itself, as an ox pulls a windlass and a magnet pulls iron. [However], our bodies move [voluntarily] without being pulled or repulsed by something else. Since the movement of our bodies is not [caused] from outside, it must of necessity be from inside. The movement of an entity which comes from inside is either natural [physical] or spiritual. [The entity with] natural movement

is that which never rests and does not alter from one state into another. As for our bodies, sometimes they move and sometimes they rest as long as the soul is with them, but they become [inactive] when the soul parts from them. Thus, it is evident that the movement of our bodies is not due to a physical [cause]; had it been physical, they would not become [motionless] by the separation of the soul from them. The movement of our bodies is caused by the soul.

[54] From this explanation it becomes clear that it is the soul which keeps our bodies alive and that the souls of our bodies subsist by themselves. The soul is a substance and self-subsistent, the mover and keeper alive of the body. The body is not a substance, nor self-subsistent, nor is it the mover of a substance, since the mover by necessity is [another] substance. The soul which moves the body is a substance [because] the definition of a substance is that it admits opposite things, and yet [its essence always] remains the same; its state does not change from one to another by admitting them. Thus, the human soul admits opposite things, such as speaking and hearing, movement and rest, bravery and cowardice, and so on.

[55] As for the statement that the action of the soul does not come into existence without a body, the answer is that the action of the soul is to know, and in order to know it does not need a body. But when the soul wants to portray [the form of] that knowledge on a [material] body, it seeks the help of the [human] body which is linked to it, and it is able to do this because of compatibility [between the two bodies]. Ask so that you may know! Comprehend so that you may be liberated!

10 On the Definition of Substance

[56] O brother! You asked, 'What is substance (*jawhar*), how many kinds of it are there, and what is each one called? Are we permitted to call God substance or not?'

[57] Know, O brother, that substance is called genus of genera or *summum genus* [that is, the supreme genus], under which comes everything because all existents are under and within it. Substance has two species: one is called simple (*basīṭ*), that is dispersed, and the other compound (*murakkab*), which is mixed. [So] when you are asked what substance is, say that it is that whose essence is one, which brings together opposite things without changing its own state. When you are asked how many kinds of substance there are, say that there are two kinds, one is simple and the other compound. If you are asked which one is simple, say that it is the soul; and if you are asked which one is the compound, say it is this entire world and all things within it. If you are asked what opposite things the soul has brought together without changing its own state, say knowledge and ignorance, goodness and badness, well-being and mischief. And if you are asked what opposite things has the world brought together, say that it has brought together the six directions of which each one is opposite to another—that is, above and below, left and right, front and back—all three [pairs] being opposite to one another, like earth, water, air, and fire, or like light and darkness, which are [also] opposite to each other.

[58] This is the definition of a simple substance and a compound substance, so that you may know that, according to our explanation of the definition, it is not

permissible to call and know God as substance. When substance has this definition, then it is defined, and that which is defined is incapable of coming out of its definition. A definition necessitates a definer who has enclosed a substance within the domain [of that definition]. So that the wise may know, [we say]: that which is [confined] in a definition or a boundary does not deserve to be [called] God. He who keeps it in its defined boundary is God who is free from substance and accident, and all things are contained within the enclosure of His creation. As God says, 'He created everything and measured it as ought to be measured' (25:2). This is the measure of substance. Study so that you may know! Recognize so that you may be liberated!

11 On the Soul's Relation with the Body

[59] O brother! You asked, 'How and where in the body is the human soul? Previously you have established that the movement of the human body is [caused by the soul] from within. Explain how [the soul] is inside [the body]? Is it like someone who is in a house, and if that is the case how is it that when its ways are closed, the soul can leave the body all at once?' Peace!

[60] Know, O brother, that one entity can be within another entity in twelve different ways: first, it is as a part in the whole, such as a hand or a foot in the human body; the second is as the whole in the part, as is the human body in its organs, which is the totality of the organs; the third is as water in a pitcher; the fourth is as an accident in a substance, such as the whiteness of hair in old age; the fifth is as one thing mixed with another, such as vinegar and honey which is called oxymel; the sixth is as a captain in a ship; the seventh is like a king in a country; the eighth is like a genus in a species such as animal in man, that is to say, man is a species of animal and animal is included in man; the ninth is like a species in a genus, as man is in animal; the tenth is as form in matter, as is the form of a signet ring [set] in silver; the eleventh is as matter in form, as is silver in the form of a signet ring; and the twelfth is as an entity in time.

[61] It is inevitable, therefore, that the soul in the body must be like one of these [twelve] ways which have been mentioned. We say that the soul in the body is not like a part in the whole, as is a hand in the human body, because the hand is of the body but the soul is not of the body. Also, the soul in the body is not like the whole in its parts, because the whole of the organs is the body, that is, the body is nothing but the organs, but the soul itself is not the body, rather it is a different substance. Also, the soul in the body is not like water in a pitcher or jar, [because] the jar or pitcher is a place for water, but the soul does not need a place [in which to locate itself]. Also, the soul in the body is not like a captain in a ship, in that the captain is in one place and the rest [of the ship] is devoid of him, but in the human body there is no place devoid of the soul; if a place were to be devoid of it, that place would not be alive and moveable. Also, the soul in the body is not like an accident in a substance, because the soul itself is a substance and not an accident; and when an accident leaves a substance, the substance remains in its state, but the body does not remain in its state when the soul leaves it. Also the soul in the body is not like vinegar and honey in oxymel, because vinegar and honey have

both changed from their states; wherever such a thing is mixed its state changes, as when you mix vinegar and water neither remains in its previous state, but the soul and the body remain in their state despite being mingled. Also, the soul in the body is not like a species in a genus as man is in animal, in that both are alike in eating and reproduction, but the soul leaves the body and is [therefore] not its species. Also, the soul in the body is not like a genus in a species as animal is in man, since genus and species are linked together in many aspects except in their form which is different, but the soul has no connection with the body as a genus because the soul is subtle and the body is dense. Also, the soul in the body is not like an entity in time, because time is prior to an entity which is in time and comes into being in time, but the body has not been and is not prior to the soul.

[62] We say, therefore, that the soul in the body is like a subtle from in dense matter, as is the form of a signet ring in silver, because the soul is subtle like the form and matter is dense like the body, and the soul is not the body. Ask so that you may know! Learn so that you may be liberated!

Faquir M. Hunzai, translator

Dīwān

PHILOSOPHICAL POETRY

The First Poem

God in his unity
most ancient of all.
no multiplicity.
alone of everything
uncreated.
What say you? Why did He
make the universe
out of pearl?
neither matter for form
height nor breadth.
You agree: in every case
cause precedes effect
as ONE is prior to numbers
or part to the whole
and since heaven and earth (all agree)
are both effects
why consider heaven alone

This translation is based on Nāṣir-i Khusraw *Dīwān*, translated by P. L. Wilson and Gh. R. ʿAavānī (Tehran: Imperial Iranian Academy of Philosophy, 1973), pp.31–43.

a realm of knowledge and power
(like its own antecedent cause)?
Whatever He brings today
from potency into Act
could just as well be
yesterday or tomorrow
since He is not in need
nor impotent. You claim
that between cause and effect
between nothingness and creation
some interval of TIME must intervene
but TIME itself is born
of the rolling spheres.
How can TIME exist?
a non-existent entity?
a beginningless void?
before the spheres themselves?
If you think of nothingness
subsisting in itself
then Unity must have an opposite
a partner in manifestation.
If 'nothingness'
is merely a name or sound
would this not prove that even names
are not without their due effects?
God is above all
as ONE above the numbers:
only thus is TIME's existence known
that of PLACE refuted
genesis necessitated
and Eternity proven.
Do not if you are wise
attribute to HIM
any action but *creatio* ex *nihilo*
of a single being in the wink
of an eye
or less.
Do not speak of His Action
in such a way that His Essence
might be passive like our own
moulded in time by act
by the least of intentions.
ABSOLUTE UNITY:
seek nothing outside His Essence
for He is All-comprehensive
while the essences of things
are particular, determined.
If you claim He transcends all vision
do not attribute qualities to Him

for this would make Him
dual in essence
no longer singular, unique and ONE.
True, you see in this universe
a myriad of things made of earth,
wind, water, fire, metals and seas.
If you could float down
like Harut the fallen angel
from celestial spheres
then could you not
lift yourself up again
like the Morning Star?
EMANATION FROM ESSENCE
NOT FROM BEING:
the cause or the creation of one thing
must be ONE.
The First Emanation is Intellect
then Soul, then Body,
plants, the abundance of beasts,
the Rational Animal.
Each Archetype contingent in itself
but (in reality) an impossible being;
each one manifest in itself but
(in reality) a hidden non-existent.
What say you now? how this painted screen
is set up in the vasty air
like an enamelled pavilion pitched
in a desert of fire?
Does it move by itself or
has someone set it spinning?
keeps it revolving like *this*
around the zenith on high?
How do you define 'movement'?
Locomotion? Turning from one state
to another lowly or sublime?
Then explain to me please
its condition and locus
if you know. If you don't know
stay off the path of Wisdom
till your blindfold is untied.
When by way of demonstration
and deduction you speak
of NINE SPHERES—
what say you again?
what lies beyond these verdant fields?
If you answer 'VACUUM'
I say you're wrong—impossible
that solid forms should hang
in a void. If you say

'PLENUM'—no no—one cannot conceive
a physical body without limit or end
like a sublime substance.
Then what keeps this ball of dust
suspended—*so*—between water and fire
thunderbolt and raging tempest?
If the elements are opposites in nature
why do the four of them
seem to embrace in an excess of unity
in a single place like
loving brothers? or if you say
they're not opposites 'in essence'
why have they been given NAMES
which express their opposition?
BEGIN NOW
KNOW YOURSELF and turn
your steed away from the
whirling spheres
and this dust stained toy.
How can you taste Divine Mysteries
with the DEVIL in you
slashing about with his sword
duelling the inner ADAM?
Your vision of the
spiritual essences of things
reminds me of a blind man
dropped in the middle of the
soul-nourishing Garden of the Spirit
trying with his sightless eyes
to visualise the shapes and colours
of its delights.

Speech

YOU whirligig windowless jasper dome
with the hump of an old wife, power of youth
we your brood and you the unloving mother
you our mother! and yet so vengeful.
Black silent clay, this body's your baby
(not pure Intelligence nor rational Substance)
the body—abode of noble sublimities
and you the mother, mother of the house . . .
When I finish my work in this house today
I shall be off alone and tomorrow the house is yours.

MY SON this corpse of yours, this prison
will never be lovely even draped in silk brocades;
embellish your soul with the jewel of SPEECH

for the soul is ugly even in silk brocades.
Can you not see God's chains on your ankles
(only awakened souls can see them)?
Be a man in your chains and cinch your belt
nor dream your cell the realm of DARIUS:
those who act in moderation find
kingdoms wider far than his.
Patience! no one finds heart's desire
but a man of patience;
and for sexual lust open the Qur'ān
to the story of Adam and Eve.
Stay out of harm's way and do no hurt
but justly, eye for eye;
stick to no petty grudge like the brambles
nor like the datepalm bend in humiliation
for dung is thrown in the pit because it stinks
sweet incense *burned* for its refreshing fragrance.
Don't run around with everyone nor shut yourself up alone—
walk wisdom's way—be neither fly nor gryphon:
if there's no one around worth talking to
then 100 times better alone than with idiots
(the SUN's alone—who blames it
or calls it less than the seven PLEIADES?)
Don't screw up your face at *more or less*;
do with what's given and be equitable with all.
The states of this vagabond world are fleeting
cold after heat, joy after sorrow—
better not to have grabbed for ephemeralities.
Listen—GOOD ADVICE—don't be a bilious fool.
Who cares if the earth is littered with pebbles or gold:
you'll lie in your grave beneath a shack or a palace
(remember the man who built a castle in SANAA
now fallen to ruins in a ruined city).
The world's a cunning devil whom the wise
have never cultivated for companionship;
if you've an ounce of sense don't swagger
in its sulphurous wake like a drunken clot.
The world's a bottomless mudchoked well—
don't lose your purified soul in its cloudy depths
(your soul purified by SPEECH—as the wise
through LOGOS have flown from well's-bottom to the stars).
Take pride in speech as the Prophet (who willed
not even a camel to his heirs) treasured his eloquence;
come to life in speech as Jesus
raised the dead with a word;
make yourself known through speech
for no one is known if not by what he says . . .
but if you've no ideas sew up your trap
for a word unspoken's better than an asinine remark.

Carve your utterance straight as quarrel's shaft
then *shoot*—don't fumble the bow.
Pay more attention to words than good looks
for man is SUBLIMED through speech not stature
(the almond gives better fruit than willows
or poplars which are taller;
a sober man may look like a tramp
but his words will brand him no drunk).
The ocean of LOGOS are the lovely words of God
sparkling with gemstones, glowing with pearls.
The outward form of Revelation: bitter as a gulp
of seawater—sweet pearls its innards to the wise.
If sunken treasure lies in ocean deeps
look for a diver—why run vainly down the strand?
Why has the Creator sunk these chests
of gems in briny weeded troughs?
Tell me for the Prophet's sake! who told HIM
to entrust the hermeneutic to the wise, words to the rabble?
The diver surfaces with a handful of slime
perhaps because he sees in you an enemy . . .
look for the pith of Revelation, don't follow the herd
content with husks like asses with their braying.
On the NIGHT OF POWER the mosques are bright as day
with your candles—but your heart is pitchy as 12 o'clock;
don't waste wax—for tapers cannot banish
darkness from an ignorant heart.
You have not learned piety but from sheer pride
you solve riddles at midnight in an ebon well . . .
if you're not a *snake* why do the believers
tremble in your hands and the Christians fear you?
Cease this rambling and giggling at the fortunes of life
for nothing on this dusty globe belongs to you.
How often have the spinning spheres distracted the wise
and thrown their perfect peace in turbulence?
DARIUS left behind his slaves, his concubines
his cattle and gold and departed with a decaying bag of skin.
Earth is a vulture, no creature safe
from its beak, neither lord nor butler.
A day comes in which is no shelter nor refuge
from the arbitration of a just and equitable Judge;
at that hour all shall be paid for their deeds
both the just and the unjust receive justice;
on that day of tumult in that turbulent crowd
before the martyrs of God I shall take refuge with
THE DAUGHTER OF MUHAMMAD
so that God the Almighty may decide
between me
and the enemies
of the household
of the Prophet.

The Angelic Presence

You, whose name has not been formed by anyone,
whose proof not even intellect can grasp,
to label you would be a loathsome act
for you are far removed from genus and species:
neither a 'subject' nor an 'attribute',
neither a Substance nor an Accident.
The moralist can't order you about
nor any censor tell you what to say.
The dance of the Sun's disc through the skies
is your command and gives birth to the shades
of animals; you stir the painter's pot,
the whirling spheres, mixing and mingling all
your most heart-catching colours in the stars.
The very mention of your name in the Nest
of Glory cuts off the wing of Gabriel;
on the Throne of Sanctity your lowliness
unveils the jewels which grace the bride of heaven.
Creation testifies that you were here before it,
and pre-eternity swears to your permanence.
O luminous sun, veiled by your shadow of light,
goal of all lovers, beyond their petty loves,
the paradoxical treasure of Qarun
(which is never where you find it) symbolises
your single pearl, concealed within two jewels—
two jewels which created the world, two gems
which chastised Adam.
                                        The Universe is like
a rolling sea, our planet a tiny skiff
and Nature the anchor; its waves are trees, the stones
which wash up on the beach are animals;
but one, the pearl, the crimson carnelian
is YOU—the lonely beast endowed with speech.
And who is the diver? the Active Intellect
(worthy to be the mind of the Prophet himself).
What is the End? the same as was the beginning.
What is the goal? to seek that which is best.
Behold the Good, if you have eyes, listen
to Truth, if you have ears to hear it with.
Lust's falcon has snatched you up in its beak, a dove
from Time's snare—have you forgotten, my brother,
Adam our father's sin and repentant tears?
I give you a gift wrapped in veils of allusion
hoping you can slice away its seals
with meditation's sword: Adam ate
no bread in Eden; man was not the eater
of grain till his feet crossed the threshold of earth.
All this had happened to Adam when Satan's dam
had not yet come to birth.

What do you say
of Satan's refusal to worship man? Was he forced
not to bow, or did he have free choice to refuse?
If the power was his, to prostrate or not, then God
was impotent; but if God had pre-ordained
him to refusal, then God must be unjust.
No, give up thinking of work which is not your work
and cease to tread a path which is not your way.
No longer seek in vain the Water of Life
in the midst of your own darkness, like some lost
and bootless Alexander; for there where Khizr
found the fountain, the demon is no more
companion of the angel of our soul.

Free Will and Determination

Who forced you to go in for all this
eating and running around and sleeping and waking up
and what's the good of it? If this fate
didn't tickle your palate, why
have you spent your life guzzling and snoring?
How have you become such a disaster to yourself?
Tell the truth (wisemen always tell the truth):
If you yourself destined yourself to such a fate
then you must be your own Maker!
but this is manifestly bad doctrine. No,
the truth is that God's chains are upon you
and this abode is your pasturing place.
But munching grass and chewing cud
—damn!—this is work for cows!
How then do you explain your curious love
for the pasture? Ah, gourmet of hay,
all your fear and sorrow is the fear
of *decrease*—which cannot be avoided.
How in this hurlyburly world do you expect
to find permanence? Becoming and Change
to the wise are signs of Annihilation.
Your state changes, the stars shift about
day gives way to night—are these
not witnesses of the world's impermanence?
My dear tourist; this earth is like
a room in a onenight hotel, your journey
towards the Abode of Eternity.
Do not regret your passing from this place—
even if the house is torn down
religion prospers. Do not debase yourself
for finally some day however late at last
you must depart this caravanserai.
Make your provision for the road

obedience to God, devotion
the coin you spend on this difficult journey.
Gird yourself in armour of godliness and wisdom
for there lurks along the path a hideous dragon.
When you reach the fork, choose the best way
for one street leads to felicity, the other to Hell.
When the Prophet himself has come to you
with promises and threats, how can you claim
that Good and Evil are written, kismet, Fate?
Why try to shift the burden of sin and sloth
onto the shoulders of Destiny? Nonsense!
If God destined you to sin
then—according to you—the sin is God's
the evil-doer is God (hideous belief!)
even if you don't dare to draw
the logical conclusion, in fear of getting
knocked on the head. Yes, that's your doctrine
even if your tongue proclaims Him Judge
and Wisest of Wise. God knows
your tongue and heart do not agree—but you
lie baldfaced to the Lord of the Universe.
The wiseman treads midway
between Fate and Freewill
the path of the learned threads between hope and fear.
Seek you the Straight Way likewise
for either extreme leads to pain and suffering.
Straight indeed is that Way in religion
approved by Intellect, the gift of God to Man.
Justice is the cornerstone of the Cosmos
—and consider!—by what faculty is justice
distinguished from tyranny except by Reason?
If man follows the tracks of Reason
it would not be wrong to expect to see
pearls spring up in his footprints from the soil.
Reason—Wisdom—only for this
and its radiant dignity does the Lord
of the Universe applaud and deign to address
his creature Man. Wisdom is the prop
for every weakness, relief from every sorrow
comfort in every fear, balm for each ill
noble companion, bulwark in the way of the world
and in religion a trusty guide, a stout staff.
Even if the whole Universe were free
it would be in bondage—but the wiseman
even in chains would be at liberty.
The Sage! Study him well with an awakened eye
and see by contrast with what black plague
this ignorant world is afflicted.
This one tells you 'All actions are performed
by God—the servant's duty is silence

submission and contentment.' That one replies
'All good is from God, all evil, O World
your work alone'. But both parties
Agree on one thing at least, that a Great Day
is coming, a day of reward and punishment.
But if the work is not mine, how
shall I be rewarded? Look: Illogic!!!
Where's the justice in chastising the innocent?
You may see it but I am nonplussed. No,
this arbitrator of *your* judgement day
is the Drunkard of Sodom, not the Wise Being
who has built the vault of Heaven.
True wisdom would never lead us astray
in such error—then follow Wisdom's manifest Way.
Know the God of the Universe and be grateful—
these two precepts are worth more to you
than all the powers of Solomon.
Learn to be wise. Do not prattle
but speak in measure. Know that on the Last Day
these things have value, these are priceless.
The True Man is robed in Faith and virtue
—even fine silks cannot disguise
the art-less and wicked. Endeavour
to become a man by SPEECH—know
that save for such a man all creatures
are but weeds and thorns. GOOD SPEECH
is to man's heart as air and water
to his body—a source of life.
Listen then O noble heart to the PROOF
for to the truly noble, his words are nobility.

Being and Becoming

Whatever EXISTS, shall be worn away and die;
that which IS TO BE, then—whence does it spring?
HE has not come into being, but is eternal;
that which BECOMES cannot be everlasting.
What is never born does not increase, and that
which does not increase, how can it die?
The world forever wears away and disappears
for if it did not die it could not grow.
No one can undo the knot tied by God's hand.
Four wives and seven husbands procreate
without cease and all things of the world but God
are like these women. Decrepit filthy earth,
how does it manage to seize and enchant our hearts?
What do you think, my sage? When does the wheel
of this watermill ever cease to turn? Tell me how
that which is not can ever be, or that which is

can cease to be? Don't waste your time in chat
(fashionable as it may be with So-and-So);
how did you develop a taste for food
that gives you indigestion? Rather ask:
if the world goes on forever, what can it do
for you? or if it dies, what can *you* do?
He who wants to know more of what I teach
ought first to purify his soul, for honey
cannot stick to a hand that's purified.
Wisdom asks no one but the wise
to busy himself with such matters.
Furs and silks are still lovely even on a hag
but they cannot improve an ugly woman's face.
He who cleanses his soul of error and sin
in the fire of intellect, deserves to dole out
measure by measure the contents of my sack,
but if you lack the wherewithal, refrain
from spattering heaven's cupola with mire.
He whom love of the world has inflamed will never
be able to comprehend the truths I speak;
O confidence-man, O trickster, what can you gain
from poetry such as mine? You cannot trust
yourself—how then shall anyone trust you?
Prepare your heart, as I instruct and hope,
for the work at hand, so that this axe of mine
can trim the branches from your ignorance-tree
(but mildly and without pain); and turn your face
from those who deal in superstitious slander.
Good counsel scratches out the eye of ignorance
as sure as a fool in public will lose his pants!

Planets, Metals, Etc.

Reveille! Time to get up! from the couch of sloth! my son!
and gaze upon the globe with the orb of sagesse!
Eating and sleeping is the work of a creature with whom
you my ignoramus cannot hope to compare: the ASS.
Why do you suppose God gave you a brain?
for eating and snoring contests with donkeys?
Tie round your fat head the turban of Wisdom
then one night raise your eyes to the lapis lazuli vault
of heaven like an emerald sea's surging waves
which cast bright pearls from stygian trenches:
dark night crawling with stars like the armour
of Alexander's legions glinting through tenebrous shades.
See the Pleiades like seven sisters sitting side by side
Venus palefaced as a terrified girl and Mars
with the baleful eye of a he-lion. Ponder:
Did the Dog-star grow silvery grey or Capella

begin to glow like a scarlet carnelian by themselves?
Each night the spheres spin their cerulean twine
about the throats of thousands upon thousands
of blossoming narcissus and lay their distant fires
around the harvest of the water lilies. But—
if these lights are really fires, how has this harvest
never been seen to increase or diminish?
Without oil, wick or wood fire never gives
light and radiance. If fire is that which needs fuel
that which needs no fuel cannot be fire.
The Sun is the *maker* of fire; distinguish, my boy,
between the maker and the fire itself.
Or if that which you see is an army, who
is its general? Socrates spoke of seven
commanders of these troops, prudent and energetic.
The Moon (said he) is green and from it grows
salt in the bowels of the earth, silver in stone.
Mars breeds ill-tempered iron and from the womb
of the Sun (so he maintained) all gold is born.
'Jupiter' he claimed 'is the father of tin
and all copper has Venus for its dam.
Quicksilver is the daughter of Mercury
and Saturn the mother of gloomy lead.'
Thus did the Greek associate with seven worlds
These seven melting metals . . .

Peter L. Wilson and Ghulam-Reza Aʿavānī, translators

References

Classical and Modern Biographical Sources

Corbin, H. "Nāṣir-i Khusraw and Iranian Ismāʿīlism." In *The Cambridge History of Iran*, ed. R. N. Frye. Cambridge: 1975. Vol. 4: 520–42.

Corbin, H., Nasr, S. H., and Yahya, O. *History of Islamic Philosophy*. London: 1993, pp. 138–40.

Daftari, F. *The Ismāʿīlīs: Their History and Doctrines*. Cambridge: 1990, pp. 215–18.

Dawlatshāh, ʿAlāʾ al-Dawlah. *Tadhkirat al-shuʿarāʾ*. Ed. E. G. Browne. London: 1901, pp. 61–64.

———. *Memoirs of the Poets*. Trans. P. B. Vachha. Bombay: 1909, pp. 29–33.

Ethé, W. "Neupersische Litterature." In *Grundriss der iranischen Philologie*. Ed. by W. Geiger and E. Kuhn. Strassburg: 1895–1904. Vol. 2: 278–82.

Nasr, S. H. "Nāṣir-i Khusraw." In *Encyclopedia of Religion*, new ed. London: 1987: Vol. 10 pp. 312–13.

Primary Sources

Ivanow, W. *Rawshanāʾ-ī nāmah*, Six chapters. Leiden: 1949.

Nāṣir-i Khusraw: *Forty Poems from the Divan*. Trans. by P. L. Wilson and Gh. R. Aavani. Tehran: 1997.

———. *Gushāyish wa rahāyish* (Knowledge and Liberation). Trans. F. M. Hunzai. London: 1998.

———. *Gushāyish wa rahāyish.* Trans. P. Filippani-Ronconi, into Italian as *Il libra dello scioglimento e della liberazione*. Naples: 1959.

———. *Kitāb Jamiʿ al-Hikmataīn: Le Livre réunisant les deux sagesses*. Ed. H. Corbin and Moʿin, M. Tehran: 1953.

———. *Naser-e Khosraw's Book of Travels* (*Safar-nāmah*). Trans. by W. Thackston. Albany: 1985. Trans. into Russian by A. E. Bertels, Leningrad: 1933; into Urdu by M. Tharvat Allah, Lucknow: 1937 and M. A. Kampuri, Delhi: 1941; into Arabic by Y. al-Khashshab, Beirut: 1970; and into Turkish by A. Tarzi; Istanbul: 1950.

———. *Wajh-i dīn*. Ed. by Aavani, Gh. R. and Introduction by S. H. Nasr. Tehran: 1977.

———. *Wajh-i dīn*, trans. into Urdu by ʿAllāmah Naṣīr Hunzaī. Karachi: 1968.

Schimmel, A. *Make a Shield from Wisdom: Selected Verses from Nāṣir-i Khusraw's Divan*. London: 1993, pp. 1–10.

Secondary Sources

Browne, E. G. "Nāṣir-i Khusraw, Poet, Traveller and Propagandist." *Journal of Royal Asiatic Society*, 1905, pp. 313–52.

———. *A Literary History of Persia from Firdawsi to Saʿdī*. London: 1902–1924.

Corbin, H. *Etude Préliminaire pour le "Livre réunissant les deux sagesses" de Nāṣir-e Khosraw*. Tehran: 1953, pp. 25–39, 128–44.

Ivanow, W. *Nāṣir-i Khusraw and Ismailism*. Bombay: 1948.

———. *Problems in Nāṣir-i Khusraw's Biography*. Bombay: 1956.

Al-Khachckāb, Y. *Nāṣir-e Khosraw, son voyage, sa pensée religieuse, sa philosphie et sa poésie*. Cairo: 1940.

Rypka, J. *History of Iranian Literature*. Ed. K. Jahn. Dordrecht: 1968, pp. 185–89.

Nasr, S. H. *The Islamic Intellectual Tradition in Persia*. Ed. by M. Amin Razavi. London: 1996, pp. 103–105.

———. *Ismāʿīlī Contributions to Islamic Culture*. Ed. by S. H. Nasr. Tehran: 1977: pp. 102–105.

9

NAṢĪR AL-DĪN ṬŪSĪ

The full name of this prominent Shiʿite philosopher and scientist, whose family hailed from Kashan and who was born in Rayy in 597/1201 and died in 672/1274 in Kāẓimayn near Baghdad, was Abū Jaʿfar Muḥammad ibn Muḥummad ibn al-Ḥasan Naṣīr al-Dīn Ṭūsī. The scope of Ṭūsī's contributions went well beyond philosophy and covered an array of fields such as *kalām*, mathematics, astronomy, ethics, and Sufism, not to mention his political contributions.

Ṭūsī, who began his career as an astronomer, soon found himself at the court of Mongol rulers who helped him to build his famous observatory at Maraghah. He was a Twelve Imām Shiʿite, as can be seen both in his political attitude and in his metaphysical and theological perspectives, as exemplified in his work *al-Fuṣūl* (chapters), written in Persian, and *Kitāb al-tajrīd* (The Book of Catharsis), the most important text of Twelve-Imām theology. Philosophically, Ṭūsī belonged to the school of Ibn Sīnā and comments on a variety of Ibn Sīnan topics, defending him against his opponents. Ṭūsī is in fact the reviver of Peripatetic philosophy in the eastern lands of Islam. It was thanks to him that Ibn Sīnā's philosophy became once again part and parcel of Islamic philosophy and a living school of philosophy that has survived to this day. The great influence of Ibn Sīnā on later Islamic philosophers such as Mīr Dāmād and Mullā Ṣadrā was in fact mostly through the works of Ṭūsī, especially his commentary on the *Ishārāt*. This monumental work begins with Fakhr al-Dīn Rāzī's criticism of Ibn Sīnā's text. Ṭūsī, who responded to every criticism of Rāzī with an intellectual rigor rarely paralleled in any philosophical text, not only revived Ibn Sīnā's thought but also created a work that has remained one of the main texts for the teaching of Islamic philosophy in traditional circles to this day. The commentary of Ṭūsī is considered by the *ḥakīms* of Persia as one of the four or five most significant texts of Islamic philosophy, and he must be considered as one of the most important philosophers of Persia.

Ṭūsī's devotion to Shiʿism is evident in his theological works while his writings on Sufism and gnosis (*ʿirfān*), such as his work written in Persian *Awṣāf al-*

ashrāf (Descriptions of the Noble), as well as his reverence for such figures as Ḥallāj, reveal his attraction for Sufism. He corresponded with such Sufi masters as Jalāl al-Dīn Rūmī and Ṣadr al-Dīn Qūnawī. As for jurisprudence, he commented on a variety of issues, particularly, the laws of inheritance as is evident in his *Kitāb al-raml* (Book of Geomancy). His work *Akhlāq-i nāṣirī* (Nasirean Ethics), written under the influence of Miskawayh, is a classic work on ethics and is in fact perhaps the most important work of philosophical ethics in Islam.

Ṭūsī's works and research in astronomy and medicine, as well as physics, are also of the highest order and his contributions are significant. He is in fact one of the most important of Muslim scientists, but this aspect of his activities is beyond the scope of this book.

Ṭūsī stayed for over three decades, from 624/1227 to 654/1256, among the Nizārī Ismāʿīlīs in different places in Quhistan and Alamut. It was during this time that he embraced Ismāʿīlism (at least outwardly) and composed several works pertaining to Ismāʿīlī thought, including a major opus entitled *Taṣawwurāt* (Conceptions), also known as *Rawḍat al-taslīm* (The Paradise of Submission). *Taṣawwurāt*, which consists of twenty-eight "Conceptions," treats such topics as ontology, epistemology, cosmology, eschatology, imamology, and soteriology. The philosophical structure of the book is essentially Neoplatonic and presents the doctrine of *taʿlīm* and *qiyāmah* (resurrection) and the inner meaning of religion. According to this work, there are three types of people. First, there are those whom Ṭūsī calls "the people of contradiction" (*ahl al-taḍādd*); they are of an exoteric nature and live only in the world of appearances. Second are "the people of gradation" (*ahl al-tarattub*), men of esoteric nature who have transcended the outward level of the *Sharīʿah* and are among the spiritual elites who have achieved unity with the inner meaning of religion. This station is achievable only through the knowledge given by a divinely guided teacher (*muʿallim-i rabbānī*) and by living a virtuous life based on metaphysical knowledge and not the endeavor of the human mind alone. Third are people of union (*ahl al-waḥdat*), the super-elite who have achieved unity with the *ḥaqīqah* (truth), thereby experiencing perennial wisdom—the inner meaning behind the inner meaning of all religions.

The selections from Ṭūsī include first a portion of his autobiographical notes from the *Sayr wa sulūk* (Contemplation and Action) dealing mainly with his early education and search for truth. The *Sayr wa sulūk* takes the form of an extended letter written by Ṭūsī and addressed to the chief *dāʿī* of the Ismāʿīlī mission in Iran. The letter is clearly intended to be confessional, that is, to present an account of Ṭūsī's personal search for knowledge of the Divine which led him to embrace the Ismāʿīlī faith, together with a declaration of his religious convictions. But the philosophical and theological content of the work gives it special importance in the collection of Ṭūsī's writings that have come down to us, because the author has an expository purpose too which manifests itself in his highly skillful and explicit exposition of the Ismāʿīlī doctrine of *taʿlīm* and *qiyāmah*.

In the second section of this chapter, we have included part of *Taṣawwurāt* which deal with three themes: (1) the doctrine of the intellect, soul, and epistemology, which is basically Ibn Sīnan in concept but integrated into the *qiyāmah* doctrine; (2) the issue of good and evil with which Ṭūsī deals metaphysically, according to which good has substantial reality whereas evil is nothing but the privation of good; and (3) the esoteric hermeneutics of the verses of the Qur'ān on the origin of the creation by God, and the narrative of Adam and Iblīs, which represent the *qiyāmah* doctrine. All these themes are interlinked. They deal with the acquisition of both theoretical and practical knowledge for the perfection of the human soul.

—M. Aminrazavi

Sayr wa Sulūk

CONTEMPLATION AND ACTION

As a result of predetermined decree and design (*bi ḥukm-i taqdīr wa ittifāq*), I was born and educated among a group of people who were believers in, and followers of, the exoteric aspects of the religious law (*sharīʿat*). The only profession and vocation of my near relatives and kindred was to promulgate the exoteric sciences. From the time that [the faculty] of discrimination began to stir within myself, I grew and thrived listening to their opinions about both fundamental principles and derived rulings (*uṣūl wa furūʿ*) [of Islam]. I assumed that, apart from this way, there could be no other religious teaching or method. But my father, a man of the world who had heard the opinions of different kinds of people and had [received] his education from his maternal uncle who was one of the attendants and students of the chief *dāʿī* (*dāʿī al-duʿāt*), Tāj al-Dīn Shahrastāni, was less enthusiastic about following these regulations. He used to encourage me to study [all] the branches of knowledge, and to listen to the opinions of the followers of [various] sects and doctrines.

Then it happened that one of the students of Afḍal al-Dīn Kashānī—may God have mercy on him—came to the region. His name was Kamāl al-Dīn Muḥammad Ḥāsib, who had acquired a first-rate knowledge in a variety of philosophical subjects, especially in the art of mathematics; he had previously been a friend and acquaintance of my father. My father suggested that I should learn from him and frequent his company; so I began to study mathematics with him.

Frequently, in the course of speaking—may God have mercy on him—he would deprecate the exotericists, and explain the unavoidable inconsistency of those who blindly follow the rules of the *sharīʿat,* and I would find his discourse appealing, but whenever I wanted to get to the bottom of what he was saying, he would refuse, remarking, "That which is the core and essence of the truth cannot yet be mentioned to you, for you are young and do not have experience of the world. If you grow up and are successful, seek for it until you attain it." Occa-

From Ṭūsī's "*Sayr wa sulūk: Contemplation and Action,*" edited and translated into English by S. J. Badakhchani (London, I. B. Tauris and The Institute of Ismaili Studies, 1998), pp. 26–47.

sionally, as a piece of advice, he would say, "It is possible that the truth [may be found] among people who are, in the eyes of the group that you know, the most contemptible people," and he would quote this verse [in which the unbelievers say to Noah]: "We see not any following thee but the vilest of us, in their apparent opinion" (11:27). Then he would say, "You should not pay any attention to whether or not someone has an ugly appearance. If, for example, you find truth with the idolaters, you should listen to them and accept it from them."

In short, it became clear to me from being in his company that whatever I had heard or seen up to that time [on religious matters] was without foundation. I understood that the truth was in the possession of another group and that I would have to strive hard to attain it.

Not long after this, worldly affairs required him [Kamāl al-Dīn] to move away from the region. [Also at this time] my father departed from this world, and I left my home in search of the truth, intending to acquire the knowledge which guides people to the happiness of the next world. Following the instructions of my father, I studied every subject for which I could find a teacher. But since I was moved by the inclination of my thoughts and the yearning of my soul to discriminate between what was false and what was true in the differing schools of thought and contradictory doctrines, I concentrated my attention on learning the speculative sciences such as theology (*kalām*) and philosophy (*ḥikmat*).

When I first embarked upon [the study of] theology, I found a science which was entirely confined to practices of the exoteric side of the *sharīʿat*. Its practitioners seemed to force the intellect to promote a doctrine in which they blindly imitated their ancestors, cunningly deducing proofs and evidence for its validity, and devising excuses for the absurdities and contradictions which their doctrine necessarily entailed.

In short, I derived some benefit from enquiring into this science, to the extent that I came to know something of the divergence between the sects. I came to understand that [with regard to] the knowledge of truth and the attainment of perfection on which happiness in the hereafter depends, men of intellect agreed in one way or another, summarily but not in detail, on the affirmation of such a truth and a hereafter. However, there was a primary disagreement about whether one could reach the desired objective solely through intellect and reason, or whether, in addition to these, a truthful instructor (*muʿallim-i ṣādiq*) was required. All people are accordingly divided in this respect into two branches: those who believe in reason (*naẓar*), and those who [in addition to reason] believe in instruction (*taʿlīm*). Moreover, those who believe in reason [alone] are divided into different schools—which is in itself a lengthy subject—whereas those who believe in [the necessity of] instruction are a group known as the Ismāʿīlis. This was my first acquaintance with the religion of the *Jamāʿat*.

As the science of theology proved fruitless, except for an acquaintance [it allowed] with the positions of the adherents to [various] doctrines, I became averse to it, and my enthusiasm to learn [more about] it lost its momentum. Then I started [to study] philosophy. I found this science to be noble and of great benefit. I saw that among the groups [into which] mankind [is divided], the practitioners of this discipline were distinguished by their allocation of a place for the intellect in the recognition of realities, and by their not requiring blind imitation (*taqlīd*) of a particular stand. Rather, in most cases they build the structure of religion in accordance with the intellect, "except what God wills" (7:188). However, when the discussion reached the desired objective—that is, the recognition of the True One (*ḥaqq*), the exalted, the most high, and knowledge of the origin and the return (*mabdaʾ wa maʿād*)—I found that they were on shaky foundations in these matters, for the intellect (*ʿaql*) is incapable of encompassing the giver of intellect (*wāhib-i ʿaql*) and the origins (*mabādī*). And because they rely on their own intellect and opinion, they blunder, they speak according to their own conjectures and whims in this field, using the intellect [to arrive] at knowledge of something which is not within its scope.

To sum up, my heart was not satisfied with what they said in these matters, while my desire to attain the truth was not diminished. In my exposition, I shall mention some more aspects of this matter. Many benefits, however, were obtained from this investigation into philosophy, one of them being that I came to know that if in any existing thing a perfection is potential, it cannot change from potentiality into actuality by itself without being affected by something outside itself, because if its essence were sufficient to bring that perfection from potentiality into actuality, the change would not be delayed. Indeed, the attaining of that perfection would have been simultaneous with the existence of the essence. We can take bodies as an example of this: motion is [always] potential in them. Without the effect of something else, that motion is never actualized; otherwise all bodies would be in [perpetual] motion. But when another thing exerts an effect on a body, that potential motion (*ḥarakat*) becomes actual. In this case the other is called the "mover" (*muḥarrik*) and the body is called the "moved" (*mutaḥarrik*).

Once this proposition had been established and my soul was satisfied of its truth, my attention was drawn to the point that was made in the science of theology, about the primary disagreement among mankind being whether knowledge of the truth is attainable solely through the intellect and reason, without instruction from any teacher, or whether, in addition to intellect and reason, an instructor is needed. Then I applied the [above] proposition to this situation and found that the truth lay with those who believe in instruction (*taʿlīmiyān*), for knowledge and understanding in man is in itself [merely] potential, and its perfection can only be actualized in men of sound natures, [in whom] intellect and reason are to be found, when something external has exerted an effect on them. Thus, this perfection too can inevitably only be actualized by means of the effect of some other thing. [Accordingly], when that other bestows a perfection, the perfection [here] being knowledge (*ʿilm*), the bestower, in accordance with the previous law, is called the "instructor" (*muʿallim*) and the one on whom it is bestowed the "instructed" (*mutaʿallim*), by analogy with the "mover" (*muḥarrik*) and the "moved" (*mutaḥarrik*).

It thus becomes clear that without the instruction (*taʿlīm*) of a teacher (*muʿallim*), and the bringing to perfection (*ikmāl*) by an agent of perfection (*mukammil*), the attainment of the truth is not possible; that mankind, with its great number and differences of opinion, is mistaken in its claim that the truth can be reached solely through the intellect and reason; and that the believers in instruction (*taʿlīmiyān*) are therefore correct.

Once this proposition had become clear, I began to investigate the religion (*madhhab*) of this group. But since I did not know anyone who could describe the nature of their doctrine objectively, and could only hear about their beliefs from people hostile to them, and since I knew that I could not rely on a person's prejudices about his enemy, I was unable to get to know [this group] as I should, and out of fear I was unable to disclose my secret.

In short, I spent [quite] a period of time thinking about this. Then, in the course of my search, I frequently heard from travellers to the [surrounding] countries about the scholarly virtues of the auspicious master, Shihāb al-Dīn—may God be pleased with him—and his deep insight into different fields of knowledge. Then I sought a suitable opportunity and, through the intermediary of a friend who had an association with him, I sent him a letter containing two or three questions about those points in the discourse of the philosophers which I had found to be contradictory and about which I also had some observations of my own. Then I was granted the honour of a reply from him—may God be pleased with him—in the handwriting of the master, the chief scribe, Ṣalāḥ al-Dīn Ḥasan—may his glory endure—and in answer to the questions he said: "For a reason which can only be explained face to face, I am not [in a position] to convey any scholarly communication [in writing]."

Shortly after this, I took the opportunity, while on a journey from Iraq to Khurāsān, to pass through the glorious territory of [Gird] Kūh—may God, the exalted, protect it—and for two or three days [was able to] be in Shihāb al-Dīn's company and hear something of the *daʿwat* doctrines from his own mouth. I copied down his talks and derived much [benefit] from them. Since the requisites for staying with him and remaining in that place had not been prepared—for several reasons which I need not go into—I journeyed on from there to Khurāsān. A few days later, I happened to see a copy, in mediocre handwriting and antiquated paper, of the *Fuṣūl-i muqaddas* (Sacred Chapters) of [the Imām] ʿAlā Dhikrihi al-Salām, in the possession of an unworthy person who did not know what it was.

Obtaining [the text] with a ruse, I occupied myself day and night with reading it, and to the extent of my humble understanding and ability, I gained endless benefits from those sacred words which are the light of hearts and the illuminator of inner thoughts. It opened a little my eye of exploration (*chishm-i taṣarruf*) and my inner sight (*dīda-yi bāṭin*) was unveiled.

Thereafter, my only desire was to introduce myself among the *Jamāʿat* when the opportunity presented itself. At that time, in accordance with my inward motivation, I made such strenuous efforts that finally I succeeded. Through the good offices of the exalted royal presence of Nāṣir al-Ḥaqq wa'l-Dīn—may God exalt him—and his compassionate regard for my improvement, I was granted the good fortune of joining the *Jamāʿat* and entry among the ranks of the novices (*mustajībān*) of the *daʿwat,* and thus my situation reached the point where it is now.

Nothing can be gained by the illuminated mind in listening to this story except weariness. However, due to the previously mentioned circumstances concerning his [Nāṣir al-Dīn's] cordial nature and sympathy for me, its narration seemed to me to be prudent. If God the exalted is willing, it will be covered with the veil of forgiveness and heard with consideration. This [exposition so far] has been a description of the exoteric situation.

From an esoteric perspective, however, when I had reached a position where I could understand—by the proof that has already been cited—that it was the followers of instruction who were correct, I concluded with no additional troublesome thinking that the true instructor can only be he who is the instructor of the followers of the truth. This person, through whose teaching souls move from potentiality to actuality, must therefore be the instructor of the *Taʿlīmiyān* [i.e., the Ismāʿīlīs].

Then my mind became preoccupied with considering what particular characteristics would distinguish that instructor from other teachers, and what his instruction would be like. With due submissiveness, I beseeched God the exalted—may His greatness be magnified—to clarify and unveil this question, so that my heart might be appeased. Then I referred [myself] to the intellectual principles which I had already verified and the premises which had been made clear in the *Fuṣūl-i muqaddas*. I combined them, asked questions from here and there, and held discussions and debates with [other] novices (*mubtadiyān*), until gradually, through the stages which I will explain, the scheme of beliefs (*ṣūrat-i iʿtiqādī*), as will be mentioned later on, became clear in my mind.

First, it appeared to me that the instructor through whose mediation the potential perfection of the instructed soul is actualized must [himself] be in a state of actual perfection, because he who is not actually perfect cannot perfect others; and if that perfection had been potential in him and become actualized afterwards, he also would have been in need of another instructor. As necessity dictates (*az jihat-i qaṭʿ-i iḥtiyāj*), this would either result in an infinite regression (*tasalsul*), or end up with a teacher who has always been in a state of actual perfection. The evidence for the existence of such a person among humankind can be deduced both from philosophy (*ḥikmat*) and revelation (*sharīʿat*).

As for philosophy, it has been stated by philosophers that the possessor of sacred powers (*quwā-yi qudsiyyah*) has absolutely no need to acquire knowledge (*iktisāb*). Indeed, merely by focusing his soul and without having to go through the process of acquisition and active seeking, realities and knowledge become clear [to him] in their totality. As for revelation, it is maintained by the followers of the exoteric (*ahl-i ẓāhir*) that the possessor of bestowed knowledge (*ʿilm-i ladunī*) receives it without the mediation of any instruction.

Consequently, the mind does not reject the necessity of the existence among human beings of an instructor who is the first among instructors and is absolutely perfect. The instructor [is necessary] in order that some may gain perfection through him, and others through the latter, so that the effusion of the primordial bliss (*saʿādat-i nakhust*) might encompass the next level gradually, according to the order and degree which are ordained by the wisdom of the first origin (*ḥikmat-i mabdaʾ-i awwal*).

When I passed this stage and another veil had been removed from my mind, I realized that the perfection to which the seeker directs himself is knowledge of the True One, the exalted, the most high, who is the origin of [all] beings. Between Him and the first instructor, whose knowledge of the True One, the exalted, the most high, is always actual, there cannot exist any intermediary, because if an intermediary is posited, he would first have to come to know the intermediary, and then through him the True One. Knowledge of the True One would also, therefore, be a [mere] potentiality in him, [waiting to be actualized] through someone else. If this were so, this other person would have to be the first instructor, not him. But since we have already supposed him to be the first instructor, so the first instructor is the nearest person to God—may He be praised and exalted.

It only remained for me [to understand] what his knowledge of God—may He be exalted—would be like. While contemplating this, I remembered that in philosophy, in the section on the soul (*kitāb-i nafs*), it has been proved that the most self-evident knowledge, the surest intelligible thing, is the knowledge that non-material beings have of themselves, in which reasoning and acquisition of knowledge play no part. Moreover, it has been demonstrated in logic, in the apodeictics (*kitāb-i burhān*), that the only certain acquired knowledge (*ʿilm-i yaqīnī-yi muktasab*) is that in which the effect becomes known through [its] cause. Whatever does not become known through a proof proceeding from cause to effect is not absolutely certain. In the case under consideration, where the discussion is about the philosopher's knowledge of the first cause (*ʿillat-i ūlā*), he would have to admit that there can be no certainty about that which has no cause.

Again, when the philosopher discusses the degrees of existents, he posits the First Intellect (*ʿaql-i awwal*), which is the first effect, as the closest being to the First Cause. Necessarily, [the First Intellect's] knowledge of the First Cause is possible only because it is the first effect. But when [the First Intellect] cannot be certain [in this knowledge], how could others expect certainty about it? Here, then, the philosopher has completely shut to himself the door on [reaching] the knowledge of God, which is in truth a disturbing and deplorable situation. This is one of the problems I mentioned at the beginning, which resulted in my dissatisfaction with the principles of the philosophers for arriving at the knowledge of the True One.

The aim of setting out these arguments here is not to show the weakness of the philosophers; it is rather to show how my recollection of these points demonstrates that the level [of knowledge] of the first instructor cannot be the level of the First Effect [the First Intellect]. In fact, his rank must be higher than that of the First Effect, in order that his knowledge of the True One, the exalted, the most high, may be the noblest knowledge.

Here it is necessary to consider whether or not there can be any intermediary at all between the First Effect and the First Cause. Among most people of discrimination and reason, it is commonly held that there can be no intermediary between the First Effect and the First Cause. Now the *Taʿlīmiyān* believe that all beings issue forth from God, the exalted, who is the first origin (*mabdaʾ-i awwal*), through the mediation of something which, in the terminology of the later scholars of this *Jamāʿat*, is called His command (*amr*) or His word (*kalimah*). [According to them] the First Cause of the Universal Intellect (*ʿaql-i kull*), which is the First Effect, is God's command, because God is altogether beyond (*munazzah*) cause or effect.

It is of [crucial] importance to grasp this point, to verify [its] truth and eliminate falsity, because those who do not realize that it is true remain veiled from the knowledge of the True One. Indeed, whoever thinks over this discussion in fairness will realize that he must come to exactly this verdict, as explained by the followers of instruction (*aṣḥāb-i taʿlīm*) about this matter of which he is ignorant. And this is because the philosopher says that "from the Real One (*wāḥid-i ḥaqīqī*) comes forth only one entity." For example, if two existents were to issue from it at the same time, the aspect from which the first existent issued would be different from the aspect from which the second issued. Thus, if these two different aspects were included in [the absolute unity of] His essence (*māhiyyat*), He would no longer be the Real One. And if the two aspects were external to [the real one], then the discussion about their origin would be concerned with how it is possible for two postulated existents to emerge [from it]. Since both these arguments are invalid, it is obvious that two existents cannot possibly come forth from the Real One at the same time. It follows therefore that the First Effect is one, and this is the First Intellect.

This explains the philosopher's view, but after this he forgets [the principle] which he knew that when only one existent comes forth from the Real One, it comes forth in every respect from the one aspect [of its unity], for if the production of two existents necessitates that there be two aspects, the production of one existent requires that there be one aspect. Thus, if they do not admit this [one] aspect, through which the First Effect has come forth from the first origin, it must mean that no existent has issued from it, and hence nothing has come into existence [at all]. It is thus demonstrated on the basis of the philosopher's own arguments which he must admit, that the existence of this [one] aspect is necessarily proven, but because of his negligence of this point, the path to the recognition of God has been barred to him.

However, the instructor who had not neglected this aspect named it the "command" (*amr*) or the "word" (*kalimah*), in accordance with the verse of the Qur'ān: "Verily, His command, when He desires a thing, is to say to it 'Be' and it is" (36: 82). This verse makes it clear that the issuing forth of existents from God depends on the expression "Be" (*kun*), and the word "verily" (*innamā*) in Arabic serves the purpose of pinpointing [the scope of the expression], thereby making clear that the command is an expression for that word. The proof for the existence of this aspect, which only the people of *taʿlīm* have established, can also be deduced from philosophy and revelation (*sharīʿat*). However, those who cling to only the exoteric aspects of these two methods remain deprived of, and veiled from, the knowledge of it.

There is no doubt that this aspect, the command or the word [of God] is not something additional to His sacred Essence, in so far as He is He, the exalted—otherwise another intermediary would be required for the origination of that one [i.e., the First Intellect]—but from the point of view where [the command] is the cause of an effect, it is something additional. This additional entity, in reality, is the cause of the First Effect, because cause and effect are two concatenating (*iḍāfī*) entities, in so far as there can be no cause without a corresponding effect, and no effect without a corresponding cause. Whatever is relative is within the scope (*ḥayyiz*) of opposition, because opposition can only exist between two things, and duality is plurality.

Thus, where there is [a concatenation of] cause and effect, there is no escape from plurality, but plurality cannot be allowed for the first origin of existents, since plurality cannot exist without unity. Such being the case, the first origin, the True One—may His name be exalted—cannot, in so far as He is the first origin, be attributed with cause or effect, existence or non-existence, temporality or eternity, necessity or contingency, nor any of the other kinds of opposition, contradiction or concatenation. He is more glorious and exalted than to be the fount of two opposites, the origin of two contraries, the source of unity and plurality, the cause of the absolute and the non-absolute (*tanzīh wa lā tanzīh*). He is beyond any attribute by which something could be qualified, whether it be non-existent or existent, negative or positive, relative or absolute, verbal or in meaning (*lafẓī yā maʿnawī*). He is beyond [all this], and also beyond the beyond (*tanzīh*), and so forth.

There is no doubt that no one maintains such pure unity (*tawḥid-i ṣirf*), such unconditioned absoluteness (*tanzīh-i maḥḍ*) [of God], except the *Taʿlīmiyān*; and none of the adherents of [the other] sects, nor any of their leaders, except the instructor of this group, has been able to go to the extent of unveiling this secret. This is because others talk about possibilities (*na shāyad buwad wa shāyad buwad*), whereas he speaks from the position of "I recognize You through You, and You are my Guide to Yourself."

From this [discussion], it becomes clear that, in the terminology of the philosophers, it is an error to speak of the First Cause in relation to God, but it is correct to apply it to His command which is the source of all existents. In fact, whatever attribute has been ascribed to the First Cause by distinguished philosophers and people of knowledge (*ahl-i maʿrifat*) among the men of intellect, is a reference to His command, one facet of which is directed to the world of pure, eternal unity, the other to the world of multiplicity and contingency; but God as such is free from, and exalted above, both these facets. As has been expressed in the words of [one of] the leaders of the truthful people (*pīshwā-yi muḥiqqān*)—may the mention [of their names] be greeted—"Whatever pertains to God, pertains to us." However, the man of truth must not succumb here to either exaggeration (*ghulūw*) or underestimation (*taqṣīr*), because the pitfalls are many and the straight path, the true religion of God, which proceeds between underestimation and exaggeration, is narrower than a hair and sharper than a sword-edge.

In connection with this [matter], a story from my own past experience has come to my mind. Although it may prolong this discourse, I shall relate it, so that, God willing, in accordance with the vindication proffered at the beginning, I may receive the necessary guidance. At that time, when I had not yet joined the *Jamāʿat*, and had not yet acquired much understanding of the true religion (*madhhab-i ḥaqq*), I was engaged in a dispute with a jurist (*faqīh*) in Jājarm. In the course of the debate, the jurist denigrated the Ismāʿīlīs. I asked the reason for this, and he said that they considered the Imam to be God, because they refer to their Imām with the words "our lord" (*mawlānā*) which, in their opinion, could not be used except for God. Sometimes they say "our lord ʿAlī" or "our lord Muḥammad," and sometimes [when addressing God] they say and write, "O Allah, our Lord (*Allāhumma mawlānā*)," and so on. They seek from "our lord" what should be sought through prayer from God.

I said that if he were to consider the matter fairly, [he would find that] the foundation of their belief (*qāʿida-yi madhhab*) is that, since God cannot be recognized except through the Imām, the relationship of the Imām to God in respect to his guidance is like that between a name and what it names. Do not ordinary people (*ahl-i ʿurf*) use the same word both for the name and the named? They call Zayd "Zayd" and also call his spoken or written name "Zayd". It is because of this that one group have imagined the name to be the same as the named. Thus, if the Ismāʿīlīs use the name of God [i.e., *mawlānā*] for that person who is the guide to God, they are not deviating from the rules of the philologist or from customary practice. For this reason, they are not guilty of exaggeration, and vilification is not appropriate for them. The jurist could give no reply to this argument, and because this vindication [of the Ismāʿīlīs] was altogether pertinent, he acted fairly and accepted my explanation.

In terms of the implication of these principles, it became clear that there is a degree higher than those of effects. This is the degree of the [divine] command, which is the first of [all] causes and the origin of [all] degrees. On the one hand, it is an intermediary between the Creator and what is created, while, on the other, it is the final degree, the [point of] return of [all] beings, and the last of [all] existents.

The Knowledge of the first, the command of the True One—praise be to Him—in so far as He is He, in other words from the aspect of absolute unity, is the knowledge of God by God (*maʿrifat-i khudā bi khudā*), within the limits of the knowledge [implied in the verse]: "God bears witness that there is no God except He" (3:18). This is the noblest degree of certainty, the most perfect mode of knowledge, unlike the knowledge of cause through effect which does not give certainty. For the truth about knowledge is, as they have said: "We have not known You as You should be known," [and in the words of the Qurʾān]: "They measure not [the power of] God in its true measure" (6:91).

In the sciences of the truth (*ʿulūm-i ḥaqīqī*), it has been perceived that beyond the world of the senses there is another world, that of the intellect, which is related to the former in the same way as the soul is to the body. This is why it is called the spiritual world and the other the physical world. Corresponding to each sensible thing in this world is an intelligible entity in that world, and corresponding to each person here is a spirit there, and corresponding to every manifest thing (*ẓāhir*) here, is a hidden one (*bāṭin*) there. Similarly, corresponding to every intelligible entity there is a sensible one here, and corresponding to each spirit there is a person here, and corresponding to each hidden entity there is a manifest one here. That intelligible entity is the source (*maṣdar*) of this sensible one, and this sensible thing is the manifestation (*maẓhar*) of that intelligible one.

For example, if there were a sensible thing here which did not have an intelligible entity corresponding to it there, its appearance would be a deception, like a mirage or the hallucinations from which the delirious or the melancholic suffer. Just as a derivation (*farʿ*) cannot exist without a basic principle (*aṣl*) [from which it is derived], one should suppose that an intelligible which did not have a sensible here corresponding to it would be purely fanciful or imaginary with no reality at all, for no existent can be left floating free (*muʿaṭṭal*). Both the perceptible realm (*shahādat*) and the imperceptible realm (*ghaybat*), the creation and the command, that is to say the two worlds, the physical and the spiritual, have been disclosed in the word of the revelation.

As for the word of the exalted Creator—which is the sustainer of existents in the world and that by which each of them reaches its perfection, originating from it and returning to it—if it had no connection (*ta'alluq*) to the sensible world, the latter would have never come into existence. Since there is such a connection, which is of the same kind and therefore has to be perceptible to the senses, the command and the word must inevitably be manifest in this world, and the locus of its manifestation (*maẓhar*) must be in the form of an individual human being who appears to be like other humans, [one who] is born, grows old and succeeds to the one before him in a continuous line, so that it [the command] will be preserved in perpetuity [among mankind]: "And had We made him [the Prophet] an angel, We would have certainly made him a man, and disguised [him] before them in garments like their own" (6:9).

In the world of pure spirituality, it [the command] is the possessor of infinite knowledge and power; all forms of knowledge and perfections pour forth from it upon the intellects and souls: "We were shadows on the right-hand side of the Throne and praised Him, so the angels praised Him." This being is the command or the word of God; its rank is higher than that of possible things and effects, both of which are obedient and subservient to His command: "None is there in the heavens and the earth but he comes to the All-merciful as a servant" (19:94). As for God as such, He is above both the worlds; He is free and absolved from [the oppositions of] unity and multiplicity, similarity and differentiation, reality and relativity (*ḥaqīqat wa iḍāfat*): "Glory be to thy Lord, the Lord of majesty. [He is] above what they describe" (37:180). Any perfection that exists potentially in souls and individuals in the two realms is brought from potentiality to actuality by [His command], by the light of its instruction and the illumination of its guidance: "[Our lord is He] who gave everything its existence, then guided it" (20:50). Since in the beginning the existents came forth from the Command and by it they attain their perfection, it is their origin (*mabda'*) and to it is their return (*ma'ād*); it is the first (*awwal*) and the last (*ākhir*), and in it the circle of existence is completed: "He is the first and the last, the manifest and the hidden; He has knowledge of all things" (57:3).

[The command], therefore, has necessarily three aspects: first, it is a person like any other; second, it is the cause, the instructor, the perfect one, and the others are its effects, the instructed, those who are lacking in perfection; and third, it [the command] is itself, and nothing other than it is worthy of being the cause of existence. The case is such that the three realms, which the people of the *da'wat* have named the realm of similitude (*mushābahat*), the realm of differentiation (*mubāyanat*) and the realm of unity (*waḥdat*), refer to these three aspects.

The proof that the human species is distinguished from other simple and composite species of the sensible world by the manifestation of [the command] among them is this: according to philosophers, the human being is the noblest in the whole of existence, because he is nobler than the other three kingdoms [i.e., mineral, plant and animal], and the three kingdoms are nobler than the elements [i.e., earth, water, air and fire], and the elements are nobler than their own corporeal bases, that is to say, matter and form. Thus, the noblest source has revealed itself in the noblest manifestation.

On the evidence of the revealed law (*sharīʿat*) and the exoteric side of revelation (*tanzīl*), the trust (*amānat*) which the heavens, the earth and the mountains were unable to accept, was accepted by mankind: "We offered the trust to the heavens and the earth and the mountains, but they refused to carry it and were afraid of it; and man carried it. Surely he is unjust, ignorant" (33:72). It was [only] after accepting this trust that mankind deserved the prostration of the intimate angels (*malāʾika-yi muqarrabīn*), who are the noblest in creation: "And when we said to the angels, 'Bow yourselves to Adam,' they bowed themselves, except Iblīs" (2:34). They testified to the descent of the manifestation of the person of divine knowledge (*shakhṣ-i maʿrifat-i bārī*) among the individuals of the human species when he appeared before them, and not among any other species of existents. And since his appearance in this world is because he is its perfection, as long as the world remains it can never be devoid of him: "If the earth were devoid of the Imam even for a short time, it would be convulsed with all its inhabitants."

It is also necessary that the people should have access to the lights of his guidance; otherwise they would be deprived of attaining perfection, and the usefulness of the manifestation would be rendered futile. Since it is necessary in the world of similitude that human beings should succeed one another through a recognized relationship (*ʿalāqah*), once this relationship which indicates continuity and succession (*ittiṣāl wa taʿāqub*) is disregarded, the means of knowing him will also be closed to the people. The relationship can only be of two kinds, spiritual and physical. The spiritual relationship is the clear appointment (*naṣṣ*) of one by the other, and the physical relationship is that of the child to the father by way of succession. Through these two relationships, the close affinity between these individuals becomes known, and [the meaning of the revealed] evidence (*athar*), "He made it a word enduring among his posterity" (43:28), and of the decree (*ḥukm*), "the offsprings, one of the other "(3:34), becomes clear. By testifying to these two proofs of birth and clear appointment, all the inhabitants of the world have access to the individual who is the locus of the manifestation of that light.

However, for the elite (*khawāṣṣ*) there is another sign, which is one of the vestiges of the world of unity (*ʿālam-i waḥdat*), and this is his uniqueness in the claim of "I know God through God and I lead people to God." This claim and call are vouchsafed to no one but him, so that from all the realms of being there may be testimonies to His eternal unity and the proof (*ḥujjat*) of God among the people may be fulfilled: "Say, to God belongs the conclusive proof" (6:149). Thus, with these premises and propositions, the rank of the first instructor and the particular characteristics by which he is distinguished, such that he is absolutely perfect whereas others are imperfect and in need of [his power] to perfect them, becomes clear.

It remains to see what his teaching is, and how people can attain perfection through it. At this point, after much deliberation and thought, and going back to an examination of the sayings of the eminent ones [i.e., the Imams], the following points impressed upon my mind.

Firstly, as the philosophers have explained, absolute certainty cannot be achieved by reasoning from effect to cause; but since the highest state [of knowledge] for the speculative rationalists (*ahl-i naẓar*) is to know cause from effect, no rationalist can come to know God.

Also, since knowledge, according to the rationalists, is a picture (*mithāl*) or form (*ṣūrat*), produced from what is known in the mind (*dhāt*) of the knower, and since any picture or form which is thus produced is different from that which is known, the subject's knowledge must, in reality, be the estimated form (*ṣūrat-i mawhūm*) and not what is actually known. For this reason it has been said, "Everything which you distinguish by your estimation, even in its most precise meanings, is turned away from Him and returned to you; it is fabricated by you and created like you."

Since worship depends on knowledge and [human] knowledge is like this, what must worship be like? "Surely you and that which you worship apart from God are fuel for hell; you shall go down to it" (21:98). Such is the ultimate stage the rationalist reaches in his quest for perfection.

The followers of *taʿlīm*, however, believe in the principle (*qāʿidah*) that everyone, whatever his degree may be, knows his own instructor, who in turn knows his own instructor, [and so on] to the first instructor, who knows God through God. As a result, everyone also comes to know God through God.

In the *Fuṣūl-i muqaddas* it is written: "Everyone must know [God] through knowing me, since a person becomes a knower (*ʿārif*) through my knowledge and becomes a monotheist (*muwaḥḥid*) through my monotheism. Then the reality of knowledge (*maʿrifat*), union (*ittiḥād*) and oneness (*waḥdat*) comes completely into existence, and the reality of worship becomes evident." The evidence for such a judgement in the revealed law and the exoteric aspect of revelation is the text (*naṣṣ*) of the Qurʾān: "Those are they whom God has guided, so follow their guidance" (6:90). And there is also the fact that in the realm of religious law, knowledge of God is not judged by the mere profession of the formula "There is no god but God," unless the confession of "Muḥammad is His Messenger" is added to it.

From the point of philosophy and rational thought, since both the worlds, the manifest (*ẓāhir*) and the hidden (*bāṭin*), are connected with one another, whatever is real (*bi ʿayn*) there has its trace (*athar*) here, and whatever is real here has its trace there. One can therefore make deductions about the state of that world from the state of this world.

Reflection about this world makes it clear that matter is perpetuated through form, for no matter (*māddah*) can exist without form (*ṣūrat*), and that the multiplicity and differentiation of matter too is caused by the multiplicity and differentiation of form, because matter [whatever form it takes] is, in reality and essence, always the same. Consequently, whenever differentiation between these forms is eliminated, they become one with each other. For example, between the form of water and the form of air there is differentiation and multiplicity. But if water is stripped of its watery form and takes an aerial form [as steam], it becomes one with air and there remains no differentiation between them.

It is the same in that [hidden] world where souls, despite their various ranks, emanate from one origin and share in the same essence (*māhiyyat*), but they are perpetuated [individually] by virtue of the forms they acquire, which is the cause of their coming into this world. So if the form which is represented in the soul of the disciple is identical to that which is represented in his instructor's soul, and if his position is such that he knows through the knowledge of his instructor, and the instructor is in agreement with his return, there will be no differentiation and multiplicity between their souls; and when the veil is removed, he will reach his instructor and be united with his oneness, and then he [the disciple] will have reached [his place of] return.

However, if there is differentiation in the forms of the two souls, such that [in] acquiring the form of his soul the disciple follows his own opinion and desire, or blindly imitates someone else who has followed his own opinion and desire, he remains in the darkness of purgatory (*barzakh*), covered by the veil of multiplicity, which is the shadow of existence, [as mentioned in the verse], "No indeed; but upon that day they shall be veiled from their Lord" (83:15).

In this world, no one who seeks something can reach his goal unless, first of all, he has some capital of the same kind as that which he seeks and subsequently makes the necessary effort. For example, unless a farmer sows seed and cultivates the land, he cannot reap any harvest; if a merchant has no capital and does no business, he makes no profit; unless a hunter provides himself with bait and goes after the prey, he cannot catch anything; and so on and so forth. Similarly in this world, unless the seeker after perfection attains a favour from the primordial decree (*ḥukm-i mafrūgh*), which is equivalent to the merchant's capital—that is, having a pure soul and a sincere heart, as it is said in [the verse], "Except for him who comes to God with a pure heart" (26:89)—and [unless he] has acquired something from the subsequent decree (*ḥukm-i mustaʾnif*), which is equivalent to the merchant's profit—that is, an act of submission (*taslīm*) based on the insight (*baṣīrat*): "And whosoever submits his will to God, being a doer of good, has grasped the firmest handhold" (31:22)—and unless he yokes both of these together and immerses the subsequent in the primordial, he cannot attain the degree of perfection [indicated in the verse]: "Theirs is the abode of peace with their Lord, and He is their protector (*walī*)" (6:127).

Here [in the physical world] this capital is a kind of premium; there [in the spiritual world] the believer's descent was created from the light of the True One: "The believer has been created from the light of God, and knowledge is a light which God has cast into the heart." If in the beginning, the believer had not been created from the light of God, he would not get as far as the return (*maʿād*) implied in [the words], "When God gives the command, He knows it," since in the return things go back to whence they started.

To sum up, from the above premises and the testimonies of intellect and religious law (*ʿaqlī wa sharʿī*), it became evident to me that the final steps on the path of the seekers after truth is to be blessed with success in knowing their instructor and to become knowledgeable through his knowledge, as it is expressed in the *Fuṣūl-i muqaddas*: "Knowledge of God is [through] knowledge of the Imām."

Sayyid J. H. Badakhchani, translator

Rawḍat al-taslīm or *Taṣawwurāt*

THE GARDEN OF SUBMISSION, OR NOTIONS

The Doctrine of Intellect, Soul and Epistemology

Eighth Conception: Concerning Knowledge of the Human Soul

It is clear that body as such is not in action or motion. For if a body was in action and motion by itself, then inevitably all the bodies belonging to one category would have had similar action and motion. But we observe that, that is not the case. We see bodies which exhibit no action and motion, and bodies which exhibit actions and motions. So we conclude that those actions and motions are due to a power which is supra-physical.

We find that the motions of some bodies are uni-directional, for example, the motion of fire is from the center to the circumference, the motion of water is from the circumference to the center. So we conclude that water and fire exhibit that motion by [their] nature (*bi-ṭabʿ*). We call that motion natural motion. We find the motion exhibited by some bodies is of many kinds and is in different directions. The motion exhibited by some bodies is, semi-voluntary and without consciousness and perception. We call [the mover of such body] vegetative soul (*nafs-i nabātī*). The motion exhibited by some bodies [21] is semi-voluntary, with consciousness, and perception, but in the consciousness and perception there is no discrimination. We call [the mover of such bodies] animal soul (*nafs-i ḥayawānī*). The motion exhibited by some bodies is voluntary with free will, consciousness, and perception, and with consciousness and perception there is total discrimination. We call [the mover of such bodies] human soul.

These two souls, i.e., the vegetative and animal, are divisible and subject to disintegration, so with the annihilation of their material body they are annihilated. But the human soul is indivisible and not subject to disintegration, therefore after its detachment from [its] material body it continues to exist. Although it is not a pre-eternal (*azalī*) substance, it is nevertheless a post-eternal (*abadī*) substance. The *azalī* is that which neither has a beginning 'from this side' [i.e., the past], nor has an end on 'the other side' [i.e., the future]. Whereas *abadī* is that which manifests a beginning 'from this side', but has no end 'on the other side'. The imagi-

This translation is based on Naṣīr al-Dīn Ṭūsī's *Taṣawwurāt*, edited by S. J. Hosseinī Badakhshānī, *The Paradise of Submission*, unpublished Oxford University, 1989. Pp. 20–33, 35–39, 46–51. The numbers in parentheses refer to the pagination of the W. Ivanow edition (Leiden, 1952) and the items in square brackets are additions of the translator.

I have compared this translation with J. Badakhshani's translation of the same treatise and would like to acknowledge that changes have been made here based on his translation. I would like to express my debt of gratitude to him and the Institute for Isma'ili Studies for making Dr. Badakhshānī's translation available to me.

native soul (*nafs-i khayālī*) is intermediary between the animal soul and the human soul. It faces the senses and sensibles [on the one end] and the intellect and the intelligibles [on the other end]. If it unites with the animal soul, then it can imagine by the organ of the material body and is needy of [that] organ; so by its destruction, it is destroyed. But if it unites with the human soul, it can preserve (*ḥifẓ*) the meanings without the physical organ and is independent of that instrument; so it continues to exist due to the subsistence (*baqāʾ*) of the [human] soul, and participates with the soul in its felicity (*saʿādat*) as well as in its wretchedness (*shaqāwat*).

When the [human] soul detaches from [its] material body, corporeality (*hayʾat*) remains in it from the [faculty of] imagination (*khayāl*). The reward and punishment are determined [for it] according to the measure of whatever the imaginative soul has known and done; the imaginative soul brings the remembrance of reward and punishment with it. The identity of the souls in the next world will be due to it [i.e., *hayʾat*]. A human being in this world is a spiritual being garbed by corporeality but in the next world he will be corporeal garbed by spirituality.

The human soul is neither body nor a faculty in the body because body accepts division but soul does not. Its substance which is nonmaterial and separate (*mufāriq*) is from the realm of the Intellect. Its connection with the body is of the type whereby it moves, transforms, controls and governs it unlike the connection of vegetative and animal souls [with their bodies]. The latter two seek nutrition, growth and procreation, mix with the humors; so inevitably they become corrupted by the corruption of the humors. Nay, the human soul intellects its own essence (*dhāt*). Its intellection of intelligibles and abstract things (*mufāriqāt*) is not through the physical organ. Rather, it perceives all these by itself. This is the reason why it is indivisible and not subject to disintegration, for anything which [22] accepts division has magnitude and quantity, whereas the soul has no magnitude and quantity. If the soul were subject to division, then in one part it would have been ignorant, and in another it would have been the knower of the same thing. But that is not the case with the soul *qua* soul. It is the first faculty from among the human faculties to become receptive (*qābil*) to the effusion of the Intellect, [it is] an entrance (*mawrid*) for spiritual beings, and a treasury of intelligible forms. It makes the distinction between things whose comprehension of form and meaning is impossible [without it]. It has [the power] to comprehend and know the power of coagulation (*quwwat-i inʿiqādī*) which has no knowledge of its [own] state nor of the eminence of the vegetative power, and of the animal power which has no knowledge of its creation nor of the eminence and status of man, and to recognize the wisdom which exists in every form appropriate for each species.

Due to these reasons it is possible to conceive that the human soul is a simple spiritual substance. One and the same person can know many kinds of sciences, for instance, mathematics, natural sciences, logic and the divine sciences; and can remember many things from the Qur'ān, reports, poetry, parables, narratives, and traditions. None of these sciences becomes mixed up with the other sciences [in him]. He can give lengthy commentary [on each of these sciences] and all [these sciences] come to the ears of the audience part-by part. Let us [compare] it, for example, with a house. If it has the capacity to give place to fifty people and they desire to give place to one hundred people in that house, it is not possible. [If they do so] then they have to go through a great deal of pain to squeeze them in [that place]. Whereas the soul never gets crowded with the forms of the objects of knowledge and hearing the intelligibles, rather the more [forms of objects of knowledge and intelligibles] it acquires, the greater becomes its skill for operation, the wider and deeper becomes its space for motion, and more intense becomes its joy and happiness due to that.

When you say, 'my head', 'my eyes', 'my ears', 'my heart', 'my tongue', 'my hands' etc., those are not the essence of the human soul; they are in fact its additions (*iḍāfāt*). For instance, [the human soul] is like a king, and all these are its subjects, army, family, servants; [23] or it is like a perfect artisan, and they are all like his instruments and tools. Just as neither a king can function without an army, nor an artisan without his instruments, likewise the soul cannot function without [its instruments]; i.e., it must have a human physical body so that it manifests through it. It must have a head and brain so that it can think and make distinction among things; it must have eyes in order for it to see, ears to hear, 'heart' in order to know, tongue in order to speak, hands in order to handle [things], legs to walk, etc.

Also, the human soul is the first perfection of the natural, organic body having potential life. The soul is the prime mover of the parts [of the body], the transformer of the states and enshaper of the bodily matter. At the beginning [of its attachment to the body] it is material power just as there is a potential human person in the sperm—[i.e.], its final human perfection is in potentiality—its particular act is to become a separate form (*ṣūrat-i mujarrad*) gradually and progressively, and its entified life (*ʿāyin-i ḥayāt*) becomes actualized through Him the Exalted.

All the soul substances are from one genus. The difference among them is due to their [difference] in knowledge, character traits, habits, and acts. The soul at inception is simple. Then it accepts the imprints of knowledge, opinion, analogy, moral traits, habits, and acts. Each one of these states becomes a form in the substance of each soul, and the soul becomes the matter for that form.

The eminence of the soul lies in its knowledge. We observe that a soul which becomes receptive to any kind of knowledge becomes more eminent than those souls which have not benefitted from that knowledge. It is known that when a soul receives knowledge perfectly, it becomes more powerful [than those which do not receive that knowledge perfectly]. Gradually it reaches the level of the souls of the great *ḥujjats*.[1] They surpass the other souls due to their receptivity to the lights of the exalted Word, and the purity of the substance of their [souls]. They become distinguished from the other souls due to the direct Divine teaching of the Lord. They liberate the souls of people drowned in the ocean of matter, darknesses [of ignorance] and entangled in the chain of nature by benefitting them [from their knowledge] and making them take advantage [of that knowledge].

1. The Nizārī Ismāʿīlī *daʿwah* organization consisted of three degrees. They were in decending order: *imām, ḥujjat* (proof), and *dāʿī*.

God, may He be Exalted, has created everything. He has decreed that the sustenance [of a thing] on which depends its firmness and perpetuity should be from its own genus. The human body is composed of these [24] four elements; so its sustenance is also from these things which are these four elements. The human soul from the point of being potential intellect, and [its] intellect an actual soul, is from the realm of the Intellect. So its sustenance is from knowledge, and action [according to knowledge]. Its proof is this: if someone eats an abundant amount of healthy and delicate food with enjoyment till the end of his life but does not acquire knowledge, he will not become learned. But if he takes a small portion of food, enough to keep him alive, and acquires knowledge he becomes learned. Peace.

Ninth Conception: Concerning Knowledge of the Human Intellect

It is the belief of some people that the innate intellect (*ʿaql-i gharīzī*) due to which human beings are distinguished from the other animals—which joins man at the beginning of puberty when the days of his childhood are over, and he remains intelligent due to it till the end of his life—is equal in all mankind. They also agree that any [property] which is equal [in all] those who possess it, its possessors have no differences among themselves. Although they mutually agree upon [the above matter] yet they contradict their own opinion by continuously disputing with each other on intelligibles, and they exhibit their opposition to each other.

They do not realize that if [human] intellects had been equal, then an intelligent person would not have opposed another. Their argument on the equality of all intellects is based on the proof that *taklīf* (religious prescription) is equally obligatory [on all believers having rationality]. They do not know that if there had not been gradation and hierarchical eminence (*tafāḍul*) in the intellects, then one person would not have been the giver of *taklīf* and the other obligated to accept that *taklīf* for himself; one a giver (*muʾaddī*) and the other a receiver, one a giver of law and the other obligated to accept the law, one a teacher and the other a pupil, one a master and the other a disciple. If there had not been various measures and differences in the [human] intellects, then a common person who cannot make a distinction between head and foot or sandals and gloves and a great philosopher who knows many things would have been equal.

It is also known that when [people] give reports [about something] everything in that [report] is neither absolutely correct nor absolutely false; some of it is true and some false. Whoever gives the verdict that [all human] intellects are equal, [then] from that verdict it becomes necessary that in any report they give about it there is a possibility of truth and falsehood. Therefore the two should be left as they are, and the truth and falsehood in that [report] should not be highlighted.

So there is gradation and hierarchical eminence in the [human] intellects. [25] At its inception it is the state of potentiality. [The philosophers] affirm that in the process of its actualization from the state of potentiality [to actuality] it goes through four stages: (i) material intellect (*ʿaql-i hayūlānī*); (ii) intellect *in habi-*

tus (*ʿaql biʾl-malakah*); (iii) active intellect (*ʿaql biʾl- fiʿl*); (iv) acquired intellect (*ʿaql biʾl-mustafād*).

Material intellect is a faculty which [has the potentiality to] accept forms without matter. Though it does not accept those forms, it has the capability for [acceptance]; for instance a small child cannot be a teacher but he has the capability and possibility to become a teacher.

Intellect *in habitus* is a faculty which, as mentioned earlier, when it accepts abstract forms those forms become rooted in it so that it can easily move from a priori (*ḍarūriyyat*) to speculative (*naẓariyyāt*) and from speculative to a priori ideas.

Active intellect is a faculty which accepts abstract forms. The capability to move from a priori to speculative and from speculative to a priori [ideas] is actualized in it; it is no more passive. So at any time it desires to refer to those [ideas], it is able to do so.

Acquired intellect is a power which has attained all the perfections mentioned earlier. Between it and the intellect which transforms it from potentiality to actuality a relationship is created, so every intelligible form which is in that one is manifested in this one, neither more nor less like a polished mirror when placed before a person.

Vegetative soul, animal soul, human soul and human intellect are from one root and one source but appear as four different [powers]. This may be compared to a person on a dark night standing two or three *farsangs*[2] away from a mountain on which a fire has been lit. Watching it from a distance he assumes that it is a star and not fire. Here the reality of this distance [from the source of fire] without any trace of [his] nearness [to it] could be applied to the vegetative soul [vis à vis its source].

When this person walks toward that mountain he at times assumes [this fire] to be a fire and not a star, and at times he assumes it to be a star and not fire. Here [the simile of that man's] distance [from the source] but having some trace of his nearness [to it] could be applied to the animal soul [vis à vis its source].

When this person reaches very near to that mountain, he knows without any doubt that that [glow] is a fire and not a star. Here the reality of nearness [to the source of fire] with some trace of his distance [from it] could be applied to the human soul [vis à vis its source].

When the man reaches the top of that mountain, he sees clearly the environs of that mountain including everyone and everything in it by the light of that fire. [26] Here [the reality of] his very nearness [to the source] without any trace of distance [from it] could be applied to the human intellect. That is why they have said, "The intellect is the light of human soul."

Thus it is known that each one of the four [powers, i.e.,], vegetative soul, [animal soul, human soul,] and human intellect does not issue forth from a different source, but all of them come from the same root. They are [like] the four branches of a tree, or four streams of a brook, or four flames of a wick. The difference among them is due to their different acts and motions, and their nearness or distance in relation to the universal origin of existence.

2. *Farsang* or *farsakh*: a measure of distance about three miles.

The [definition] of sense (*ḥiss*), sensation (*ḥāssah*), sensible (*maḥsūs*), estimation (*wahm*), and imagination (*khayāl*): sense is a corporeal faculty (*quwwat-i jasadānī*), sensation is a spiritual faculty, and sensible is something which the sense perceives. The lower dimension of imagination is the senses, its higher dimension is the estimation. The lower dimension of estimation is the imagination; its higher dimension is [the human] soul; the lower dimension of [human] soul is estimation; its higher dimension is the intellect. The lower dimension of intellect is the [human] soul; its higher dimension is the Command. Peace.

Tenth Conception: Concerning the Purpose of the Attachment of Particular Souls to Human Bodies, and a Short Account of the Composition of the Human Body

One of the reasons for the attachment of particular souls to human bodies is [that it manifests itself through the body]. Although in terms of reality the active agent (*fāʿil*) produces the act, but in terms of relativity the effect of the act is manifested in the receptacle which is passive; in terms of the primordial decree the agent is the [divine] Command, but in terms of the subsequent decree (*mustaʾnif*) the effect of [its] act is manifested in the creation which is passive. In terms of meaning (*maʿnī*) the agent is the spirit but in terms of form (*shakl*) the effect of [its] act is manifested through the body which is passive. In other words, an active agent manifests itself through a receptacle, the [divine] Command through the creation, and the spirit through the body.

One of the benefits of this attachment is that the form of good in a good soul, and the form of evil in an evil soul which exists potentially in them. These two souls *qua* souls are similar to mental existence, and so long as they do not manifest themselves in external existence, they cannot be distinguished [from each other]. The distinction between each one of the two souls, the progression of the good soul from the degree of possibility to necessity, and the declining of the evil soul from the level of the possibility to the lowest level of impossibility (*imtināʿ*) is through attachment to a body. The acquisition of knowledge, the attainment of experience and discipline (*riyāḍat*), the necessity of attaining eminence [27] and position, the administration of matters pertaining to livelihood, crossing the levels of perfections from [its] Origin to [its] return (*maʿād*), are possible only through this body which is composed of blood, flesh, and other matters.

There are some souls which, due to their innate eminence, perfection, and goodness, are fortunate to receive and accept directly the unlimited divine munificence (*jūd*),[3] effusion, and generosity. They receive [all those graces directly] by their essence (*dhāt*) without any instruments, and without time so, for them to give and to take has the same meaning. They are the divinely guided people possessing knowledge (*ʿālimān-i rabbānī*). The benefit of their attachment to the bodies is to train their souls by the [divine] light and guide them toward [their] perfection and completion so that they become prepared to receive perfection.

3. The text reads *wujūd* (existence).

Their likeness is that of a teacher who brings himself down from the level of the teacher to the level of the pupil and teaches him first the alphabet, then gradually and systematically makes him cross the degrees [of knowledge] until he becomes a learned scholar and reaches the level of the teacher.

There are some souls which in their innate disposition are not perfectly good, but have the preparedness to become perfect[ly good]. These are the pupils treading on the path of salvation. The benefit of their attachment to the bodies is that through the training of the possessors of perfection they become capable of perfection, and whatever degrees of perfections are there in them in the state of potentiality become actualized through them.

There are souls which are evil; [nay] they are at the extreme level of evil and do not become receptive to any goodness, eminence, and perfection—i.e., they are rogues and villains who are not illumined by the light of knowledge, and do not take refuge beyond themselves in someone who could be their trustworthy (*wāthiq*) pillar.[4] The benefit of their attachment to the body is that the trace [of evil] which is concealed in them becomes manifest so that the good becomes distinct from bad, and pure from impure.

Another benefit: If the particular souls had not attached [themselves] to human bodies, then the edifice of the universe, the structure of existent things, the establishment of the divine proof, the execution of the divine Tradition (*sunnat-i rabbānī*) would not have been possible.

Another benefit: The macrocosm from the circumference of the highest sphere till the depth of the earth is one person called the Universal Man (*insān-i kullī*). The sign of a person reaching the degree of puberty is that he can reproduce like himself. When the macrocosm, which is the universal Man, reached the height of its puberty it reproduced someone like itself who is the particular man (*insān-i juzwī*. He is the microcosm in the macrocosm in form, and macrocosm in the microcosm in meaning (*maʿnī*, [or essence]).

It is known that no [28] existent thing is nobler than man in its perfection of creation and nobility in relation to the whole universe which he resembles. That is because man is a totality comprising the subtleties of the lights of the First Intellect; the traces (*maʾāthir*) of powers of the Universal Soul, the astonishing compositions of the spheres, various kinds of constellations, the motions of the stars; the traces (*āthār*) of the natural elements, variety of mineral substances, variety of vegetative forms, amazing structures of animals; stations of angels, *jinn*, man, devils; signs of land, sea, mountain, plain, inhabited land, desert, garden and spring, summer autumn, winter [seasons are] within himself.

They have struck the similitude of the human body—composed of four elements, which when separate and distinct from each other in form reject each other

4. The reference is to a long conversation of Imam ʿAlī ibn Abī Ṭālib with one of his foremost disciples Kumayl ibn Nakhaʿī, in which the Imam besides other matters, discusses the characteristics of three categories of people. Cf. *Nahj al-balāghah*, text in Arabic, with commentary by Shaykh Muḥammad ʿAbdūh, (Beirut, n.d.), vol. 4, p. 35; English trans. by S. M. Jafery (New York, 1985), p. 600.

vehemently, but when combined and mixed with each other, are broken down in form by each other and become harmonious—to a Virtuous City (*madīna-yi fāḍilah*). Man is like a city, constructed of different things, having a fortified [physical] structure and a firm form. From head to foot all the parts [of his body], limb joints, blood vessels, bones, and nerves [resemble] the courtyards, streets, houses, treasuries, bazaar, shops, roads, etc., which a city should have. The intellect and soul are like a king and his minister; the external and internal senses, the faculties of feeding, attraction, digestion, expulsion, and any other faculty which belongs to the nature [of each one those faculties]. The acts of those faculties through motion specific to each one of them which finally manifests itself through each one in the body correspond to the pillars of the state, such as physician, teacher, people of other professions and degrees such as chamberlain, lawyer, porter, army, servant, domestic servant, subject, spy, postman, messenger, craftsman, merchant, and every builder through whom the structure and splendor of that city is completed, and the preservation of that city is possible due to their existence and through them.

The structure of the body and the form of the soul [attached to it] are the epitomes of the universe which the pre-eternal Pen has inscribed on the post-eternal Tablet by the primordial Command. Just as the human soul is nobler than all the other souls, likewise the matter from which its body has been composed is also subtler than all kinds of matters.

[29] The wisdom of God the Exalted has decreed it so that all of man's dispositions (*taṣarrufāt*), movements, and acts should be intellectual; that in each one of [these acts] there should be discernment, and in each discernment verification (*taḥqīq*). Therefore, the matter of his body has to be more perfect in equilibrium; the form of his creation, and the mode of his physical structure, posture, stature, and constitution should be nobler in relation to the other existents.

The human soul before its attachment to the body is a substance which contains things in the state of potentiality which are actualized through [the influence of] the spheres and stars. When the [human] sperm, which is potentially the whole human person, reaches the womb, it settles down there.

In the first month it is under the governance [*tadbīr*] of Saturn, because the spirituality of Saturn is the first one to have effect in the realm of natures [of the fertilized egg]. So the whole aqueous content [of the fertilized egg] becomes coagulated.

In the second month it is under the governance of Jupiter. The nature of Jupiter is constituted of heat and humidity which further the development and growth of the fertilized egg. [The nature of] its aqueous parts is dissolved and transformed to a clot of blood. Jupiter['s influence] in a period of time makes the faculty of growth and feeding commence [in the clot of blood].

In the third month it is under the governance of Mars. The nature of the blood clot is dissolved and transformed to a fetus. In the period of the influence of Mars, if the heat increases and [the fetus] accepts a little dryness, then its power of growth becomes stronger, and the passage for food for the fetus becomes open.

In the fourth month it is under the governance of the sun. Through [the influence of] the nature of the sun the marks of [various physical parts and organs] are manifested in the fetus. It rises from its place, the animal spirit originates in it, the embryo comes in motion, its limbs and organs become distinct, and the head, heart, and the rest of the parts of its body become manifest.

In the fifth month it is under the governance of Venus. By [the influence of] the nature of Venus and the domination of its spiritual powers on it, the creation [of the fetus] becomes complete, its physical structure reaches its perfection, the position of eyes and ears becomes manifest, the mouth opens, and the head between the two ears emerges.

In the sixth month it is under the governance of Mars. Through [the influence of] the nature of Mars, it acquires another sense and performs another kind of movement; its physical parts become distinct from each other; it acquires the sense of its whereabouts; it opens its mouth, moves its lips, licks with its tongue, and sniffs with its nose. At times it sleeps; at times it is awake.

In the seventh month it is under the governance of the moon. [The influence of] the nature of moon works in it; the senses attain perfection, its stature becomes erect, the parts [of its body] become strong, the joints become firm, its movement becomes continuous, it feels the narrowness of its place and aims [30] to get out. If it is born in this month, it will survive and will be fully developed.

In the eighth month it comes again under the governance of Saturn. The heaviness and repose become manifested in the fetus. If it is born in this month it will not survive, because the eighth domicile is of the [constellation] of Pisces, and Saturn [in this domicile] brings all the powers [of the fetus] to a static state by its coldness and humidity so [if the fetus is born] it does not survive.

The ninth month is once again the turn of Jupiter. [Under its governance] the signs [of life], motion and spontaneity becomes manifest in the fetus. [Jupiter's] ninth domicile is the Pisces toward which it travels, and the fetus certainly exits from the womb and is born.

The parts of the body [of the fetus] which are firm and hold together become organs and limbs; those which are fluid are four kinds of humors; and what rises from the four kinds of humors in the form of vapor in extreme subtlety, purity, and transparency and permeates all parts of the body [it is called animal spirit (*ruḥ-i ḥayawānī*)].

The animal spirit originates from the heart; then it fills the nasal cavity; then the orifices of the eyes, the audible tubes of the ears, the passage of the tongue, and the rest of the organs from head to foot.

The external senses are five: touch, taste, smell, hearing, sight. From these [five], three, i.e., touch, taste and smell, are attained [by the baby] when it is in the womb, and the other two, i.e., hearing and sight, are attained by it when it is born. The interior senses are also five: sensorium, the form-giving faculty (*muṣawwirah*), [the faculty of] reflection (*mufakkirah*), estimation, and memory. They join the baby before it is born; each one manifests itself gradually and progressively in its own time; so does the discerning rational soul. It [manifests itself] in the brain first; from there it spreads to most of the remaining parts and organs of the body.

The sensorium is located at the beginning of the front part of the first cavity of the brain. It is called sensorium because it has contact with every sense and each sense associates with it; for example, what the eyes see, the ears hear, the [sense of] touch feels, the [senses of] taste and smell experience, come to [the sensorium] first. [Hence] it is called the resort (*mawrid*) of the senses and treasury of sensible forms.

The form-giving faculty is located at the beginning of the first part of the second cavity of the brain. If this power is obedient to and supports the human intellect, it is called reflective [faculty]; if it is occupied with the body and bodily things and obedient to imagination and estimation, it is called imaginative faculty (*mukhayyilah*).

The [sensible] forms [received by the senses] are all entrusted to the [31] which then passes them on to the [faculty of] imagination located in the forefront of the third cavity of the brain. What the form-giving faculty has entrusted to it is either present [in it], or it retains it.

The estimative faculty is located in the fourth cavity of the brain which is in the middle of the head; the faculty of memory is located in the hind part of the brain. It retains all the forms entrusted to it so that at the time of need it reminds one [of them] through the [power of] remembrance (*dhākirah*).

The faculty of imagination guards the physical forms. The animal also associates with man in having this [faculty]. But [the physical forms are retained in the faculty of imagination] so long as the animal's spirit, which is subtle vapors of the humors, permeates through his body. Due to the continuation and persistence of his soul, a form (*hayʾat*) from his imaginative faculty remains with it forever, continuously, eternally.

The similitude of the *sensus communis* is that of the master of postal information; to him each one of the possessors of information brings a letter mentioning about something, and he collects all [this information]. The similitude of the form-giving faculty is that of the carrier of a mail bag; the master of postal information gives him the letters to be put in the mail bag. The similitude of the reflective faculty is that of a king to whom the carrier of a mail bag brings the bag of letters and entrusts it to him so that he reads them and becomes aware of the good and bad written in them. The similitude of the faculty of memory is that of a treasurer to whom the king entrusts those letters so that he stores them in the treasury. The similitude of the faculty of remembrance is that of a person who, when the king needs that information another time, submits it to him.

When a child is born, his life and death, comfort and pain, affluence and poverty, honor and disgrace, and the other contradictory [matters], which will take us too long to enumerate, are destined for him on his horoscope decreed by the conjunctions of the stars, the influence of the planets, the influence of the fixed stars and their good and bad effects, which by the divine Decree are for him. But the Will (*irādat*) of God, the Almighty and Exalted, which is the creator and governor of the spheres and stars, is above all [that is decreed by the horoscope, and the latter is] connected to His Command and Wish. Peace be upon the one who heeds guidance.

Eleventh Conception: Concerning the Essential Differentia of each Genus and the Engendered Beings: The Mineral, the Vegetable, the Animal, and the Human

Minerals on account of having coagulative [power] (*inʿiqād*) are associated with mineral substances. The essential *differentium* of mineral substances is their power of coagulation. Mineral substances are associated with plants on account of [32] [both having the power of] coagulation and some [common] properties. The essential *differentium* of the plant [kingdom] is the power of growth. Plants are associated with animals on the basis of [both having the power of] coagulation, some [common] properties, and the [power of] growth. The essential *differentium* of the animal is sense perception and motion. An animal is associated with man on the basis of having [the power of] coagulation, some [common] properties, the [power of] growth, senses and motion. On the essential *differentia* of man there are three views pertaining to three categories of people: the multitude, the elite, and the highest elite.

First view: When the multitude found man [having the power of] speech, they assumed that the eminence of man over the animal was due to this ordinary, external speech; so they concluded that his essential *differentium* was this external speech.

Second view: The elites have said that those who have accepted this ordinary external speech as the essential *differentium* of man have done so on the basis of one aspect which is judgment from the point of the observer, and not from the point of the object of observation; the latter has been withheld and its states not discussed. [According to them] the essential *differentia* of anything are in reality that in which no other thing can associate with it. But we see that this ordinary external speech assumed to be the essential *differentium* of man is not true because a parrot, which is from the animal [kingdom], can be taught this external speech. So beyond this external speech there should be another virtue (*faḍīlat*) which cannot be shared with anyone, and that virtue is discerning reflection (*tamyiz-i fikr*). Therefore, [the essential *differentium* of man] is in reality the power of discernment, and not this external speech. So they concluded that the discerning reflection is the essential *differentium* of man.

Third view: The highest elites have said that those who have sought another virtue as the essential *differentium* of man beyond this external speech which they have judged to be discerning reflection, that is so to a certain extent. But they too have not understood the ambiguities of the mystery of this issue and have not been able to go beyond the opinion of those who consider that the essential *differentium* of anything is that in which no other thing can associate with it. [They say], "We observe certain animals which have the power of discernment due to which they know something about the beginnings and consequences of their work, [and] in what lies their well-being and corruption." For example, a bird knows that the perpetuity of its species lies in its egg, that whatever is in the egg is in the state of potentia, and by heat becomes actualized, and that heat [33] is attained when it puts the egg under its wings. The turtle has no wings, but it knows that whatever is in the egg is in the state of potentia and can be actualized by heat. So it repeatedly and continuously blows warm breaths over it until it finds the baby turtle has come into being in the egg. It knows its time [for coming out, so when the time is ripe] it breaks the egg and brings the baby turtle out.

An intelligent person knows that [such an act of a bird is due to] essential discerning reflection which resembles man's discerning [power]. So this discerning reflection is not absolutely specific to man. Since it is not specific to him, it is not his essential *differentium*. Therefore his essential *differentium* has to be his greatest specific quality (*khāṣiyyat*). This greatest specific quality is to impart knowledge by the act of imparting, and to accept [knowledge] by the act of listening. Accordingly a real human being and his essential *differentium* is that he acquires knowledge from those who are above him [in knowledge] according to the principle of acceptance, and imparts it to those who are below him [in knowledge] according to the principle of effusion (*fā'iḍ*). Peace.

Good and Evil

Fourteenth Conception: Concerning Good and Evil, that Evil Does Not Exist in Initial Origination, the Nature of the Evil that Appears in this World

Since people see good and evil in this world, some assume that good has a source and evil has a source. Zoroastrians believe that Yazdān is one source and Ahrīman is one source. They relate light and goodness to Yazdān, and darkness and evil to Ahrīman. There is corruption in this concept. The one who says that there are two sources should be asked, "According to your opinion there are two sources. Tell us, are these two sources equal without being more or less than the other in existence, might and [power of] encompassing? Or one is prior in goodness and one is prior in evil?" If they are not equal, then it necessitates that one is perfect and the other is deficient. The perfect is [obviously] encompassing and the deficient is encompassed; so the one which is greater and encompassing is prior in being the source to the one which is deficient and encompassed. Therefore the two sources for good and evil according to their claim do not exist; everything has [or comes from] one source which is His Exalted Command.

It is known that goodness is a concomitant of perfection and perfection is a concomitant of goodness, while evil is a concomitant of deficiency and deficiency is a concomitant of evil. So where there is absolute perfection there is sheer goodness; where there is absolute deficiency there is sheer evil, and where perfection and deficiency are mixed there good and evil are also mixed. For example, the First Intellect is nobler in substance, more perfect existentially, and higher in rank than all the existent beings; so absolute perfection belongs to it, and wherever it is there is sheer goodness.

The Universal Soul is more deficient in substance, existence and rank than the First Intellect. One of its dimensions is toward perfection and the other dimension toward deficiency. The mixture of perfection and deficiency belongs to it, because the Universal Body is deficiency itself. To it belongs the absolute deficiency; so wherever it is, there is sheer evil. According to this measure there are three realms: (1) the intellectual realm which is sheer good; (2) the spiritual realm (*ʿālam-i nafsānī*) which is a mixture of good and evil; and (3) the physical realm which is sheer evil. Each one of these realms has its people. The people of the intellectual realm are the people of unity (*ahl-i waḥdat*); the people of the spiritual realm are the people [36] of gradation (*ahl-i tarattub*); and the people of the physical realm are the people of contradiction (*ahl-i taḍādd*). The rule of contradiction is: the people of the world contradicting each other; the rule of gradation is: the people having the divine Law (*sharʿ*) agreeing with each other; and the rule of unity is: unification among the people of resurrection (*ahl-i qiyāmat*).[5]

Whoever turns his face away from the people of the world contradicting each other [and turns toward] the people having the divine Law agreeing with each other, and then from the people having the divine Law agreeing with each other to the people of resurrection united with each other no trace of evil in itself remains due to his relation with the latter. His physical acts become analogous to spiritual traces (*āthār*) and his spiritual traces become analogous to intellectual lights.

Also, goodness effuses essentially from the donor of goodness (*wāhib al-khayr*), whereas evil comes about accidentally in the way. For instance, imagine goodness like a grain of wheat thrown into the soil and watered, and evil like the foam which comes into existence from the dust particles in the passage of water which settle on the surface of water. It is known that foam manifested from the passage of water is not the essence and substance of water. At times it happens that the dominance, scale and power of [foam] on the water reaches such a degree that water is not seen, and it is assumed that there is no water and everything is foam. [Likewise] at times it happens that the dominance, scale and power of evil over good reaches to such a degree that good is not seen, and it is assumed that there is no goodness and everything is evil, and before long the light of goodness declines and corruption is manifested in the world. One of its reasons is the good is weak at the start, but powerful in the end, while evil is powerful at the start but weak in the end. When the good which is weak at the start begins evil which is contrary to it becomes manifest with its initial power. Since the good is weak [initially], evil appears powerful, but in the end in reality the power of the good which begins gradually reaches its [highest] limit, and evil diminishes and becomes extinct.

Destiny (*qadar*) is the first [divine] measure (*taqdīr*) which proceeds through the primordial Command to the First Intellect. Decree (*qaḍāʾ*) is the primordial prescription which is inscribed by the primordial Command on the First Tablet. The meaning of the first [divine] measure in terms of similitude is when someone wants to build a house, he first lays the foundation of the walls and the rooms. The meaning of the decree in terms of similitude is that house and whatever is necessary for it become constructed. Two angels one called Sāʾiq[6] and the other

5. The anthropology developed by Ismāʿīlī thinkers of the Alamut period of Ismāʿīlism represent three levels of people: (1) the people of contradiction (*ahl al-taḍādd*) who exist only in the realm of the external (*ẓāhir*) dimension of the Islamic *Sharīʿah*; (2) the people of gradation (*ahl al-tarattub*) who have gone beyond the external dimension of the *Sharīʿah* to the inner dimension (*bāṭin*) of the *Sharīʿah*; they consist of many grades or degrees; (3) the people of union (*ahl al-waḥdah*) who have arrived at the realm of *ḥaqīqah* of all *sharāʾiʿ* and realized the inner meaning, the *bāṭin* behind the *bāṭin* and see only the truth of all *sharāʾiʿ* and the spritual reality of the divinely guided teacher, i.e., the Nizārī Ismāʿīlī Imam. Cf. F. Daftary, *The Ismāʿīlīs*, op. cit., pp. 324–410. Quite similar concepts of cosmology and anthropology including similar terminology is seen in the Kubrawiyyah Sufi Order of Central Asia, cf. Kubrawī Sufi ʿAzīz al-Dīn Nasafī's (d.c. 700/1300–1) *Kitāb insān al-kāmil* (Tehran, 1941), pp. 178–179.

6. The text reads '*sābiq*' which is obviously an error of the copyist.

called Shāhid are appointed as guardian angels over destiny and decree so that they raise all the existent things to perfection and the end which is specific to each one, and for which they have been created. Their aim is universal goodness; the good is concealed in their motion. This evil which comes in the way is not due to decree [37] and destiny, but to the sensory, imaginative and estimative veils which lie before the reflective consideration (*naẓar-i fikrī*) and insight due to which our choice (*ikhtiyār*) [of action] does not come out right.

Since our knowledge and foresight cannot encompass the consequences of affairs, and we are not able to choose the real (*ḥaqq*) by our opinion and analogy (*qiyās*), therefore by choosing that which is not real evil comes into existence. For instance the need [to learn from a teacher] is specific to the pupil and his good lies in that. To be independent [of being a pupil] is specific to a teacher and his good lies in that. If we do not submit ourselves as pupil [to a teacher] and desire to become a teacher, then we forfeit our need specific to us in which lies our good, and conceive of becoming independent [from being a pupil] which is not specific to us and in which lies our evil; then we come out of that good and fall into evil. We take refuge in God from that.

Also, you must know about universal evil and particular evil. The example of particular evil is fire sets in the house of an ascetic and burns his gloves and clothes. [The example of] universal evil is the existence of fire is removed from the world. Also, particular evil is there is a flood which destroys the houses of people, with the children, the weak and the poor. [The example of] universal evil is the existence of water is removed from the world. So the term evil is not applied to the essence and act of fire and water in reality, but figuratively, relatively and accidentally.

Also, existence in this world must have a cause, while nonexistence requires no cause. Wealth requires a cause while poverty must have no cause. Day, for example, has a cause but night has no cause. Day has a cause, and that cause is the sun which shines from the horizon of the sky, while night has no cause because when the sun sets the night comes by itself. So, just as privation of existence is nonexistence, privation of wealth is poverty and privation of day is night, likewise privation of good is evil.

Now, [if someone says], "Just as particular intellects of the people possessing intellects are the effects of the First Intellect which has come into existence by the divine Command, similarly the particular ignorance of the ignorant people is the effect of the primordial ignorance—the concomitant of contradiction—which is the counterpart of the Intellect" [In response to this it should be said], "That [statement] is cunning; it is satanic, it seems intelligent but is not intelligent."[7] The reason why there is contradiction and gradation in souls is that a soul may fall besides the gradation [leading] toward perfection in such a way that when it is actualized from potentiality, it becomes the best creation; a soul may fall besides

7. This quotation seems to refer to a tradition of the sixth Shiʿite Imam Jaʿfar al-Ṣādiq (d. 148/765), cf. *al-Uṣūl min al-kāfī* by al-Kulaynī, ed. with commentary by Ḥājj Sayyid Muṣtafawī (Tehran, 1385 H.S.), p. 11, tradition no. 3.

contradiction [leading] toward deficiency in such a way that when it is actualized from potentiality, it becomes the worst creation; and a soul [38] may fall in the middle [position], its one dimension facing toward the good and another dimension facing toward the evil. Just as there is contradiction and gradation among souls, likewise in physical matter too there is contradiction and gradation due to which some [physical matter] falls on the high side, some on the low side and some in the middle.

Thus according to the principle, "Everything returns to its root" some matter may be good and some souls good; the former is fit for the latter and the latter takes possession of it. There may be evil matter and evil soul; the former takes possession of the latter, and the latter is fit for it. There may be matter halfway between good and evil and similarly such a soul; the former becomes receptive to the latter, and the latter governs the former.

If someone says, "Since evil souls manifest evil due to the evil substance of which they are constituted, so why do the "rightful people" (*muḥiqqān*), peace be upon their remembrance, struggle (*jihād*) against them and give them religious prescription (*taklīf*) in order to make them good?" Its answer is this: as already said in the introduction, good souls are [constituted] of true substance, and evil souls of unreal (*bāṭil*) substance. In this world, which is the realm of similitude (*kawn-i mushābihāt*), good and evil both look alike in form and appearance. When the "rightful people" invite (*daʿwat*) [the people to the divine Command] they do not claim, "We transform evil to good." Rather they give the divine Command to the people of the world on the basis of which the good people become distinct from the evil ones; and the good ones according to the rule, "the *muʾmin*s (believers) are created from the [light of] the Real so when they are commanded by the Real by it, they truly know it," so they separate from the evil ones; and the evil ones according to the rule, "They struggled against it wickedly and arrogantly though their souls acknowledged them" [Qurʾān, 27:14], separate from the good ones. Thus when this distinction takes place, the evil ones will have no excuse or argument according to the rule, "So that mankind might have no argument against Him the Exalted, after the [coming] of the apostles" [Qurʾān, 4:165]. The "rightful people," peace be upon their remembrance, in the beginning according to the rule, "Invite to the way of your Lord with wisdom and goodly exhortation" [Qurʾān, 16:125], make them attentive to the divine proof. After that, according to the rule, "Have the disputation with them in the best manner" [Qurʾān, 16:125], they lay the rule of the sword on them, and by combat and warfare bring them out from the realm of ambiguity.

The invitation [to the divine Command] and religious prescription of the "rightful people" is not for evil ones so that evil is transformed to good, but for good ones. The latter at first in this world due to the acquisition of sins, mistakining something not right [according to the divine Command], fall out of their innate original nature (*fiṭrat*); so by [following] that invitation and religious prescription—the similitude of which is the nature of an elixir which affects the substance of copper and transforms it to standard pure gold—those acquisitions by their memory which are not right [according to their original innate nature] are erased from their memory, and they attain their original innate nature. What the evil person derives from their invitation and religious prescription is, "He has no invitation in the world [39] nor in the next world" [Qurʾān, 40:43].

Also, if someone asks, "Man's act is finite. Why should he get eternal retribution from the Almighty God? That is to say, Why a [man for the] finite sin is punished infinitely?" Its answer is: from the Almighty God no infinite punishment is given for the finite sin. But since the souls of good people by nature deserve reward, they remain forever and eternally in joy, delight, pleasure and good fortune; while the souls of evil persons by nature deserve punishment; so they remain forever and eternally in great repentance and abundant misfortune. We take refuge in God from them.

By these arguments and premises, it is evident that evil does not exist in the [primordial] divine origination (*ibdāʿ*, or divine Command); that there are no two sources for good and evil. Whoever affirms these two contradictory sources and recognizes Yazdān as the source of light and good, and Ahrīman as the source of darknesses and evil, has accepted Yazdān and Ahrīman as two opposing [sources]. But wherever the [two] opposing [powers] meet like two antagonists, they need an arbitrator over them. Thus, both these ideas are a great error and a clear [sign of] misbelief (*kufr*) [in those who harbor them]. Peace.

Esoteric Hermeneutics (*Taʾwīl*)

Sixteenth Conception: Concerning the Act of Adam and Iblīs

The belief of the majority of people and the people of Islam is that there was a time when God the Exalted had not created this universe. Then He created it [as it is said], "Surely your Lord is God, Who created the heavens and the earth in six days" [Qurʾān, 7:54]. They say, the first man whom God the Exalted created was Adam. Then He brought forth Eve who was his spouse from his left side, then the progeny of Adam came into existence through the sexual union of Adam and Eve. God at first sent Adam and Eve to Paradise, and permitted them to eat every pleasant thing therein except the wheat, which He prohibited them [to eat] and said, "You two do not approach this tree" [Qurʾān, 7:19].

Iblīs was originally a great angel, and held the position of teaching the angels. When God created Adam, He said [to the angels], "I am going to place in the earth a caliph" [2:30], i.e., "I am going to make one [of the angels] my caliph in the earth." He commanded the angels, "Prostrate before Adam" [2:34]. "They said, "What! Wilt Thou place in it someone who shall make mischief in it and shed blood, and we celebrate Thy praise and extol Thy holiness?" [2:30]. He, the Sublime and Exalted, said, "Surely I know what you do not know" [2:30]. "They said, "Glory be to Thee! We have no knowledge but that which Thou hast taught us" [2:32]. [47] So they prostrated before Adam and remained as angels. But Iblīs refused [to prostrate] and was proud, and said, "Shall I prostrate before the one whom Thou hast created of dust?" [17:61], and said, "I am better than he; Thou hast created me of fire, while him Thou hast created of dust" [7:12]. He did not prostrate before Adam, so he fell from being an angel to devil and has remained accursed by Him the Exalted, till the Day of Resurrection.

[Iblīs] after that [incident] entered Paradise and appeared in the guise of a sincere teacher before Adam and Eve, and beguiled them and said, "Eat this wheat. They were deceived by his talk and ate that wheat; so they were seized by God's punishment and fell from Paradise. But when they repented and said, "Our Lord! We have been unjust to ourselves, and if Thou forgive us not, and have (not) mercy on us, we shall certainly be the losers" [Qur'ān, 7:23]. God the Exalted accepted their repentance and sent both of them back to Paradise. After that they never fell from Paradise.

All [these narratives] are mysteries (*rumūz*) and allusions [to something] which is implicit in the exoteric dimension of the Revelation (*tanzīl*). Those people whose reflective insight (*naẓar-i baṣīrat*) does not transcend the realm of similitude (*kawn-i mushābihāt*) and reach the realm of distinction (*kawn-i mubāyanāt*) cannot transcend the rules [of the former realm]; so they stick to them. Those whose reflective insight has transcended the realm of similitude and reached the realm of distinction, they confirm all these [mysteries and allusions] according to the rule of the exoteric dimension of the *tanzīl* as well as according to the rule of its inward dimension (*bāṭin*) and esoteric interpretation (*ta'wīl*) [of the *tanzīl*.] They confirm [the meaning] of each one of these mysteries and allusions from the point of reality and [also] the spiritual meanings (*ma'nawiyyāt*), by the permission of God the Exalted, and by His good will.

For example, regarding the nonexistence of the world, i.e., there was a time when it did not exist, then it came into existence, they say, "We affirm that there was a time when there was no world, then it came into existence. We also affirm that there was no such time when there was no man in this world since its inception. We also affirm that man has been in the world since its beginning."

Now regarding the world we say, "When you say 'there was a time when there was no world, then it came into existence' which world do you mean? If you mean this world whose heavens are elevated and decorated by the sun, the moon, the spheres and the stars; whose earth is outstretched, and in which mountains, oceans, plants, animals, and humankind have become manifested, then it cannot be said about it that there was a time when it did not exist, then it came into existence. Because if you say that there was a time when this world did not exist, you have said that the Creator at that time [when it did not exist] was not a Creator; or [you have said that] the Creator was [the Creator] but [48] *in potentia* and later on [when the world came into existence] He emerged [from potency] into actuality, such a statement is misbelief (*kufr*). We take refuge in God from it."

So it should be said that He the Exalted was always the Creator. Now if you say that He was [always] the Creator, then the creation, i.e., this world becomes requisite. So there was never a time when the world did not exist.[8]

8. The issue pertains to the conflict of two points of views on the creation of the universe, one by Muslim metaphysicians, including Fārābī, Avicenna, Ṭūsī etc., who viewed the world as eternal but contingent on God from the metaphysical point of view, and the other held by Muslim *mutakallimūn*

If someone says, "According to this argument both the world and God are eternal, that means associating a partner with God (*shirk*)." To this we reply, "We deny neither the eternity of the world nor its being created. The world with respect to itself is created, with respect to its Completer and Perfector it is eternal; its creation is its contingency and deficiency; its eternity is its emergence from contingency to necessity, from deficiency to perfection. Since the real state of the world cannot be comprehended by the people, so they give imaginative and estimative [views and say,] 'there was a time when the world did not exist; then it came into existence'. The world appears different to everyone; for example, the world in relation to a worm in the stone, to a bird flying in the middle of the air, to an embryo in the womb, to a child, to a mature child, to a mature ignorant child, to one of the scholars whose knowledge is speculative (*naẓarī*), or it is instructional (*taʿlīmī*), or inspirational (*taʾyīdī*), to each one of them it appears different, and each one of them can describe the world only according to his existential limit."

But this world about which it can be said 'there was a time when it did not exist; then it came into existence', they say that it consists of eighteen thousand worlds. The change of a [religious] cycle to another cycle, a prophetic tradition (*sunnat*) and community (*millat*) to another prophetic tradition and community, a creed to another creed, each one is a world. Among these [worlds] when one changes to another, it can be said: that cycle, that prophetic tradition and community did not exist before but now it has come into existence. It is [saying], there was a time when this world did not exist; then it came into existence. Now the first person of that world who is the transformer of the previous prophetic tradition is the founder of that community.

[The meaning of] 'this world has been created in six days' [Qurʾān, 7:54] is: These six days are the cycles of the Founders of [six] *sharīʿah* (divine Laws) beginning from Adam to Muhammad the Chosen, peace be upon him. Each day is equivalent to one thousand years [as God said], "Surely a day with your Lord is as a thousand years of what you number" [Qurʾān, 12:47]. It is this world about which it can be said that there was a time when it did not exist; then it came into existence.

[People say] the first inhabitants in the first world were not human. But there was never a time when humankind was not there in this world. Because the goal of the motions of the spheres is the mixture of the elements of the kingdoms [i.e., mineral, plant and animal]; the goal [of the creation of] the [three] kingdoms is the human species. The creation in [the form of] gradation is decreed in such a way that the first to become manifest is mineral, followed by animal and then man. For if mineral had not been there, plant would not have been there; [49] if mineral, plant and animal had not been there, there would not have been man. [So] 'there was never a time when the world did not exist' [means], [there was never a time] when mineral, plant, animal and human species were not there. Therefore,

---

such as Abū Ḥāmid Gazzālī and the others who viewed it to be created from the point of view of dogmatic theology (*kalām*). Cf. M. Fakhry, *A History of Islamic Philosophy*, (New York, 1983), pp. 222–26.

according to this rule the human species has always been there [in the world] since its beginning and will always be there till post-eternity (*abad*).

As for [the issue of] Adam, whether the first man in the world was Adam, or he was not they say, "According to the narrative concerning him, as well as the world and the [three] kingdoms, it has been gradually known that the human species has always been there, and will always be there in the world, but the first man in the first world was not Adam, and yet the first man in the first world has been Adam. With regard to that I say: the [religious] cycles are the worlds; the change of one cycle [to another cycle] is [like] the change of one world to another. So when a [new] cycle which is another world begins, the founder of the religion of that cycle, whose structure, mode, language, script, speech, conduct, activity, course, in sum and in detail, are different [from the previous cycle], is called the first man who did not exist in the world [i.e., in the previous cycle], but he came into existence later on and became manifest. As long as that cycle is his cycle, all the people [of his cycle] are named after his cycle and relate themselves as his children. The founder of the community in these seven thousand years who became manifest has been Adam, so [the people of this period] are called Ādamiyān (i.e., the followers of Adam) after Adam."

In the cycle of every prophet, the outward dimension (*ẓāhir*) of his *sharīʿat* is called the 'cycle of concealment' (*dawr-i satr*). The cycle of every Resurrector (Qāʾim) who manifests the [hidden] realities (*ḥaqāʾiq*) of the *sharāʾiʿ* of the prophets is called the 'cycle of unveiling' (*dawr-i kashf*). The cycles are destined in terms of millennia, and every cycle lasts a thousand years.

When such millennial periods start, after every seven thousand years there is a Resurrection. When seven times seven, i.e., forty-nine thousand years pass away and the fiftieth thousand begins, then arises the Great Resurrection. In the course of these thousands of years, the cycle of concealment and the cycle of unveiling follow each other as night and day.[9]

[The meaning of the narrative] of Adam and Iblīs is this: At the beginning of these seven thousand years which had come to an end, the Qāʾim of that cycle, by

9. This concept is the continuation of the cyclical theory of the epochs of the world held by the Ismāʿīlī thinkers of the Fāṭimid period of Ismāʿīlism. According to this concept, religious history was envisaged in terms of seven eras marked by the appearance of the seven speaker-prophets (*Nuṭaqāʾ*, sing. *Nāṭiq*). The seven *Nāṭiq*s were: Adam, Noah, Abraham, Moses, Jesus, Muḥammad, and Qāʾim. The first six speaker-prophets were sent to reveal the divine *sharīʿah* which conveyed a single, unified divine message, although each of them was forced to translate that message to fit particular circumstances of time, place, local language, and exigencies of a specific social group. The seal of the six *sharāʾiʿ* was Muḥammad. These six cycles in the Ismāʿīlī sacred history are called the 'cycles of concealment—that is the epochs when the positive *sharāʾiʿ* are preached to people but their hidden truths are reserved for a few elite. The seventh cycle would be of the Qāʾim (or Messiah). He would not reveal a new *sharīʿah*, for his function would be to unveil the inner meanings hidden in the previous *sharāʾiʿ*. It would be the period of *qiyāmat* (resurrection) when all the aspects of the positive *sharīʿah* will be removed from the people except the intellectual aspects (such as killing the innocent, etc.], and the inner truths of all the six *sharāʾiʿ* would be revealed by the Qāʾim (or Messiah) to those who accept his *daʿwat*. Cf. H. Corbin, *Cyclical Time and Ismaili Gnosis*, English trans. R. Manheim and J. W. Morris, (London, 1983), esp. pp. 84–99.

divine order and wisdom, closed the door to the invitation (*daʿwat*) for the Resurrection (*qiyāmat*) which was being carried out at that time, and inaugurated the cycle of concealment, [i.e.,] the cycle of *sharīʿat*, and was designated as prophet by divine revelation and sublime inspiration. He established sensory similitude (*mithāl-i ḥissī*) for every intellectual truth (*mamthūl-i ʿaqlī*), and spread the slogan of positive *sharīʿat* in the world. This was difficult for the teachers of the Qāʾim of that cycle, i.e., the angels, to accept so they objected to it and wanted to get rid of the chains and fetters [of the positive *sharīʿat*] according to the measure of what they had heard about the knowledge of the Resurrection. [50] When the order of the Qāʾim, peace be upon his name, arrived that "I know what you do not know" [Qurʾān, 2:30], they understood their [position] and found it necessary to apologize and ask for his forgiveness; and by accepting those commands and interdictions (*awāmir wa nawāhī* of the *sharīʿat*) they reached to that eminence and praiseworthy place intended for them.

Ḥāris-i Murrah, i.e., Iblīs was one of the teachers [of the angels] of the end of the cycle of unveiling who had survived until the beginning of the cycle of concealment. Since he held the teaching position of the angels, i.e., the people of the *daʿwat* of Resurrection, and did not have in him the receptivity to learn from Adam, he said, "This positive *sharīʿah* is a set way and the *qiyāmat* whose doors have been closed is the universal goal [of everyone]. I have reached that goal and attained [my] end, so why should I return from the goal and the end [which I have already attained] and once again become occupied with crossing the stages and degrees [of that goal, i.e., the *qiyāmat*]." So he did not accept the *sharīʿat*, and said, "I have comprehended the gist and essence of the *daʿwat* of Adam so I have no need of it, therefore I am coming out of the noose of obedience [to the *sharīʿat*] and [its] prescription."

Then he said, "I am better than Adam, Thou hast created me of fire and him of dust" [7:12]. By fire he meant the divinely assisted [or inspirational] knowledge (*ʿilm-i taʾyīdī*), and by dust the speculative and instructional knowledge (*ʿilm-i naẓarī wa taʿlīmī*), that is, [his knowledge was] fire [i.e.,] divinely assisted (or inspired) knowledge, while Adam's knowledge was speculative and instructional. Fire on account of its rising and circumscribing [quality] corresponds to inspiration (*taʾyīd*), dust to speculation (*naẓar*), and water to instruction (*taʿlīm*).

He ordered Adam not to seek the proximity of that tree, that is, 'Do not eat the wheat'. By 'tree' it is meant 'the tree of Paradise' (*dirakht-i khuld*) and 'the eternal kingdom' (*mulk-i yulbā*), that is, the knowledge of the Resurrection. By 'Do not eat wheat' is meant, do not start penetrating into the knowledge of the Resurrection; do no express it by speech because its time is not yet ripe.

[Adam] was disobedient, and was deceived by the words of Iblīs and ate the wheat. It implies, when Iblīs refused [to prostrate before Adam] and was proud, he was cursed but he paid no attention to that curse. After that [episode] he came toward Adam and gave him speeches and proofs about the *daʿwat* of the Resurrection of that Qāʾim. Adam on account of being weak at the start, accepted what [Iblīs said], and on top of that he repeated that [knowledge] to those who did not deserve it. Due to this reason, he fell into the whirlpool of punishment of the Qāʾim, peace be upon his remembrance. When he realized that he had committed an error, he acknowledged his error, and took refuge in God's vast compassion. His apology and repentance were accepted.

Eve about whom they say she was the spouse of Adam, means the spiritual meaning (*maʿnī*) of that *sharīʿat*. She was informed about the principles of the inner dimension (*bāṭin*) and spiritual meaning [of the *sharīʿat*]. The work of the *sharīʿat* [51] of that cycle could only be completed by Adam and her. She at the beginning also accepted the words of Ḥāris, but eventually she turned to God with penance and repentance.

The [meaning of the] Paradise from which Adam and Eve fell, and the Paradise which they reached from which they never fell is, the real (*ḥaqq*) which has a beginning and an end. As a rule we see contradiction [in everything] in the beginning; so one can say that there is [something] unreal (*bāṭil*) [in everything]. Finally, as a rule, we see gradation; so it could be said that the real exists and the unreal does not exist. Anything real is weak at the start, but powerful at the end, but the unreal is powerful at the start and weak at the end. Due to this reason, the unreal appears similar to the real but in the end it does not, and its existence does not remain at all. Now the Paradise where Adam [and Eve] inhabitated [in the beginning] and from which they fell was a Paradise which appeared real at first, but it was the realm of similitude constituted of something which was real and unreal. The Paradise where [they] reached from which [they] never fell was something real at the end which was the real distinction between something real and unreal. Anything which is unreal has eventually no existence in that realm [of the real]. The esoteric interpreters [of the Qurʾān], (*asḥāb-i taʾwīl*) have given this genre of interpretations to the similitudes and indications (*dalālat*) recorded about the narrative of Adam and Iblīs. Peace.

—Latimah Parvin Peerwani, translator

References

Classical and Modern Biographical Sources

al-Ḥurr al-ʿĀmilī. *Amal al-ʿāmil fī fikr ʿūlamāʾ jabāl ʿĀmil*. Tehran:1306, p. 506.
Ibn Shakīr. *Fawāt al-wafayāt*. Bulak: 299. ii, 149.
Khwandmīr, Gh. *Ḥabīb al-siyar*. Bombay: 1857; ii, 80; iii: 54.
al-Khʷansārī, M. B. *Rawḍāt al-jannāt*. Tehran: 1306: iv. 66 sqq.
al-Kintūrī, I. H. *Kashf al-ḥujub waʾl-asrār ʿan al-kutub waʾl-asfār*. Bib. Ind. N.S., N°. 1403.
al-Majlisī, M. B. *Biḥār al-anwār*, xxv. Tehran: 1315: i. 4.
Marʿashī al-Shūshtarī, N. A. *Majālis al-muʾminīn*. Tehran: 1268, in the 7th *Majlis*.
Quatremère, *Histoire des Mongols de la Perse*. Paris: 1836.
Rashīd al-Dīn Faḍl Allāh, *Jāmiʿ al-tawārikh*. Ed. by M. T. Dānesh-Pazhūh and M. Modarresī, Tehran: 1960.
al-Tafrishī, M. *Naqd al-rijāl*. Tehran: 1318, p. 331.
al-Waṣṣāf. *Tajziyat al-amṣār*. Bombay: 1269.
Abraham ben Samuel Zucuto. *Sefer yukhasin*. Cracaw: 1581: 152.

Primary Sources

Ṭūsī, Naṣīr al-Dīn. *The Metaphysics of Ṭūsī*. Trans. P. Morewedge. New York: 1999.

———. *Sayr wa sulūk* (Contemplation and Action), trans. S. J. Badakhchani. London: 1998.

Secondary Sources

Browne, E. G. *A Literary History of Persia*. London: 1906.

———. *A History of Persian Literature under Tartar Dominion*. Cambridge: 1920, s. indices.

Carathéodory Pasha, A. *Traité de quadrilatère*. Constantinople: 1891.

Carra de Vaux, B. *Gazali*. Paris: 1902: 167 *sqq*.

———. "Les sphères célestes selon Naṣīr-Eddin Aṭṭūsī." In *Recherches sur l'histoire de l'astronomie ancienne*, ed. P. Tannery. Paris: 1893, pp. 337–61.

Corbin, H. "Naṣīr al-Dīn Ṭūsī and the Shiʿite *kalām*." In *History of Islamic Philosophy*. London: 1993.

Daftari, F. *The Ismāʿīlīs: Their History and Doctrines*. Cambridge: 1990, pp. 324–410.

d'Ohsson. M. *Histoire des Mongols depuis Tschingiz Khan jusqu'à Timour Bey*. The Hague: 1824, sq.

Hammer-Purgstall. *Geschichte der Ilchane*. Darmstadt: 1842, sq.

Horten, M. *Die philosophischen Ansichten von Rāzī und Ṭūsī*. Bonn: 1910.

———. *Die spekulative und positive Theologie des Islam nach Rāzī und ihre Kritik durch Ṭūsī*. Leipzig: 1912.

Howorth. H. H. *History of the Mongols*. London: 1876, *sqq*., iii., s. indices.

Madelung, W. "Naṣīr ad-dīn Ṭūsī's Ethics between Philosophy, Shiʿism, and Sufism." In *Ethics in Islam*, ed. by R. G. Hovannisian. California: 1985, pp. 86–101.

Nasr, S. H. "Afḍal al-Dīn Kāshānī and the Philosophical World of Khwājah Naṣīr al-Dīn Ṭūsī." In *The Islamic Intellectual Tradition in Persia*, ed. by M. Aminrazavi. London: 1996, pp. 189–207.

———. "Muḥammad ibn Muḥammad Naṣīr al-Dīn Ṭūsī." In *The Islamic Intellectual Tradition in Persia*, ed. by M. Aminrazavi. London: 1996, pp. 207–16.

Peiper. *A Stimmen aus dem Morgenland*. Hirschberg: 1850.

Scaliger, J. *Thesaurus temporum Eusebii Pamphili Chronicorum Canonum*. Leiden: 1606, Suppl. 2, Book 2, p. 145 *sq*.

Siddiqui, B. H. "Naṣīr al-Dīn Ṭūsī." In *A History of Muslim Philosophy*, ed. by M. M. Sharif. Wiesbaden: 1963. Vol. 1: pp. 564–80.

Strothmann, R. *Die Zwolfer-Schiʿa*, Leipzig: 1926.

GENERAL BIBLIOGRAPHY

Brockelmann, Carl. *Geschichte der arabischen Litteratur.* 1st ed., Weimar, 1898–1902; 2nd ed., Leiden: 1943–1949. *Supplementbande*. Leiden: 1937–1942.

Browne, Edward G. *A Literary History of Persia.* London-Cambridge: 1902–1924.

Cahen, Claude. *Introduction à l'histoire du monde musulman médiéval: VIIe-XVe siècle.* Paris: 1982.

The Cambridge History of Iran: Volume 4, *The Period from the Arab Invasion to the Saljuqs*, ed. R. N. Frye. Cambridge: 1975.

The Cambridge History of Iran: Volume 5, *The Saljuq and Mongol Periods*, ed. J. A. Boyle. Cambridge: 1968.

The Cambridge History of Iran: Volume 6, The Timurid and Safavid Periods, ed. P. Jackson and L. Lockhart. Cambridge: 1986.

Corbin, Henry. *En Islam Iranien: Aspects spirituels et philosophiques.* Paris: 1971–1972.

———. *History of Islamic Philosophy*, with S. H. Nasr, O. Yahya, trans. L. Sherrard, Paris: 1992.

———. *Epiphanie divine et naissance spirituelle dans la Gnose Ismaélienne*, Rome: 1957.

———. 'Imamologie et philosophie', *Le Shiʿisme imamite*, Paris: 1970, pp. 143–174.

———. 'Nāṣir-i Khusraw and Iranian Ismāʿīlism' in *The Cambridge History of Iran,* vol. 4, Cambridge, 1976, pp. 520–542.

Daftary, Farhad. *The Ismāʿīlīs: Their History and Doctrines*. Cambridge: 1990.

———. 'The Bibliography of the Publications of the late W. Ivanow', IC, 45 London: 1971, pp. 55–67, and 56 London: 1982, pp. 239–240.

Encyclopaedia Iranica, ed. E. Yarshater. London-Boston: 1982.

Encyclopaedia of Iran and Islam, ed. E. Yarshater. Tehran: 1976–1982.

Encyclopaedia of Islam, ed. M. Th. Houstma et al. 1st ed., Leiden-London: 1913–1938.

Encyclopaedia of Islam, ed. H. A. R. Gibb et al. New ed., Leiden-London: 1960–.

Handwortenbuch des Islam, ed. A. J. Wensinck and J. H. Kramers. Leiden: 1941.

Ivanow, Wladimir. *A Guide to Ismailis Literature.* London: 1933.

———. 'Early Shiʿite Movements,' *JBBRAS*, NS, 17 (1941), pp. 1–23.

———. 'A Forgotten Branch of the Ismāʿīlīs', *JRAS* (1938), pp. 57–79.

———. *Studies in Early Persian Ismailism.* Bombay: 1955.

———. "Haft bāb-i Bābā Sayyidnā," ed. W. Ivanow, in his *Two Early Ismaili Treaties*, pp. 4–44. English trans. M. G. S. Hodgson, in his *Order of Assassins*, 99. 279–324. Gravenhage: 1955.

———. *A Brief Survey of the Evolution of Ismailism,* Bombay-Leiden: 1952.

———. *Ismaili Literature, a Bibliographical Survey,* Tehran: 1963.

Justi, Ferdinand. *Iranisches Namenbuch*. Marbug: 1895.

Lewis, Bernard. *The Origins of Ismāʿīlism: A Study of the Historical Background of the Fatimid Caliphate*. Cambridge: 1940.

Madelung, Wilfred. 'Aspects of Ismāʿīlī Theology: The Prophetic Chain and the God Beyond Being', in *Ismāʿīlī Contributions to Islamic Culture,* Tehran: 1977, pp. 51–65.

———. 'Shiʿism: Ismāʿīlīyah, *Encyclopedia of Religion*, NY: 1987 vol. 13, pp. 247–260.

———. "The Sources of Ismāʿīlī Law," *Journal of Near Eastern Studies,* 35 (1976), pp. 29–40.

Marquet, Yves. *La Philosophia des Ikhwān al-Ṣafā',* Algiers: 1975.

Nasr, S. H. (ed.) *Ismāʿīlī Contributions to Islamic Culture*, Tehran: 1977.

Pearson, James D. *Index Islamicus, 1906–1955*. ed. W. Heffer, 1986 printing Mansell. Cambridge: 1958.

Poonawala, Ismāʿīl. *Bibliography of Ismāʿīlī Literature*, Malibu: 1977.

Sauvaget, Jean. *Introduction à l'histoire de l'Orient musulman: Elements de bibliographie*, Paris: 1943.

Sezgin, F. *Geschichte der arabischen Schrifttums*. Leiden: E. J. Brill, 1967–.

Shorter Encyclopaedia of Islam, ed. H. A. R. Gibb and J. H. Kramers. Leiden: 1953.

Stern, Samuel M. *Studies in Early Ismāʿīlism.* Jerusalem-Leiden: 1983.

Storey, Charles A. *Persian Literature: A Bio-bibliographical Survey*, London-Luzac: 1927. Persian trans. Y. Ariyanpur et al., *Adabiyyāt-i Fārsī*. Terhran: 1362–/1983–.

Walker, P. E., *Ḥamīd al-Dīn Kirmānī*, London: 1999.

———. *Early Philosophical Shiʿism*: *The Ismāʿīlī Neoplatonism of Abū Yaʿqūb al-Sijistānī*, Cambridge, Cambridge University Press, 1993.

INDEX